INSIDE AutoCAD

The Complete Guide to AutoCAD ®

Daniel Raker and Harbert Rice

 New Riders Publishing, Thousand Oaks, California

INSIDE AutoCAD

The Complete Guide to AutoCAD ®

By Daniel Raker and Harbert Rice

Published by:
New Riders Publishing
Post Office Box 4846
Thousand Oaks, CA 91360, U.S.A.

First Edition, 1985
Second Edition, 1986
Third Edition, 1987
Fourth Edition, 1988
Fifth Edition, 1989

9   0

Printed in the United States of America

Library of Congress Cataloging-in-Publication Data

```
Raker, Daniel.
Inside AutoCAD.

Includes index.
1.  AutoCAD (Computer program)  2. Computer graphics
I. Rice, Harbert.  II. Title.
T385.R35  1989   620' .00425'02855369  99-31548
ISBN 0-934035-49-0
```

Cover digital video images produced by Digital Arts, Los Angeles, CA from Space Station and Voyager drawings by Charles Huckeba. The Voyager drawing was adapted from a drawing from the Autodesk File by John Walker (New Riders Publishing).

Warning and Disclaimer

This book is designed to provide tutorial information about the AutoCAD and AutoShade computer programs. Every effort has been made to make this book complete and as accurate as possible. But no warranty or fitness is implied.

The information is provided on an "as-is" basis. The authors and New Riders Publishing shall have neither liability nor responsibility to any person or entity with respect to any loss or damage in connection with or arising from the information contained in this book.

Acknowledgments

The authors wish to give special thanks to Patrick Haessly for his help and efforts in putting this fifth edition together. Pat reworked all the old exercise material, developed all the new material for Release 10, and helped develop the new graphics techniques used in the book. His technical expertise with AutoCAD, extra effort and long hours make this edition the finest edition yet for the book. Special thanks also are due to Christine Steel for her long hours and extra effort in copy editing and laying out this edition, making it our cleanest edition.

The authors wish to thank Rusty Gesner for his technical editing, for contributing yet more special tips and tricks, and pitching in at the last moment to help index the book. Thanks to John Riggs for producing all the graphics, plus reviewing all the exercises. Thanks to Carolyn L. Porter for redesigning the book for Ventura layout and overseeing production. Thanks to Todd A. Meisler for reproducing the graphics, and for actually putting the book together. Thanks also to Solano and Max DeKeles for their support.

The authors wish to thank Autodesk for its continuing encouragement and support for this fifth edition of INSIDE AutoCAD. Our special thanks to John Walker, Dan Drake, Duff Kurland, Eric Lyons, Mauri Laitinen, Joe Oakey and many others from Autodesk for their help and support over the years. Autodesk, Inc. supplied AutoCAD and AutoShade.

Xerox Corp. supplied Xerox Ventura Publisher, Microsoft supplied Microsoft Word. Symsoft provided a copy of Hotshot Plus. Video Seven, Inc. provided a Vega VGA Video Display. Sun Microsystems Inc. provided a complete Sun 386i system. KETIV Technologies helped acquire numerous pieces of equipment and supplies for this fifth edition.

About the Authors

Daniel Raker

Daniel Raker is president of Design & Systems Research, Inc., a Cambridge, Massachusetts-based management consulting firm specializing in computer graphics applications and market research. He is founder of the MicroCAD Institute ™. With offices in major US cities and affliates in a half dozen countries, the MicroCAD Institute is a leading training organization serving professional users of computer-aided design systems.

Mr. Raker is the editor of Design Systems Strategies published by the Design & Systems Research Publishing Co. (formerly A/E Systems Report). In addition to the newsletter, Mr. Raker's column "CAD Angles" appears monthly in Plan and Print magazine.

Mr. Raker's experience in computer graphics comes from General Telephone and Electronics (GTE) Laboratories where he worked as an assistant research director, and from the Harvard University Laboratory for Computer Graphics where he held the position of Director of Services and was responsible for applications development, and graphics education and training. Mr. Raker earned his Bachelor of Arts degree from Harvard College.

Harbert Rice

Harbert Rice is the president of New Riders Publishing in Westlake Village, CA. He divides his time between publishing and writing books on computer engineering software and desktop publishing software. Mr. Rice writes about computer graphics software from practical interests in using microcomputers to publish technical books, and a long-standing interest in pattern recognition software.

Before moving to the west coast and forming New Riders, Mr. Rice was a Vice President of the Ziff-Davis Publishing Co. Based in Burlington, MA, he headed up a computer group providing engineering databases to utility companies. His publishing group distributed data electronically from central site minicomputers.

Originally trained as a plant biochemist, Mr. Rice earned his PhD from Harvard University. While at Harvard, he became interested in using computers to model non-linear systems. Mr. Rice gained his computer software experience at ERT, an engineering consulting subsidiary of COMSAT Corp., and the Raytheon Company in Burlington, MA. where he held research and development positions. He applied pattern recognition methods to large scale computer simulation problems, and co-developed a series of system identification programs called the Group Method of Data Handling (GMDH) program. GMDH forms a type of engineering model popularly called a neural-net model. This software is used on mainframe and minicomputers to extract non-linear engineering models from test and experimental data.

CONTENTS

CHAPTER 3

Drawing Fundamentals

HOW TO MAKE ACCURATE DRAWINGS

CHAPTER 4

Getting Around

MAKING A SMALL DISPLAY SCREEN DO THE WORK OF A BIG PIECE OF PAPER

CHAPTER 5

Graphic Entities

LINES AND THE SHAPES THEY MAKE

CHAPTER 6

Introduction to Editing
IF AT FIRST YOU DON'T SUCCEED, TRY EDITING

CHAPTER 7

More Editing
PRELUDE TO 3D EDITING

CHAPTER 11

Dimensioning
ADDING "SMARTS" TO YOUR DRAWING

CHAPTER 12

Attributes and Data Extraction
ASSIGNING INFORMATION TO GRAPHIC ENTITIES IN YOUR DRAWINGS AND GETTING IT OUT AGAIN

PART TWO   AutoCAD 3D

CHAPTER 13

Getting Started with 3D

CHAPTER 14

Using 3D Entities

CHAPTER 15

Controlling Dynamic 3D Displays
HOW TO DISPLAY AND PRESENT 3D DRAWINGS

CHAPTER 16

Inside AutoShade
ENHANCING 3D WITH SHADED RENDERINGS

CHAPTER 17

Drawing Output

PART THREE   Customizing AutoCAD

CHAPTER 18

Customizing Macros and Menus
AutoCAD YOUR WAY

CHAPTER 19

Tailoring Your Menu System

ANATOMY OF AutoCAD'S MENU

CHAPTER 20

Using AutoLISP for Drawing Automation

APPENDIX A

AutoCAD Commands

APPENDIX B

MS-DOS and Configuring AutoCAD

APPENDIX C

AutoCAD Menus and System Variables

INDEX

Index

Introduction

Lay of the Land — What We Want to Do

Our aim in INSIDE AutoCAD is to introduce you to AutoCAD, the most powerful and most popular computer-aided drafting program. We want to help you unlock AutoCAD's power to do your design and drafting work quickly and easily. INSIDE AutoCAD will show you how AutoCAD works and how you can benefit from working with AutoCAD.

INSIDE AutoCAD breaks the AutoCAD program down into easily managed drawing operations. You can master each operational group in a few hours. Using INSIDE AutoCAD, you will learn what work AutoCAD can do for you, and what you must do on your own.

How INSIDE AutoCAD Is Organized

INSIDE AutoCAD is organized for the beginner as well as the experienced AutoCAD user. The book does not require any programming and it keeps computer jargon to a minimum. The book is made up of three parts.

Part One shows you how to create and display two dimensional (2D) drawings. It takes you sequentially from setting up AutoCAD, through building and editing 2D drawings.

Part Two shows you how to create and edit 3D drawings, including how to use 3D surface meshes and how to pass an AutoCAD 3D wireframe drawing to AutoShade for rendering.

Part Three shows you how to take control of AutoCAD and make it into your own drawing system. Starting with making your own menus and macros, it demonstrates how to customize AutoCAD for your own use, including using AutoLISP to automate your drawings.

INSIDE AutoCAD has three helpful appendices. Appendix A provides a complete listing of all the AutoCAD commands covered in the book. Appendix B provides additional help setting up AutoCAD and dealing with problems and errors. Appendix C provides help in setting up AutoCAD's tablet menu. It also provides a quick reference of AutoCAD's system variables.

The Exercises

We've organized the book so that you can get just the information you want. Chapters are divided into a series of exercises, each teaching one or more AutoCAD commands. Explanatory text accompanies each exercise, putting the command into context, explaining its behavior, and explaining how to use the command with its different options. Most AutoCAD drawing and editing commands have several modes and options. Part of the trick to learning AutoCAD is to find the commands and command options that meet your needs.

In many chapters, we've provided *additional techniques* exercises. These exercises combine using several AutoCAD commands to accomplish some real-world task, like inserting a border and titleblock into a drawing. These technique exercises will give you a better feel for how AutoCAD is really used, and how commands interact with each other in practice. One or two chapters provide pure techniques. In the advanced 2D editing chapter, for example, we show you how to use point filters and how to place editing check marks in your drawings. These are pure tips and tricks. If you are looking for help to get some common drafting task done, like scaling your drawing during setup, look for these task-specific exercises. They are indexed by the name of the task.

The Optional IA DISK

To help you save time and effort, we have added an optional IA DISK to this edition of INSIDE AutoCAD. The disk is a time-saver, and a typing-saver. At the start of each chapter, there is a drawing setup sequence (shown in a settings table). It takes time to go through a drawing setup, particularly when we get to more advanced drawing and editing functions in 3D. The disk contains starting drawing files and any supporting files you need for all the chapters (except the first two setup chapters.) The disk also contains pre-built menu macros and AutoLISP routines used in the customization chapters in Part Three.

You don't need the disk to work through the book. We've designed all the example exercises so that you can do them from scratch. But we know that you may be pressed for time. If you wish to jump into the middle of the book and do an exercise that uses a drawing created in an earlier chapter, you can copy the starting drawing from the IA DISK and be ready to go. Using drawings from the IA DISK insures accuracy and lets you avoid spending time preparing drawings and supporting files, like symbol drawing files. The IA-DISK lets you concentrate on learning what you need to know about AutoCAD when you want to know it.

You'll find an order form for the INSIDE AutoCAD (IA DISK) drawing disk inside the back of the book. See the instructions in chapter 1 on backing up and installing the disk so that the drawing and supporting files are ready to use.

How to Use INSIDE AutoCAD

INSIDE AutoCAD is a hands-on tutorial. If you just read the text and look at the drawing examples, you will learn a great deal about AutoCAD. To solidify your working knowledge of AutoCAD, you need to sit down at an AutoCAD-equipped computer and work through the drawing sessions.

We suggest that you take each part of the book in sequence. However, if you are in a hurry to get started, the following Quick Start Guide provides suggestions for getting started with key techniques.

Quick Start Guide

If You Want to:	Turn to this Chapter:
Set Up Hard Disk	Chapter 1
Install the IA DISK	Chapter 1
Set Up AutoCAD	Chapters 1, 2 and 3
Use the User Coordinate System (UCS)	Chapters 3 and 13
Use Multiple Views (Viewports)	Chapters 4 and 13
Learn 2D Drawing Commands	Chapter 5
Use 2D Drawing Commands in 3D	Chapter 13
Learn 3D Drawing Commands	Chapter 14
Edit 2D Drawings	Chapters 6, 7 and 8
Edit 3D Drawings	Chapters 13 and 14
Use Blocks in Drawings	Chapters 9 and 13
Dimension Drawings	Chapter 11
Add Attribute Tags	Chapter 12
Control 3D Views and Perspectives	Chapter 15
Render 3D Drawings with AutoShade	Chapter 16
Plot 2D and 3D Drawings	Chapter 17
Customize AutoCAD Menus and Macros	Chapters 18 and 19
Use AutoLISP to Automate Drawing	Chapter 20

What the Exercises Look Like

INSIDE AutoCAD is a self-teaching guide to the AutoCAD program. What you see below is an example of a formatted exercise. Don't try to work through this exercise; it's only a sample to illustrate the book's exercises. Each exercise has an illustration that will show you what you should see on the screen when you do the exercise. AutoCAD's screen display text is printed in computer-style type on the left of the exercise. Comments and instructions are given on the right.

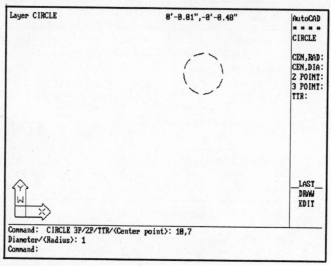

Example Exercise Illustration

Example Exercise Format

Select: **[DRAW] [CIRCLE:]**	Select circle command.
3P/2P/TTR/<Center point>:	Pick a point centered in the upper right quarter of the screen.
Diameter/<Radius>:	Drag a radius of about 1 inch.
Command: **SAVE**	Save the drawing with the file name WORK.
File name <WORK>: **WORK**	

When you see the word *select*, it means that you select a screen menu, or select an AutoCAD command with your pointer. In the example above, you select the [DRAW] menu to get to the [CIRCLE:] command. The bracketed items are called menu items, labels, *or boxes*. To select a menu item, you highlight its label and hit your pointer pick button. All menu selection sequences assume you start from the first (root) page of the screen menu. You also can execute commands by typing them followed by a <RETURN>. **SAVE** (in the example above) is a command. Each exercise shows all necessary commands (and command prompts) in computer text at the left. The responses for you to input as you work through the exercises are shown in **bold** face type.

The right-hand section provides our *in-line* comments. These comments will give you extra pieces of information to help guide you through AutoCAD's drawing and editing commands. All you need to do to follow an exercise sequence is to follow the left-hand command sequence, refer to the in-line instructions and type (or pick) any input shown in **bold**.

You can usally make your selection by simply clicking your pointer on a command menu box. Often, it may be quicker to simply type the command. In some cases, you may work with dialogue boxes where you make your selections by clicking your pointer on the appropriate box. This is shown by the [ ] following the item that you want to select. When you have made your selection or selections, you click on [OK] to execute the command, or [Cancel] if you want to cancel the command. The following illustration shows a typical dialogue box.

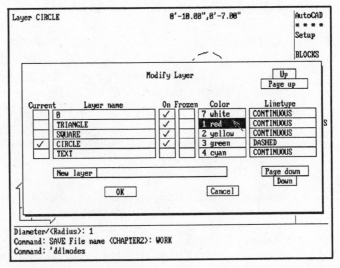

Typical Dialogue Box

Drawing Examples

To help guide you through the tutorial exercises, each tutorial example has one or more drawings. Many exercises have intermediate drawing displays, corresponding to the key steps used to create the drawing. (Remember we had to do the exercises to create the book!) We have annotated these drawings, particularly for work in 3D, to help you locate your drawing points. The following illustration shows you what these detailed screen shots with drawing points will look like.

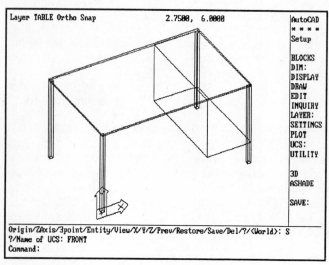

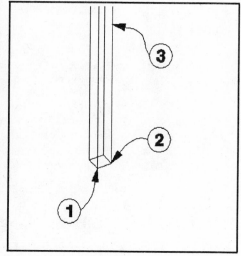

Sample Illustration   *Detail With Pick Points*

➡ *NOTE: Our illustrations were developed on an EGA (Enhanced Graphics Adaptor) display. If you are using a different display, particularly a CGA (Color Graphics Adaptor) display, you may need to to do more zooms to get better views of your screen display when you work through the exercises. For clarity, we omit the AutoCAD grid from most of our illustrations, but you should keep you grid on.*

Two Key Tricks to Learning AutoCAD

There are two basic tricks to learning AutoCAD. The first is to learn the AutoCAD menus and commands that you need for your own application. The second is to practice drawing by *experimenting* with these AutoCAD commands. We encourage you to play around with different commands. To help you learn the AutoCAD menus and commands, portions of the screen menus, pull-down menus and dialogue boxes are shown in the chapters. Appendix C contains a complete screen menu map to AutoCAD commands.

Note to Instructors

If you are using INSIDE AutoCAD for classroom instruction, you will want to know what AutoCAD commands and techniques each chapter covers. Early in each chapter, we tell what tools, techniques, and groups of commands will be covered. Appendix A provides a chapter-by-chapter list and the Index contains an alphabetical list of all AutoCAD commands used and explained in the book. You can use either the chapter-by-chapter listing or the alphabetical listing to find the commands covered.

You may also want to know that each chapter has one or more suggested stopping points. If you need to break a chapter's exercise sequences, you can use these stopping points; they show how to stop and resume with the exercise drawings. If you don't need to break the sequences, just proceed straight on through the chapter.

What You Will Need

To work with INSIDE AutoCAD, you need a workstation that can run AutoCAD Release 10, or a later release.

AutoCAD Versions and INSIDE AutoCAD

INSIDE AutoCAD's fifth edition is designed for use with AutoCAD Release 10 with full 3D. Appendix B gives the book's assumptions for your hardware and operating system. The checklist that follows gives the book's assumptions for working with the tutorial examples. We assume that you can:

- Load your operating system from a system disk, or your hard disk.

- Load a configured AutoCAD program.

- Select your responses to AutoCAD's prompts by typing from your computer keyboard or

- Select your responses from AutoCAD's screen menus or tablet menu by using a pointing device like a digitizer stylus, puck, or a mouse.

If you have a release that is earlier than AutoCAD Release 10, don't be alarmed. Most of INSIDE AutoCAD is perfectly usable with Release 9. Editions of INSIDE AutoCAD for Release 9 and earlier versions of AutoCAD are available from New Riders Publishing. If your AutoCAD version differs from the one assumed here in the book, you will notice slight differences in screen displays, menus and command prompting sequences. None of these difference will keep you from getting the full benefit of training and support that INSIDE AutoCAD provides.

System Setup and the IA DISK

Chapter 1 explains how to set up your hard disk directories for use with INSIDE AutoCAD. We've designed the book's setup and exercises so that they won't interefere with any AutoCAD settings or other work that you may already be doing with AutoCAD. Chapter 1 also will show you how to install the drawing and support files on the IA DISK.

To help you along in the exercises that reference the IA DISK, we've marked certain exercise sections with special symbols. These show you what to do if you have the disk.

Disk Symbols

 Do this if you have the IA DISK.

 Do this if you don't have the IA DISK.

References, Tips and Occasional One-Liners

Besides the working drawing sessions, INSIDE AutoCAD also contains AutoCAD menus and command references, and tips which we have collected from other AutoCAD users. The references are option lists that explain AutoCAD's program assumptions or give settings for different drawing commands. These AutoCAD references and users' drawing tips are set off in the text to make it easy for you to find the options and tips. Our one-liners are set off as an occasional respite.

"It is time to bait, or cut fish."

—Fortune Cookie

Working in AutoCAD 2D
HOW TO GET PROFESSIONAL DRAWINGS

Basic Drawing Tools

Two dimensional (2D) drawings are the workhorses of drafting and design. To get good 2D drawings from AutoCAD, you need to know the basics of setting up drawings, creating and editing objects, inserting drawing symbols, and dimensioning your drawings. Part One of INSIDE AutoCAD gives you the basics you need to get accurate professional looking drawings. You will find all the commands, drawing and editing techniques, tips, and tricks you need to produce the high quality 2D drawings that you want and expect from AutoCAD.

How Part One Is Organized

Part One has twelve chapters formed from four easy-to-remember groups.

- **Setup and Display Controls**. Chapters 1 through 4 show you how to setup everything from your hard disk to controlling your drawing and viewing displays.

- **Drawing and Editing**. In chapters 5, 6, 7, and 8, you learn how to create and edit 2D drawings. Chapter 5, shows how to use *every* 2D drawing command. Chapters 6 and 7 teach you how to edit your drawings with both basic and more exotic editing commands. Chapter 8 is a pure editing techniques chapter.

- **Using Blocks (Symbols) and Hatches**. Chapter 9 shows you how to use blocks, and how to update your drawings quickly and easily. Chapter 10, shows how to use the same block insertion techniques to add hatches and patterns to enhance your drawings.

- **Dimensioning and Attribute Tags**. Chapters 11 and 12 show how to add dimensions and other non-graphic information to drawings. Chapter 11 guides you through AutoCAD's dimensioning settings and commands, including associative dimensions. Chapter 12 describes how to add non-graphic text tags to your drawing, and how to extract this information in a text report to extract bills of materials, specifications, schedules, and other data lists.

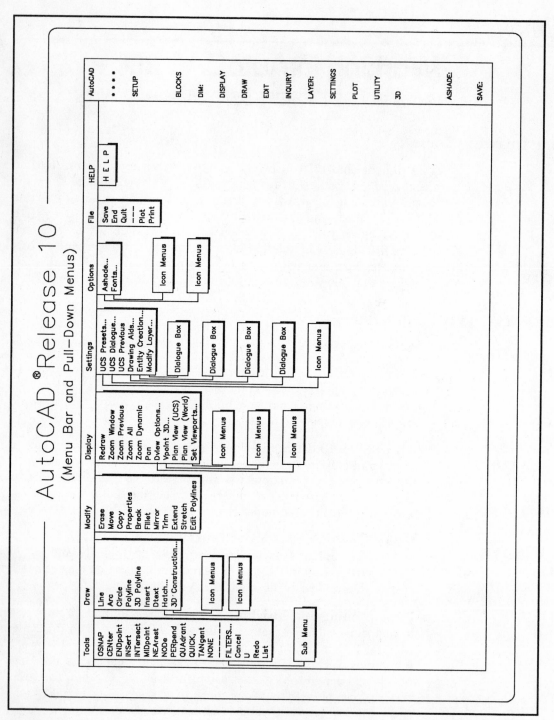

AutoCAD Release 10 Pull-Down Menu, Courtesy of Autodesk, Inc.

Getting Started

GETTING TO KNOW HOW AutoCAD WORKS

Lay of the Land

This book is a tutorial about AutoCAD. In this chapter we cover the basics on how to set up the program, how to turn it on, and how to draw. By the end of the chapter you will have created an electronic CAD drawing file, played around by drawing a few lines, typed some text, and saved your drawing.

The Benefits of Learning How AutoCAD Works

The benefits of learning how to set up and store an electronic drawing file are obvious. Your real drawing benefits will come from learning about AutoCAD's command structure and how you can interact with AutoCAD to produce the drawings you want. By learning to communicate with AutoCAD, you will unlock AutoCAD's power and versatility for your own use.

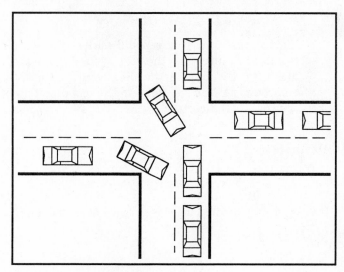

Manhattan Street Intersection

Think about learning AutoCAD in the same way that you learn to navigate your way around a big city. You know where you want to go, you just need to get a few basic routes down pat, then you can explore the byways at your leisure. We guarantee that your learning period with AutoCAD is going to be a lot easier and much shorter than learning how to get around a place like Manhattan.

Setting Up AutoCAD

Before you start, you need to get a few chores out of the way. INSIDE AutoCAD comes with an optional disk called the IA DISK. The book and disk are designed for use on your AutoCAD workstation. Setting up for INSIDE AutoCAD requires that you set aside space on your hard disk to create a directory called IA-ACAD. By doing this, we can insure that any AutoCAD settings used for the book won't interfere with any other AutoCAD settings or projects that you or your co-workers may have under way.

Directories

INSIDE AutoCAD assumes that you are using the DOS operating system, running AutoCAD on a hard disk called C:, and that you have a directory structure similar to the one shown in the following exercise. If your drive letter or subdirectory names vary from those shown, you need to substitute your drive letter and directory names wherever you encounter the C: or the directory names in the book.

Making the IA-ACAD Directory

The book assumes that you will work in the IA-ACAD directory. You need to make this directory, then copy your AutoCAD configuration files to this directory. By copying the files, you set up a self-contained AutoCAD environment. You should be in the root directory of your hard disk. Make the IA-ACAD directory.

Making the IA-ACAD Directory

```
C:\> MD \IA-ACAD
```

Take a look at your directory names. Get into the root directory of drive C: and type:

```
C:\> DIR *.
Volume in drive C is DRIVE-C
Directory of  C:\
```

```
ACAD     <DIR>  12-01-88   11:27a      AutoCAD program, configuration and standard
                                       support files.
DOS      <DIR>  12-01-88   11:27a      All of the DOS files.
IA-ACAD  <DIR>  12-01-88   11:27a      INSIDE AutoCAD config. and support files.
```

Your disk will show other directories, like:

```
123      <DIR>  12-01-88   11:27a      Lotus 123 directory.
DBASE    <DIR>  12-01-88   11:27a      dBASE III files.
5 File(s)   8753472 bytes free         Your list will be different.
```

Setting Up AutoCAD Configuration Files

AutoCAD requires a set of overlay and configuration files, which get created when AutoCAD is first run. The book assumes that AutoCAD's support files are in the \ACAD directory. By copying these configuration and overlay files to the \IA-ACAD directory, you establish a separate AutoCAD configuration for working through the book.

Copying AutoCAD Files to the IA-ACAD Directory

```
C:\> CD \ACAD <RETURN>                 Change to the ACAD directory.
C:\ACAD> COPY ACADP?.OVL \IA-ACAD\*.*
ACADPL.OVL                             Plotter overlay file.
ACADPP.OVL                             Printer/plotter overlay file.
2 File(s) copied

C:\ACAD> COPY ACADD?.OVL \IA-ACAD\*.*
ACADDS.OVL                             Display (video) overlay file.
ACADDG.OVL                             Digitizer (or mouse) overlay file.
2 File(s) copied

C:\ACAD> COPY ACAD.CFG \IA-ACAD\*.*
1 File(s) copied                       General AutoCAD configuration file.
```

➡ *NOTE: If your AutoCAD directory is not named \ACAD, you will have to make sure that you can find the AutoCAD support files and copy them to the \IA-ACAD directory. See Appendix B for more help on setting up AutoCAD's system environment.*

Installing the IA DISK

Now you are ready to install the IA DISK files. If you have the optional disk, install it. If you don't have the disk yet, see the order form in the back of the book on how to get a copy. We recommend getting the disk. Besides saving you typing and drawing setup time, the disk provides starting drawings for the book's chapters, letting you bypass material and jump into the book where you want. For example, if you want to learn about editing, then you can skip the basics and start editing with a preset drawing from the disk.

Installing the IA DISK

Put the IA DISK in your disk drive A: Change directories, and type A:IA-LOAD.

```
C:\> CD \IA-ACAD
C:\IA-ACAD> A:IA-LOAD
```

All that's left to do is create a simple batch file to help start AutoCAD. This IA.BAT file avoids conflict with your current AutoCAD setup and keeps the book's files in one place. The batch file calls AutoCAD directly from your ACAD directory to avoid conflict with any possible ACAD.BAT batch file that you might have.

Starting AutoCAD

Use the following exercise to create a batch file named IA.BAT. You can start AutoCAD from any directory by typing \IA. The batch file will automatically change to the IA-ACAD directory, start AutoCAD, and return you to the root directory when you exit AutoCAD. If you want to learn how to enhance your batch file, turn to Appendix B. Appendix B also contains information on automating your drawing setup and configuring AutoCAD.

Creating the IA.BAT Batch File

Return to the root directory.

```
C:\COPY CON IA.BAT        To create a file from the keyboard.
CD \IA-ACAD               To change directory to IA-ACAD.
SET ACADCFG=
\ACAD\ACAD %1 %2          To call the AutoCAD program.
CD \                      To return to the root directory after exiting AutoCAD.
^Z                        Type a <Ctrl Z> to end the IA.BAT file.
1 File(s) copied
```

You can start an INSIDE AutoCAD session from anywhere in your hard drive simply by typing \IA. With these file handling chores out of the way, it is time to start up AutoCAD.

Starting AutoCAD

```
C:\>  \IA
```

As soon as you type \IA from the operating system, the batch file takes control of your computer. The directory is changed to IA-ACAD and the AutoCAD program displays the Main Menu for you. The Main Menu gives you the choice of creating or editing drawings, plotting drawings, installing (configuring) AutoCAD, and a whole list of special utilities.

If you are like most CAD enthusiasts, you face the first screen with anticipation. The first time around, we all really want to get at drawing. There is that nagging urge to get in the drawing editor, thinking, "Can I get away with entering a few commands just to see what happens?" Before you satisfy that urge, you need to prepare a prototype drawing to insure that your INSIDE AutoCAD sessions are set to the default settings.

When you begin a new drawing, AutoCAD looks for a drawing called ACAD.DWG. AutoCAD uses this drawing to establish the default working environment for your new drawing. INSIDE AutoCAD assumes your prototype drawing is the same as when you took AutoCAD out of the box. In order to make sure this is true, you need to create a new ACAD.DWG in your IA-ACAD directory. The following exercise creates the new prototype drawing. The equal sign following the drawing name tells AutoCAD to make the ACAD.DWG with its original default settings. You will learn more about the ACAD.DWG in the next chapter.

```
              A U T O C A D
Copyright (C) 1982,83,84,85,86,87,88 Autodesk, Inc.
Release 10.0 (10/25/88) IBM PC
Advanced Drafting Extensions 3
Serial Number:  ##-######

Main Menu

   0.  Exit AutoCAD
   1.  Begin a NEW drawing
   2.  Edit an EXISTING drawing
   3.  Plot a drawing
   4.  Printer Plot a drawing

   5.  Configure AutoCAD
   6.  File Utilities
   7.  Compile shape/font description file
   8.  Convert old drawing file

Enter selection: 1

Enter NAME of drawing: ACAD=
```

Main Menu With Option 1 Selected

Creating a Prototype Drawing

```
Enter selection: 1          From main menu.
Enter NAME of drawing: ACAD=          Type in.

                            The AutoCAD drawing screen appears.

Command: END                Type in command.
```

The Drawing Editor

We can come back later and explore the Main Menu options; for now let's jump right back into the drawing editor. You get into the drawing editor by selecting option 1 from the Main Menu. Load a new drawing file by giving it a name. Call your first drawing CHAPTER1. AutoCAD will set up a drawing file on disk C: called CHAPTER1, put you into the drawing editor, clear the screen of text, and set you up for drawing.

Loading a New Drawing File

```
Enter selection: 1
Enter NAME of drawing: CHAPTER1
```

➡ *NOTE: AutoCAD drawings have names like CHAPTER1.DWG, but AutoCAD assumes the file name .DWG extension (.DWG). You can use characters, numbers, and most symbols, but no spaces in your drawing names.*

Getting Familiar with the Screen Menus

AutoCAD's first drawing screen displays a graphics drawing area and its screen menu down the right side of the screen. The first screen menu is called the root menu. It has "AutoCAD" at the top of the menu. If you look at the bottom of the AutoCAD screen, you'll see a *Command:* prompt line. This is AutoCAD's communication channel. You will learn to keep an eye on the command prompt to read messages from AutoCAD.

As you move your pointing device across the desk top or pad, the crosshairs on the screen move too. Make your pointer move the crosshairs towards the items listed in the root menu. When the crosshairs pass into the menu area, a menu item lights up. Now move the pointer up and down to highlight different menu items.

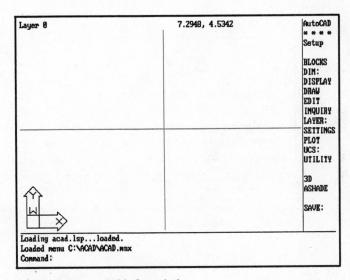

AutoCAD Screen With Crosshairs

Using the DRAW and LINE Menus

You can select a menu item from the screen by pressing your pointer's pick button. Select [DRAW]. As soon as you do, you get a new menu. Now select [LINE:]. When you do this, both the screen menu and the prompt line change. Move your pointer to the center of the screen's drawing area and pick a point by clicking your pointer's button. The prompt line will change again. Play around and draw a few lines, using the following exercise sequence as a guide.

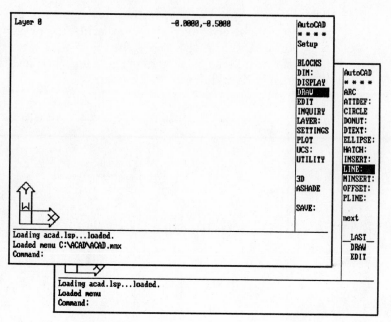

DRAW to LINE Screen Menus

Drawing Your First Line

Select **[DRAW]**	Draw screen menu appears.
Select **[LINE]**	Select from screen menu.

The line command starts and prompts for the first point.

Command: LINE From point:	Pick the first point at ①.

Move the crosshairs and see the beginning of a line trailing behind them.

To point:	Pick a second point at ②.
To point: **<RETURN>**	End the Line command.

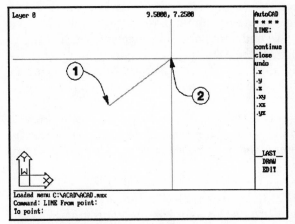

Beginning a Line

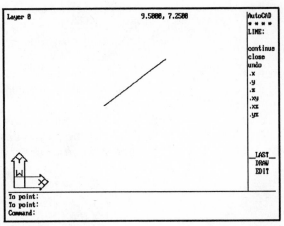

The Completed Line

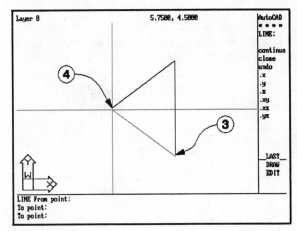

Continuing the Line

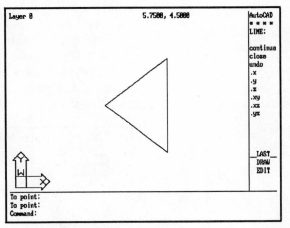

The Completed Continuing Line

Continue your line by repeating the LINE command with a <RETURN>.

Continuing the LINE Command

Command: **<RETURN>**   Repeat the previous command.

Draw a second set of connecting lines.

LINE From point: **<RETURN>**   Start the line at the last point of the first line.
To point: Pick a point at ③.
To point: Pick a point at ④.
To point: **<RETURN>**   End the line command.

Rubber Band Cursor

You've seen that AutoCAD's LINE command is simple and straightforward. Issuing the line command to AutoCAD begins the process of recording the two endpoints of a line segment. Once a line is created from two endpoints, AutoCAD assumes that you want to continue drawing lines. Not only that, AutoCAD assumes that you want to continue drawing lines from the last endpoint of the previous line.

You can keep on drawing segments every time you see a To point prompt. AutoCAD helps you visualize where the next segment will be located by *rubber banding* or trailing a segment between your last point and the cursor.

➤ *TIP: A CANCEL, <RETURN>, or a <SPACE> (hitting the space bar) ends the LINE command and returns the command prompt.*

Using AutoCAD's Pull-Down Menus

AutoCAD has a set of pull-down menus in addition to the screen menus found on the right side of the screen. These pull-down menus are quite similar to the screen menus. If your video hardware supports pull-down menus, you will see a menu bar when you move your pointing device to the top of the graphic screen. The menu bar presents a list of titles indicating the selections available in each pull-down menu.

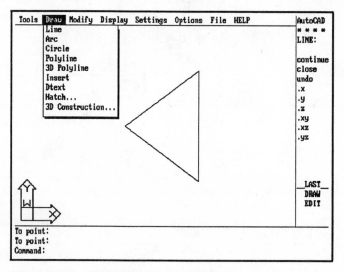

The Pull-Down DRAW Menu

Pull-down menus require a video board which supports the AUI (Advanced User Interface). If you are uncertain about whether your workstation supports pull-down menus, try the following test by typing the names shown in bold.

Testing for Support of Pull-Down Menus

Command: **SETVAR**	Access the system variables.
Variable name or ?: **POPUPS**	Get the Popups value.
POPUPS = 1 (read only)	

If you got a 1, you can use AutoCAD's pull-down and icon menus. If you got a 0, you need a new video driver from your board manufacturer, or you need a new video board and driver that support the pull-down menus. Release 9 requires an ADI 3.1 driver and Release 10 requires an ADI 4.0 (or later) driver. If you got *Unknown variable name,* you don't have a Release 9 (or later) version of AutoCAD.

Using the DTEXT and ZOOM Pull-Down Menus

To open a pull-down menu, you *highlight* the menu bar title and press the pick button on your pointing device. At this point you are presented with a list of selections that are executed exactly like the screen menus. Once you make a selection, the pull-down menu is closed and the selection is executed.

Try the following exercise. Type in the text and coordinate values shown in bold followed with <RETURN>s. If your workstation does not support pull-down menus, you can select the same menu items from the screen menu.

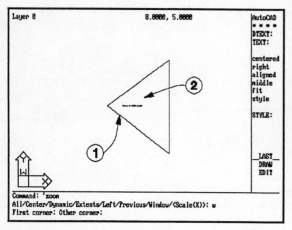

Small Text Prior to Zoom Window   Magnified Text After Zoom

Using the Pull-Down DRAW Menu

Pull-down **[DRAW]** Select **[DTEXT:]**   Select from pull-down menu.
Command: DTEXT Start point or Align/Center/Fit/Middle/Right/Style: **C** Center text.
Center point: **7.25,4.5**   Enter coordinates.
Height <0.20000>: **.05**   Set the text height.
Rotation angle <0>: **<RETURN>**
Text: **Welcome To INSIDE AutoCAD**   <RETURN> twice to finish the DTEXT command.
            So where is the welcome? Let's zoom in to see it.

Pull-down **[DISPLAY]** Select **[Window]**   Select from pull-down menu.
Command: 'zoom   Magnify an area to read the text.
All/Center/Dynamic/Extents/Left/Previous/Window/<Scale (X)>: **W**
First corner: Pick a point at ①.
Other corner: Pick a point at ② and you see it.

Command: **<RETURN>**   Repeat the zoom command.
ZOOM
All/Center/Dynamic/Extents/Left/Previous/Window/<Scale(X)>: **ALL**

            Return to the full magnification.
Regenerating drawing.

➥ *TIP: When you select menu items from the screen, it is a good idea to glance at the command prompt line at the bottom of your screen to make sure that you and AutoCAD are communicating. Then watch the center of the graphics screen for the action.*

You have loaded a new drawing file, and created some lines and text using AutoCAD's screen menus. Why not complete your first pass through the drawing editor by saving your first effort?

Saving a File

AutoCAD provides two saving commands. Both save your work to a .DWG file and secure it by renaming your previous drawing file on disk with a .BAK extension.

■ The SAVE command makes a .DWG file and returns you to the drawing editor to work on your current file. Saving gives you the option of saving your current drawing editor session under the current name or under a file name of your choice.

■ The END command makes a backup file from your previous (last) file, stores the up-to-date copy of your file, and exits the drawing editor. The END command assumes the current drawing file name.

Using SAVE to Save Your File

```
Command: SAVE                          Type or select from screen menu.
File name <CHAPTER1>: <RETURN>         Save your drawing.
```

As we promised, you have just navigated the most basic route with AutoCAD. You have loaded a new drawing file, done some drawing, and saved it to a new file name. Now let's turn our attention to the drawing editor and take a more leisurely look at AutoCAD's screen.

How AutoCAD Communicates With You (and Vice Versa)

Why is it so easy to draw in AutoCAD? You boot the program, get into the drawing editor, and start entering points. It doesn't matter whether you enter points by picking them with your pointer, or whether you enter the points at the keyboard (as you did to center your "Welcome" text). The answer, of course, is that AutoCAD knows its geometry and has a default Cartesian coordinate system set up and ready for your use.

World Coordinate System

When you enter the drawing editor, you enter a coordinate system called the World Coordinate System. When AutoCAD asks you to enter a point, you either locate the point with your pointing device or enter the point's coordinates from the keyboard. The system's coordinates consist of a horizontal X displacement, a vertical Y displacement (and a positive Z displacement for 3D). These are called absolute coordinates. Although it is conventional to specify absolute coordinate points with parentheses (3,4), when you type coordinates for AutoCAD at the keyboard you separate the X and Y values with a comma and omit the parentheses: **3,4**. Both the X and Y are measured from a zero base point that is initially set at the lower left corner of your screen. This base point's coordinates are 0,0.

The UCS — User Coordinate System

If you look at the lower left corner of your screen, you will see that there is an icon at point 0,0. This is the UCS (User Coordinate System) icon. UCS means, of course, that you can establish your own coordinate system and shift your base point in your drawing by changing the position of the UCS icon. You will make extensive use of the UCS when you work in 3D, but for now we will leave it at the default position.

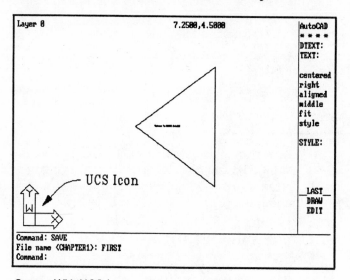

Screen With UCS Icon

The default X-axis is horizontal, left to right, and the Y-axis is vertical, down to up. If you look closely at the UCS icon, you will see that the X arrow points to the right on the X-axis, and the Y arrow points up the Y-axis. The "W" on the Y arrow means that you are in the default world coordinate system. The UCS icon will display a "+" when it is shown at the UCS origin (0,0). The UCS icon displays other information about where you are in 3D. For example, the box in the corner indicates the Z-axis direction which we will cover in the 3D section. If you find the UCS distracting when you are working in 2D, you can always turn it off. Here is how you turn it off and on.

Turning the UCS Icon Off and On

```
Command: UCSICON                              Turn icon off.
All/Noorigin/ORigin/OFF/<ON>: OFF
Command: UCSICON                              Turn it on again.
All/Noroigin/ORigin/OFF/<OFF>: ON
```

The Status Line

If you look at the top of your graphics screen you will see a line of text. This line is called the status line. Here you'll find information about how AutoCAD is set up, and how it will react when you issue certain commands. Think of the status line as a medical monitor that gives AutoCAD's vital signs to you. The illustration called Status Line shows the layer name and other types of settings that you see on the status line. We won't go into all the signs, but we will have you check a few to see how they work.

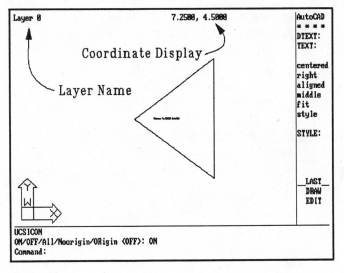

Status Line

If you look at the status line area, you will see several numbers to the right. These numbers represent the latest crosshairs coordinate position. When you move the pointer around, these numbers don't change. They're stuck at the last point that you officially entered as part of a command.

Using the COORDS Toggle for Cursor Digital Readout

To make the status line, X,Y, readout follow your cursor's positions, type <^D> (Control key and D pressed at the same time — read "Control-D").

The <F6> function key does the same thing on many systems. This status command calls for the continuous update and display of the cursor's position, giving you a digital readout. We refer to it as the COORDS toggle.

Now move your cursor around the screen. The X,Y readout will keep up with you and always let you know where you are. Move the cursor's position to the lower left corner and you will see the coordinates approach 0,0. You can disable the digital display by hitting <^D> (or <F6>) again.

The Command Line — Keeping Track of AutoCAD

As you work with the AutoCAD program, you'll come to know what it expects from you and how it will react when you do something. Many AutoCAD commands set up new drawing environments to receive additional commands. To help you keep track of your drawing environment, AutoCAD uses the bottom part of the screen to tell you how it's doing. This communication channel is called the *command line*. The command line is usually three lines depending on your video hardware, and shows you AutoCAD's prompts and your responses. It keeps track of your latest communication with AutoCAD.

➡ *NOTE: If you have a dual screen system, the command line will not show your responses — only AutoCAD's prompts to you. Your responses appear only on the text screen.*

AutoCAD has a flexible command and menu structure. You can issue an AutoCAD command by typing the command name at the keyboard in response to the command prompt. You have already executed several system commands at the keyboard in this fashion, turning the UCS icon off and on, and testing whether your system supports pull-down menus by issuing the SETVAR command.

As you type, the letters appear following the command prompt. In order to execute any typed command, you must press the <RETURN> key on your keyboard to let AutoCAD know that you're finished typing. On some systems this is the <ENTER> key, on others it is a broken arrow <↵>. If AutoCAD doesn't understand what you've typed after you press <RETURN> it will let you know.

Command Line Exercise

```
Command: LI
Unknown command.  Type ? for list of commands.
Command:

Command: LINE              Execute the line command.
From point:               Pick any point.
From point:               Pick any point.
From point: <RETURN>      End line command.
```

The FLIP Screen

Besides the command line, AutoCAD uses a screen full of text instead of the graphics screen to show you more information. On a two screen system this text is shown on your second monitor. On a single screen system, use the <FLIP SCREEN> function key on your keyboard to display the text screen. It is usually the <F1> key, or occasionally the <HOME> key. Press the key and the graphics drawing area goes away (along with the screen menu) and a text page appears.

```
File name <CHAPTER1>: FIRST

Command: UCSICON

ON/OFF/All/Noorigin/ORigin <ON>: OFF

Command:
UCSICON
ON/OFF/All/Noorigin/ORigin <OFF>: ON

Command:  <Coords on> LINE From point:
To point:
To point:
To point:

Command: LI
Unknown command.  Type ? for list of commands.
Enter "Ins" key to select menu item.

Command: LINE
From point:
To point:
To point:

Command:
```

Flipped to Text Screen

Flip Screen Exercise

```
Command: <F1>             Use your FLIP SCREEN key.

                          The graphics screen goes away and a page of text appears.

Command: <F1>             Flip back to graphics.
```

If you look closely at the text, you will see the last sequence of commands you typed (or picked from the screen menu). AutoCAD keeps track of the previous commands you have entered as well as your command prompt line dialogue. The last three lines of text appear on the graphic screen command line.

Using this screen full of information, you can look back through a set of command lines to see where you've been. If you get interrupted with a phone conversation, using the <FLIP SCREEN> is an easy way to pick up your place. Some commands (like HELP) automatically flip you to the text screen. At other times you can use the <FLIP SCREEN> just to get information.

What to Do About Errors. How to Get HELP!

AutoCAD is very forgiving. The worst thing that can happen when you mis-type a command name is that AutoCAD warns you that it does not understand what you want to do. It gives you another chance or prompts you to get help.

What if you catch a typing error before you hit <RETURN>?

Using the <BS> (backspace) key on the keyboard erases the characters. Typing <^X> (control key and X key pressed together) displays *Delete*, ignores all previous characters on the line, and gives you a blank new line to enter what you intended.

What if you start the wrong command and it is already showing on the command line?

Using a <^C> (hitting the control and C keys together) once or twice will cancel any command and return you to the command prompt.

Using the ERASE Command

What do you do if you draw something that you don't want, or put an object in the wrong place?

You can remove it using the ERASE command, and draw what you want. When you use ERASE, the crosshair changes to a *pick box*. You move the pick box until it touches the entity that you want to remove. You select the entity by clicking on it with your pointing device's pick button. There are other ways to select entities and other ways to salvage errors without erasing. We will explore them in later chapters. For now, follow the next exercise. It will be enough to get you out of a jam if you get stuck with a screen full of lines that you don't want. Try erasing the "Welcome ..." text on your screen. You will find ERASE on the [EDIT] screen menu.

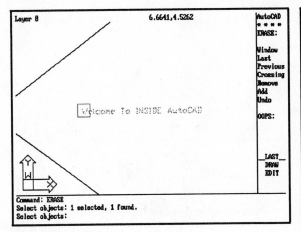

Text With Pick Box

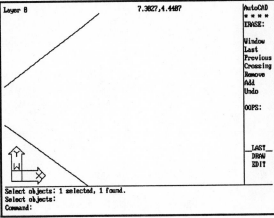

Text is Gone

Using ERASE to Erase an Entity

```
Command: ZOOM                                Use a window to zoom in on the text.
All/Center/Dynamic/Extents/Left/Previous/Window/<Scale(X)>: W
First corner:                                Pick first corner point.
Other corner:                                Pick second corner point.

Select [AutoCAD]                             Return to the root menu.
Select [EDIT]                                Displays the EDIT menu.
Select [ERASE:]                              Starts the ERASE command.
Command: ERASE                               The crosshair turns into a pick box.
Select objects:                              Pick the text.
1 selected, 1 found.
Select objects: <RETURN>                     The text is gone.
```

Using the UNDO Command

Sometimes you will discover you have executed a lot of commands and that your drawing isn't turning out quite right. Think of this as a *fork-in-the-road* problem. If you had turned left back at that command instead of right, things would have turned out OK. Well, you can use AutoCAD's UNDO command to step back one command at a time. Using UNDO can be more helpful than just erasing, because the command undoes not only entities, but zooms and screen settings that you may have changed.

Error Handling Exercise

```
Command: U                      Undoes the erased text from previous exercise.
DTEXT                           UNDO shows what command was undone.

Command: REDO                   Undoes the UNDO. The text is removed.

Command: LINE                   Try cancelling a command.
From point:                     Pick any point.
From point: *Cancel*            Type <^C> to cancel line and return to the command prompt.
Command:
```

If you get lost, what do you do?

Type **?** or HELP. AutoCAD always gives you more information.

Help!

Help is almost always available in AutoCAD. You can get a complete listing of available commands or more information about a specific command.

If you are at the command prompt, you can either type HELP or **?** to invoke AutoCAD's friendly help. Either will prompt you for what you want help with. Enter a <RETURN> for a list of all the available commands as well as point input information. Entering a command name will get you detailed information about a specific command and refer you to the AutoCAD User Reference for more detail. When HELP has shown you all it knows, it returns you to the command prompt.

You can usually type '**?** or 'HELP while you are in the middle of another command to receive help about the command. This type of help is called *transparent* help.

Try getting some help by looking at the COPY command.

```
┌─────────────────────────────────────────────────────┐
│ AutoCAD Command List  (' = transparent command)     │
│                                                     │
│ APERTURE   CHANGE    DIVIDE     EXPLODE    IGESOUT   │
│ ARC        CHPROP    DONUT      EXTEND     INSERT    │
│ AREA       CIRCLE    DOUGHNUT   FILES      ISOPLANE  │
│ ARRAY      COLOR     DRAGMODE   FILL       LAYER     │
│ ATTDEF     COPY      DTEXT      FILLET     LIMITS    │
│ ATTDISP    DBLIST    DVIEW      FILMROLL   LINE      │
│ ATTEDIT    DDATTE    DXBIN      'GRAPHSCR  LINETYPE  │
│ ATTEXT     'DDEMODES DXFIN      GRID       LIST      │
│ AXIS       'DDLMODES DXFOUT     HANDLES    LOAD      │
│ BASE       'DDRMODES EDGESURF   HATCH      LTSCALE   │
│ BLIPMODE   DDUCS     ELEV       'HELP / '? MEASURE   │
│ BLOCK      DELAY     ELLIPSE    HIDE       MENU      │
│ BREAK      DIM/DIM1  END        ID         MINSERT   │
│ CHAMFER    DIST      ERASE      IGESIN     MIRROR    │
│                                                     │
│ Press RETURN for further help.                      │
│                                                     │
│                                                     │
└─────────────────────────────────────────────────────┘
```

Help Screen

```
┌─────────────────────────────────────────────────────┐
│ The COPY command is used to duplicate one or more    │
│ existing drawing entities at another location (or    │
│ locations) without erasing the original.             │
│                                                     │
│ Format:    COPY Select objects: (select)             │
│            <Base point or displacement>/Multiple:    │
│            Second point of displacement: (if base    │
│            selected above)                           │
│                                                     │
│ You can "drag" the object into position on the       │
│ screen. To do this, designate a reference point on   │
│ the object in response to the "Base point..." prompt,│
│ and then reply "DRAG" to the "Second point:" prompt. │
│ The selected objects will follow the movements of    │
│ the screen crosshairs. Move the objects into         │
│ position and then press the pointer's "pick" button. │
│                                                     │
│ To make multiple copies, respond to the "Base point" │
│ prompt with "M". The "Base point" prompt then        │
│ reappears, followed by repeated "Second point"       │
│ prompts. When you have made all the copies you need, │
│ give a null response to the "Second point" prompt.   │
│                                                     │
│ See also:  Section 5.2 of the Reference Manual.      │
│                                                     │
│ Press RETURN to resume COPY command.                 │
└─────────────────────────────────────────────────────┘
```

Copy Help Screen

Using HELP to Get Help

Command: **HELP**   Or type ?
Command name (RETURN for list): **<RETURN>**   Text screen appears:

A HELP screen appears with an alphabetical listing of commands.

Press RETURN for further help. **<RETURN>**

Another screen of HELP appears... and another... and another.

Command: **COPY**   Start the copy command.
Select objects: '?   Type apostrophe and ? to call for transparent help.

Help screen for copy is displayed.

Resuming COPY command.
Select objects: *Cancel*   Cancel the copy command.

Hit the flip screen function key to get back to the graphics screen.

Quitting the Drawing Editor

Of course there are those occasions when you may get hopelessly muddled up in a drawing. In that case, you can make a dignified retreat by quitting your drawing. Unlike the SAVE command, if you quit your drawing using the QUIT command, AutoCAD does not update your drawing (.DWG) file. AutoCAD ends your drawing session and returns you to the Main Menu.

Follow the prompts below to clear the screen and to get out of the drawing editor. AutoCAD will diplomatically ask if you want to discard all your changes to your drawing.

Using QUIT to Quit a Drawing

```
Command: QUIT
Really want to discard all changes to drawing? Y        Returns to the Main Menu.
```

How AutoCAD's Commands and Menus Work

Where are we? Where are we going? Let's take that second look at AutoCAD's Main Menu, then get an overview of how AutoCAD's command and menu systems work.

The Main Menu

```
           A U T O C A D
Copyright (C) 1982,83,84,85,86,87,88 Autodesk, Inc.
Release 10 (10/7/88) IBM PC
Advanced Drafting Extensions 3
Serial Number:  ##-######
Current drawing:  CHAPTER1

Main Menu

  0.  Exit AutoCAD
  1.  Begin a NEW drawing
  2.  Edit an EXISTING drawing
  3.  Plot a drawing
  4.  Printer Plot a drawing

  5.  Configure AutoCAD
  6.  File Utilities
  7.  Compile shape/font description file
  8.  Convert old drawing file

Enter selection:
```

AutoCAD's Main Menu

Here's a listing of what each Main Menu selection does.

Main Menu Options

Option **0** (Exit AutoCAD) gets you back to the operating system. You will use this option every time you finish an AutoCAD session. An \IA <RETURN> starts the batch file that gets you in, option **0** gets you out.

Options **1** (Begin a NEW drawing) and **2** (Edit an EXISTING drawing) are where you create, edit, and store your drawings in AutoCAD. You will spend the majority of your AutoCAD hours inside the drawing editor. The drawing editor is the AutoCAD equivalent of your drafting board — the interactive part of the program that lets you create and modify drawings.

There are two ways to get into the drawing editor. If you are starting a new drawing file, type 1 <RETURN> in response to the Main Menu selection prompt. AutoCAD will prompt you for the name of a NEW drawing file. If you want to edit a drawing that already exists, type 2 <RETURN> and AutoCAD will prompt you for the name of the existing disk file you want to work with.

Options **3** (Plot a drawing) and **4** (Printer Plot a drawing) are where you print and plot your drawings.

Option **5** (Configure AutoCAD) steps you through AutoCAD's interactive utility to let the ACAD program know what hardware you are using. You can find more details about this option in Appendix B.

Option **6** (File utilities) lets you perform disk file maintenance operations just as if you were using the operating system. You can use the AutoCAD file utility to perform housekeeping chores on your files. If you feel more comfortable using the commands directly from the operating system prompt, there is no harm in doing so — they perform the same tasks:

```
AutoCAD File Utility Options          MS-DOS Equivalent
0. Exit File Utility Menu
1. List Drawing files                 DIR *.DWG
2. List user-specified files          DIR
3. Delete files                       DEL
4. Rename files                       REN
5. Copy file                          COPY
```

You also can access the AutoCAD file utility from within the drawing editor by typing FILES at the command prompt.

Options **7** (Compile shape/font description file) and **8** (Convert old drawing file) are special situations and will not be covered in this book. See CUSTOMIZING AutoCAD (New Riders Publishing) or the AutoCAD User Reference for details.

Let's get back into the drawing editor for an overview of AutoCAD's commands and menus. You can reload your previous drawing file from the main menu. (If you exited to the operating system, start up AutoCAD again by typing \IA.)

Loading an Existing Drawing

```
Enter selection: 2
Enter NAME of drawing (default CHAPTER1): <RETURN>
```

How AutoCAD's Menus Work

AutoCAD has more than 130 commands and numerous subcommands. Most of these commands relate to specific functions such as drawing, editing, or dimensioning. Because many of us are somewhat handicapped when it comes to typing, AutoCAD provides an ACAD.MNU file which contains six alternate ways to enter commands with menus:

- Screen Menu

- Pull-Down Menu

- Dialogue Box

- Icon Menu

- Tablet Menu

- Button Menu

You have already used the screen menu and the pull-down menus. Menus provide a convenient way to organize and group commands into screen *pages* so they can easily be selected and executed. A screen, icon or pull-down *menu page* is a listing of commands or *keys*. These groupings are for convenience only and have no effect on AutoCAD's command structure. AutoCAD doesn't care how you tell it what to do.

When you select a menu item, it changes menu pages or sends a command, or a series of commands, to AutoCAD for execution. This command execution is the same as if you had typed the commands. A *KEY* is our name for an item which activates another AutoCAD submenu. It also can include commands.

AutoCAD's standard menus give you a variety of ways to execute the same AutoCAD commands. These standard menus are used throughout the book. You should try all the menu options available to you to see which menu method you prefer. Later in the book, you will learn how to change these standard menus and create your own menu selections.

The Screen Menu

The most commonly used menu is the screen menu. You saw the screen menu on the right side of the display screen when you first entered the drawing editor. Feel free to experiment with the menu as you read this. If you get lost, just select [AutoCAD] at the top of any screen menu. This returns you to the root menu.

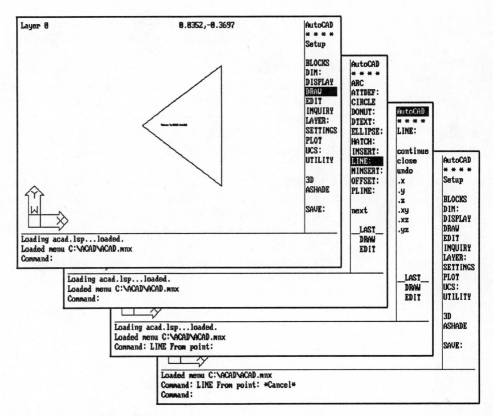

Screen Menu Paging

Recall that you make your screen menu selections by highlighting the item with your pointing device and pressing the pick button or by using the keyboard.

Keyboard Access to the Screen Menu

You can access the screen menu from the keyboard. The keyboard offers two methods of screen menu selection. The first method is to hit the <MENU CURSOR> key (usually <INS>) to highlight a menu selection. Use the <CURSOR UP> and <CURSOR DOWN> keys to move the highlighted bar to the menu item you want and press the <MENU CURSOR> again to execute the selection.

The second method is to start typing characters of the menu selection at the command prompt. As you type, the menu label beginning with the characters you type becomes highlighted. Most selections are highlighted by typing one or two characters, then you press the <MENU CURSOR> or <INS> key to execute the selection.

As you move through the screen menus, you will notice some selections are followed by colons, [DIM:], [LAYER:], and [SAVE:]. These selections will not only call a new page menu but will also start the command. Any selection which automatically starts a command has a colon after the menu label. Many commands require subcommands in order to complete their chores. These subcommands are listed in lower case letters. As you flip through menu pages, remember you can always return to the root menu by selecting AutoCAD at the top of the menu page. If you get really lost, look at the screen menu map in Appendix C.

At the bottom of most menu pages are shortcut key selections that let you return to your [LAST] menu page or to the [DRAW] and [EDIT] menu pages. Some menu pages offer more selections than can fit on one page. The [next] and [previous] selections access all the selections available.

Finally, each menu page has [* * * *] below the [AutoCAD] selection which is visible in every menu page. This selection presents you with a menu page of options called osnaps. These are aids for drawing objects. We will cover the OSNAP options later in chapter 3 when we look at Drawing Basics.

Screen Menu Conventions

Here are the screen menu conventions:

- Selections without a colon following them are keys to other menu pages.

- Selections followed by a colon begin the AutoCAD command and usually present a selection of subcommands.

- Subcommands are always listed in lower case letters.

- Selecting [AutoCAD] at the top of the menu page will always return you to the root menu.

- [* * * *] selection will present a selection of osnap options.

- The bottoms of most menu pages have a selection of shortcut keys: [__LAST__], [DRAW], and [EDIT].

- Some menu pages present you with [next] and [previous] selections in order to display all the menu item selections available.

➥ *NOTE: The root menu has an item called [ASHADE]. This selection initiates a set of AutoLISP tools and a menu page that creates a film roll for use in Autodesk's AutoShade program. AutoShade is a separate program that takes a three dimensional AutoCAD drawing and converts it to a realistic picture. The book covers AutoShade in the chapters on 3D.*

Pull-Down Menus

AutoCAD's pull-down menus are similar to screen menus. You have already tested your video hardware for pull-down support. If you have pull-down menus, you will see a menu bar when you move your pointing device to the top of the graphic screen. (If you do not have a pointing device, you cannot access the pull-down menus.) The menu bar presents a list of titles indicating the selections available in each pull-down menu. You can have up to ten pull-down menus available, but the standard AutoCAD menu bar uses only eight. All eight choices are shown in the Menu Bar illustration.

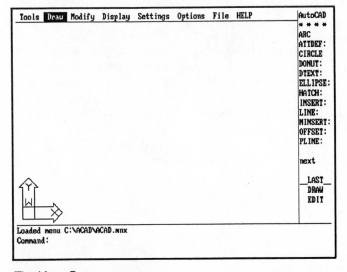

The Menu Bar

Many pull-down menu selections open a screen menu page to help with subcommand selection. Some AutoCAD pull-down menus present dialogue boxes for commands with multiple settings, and groups of related commands. Pull-down menus offer quicker menu selections than screen menus since you don't have to flip through multiple menu pages. The complete set of pull-down menus is shown in the illustration on the facing page at the beginning of the chapter.

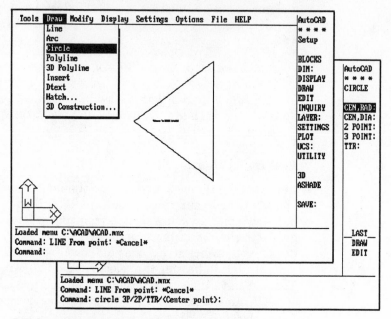

Pull-Down Menu Calling a Screen Menu

Dialogue Boxes

AutoCAD's dialogue boxes offer a unique and convenient way to view and execute certain AutoCAD settings. Like pull-down menus, dialogue boxes require AUI video support. Although dialogue boxes are actually brought up by commands, such as DDEMODES, you usually access them through a menu selection. When a dialogue box pops up on the screen, it shows a list of settings and their current values. You change these settings by highlighting the value and pressing the pick button on your pointer. You can either turn a check mark on or off, or type a new value.

Although dialogue boxes duplicate the functions of existing commands, they provide clearer and more convenient control over complex commands or groups of commands. The following illustration shows the dialogue box for creating a drawing entity.

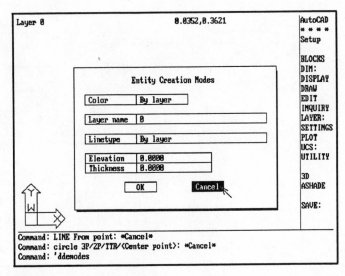

Entity Creation Dialogue Box

The Icon Menu

If your hardware supports pull-down menus, it also supports a third type of screen menu called an Icon Menu. An icon menu displays menu selections as graphic images on the display screen. AutoCAD uses slide files to construct these icon menus, displaying four, nine or sixteen images at one time. After displaying an icon menu, you select a menu item by highlighting the small square to the left of the image and pressing the pick button on your pointing device. AutoCAD executes the corresponding selection like any other menu selection. Icon menus can page through other icon menus the same way screen menus page through other menu pages. AutoCAD has a number of preset icon menus for various commands such as hatch patterns and text styles.

Menus are a powerful tool within AutoCAD, giving you flexibility in command entry. With a little practice, you will soon find your preferences. Many users prefer to use a tablet menu.

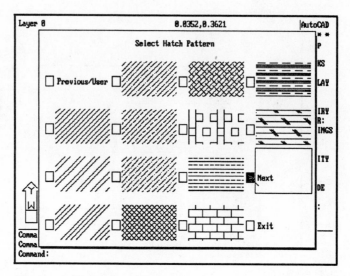

The Hatch Pattern Icon Menu

The Tablet Menu

AutoCAD comes with a standard tablet menu that performs the same functions as the screen menu. The complete tablet menu is shown in the accompanying illustration. The tablet menu offers a few advantages over the other menu options. Tablet menu selections are always available without flipping through menu pages. Many selections from the tablet menu call the appropriate screen menu pages to help you in your subcommand selection. The tablet menu also includes graphic images to help you identify the selection.

➡ *NOTE: Bringing up AutoCAD's standard tablet menu requires running through a small set of configuration steps. See Appendix C to help you configure the AutoCAD standard tablet menu.*

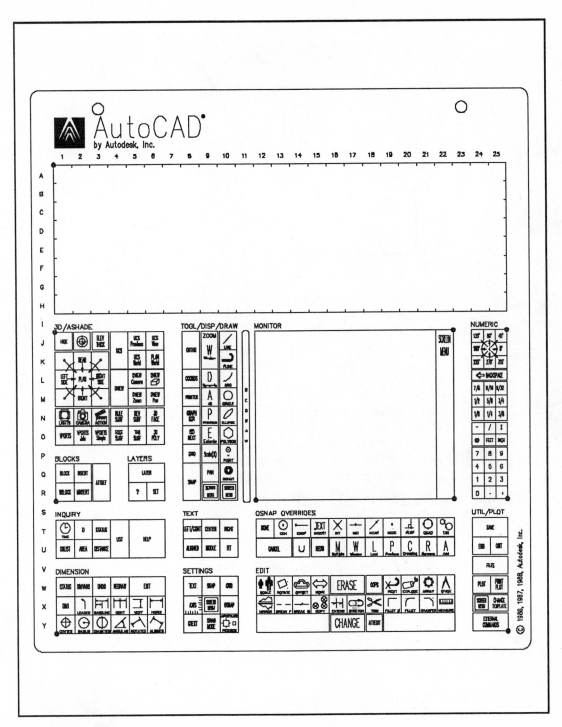

AutoCAD Tablet Menu

The Buttons Menu

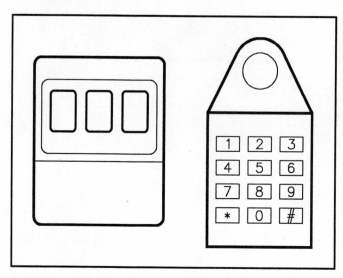

Mouse and Tablet Cursor

We all use some type of pointing device with AutoCAD, usually a tablet cursor or a mouse. AutoCAD reserves one button on the cursor or mouse for picking points and selecting screen and tablet menu items. This is the button that tells AutoCAD to pick a point or select an object where the pointing device is positioned on the screen. A mouse usually has two or three buttons, and a tablet cursor can have up to sixteen buttons. The position of the pick button varies with the device. You can assign the remaining buttons to execute menu selections by creating a button menu. For details on creating button menus, see CUSTOMIZING AutoCAD (New Riders Publishing).

One More Utility — Ending Your Work

You have already seen that AutoCAD provides a quick way out of the drawing editor through QUIT. Quitting is fast, but does not save anything. The illustration called Menu Options shows the menu options that you can use to end a drawing by executing the END command.

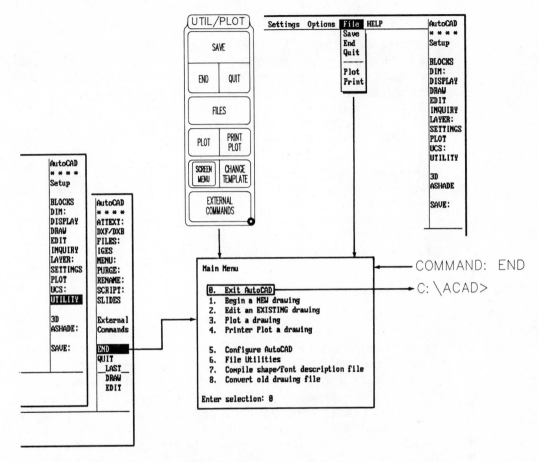

Summary of the Menu Options to END a Drawing

Save your work now using the END command. Remember ending makes a backup file from your previous file, stores the up-to-date copy, and exits the drawing editor. The END command assumes the current drawing file name.

Using END to Save a Drawing

Command: **END**   You've completed your first AutoCAD session.

Exit AutoCAD with a 0 from the Main Menu.

Drawing File Naming Conventions

As you work in AutoCAD, it helps to think ahead about how you are going to name and organize your drawing files. If you already have a naming convention, try adapting it to AutoCAD. While you can have up to 31 characters in your drawing names with some operating systems, MS-DOS is still limited to eight characters. Try to anticipate how you are going to sort your files in MS-DOS. PROJ01 and PROJ02 sort in order with PROJ??, but PROJ1 sorts after PROJ02!

As you invest time in your drawings, they become more valuable and you need to save them using AutoCAD's SAVE function. Try to use SAVE to record your work-in-progress. Adopt a temporary naming convention that lets you save as you go, PTEMP01, PTEMP02, etc. Get into the habit of using SAVE often. Your work isn't secure until it is saved to file on your hard disk (and copied to a backup disk or tape).

Summing Up

You've had a chance to set up AutoCAD and play around with the drawing editor by entering a few commands. Surprise! It does not bite, and it does not laugh when you make mistakes. AutoCAD is cooperative. It only takes action when you tell it to do something. AutoCAD lets you know that it's waiting for your input with the command prompt or other prompts on the prompt line. Help is always available to you if you type HELP or **?** at the command prompt, or if you type 'HELP or '**?** when you are in commands. If you get stuck drawing, you can always undo a command, erase your drawing, or quit the drawing and start over.

Now that you know your way in and out of AutoCAD, you can move on to learning how to organize AutoCAD's drawing environment.

CHAPTER 2

Setting Up
PREPARING AN ELECTRONIC DRAWING SHEET

Preparing a new drawing in AutoCAD is much like preparing to draw on a drafting board. Before you ever draw the first line you have to organize and make decisions on how you want the drawing to look. You need to determine your units and sheet size. Once you set your sheet size, you gather your drawing tools together and begin the drawing.

Organizing Your Drawing Setups

While organizing an electronic drawing is similar to organizing a manual drawing, there are differences. You have to adjust your way of thinking about scale, layers, and drawing entities. Before you prepare an electronic drawing sheet, take a moment to become familiar with the *thinking* behind scale, layers and entities.

How Electronic Scale Works

Inside AutoCAD, drawing elements are stored in real world units. AutoCAD can track your drawing data in meters, millimeters, feet, inches, fractions, decimals, or just about any unit system that you want.

How do you work out your scale? First, you establish your unit system. Then, you determine a *scale factor* to establish AutoCAD settings to draw at actual size (full scale) that will produce a plot at the size you want. You set your *electronic sheet* so that you can draw at *full scale*. When drawing on a drafting board you often need to reduce the image to fit a specific sheet size or scale. The text, symbols and line widths are always the same regardless of sheet size or scale. In AutoCAD this process is reversed, you draw the image at actual size and you adjust the text, symbols and line widths proportionally.

Scale is the hardest thing to get used to in electronic drawing. You draw in *full scale* all the time on a small video screen. A bolt which is two inches looks two feet when it's blown up on the screen, but it's really two inches no matter how you show it, or plot it. To help you get comfortable with *electronic scale*, we will take you through some setups with different units and scales.

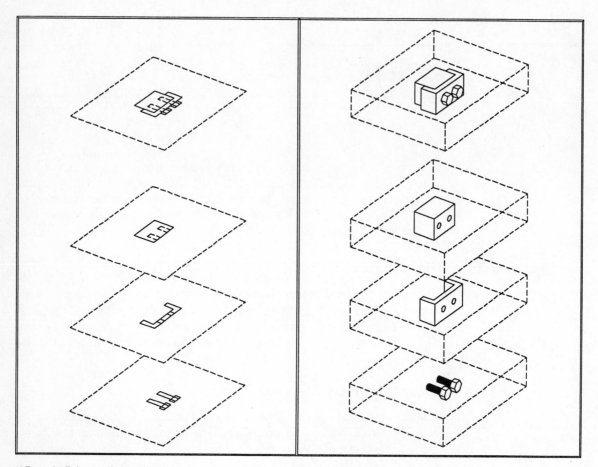

2D and 3D Layer Concepts

How Electronic Layers Work

When you are manually tied to a sheet of paper, it is easy to neglect the fact that almost everything you design and draw is separated into layers. Printed circuit boards have layers. Buildings are layered by floors. Even schematic diagrams have information layers for annotations. In AutoCAD, unlimited electronic layers give you more flexibility and control in organizing your drawing.

Think of AutoCAD's electronic layers in 2D as sheets of clear acetate overlaid one over the other. When you are working in 2D, you are looking down through the sheets. You can see your whole drawing built from the superimposed sheets. You can pull a single sheet out to examine or work on one layer, or you can work with all the layers at once.

In 3D, layers become more of an organizational concept. Any layer may contain any group of objects, which may be superimposed in space to coexist with other groups on other layers. Think of 3D layers as containing *chunks* of objects. You can look at all layer groups together, or you can look at any combination, by specifying the layers.

Each layer has a color and linetype *associated* with it. When you set up your AutoCAD layers, you need to determine what parts of your drawing you are going to place on each layer, and what color and linetype you are going to use on each layer. Of course, if things get complicated, you can make more layers!

Electronic Entities and Properties

When you use AutoCAD's drawing tools to draw on one of these electronic layers, you create a *drawing entity*. A line segment is an entity, circles and text are entities. Besides its geometric location, each entity has an associated color and a linetype. AutoCAD calls these associations *properties*.

Part of the getting-organized process is to determine what colors and linetypes you are going to use when you construct your drawing entities. The simplest (and in many cases the best) organization is to use your layers to control your entities. If you are going to draw a red gizmo with dashed lines, then you draw it on the red-dashed-line layer. Many of these decisions are determined by drawing standards that you may have already established. (If you are not using color in your plotted and printed output, you still need to consider how you are going to use it to control line weight in your plots.) If things get muddled and your layer organization begins to break down, AutoCAD gives you a set of tools to change the properties of any entity.

The Benefits of Tailoring AutoCAD's Settings

While you can use AutoCAD fresh out of the box, spending some time setting up AutoCAD to fit your own needs will save you hours and make AutoCAD more fun to use. While it takes a little more time to set up to get the right units, scale, linetype, and text, you can save these settings from drawing to drawing. Setting up is like the old adage: "Once right is better than twice wrong." You will save many hours of work later on.

Setting Up Tools

You will find the setup tools that you will use on the [Setup] and [SETTINGS] screen menus, or the pull-down [Settings] menu.

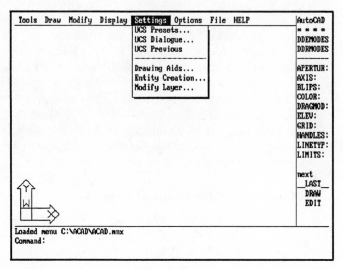

Settings Screen and Pull-Down Menus

Setting Up a Drawing

To get started, you need to start AutoCAD and create a new drawing with the main menu.

Creating the Chapter 2 Drawing

Load AutoCAD with your IA.BAT batch file to get the Main Menu.

```
Enter selection: 1
Enter NAME of drawing: CHAPTER2
```

When you begin a new drawing starting with the main menu, you can draw immediately because AutoCAD has already made several assumptions about units, scale, and linetype. These settings are called *defaults*.

ACAD.DWG — AutoCAD's Prototype Drawing

AutoCAD sets up many default command settings by reading a prototype drawing stored on your hard disk. AutoCAD's standard prototype drawing is called ACAD.DWG and it comes with your AutoCAD software which you duplicated in your IA-ACAD directory in chapter 1.

The standard ACAD.DWG assumes you want to enter drawing entities on layer 0. Layer 0 has white, continuous lines (or black on white in some systems). ACAD.DWG also assumes a default unit system that uses decimal units with 12 units in the X direction and 9 units in the Y direction.

When you set up your drawing, you are actually modifying settings that were passed by AutoCAD from the prototype drawing into your new drawing. As you work through your drawing setups, AutoCAD lets you know what defaults are set by showing you default values in brackets <default example> in the command prompt. You can accept a <default prompt> that AutoCAD offers by just hitting a <RETURN>. You also can change the prototype drawing that AutoCAD reads. You will see how to change a prototype drawing and tailor it for your own use in the book's last part (Part Three) on making AutoCAD more productive.

Determining a Scale Factor and Drawing Limits

We'll start tailoring AutoCAD settings by taking a case study approach to scale. First, we will take you through setting up an architectural drawing. Second, we will work through an engineering drawing. Last, we will show you how to set up layers, using a simple one-to-one scale drawing.

Scale Factor Settings

When you determine a drawing scale factor, it affects several AutoCAD settings. These include:

■ Sheet size (limits).

■ Line width.

■ Text height.

■ Symbol size.

■ Linetype scale.

Sheet size is the most important. AutoCAD calls the sheet size settings *limits*. You set your sheet size *limits* during your initial drawing setup. You set the other drawing effects settings later.

Determining a Scale Factor for Sheet Size

Take an architectural calculation as your first case. You have a floor plan that is 75 feet x 40 feet, and you want a drawing scale at 1/4 inch = 12 inches. What is your scale factor, and what size electronic sheet are you going to use? The size of your electronic sheet is set by the *limits* that you choose. These are the X,Y values of the upper right corner of your electronic sheet.

The *scale factor* is the multiple of your drawing scale. If you already have selected a drawing scale, it is easy to determine the scale factor. For example, if you have selected a drawing scale of 3/8" = 1'-0", your drawing scale factor is 32.

```
3/8:12/1 so 1:96/3 for a scale factor of 32.
```

In the current case you are working at 1/4" = 1'-0" so your scale factor is 48.

```
1/4:12/1 is 1:48/1 for a scale factor of 48.
```

You determine your electronic drawing limits by running some test calculations on possible plotting sheet sizes. You set your limits by multiplying the sheet size that you select by your scale factor. Here are a sample set of calculations.

```
Size of floor plan                            75' x 40'
Scale                                         1/4" = 12".
Determine scale factor                        48
Test a 17" x 11" sheet
    17" x 48 = 816" or 68' and 11" x 48 = 528" or 44'
    A 17" x 11" sheet equals 68' x 44' at 1/4" to 12" scale.
    This sheet size is too small.
Test a 36" x 24" sheet
    36" x 48 = 1728" or 144' and 24" x 48 = 1152" or 96'
    A 36" x 24" sheet equals 144' x 96' at 1/4" to 12" scale.
    This should work with plenty of room for dimensions,
notes and a border.
```

In this example, you determine your limits by the number of units that will fit across a standard sheet (D size, 36" x 24", for 144' across 36" at 1/4" = 12").

How do you get these settings into AutoCAD? You can set them explicitly, or you can use a series of AutoCAD setup routines that will automatically set your units and limits by stepping you through the limits calculations for your sheet size and scale.

You get to these automatic routines by selecting [Setup] from the screen menu. Try stepping through the setup sequences provided in the following exercise. When you are done, look at the limits to see if they match your calculations.

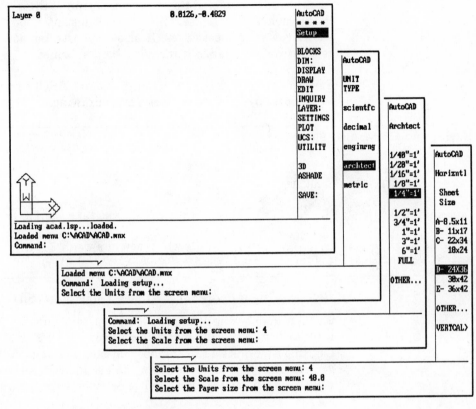

Architectural Setup Menu Sequence

Using the [Setup] Menu to Prepare an Architectural 1/4" Scale Drawing

Select **[Setup]**	Displays unit type screen menu.
Select **[archtect]**	Displays architectural scales menu.
Select **[1/4"=1']**	Displays sheet sizes menu.
Select **[D- 24X36]**	Completes the setup.
Select **[SETTINGS]**	Displays settings menu.
Select **[LIMITS:]**	Sees if limits are set correctly.

Command: LIMITS
ON/OFF/<Lower left corner> <0'-0",0'-0">: **<RETURN>**
Upper right corner <144'-0",96'-0">: **<RETURN>**   They match your calculations.

As AutoCAD completed this automatic setup, it drew a reference border that matched your limits. This border is not intended to be plotted, but shows you your sheet edges. It also demonstrates how a custom setup routine can automatically include a border format.

Save this setup by saving to a new file name, ARCH, then move on to the second case by quitting to start a fresh drawing.

Saving an Architectural Sheet

```
Command: SAVE
File name <CHAPTER2>: ARCH

Command: QUIT                          Quit the drawing and start over fresh.

Enter selection: 1                     Begin a new drawing.
Enter NAME of drawing (default CHAPTER2): <RETURN>
```

Determining a Scale for a Known Object and Sheet Size

Take an engineering example as a second case for setting limits. Say you want to draw a 24-inch manhole cover on an 8 1/2" x 11" plotting sheet. OK, this isn't quite a full engineering case, but you get the idea. How do you compute your scale factor and determine your electronic limits? You need to do a little trial and error to determine the drawing scale factor.

Here are the sample calculations.

```
Size of manhole cover                              24" diameter.
Sheet size                                         11" x 8 1/2".
Test 1/2" = 1" scale  (1 unit = 2 units) scale factor of 2.
   11" x 2 = 22" and 8 1/2" x 2 = 16"      22" x 16"
limits.
   This scale factor is too small.
Test 1/4" = 1" scale  (1 unit = 4 units) scale factor of 4.
   11" x 4 = 44" and 8 1/2" x 4 = 34"      44" x 34"
limits.
   This should work.
```

To fit your manhole cover on the sheet, you need a scale factor of 4 and your limits are 44" x 34".

Setting Units, Limits, and Other Drawing Effects

You have used AutoCAD's automatic setup menu. Try stepping through a setup sequence for the engineering sheet using AutoCAD's individual settings commands for units and limits.

Setting Units

Generally, you set your units following your normal drawing practice. If you normally use architectural units, then use AutoCAD's architectural units. Select your unit system by using the UNITS command. Setting units does two things for your drawing. First, it sets up the input format for entering distances and angles from the keyboard. Second, it sets up the output format AutoCAD will use when displaying and dimensioning distances and angles.

Select [SETTINGS] from the screen menu, select [next], then select [UNITS:]. Your screen will flip to text mode. AutoCAD will prompt you for units information. For the current case, select Engineering units. Engineering units are feet and inches with the inch as the smallest whole unit. Engineering fractions are decimals.

Next, AutoCAD will prompt you through setting angle measurements and angle display, giving examples for each system setting. The default screen setting for zero angle is usually to the right or *east*. The default setting for angle measurement is *counterclockwise*. Use both default settings in your setup.

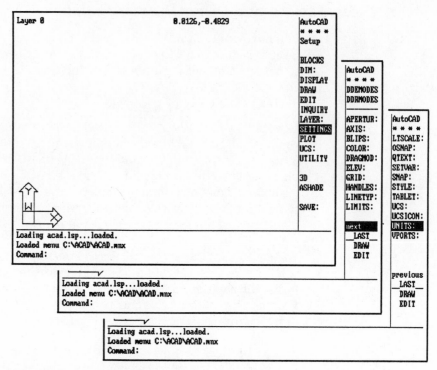

Menu Selection Sequence for Units

Using UNITS to Set Engineering Units for a Drawing

Select **[SETTINGS] [next] [UNITS:]**   AutoCAD flips to text screen.
System of units: (Examples)

1. Scientific   1.55+01
2. Decimal   15.50
3. Engineering   1'-3.50"
4. Architectural   1'-3 1/2"
5. Fractional Units   15 1/2

Enter choice, 1 to 5 <2>: **3**
Number of digits to right of decimal point (0 to 8) <4>: **2**

System of angle measure: (Examples)

1. Decimal degrees   45.0000
2. Degrees/minutes/seconds   45d0'0"
3. Grads   50.0000g
4. Radians   0.7854r
5. Surveyor's units   N 45d0'00" E

```
Enter choice, 1 to 5 <1>: <RETURN>
Number of fractional places for display of angles (0 to 8) <0>: 2
Direction for angle 0.00:
East      3 o'clock  =  0.00
North    12 o'clock  =  90.00
West      9 o'clock  =  180.00
South     6 o'clock  =  270.00
Enter direction for angle 0.00 <0.00>: <RETURN>

Do you want angles measured clockwise? <N>: <RETURN>

Command: <F1>                    Flip screen to get back to the graphics.
```

Usually you set units only once for a set of drawings. You can change units in midstream should the need arise. We know of one firm that makes mechanical components for an international clientele. The AutoCAD designer in the firm makes presentation drawings for European customers in decimal units, and then rescales and replots the shop drawings in engineering units for the U.S. based factory employees.

Here is a list of your unit system options.

UNIT Options

SCIENTIFIC — Uses scientific decimal notation and a generic whole unit as the smallest drawing unit.

DECIMAL — Uses simple decimal notation and a generic whole unit as the smallest drawing unit.

ENGINEERING — Uses feet and inches with the inch as the smallest whole unit. Fractions are decimals.

ARCHITECTURAL — Uses feet and inches with the inches as the smallest whole unit. Fractions are true fractions.

FRACTIONAL — Uses whole numbers and fractions. Fractional units represent inches by default, but the inch (") marks are not shown.

You can use fractional units for units other than inches by adjusting the dimensioning and plot setups.

Setting Limits

Set your drawing file sheet boundaries with the LIMITS command. You don't actually limit how big your drawing can be. Think of AutoCAD's limits as an *electronic fence* which AutoCAD can use to warn you if you draw outside your boundary. This boundary makes an ideal way to represent a sheet size. It gives you a frame of reference for zooming or plotting. If you run off your electronic sheet, you can expand the sheet by resetting the limits.

Select [SETTINGS] on the screen menu. When you select [LIMITS:], AutoCAD shows you <0'-0.00",0'-0.00"> as a default prompt. The lower leftmost corner is home base. It is telling you that the lower leftmost boundary of your drawing file is X=0,Y=0. You can enter a new lower left corner by typing new X,Y coordinates. To accept the default, hit <RETURN>. Then, enter your estimated limits of 44",34" for the upper right corner.

Setting Limits for an Engineering Drawing Sheet

```
Select [SETTINGS] [LIMITS:]
ON/OFF/<Lower left corner ><0'-0.00",0'-0.00">: <RETURN>
Upper right corner <1'-0.00",0'-9.00">: 44",34"
```

➡ *NOTE: The exercise sequence shows " (double quotes) for entry of inches. You do not need to type the " marks. AutoCAD will assume inches unless you type ' for feet. In fact, you do not need to type the inches if they are zero. 2'0" or 2'0 or 2' or 24" are all equivalent in engineering units.*

How can you see your limits? One easy way to see your drawing limits is to set a drawing grid, then extend your screen image using the ZOOM command. Select [GRID:] from the [SETTINGS] menu, getting your grid values from the exercise sequence below. After you set your grid, select [ZOOM:] from the [DISPLAY] menu, getting your zoom value from the exercise sequence.

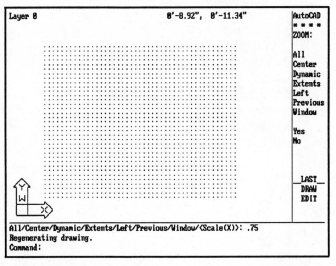

Limits Shown by Grid

Seeing Your Limits with a Grid

Select **[SETTINGS] [GRID:]**   Set grid to 1".
Command: GRID
Grid spacing(X) or ON/OFF/Snap/Aspect <0'-0.00">: **1**

Select **[DISPLAY] [ZOOM:]**   Zoom all.
Command: 'ZOOM
All/Center/Dynamic/Extents/Left/Previous/Window/<Scale(X)>: **A**
Regenerating drawing.

Select **[DISPLAY] [ZOOM:]**   Zoom .75 times.
Command: 'ZOOM
All/Center/Dynamic/Extents/Left/Previous/Window/<Scale(X)>: **.75**
Regenerating drawing.

Your screen should look like the Limits Shown by Grid illustration. The area covered by the grid is your defined limits, representing an 11" x 8 1/2" plotting sheet. If you drew outside the grid, you would actually be drawing off the *electronic paper*.

➡ *TIP: Don't set square limits (for example 100 x 100), unless you have an explicit reason. Your screen and most engineering sheets have a 4X:3Y ratio. You might as well take advantage of the full drawing area.*

➡ *TIP: When you set drawing limits to match your plotting sheet size, remember that plotters hold a portion of the sheet's edge during plotting. Make sure your drawing allows enough room at the borders for your plotter. An inch and a quarter is a safe margin for most plotters.*

Try drawing a 24-inch diameter circle to represent the manhole cover and see if it fits within your limits. Select [CIRCLE:] from the [DRAW] menu, and pick a center point near the center of your screen. Draw the circle using a 12-inch radius.

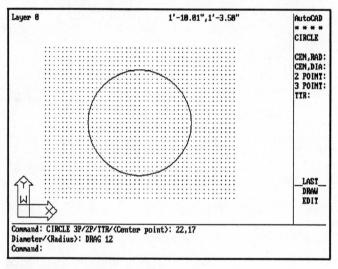

Manhole Drawn With a Circle

Testing Your Drawing Scale Factor

Select **[DRAW] [CIRCLE]**	Displays the circle menu.
Select **[CEN,RAD:]**	Draw a circle at 22,17 with a 12" radius.

```
Command: CIRCLE 3P/2P/TTR/<Center point>: 22,17
Diameter/<Radius>: DRAG 12
```

Your manhole should fit neatly on your drawing, as shown in the Manhole Drawn With a Circle illustration.

Setting Other Drawing Effects

Settings such as text height and symbol scale are a matter of drawing standards. If you have an established standard, you should adjust AutoCAD's settings to your normal standard. Just as you had to increase your electronic sheet size to accommodate the manhole cover, you adjust your text, symbols, and line width proportionally to your sheet size. Once you have a drawing scale factor, this is a simple procedure. You determine the size you want to see text, symbols, etc. when the drawing is plotted, then multiply that size by the scale factor.

Here are some examples for the manhole cover.

```
Plotted Size          x   Scale Factor   =   Electronic Size
Text height 0.2"      x   4              =   0.8"
1/2" Bubble           x   4              =   2"
1/16" Line width      x   4              =   1/4"
```

AutoCAD also provides a variety of linetypes, such as hidden and dashed linetypes. You adjust linetypes by the scale factor, controlling linetype scale with the LTSCALE command. Like text and symbols, LTSCALE should be set for the plotted appearance, not how it looks on the screen. Linetype scale is largely a matter of personal preference, but setting it to your scale factor is a good starting point.

Try applying some of the examples to the manhole drawing. Since we haven't covered symbols yet, create the bubble with a circle and the number 1. You will find [LINETYPE] and [LTSCALE] on the [SETTINGS] menu. Use the following illustration of Manhole With Text, Symbol, and a Linetype as a guide for the exercise.

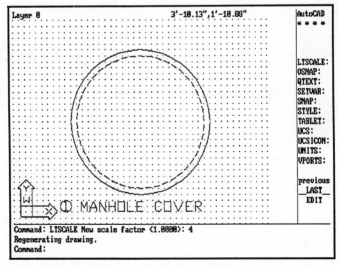

Manhole With Text, Symbol and a Linetype

Setting Text Height, Symbol Size, and Linetype Scale

```
Command: ZOOM
All/Center/Dynamic/Extents/Left/Previous/Window/<Scale(X)>: A
Regenerating drawing.

Command: DTEXT
Start point or Align/Center/Fit/Middle/Right/Style: M
Middle point: 22,3                      Pick point.
Height <0'-0.20">: 1.6
Rotation angle <0.00>: <RETURN>
Text: MANHOLE COVER
```

Move text cursor by picking point 9,3 with your pointer.

```
Text: 1
Text: <RETURN>
```

Command: **CIRCLE**   Draw a circle at 9,3 with a 1" radius.

```
Select [SETTINGS] [LINETYP:]             Select linetype from settings menu.
Command: LINETYPE                        Set linetype to hidden.
?/Create/Load/Set: S
New entity linetype (or ?) <BYLAYER>: HIDDEN
?/Create/Load/Set: <RETURN>
```

Command: **CIRCLE**   Draw a circle at 22,17 with an 11" radius.

The circle should appear with a hidden linetype. Adjust the linetype scale to get a proportional appearance.

```
Select [SETTINGS] [LTSCALE:]             Select Ltscale from settings menu.
Command: LTSCALE New scale factor <1.0000>: 4        Set line scale to scale factor.
```

As you can see from the exercise, it is relatively simple to adjust text height and linetype scale by using a drawing scale factor. The important thing to remember is that this drawing scale factor is *external* to AutoCAD. It is not an internal AutoCAD setting. You apply a scale factor to get your initial drawing limits, then you apply it to individual commands, like DTEXT, to adjust your text proportionally by setting your text height.

➡ *TIP: An [LTSCALE] range of 0.3 to 0.5 times your drawing scale factor yields the best plotted output.*

Getting a Quick Printer Plot

If you have a printer configured for plotting in AutoCAD, you can do the following exercise to get a hard copy of the manhole drawing. Don't be too concerned about the sequence of the exercise. We will explain plotting in detail in the plotting chapter. The plotted drawing will show how all the calculations that you made provide a plotted drawing at 1/4-inch scale.

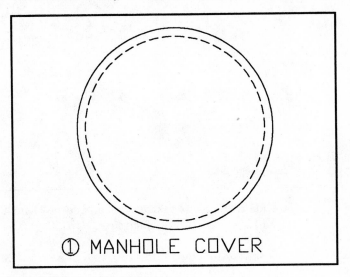

Plotted Manhole Drawing

Making a Quick Printer Plot

```
Command: PRPLOT
What to plot -- Display, Extents, Limits, View, or Window <D>: L

Plot will NOT be written to a selected file
Sizes are in Inches
Plot origin is at (0.00,0.00)
Plotting area is 7.99 wide by 10.29 high (MAX size)
Plot is NOT rotated 90 degrees
Hidden lines will not be removed
Scale is 1=1

Do you want to change anything? <N> Y
Write the plot to a file? <N> <RETURN>
Size units (Inches or Millimeters) <I>: <RETURN>
Plot origin in Inches <0.00,0.00>: <RETURN>

Standard values for plotting size
```

```
Size     Width    Height
MAX      7.99     10.29

Enter the Size or Width,Height (in Inches) <MAX>:
Rotate 2D plots 90 degrees clockwise? <N> Y
Remove hidden lines? <N> <RETURN>

Specify scale by entering:
Plotted Inches=Drawing Units or Fit or ? <1=1>: 1=4
Effective plotting area:  7.99 wide by 8.50 high
Position paper in printer.
Press RETURN to continue: <RETURN>

Processing vector: nn        AutoCAD cycles through whole drawing.

                             Plotting takes place.

Printer plot complete.
Press RETURN to continue: <RETURN>
```

You should be able to take a scale and see a 24-inch circle at 1/4 scale and .2-inch-high text with a .25 circle.

Save your setups by saving to a new file name, MECH. Then, quit the drawing to start a new drawing.

Saving Your Engineering Setup

```
Command: SAVE
File name <CHAPTER2>: MECH

Command: QUIT            To start a fresh drawing.
```

Stopping Point

If you are pressed for time, this is a good stopping point. You can exit AutoCAD, and resume by starting a new drawing. The next section shows how to set up and control layers using a simple 1:1 (full scale) engineering drawing.

Setting Up Layers, Colors and Linetypes

Set up a new drawing using Engineering units. Set your limits for an 8 1/2" x 11" sheet with a drawing scale factor of one (full scale). You will use this setup to create a set of layers and to set colors and linetypes.

Setup Drawing for Layers

```
Enter selection: 1          Begin a new drawing.
Enter NAME of drawing (default CHAPTER2): <RETURN>

Command: UNITS             Set units to engineering with 2 decimal points of accuracy.
                           2 fractional places for angles. Default all other settings.

Command: LIMITS            Set your limits for 8.5" x 11".
ON/OFF/<Lower left corner ><0'-0.00",0'-0.00">: <RETURN>
Upper right corner <1'-0.00",0'-9.00">: 11,8.5

Command: ZOOM              Zoom all.
```

Layers

Layers help you control your drawing. If your drawing becomes too dense or complicated, you can turn selected layers off. If you neglected to anticipate drawing certain parts, you can create new layers for those parts.

We have compared layers to acetate sheets. In effect, you build your drawing by building a *family* of sheets. Each sheet has a name, color and linetype. You can work on any layer, but you can only work on one layer at a time. The active layer is called the *current* layer. When you draw an entity, it is attached to the current layer.

Your current layer is always displayed on the status line. Since you have started a new drawing, your current layer is the default layer 0 from the prototype drawing.

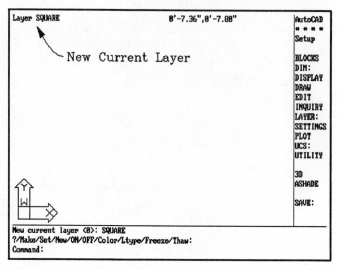

The Status Line Shows the Current Layer

You set up and control your layers using the LAYER command. You use LAYER to switch from layer to layer by setting the current layer, and to turn layer visibility on and off. You also can control your layers using the [Modify Layer...] dialogue box found on the pull-down [Settings] menu.

You can see the properties associated with your layers by having AutoCAD display the layer status. Type the LAYER command or page back through the screen menu to the root menu and select [LAYER]. Then respond to the prompt by typing a question mark. The <*> in the default layer name prompt is a *wildcard*, meaning "Tell me about every layer."

Displaying Layer Information

```
Command: LAYER              Type or pick from screen menu.
?/Make/Set/New/On/Off/Color/Ltype/Freeze/Thaw: ?
Layer name(s) for listing <*>: <RETURN>
```

AutoCAD responds by flipping to the text screen and displays:

```
Layer name     State    Color        Linetype
----------     ------   -----------  --------------
0              On       7 (white)    CONTINUOUS

Current layer: 0
?/Make/Set/New/On/Off/Color/Ltype/Freeze/Thaw:
```

As you might have anticipated, you have AutoCAD's default drawing properties: layer 0 with white, continuous lines. Layer 0 is fine for playing around, and it has some special properties that you will see later, but for most drawing work you will want to set up your own layers.

9-28

Layering Conventions

Well, how do you go about setting up layers? Like setting drawing effects, setting up layers is a matter of standard practice and style. The most common sense approach to layers is to use them to separate different *types* of objects in your drawing. For example, put drawing components on one layer and their dimensions on another. Try to anticipate the number of *types* that you want to separate. Here is an example set:

Objects on Layer	Layer Names
Components	OBJ01
Dimensions	DIM01
Symbols & Annotations	ANN01
Text	TXT01
Title Sheets	REF01

You can create an unlimited number of layers, but for most applications ten to twenty layers is more than enough. When you name your layers, it helps to apply DOS-type naming conventions and use *wildcards* to organize them. Layer names can be up to 31 characters long. (However, the status line will only show the first eight characters of the layer name.) You can use letters, digits, and the dollar ($), hyphen (-) and underscore (_) characters. AutoCAD converts all layer names to upper case.

Using the LAYER Command

Think about what having separate layers means operationally. You need a way to let AutoCAD know which layer you want to draw on. You control the LAYER command by telling AutoCAD which layer property you want to use, like setting a layer current or turning a layer on to make it visible. Then AutoCAD prompts you for the name(s) of the layers you want this property applied to. You can only operate on one property at a time, but you can apply this property to several layers in one pass with wildcards or by naming several layers.

The LAYER command sets the following properties:

LAYER Properties

On — Makes the layer visible.

Off — Makes the layer invisible.

Color — Defines a single default color so that anything drawn directly on that layer will take on this color unless you specifically override the default layer color.

Ltype — Defines a single default linetype. Lines (and other drawing elements) drawn on a layer will take on the linetype unless you specifically override it.

Freeze — Makes the layer invisible and all entities are ignored during a regeneration, increasing the performance of AutoCAD searches and screen displays.

Thaw — Removes the freeze option.

The LAYER command also offers these options:

LAYER Options

? — Lists all the layers in your current drawing including status and default properties.

Make — Creates a new layer and sets it current.

Set — Makes the layer current or active for drawing.

New — Creates a new layer.

Creating New Layers

As you can see from the list, AutoCAD provides two options for creating layers. The Make option creates one layer and automatically sets it as the current layer. If you want to make more than one layer, use the New option.

Right now there is only one layer in the drawing file. Put in several more, set them up and then save them for future use. The target layers are shown in the following Layer Configuration Table.

Layer name	State	Color	Linetype
0	On	7 (white)	CONTINUOUS
TRIANGLE	On	1 (red)	CONTINUOUS
SQUARE	On	2 (yellow)	CONTINUOUS
CIRCLE	On	3 (green)	DASHED
TEXT	On	4 (cyan)	CONTINUOUS
PARAGRAM	On	5 (blue)	HIDDEN
Current layer: 0			

Layer Configuration Table

The following exercise shows how to create the new layers.

Creating New Layers

```
?/Make/Set/New/On/Off/Color/Ltype/Freeze/Thaw: N          Type NEW or just N.
New layer name(s): TRIANGLE,SQUARE,CIRCLE,TEXT,PARAGRAM
?/Make/Set/New/On/Off/Color/Ltype/Freeze/Thaw: ?          Displays layer information.
Layer name(s) for listing <*>: <RETURN>                   See the list.
```

Your text screen should look like the Default Properties for New Layers illustration.

```
Layer name      State     Color        Linetype
----------      -----     -----        --------
0               On        7 (white)    CONTINUOUS
TRIANGLE        On        7 (white)    CONTINUOUS
SQUARE          On        7 (white)    CONTINUOUS
CIRCLE          On        7 (white)    CONTINUOUS

TEXT            On        7 (white)    CONTINUOUS
PARAGRAM        On        7 (white)    CONTINUOUS

Current layer: 0

?/Make/Set/New/ON/OFF/Color/Ltype/Freeze/Thaw:
```

Default Properties for New Layers

➡ *NOTE: When you create a new layer, typing an N is enough to initiate the New subcommand. In fact, the upper case character is enough for any of the subcommands except On/Off, where you need at least an ON or an OF.*

➡ *TIP: Try thinking ahead about your layer assignments. You can (and should) type as many names as you want on the New layer name(s): line. Separate layer names with commas; a <RETURN> ends your input. If you input a space, AutoCAD thinks you are trying to end the input line just like a <RETURN>.*

Take a look at the layers information. Since you didn't invoke any settings for properties for the new layers other than a new name, AutoCAD automatically sets the properties with layer 0 defaults. Each layer is color 7 (white) with a continuous linetype. Change the layers to get the desired configuration. Start with color.

Setting Layer Color

A layer has only one color, but several layers can have the same color. Color is assigned to layers by names or numbers (up to 256 different colors — limited by your hardware, not AutoCAD). AutoCAD uses the following naming and numbering conventions for seven standard colors:

```
         AutoCAD's Seven Standard Colors
         1 - Red              5 - Blue
         2 - Yellow           6 - Magenta
         3 - Green            7 - White
         4 - Cyan
```

When you assign a color to a layer, you can use a color number or a color name for the standard seven colors. Each color setting requires that you give a separate execution of the color subcommand. You can make several layers the same color by giving more than one layer name on the prompt line. AutoCAD will prompt you with the current layer name as a <default>.

Setting Layer Color

```
?/Make/Set/New/On/Off/Color/Ltype/Freeze/Thaw: C
Color: 1
Layer name(s) for color 1 (red) <0>: TRIANGLE
?/Make/Set/New/On/Off/Color/Ltype/Freeze/Thaw: C
Color: YELLOW
Layer name(s) for color 2 (yellow) <0>: SQUARE
?/Make/Set/New/On/Off/Color/Ltype/Freeze/Thaw: C
Color: 3
Layer name(s) for color 3 (green) <0>: CIRCLE
?/Make/Set/New/On/Off/Color/Ltype/Freeze/Thaw: C
Color: CYAN
Layer name(s) for color 4 (cyan) <0>: TEXT
?/Make/Set/New/On/Off/Color/Ltype/Freeze/Thaw: C
Color: 5
Layer name(s) for color 5 (blue) <0>: PARAGRAM
?/Make/Set/New/On/Off/Color/Ltype/Freeze/Thaw:
```

Setting Layer Linetype

The LTYPE subcommand sets your layer linetype. Use the **?** option to see the linetypes that have been set up within the drawing file. <CONTINUOUS> is always offered as a default. When you specify a non-continuous linetype, AutoCAD first looks in its linetype library (the ACAD.LIN file) to see if it has a linetype definition that matches your request. If it finds your linetype, everything is OK. If not, you have to select another.

```
DASHED      — — — — — — — — — — — —
HIDDEN      ————————————————————————
CENTER      ___ _ ___ _ ___ _ ___ _ ___
PHANTOM     ___ __ __ ___ __ __ ___ __ __
DOT         ..................................................
DASHDOT     ___ . ___ . ___ . ___ . ___ .
BORDER      __ __ _ __ __ _ __ __ _ __ __ _
DIVIDE      __ . . __ . . __ . . __ . . __
CONTINUOUS  _____
```

Standard AutoCAD Linetypes

Set the layer linetypes shown previously in the Layer Configuration Table.

Setting Layer Linetype

```
?/Make/Set/New/On/Off/Color/Ltype/Freeze/Thaw: L
Linetype (or ?) <CONTINUOUS>: DASHED
Layer name(s) for linetype DASHED <0>: CIRCLE
?/Make/Set/New/On/Off/Color/Ltype/Freeze/Thaw: L
Linetype (or ?) <CONTINUOUS>: HIDDEN
Layer name(s) for linetype DASHED <0>: PARAGRAM
?/Make/Set/New/On/Off/Color/Ltype/Freeze/Thaw:
```

You now have a complete set of layers. You can modify their other properties by indicating the layers that you want to modify. Look at modifying layer visibility.

Setting Layer Visibility (On and Off)

Try turning a layer on and off. Both ON and OFF work the same way. The exception is trying to turn the current layer off. AutoCAD will ask if you really want to do such a foolish thing. Remember you have to see what you are drawing!

Turn the TEXT layer OFF, then ON again.

Setting Layer Visibility

```
?/Make/Set/New/On/Off/Color/Ltype/Freeze/Thaw: OFF
Layer name(s) to turn Off: TEXT
?/Make/Set/New/On/Off/Color/Ltype/Freeze/Thaw: <RETURN>

Command: LAYER
?/Make/Set/New/On/Off/Color/Ltype/Freeze/Thaw: ON
Layer name(s) to turn On: TEXT
?/Make/Set/New/On/Off/Color/Ltype/Freeze/Thaw:
```

➥ *TIP: Remember you can use a wildcard * or ? to turn collections of layer names on or off. However, you can't use wildcards with the Make, Set, or New options.*

Setting the Current Layer

You can only draw on the current layer. To tell AutoCAD which layer you want as the current layer, use the Set subcommand. The Set subcommand will show the current layer name as the default in the prompt. If you want to leave the current layer alone, just hit a <RETURN>. Setting a new current layer automatically makes the *old* current layer inactive.

Make the SQUARE layer the current layer.

Setting the Current Layer

```
?/Make/Set/New/On/Off/Color/Ltype/Freeze/Thaw: S
New current layer: SQUARE
?/Make/Set/New/On/Off/Color/Ltype/Freeze/Thaw: ?          Display Layer information.
?/Make/Set/New/On/Off/Color/Ltype/Freeze/Thaw: <RETURN>
```

Look at the layer name on the screen to see if the settings have been made correctly.

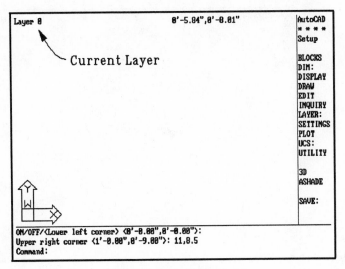

The Status Line Shows the New Current Layer

You can change the layer setting at any time while you are in the drawing. If you alter the properties of layers on the screen (like linetype or color), AutoCAD will regenerate the screen image to reflect these changes when you exit the layer command.

Testing Your Drawing Layers

During the last few minutes you have created a working drawing file with real units, limits, and a foundation of layers. It would be nice to know that all these layers really work. Set your CIRCLE layer current, and draw a circle to see how entities adopt the layer settings.

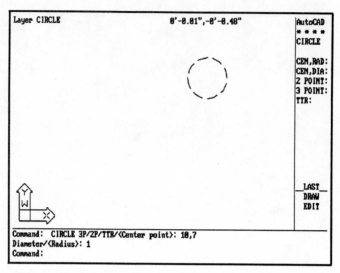

```
Layer CIRCLE                        0'-0.01",-0'-0.48"      AutoCAD
                                                            * * * *
                                                            CIRCLE

                                                            CEN,RAD:
                                                            CEN,DIA:
                                                            2 POINT:
                                                            3 POINT:
                                                            TTR:




                                                            LAST
                                                            DRAW
                                                            EDIT

Command:  CIRCLE 3P/2P/TTR/<Center point>: 10,7
Diameter/<Radius>: 1
Command:
```

Circle on Circle Layer

Testing Your Drawing Layers

```
Command: LAYER                  Set layer CIRCLE current.
?/Make/Set/New/On/Off/Color/Ltype/Freeze/Thaw: S
New current layer <SQUARE>: CIRCLE
?/Make/Set/New/On/Off/Color/Ltype/Freeze/Thaw: <RETURN>

Command: CIRCLE
3P/2P/TTR/<Center point>:  Pick a point centered in the upper right quarter of the screen.
Diameter/<Radius>:         Drag a radius of about 1 inch.
```

You should have a green dashed circle. Save your drawing by naming it to a new file called WORK. You will use the drawing as the setup drawing in the next chapter on drawing basics.

Saving the WORK Drawing

```
Command: SAVE
File name <CHAPTER2>: WORK
```

Now that you have put WORK safely to rest, you can use the existing drawing file to see how you can modify layers with a dialogue box.

Using the Modify Layer Dialogue Box

If your display supports pull-down menus, you can use the layer dialogue box to do all the layer setups that we have just done. You can create new layers, rename layers, and do all the other options the LAYER command offers. Using the dialogue box offers the advantage that you can see all the layer information and the settings as they are made. This is a convenient way to set layer data.

If your workstation supports pull-down menus, check your settings with the Layer Dialogue Box, DDLMODES. You can get the dialogue box by selecting [Modify layer...] from the pull-down [Settings] menu. Or you can access DDLMODES as a transparent command by typing 'DDLMODES. Use the following exercise to practice changing color and linetype for the TRIANGLE layer. Then, cancel the changes to keep the basic drawing setup.

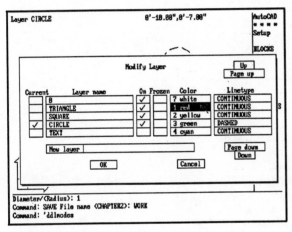

Dialogue Box Showing Current Settings

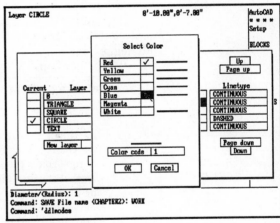

Color Dialogue Box

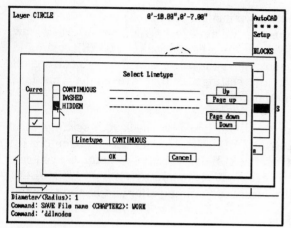

Linetype Dialogue Box

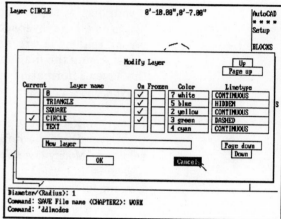

Dialogue Box Showing New Settings

Select [Modify Layer...] from the pull-down [Settings] menu to get the dialogue box.

Using the DDLMODES Layer Dialogue Box

Pull down **[Settings]**	
Select **[Modify Layers...]**	The dialogue box is displayed.
Select **[1 red]**	The color dialogue box opens.
Select **[Blue]**	Change color to blue.
Select **[OK]**	Close the color dialogue box.
Select **[CONTINUOUS]**	The linetype dialogue box opens.
Select **[HIDDEN]**	Change linetype to hidden.
Select **[OK]**	Close the linetype dialogue box.
	The dialogue box shows the changes to the TRIANGLE layer.
Select **[Cancel]**	Cancel the layer changes.

If you can modify a layer so easily, it will come as no surprise that you can modify the color and linetype properties associated with any drawing entity.

Color and Linetype Drawing Effects

You can control what color or linetype an entity will get by drawing it on an appropriate layer. You also can set color and linetype explicitly by *overriding* a layer and setting an entity's color and linetype with separate commands.

How an Entity Gets its Color

The COLOR command is in charge of making sure an entity gets the color you want. When a new entity is created, AutoCAD checks the current setting of COLOR, finds out what COLOR says, and then assigns the color setting to the new entity.

You can set color to any valid color name or number. (Remember you can have 1 to 255 colors, but only the first seven have names.) In addition, you can set color BYLAYER. This is the default condition, which is why AutoCAD initially assigns colors by layer. When color is set to BYLAYER, AutoCAD doesn't give new entities a specific color. Instead, it gives new entities the default color property of whatever layer the entity is on. Colors set specifically by the COLOR command instead of BYLAYER are referred to as *explicit* colors.

➡ *NOTE: There is also BYBLOCK color. We will cover BYBLOCK assignments when we get to the blocks chapter.*

Take a look at the color setting right now. Change the color to red using the COLOR command. Select [COLOR:] from the [SETTINGS] menu. You will see that the default color is set to BYLAYER. After you change the color, draw another circle to see how the explicit color settings override the layer setting.

Using the COLOR Command

```
Select [SETTINGS] [COLOR:]              Select color from the settings menu.
Command: COLOR
New entity color <BYLAYER>: RED

Command: CIRCLE                         Draw a circle below the first circle.
```

Your drawing should show a red dashed circle in addition to your green dashed circle.

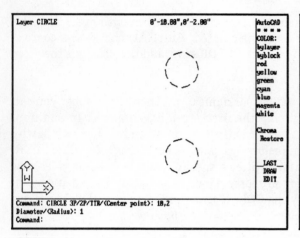

Second Circle is Color Red

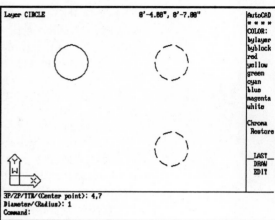

Third Circle is Red and Continuous

How an Entity Gets its Linetype

After this colorful discussion, you might have guessed that linetype default and entity settings have a similar control. Take a look at the LINETYPE command. The Set option lets you set an explicit linetype that overrides the layers setting for all entities that you create after you change the setting. Linetype can also be set to BYLAYER to use the layers default.

LINETYPE Options

? — Displays a listing of all the linetypes currently defined in the drawing.

Create — Allows user to create a linetype.

Load — Loads linetype from a user specified file. The ACAD.LIN file has nine linetype definitions.

Set — Establishes a linetype to be used on all the following entities that are created until set to another type.

Using the LINETYPE Command

```
Command: LINETYPE
?/Create/Load/Set: S
New entity linetype <BYLAYER>: CONTINUOUS

Command: CIRCLE            Draw another circle.
```

You should have three circles. The last one is a red continuous line.

➡ *NOTE: Explicit color and linetype settings stay in effect even when you change current layers. We do not recommend mixing explicit color and linetype settings with layer settings.*

➡ *NOTE: You can create your own linetypes using the LINETYPE command. See CUSTOMIZING AutoCAD (New Riders Publishing) on how to customize linetypes.*

Changing Entity Properties

Both the COLOR and LINETYPE commands change the properties for new entities drawn *after* you change the color and linetype settings. However, you can change the properties of existing entities by using the CHPROP (CHange PROPerties) command. When you select objects to change, AutoCAD prompts you for the appropriate properties to modify. You can change the following properties with CHPROP:

- Color

- Layer

- Linetype

- Thickness

Thickness is a property associated with 3D. You will learn about thickness in the 3D chapter.

Try changing a circle using CHPROP.

Using CHPROP to Change Layers and Color

```
Command: CHPROP                            Select or type.
Select objects:                            Select the green (first) circle.
1 selected, 1 found.
Select objects: <RETURN>
Change what properties (Color/LAyer/LType/Thickness)? LA
New layer <CIRCLE>: SQUARE                 Circle has layer SQUARE properties.
Change what properties (Color/LAyer/LType/Thickness)? C
New color <BYLAYER>: 1                      Circle turns red.
Change what properties (Color/LAyer/LType/Thickness)? <RETURN>
```

Obviously, you cannot always determine how an entity will be created by looking at the layer name on the status line. You need a way to check.

Using the STATUS Command

If you are working on a drawing and you override your color and linetype layer conventions, you can check your drawing properties with the STATUS command. The status command is a flip screen function. Try it now; type STATUS in response to the command prompt.

```
3 entities in CHAPTER2
Limits are       X:   0'-0.00"   0'-11.00"  (Off)
                 Y:   0'-0.00"   0'-8.50"
Drawing uses     X:   0'-3.00"   0'-11.00"
                 Y:   0'-1.00"   0'-8.00"
Display shows    X:  -0'-0.00"   1'-2.44"
                 Y:  -0'-0.50"   0'-9.50"
Insertion base is X:  0'-0.00"   Y:  0'-0.00"   Z:  0'-0.00"
Snap resolution is X: 0'-1.00"   Y:  0'-1.00"
Grid spacing is  X:   0'-0.00"   Y:  0'-0.00"

Current layer:    CIRCLE
Current color:    1 (red)
Current linetype: CONTINUOUS
Current elevation: 0'-0.00"  thickness:  0'-0.00"
Axis off  Fill on  Grid off  Ortho off  Qtext off  Snap off Tablet off
Object snap modes: None
Free RAM: 14250 bytes       Free disk: 3635200 bytes
I/O page space:  17K bytes  Extended I/O page space: 768K bytes

Command:
```

Status Screen Display

Using STATUS to Get a Drawing Status Report

Command: **STATUS**   Flips to text mode and shows a screen full of information.

Hit the FLIP SCREEN key to get back to graphics.

The status report shows your drawing limits at the top of the screen. About halfway down, it lists the current layer, current color, and current linetype. The status text screen carries additional information about your settings. These settings will become more important to you as you read through the book. For now, just feel comfortable knowing that you can look at the information and that AutoCAD is keeping track of all that stuff for you.

The Entity Modes Dialogue Box

There are other properties associated with entities; AutoCAD provides the DDEMODES dialogue box to set five entity properties. We will use this dialogue box later in the book when we begin working with blocks and drawing symbols. If you are curious about this box and want to look at it, you can select [Entity Creation...]from the [Settings] pull-down menu.

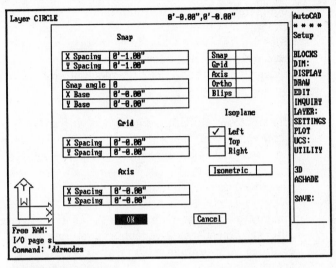

Modes Dialogue Box

If entity properties, like *quarks*, seem a bit confusing, don't worry. They *are* confusing. We recommend that you start with simple controls. Use layers with the default BYLAYER setting to control your drawing color and linetype. Wait until you start editing complex drawings, then use COLOR, LINETYPE, and CHPROP if you need more flexibility.

If you want to save this drawing setup for future practice, end the drawing.

Saving the Drawing

Command: **END**   You've completed your second AutoCAD session.

Exit AutoCAD with a 0 from the Main Menu.

Summing Up

What you've seen so far is typical of AutoCAD setup commands. AutoCAD begins new drawings by reading many default settings from a prototype drawing named ACAD.DWG. Setting up a drawing file requires setting units, limits, and a working set of layers as a good foundation for future drawing. AutoCAD tries to save you time by offering <defaults> and wildcard options (* and ?) in place of elaborate keyboard entry during your setup.

The key to establishing a good drawing setup is getting a drawing scale factor to set your drawing limits for your electronic sheet size. You also can use AutoCAD's automatic setup routines to select your final sheet size and to set your limits. You can scale text, linetype, and symbols using your drawing scale factor.

The key to establishing a good set of layers is to create your layers to draw different object types. Adopt a layer naming convention that lets you organize your names with wildcards. The current layer is the active drawing layer. The status line always shows the current layer. Default drawing properties for color and linetype are set BYLAYER. You can explicitly override BYLAYER color and linetype with the COLOR and LINETYPE commands. You also can change properties associated with existing entities by using the CHPROP command. If you are uncertain about what properties are current in your drawing, use STATUS to help you keep track.

Setting up is well and good, but it is time to move on to some drawing basics.

CHAPTER 3

Drawing Fundamentals
HOW TO MAKE ACCURATE DRAWINGS

Given a straight edge and a rule, a draftsperson can locate a point on a drawing sheet with some degree of accuracy and use that point as a location for drawing more objects. In this chapter you will learn about AutoCAD's electronic tools that replace the draftsperson's manual tools for locating points and maintaining drawing accuracy.

Some benefits from getting to know AutoCAD's electronic tools immediately stand out: no eraser shavings, always having the right scale ruler, never having to borrow your 30-60 triangle back from your neighbor. Other benefits, however, are not as apparent: 100 percent accurate straight edges and triangles, mathematically defined curves, and electronically flexible graph paper to trace over as a guide.

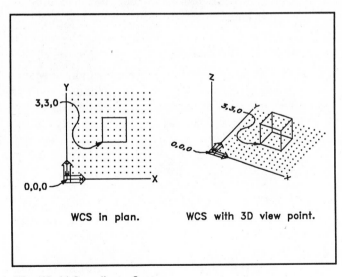

The World Coordinate System

Electronic Drawing Aids

Obviously, the first step in getting accurate drawings is to locate your drawing points. How do you locate your drawing points accurately? You have three ways to control your electronic drawing input. First, you can type your coordinates in. You know some coordinate values to start a drawing. However, you rarely have such complete information that you can type in all your drawing points. Besides, this would be grueling, tedious work and prone to typing errors.

Most of the time you *pick* your drawing points. AutoCAD provides two alternatives to let you control the movement of your pointer and to help you select your pick points. These are *grid* and *snap* functions, and a second set of functions called *object snap* functions. AutoCAD shortens the name of these object snap functions to OSNAP.

How Grid and Snap Work

If you pick your drawing points without some form of control, AutoCAD rounds the pixel location of your pointer and you cannot be sure that you have accurately located the point that you want. Grid acts as a visible template on your screen showing you where a set of points are located. Snap acts as an *invisible* template that limits the points that you can select with your pointer. You control your pointer by *coordinating* your grid and snap. If you set them equal, then you can only select grid points. If you set your snap points to half your grid, then you can only select grid points or points halfway in between grid points. You control the accuracy of your point selection with snap.

Object Snap Points

As you place objects and your drawing becomes more complex, not all drawing points are going to be grid and snap points. Points on arcs and circles are obvious examples. AutoCAD offers OSNAP as a means of controlling pick points on objects. It helps to think of drawing objects as having *attachment* points. Lines have endpoints, circles have center points and tangent points. When you draw you often *attach* lines to endpoints or tangent points.

AutoCAD's OSNAPs are *geometric filters* that let you select your drawing attachment points. For example, if you want to draw to an intersection of two lines, you toggle the object snap *intersection*, and pick the intersection. You will get the intersection of your two lines, not something close to the intersection, but *the* intersection! While it takes a little time to get used to setting osnaps, it is the best way to maintain geometrically accurate drawings.

Tools for Making Accurate Drawings

You will find your grid, snap and osnaps on the [SETTINGS] screen menu, and the [Settings] and [Tools] pull-down menus. You set these drawing aids functions by toggling settings and setting values.

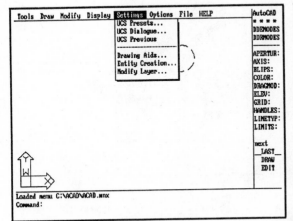

Settings Screen and Pull-Down Menus

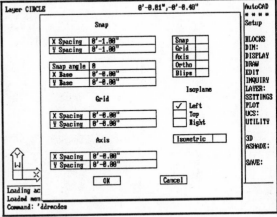

DDRMODES Settings Dialogue Box

Setting Up for Using Drawing Aids

We are going to use the WORK drawing as the drawing for learning how to use AutoCAD's drawing aids. If you are using the IA DISK, copy your CHAP-03.DWG to WORK.DWG. To get started you need to get back into the AutoCAD drawing editor. Call up the drawing file you set up in the last chapter and stored on disk as WORK. As you make your way through the drawing exercises, you can select the screen menu and pull-down menu items, or type the commands as you need them.

Reloading the WORK Drawing File

 Copy the CHAP-03.DWG to WORK.DWG.

 You need the WORK drawing from chapter 2.

Load AutoCAD with your IA.BAT batch file to get the Main Menu.

```
Enter selection: 2          Edit an EXISTING drawing.
Enter name of drawing: WORK
```

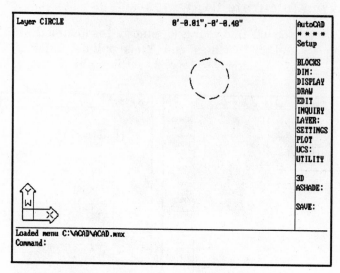

WORK Drawing

Your screen should look like the WORK Drawing illustration, showing a single circle in the upper right of your graphics drawing area. Verify that your drawing settings are the same as those shown in the WORK Drawing Settings table. Your current layer is CIRCLE.

UNITS	Engineering, 2 decimal points, 2 fractional places for angles, defaults all other settings.		
LIMITS	0,0 to 11,8.5		

Layer name	State	Color	Linetype
0	On	7 (white)	CONTINUOUS
TRIANGLE	On	1 (red)	CONTINUOUS
SQUARE	On	2 (yellow)	CONTINUOUS
CIRCLE	Current	3 (green)	DASHED
TEXT	Off	4 (cyan)	CONTINUOUS
PARAGRAM	On	5 (blue)	HIDDEN

WORK Drawing Settings

Let's start by drawing a few points.

Controlling Drawing Points

Using the POINT command is the simplest way to input a drawing point. Select [POINT:] from the [DRAW] screen menu, and type in the coordinate values shown below. To see the *actual* point, you need to redraw your screen after you enter the point.

Using the POINT Command

Select: [DRAW] [next] [POINT:]   Now let's make the point.
Point: **3,6.25**   Place the point in the upper left 1/4
of your screen.

A small blip appears at that point.

Command: **REDRAW**   Leaves only a dot.

First, a mark appeared on your screen at the coordinate values you input. This mark was actually larger than the point that you placed. It was the construction marker (blip) for the point. Your redraw cleared the construction marker and left a small white dot on the screen. This is a true drawing point you can osnap to. You can be certain of its location because you input the absolute coordinate values.

How Accurate Are Pick Points?

When you pick a point on the screen with your pointer, it is much more difficult to get accurate points. To help track your pointer, turn on your COORDS by hitting the <F6> key or type <^D>. Take a look at the status line and see what the digital readout of your coordinates says. Move your pointer around; the status line should display the current X,Y location of your crosshairs.

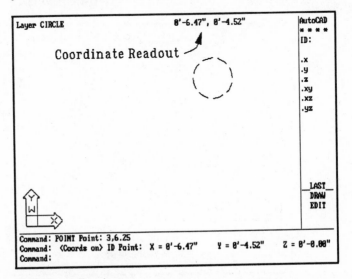

Coordinate Readout

Now, try the following exercise to see how accurately you can pick your drawing points. To test your pick point, use an inquiry display command called ID. Select [ID:] from the [INQUIRY] screen menu or type it in. Then, try to pick the point given in the exercise.

Using ID to Test Pick Points

Make sure your Coords are toggled on with <^D> or <F6>.

```
Select: [INQUIRY] [ID:]      Use coordinate readout to position your crosshairs.
Point:                        Try picking a point at exactly X = 0'-6.50", Y = 0'-4.50".
X = 0'-6.47"     Y = 0'-4.53"     Z = 0'-0.00"
                              Your pick points may be different.
```

The ID command shows the X, Y and Z position of your pick point. Try a few more points. You will quickly find it's nearly impossible to pick the point you want accurately. Without some form of controlling your picks, a drawing can quickly turn into a sea of inaccurate points.

Grid and Axis Displays

The first step to getting accurate points is to set up templates that help you see points on the screen. One way to help keep track of accurate screen locations is to use an AXIS ruler. An axis acts like a manual ruler, giving you tick marks across the bottom and right side of your screen.

To select [AXIS:] go back to the root menu. Select [SETTINGS] again. Then select [AXIS] and turn it on by setting it to .25.

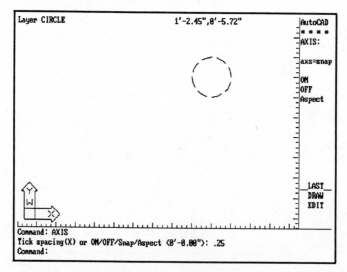

AutoCAD's AXIS

Using AXIS to Create Ruler Lines

Select: **[SETTINGS] [AXIS:]**
Tick spacing(X) or ON/OFF/Snap/Aspect <0'-0.00">: **.25**

Notice that the lower and right boundaries of the screen now have a built-in ruler with tick marks at .25-inch spacing and a longer tick at every inch. You can use the ruling lines to help you locate your crosshairs movement. To control point input, you coordinate your axis spacing. Although axis helps keep track of where you are, it does not affect point entry itself. If you set your snap spacing equal to your axis spacing (0.25), then each 0.25-inch increment in the X and Y directions on your screen is a snappable point.

You can turn the axis off. Since it doesn't get in the way, many users leave it on so it will be there when they need it.

Turning Axis Lines Off

Select: **[SETTINGS] [AXIS:]**
Tick spacing(X) or ON/OFF/Snap/Aspect <0'-0.25">: **Off**

An axis provides reference marks only at the screen edges. Using a grid is the easiest and most popular way to locate drawing points.

Setting Up a Grid

A grid is a frame of reference, a series of construction points that appear on the screen but are not part of the drawing file itself. Set up a grid with the GRID command. It also is located on the [SETTINGS] screen menu. Set up a 1-inch grid, then prove to yourself that grid points are not active points by moving your crosshairs around and trying the "how accurate I can be" exercise again.

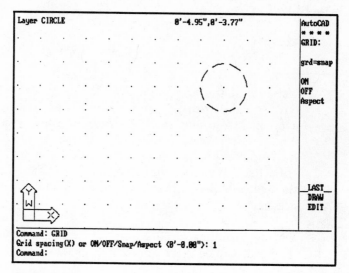

My First Grid

Using GRID to Set Up a Grid

Select: **[SETTINGS] [GRID:]**
Grid spacing(X) or ON/OFF/Snap/Aspect <0'-0.00">: **1**

Your screen should look like the My First Grid illustration. When you move your pointer around, you will find that its movement is unimpeded.

➡ *TIP: Turning a grid on not only helps you visualize distances on the screen, it also shows your drawing limits.*

You are not limited to creating rectangular grids. You have several options in setting up your grid. You can, for example, change your grid spacing to give different X,Y aspect ratios. The illustration below shows a grid with a 2X:1Y aspect ratio. When you set your grid spacing, avoid setting dense grids. A too-dense grid gets in the way. Here are your options for setting the GRID command.

GRID Options

On — Turns grid on.

Off — Turns grid off.

Snap — Changes the grid spacing to match the current snap setting.

Aspect — Allows different spacing for the vertical and horizontal rules.

spacing (X) — A value followed by an X creates a grid that is a multiple of the current snap setting.

➡ *NOTE: A <^G> (Control-G) or <F7> acts as an On and Off toggle for the grid.*

➡ *TIP: A dense grid takes longer to redraw. If your grid takes too long to redraw, try a coarsely spaced grid coordinated with a finely spaced axis.*

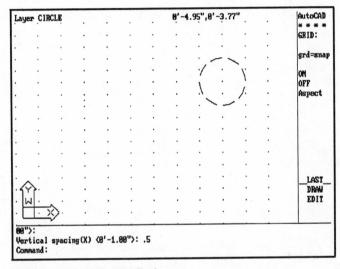

Grid with 2X:1Y Aspect Ratio

A grid provides a good set of reference points, but you still can't *pick* the point you want accurately. This is about to change. This may be the last time you'll see freely moving crosshairs. What you need to whip the pointer into shape is *snap*.

Setting Snap Points

SNAP sets up the smallest increment AutoCAD will recognize when you move the pointer around. When you set SNAP on and set a spacing value, you will notice that your screen cursor has a jerky motion. Try thinking of snap as setting your basic drawing increment. When you set your snap spacing values, all drawing pick points are multiples of your snap values.

It is good practice to set your snap at some fraction of your grid spacing. Try setting your snap at 0.5-inch, or half your grid spacing. To get to [SNAP:] from the grid screen menu, select [LAST] (to get back to the [SETTINGS] menu), then select [SNAP].

Using SNAP to Set Snap Points

Select: **[SETTINGS] [next] [SNAP:]**
Snap spacing or ON/OFF/Aspect/Rotate/Style <0'-1.00">: **.5**

The only thing that should change on your screen is the status line. It should now say "Snap," indicating that snap is on. The digital readout should be rounded to half inches. Try moving the pointer around. The crosshairs jump to the next snap increment.

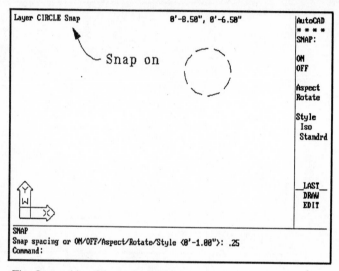

The Status Line Shows Snap On

➡ *NOTE: Snap has a toggle <^B> or <F9>. You'll find this toggle helpful when you are trying to get to a point that is not snappable. Use <^B> in the middle of other commands when you want to turn snap off (or on).*

Using Snap Points to Draw Objects

Once you set your snap, you can draw accurately as long as what you want to draw is on a snap point. The status line will show the correct crosshairs position as it rounds the X,Y values up to 0.5 inches. Draw a 2-inch x 2-inch square with the lower left corner at 0'-7.50",0'-1.00". Use the coords readout to help you pick the points given in the exercise below.

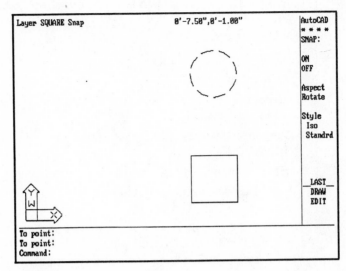

A Square Drawn With SNAP

Using SNAP to Draw a Square

Command: **LAYER**	Set Layer SQUARE current.

Command: **LINE**
Toggle Coords <F6> or <^D> once or twice to show crosshairs position as X,Y.

From point:	Pick absolute point 7.50,1.00".
To point:	Pick absolute point 9.50,1.00".
To point:	Pick absolute point 9.50,3.00".
To point:	Pick absolute point 7.50,3.00".
To point:	Pick absolute point 7.50,1.00".
To point: **<RETURN>**	End Line command.

When you are done, your screen should look like the illustration, A Square Drawn With Snap.

As you work with grid and snap, you will find that you need to adjust your grid and snap settings as you zoom to work with greater drawing details. If you start with a snap at 1 unit and a grid at 5 units on a whole drawing, you may need to reset your snap to 0.25 units and your grid to 1 unit when you zoom to work on a portion of the drawing. You can coordinate your snap and grid spacing to suit your needs. Make it a practice to set your grid and snap and leave them on most of the time. If you don't pick your drawing points with snap (or osnap) on, you won't get accurate drawings.

You have several options in setting your snap spacing. Here is the list:

SNAP Options

On — Turns snap on.

Off — Turns snap off.

Rotate — Changes the angle of the snap. Also changes the GRID and AXIS appearance.

Aspect — Allows a different increment spacing for the vertical and horizontal snap.

Style — Provides a standard or isometric snap.

spacing — A value indicating the snap setting.

Note that Style provides a standard snap and an isometric snap. You can use isometric snaps to control isometric drawing planes. We will show you how isometric snaps work later in this chapter.

➡ *TIP: You can use snap Rotate to set your drawing's Base Point to something other than 0,0 even if you leave the angle at 0 degrees.*

Using Ortho Mode as a Special Snap

When you are drawing horizontal and vertical lines, you can place an additional constraint on your pointer movements by setting a special *ortho* mode on. Ortho stands for *orthogonal*, and limits your pointer movement to right angles from the last point. This means that any lines you enter with the pointer when ortho is on will be aligned with the snap grid axes. In effect, you can only draw right angles.

Ortho is easy to use and handy any time your are faced with drawing sets of horizontal and vertical lines. Try turning ortho on and drawing another square around the square you just drew. To turn ortho on, type the ORTHO command, or use either <^O> or <F8> as toggles. After you draw the square, erase it and toggle ortho off. You will use this drawing later on to try out osnaps.

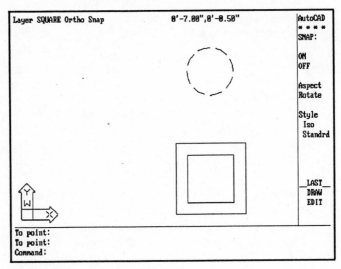

A Square Drawn With ORTHO

Using ORTHO to Draw a Square

Toggle ORTHO on with <^O> or <F8>.

```
Command: LINE
From point:                          Pick absolute point 7.00,0.50.
To point:                            Pick absolute point 10.00,0.50.
To point:                            Pick absolute point 10.00,3.50.
To point:                            Pick absolute point 7.00,3.50.
To point:                            Pick absolute point 7.00,0.50.
To point: <RETURN>                   End Line command.
```

Toggle ORTHO off with <^O> or <F8>.

```
Command: ERASE                       Erase the 4 lines you just drew.
```

When you turn ortho on, "Ortho" appears on the status line and "<Ortho on>" shows on the prompt line. As you draw the square, you find that your cursor is limited to vertical and horizontal movement, making it easy to get true 90-degree corners.

Interrupts

Since ortho is either on or off, we recommend that you control ortho with the control or function key toggles. We call the use of the <^B> or <F9> toggles for snap, and the <^O> or <F8> toggles for ortho, *interrupts*. You can interrupt a drawing command, for example, to get a snappable point.

You can use ortho as an interrupt just like snap. When you enter coordinate points from the keyboard, the entry overrides ortho and snap pointer controls.

Coordinate Entry

When you drew the square in the previous exercise, you picked points based on an X and Y distance from 0,0, controlling your distance with your snap increment. These X,Y distances were *absolute* coordinates. You could have typed in the coordinates just as you typed in the coordinates when you placed a drawing point.

You often use coordinate entry when you are setting up drawings or when you are drawing at known distances relative to known points. Say you have a point and you want to place a line segment relative to that point. You can type in your coordinates as *relative* coordinates. Here are three methods for coordinate entry.

- *Absolute coordinates* treat coordinate entry as X and Y displacements from 0,0. Recall that you set the 0,0 point for the UCS icon. The default position for 0,0 is at the lower left of your drawing screen.

- *Relative coordinates* treat the last point of coordinate entry like a temporary 0,0. If you want to add a horizontal line segment that is two units in the X direction, you type @2,0. The @ sign tells AutoCAD that you are using relative coordinates. If your displacement is positive, you don't need to use a + sign. Negative displacement is left and down on the screen. Use a - sign for negative displacements.

- *Polar coordinates* also treat the last point as 0,0, but you measure your point displacement with a distance and angle. Like relative coordinates, the @ sign tells AutoCAD that you are giving a polar coordinate: @2<60 is 2 units at 60 degrees. The distance and angle values are separated by a < sign (left angle bracket). Your angles are relative to 0 degrees as a horizontal extending to the right of the last point. Ninety degrees is vertically above, 180 degrees is horizontally left. A zero distance is the same as the last point. Positive angles are measured counterclockwise. See the illustration below.

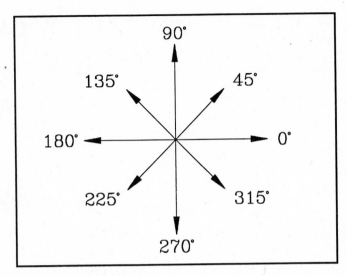

Default Angle Directions

Absolute Coordinate Entry

Try creating a triangle in the upper left portion of your screen. Type in the absolute coordinates given in the following keyboard sequence.

Using Absolute Coordinates to Draw a Triangle

```
Command: LAYER            Set layer TRIANGLE current.
Command: SNAP             Turn Snap off.

Command: LINE             Draw triangle by typing coordinates.
From point: 1.25,5.25
To point: 4.75,5.25
To point: 3,7.5
To point: 1.25,5.25
To point: <RETURN>
```

If you type an incorrect coordinate such as 1.5.5 instead of 1.5,5.5 in response to the From point prompt, AutoCAD will respond with an "Invalid point." It will repeat the prompt so that you can type the correct coordinates. When you are done, your screen should look like the Triangle Drawn With Absolute Coordinates illustration.

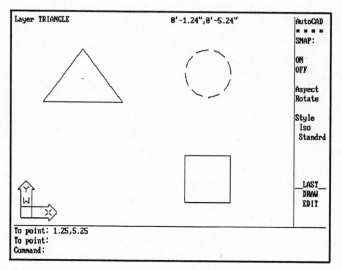

Triangle Using Absolute Coordinates

The @ Sign for Relative Coordinates

You also can enter relative coordinates from the keyboard. Relative coordinates are useful when you know exactly where you want to place drawing elements in relation to your last drawing point. The @ sign before the X,Y values tells AutoCAD that the coordinates of the new point are relative to the last point. When you enter @3,4 from the keyboard, the new point will be 3 units in the positive X direction, and 4 units in the positive Y direction from the last point.

➡ *NOTE: The @ sign has one other function. When entered by itself, it indicates the last point picked in the drawing. You might say that entering @ alone is equivalent to @0,0.*

Try relative coordinate entry by drawing a parallelogram. Rather than using the same old line command, try a different drawing command called PLINE, which creates polylines. Polylines are continuous lines with special properties like width and curvature. You will use polylines extensively later on in the book. Select [PLINE] from the [DRAW] screen or pull-down menus, and use the following exercise sequence for your input values.

Your screen should look like the Parallelogram Drawn With Relative Coordinates illustration.

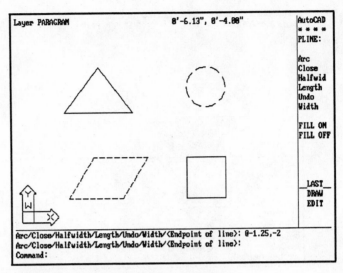

Parallelogram Using Relative Coordinates

Using Relative Coordinates to Draw

Command: **LAYER**   Set layer PARAGRAM current.

Select: **[DRAW] [PLINE:]**
From point: **1.5,1**   Absolute coordinates locate the first point.
Current line-width is 0'-0.00"
Arc/Close/Halfwidth/Length/Undo/Width/<Endpoint of line>: **@2.75,0**
Arc/Close/Halfwidth/Length/Undo/Width/<Endpoint of line>: **@1.25,2**
Arc/Close/Halfwidth/Length/Undo/Width/<Endpoint of line>: **@-2.75,0**
Arc/Close/Halfwidth/Length/Undo/Width/<Endpoint of line>: **@-1.25,-2**
Arc/Close/Halfwidth/Length/Undo/Width/<Endpoint of line>: **<RETURN>**

Using Polar Coordinates

Drawing with polar coordinates is similar to drawing with relative coordinates except you supply a distance and angle from the last point in the form of @3<60. This tells AutoCAD to enter a new point that is 3 units at 60 positive degrees away from the last point.

Tracking and Picking Polar Coordinates

You can track your pointer movements for polar input by toggling COORDS with <F6>. Coords has three modes. The default mode is static coordinates or off. Static coordinates displays an X,Y point and is updated only when a new point is picked. When you toggle <F6> once, you get the second mode where the X,Y display is constantly updated.

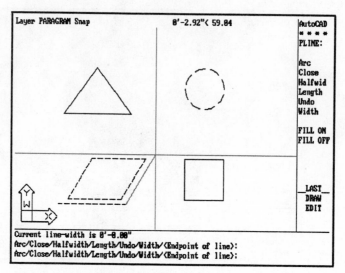

Displaying Polar Coordinates

This second updated mode has a split personality in most commands. When the crosshairs pull a rubber band line around, such as a LINE command To point, the second mode switches your coords digital readout to show a polar readout. Instead of an X,Y readout, AutoCAD gives you the distance and angle of your current cursor position relative to the From point. You'll see the distance increase in the digital readout as you move the cursor away from the From point. The angle is displayed with 0 degrees pointing to the right and progressing to 360 degrees in a counterclockwise direction.

The third mode is only an option within a command and only when rubber banding. If the coords on display is showing a polar readout, pressing <F6> once more locks it into X,Y mode. If this sounds confusing, it is! Do what we do, which is toggle until we get the readout display that we want.

Try drawing another parallelogram outside the first using PLINE and polar coordinates. Input a starting point, then pick your next two drawing points using polar tracking. Input the last two points with keyboard entry. Use the illustration below as a guide.

When you are done, erase this second parallelogram. You will need the drawing later.

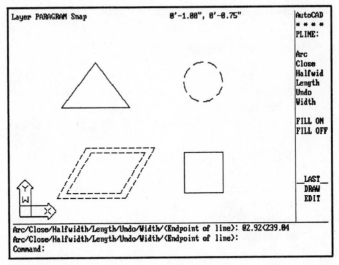

Parallelogram Using Polar Coordinates

Using Polar Coordinates to Draw

Command: **SNAP**   Set Snap to 0.25.

Select: **[DRAW] [PLINE:]**

Toggle Coords <F6> to show polar coordinates.

From point: **1,.75**   Absolute coordinates locate first point.
Current line-width is 0'-0.00"
Arc/Close/Halfwidth/Length/Undo/Width/<Endpoint of line>: Pick polar point
@3.50<0.00.
Arc/Close/Halfwidth/Length/Undo/Width/<Endpoint of line>: Pick polar point
@2.92<59.04.
Arc/Close/Halfwidth/Length/Undo/Width/<Endpoint of line>: **@3.50<180.00**
Arc/Close/Halfwidth/Length/Undo/Width/<Endpoint of line>: **@2.92<239.04.**
Arc/Close/Halfwidth/Length/Undo/Width/<Endpoint of line>: **<RETURN>**

Command: **ERASE**   Erase last to remove polyline.

➡ *NOTE: Don't let the coords readout fool you. It displays with as much
or as little precision as you set in the UNITS command. A polar
readout is rarely precise at odd angles. For example, 2.10<60 is more
likely 2.0976325 at 60.351724 degrees.*

Even when snap is on, keyboard entry will override your snap settings. Let's turn and look at the world sideways.

Creating Your Own Coordinate System

So far you have been using AutoCAD's world coordinate system, the default coordinate system. You can create you own coordinate system using the UCS and UCSICON commands. While these commands were developed for 3D, you can use them for 2D drawing applications.

We will show you two applications. The first uses UCS to change the location of the 0,0 point and the direction of X and Y in your drawing. The second application changes the location of 0,0, keeping the X and Y directions the same as the default directions. Drafting in 2D, you frequently encounter cases where you have drawing data relative to 0,0 positions. Large sets of offset data are a common example. To handle this type of drawing, you can set your UCS, input the drawing data, then return your UCS to its original (default) setting.

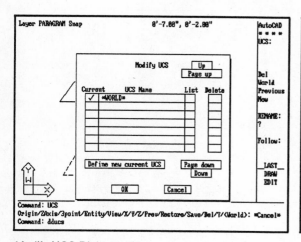

Modify UCS Dialogue Box

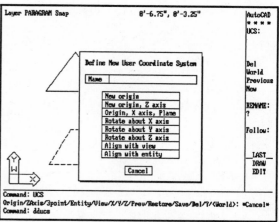

Define a New Current UCS Dialogue Box

You can modify the UCS from the [SETTINGS] screen menu or from several items in the [Settings] pull-down menu. The [UCS Dialogue...] pull-down selection uses the DDUCS command with its two UCS dialogue boxes.

Make sure your UCSICON is on, then type or select UCS. Rotate your drawing 90 degrees by making the lower right corner the 0,0 origin.

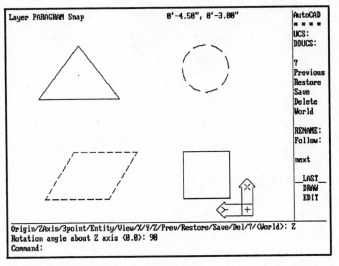

The New User Coordinate System

Using UCS to Create a User Coordinate System

```
Command: UCSICON
ON/OFF/All/Noorigin/ORigin <ON>:OR        Set UCS icon to origin.
```

```
Command: UCS                              Move Origin to lower right corner.
Origin/ZAxis/3point/Entity/View/X/Y/Z/Prev/Restore/Save/Del/?/<World>: O
Origin point <0,0,0>: 10.25,.5            The current coordinates of the new UCS.
```

```
Command: UCS                              Rotate about the Z axis 90 degrees.
Origin/ZAxis/3point/Entity/View/X/Y/Z/Prev/Restore/Save/Del/?/<World>: Z
Rotation angle about Z axis <0.0>: 90
```

To see the effect of the changed origin, move your crosshairs and look at your coordinate display. The coordinate display should show 0,0 at the lower right corner, a vertical X direction and a horizontal Y direction.

While offsetting the origin is straightforward, you might ask what the Z axis has to do with 2D drawing. Imagine that you're standing on the X axis, looking down at your drawing, with your left arm extended to the left to grip a pole rising up from 0,0. Walk forward through 90 degrees, kicking the X axis along with you. You just rotated about the Z axis 90 degrees.

Try out the effect by making a border around your drawing. Use the following sequence as a guide.

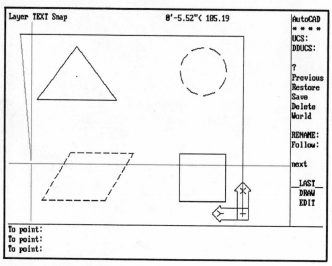

Layer TEXT Snap   8'-5.52"< 185.19

Border in Progress

Drawing a Border in a UCS

```
Command: LAYER               Set layer TEXT current.

Command: LINE
From point: 0,0              Lower right corner of border.
To point:                   Pick polar point @7.50<0.00.
To point:                   Pick polar point @9.75<90.00. Notice "up" is left now!
To point:                   Pick polar point @7.50<180.00.
To point:                   Pick polar point @9.75<270.00.
To point: <RETURN>          End the line.

Command: UCS                Set UCS back to World, the default.
Origin/ZAxis/3point/Entity/View/X/Y/Z/Prev/Restore/Save/Del/?/<World>: <RETURN>
```

Try changing the location of your origin to about midway up your drawing, then input some text.

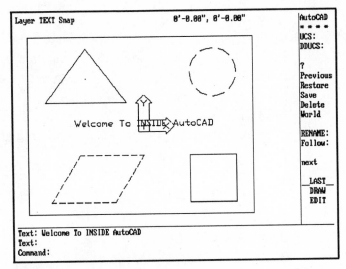

Text Added at the Current UCS's Origin

Using UCS to Demonstrate Changed Origin Point

```
Command: UCS                                    Set UCS to center of drawing.
Origin/ZAxis/3point/Entity/View/X/Y/Z/Prev/Restore/Save/Del/?/<World>: O
Origin point <0,0,0>: 5.5,4.25                  The current coordinates of the new UCS.


Command: DTEXT
Start point or Align/Center/Fit/Middle/Right/Style: C
Center point: 0,0
Height <0'0-0.20">: .25
Rotation angle <0.00>: <RETURN>
Text: Welcome To INSIDE AutoCAD                 Our favorite text.


Command: UCS                                    Set UCS back to the world coordinate system.
Origin/ZAxis/3point/Entity/View/X/Y/Z/Prev/Restore/Save/Del/?/<World>: <RETURN>
```

As you can tell by looking at the command prompt line, the UCS command is one of the more complex commands and has several options. We will show you how to use these options when we take up 3D in section two. Here is a subset of the options that will get you through most 2D applications.

UCS Options (for 2D Applications)

Origin — Establishes the X Y axes at a new point of origin.

Z — Provides the option of rotating the X Y axes about the Z axis.

Prev — Lets you step back, up to ten previously used coordinate systems.

Restore — Sets the coordinate system to a previously saved UCS.

Save — Stores a coordinate system under a user-specified name.

Del — Removes a saved coordinate system.

? — Displays a list of saved coordinate systems by name, point of origin and orientation.

<World> — Sets the UCS to the world coordinate system.

Here are the UCSICON command options to control the display of the UCS icon.

UCSICON Options

ON — Makes the UCS icon visible.

OFF — Removes the UCS icon.

All — Displays the UCS icon in all viewports.

Noorigin — Displays the UCS icon in the lower left corner of viewport.

ORigin — Displays the UCS icon at the point of origin (0,0).

We will show you how to make your screen display multiple viewports of your drawing and control this type of drawing display in the next chapter.

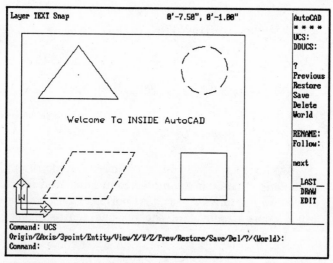

Geometric Shapes Drawing

Checking Your Drawing Aids Settings

Take a look at your drawing. Your screen should look like the Geometric Shapes Drawing. Each shape should have the color and linetype of the layer it was created on. While you have used individual axis, grid, and snap commands to help you construct these shapes, you can also set these drawing aids using the transparent DDRMODES command. Check your settings by looking at the Modes Dialogue Box illustration.

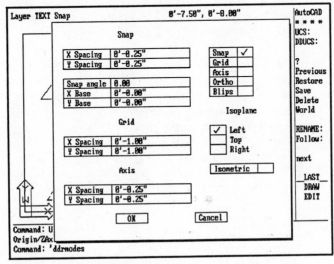

The Modes Dialogue Box

Saving the BASIC Drawing

Command: **SAVE**   Save the drawing as BASIC.

Change any settings to match the dialogue box, then save your drawing by renaming it BASIC. We are going to use this drawing again in the next chapter on display controls.

Stopping Point

If you want to take a coffee break, this is a good stopping point. For the rest of the chapter, we are going to use the WORK drawing as a scratch drawing to show you how isometrics and OSNAPS work. If you want to pick up isometrics later, skip on to osnaps.

Isometrics

Isometric views are often used in 2D drawings to represent 3D objects. Angles and lines are aligned in an isometric view to give the *impression* that some lines are boundaries for the front, top, and side views of an object. Perspective in an isometric drawing is simplified. Isometric projections have no vanishing point, and are usually drawn with a restricted number of angles. Rectangular objects, for example, are usually drawn with 30, 90, or 150 degree angles. The key to drawing isometrics is to keep your lines and angles aligned so that you do not draw entities that would ruin the 3D illusion.

AutoCAD provides a series of drawing aids to save time when drawing isometric projections. Setting the SNAP STYLE to the ISO option sets up a drawing environment with grid and snap that helps you draw in three basic isometric planes. (See the illustration below.) The snap style option toggles between isometric drawing control and the standard snap/grid control. Once you are in isometric mode, you control which *face* (top, left, or right) you are drawing on by using the ISOPLANE command.

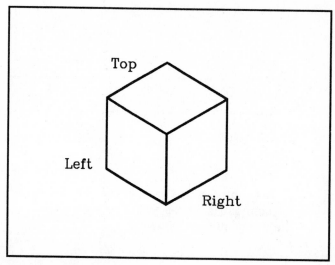

Isometric Planes

Set up for some isometrics by making a new ISO drawing layer and freezing the old SQUARE layer. You will be drawing an isometric cube where the square was displayed.

Setting Up for Isometric Drawing

```
Command: LAYER                   Turn the SQUARE layer off and make a new layer named ISO.
?/Make/Set/New/ON/OFF/Color/Ltype/Freeze/Thaw: OFF
Layer name(s) to turn Off: SQUARE
?/Make/Set/New/ON/OFF/Color/Ltype/Freeze/Thaw: M
New current layer <TEXT>: ISO
?/Make/Set/New/ON/OFF/Color/Ltype/Freeze/Thaw: C
Color: 6
Layer name(s) for color 6 (magenta) <ISO>: <RETURN>
?/Make/Set/New/ON/OFF/Color/Ltype/Freeze/Thaw: <RETURN>

Command: ZOOM                            Zoom into the area where the square was.
All/Center/Dynamic/Extents/Left/Previous/Window/<Scale(X)>: W
First corner:           Pick a point at approximately 0'-6.00",0'-1.00".
Other corner:           Pick a point at approximately 0'-10.00",0'-3.50".
```

As soon as you set your snap style to ISO, your screen crosshairs will be skewed. You control your drawing by setting a grid and snap, then toggling the ISOPLANE command to draw on each face. The toggle for ISOPLANE is Control E <^E>. The left plane is the default plane. Here are the ISOPLANE options.

ISOPLANE Options

Left — Creates isometric crosshairs at 90 degrees and 150 degrees.

Top — Creates isometric crosshairs at 30 degrees and 150 degrees.

Right — Creates isometric crosshairs at 90 degrees and 30 degrees.

<Toggle> — Rotates the crosshairs from left to top to right planes in a continuous loop.

Set a grid and snap, and toggle your way around the planes. Use the following illustrations as guides.

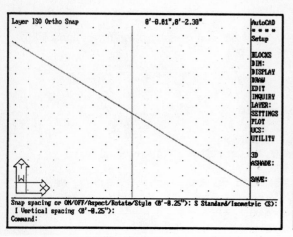

Default Left Isometric Plane

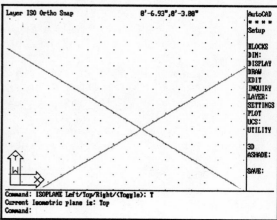

Top Isometric Plane

Creating and Testing an Isometric Screen

```
Command: GRID                                     Set to .25.


Command: SNAP                                     Set Snap to isometric mode.
Snap spacing or ON/OFF/Aspect/Rotate/Style <0'-0.25">: S
Standard/Isometric <S>: I
Vertical spacing <0'-0.25">: <RETURN>


Command: ISOPLANE                                 Toggle from the left to the top plane.
Left/Top/Right/<Toggle>: <RETURN>
Current Isometric plane is: Top


Command:  <Isoplane Right>                        Use <^E> to get into the right plane.


Command: ISOPLANE                                 Specify the left plane.
Left/Top/Right/<Toggle>: L
Current Isometric plane is: Left
```

Now that you know how to get around the isometric planes, try drawing a simple 1-inch cube.

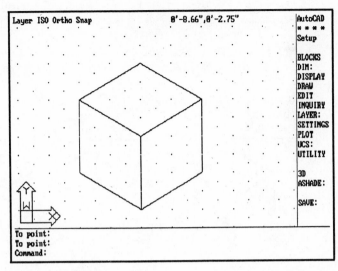

An Isometric Cube

Using Isometric Tools to Create a Cube

Command: <Ortho on>	Turn Ortho on with <^O>.
Command: <Coords on>	Set Coords to polar with <^D>.
Command: **LINE**	Draw the left and right side of the cube.
From point:	Pick absolute point 7.79,1.25.
To point:	Pick polar point 1.00<150.00.
To point:	Pick polar point 1.00<90.00.
To point:	Pick polar point 1.00<330.00.
To point:	Pick polar point 1.00<270.00.

Toggle to the Right plane with two <^E>s.

To point: <Isoplane Top> <Isoplane Right>	Pick polar point 1.00<30.00.
To point:	Pick polar point 1.00<90.00.
To point:	Pick polar point 1.00<210.00.
To point: **<RETURN>**	
Command: **ISOPLANE**	Set Isometric plane to the top.
Left/Top/Right/<Toggle>: **T**	
Current Isometric plane is: Top	
Command: **LINE**	Draw the top of the cube.
From point:	Pick absolute point 6.93,2.75.
To point:	Pick polar point 1.00<30.00.
To point:	Pick polar point 1.00<330.00.
To point: **<RETURN>**	

When you are done, your screen should look similar to the illustration, An Isometric Cube.

➥ *TIP: If you need to draw circles in an isometric drawing, use the ELLIPSE command. It works well for isometric circles.*

If you enjoyed this exercise, try some more of the isometric shapes shown below. Otherwise, it is time for osnaps.

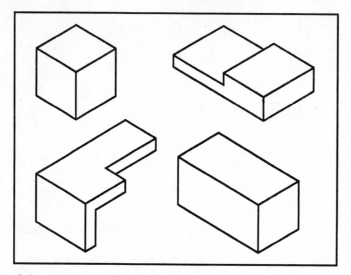

Cube and Assorted Isometric Shapes

Osnaps — Snapping to Entities

Snapping to snap increments is great when you want to make original entries for lines, arcs, and text. But when you want to edit existing lines or add graphic entities as extensions to existing entities, you need a way to identify where you want your new or edited versions to *attach* to your existing drawing.

For example, let's say you want to start a new line at the exact endpoint of one of the lines on the screen. Assuming that you haven't changed the snap setting from when you entered the line, you probably can pick the endpoint pretty well. But what if you have changed the snap increment? Or what if you want to pick a tangent point to a curve? Or pick the intersection of two lines that doesn't fall on a snap point? You need OSNAP!

Using OSNAP to Pinpoint a Crosshairs Location

AutoCAD's OSNAP command and filters calculate the *attachment* points you need to make accurate drawings. You tell AutoCAD which OSNAP mode(s) to use and pick an approximate point. But in a dense drawing, there might be several suitable attachment points close to your pick point. When osnapping an INTersection, AutoCAD may not calculate the intersection you want. So OSNAP gives you a tolerance or *target* area for identifying existing locations. This tolerance is controlled by an *aperture* box, an electronic bull's-eye that homes in on pick points. AutoCAD only considers the osnap for objects that fall within the aperture. Just how large you set the aperture depends on what you are selecting, how you are zoomed, your display resolution, and your drawing density.

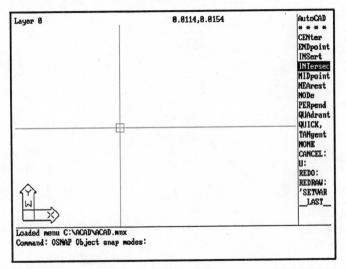

OSNAP Turns the Crosshairs Into a Target

The OSNAP Targets illustration below shows you all the filters for picking different attachment points on objects. The basic geometric shapes that you created in your WORK drawing will let you exercise all these osnap options.

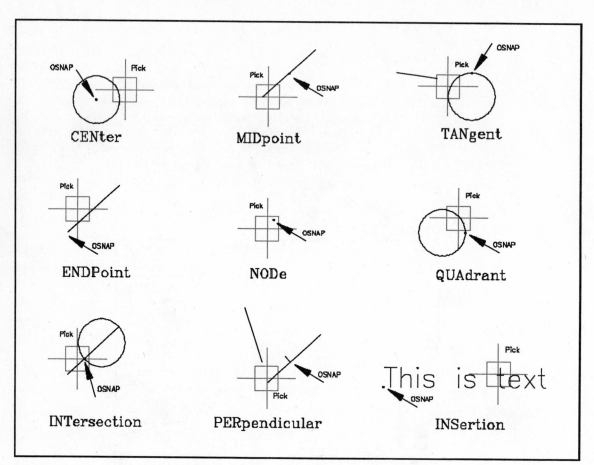

OSNAP Targets and the Points They Pick

Setting the Aperture and Picking a Point

Let's get started by setting the aperture to control the size of the crosshairs bull's-eye that osnap uses to zero in on target objects. Use the [APERTUR:] selection from the [SETTINGS] screen menu. While you are at it, change your current layer to layer 0, using it as a scratch layer.

Using APERTURE to Set the Osnap Target

```
Command: LAYER                Set layer 0, turn on the SQUARE layer and freeze ISO layer.
?/Make/Set/New/ON/OFF/Color/Ltype/Freeze/Thaw: S
New current layer <ISO>: 0
?/Make/Set/New/ON/OFF/Color/Ltype/Freeze/Thaw: ON
Layer name(s) to turn On: SQUARE
?/Make/Set/New/ON/OFF/Color/Ltype/Freeze/Thaw: F
```

```
Layer name(s) to Freeze: ISO
?/Make/Set/New/ON/OFF/Color/Ltype/Freeze/Thaw: <RETURN>

Select: [SETTINGS] [APERTUR:]
Object snap target height (1-50 pixels) <10>: 5
```

A pixel is the smallest *dot* that can be displayed on your screen. Four or six pixels (the default value is 10) gives a good target size. The size is measured from the center, so five pixels makes a 10-pixel high aperture box. Try a few different values to see how comfortable you feel with larger and smaller apertures. There are advantages and disadvantages to setting large and small apertures.

➡ *NOTE: A small aperture size finds points faster and more accurately in crowded drawings, but the crosshairs are harder to line up. A large aperture is easy to line up, but is slower and less accurate in a crowded drawing.*

Interrupts vs. Running Mode

Use osnaps as single pick filters (interrupts), or set a *running* osnap mode that remains in effect until you turn it off. You can select osnaps as interrupts (AutoCAD calls them *overrides*) from the [Tools] pull-down menu, or the [*****] item that appears near the top of the screen menus. The osnap options are the same for both interrupts and running modes.

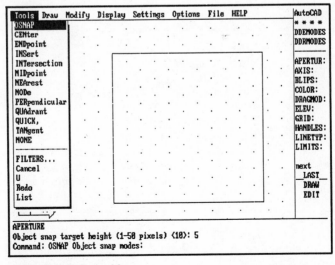

OSNAP Pull-Down Menu

Using OSNAP as a Single Pick Filter

To learn how interrupts work, use NODe and ENDpoint to draw a line from the point entity (your first point) in the triangle to the corner of the triangle. NODe osnaps to a point entity, not the triangle's geometric node. The resulting drawing will look like the OSNAP NODe and OSNAP ENDPoint illustrations. Pick the osnap options from the [Tools] pull-down menu, tablet menu, screen menu, or type them at the keyboard. Here's the prompt sequence.

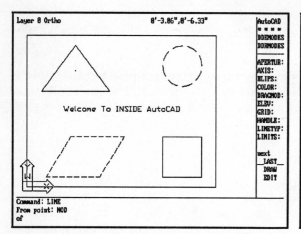

OSNAP NODe

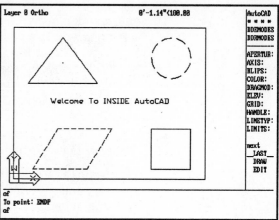

OSNAP ENDPoint

Using OSNAP for NODe and ENDPoint

Command: **SNAP**	Set Snap to standard.
Command: **SNAP**	Turn Snap off.
Command: **ZOOM**	Zoom all.
Command: **GRID**	Turn Grid off.
Command: **LINE**	
From Point: **NOD**	Now type NOD for node.
of	Put target on point entity in the triangle and pick.
From Point: **ENDP**	Now type ENDP for endpoint.
of	Put target near corner of triangle and pick.
To point: **<RETURN>**	

Congratulations! You've successfully osnapped. Your drawing should look like the Completed OSNAP illustration.

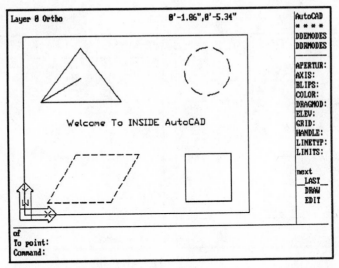

Completed OSNAP

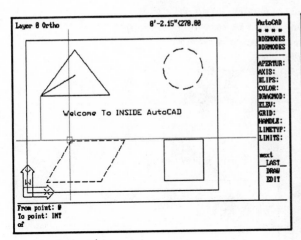

OSNAP INTersection

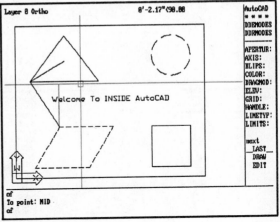

OSNAP MIDpoint

Continue the exercise to see how the remaining osnaps work. The accompanying illustrations show the completed osnaps.

Completing the OSNAP Options.

```
Command: LINE
From Point: @          Start line from last point.
To point: INT          Type INT for intersection.
of                     Now pick the intersection of the parallelogram.
To point: MID          Type MID for midpoint.
of                     Place the target anywhere on the base line of the triangle.
```

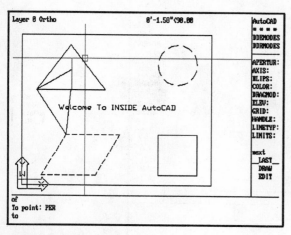

OSNAP PERpendicular

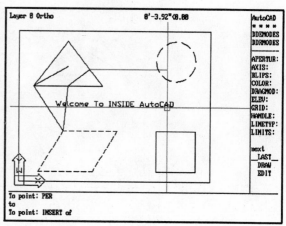

OSNAP INSert

```
To point: PER          Type PER for perpendicular.
of                     Pick anywhere on the right side of the triangle.
Select: [****] [INSert] Now try the screen menu of OSNAPs.
To point: INSERT       The menu changes back.
of                     Place the target anywhere on the text.
```

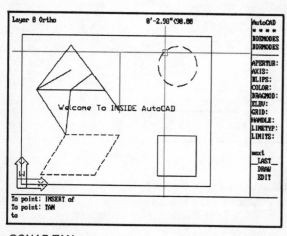

OSNAP TANgent

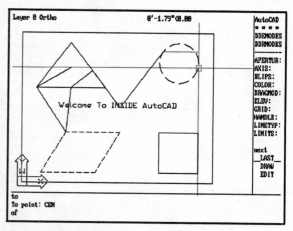

OSNAP CENter

```
To point: TAN          Type TAN for tangent.
of                     Place the target on the upper left side of the circle.
To point: CEN          Type CEN for center.
of                     Place the target anywhere on the circle.
```

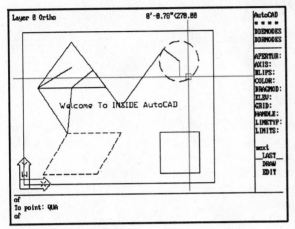

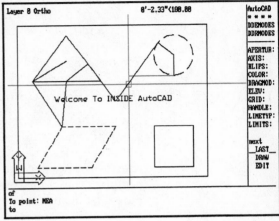

OSNAP QUAdrant   OSNAP NEAr

```
To point: QUA                Type QUA for quadrant.
of                           Pick the bottom of the circle.
To point: NEA                Type NEA for near.
of                           Pick anywhere on line from the text to the circle.
To point: <RETURN>
```

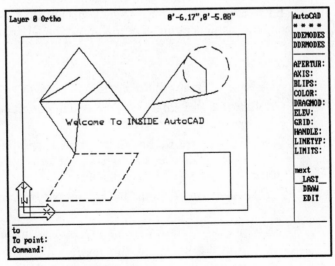

Completed OSNAP

➡ *TIP: If you type the OSNAP modifier, you just type the first word or first three or four characters like **ENDP**oint or **PER**pend. AutoCAD will fill in the **of** or **to**. When using ENDPoint, get in the habit of typing ENDP, not END, to avoid accidentally ENDing your drawing.*

You drawing should look similar to the Completed OSNAP illustration.

Using QUIck to Optimize OSNAP

AutoCAD goes through a lot of work trying to find the correct object to osnap to when you are using an OSNAP command. In fact, AutoCAD searches every object on the screen to find all objects crossing the aperture box to find the *best* fit to your osnap request. Then it calculates potential points for these objects. This can take a little time when you have a lot of objects in the file.

You can optimize or shorten the osnap search process by keeping the aperture reasonably small to keep extraneous objects out of the target. Or you can use the QUIck osnap option. QUIck lets AutoCAD take the most recent object that meets your osnap criteria instead of doing an exhaustive search. You invoke QUIck by using it as a prefix for other osnap option(s).

QUIck may sometimes let you down if the first fit that AutoCAD finds is not the one you want. In that case, simply CANCEL what you are doing and start the osnap process again without the quick modifier. Here is the complete osnap options list, including the QUIck modifier.

OSNAP Options

CENter — Snaps to the center of an arc or circle.

ENDPoint — Snaps to the nearest endpoint of a line, arc, solid, trace, 3Dface, or polyline vertex.

INSert — Snaps to the origin of text, attributes and symbols (block or shape) that have been inserted into the drawing file. More about blocks, shapes, and attributes later.

INTersection — Snaps to the nearest intersection of two entities in the drawing file.

MIDpoint — Snaps to the midpoint of a line or arc.

NEArest — Snaps to the nearest point on an entity. This will generally be an endpoint or a perpendicular point.

NODe — Snaps to a point entity.

PERpendicular — Snaps to a point for the picked entity that would form a perpendicular (normal) line from the last point to the picked entity. The point need not even be on the entity.

TANgent — Snaps to a point on a picked arc or circle that forms a tangent to the picked arc or circle from the last point.

QUAdrant — snaps to the closest 0-, 90-, 180-, or 270-degree point on a picked arc or circle.

QUIck — Forces all other OSNAP options to quickly find the first potential target, not necessarily the best. QUIck finds the potential point that is on the most *recent* qualified object in the target box.

NONe — Removes or overrides any running osnap.

In the exercise examples above, you used OSNAP as an interrupt in the middle of the line command to fine tune your line endpoints. The osnap interrupt mode temporarily sets up an osnap aperture condition to complete a task at hand.

Using a Running Mode OSNAP

Setting up osnap conditions to be in effect throughout an AutoCAD editing session is called a *running mode*. To set a running mode, you select [OSNAP] from the [SETTINGS] screen menu. Running mode osnaps remain in effect until you replace them with another running mode setting or temporarily override them with an interrupt.

Use the interrupt mode whenever the need arises. Set up a running osnap condition only when you know that you will be spending a good deal of time connecting drawing elements where osnap will be helpful.

➡ *NOTE: If a running osnap is on, the crosshairs will have a bull's-eye aperture during your point entry and object selection.*

Try putting a diamond in the square using a running osnap mode.

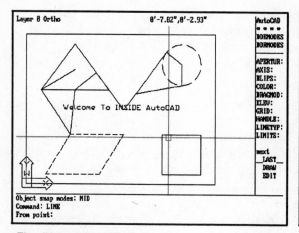

First Pick for Diamond

Second Pick for Diamond

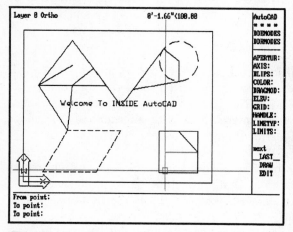

Third Pick for Diamond

Final Pick for Diamond

Using a Running OSNAP to Put a Diamond in a Square

```
Command: OSNAP
Object snap modes: MID       Type MID for midpoint.

Command: LINE
From point:                  Pick a point on the top line.
To point:                    Pick a point on the right line.
To point:                    Pick a point on the bottom line.
To point:                    Pick a point on the left line.
To point:                    Pick a point on the top line.
To point: <RETURN>
```

➡ *NOTE: OSNAP running conditions cannot be toggled like snap and grid. Turning osnap off with NONe wipes out the previous settings. Try to plan ahead to get OSNAP help. You can always type the osnap interrupt modes, or select them from the screen menu, but that does take some time.*

If you want to practice more osnaps, keep drawing. You have all the geometric points you need.

REDRAW and BLIPMODE Keep Screen Clutter Down

As you worked through the osnap exercises, you probably noticed that when you entered a point on the screen (either with a pointer or keyboard entry), AutoCAD placed a small cross (blip) on the screen. As you draw, filling up the screen area with real drawing entities (like lines and circles), you also get a screenful of clutter from construction markers. A few blips are great for keeping an eye on where you've been (or might want to go again), but they are a bother when they accumulate.

The simplest way to clean up the screen and get rid of blips is to use the REDRAW command. This clears the screen and redraws real drawing elements, leaving old blips behind.

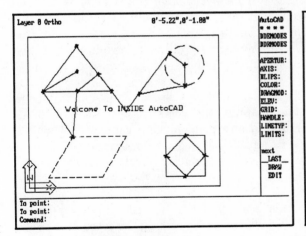

Display Screen Before REDRAW

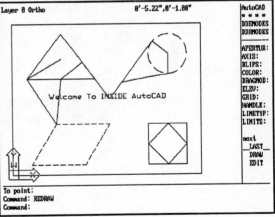

Display Screen After REDRAW

Using REDRAW to Clear Up the Screen

```
Command: REDRAW
```

> ➥ *TIP: You can do a redraw without typing or picking the command. Toggling grid twice with <^G> or <F7> causes a redraw. You also can issue a transparent redraw with 'REDRAW.*

If you find you just don't need blips, you can use the BLIPMODE command to suppress construction markers. You can keep AutoCAD from drawing these temporary markers by typing BLIPMODE OFF or selecting [BLIPS] from the [SETTINGS] screen menu.

Well, you have a clean screen so to speak. Save your drawing by ending your editing session.

Ending the WORK Drawing

Command: **END**   You don't need this drawing any more.

Summing Up

You have seen that one of the tricks to accurate drawing is to use relative and polar points, with coords for reference. Use Grid (and Axis) to give you a frame of reference. You can toggle Grid on and off. Use Snap to limit your crosshairs movement to pre-set increments. Snap can be used to set Rotated or ISOmetric Grids. If you need to draw at 90-degree increments, toggle Ortho on. If you need to change your coordinate system, you can change your UCS. Many users find it helpful to jot down notes or make up a checklist to keep track of these display settings.

To construct geometrically accurate objects, use coordinate entry and use OSNAP to set up a target for snapping to objects. You can invoke OSNAP temporarily as an interrupt to any point-picking command. Using a running OSNAP mode sets up a full-time mode and aperture that you can override. Try to find a good aperture setting to control the reliability and speed of your osnap searches.

Throughout the rest of this book, you will see coordinates given in response to prompts with the exercises. Try picking the coordinates with the pointing device first if you are sure the pick is accurate. Remember crosshairs position is only accurate with snap on, or with osnap. Use OSNAP at every opportunity you can. Using osnap is a habit that you want to cultivate. Your drawing productivity will improve and you can be confident that your work is accurate. Now that you've had a chance to play around with osnaps, you can move on to learning How to Get Around in AutoCAD.

CHAPTER 4

Getting Around

MAKING A SMALL DISPLAY SCREEN DO THE WORK OF A BIG PIECE OF PAPER

Whether you've set your drawing limits to represent 2 by 3 feet or 2000 by 3000 feet, your display screen is not large enough to give you a one-to-one view of your drawing file. In this chapter, you will learn to use AutoCAD's set of electronic tools to control where you are in your display, where you are going, and how you will get there. Your display becomes a *viewport* into your drawing, zooming in, out, and around. Then you will learn to use *multiple viewports* to see several parts of your drawing simultaneously.

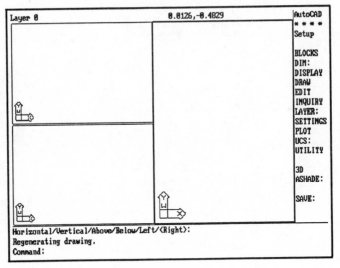

Screen Divided Into Three Viewports

The Benefits of Getting Around

AutoCAD's display controls make your drawing life easier. AutoCAD's basic display controls, like *zoom* and *pan*, function just like they do in photography. The ZOOM command lets you magnify your drawing to do detailed work. PAN lets you slide your drawing from side to side so that you can work on long objects without having to return to a full screen view to find where you are. Simple controls, like *redraw* and *regen*, let you clean up your screen or display the most current view of your drawing.

To make life at the screen even easier, you can create multiple views of your drawing. AutoCAD calls these multiple views viewports. While viewports were developed to let you display different geometric views and scales of your drawing for work in 3D, you can also use viewports in 2D. For example, you can see your entire object in a single window while you zoom in to work on a drawing detail in a second window. Or you can keep a parts schedule in one window while you check your drawing annotations in another. You can even set many of AutoCAD's settings, such as snap and grid, differently in each viewport. When you are done, you can name and save your viewport configurations and their settings with your drawing.

Tools for Display Control

You will find view control tools on the [DISPLAY] screen menu and the [Display] pull-down menu.

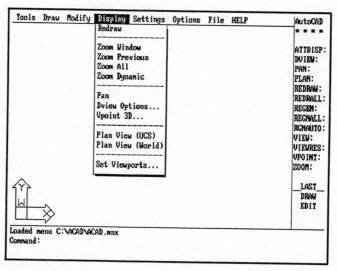

Display Screen and Pull-Down Menus

Display Control Setup

To work with the display control commands, use the BASIC drawing file you saved in chapter 3. If you are using the IA DISK, copy the CHAP-04.DWG to BASIC.DWG. Your screen should look like the BASIC Drawing illustration.

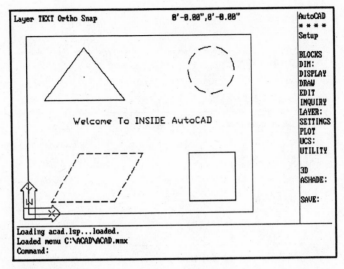

BASIC Drawing

Display Control Setup

 Copy the CHAP-04.DWG from disk to the name BASIC.DWG.

 You will need the BASIC drawing from chapter 3.

`Enter selection: 2`   Edit an EXISTING drawing called BASIC.

Verify the drawing has the settings shown in the BASIC Table.

If you are uncertain about the status of your drawing, verify that the drawing has the settings shown in the following settings table.

AXIS	GRID	SNAP	ORTHO	UCS	UCSICON
Off	On	On	On	World	On

UNITS	Engineering, 2 decimal points, 2 fractional places for angles, defaults all other settings.
LIMITS	0,0 to 11,8.5

Layer name	State	Color	Linetype
0	On	7 (white)	CONTINUOUS
TRIANGLE	On	1 (red)	CONTINUOUS
SQUARE	On	2 (yellow)	CONTINUOUS
CIRCLE	On	3 (green)	DASHED
TEXT	Current	4 (cyan)	CONTINUOUS
PARAGRAM	On	5 (blue)	HIDDEN

BASIC Drawing Settings

You don't need an elaborate drawing to get a feel for display controls; the simple geometric shapes in the BASIC drawing will work well enough to get you around the display screen.

Controlling Screen Display with ZOOM

Suppose you want to look more closely at the intersection of the triangle on the screen. To do this you need to *zoom* in on the drawing. You have to be able to communicate to AutoCAD exactly what part of the current screen you want to enlarge. The most common way to tell AutoCAD what you want to see is to show a box or *window* around the area of interest. Remember, ZOOM Window only zooms in on your drawing, not out.

Using ZOOM to Look More Closely

Step through a zoom window example. Use the Zoom Window Box illustration as a guide to picking your window corners. You don't need to pick exact coordinates, just show a rough area you want to see in more detail. If you don't want to pick freehand, use the digital readout to get close to the lower left (first) and upper right (second) corners given in the exercise sequence.

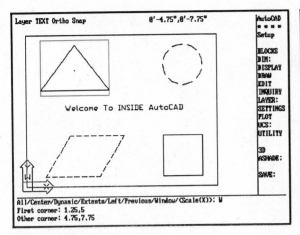

ZOOM Window Box

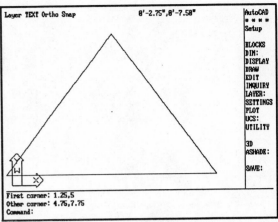

Magnified Screen

Using ZOOM Window

```
Command: ZOOM
All/Center/Dynamic/Extents/Left/Previous/Window/<Scale(X)>: W
First corner:          Pick absolute point 1.25,5.00.
Other corner:          Pick absolute point 4.75,7.75.
```

Notice that after you pick the first corner, instead of the normal crosshairs, your cursor changes to a *rubber band* window. As soon as you pick the other corner, AutoCAD repaints the screen and fills it with the area you enclosed in the window. The corners that you picked guide AutoCAD in setting up the zoomed-in display. This display will not be exactly the same shape as your original window because AutoCAD maintains its X and Y screen ratio regardless of your corner locations.

Try zooming closer to the upper point of the triangle, picking two more window corners, and letting AutoCAD redraw the screen. Use the Second ZOOM Window illustration as your guide.

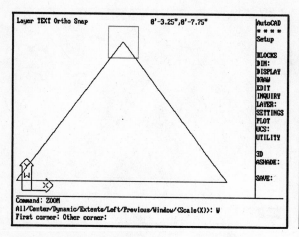

Second ZOOM Window

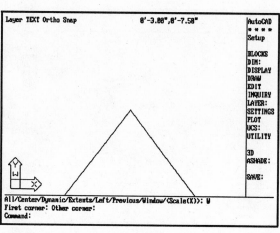

Magnified Top of Triangle

Picking a ZOOM Window

```
Command: ZOOM                Zoom to upper point of triangle.
All/Center/Dynamic/Extents/Left/Previous/Window/<Scale(X)>: W
First corner:                Pick the lower left corner.
Other corner:                Pick the upper right corner.
```

OK, you can get in. How do you get back out? Use ZOOM All.

ZOOM All is the easiest way to get back to the full display of your drawing file.

Using ZOOM All

```
Command: ZOOM
All/Center/Dynamic/Extents/Left/Previous/Window/<Scale(X)>: A
Regenerating drawing.
```

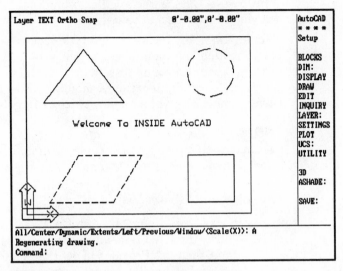

ZOOM All

Your screen should look like the ZOOM All illustration. When AutoCAD sees a ZOOM All, it regenerates and repaints the screen with everything in the drawing file. If you have drawn within your drawing limits, ZOOM All takes you to your limits. If you have exceeded your limits, ZOOM All displays everything in your drawing file.

Other ZOOM Options

ZOOM Window and ZOOM All will get you in and out, but you have several other zoom options at your fingertips. Here's the complete list.

ZOOM Options

All — Zooms out to limits, or everything in the drawing file, whichever is inclusive. All always regenerates the drawing, sometimes twice.

Center — Magnifies the screen around a center point with a given height or factor.

Dynamic — Temporarily displays the whole drawing, letting you graphically select any portion of the drawing as your next screen view.

Extents — Gives the tightest zoom view of everything in the drawing file.

Left — Uses a lower left corner and a height or magnification factor.

Previous — Restores the last ZOOM setting. Remembers up to 10 previous magnifications.

Window — Uses a rectangular window to show what part of the drawing file will be on the screen.

<Scale(X)> — Uses a numeric zoom factor to determine magnification. A magnification factor of 1 displays a view of the drawing limits. A value less than 1 zooms out, and greater than 1 zooms in. The magnification X modifier gives zooms relative to your current view. 2X gives a display twice as large as the last display.

➡ *NOTE: Zooms will occasionally require a drawing regeneration. Zoom All and Extents always cause a drawing regeneration. If you can use a Zoom Previous, you will avoid the regeneration.*

Keeping Track of Zoom Displays

Every time you zoom in or out, AutoCAD keeps track of the previous display. In fact, AutoCAD remembers up to ten zooms. Try the Left and Center options, then use Previous to get the zoom-before-this-one on the screen. Use the following illustration sequence to work your way around the drawing. Input the magnification values given in the exercise sequence.

Using ZOOM Previous

```
Command: ZOOM                    Use the Left option to zoom an area surrounding the text.
All/Center/Dynamic/Extents/Left/Previous/Window/<Scale(X)>: L
Lower left corner point:              Pick absolute point 2.50,2.00.
Magnification or Height <0'-8.50">: 4.5


Command: ZOOM                    Zoom Center on the W in Welcome.
All/Center/Dynamic/Extents/Left/Previous/Window/<Scale(X)>: C
Center point:                         Pick a point on the W.
Magnification or Height <0'-4.50">: .5


Command: ZOOM                    Zoom Previous to return to the complete text.
All/Center/Dynamic/Extents/Left/Previous/Window/<Scale(X)>: P
Command: ZOOM                    Use Previous again to return to the start.
All/Center/Dynamic/Extents/Left/Previous/Window/<Scale(X)>: P
```

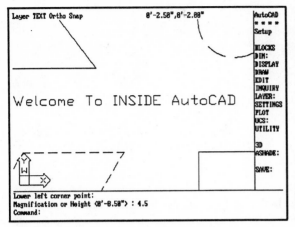

ZOOM Left

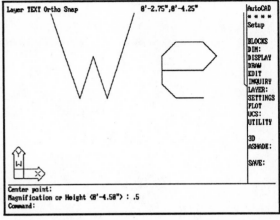

ZOOM Center

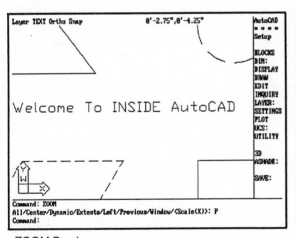

ZOOM Previous

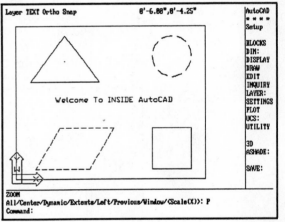

ZOOM Previous

If all went well, you should end up where you started. Your screen should show a zoomed-out view of your drawing.

➡ *NOTE: Previous does not necessarily zoom out. It zooms to the previous zoom view setting.*

Dynamic ZOOM Gives You More Display Control

You have used the basic two-step process of zooming in on your drawing with a window and zooming back out with a ZOOM All. But what if you want to magnify a small portion of your drawing while you are already zoomed in to a different section? There is another option called ZOOM

Dynamic that lets you control and display your zoom window in a single step without having to do a ZOOM All.

There are really three display subsets. When you work with a dynamic zoom, these subsets are shown on your screen. Here are the display sets:

■ The drawing Extents. Everything in the drawing file.

■ Generated data. A portion (up to all) of the drawing file that AutoCAD can keep *ready active*. This is the *virtual screen*.

■ The screen view. A portion (up to all) of the generated data that currently appears on the screen.

When you select a dynamic zoom, you can see all three of these areas graphically on the screen before making a decision on what your next screen view will be.

Take a look at the Dynamic Control Screen. You see four rectangular areas outlined on the diagram. The first three show the entire drawing area (extents), the currently generated area (the virtual screen), and the current view screen. (The extents will be the limits unless you have drawn beyond the limits.)

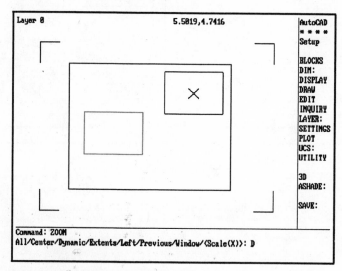

Dynamic ZOOM Control Screen

The fourth rectangular area is a dynamic window that moves with your pointer. Use this dynamic window to select the next screen view you want to see.

If you select your next screen view from within the area bounded by the *generated* data, the next screen view will appear on the screen in redraw speed. If you select your next screen view to include data from outside the currently generated data, your zoom will require a regeneration of the entire drawing file as AutoCAD calculates the part of the drawing file you want to see in your next view. When you move the pointer outside the generated drawing file area, a little hourglass appears on the lower left part of the screen indicating that regeneration will occur. If you zoom in beyond about 50X, AutoCAD must regenerate the drawing.

Try a ZOOM Dynamic. First get a zoomed-in view on the screen by magnifying your drawing 3X. Then call up the ZOOM Dynamic display. Use the following illustrations and exercise sequence to get you started.

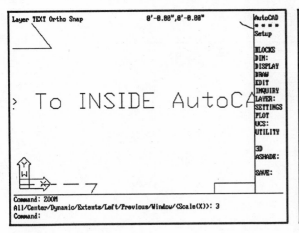

Screen Magnified 3 Times

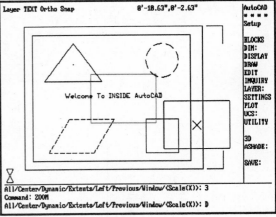

Beginning of Dynamic Zoom

Using Dynamic ZOOM

```
Command: ZOOM                    Use a Scale factor of 3 to magnify display.
All/Center/Dynamic/Extents/Left/Previous/Window/<Scale(X)>: 3

Command: ZOOM                    Now get the Dynamic Zoom Display on the screen.
All/Center/Dynamic/Extents/Left/Previous/Window/<Scale(X)>: D
```

Your screen should look like the Beginning of Dynamic Zoom illustration. When you move your pointer around, it *drags* the dynamic viewing window around the screen as if it were held by the X handle in the middle of the window. Your pointer also controls the size of the window. Press your pointer button to get an arrow that controls the size of your window.

When you move the arrow to the right, you make the window larger. Left makes it smaller.

When you have the dynamic window the size you want, hit the pointer button again to lock in the size. You can toggle between controlling the dynamic window size and its location by hitting the pointer button.

Once you have selected the next viewing screen that you want, hit the <RETURN> key while holding the dynamic viewing window in place. AutoCAD will zoom. Use the illustrations as a guide. Here is the exercise sequence.

Controlling a Dynamic ZOOM

```
All/Center/Dynamic/Extents/Left/Previous/Window/<Scale(X)>: D
```

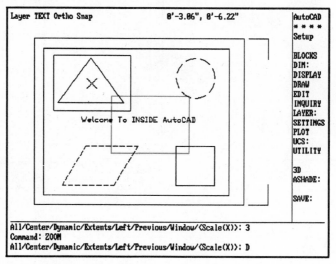

Moving Current View Screen

Move the dynamic window around with the **X** handle.
Press the pointer button to switch to dynamic window size.

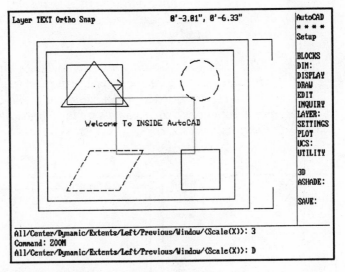

Resizing Current View Screen

Stretch or shrink the dynamic window by moving horizontally.
Press the pointer button to switch to dynamic window location control.
Line up the dynamic viewing window to enclose the circle.

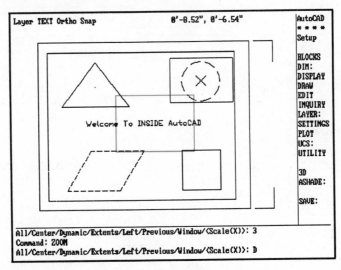

Viewing Window Enclosing the Circle

Hold the pointer in place and press the <RETURN> key.

➤ *NOTE: If the dynamic window disappears and you see only the arrows or X, you probably have sized it to nothingness. Move or hit the pointer to regain control.*

➤ *NOTE: You can also do your own style of dynamic zoom by simply using the normal zoom options and cutting them short. For example, you can start a ZOOM Previous and cut it short with a <^C> as soon as you see enough to decide where to go next. Then follow it with your intended zoom.*

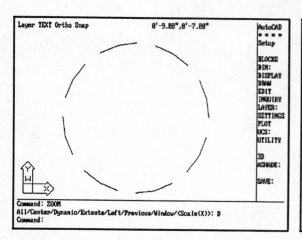

Display After Dynamic Zoom

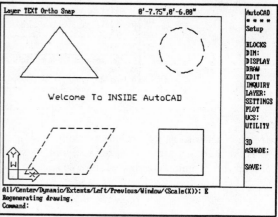

Zoom Extents

When you are done, try zooming back out with a ZOOM Extents. Extents acts like All if you have kept your drawing within your drawing limits.

Using ZOOM Extents

```
Command: ZOOM                 Zoom Extents magnifies screen to edge of border.
All/Center/Dynamic/Extents/Left/Previous/Window/<Scale(X)>: E
```

Your screen should look like the Zoom Extents illustration.

➤ *TIP: Always use a ZOOM Extents just before you end your drawing session. It will act as a check to let you know if you have drawn anything outside your limits.*

Using PAN to View Side-to-Side Windows

Frequently, you will need to move your drawing sideways (or up, or down). Say you are working on a zoomed-in area and want to see the part of the drawing file that is just a little to the left, what view control do you use? Use PAN. PAN acts just like a camera pan. It lets you move around the drawing file at your current magnification.

To make PAN work, you need to supply AutoCAD with a *displacement*. You define a displacement by giving two points. These two points determine a vector giving the distance and direction of your pan. When you give two points to identify a displacement, you specify a point where AutoCAD will pick up the drawing (first displacement point) and then specify another point where the drawing will be placed (second displacement point). Your display crosshairs trail a line from the first to the second displacement point, showing you the pan path.

Use PAN to isolate the square in the upper left corner of your screen. When you are done, your screen should look like the View After Pan illustration.

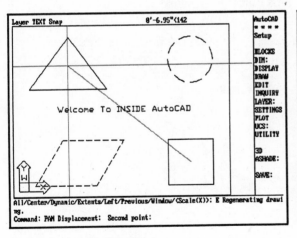

Pan Showing Displacement

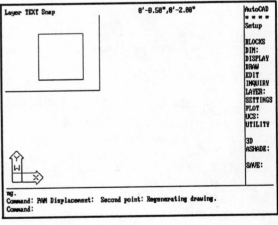

View After Pan

Using PAN for Display

```
Command: PAN
Displacement:            Pick first point at square.
Second point:            Pick second point at triangle.
```

➡ *NOTE: You can use a dynamic zoom to pan around your drawing.
Keeping your dynamic zoom window a constant size makes a dynamic
zoom function like the pan command. You can also do limited panning
with the center and left zoom options by defaulting the height.*

Using VIEW to Name and Save Working Displays

As you work on a drawing, you will find that your zooms and pans
frequently return to the same few drawing views. It would certainly save
time if you could save and recall your zooms and pans.

Suppose that you are going to concentrate your work on the square for
the next few hours. Periodically, you will want to zoom out to work in
other areas, but most of the time you will be zoomed in to the square.
Rather than having to show a window around the square every time you
want to zoom to this area, you can store this window, give it a name, and
call it up whenever you need it.

A stored window is called a *named view*. To store a window, use the VIEW
command to name and store it. You can select [VIEW:] from the [DISPLAY]
screen menu, or you can type it at the keyboard. Here's an exercise to test
AutoCAD's view command and to record SQUARE as a view.

Using VIEW to Save and Restore a View

```
Command: ZOOM              Zoom to an area just surrounding the square.

Command: VIEW
?/Delete/Restore/Save/Window: S
View name to save: SQUARE

Command: ZOOM              Zoom Previous to test the view.

Command: VIEW              Now restore it.
?/Delete/Restore/Save/Window: R
View name to restore: SQUARE
```

When you are done, your display should show the restored square.

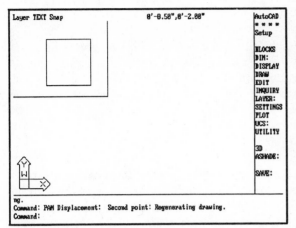

Current Display

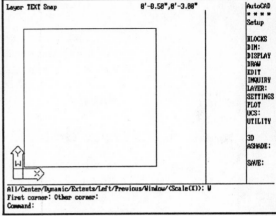

Magnified View Saved as Square

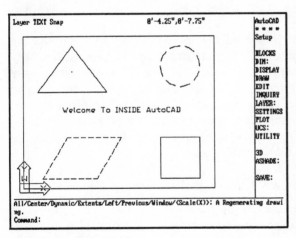

Screen After ZOOM All

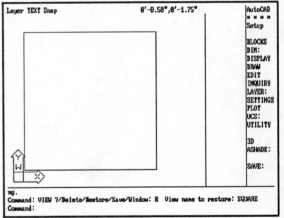

Restored View Square

The VIEW command has five options.

VIEW Options

? — Displays a list of all named views, their magnifications and center points.

Save — Lets you name the current view and store it.

Restore — Puts the view that you name up on the screen.

Delete — Prompts you for the name of a view to delete from the library of named views.

Window — Lets you name and save a view that you specify with a window (not necessarily the current display).

➡ *NOTE: You also can rename an existing view with the RENAME command.*

➡ *TIP: Two good standard views to use are "ALL" or "A" and "PLOT." If you ZOOM Center .8X, then save the view "ALL," you will give yourself a margin of safety in avoiding zoom and pan regenerations. Then use VIEW Restore All instead of ZOOM All. Use a view called PLOT for consistency in plotting.*

Keeping the Right Image Generated

As your drawing files become larger, you will need to control the screen size and resolution of your drawing. This means that you have to be conscious of just how much of your drawing you want AutoCAD to keep active at any one time. In using dynamic zooms, you have seen that AutoCAD keeps three different sets of drawing data active: the drawing extents, generated data, and the screen view.

When your drawing file is small and uncomplicated, all these subsets are usually one and the same. But as your drawing file gets larger, only portions of the file are generated, and it is more efficient to show only portions of your drawing on the screen. Going from one screen view to another within the generated portion of the drawing file with a PAN or ZOOM is usually done with redraw (fast) speed. However, calling up a screen view that contains non-generated data requires recalculation of a different area data set, and therefore takes more time.

VIEWRES Controls Smooth Curves and Regeneration

When you asked AutoCAD to call up the BASIC drawing file, AutoCAD performed two important calculations. First, it determined how much data to generate as active. In this case, AutoCAD made the entire database active since it defaults to a full view upon entering the drawing editor. Second, it determined how fine to generate curves. When circles or arcs are tiny, AutoCAD needs only a few straight lines on the screen to fool your eye into seeing smooth curves. When arcs are larger, AutoCAD needs more segments (or vectors) to make a smooth arc. AutoCAD determines how many segments are needed to draw what is to be shown on the screen.

The VIEWRES (VIEW RESolution) command controls both of these parameters. Try altering the smoothness of the circle on the screen by generating fewer segments. To see the effect, you need to change the circle's layer to a continuous linetype.

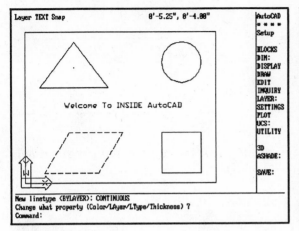

Before VIEWRES

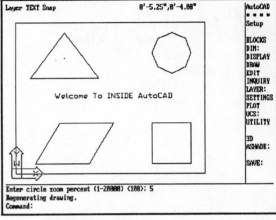

After VIEWRES

Using VIEWRES to Control Resolutions

Command: **ZOOM**   Zoom All.
Command: **CHPROP**   Change the circle's linetype to continuous.

Command: **VIEWRES**
Do you want fast zooms? <Y>: **<RETURN>**
Enter circle zoom percent (1-20000) <100>: **5**
Regenerating drawing.

Command: **VIEWRES**   Set zoom percent back to 100.

➡ *NOTE: If you turn VIEWRES Off, ZOOM Dynamic and all other pans and zooms will always cause a drawing regeneration. Although turning VIEWRES off is rarely advisable, it may be more efficient when zooming large text-filled drawings.*

Controlling Data Generation with REGEN and REGENAUTO

Notice that the VIEWRES command caused AutoCAD to regenerate the drawing in order to make the circle coarse. To regenerate the drawing, AutoCAD *reads* all the data in the drawing file and calculates the location of each element on the screen. When the drawing file is full of many lines, arcs, circles, etc., this regeneration will take a long time.

You will see that many commands, including ZOOM, PAN, and VIEW, cause this regeneration. You can also force a regeneration of the screen and drawing file with the REGEN command. Try a regeneration now by typing REGEN or selecting it from the [DISPLAY] menu.

Using REGEN to Regenerate a Drawing

```
Command: REGEN
Regenerating drawing.
```

➡ *TIP: Freezing layers keeps extraneous data from being regenerated. Thaw the layers when you need them.*

Using REGENAUTO to Control AutoCAD's Regeneration

When you zoom, pan or view, you usually want AutoCAD to make sure that everything in the drawing file is represented accurately on the screen. However, since regeneration in large drawings may take a long time, you may not want AutoCAD to regenerate when you are busy drawing or editing.

You can control whether AutoCAD regenerates the drawing with the REGENAUTO command. When REGENAUTO is Off, AutoCAD avoids regeneration unless absolutely necessary. When necessary, AutoCAD will first stop and ask if you really want to regenerate. The REGEN command always overrides REGENAUTO and forces a regeneration.

➡ *NOTE: QTEXT is a command that displays text on the screen as a box outline so that the screen will regenerate quickly. We will show you how QTEXT works in the chapter on text entities.*

Transparent PAN, ZOOM and VIEW

You can use the PAN, ZOOM, and VIEW commands, as well as REDRAW, while you are in the middle of most other AutoCAD commands. These *transparent* commands are triggered by a leading apostrophe ('). Recall that you can get transparent 'HELP the same way.

Draw a line and try a transparent 'VIEW and 'ZOOM. Look for the double angle bracket at the command prompt line. The double bracket shows that the current command is suspended.

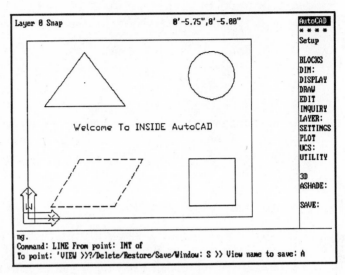

Line Suspended by Transparent View

Using Transparent VIEW and ZOOM

Command: **LAYER**	Set layer 0 current.
Command: **ZOOM**	Zoom All.

Command: **LINE**
From point: **INT**
of

                    Pick the top intersection of the triangle.

                    Before you zoom in. Save a view named A for All.

To point: **'VIEW**   Type a leading ' apostrophe for 'VIEW transparency.
                    Note the double >> prompt indicating that another command is
                    suspended.
>>?/Delete/Restore/Save/Window: **S**
>>View name to save: **A**   Saves the current View as A.

Resuming LINE command.
To point: **'ZOOM**   Window the circle.
>>Center/Dynamic/Left/Previous/Window/<Scale(X)>: **W**
>>First corner: Pick first corner point.
>>Other corner: Pick second corner point.

Resuming LINE command.
To point: Pick any point within the circle.
To point: **'VIEW**   Restore the View A for All.
>>?/Delete/Restore/Save/Window: **R**
>>View name to restore: **A** Back to the whole view, without a regen.

```
Resuming LINE command.
To point: <RETURN>

Command: ERASE            Erase the line just drawn.
```

So far, all the display controls you've used have looked in on your drawing with a single viewing screen or viewport. You can create multiple views of your drawing and display them on the screen. In effect, you can divide your screen into windows and place different views of your drawing in these viewports.

Displaying More Than One View at a Time

Viewports offer advantages over a single view display in some common 2D drafting situations. When you are faced with the problem of detailing different areas of a large drawing or you need to keep one area of your drawing, like a title block or bill of materials, in constant view, use viewports to divide your screen.

Using VPORTS

The VPORTS command controls viewports. It divides the AutoCAD graphics screen into windows. Each window contains a unique view of the drawing. These windows don't overlap on your screen like pull-down menus or dialogue boxes. They work just as if you divided your drawing screen into rectangles, making two, three, or four drawing areas out of one. You still retain your screen menu area on the right, and your command prompts at the bottom of the screen.

You can work in *only* one viewport at a time. This is called the *current* viewport. You identify the current viewport by clicking on it with your pointer. When you work within a viewport, you use your normal display controls just as if you were working with a single screen. You can zoom and pan, set a grid and snap, and the settings are retained for that viewport. The key point, however, is that you *can* draw from viewport to viewport. You can start a line in one viewport, click on an adjacent viewport as current and complete the line. AutoCAD will rubber band your line segment across the viewports.

You can select [VPORTS:] from the [SETTINGS] screen menu or the [Set Viewports...] item from the [Display] pull-down menu. When you select [Set Viewports...], you will get the following icon menu.

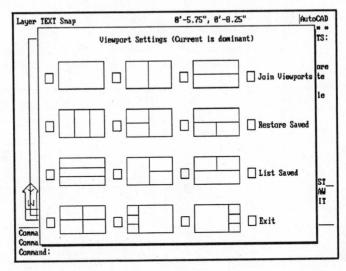

VPORTS Icon Menu

VPORTS offers several command options that you can use to build your screen display by adding, deleting and joining rectangles. Once you have the viewports you want, save and name the group. A group of viewports is called a *configuration*. Use the same naming conventions to name your configuration that you use for layer names. You can have up to 31 characters, and you can use three special characters ($, -, and _) in your names.

Here are the command options.

VPORTS Command Options

Save — Stores the current viewport configuration under a name that you have supplied.

Restore — Displays a saved viewport configuration.

Delete — Removes a named viewport configuration.

Join — Combines two adjoining viewports into a single viewport.

SIngle — Makes the current viewport into a single screen.

? — Displays a detailed description of the current viewport in the drawing.

2 — Divides the current viewport in half vertically or horizontally.

3 — Divides the current viewport into three viewports. You can choose from several configuration options.

4 — Divides the current viewport into quarters.

Try using VPORTS to divide your screen into three viewports. First, divide your screen in half, then divide the top half into three viewports. Second, join the top three viewports into two viewports so that you end up with a configuration of two up and one below. Use the illustrations and the exercise sequence below as guides.

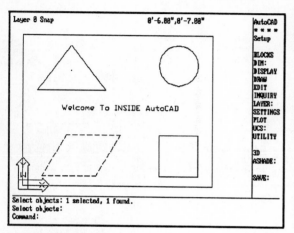

Screen Before Viewports

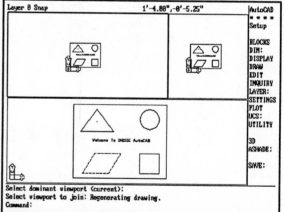

Screen With Two Viewports

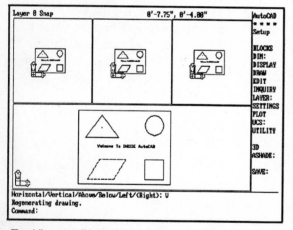

Top Viewport Divided Three Times

Screen With Two Viewports Joined

Using VPORTS to Get Multiple Views

```
Command: VPORTS                              Divide screen in half horizontally.
Save/Restore/Delete/Join/SIngle/?/2/<3>/4: 2
Horizontal/<Vertical>: H
Regenerating drawing.

Command: VPORTS                              Divide top half into 3 viewports.
Save/Restore/Delete/Join/SIngle/?/2/<3>/4: 3
Horizontal/Vertical/Above/Below/Left/<Right>: V
Regenerating drawing.

Command: VPORTS                              Join the top left and center viewports.
Save/Restore/Delete/Join/SIngle/?/2/<3>/4: J
Select dominant viewport <current>:
Select viewport to join:                    Pick top center viewport.
Regenerating drawing.
```

Well, you have multiple viewports. What do you do with them? Try a simple exercise, setting the top left viewport current, zoom to get a better view of the triangle, then draw a line from the center of the triangle to the circle on the right. Traverse the rest of the drawing, drawing to the approximate center points of the square and parallelogram, and closing the line up to the triangle. Use the next exercise sequence and illustrations as guides.

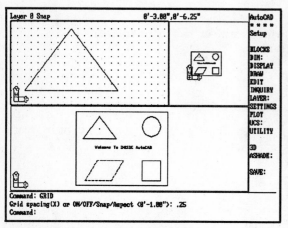

Upper Left Viewport Magnified With Grid

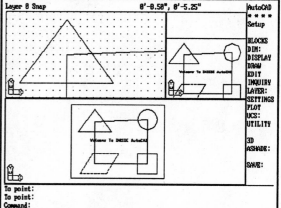

Upper Right Viewport With First Line

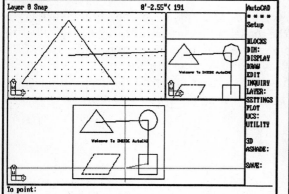

Bottom Viewport With Continuing Line

Complete Line in Viewports

Drawing With Multiple Viewports

Make upper left viewport active.

Command: **ZOOM**	Use Window option to magnify triangle.
Command: **GRID**	Set Grid to .25.
Command: **LINE**	
From point:	Start the line from the approximate center of the triangle.

Make upper right viewport active.

To point: **'ZOOM**	Do a transparent Zoom Window around triangle and circle.
Resuming LINE command.	

```
To point:                    Continue line to approximate center of circle.
```
Make bottom viewport active.
```
To point:                    Continue line to approximate center of the square.
To point:                    Continue line to approximate center of the parallelogram.
To point: C                  Line closes in the triangle.
```

When you are done, each viewport should show a portion of the completed line. Your screen should look like the Complete Line in Viewports illustration. Now, save your viewport configuration, and return your display to a standard single screen display.

Saving a VPORT Configuration

```
Command: VPORTS                  Save the viewport configuration.
Save/Restore/Delete/Join/SIngle/?/2/<3>/4: S
?/Name for new viewport configuration: BASIC

Command: VPORTS                  Set viewport to single screen.
Save/Restore/Delete/Join/SIngle/?/2/<3>/4: SI

Command: ZOOM                    Zoom all.
```

Your screen should return to a single screen display. The time it takes to name and save standard working views and viewport configurations is worth it if you are using multiple views. As your drawings become more complex, named views will save you time in editing and plotting.

Using REDRAWALL and REGENALL

When you are using multiple viewports and you want to redraw or regenerate all the ports, use the REDRAWALL or REGENALL commands. The standard REDRAW and REGEN commands only affect the current viewport. REDRAWALL can also be performed transparently.

Ending Your Display Drawing

This is the last time you will use the BASIC drawing. End the drawing if you would like to return to it for more practice. If you want to discard your work but save the setup, quit the drawing.

Exit AutoCAD

```
Command: END                     Saves your work.
```

Summing Up

There are many ways to get around an AutoCAD display screen. Display commands frame different aspects of your drawing, while viewports give you multiple views. Here are a few summary tips from experienced users.

Zoom gives you more (or less!) detail. The most common zoom-in method is the Window. It is the most intuitive and convenient way to specify what the next screen view will contain. The most common zoom-out methods are All and Previous, or named Views. When zooming out, use ZOOM Dynamic or a View named ALL to get you there in a single step. ZOOM Dynamic lets you choose your next zoom display screen. ZOOM Extents gives you the biggest view possible of your drawing file. Use ZOOM Extents at the end of a drawing session to make sure that you haven't drawn outside your limits.

A PAN displacement gives a nearby view while you are still at the same magnification. When getting from one side of the drawing file to another, use ZOOM Dynamic to get the *whole* view and help you locate your next screen view. ZOOM Dynamic is more intuitive than PAN and gives you feedback on how long it will take to generate your requested image. The VIEW command saves and restores zoomed-in windows. Take the time to use names and store views for drawing efficiency.

Watch how and how often you regenerate your drawing file. Doing a REDRAW cleans construction marks off the screen and *refreshes* the image without regenerating the drawing. Remember VIEWRES optimizes display generation by trading looks for speed. The REGEN command gets you the latest look at what's in the drawing file. Automatic drawing regeneration is controlled with REGENAUTO.

Use VPORTS to get multiple views of your drawing. Use multiple viewports when you need to do detailed (zoomed-in) work while still looking at your whole drawing, or to see a reference part of your drawing, like a schedule. Name and save your standard viewport configurations.

Let's get out of our viewing chairs and climb inside AutoCAD. Next you will find out how AutoCAD's drafting tools work, and how they speed up drawing creation.

CHAPTER 5

Graphic Entities
LINES AND THE SHAPES THEY MAKE

Lay of the Land — Basic Graphic Functions

Setup and display controls are really just tools for creating an environment in which to draw. Just as you'll find collections of tools around a manual drafting board for making lines, text, and curves, you will find AutoCAD gives you a collection of electronic tools to perform similar functions. In this chapter, you will learn about the drawing commands — the drawing tools. Each command creates an entity, the most fundamental piece of a drawing. The line command creates a line entity; the arc command creates an arc entity. These drawing entities are sometimes called *graphic primitives*. Why graphic primitives? We quote from an unamed source.

As primitives, they really are very intelligent.

— CAD Anthropologist

Actually, primitives are the primary entities from which more complex components, symbols, and whole drawings are built. For example, you might make an annotation bubble symbol from primitive line, circle, and text entities.

On paper, your drawing is static. In AutoCAD, graphic entities are *dynamic*. An AutoCAD arc has handles for hauling it around. Text has changeable height, width, and slant. Lines have two endpoints, but when two lines cross, AutoCAD can find the exact intersection. All the graphic entities are shown in the illustration below.

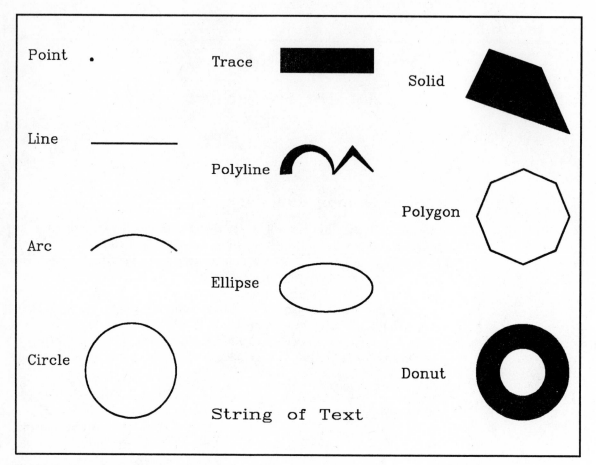

Drawing of Graphic Entities

Drawing Tools

In the course of setting up your drawing environment, you have already used a core set of drawing commands, the POINT, LINE, CIRCLE, PLINE and DTEXT commands. We will formally re-introduce you to them and to their associates, the ARC, DONUT, POLYGON, ELLIPSE, TRACE, and SOLID.

You will find all the drawing commands by selecting the [DRAW] key on the screen root menu. There are two screen menu pages of commands. Use [next] to get to the second page. The [DRAW] key also appears near the bottom of most screen menus as a convenience to get to the draw menu. You also can select drawing commands from the [Draw] pull-down menu, or from your tablet menu. In this chapter, we will show the menu item for the entity commands you will use, and assume that you have pulled down [Draw] or selected the appropriate page of the [DRAW] screen menu. The draw commands are shown in the Draw Screen and Pull-Down Menus illustration.

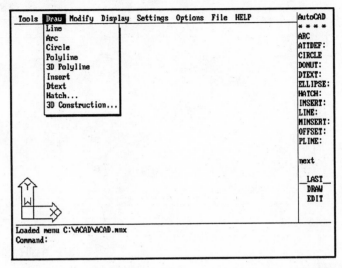

Draw Screen and Pull-Down Menus

Drawing Goals

The goals for this chapter are two-fold. The first is to learn about the different graphic entities and how they're used. The second is to begin work on a real drawing. You will use graphic entities to build a design, which we call a widget. Then, use AutoCAD's powerful editing commands (in the next chapter) to manipulate your drawing by moving, copying and changing entities quickly and easily.

By the end of the next chapter, you should have a complete widget layout on your screen. The widget may show faint resemblance to a real board layout, but it does contain *all* of AutoCAD's graphic entities. The entities that you will use are shown in the Entities Used in Widget Drawing illustration.

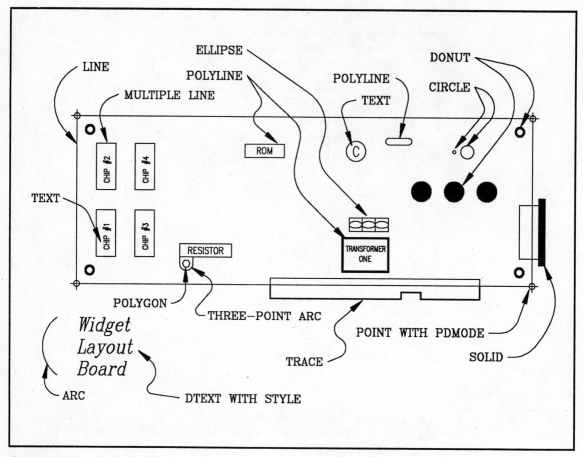

Entities Used in Widget Drawing

Setup for Drawing Entities

To get started, you need to create a new drawing. If you are using the IA DISK, use the CHAP-05 drawing and name it WIDGET. If you are not using the disk, create the WIDGET drawing with the settings shown in the table below. After you finish your setup, create three viewports, saving your viewport configuration as 3VIEW.

AXIS	COORDS	GRID	SNAP	
Off	On	.5	.1	
UNITS	Engineering, 2 decimal points, 2 fractional places for angles, defaults all other settings.			
LIMITS	0,0 to 11,8.5			
ZOOM	Zoom All.			

Layer name	State	Color	Linetype
0	CURRENT	7 (white)	CONTINUOUS
BOARD	On	2 (yellow)	CONTINUOUS
TEXT	On	3 (green)	CONTINUOUS
HIDDEN	On	1 (red)	HIDDEN
PARTS	On	4 (cyan)	CONTINUOUS

Widget Drawing Settings

Setup for WIDGET Drawing

 Enter selection: **1**   Begin a NEW drawing called WIDGET=CHAP-05.

 Enter selection: **1**   Begin a NEW drawing called WIDGET.

Check to see that your drawing has the setup shown in the Widget Drawing Settings table.

```
Command: VPORTS                          Set up for three Vports.
Save/Restore/Delete/Join/SIngle/?/2/<3>/4: <RETURN>
Horizontal/Vertical/Above/Below/Left/<Right>: A
Regenerating drawing.

Command: <RETURN>
VPORTS
Save/Restore/Delete/Join/SIngle/?/2/<3>/4: S
?/Name for new viewport configuration: 3VIEW
```

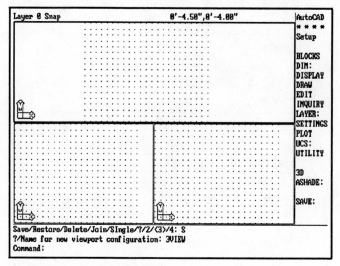

Drawing With Viewports 3VIEW

When you are done, your screen should look like the Drawing With Viewports 3VIEW illustration. Your current layer should be layer 0.

How to Use a Scratch Layer to Experiment

Each exercise in the chapter shows you how to use one or more drawing command options for each graphic entity. As you work through this chapter's exercises, you will use each drawing command. Some commands like ARC, PLINE, and DTEXT have several options that you may want to explore on your own. Make a layer named SCRATCH to experiment on; it will not be used in the basic widget drawing. If your practice entities get in the way, turn layer SCRATCH off.

Use Snaps and Osnaps

The drawing entity exercises (and the rest of the exercises in the book) show coordinate values for drawing points. These are all snappable (or osnappable) points. You can pick the points on the screen by maintaining your snap and grid, and by following your coords readout. If you are unsure about a coordinate value, you can always type in the value shown in the exercise.

Practice with Viewports

Since the basic widget drawing is rectangular, we set up three viewports: left and right zoomed views of the widget, and the whole drawing in a single (upper) view. The viewports in the exercises provide practice working with viewports, but the ports are *not* essential to the drawing. If you want, you can work with a standard single view, but you will need to do more pans and zooms.

The Point's Point

Start with the point. The lowly point is the *most* fundamental drawing entity. Points can play a helpful role in building a drawing file. You can use points as reference drawing points. The point itself is sometimes hard to see, but you can control the point display. Lay out the four reference points for the widget board using POINT, then use PDMODE to set a point *type* that is easier to see.

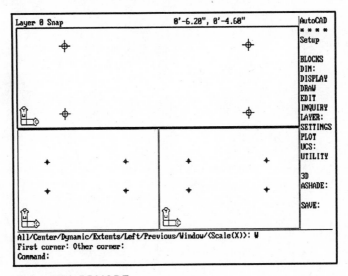

Points With PDMODE

Using PDMODE to Set a Point Type

Command: **POINT**	Now let's make the point.
Point: **2.50",3.30"**	Puts a small blip at the point.
Command: **REDRAW**	Leaves only a dot.
Command: **SETVAR**	
Variable name or ?: **PDMODE**	
New value for PDMODE <0>: **34**	Displays points as a circle with a cross in them.
Command: **POINT**	Put points at 2.50,5.80 — 9.50,5.80 — 9.50,3.30.
Command: **REGEN**	Force a regen to see the first point.
Regenerating drawing.	
Command: **ZOOM**	Use Window to fill top viewport with points.

Your screen display should look like the Points With PDMODE illustration (above). When you drew the first point, a mark appeared on the screen. This mark was actually larger than the point that you placed—it was simply the construction marker (blip) for the point. The REDRAW cleared the construction marker and left a small, white dot on the screen. That's the default point type.

Points Example Slide

Resetting your point display mode gave you the circle-with-cross points. You can set about 20 combinations of point types with PDMODE. (See the Points Example Slide above.) Control the size with the PDSIZE system variable. Set PDSIZE to a positive number to set its height in drawing units. Set it to a negative number to make point size a consistent percentage of screen height, regardless of zoom.

Setting up a reference layer with points or a few lines can help organize your drawing file to place other elements. (You *can* osnap to a point, but you can't osnap to a grid point.) When you are all through with your placements, you can turn the reference layer off.

The LINE Command — How Two Points Make a Line

You've already used the LINE command several times. Issuing the LINE command to AutoCAD begins a process of recording the two endpoints of a line segment. The two points you identify define a line segment. Recall, there are several ways to enter points.

- Using the pointer and crosshairs to pick points.

- Using SNAP, ORTHO, and OSNAP commands to control your point picking.

- Typing absolute coordinates at the keyboard.

- Typing relative or polar coordinates at the keyboard.

Once a line is created from two endpoints (however they were entered), AutoCAD assumes that you want to continue drawing lines until you end the LINE command and return to the command prompt.

How to Use LINE Options

LINE has three other useful options: Continue, Undo, and Close. The continue option lets you pick up the last point of the most recent line to start a new line segment. A <RETURN> entered in response to the From point prompt lets you continue. Undo eliminates the last line segment and backs up one point to let you try the line segment again. Close makes a polygon by taking your last endpoint and *closing* it to your first point. Undo and close are achieved by typing a **U** or a **C** at the To point prompt.

Here's a little LINE exercise. Select [LINE] from the [Draw] screen menu and start to draw the perimeter of the widget board using different types of coordinate entry. Then, try the continue and undo options before you complete the perimeter. (If all of this seems old hat, just pick the perimeter points to get the board's outline.)

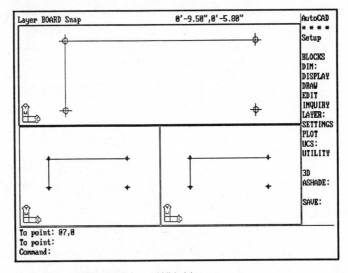

Two Sides of Board Drawn With Lines

Using the LINE Command

Make top viewport active.

Command: **LAYER**	Set Layer BOARD current.
Command: **LINE**	Use the screen menu.
From point: **2.50",3.30"**	Absolute entry.
To point: **@2.50"<90**	Polar entry.
To point: **@7,0**	Relative entry.
To point: **<RETURN>**	

Now, try the continue and undo options.

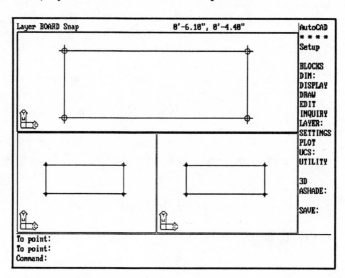

Completed Widget Layout Board

Using LINE's Continue and Undo Options

Command: **LINE**	
From point: **<RETURN>**	Continue line from last point.
To point:	Pick any random point.
To point: **U**	Undo the last line.
To point:	Pick absolute point 9.5,3.30.
To point:	Pick absolute point 2.5,3.30
To point: **<RETURN>**	End line to complete layout board.

Your screen should look like the Completed Widget Layout Board.

→ *NOTE: You can keep undoing as long as you are in the LINE command and have not exited the command with a <RETURN>, <SPACE>, or <^C>.*

Add a port to the widget's right side to see the effects of the close option.

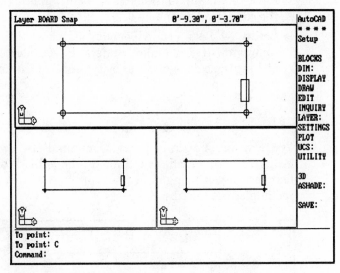

Widget Board With Port

Using the LINE Close Option

Command: **LINE**	Draw lines using absolute entry.
From point:	Pick absolute point 9.30,3.70.
To point:	Pick absolute point 9.30,4.50.
To point:	Pick absolute point 9.60,4.50.
To point:	Pick absolute point 9.60,3.70.
To point: **C**	Close to complete rectangle.
Command:	

Your screen should look like the Widget Board With Port illustration. Notice that you are no longer in the LINE command, but that the command prompt is showing. Any time you have drawn a few line segments and want to make them into a polygon, use close. A C<RETURN> is all you need from the keyboard in response to the To point prompt.

Here is a summary of the LINE options.

LINE Options

continue — Starts a new segment from the last point used as a line endpoint. (Not necessarily the crosshairs location.)

Close — Uses the From point of the first line segment in the current LINE command as the next To point, making a closed polygon out of the connected segments and ending the command.

Undo — Lets you wipe out mistakes without leaving the LINE command. If you make a mistake, you can undo the last point by picking the screen undo, or by typing **U** at the keyboard, then reissuing your next point.

MULTIPLE Commands

You can automatically repeat commands by prefixing them with the MULTIPLE command. Try filling up the left side of the board by drawing four rectangles, using multiple to prefix the line command. We call these rectangles *RAM chips*.

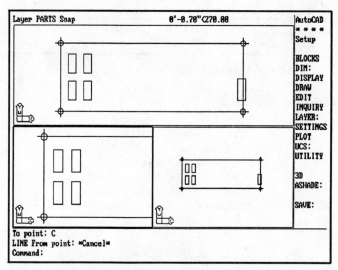

Widget Board With RAM Chips

Using the MULTIPLE Command to Draw

Make the bottom left viewport active.

Command: **ZOOM**   Zoom in on left side of board.
Command: **LAYER**   Set Layer PARTS current.

```
Command: MULTIPLE LINE
From point:                              Pick absolute point 2.80,3.70.
To point:                                Pick polar point @0.70<90.00.
To point:                                Pick polar point @0.30<0.00.
To point:                                Pick polar point @0.70<270.00.
To point: C                              Closes Line and automatically starts a new line.
LINE From point:                         Pick absolute point 2.80,4.70.
To point:                                Pick polar point @0.70<90.00.
To point:                                Pick polar point @0.30<0.00.
To point:                                Pick polar point @0.70<270.00.
To point: C
LINE From point:                         Pick absolute point 3.40,4.70.
To point:                                Pick polar point @0.70<90.00.
To point:                                Pick polar point @0.30<0.00.
To point:                                Pick polar point @0.70<270.00.
To point: C
LINE From point:                         Pick absolute point 3.40,3.70.
To point:                                Pick polar point @0.70<90.00.
To point:                                Pick polar point @0.30<0.00.
To point:                                Pick polar point @0.70<270.00.
To point: C
LINE From point: *Cancel*                Type <^C> to cancel Line.
```

Your screen should look like the Widget Board With RAM Chips illustration.

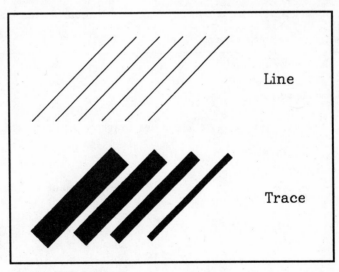

Lines and Traces

TRACE Is a Fat Line

TRACE is a distant cousin of the line. You draw traces just like you draw lines, with a From point and a To point. But AutoCAD first asks you how wide you want the trace. You can create traces as wide as you want. When drawing traces, AutoCAD lags one segment behind in displaying the trace, calculating the bevel angle between the first trace segment and the next. Try using TRACE to draw a *connector* on the lower right side of the widget.

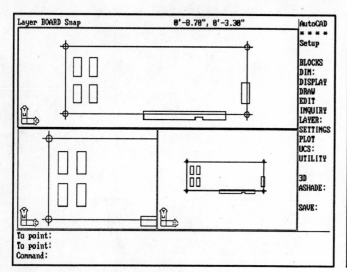

Connector Drawn With Trace

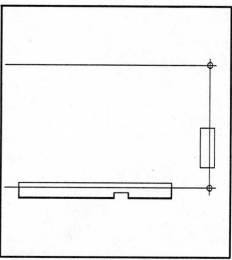

Detail of Upper Viewport

Using TRACE to Draw a Wide Line

Make the top viewport active.

Command: **LAYER**   Set Layer BOARD current.

Command: **TRACE**
Trace width <0'-0.05">: **.01**
From point: Pick absolute point 5.50,3.30.
To point: Pick absolute point 5.50,3.10.
To point: Pick absolute point 7.50,3.10.
To point: Pick absolute point 7.50,3.20.
To point: Pick absolute point 7.80,3.20.
To point: Pick absolute point 7.80,3.10.
To point: Pick absolute point 8.70,3.10.
To point: Pick absolute point 8.70,3.30.
To point: **<RETURN>**

Add an interior line with the line command.

Command: **LINE**   From 5.50,3.30 to 5.50,3.40 to 8.70,3.40 to 8.70,3.30.

Your screen should look like the Connector Drawn With Trace illustration.

Traces do have some limitations.

■ You can't curve a trace.

■ You can't close a trace.

■ You can't continue a trace.

■ You can't undo a trace segment.

OK, so TRACE isn't much like a line. But you get the idea. We recommend that you use PLINE to create thick lines, except when you need beveled ends. This bevel depends on the direction of the next trace. Sometimes the bevel can give a desired effect.

➡ *TIP: Traces are stored like four-sided solids, so osnapping to them is limited. Osnap INT and ENDP both find the corners. Osnap MID finds the middle of any side; you can use it, not ENDP, to find the original From and To points.*

➡ *TIP: You also can get thick lines just by using a thick technical pen when you plot a drawing.*

Arcs and Circles

Unlike lines, arc and circle entities require more than two simple endpoints. You can create arcs and circles in at least a dozen different ways. Regardless of the parameters (like endpoints, angles, directions, or chords) that you enter to create the entity, arcs and circles are stored by the simplest possible geometry. A circle is stored as a center point and a radius. An arc is a center point, a radius, a start angle, and an end angle. Using this geometric information, AutoCAD can regenerate curves at the best possible resolution and smoothness that your system can display or plot.

Getting to Know Circles

If you select [CIRCLE] from the screen menu, you will notice that the prompt line does not register a CIRCLE prompt. Instead, you get another screen menu listing five circle creation methods. Why so many? Different drafting tasks provide different information about where circles should go. Most often you know the center point and the radius or diameter. In these cases, you use this information to create the circle. Here are the circle options.

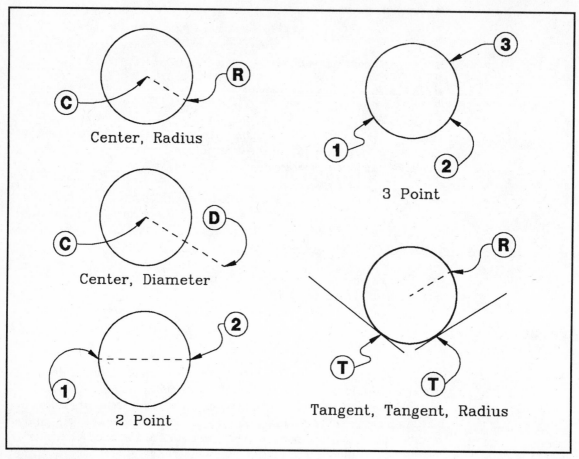

Center, Radius

Center, Diameter

2 Point

3 Point

Tangent, Tangent, Radius

Circle Examples

CIRCLE Options

2P — Lets you pick the two points of the circle's diameter.

3P — Lets you pick any three points on the circumference of a circle.

TTR — Lets you pick two tangent points and a radius. If a circle exists through these three points, AutoCAD will generate it for you.

<Center point> — Lets you pick the center of the circle and then either use the radius default or diameter option to complete it.

You now know that you can create a circle in at least five ways. Which one do you choose? If you know ahead of time whether you have a radius, diameter, or points, you can pick the correct option from the screen menu. For those who don't think that far ahead, AutoCAD lets you pick your options in midstream, using keyboard entry.

➥ *NOTE: Make sure you understand the difference between Center point/Diameter and 2P. Both let you specify a diameter, but if you pick the second point with Center point/Diameter, it merely shows the diameter's distance and the circle does not draw through the point. When you pick two points with 2P, you see a circle appear between those two points with the distance as the diameter. 2P gives you a diameter circle the way you intuitively think about diameter.*

Try using the default center point/radius, two point and diameter options to draw a capacitor and circles for a future switch, one near the center, and the second on the right side of the board. Set your PARTS layer current.

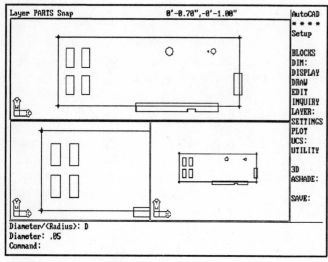

Capacitors Drawn With Circles

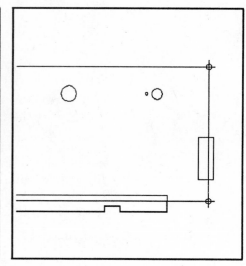

Detail of Upper Viewport

Using CIRCLE to Draw Capacitors

Command: **LAYER**   Set Layer PARTS current.

Command: **CIRCLE**   Use center point and radius for capacitor.
3P/2P/TTR/<Center point>: **6.80,5.30**   Type the center point.
Diameter/<Radius>: **0.15**   The radius.

Command: **CIRCLE**   Use 2 point for center part of switch.
3P/2P/TTR/<Center point>: **2P**
First point on diameter: **8.40,5.30**   Type point.
Second point on diameter: **8.60,5.30**   Type point.

Command: **CIRCLE**   Use diameter for outer part of switch.
3P/2P/TTR/<Center point>: **8.30,5.30**   Type the center point.
Diameter/<Radius>: **D**
Diameter: **.05**

When you pick a center point, AutoCAD gives you the option of using the
radius default or selecting a diameter. If you pick a coordinate as the
radius default as you did in the example above, you will get a circle
through the radius point. A D<RETURN> response will get the diameter
prompt. Then a coordinate pick will give you a circle by the
center/diameter option.

Typing 2P, 3P, or TTR <RETURN> will get you one or the other of those options, and AutoCAD will prompt you for the necessary points to complete the circle.

Your widget drawing is coming along. It should look like the Capacitors Drawn With Circles illustration (above).

Using Three-Point Arcs

If you thought there were a lot of ways to create circles, there are even more ways to create arcs. AutoCAD offers nearly every possible geometric method to create arcs. Start with the simple arcs.

The most straightforward way to enter arcs is with the default three-point ARC. It works about the same way as a three-point circle. The first point is the arc's beginning, the second and third points define the arc's curvature. The last point and first point define the chord of the arc. AutoCAD automatically drags the arc, unless you have turned drag off (with DRAGMODE).

Draw a resistor on the widget using the line command. Then use the three-point arc to draw the gizmo on the bottom left side of the resistor. Locate the resistor next to the RAM chips. Use your lower left viewport.

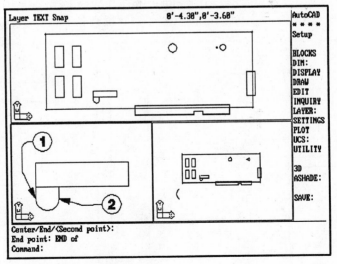

Resistor With Three-Point Arc

Using ARC Three-Point to Draw on the Resistor

Make bottom left viewport active.

Command: **ZOOM**	Use Window with corner points at 3.90,3.40 and 5.10,4.20.
Command: **VIEW**	Save view as RESISTOR.
Command: **LINE**	Draw a rectangle at the following coords.
	4.10,3.90 — 4.90,3.90 — 4.90,3.70 — 4.10,3.70 — Close.
Command **LINE**	Draw line from 4.10,3.60 to 4.10,3.70.
Command **LINE**	Draw line from 4.30,3.60 to 4.30,3.70.

Command: **ARC**
Center/<Start point>: **ENDP**
of
Center/End/<Second point>:
End point: **ENDP**
of

    Use endpoint osnap.
    Pick endpoint of first line at ①.
    Pick absolute point 4.20,3.50.
    Drag automatically comes on.
    Pick endpoint of last line at ②.

Command: **ZOOM**   Zoom Previous.

Make sure you feel comfortable with the way AutoCAD uses drag to help you decide where the three-point arc is going to fall. After the first two points are entered, drag is automatically turned on. Do you understand why the arc can flip around depending on the third point's placement? Push the pointer around until you do.

Try another arc using different options to be part of a future logo. Locate the arc just to the lower left of the board, using your right viewport.

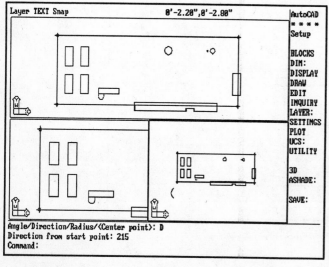

Arc for Future Logo

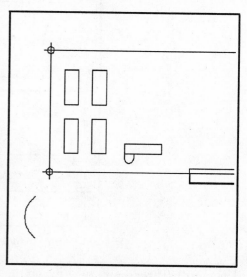

Detail of Lower Right Viewport

Using ARC With Start Point, End and Direction

Make bottom right viewport active.

Command: **LAYER**   Set Layer TEXT current.

```
Command: ARC
Center/<Start point>:                    Pick absolute point 2.20,2.80.
Center/End/<Second point>: E
End point: 2.20,1.95                     Type point.
Angle/Direction/Radius/<Center point>: D
Direction from start point: 215
```

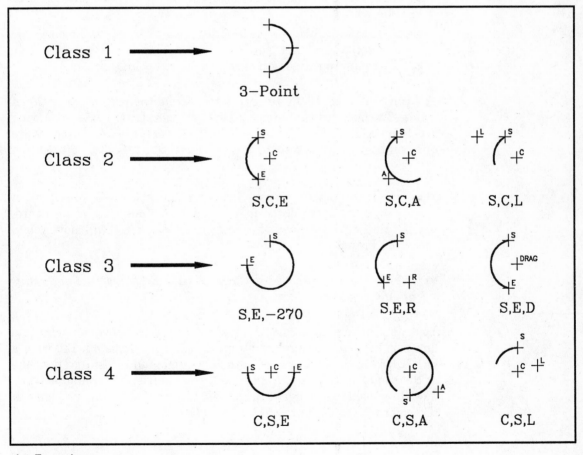

Class 1 ⟶ 3–Point

Class 2 ⟶ S,C,E   S,C,A   S,C,L

Class 3 ⟶ S,E,−270   S,E,R   S,E,D

Class 4 ⟶ C,S,E   C,S,A   C,S,L

Arc Examples

There are ten options for ARC which we've grouped by common function. (See the Arc Examples illustration above.)

ARC Options

<Start point>, <Second point>, <End point> — Creates an arc that passes through three selected points. This is the default option.

<Start point>, Center — These require an arc starting point and the center point of the radius of the arc. The third parameter determines the arc by specifying an <End point>, an Angle, or a Length of chord.

<Start point>, <End point> — These options let you define the starting and ending points of the arc first, then define how the arc will be drawn. You define the arc with an Angle, Radius, Direction, or <Center point>.

Center, <Start point> — This option allows you to first pin down the center of the arc, then the start point. The arc is completed by supplying an Angle, Length of chord or <End point>.

You can select any of the ten arc options from the screen arc or tablet menus. The options are abbreviated by mnemonic letters. If you're keying arc commands from the keyboard, you'll find the commands have common beginnings according to their class (Start, Center; Start, End, etc).

You can choose your options midstream and select one arc creation method over another by entering ARC and the options from the keyboard. A pick point will move down the start branch of arc, a C will move you to the center branch.

➡ *NOTE: You can always use OSNAP modifiers to interrupt and refine an ARC command.*

You can continue an arc or line, making use of the previous point and direction as the beginning point of the next arc command. Entering a <RETURN> at the first prompt of the line command will start a new line at the end of the last arc. A <RETURN> at the first arc prompt starts a new three-point arc tangent to the last line or arc drawn. Try some of these arc options on your SCRATCH layer.

Polyline Examples

Polylines Are More Sophisticated Lines

You have explored the most common entities, the line, arc, and circle. Given what you already know about entities, how would you create thick lines or thick, tapered lines other than by using the trace command? How would you draw a continuous series of lines and arcs? Can you make a closed polygon with three straight sides (lines) and one curved side?

Before you spend too much time on making basic graphic entities work too hard, you should consider the polyline, or *pline* for short. Instead of creating multiple lines to get a thick one, or creating independent arcs and then connecting them to lines, you can create a polyline.

Polylines vs. Lines

Polylines are different from independent line entities that visually appear to be joined with continue. AutoCAD treats a multi-segment polyline as a single drawing entity. Polylines can include both line and curve segments connected at vertices (endpoints). Information like tangent direction and line width are stored at each vertex.

Polylines offer two advantages over lines. First, since a polyline is a single entity, you can edit it by selecting any segment. Selecting any segment of a polyline selects all segments. However, if you wanted to copy one of the *RAM* chip rectangles made up of four individual lines in the widget drawing, you would have to select each line segment. Second, polyline segments are *connected*, while segments made with lines only appear to be joined. When you draw in 3D and create mesh surfaces, you must have edges that are *truly* connected. You want to use polylines to draw any polygon, particularly if you anticipate working with your drawing in 3D.

Try creating another widget rectangle, the *ROM Chip*, in the center of the board, using PLINE.

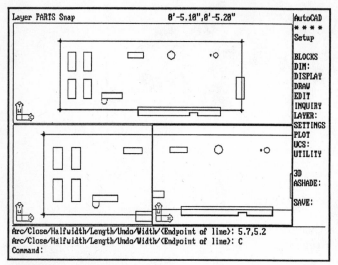

ROM Chip Drawn With PLINE

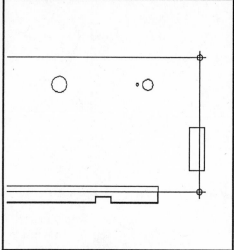

Detail of Lower Right Viewport

Using PLINE to Draw a ROM Chip

```
Command: LAYER                      Set layer PARTS current.
Command: ZOOM                       Zoom to fill the viewport with the center of the board.

Command: PLINE                      Create a ROM Chip.
From point: 5.10,5.20
Current line-width is 0.00"
Arc/Close/Halfwidth/Length/Undo/Width/<Endpoint of line>: 5.10,5.40
Arc/Close/Halfwidth/Length/Undo/Width/<Endpoint of line>: 5.70,5.40
Arc/Close/Halfwidth/Length/Undo/Width/<Endpoint of line>: 5.70,5.20
Arc/Close/Halfwidth/Length/Undo/Width/<Endpoint of line>: C
```

Your screen should look similar to the screen shot in the ROM Chip Drawn With a Polyline illustration. This new rectangle looks similar to the RAM Chips on the left. In the next chapter, you will see that this single ROM chip entity includes all four segments, while the other rectangles are actually four separate entities.

Since PLINE has the capability of drawing two basic kinds of segments — straight ones and curved ones, you will find that you get some prompts similar to the line and arc prompts. When you draw straight polyline segments, you get prompts like Endpoint, Close, and Undo. Check out the possibilities on the PLINE prompt line.

PLINE Options

Arc — Changes prompt to display arc options.

Close — Draws a straight line segment back to the first point of the polyline.

Halfwidth — Accepts values for half the polyline width for the start and end points of the following segment.

Length — Specifies a length of line to be drawn at the same angle as the previous segment. Used immediately after an arc segment, it will produce a tangent line.

Undo — Removes the last segment added to the polyline.

Width — Prompts for the starting and ending width of the following polyline segment. The ending width becomes the default width for all subsequent segments until changed with the Width/Halfwidth option.

<Endpoint of line> — Accepts the next point as the endpoint of the current polyline segment.

Selecting the Arc option presents another set of options, including some familiar arc prompts like Angle/CEnter/Radius, as well as Second pt and Endpoint of arc.

PLINE Arc Options

Angle — Prompts for the included angle of the current arc segment.

CEnter — Prompts for the center point of the current arc segment.

CLose — Draws an arc segment back to the first point of the polyline.

Direction — Allows you to override the default tangent direction.

Halfwidth —Accepts values for half the polyline width for the start and end points of the following segment.

Line — Changes prompt to display line options.

Radius — Accepts a radius value for the following arc segment.

Second pt — Accepts the second point of the point arc.

Undo — Removes the last segment added to the polyline.

Width — Prompts for the starting and ending width of the following polyline segment. The ending width becomes the default width for all subsequent segments until changed with the Width/Halfwidth option.

<Endpoint of arc> — Accepts the next point as the endpoint of the current polyline segment.

Drawing lines and arcs with PLINE is similar to drawing the equivalent elements with the basic line and arc commands. But there are several important differences. First, you get all the prompts every time you enter a new polyline vertex. Second, there are additional prompts that control the width of the segment, like Halfwidth and Width. When a polyline has width, you can control the line fill by turning FILL on or off. (We will show you how fill works a little later in this section.) Third, you can switch back and forth from straight segments to curved segments, adding additional segments to your growing polyline.

Using PLINE to Draw Arcs and Wide Lines

Try using these extra polyline features by putting two more objects on your widget. Create a *diode* by combining line and arc segments. (The diode is a little narrow object with arcs on both ends.) Locate the diode next to the capacitor circle. Then, draw a rectangle that is supposed to be a transformer using a wide polyline. Locate the transformer rectangle near the bottom center of the board. Continue working in your right viewport. When you start PLINE, the first prompt is for drawing straight segments.

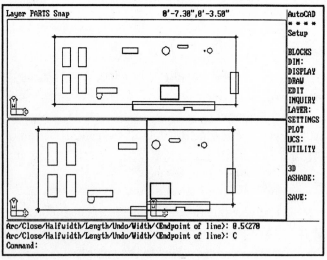

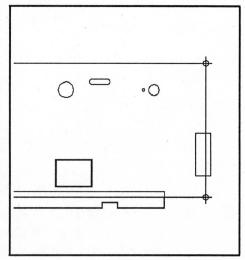

Diode and Transformer Drawn With PLINE   *Detail of Lower Right Viewport*

Using PLINE to Draw a Diode and Transformer

```
Command: PAN                                 Pan until the circle is on the left.

Command: PLINE                               Draw the diode.
From point:                                  Pick absolute point 7.30,5.40.
Current line-width is 0'-0.00"
Arc/Close/Halfwidth/Length/Undo/Width/<Endpoint of line>: @0.30,0
Arc/Close/Halfwidth/Length/Undo/Width/<Endpoint of line>: A
Angle/CEnter/CLose/Direction/Halfwidth/Line/Radius/Second
pt/Undo/Width/<Endpoint of arc>: A
Included angle: 180
Center/Radius/<Endpoint>:@0,0.10
Angle/CEnter/CLose/Direction/Halfwidth/Line/Radius/Second
pt/Undo/Width/<Endpoint of arc>: L
Arc/Close/Halfwidth/Length/Undo/Width/<Endpoint of line>:@-0.30,0
Arc/Close/Halfwidth/Length/Undo/Width/<Endpoint of line>: A
Angle/CEnter/CLose/Direction/Halfwidth/Line/Radius/Second
pt/Undo/Width/<Endpoint of arc>: CL

Command: PLINE                               Draw the transformer.
From point:                                  Pick absolute point 6.60,3.50.
Current line-width is 0'-0.00"
Arc/Close/Halfwidth/Length/Undo/Width/<Endpoint of line>: W
Starting width <0'-0.00">: .02
Ending width <0'-0.01">: .02
Arc/Close/Halfwidth/Length/Undo/Width/<Endpoint of line>: @0.50<90.00
Arc/Close/Halfwidth/Length/Undo/Width/<Endpoint of line>: @0.70<0.00
Arc/Close/Halfwidth/Length/Undo/Width/<Endpoint of line>: @0.50<270.00
Arc/Close/Halfwidth/Length/Undo/Width/<Endpoint of line>: C
```

➡ *NOTE: Because you can create complex objects with polylines, there is a companion command, PEDIT, that lets you modify a polyline without redrawing it from scratch. We will cover PEDIT in the next chapter.*

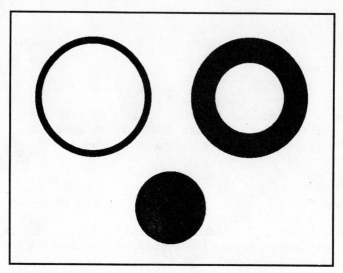

DONUT Examples

Polylines in Disguise — Donuts, Polygons and Ellipses

As you might imagine, DONUT creates a donut-looking entity. Donuts can be filled or unfilled. In fact, a donut with a 0 inside diameter is a filled-in-circle and makes a good dot. Get a cup of coffee and try the donuts! Try putting three filled-in donuts on the right of the board. Then, put a regular donut at each corner of the widget.

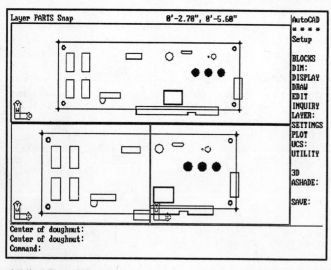

Adding Parts With Donut

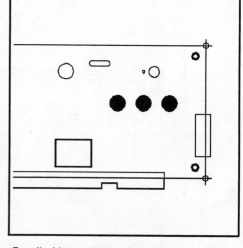

Detail of Lower Right Viewport

Using DONUT to Create Donuts

```
Command: DONUT
Inside diameter <0'-0.50">: 0
Outside diameter <0'-1.00">: .3
Center of doughnut:                      Pick absolute point 8.80,4.70.
Center of doughnut:                      Pick absolute point 8.30,4.70.
Center of doughnut:                      Pick absolute point 7.80,4.70.
Center of doughnut: <RETURN>


Command: DONUT
Inside diameter <0'-0.00">: 0.1
Outside diameter <0'-0.30">: 0.15
Center of doughnut:                      Pick absolute point 9.30,5.60.
Center of doughnut:                      Pick absolute point 9.30,3.50.
```

Make the top viewport active.

```
Center of doughnut:                      Pick absolute point 2.70,3.50.
Center of doughnut:                      Pick absolute point 2.70,5.60.
Center of doughnut: <RETURN>
```

As you can see, DONUT keeps on prompting Center of donut until you hit <RETURN> to exit the command. DONUT or DOUGHNUT, AutoCAD doesn't care which way you spell it.

The donut that AutoCAD constructs is not a new primitive. It is actually a polyline that has the following three polyline properties: it is an arc, it has width (you set the widths by entering the inside and outside diameter), and it is closed.

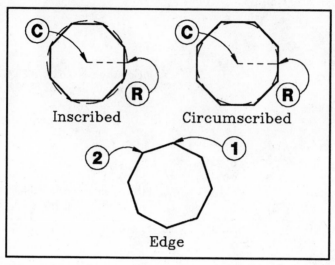

Polygon Examples

Drawing Regular Polygons with POLYGON

If you want multi-segmented polygons with irregular segment lengths, use polylines or closed lines. But if you want nice, regular polygons, take a look at the POLYGON command. POLYGON gives you two ways to define the size of your figure. You can show the length of one of the edges or define a circle. The polygon can be inscribed in or circumscribed around the circle. Add a six-sided polygon to the *gizmo* on the bottom of the resistor.

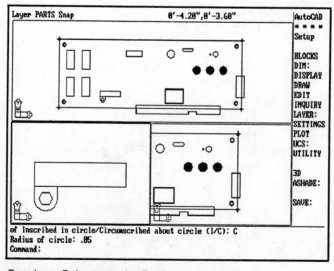

Drawing a Polygon on the Resistor

Using POLYGON to Draw Regular Polygons

Make the bottom left viewport active.
```
Command: VIEW
```
Restore view RESISTOR.

```
Command: POLYGON
Number of sides: 6
Edge/<Center of polygon>: CEN
of
```
Place target anywhere on the arc and pick.

```
Inscribed in circle/Circumscribed about circle (I/C): C
Radius of circle: .05
```

Your screen should look similar to the Drawing a Polygon on the Resistor illustration.

The POLYGON Edge method generates a polygon going counterclockwise according to the two edge endpoints you select. A polygon is actually another polyline in disguise. If you want to see a *slow* circle, do a POLYGON with 1000 edges.

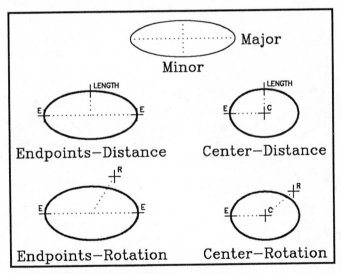

Ellipse Examples

Last — But Not Least -- the Ellipse

ELLIPSE is another polyline in disguise. AutoCAD first prompts you for the major axis, defined by two endpoints or the center and one endpoint. Then you can define the minor axis by distance or rotation, dragging the ellipse if you pick the point or angle. Use the Ellipse Examples drawing as a guide to help you make your ellipses.

Create a rectangle just above the transformer and put three ellipses in it. We call the part a *jumper*.

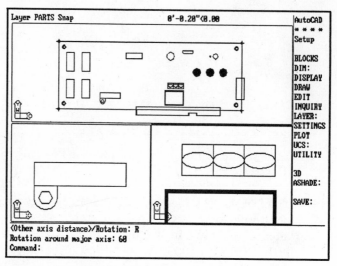

Jumpers Created With Ellipse Command

Using ELLIPSE to Draw Jumper Pieces

Make the bottom right viewport active.

Command: **ZOOM**	Position your window in close, above the transformer.
Command: **SNAP**	Set Snap to .05.
Command: **LINE**	Draw a rectangle at the following coords.
	6.70,4.10 — 6.70,4.30 — 7.30,4.30 — 7.30,4.10 — Close.
Command: **LINE**	Draw 2 more lines dividing the rectangle in thirds.

```
Command: ELLIPSE                        Draw ellipse in left box.
<Axis endpoint 1>/Center: C             Use center option.
Center of ellipse:                      Pick absolute point 6.80,4.20.
Axis endpoint:                          Pick polar point @0.10<0.00.
<Other axis distance>/Rotation:         Pick polar point @0.05<270.00.

Command: ELLIPSE                        Draw ellipse in center box.
<Axis endpoint 1>/Center:               Pick absolute point 6.90,4.20.
Axis endpoint 2:                        Pick polar point @0.20<0.00.
<Other axis distance>/Rotation:         Pick polar point @0.05<270.00.

Command: ELLIPSE                        Draw ellipse in right box.
<Axis endpoint 1>/Center:               Pick absolute point 7.10,4.20.
Axis endpoint 2:                        Pick polar point @0.20<0.00.
<Other axis distance>/Rotation: R
Rotation around major axis: 60
```

Ellipse is the last of the polyline family. If you want to try more polylines, use your SCRATCH layer as an exploratorium.

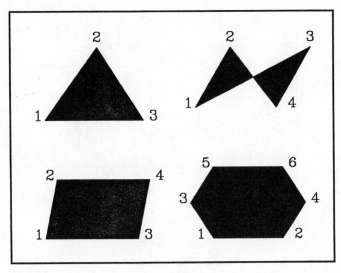

Solid Examples

SOLID Is a Polygon Filled with Ink

Using SOLID is a way to create a polygon that is filled with ink or pixels. It's that simple. A solid is a two-dimensional boundary filled with color.

Creating Solids

The SOLID command lets you create a solid filled area. This area is defined by three or four points forming either a triangular or quadrilateral shape. You can construct more complex shapes by continuing to add vertices. The order in which you enter vertices, and the spatial relationship between these points, determines what the solid will look like. You have to be careful not to get a bow tie shape from four points when you really want a quadrilateral. Nine times out of ten, users first create bow ties and butterflies instead of quadrilaterals.

Use SOLID to create a vertical solid at the outer edge of the port on the right side of the widget. Here's the prompt sequence.

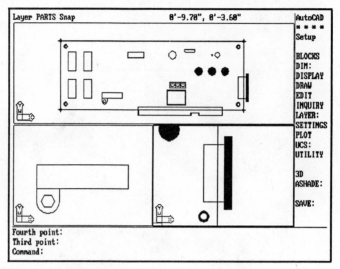

Enhancing the Port With Solid

Using SOLID to Make a Solid Shape

Command: **ZOOM**	Use Dynamic to magnify an area around the port.
Command: **SNAP**	Set Snap to 0.1.
Command: **SOLID**	
First point:	Pick absolute point 9.60,4.60.
Second point:	Pick absolute point 9.70,4.60.
Third point:	Pick absolute point 9.60,3.60.
Fourth point:	Pick absolute point 9.70,3.60.
Third point: **<RETURN>**	

Once they are created, solids and traces are identical in every way except name. They osnap and fill the same way.

Using FILL Control With Solids

When turned off, the FILL command temporarily reduces solids, polylines and traces to single-line outlines of their boundaries. When FILL is on, solids, polylines and traces are filled-in or shaded on the screen and at plotting time. Having FILL off decreases regeneration time.

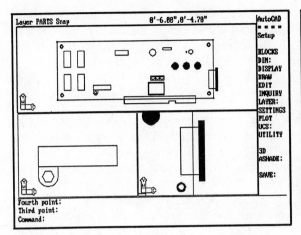

Fill On

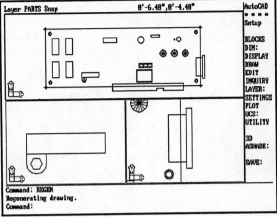

Fill Off

When you select [SOLID] from the screen menu, you will notice the [FILL On] and [FILL Off] keys. Fill is a *toggle*. It is either on or off. You can use the screen menu to select either setting. Turn the widget's filled entities on and off.

Using FILL Command

```
Command: FILL
ON/OFF <ON>: OFF
```
It doesn't affect existing entities until you regen.

```
Command: REGENALL
```

```
Command: FILL
```
Turn Fill back on.

Stopping Point

This is a good ending and resting point. There is one more entity to cover — text. If you have the time, move on. If you are pressed for time, end your drawing and come back later to the next section on text.

Saving the Widget

```
Command: END
```
End drawing and take a break.

A Word About Text and Style

Just like lines and arcs, AutoCAD's text has a set of parameters that define how text is placed and stored. You have to select a beginning point for your text, a height for the characters, and how the text is to be formatted (like a word processor). Finally, you key in the characters.

Style Settings

Before you proceed with keying in some text, you should consider style. "S" is for Style, and AutoCAD has it. Think about this: if you had to draw the letter **A**, you would need 7, 19 or more line strokes, depending on the font. AutoCAD stores characters in a compact code reflecting these strokes in special files called shape files. In translating text from the shape files to your screen or plotter, AutoCAD passes the text through several *filters* to get it to come out the way you want. The Style filter is one of the filters that AutoCAD uses in translating text from a shape into strokes on the plotter or characters on the screen. Style is a collection of instructions in the current drawing and does not change the original shape file font definition.

Rather than forcing you to go through the process of defining styles, text fonts, and other text parameters, AutoCAD supplies you with several default settings. The default style is called STANDARD. This style is defined with the simple TXT font and default width, angle, and orientation.

Using STYLE to Create and Maintain Text Styles

Use the STYLE command to create new styles or change the parameters for existing styles. Setting your style is really part of the setting up process. We recommend that you set your styles early in the drawing before you get into any intensive text input.

Use the following exercise to respecify the font used with your STANDARD style. If you are starting a drawing session, reload your WIDGET drawing.

Using STYLE to Create a Text Style

Enter selection: **2**   Edit an EXISTING drawing called WIDGET

Command: **STYLE**
                                            Select or type STYLE.
Text Style name (or ?) <STANDARD>: **<RETURN>**

```
Existing style.
Font file <txt>: ROMANS
Height <0'-0.00">: <RETURN>
Width factor <1.00>: .8                          Make it a little skinny.
Obliquing angle <0.00>: <RETURN>
Backwards? <N>: <RETURN>
Upside-down? <N>: <RETURN>
Vertical ? <N>: <RETURN>
STANDARD is now the current text style.
```

Your new style will use the ROMANS font and be slightly narrower than normal.

You will find it easy to select your text styles from a set of icon menus that are accessed from the [Options] pull-down menu. The following illustrations show two of the icon menus for selecting text styles. All of AutoCAD's standard fonts are included in the [Fonts...] icon menu. Selecting a font from the icon menu creates a new style with the same name as the font.

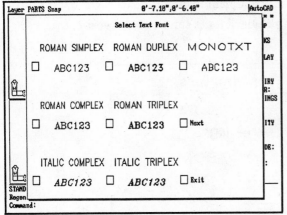

First Icon Menu for Creating Text Styles

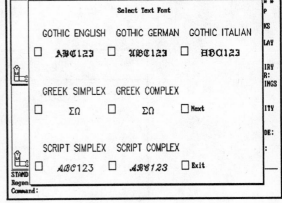

Next Icon Menu for Creating Text Styles

Here are the text style options.

STYLE Options

Name — Just a name for this collection of style parameters to help you remember how text drawn in this style will look.

Font — A set of letters and symbols with certain style characteristics. When you respecify a style with a new font, AutoCAD will regenerate your screen and replace all the occurrences of that style with the new style. This only affects the font used, not any other options in the style.

Height — The default is zero, which means the TEXT or DTEXT commands will control text height. However, if you set style height to greater than zero, text placed using this style will always default to the height you give. You will not get a height prompt in the TEXT and DTEXT commands.

Width — A multiplier, normally set to 1, that adjusts the width of characters. With a style width greater than one, you will have *squat* looking characters. With a style width less than one, the type will look *narrow*.

Slant — Normally, characters are upright with a slant angle = 0. But you can oblique your characters, making them lean forward with a positive slant or backward with a negative one. Be careful: a small angle like 15 or 20 degrees causes a dramatic slant.

Upside-down and backwards settings — If you like mirror writing or need to annotate the bottom of something, you can set up a style with upside-down or backwards writing. This also is useful for transparencies or the backs of printed circuit boards. Or just for fun!

Vertical — Any of the standard fonts can be styled vertically.

Text style parameters		
Width factor 0.75 ———►	ABC 123	R
Width factor 1.00 ———►	ABC 123	O
Width factor 1.25 ———►	ABC 123	M A
Oblique angle 0 ———►	ABC 123	N
Oblique angle 10 ———►	ABC 123	S
Oblique angle 20 ———►	ABC 123	V
Oblique angle 45 ———►	ABC 123	E R T
Upside down ———►	∀BC 123	I C
Backwards ———►	ƎSⱢ ƆᙠA	A L

Style Examples

Some examples of style are shown in the Style Examples illustration.

Notes on STYLE

Here are some notes on style.

- AutoCAD's style definitions are maintained in a tables section of the drawing database file. You can store many styles in a single drawing file. They affect only the current drawing.

- When using the STYLE command, a ?<RETURN> in response to the Text style name prompt will give you a list of the styles currently defined and stored in the drawing file.

- When you give a new name in response to the Text style name prompt, AutoCAD creates a new style in the style library.

- When you give an existing style name in response to the Text style name prompt, AutoCAD assumes you want to change or edit the existing style. It prompts you for all the style parameters using the old settings as <default> prompts.

- When you change the font or vertical option of a style that is currently defined in the drawing file, AutoCAD regenerates the screen. Any existing text of that style is updated with the new style definition. Changes to all other options are ignored for existing text.

Once you have created the styles you want for your drawing, AutoCAD offers two ways to input the text.

Dynamic Text vs. Regular Text

AutoCAD has two text commands, DTEXT and TEXT. You have already used DTEXT. Either command places text. The only difference is that DTEXT (you might have guessed it) does it *dynamically*, letting you see each character in the drawing as it is typed.

If you use TEXT, AutoCAD waits for all your text characters and then places the text on the screen when you exit the TEXT command.

It is easier to use DTEXT. Input for DTEXT is always shown left justified on the screen regardless of the chosen format. The justification is corrected when the command is finished. You also can reposition the box cursor on the screen at any point during text entry by picking a new point with your pointing device. This lets you place text throughout your drawing with a single DTEXT command.

Placing Text With DTEXT

To get started with DTEXT (and to see the new style definition), label the resistor in the lower left part of the widget.

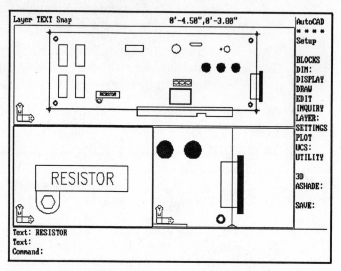

Resistor Labeled With DTEXT

Using DTEXT to Add Text Labels

Make the bottom left vport active.

```
Command: LAYER                                           Set layer TEXT current.

Command: DTEXT                                           Label the resistor.
Start point or Align/Center/Fit/Middle/Right/Style: M    Use Middle option.
Middle point:                                            Pick absolute point 4.50,3.80.
Height <0'-0.20">: .1
Rotation angle <0.00>: <RETURN>
Text: RESISTOR
Text: <RETURN>                                           Completes text entry.
```

The first thing AutoCAD wants to know about the text is how you want to format it. You have several options to format your text. Here they are.

DTEXT/TEXT Options

Start Point — Left Justified is the default setting. Just respond to the prompt by picking a point.

Align — Give the start and endpoint of the text location. AutoCAD determines the base line angle from your points and adjusts the height to fit the length of the text string you type in. Align overrides the style's height setting.

Center — Give the center point of the base line of the text along with height and angle. AutoCAD does the centering.

Fit — Like Aligned, you pick the starting point and endpoint of the text string. AutoCAD uses the text height you specify and adjusts the text width to fit. Fit overrides the style's width setting.

Middle — Like Centered, you give the center point of an imaginary rectangle around the text. AutoCAD neatly fits the text around this point.

Right — Like the left justified default, except it uses the right justification point you pick as the ending point.

Style — Lets you select from various styles you have previously set. The default is the last style used by text or set by the style command.

➡ *TIP: If you respond to the DTEXT (or TEXT) start point prompt with a <RETURN>, the new text will start one line below the last text you entered in the drawing. The new text will assume the height, style and justification of the previous text, even after you have used intervening AutoCAD commands.*

⊤EXT STRING	Starting point
TEXT STRING⊣	Right justified
TEXT ⊥STRING	Centered
⊤EXT STRING⊣	Aligned
TEXT S⊥RING	Middle
⊤EXT STRING⊣	Fit

Example Text Options

Several text options are shown in the Example Text Options illustration.

Try more text input by labeling other parts of the widget. Add text by entering a starting point and either typing or dragging answers to the height and angle prompts. The result of these text exercises is the drawing shown in the Widget Board With Text Labels illustration. Start on the left, labeling the RAM chips, then work your way around the board.

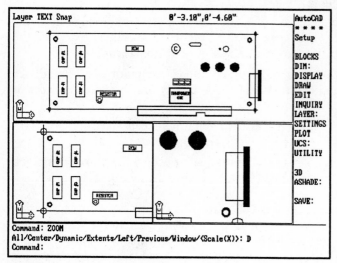

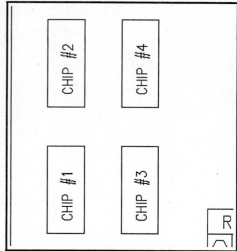

Widget Board With Chip Labels   *Detail of Lower Left Viewport*

Using DTEXT to Label the Widget Drawing

```
Command: ZOOM                          Zoom Dynamic to enclose RAM chips.

Command: DTEXT                         Change text height and rotation.
Start point or Align/Center/Fit/Middle/Right/Style: 3.00,3.80
Height <0'-0.10">: .08
Rotation angle <0.00>: 90
Text: CHIP #1

Move cursor by picking point 3.00,4.80
Text: CHIP #2

Move cursor by picking point 3.60,3.80
Text: CHIP #3

Move cursor by picking point 3.60,4.80
Text: CHIP #4
Text: <RETURN>
```

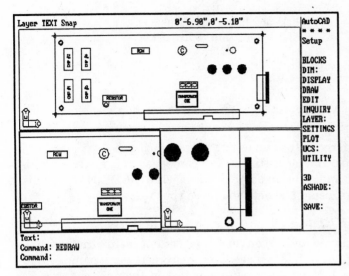

Widget Board With Text Labels

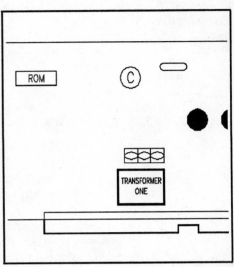

Detail of Lower Left Viewport

Command: **ZOOM**   Zoom Dynamic to the center of the board.

Command: **DTEXT**
Start point or Align/Center/Fit/Middle/Right/Style: **M**
Middle point: **CEN**
of   Pick a point on the circle.
Height <0'-0.08">: **.15**
Rotation angle <90.00>: **0**
Text: **C**
Text: **<RETURN>**

Command: **DTEXT**   Try the Fit option.
Start point or Align/Center/Fit/Middle/Right/Style: **F**
First text line point: Pick absolute point 6.65,3.80.
Second text line point: Pick polar point @0.60<0.00.
Height <0'-0.15">: **.08**
Text: **TRANSFORMER**
Text: **<RETURN>**

Command: **DTEXT**   Finish up with the Center Option.
Start point or Align/Center/Fit/Middle/Right/Style: **C**
Center point: Pick absolute point 6.95,3.65.
Height <0'-0.08">: **<RETURN>**
Rotation angle <0.00>: **<RETURN>**
Text: **ONE**
Text: **<RETURN>**

Command: **DTEXT**   Add label to ROM chip.

```
Start point or Align/Center/Fit/Middle/Right/Style: M
Middle point:                        Pick absolute point 5.40,5.30.
Height <0'-0.08">:                   Pick polar point @0.10<90.00.
Rotation angle <0.00>: <RETURN>
Text: ROM
Text: <RETURN>
```

Command: **REDRAW**   Clean up your screen to get rid of construction markers.

AutoCAD never forgets. Its <default> prompts during the text commands show your last parameter settings. You can speed parameter entry by accepting height and rotation angle defaults with <RETURN>s. You also can use snaps and osnaps to help you place your text.

What happens if you make a mistake entering text? If you use DTEXT, you can correct your errors as you type. If you do not realize that you have a mistaken text entry until you see it on the screen, don't panic — all is repairable. We will show you how to edit text in the next chapter. For now, just undo and try again.

Placing Successive Lines of Text

Try changing your text style and giving the widget drawing a title. Line up the words "Widget," "Circuit," and "Board" under one another. Here is the sequence. When you are done, change your display to a single view and zoom all.

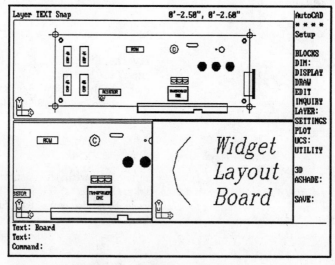

Title Added With Successive Text

Creating Successive Lines of Text

Make the bottom right viewport active.

Command: **ZOOM**   Zoom dynamic to the logo in the lower left corner of the board.

Command: **STYLE**   Create a new style for the title.
Text Style name (or ?) <STANDARD>: **TITLE**
Font file <ROMANS>: **ROMANC**
Height <0'-0.00">: **.2**   Give it a fixed height.
Width factor <1.00>: **.8**   Make it a little skinny.
Obliquing angle <0.00>: **15**   Slant it 15 degrees.
Backwards? <N>: **<RETURN>**
Upside-down? <N>: **<RETURN>**
Vertical ? <N>: **<RETURN>**
TITLE is now the current text style.

Command: **DTEXT**
Start point or Align/Center/Fit/Middle/Right/Style: Pick absolute point 2.50,2.60.
Rotation angle <0.00>: **<RETURN>**
Text: **Widget**
Text: **Layout**
Text: **Board**
Text: **<RETURN>**

Make the top viewport active.

Command: **VPORTS**   Set to a single screen.
Command: **ZOOM**   Zoom All.

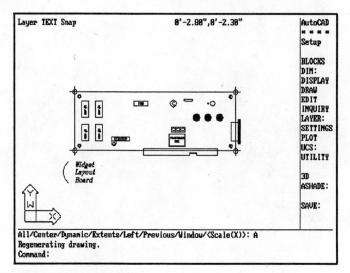

Widget Board With Text

Your screen should look like the Widget Board With Text illustration. Here are some quick tips on text entry.

➡ *TIP: Often you can set height and angle once (say when you are setting up your drawing file), and simply use these defaults for all future text use.*

➡ *TIP: To add a line to existing text, use DTEXT with Osnap mode INSert and enter only a space on the first line.*

➡ *TIP: You can enter text upside down by using an angle definition to the left of the starting point (180 degrees).*

➡ *TIP: The default height shown in the text command is rounded off to your Units setting and may not accurately display its true value.*

Using Special Text

Occasionally, you may need to use special symbols, or angle text on a drawing. This section describes how to create some common special texts. If you want to try some of the special text examples, use your SCRATCH layer to practice on.

Text Underscore and Overscore

Underscores, superscripts and special symbols are used regularly in text strings on drawings. Normally, you will not find these symbols on standard keyboards. The illustration, Special Text Examples, shows some special text. The underscored and overscored text in the illustration was typed into the DTEXT command as follows:

```
Text: %%u88%%u %%o88%%o
```

You can enter the special character switches, **%%u** (underline) and **%%o** (overscore), any time you are typing a text string in response to the Text prompt.

SPECIAL TEXT CHARACTERS		
%%%	Forces single PERCENT sign	%
%%p	Draws PLUS/MINUS symbol	88±
%%u	UNDERSCORE mode on/off	88
%%o	OVERSCORE mode on/off	88
%%c	Draws DIAMETER symbol	88∅
%%d	Draws DEGREE symbol	88°
%%nnn	Draws ASCII character	

Special Text Examples

Angled vs. Vertical Text

Most text reads horizontally from left to right. Sometimes, however, you may want text which is not horizontal.

Usually, you just use the normal DTEXT or TEXT parameters to Rotate or Align your text at any angle. But occasionally, you want your text to read vertically. You can create a style and give it a vertical orientation. A vertical orientation aligns characters one below the other. You can give all standard AutoCAD fonts a vertical orientation.

Quick vs. Fancy Text

As your drawing file fills up with drawing entities, every time you zoom or ask AutoCAD to redraw or regenerate the screen, it takes longer and longer to put all these elements on the screen. Sooner or later you'll want to cut down the regeneration time. AutoCAD offers two options for speeding up text display. First, you can do all your text work in a simple font such as TXT while you are creating the drawing. When it comes time for presentation, you can enhance the drawing by replacing the simple font with a more elegant one such as ROMANC. You save time during initial drawing editor work, but your drawings still come out well with the last-minute font change.

➡ *NOTE: Font character definitions differ in width, and font respecification doesn't affect the width of existing text, so you may find the new fancy text will not fit where you placed the old text.*

The QTEXT Option

A second option (and one we recommend to speed regeneration time) is to use AutoCAD's QTEXT command. QTEXT (for Quick TEXT) lets you temporarily replace text with a rectangle.

QTEXT is available from the keyboard or from the [SETTINGS] screen menu. It does not replace text until the next regeneration. Try *qtexting* the widget drawing.

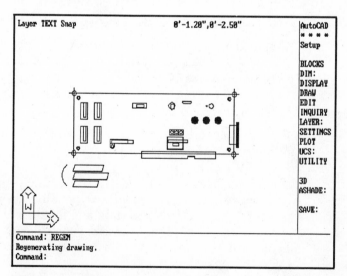

Widget After QTEXT Turned On

Looking at QTEXT

```
Command: QTEXT
ON/OFF <Off>: ON

Command: REGEN
Regenerating drawing.

Command: QTEXT              Turn QTEXT off.
```

Saving the Widget Drawing

This was the last time that you will enter drawing entities into your drawing file for the widget layout in this chapter. Your next pass through the widget will be for moving, copying, arraying and other editing commands in the next chapter. Save your drawing with an END.

Saving the WIDGET Drawing With END

```
Command: END
```

In this chapter you've covered a lot of material. Congratulate yourself on a whirlwind tour of graphic entities. You will be relieved to know that every entity that you used here works the same in a 3D drawing, although AutoCAD has a few more graphic entities especially designed for 3D which you will see in a later chapter.

Summing Up — Review of Drawing Entities

Screen and tablet menus are becoming friends, like road signs in a new town. While the number of side streets for different drawing commands may seem endless, you're beginning to understand how the primary drawing commands will get you almost all the way to your destination.

You may put aside learning additional commands and options until you need them or have some extra time to explore AutoCAD further. If you like Sunday drives into the country, AutoCAD lets you wander through some of the less frequently used commands without letting you go too far astray. We invite you to master the ten different ways to create an arc!

Here are some reminders about entities you have used.

Points are useful reference locaters for a later osnap. They can be displayed in various sizes and styles.

Lines are the pillars of the drawing community. Connected lines are the norm, a <RETURN> stops a connected line run. Continue starts a line at the last endpoint. Close makes a polygon by returning a connected line series to the first point. Take advantage of TRACE's beveled edge to get angled ends for fat lines. Otherwise, you will find PLINE superior to TRACE for every other purpose.

CIRCLE requires minimal information to generate full circles. Center/Radius is the most common circle creation method. A three-point ARC is the most convenient to create. The Start/Center series is also useful.

Polylines let you create single graphic elements composed of linear and curved segments. Donuts, polygons, and ellipses are made from polylines.

Text gets to the screen through a filtering process that controls style, justification, height, and rotation. DTEXT dynamically places text as you key characters at the keyboard. Style gives you flexibility in creating typestyles that are tailored to your needs. Keeping text on its own layer or using QTEXT keeps redraw and regeneration times to a minimum as drawing files expand.

You can think ahead about the sequence for entering SOLID vertices. But we bet you'll get a bow tie anyway!

Onward

In this chapter you began earnest work on a real drawing. While widgets may not be your thing, you have already mastered setting layers, drawing lines and circles, and inserting text. By the end of the next chapter, this drawing will be a complete, four layer, full color widget layout drawing.

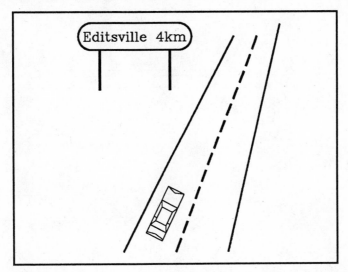

The Road Ahead

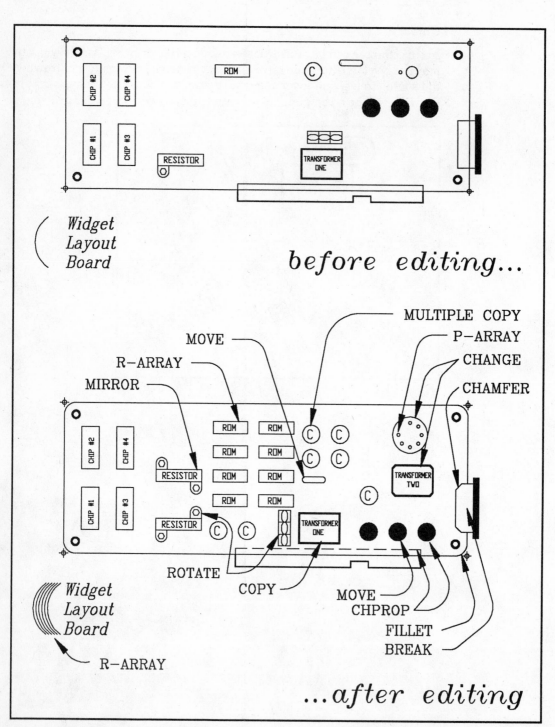

Widget Drawing Before and After Editing

CHAPTER 6

Introduction to Editing

IF AT FIRST YOU DON'T SUCCEED, TRY EDITING

You Edit More Than You Create

As you go through the book's examples, you may feel like saying, "Give me a drafting board, a straight edge, and a compass and I can beat this CAD system in a flash!"

It just isn't so. While some draftspeople may be able to create original linework faster than AutoCAD, it is safe to say that no human can revise and print new clean drawing sets faster than AutoCAD (and an organized user). The one certainty in the drawing business is *change*. Change this! Change that! Drawing revision numbers keep mounting! Becoming familiar with AutoCAD's editing functions is critical to your successful use of AutoCAD.

So far you have spent most of your tutorial time creating new drawing entities and storing them in the drawing file. Beginning with this chapter, you'll see how easy it is to modify your drawing file's contents with AutoCAD's editing commands. Sometimes you will find yourself spending more time editing existing drawings than creating new ones.

The benefits of editing are pure and simple. Editing allows you to quickly and easily stay on top of changes, and to create multiple images from minimal original entry.

Editing Activities — Changing, Copying, and Erasing

What types of activities will you encounter in editing a drawing?

Three basic activities stand out: changing, copying and erasing. You can change an existing entity's location, layer, and visual properties like color and linetype. You also can *break* entities, deleting portions of line and arc segments. You can copy entities, either one at a time or in a swoop (array) of creation. You can erase entities, getting rid of previous mistakes.

There are more advanced editing functions, like trimming, extending, stretching and scaling, as well as some editing *construction* techniques. We will cover these advanced functions in the following chapters.

The Editor's Toolkit

Most of the editing commands you will use are gathered on the [EDIT] screen menus and the [Modify] pull-down menu.

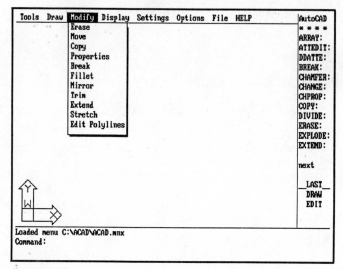

Edit Screen and Modify Pull-Down Menu

This chapter covers the basics of editing. You'll change both the spatial (location) and appearance (color and linetype) properties of existing entities. We have broken down the basic editing commands into two groups. The first group includes MOVE and ROTATE, which relocate entities, COPY and MIRROR, which duplicate entities, and ARRAY, which makes multiple copies. The second group includes the BREAK, CHAMFER, and FILLET commands. These commands delete portions of objects. In addition, we will review how to delete whole entities with ERASE.

How Editing Commands Work

Most editing commands involve a four-step process. You have to think about what kind of edit you want to do, which objects you want to edit, and how you want to edit them. The process works this way:

■ Select the editing command.

■ Select the entities.

■ Enter parameters and pick points.

■ Watch the edit occur.

Selecting an editing command puts you in an object selection mode. To get the objects you want, most commands require you to group one or more objects. This group is called the *selection set*.

The Selection Set

There are about twelve ways to collect objects for editing, including picking individual objects and using a window. If you make an error at the select objects prompt, AutoCAD will prompt you with all the available modes. As you select objects, AutoCAD sets up a *temporary* selection set and highlights the objects on the screen by briefly changing their color, blinking them, or turning their lines into dotted lines. This way you can confirm what you've selected to edit. Once you have your objects, you <RETURN> to continue with the editing command. One of the goals for this chapter is to give you practice using a variety of options to collect a selection set. Here is the list of selection tools.

Selection Set Options

object pick — The default selects by picking individual objects.

Window — Selects by grouping objects together in a window.

Last — Adds only the last object created to the selection set.

Crossing — Works like Window, except it also includes any object which is partially within (or crossing) the window. If your display hardware supports pull-down menus, Crossing will use a dashed or highlighted box.

Remove — Switches to the Remove mode, so you may select objects to be removed from the selection set (not from the drawing).

Add — Switches from the Remove mode back to normal, so you may again add to the selection set.

Multiple — Lets you pick multiple objects in close proximity and speeds up selection by allowing multiple selections without highlighting or prompting.

Previous — Selects the entire previous selection set (from a previous command) as the current selection set.

Undo — Undoes or reverses the last selection operation. Each U undoes one selection operation.

BOX — Combines Window and Crossing into a single selection. Creating your box from left to right is the same as a Window selection, right to left is the same as a Crossing selection.

AUto — Combines individual selection with the BOX selection. This selection acts just like BOX except if the pick box is on an entity, that single entity is selected.

SIngle — Works in conjunction with the other selection options. If you precede a selection with SIngle, object selection will automatically end after the first successful selection.

Setting Up for Editing

This chapter uses the WIDGET drawing that you created in the last chapter. You need to get into the drawing editor and create a new file called WIDGEDIT. You can make this starting file the same as the WIDGET drawing by setting it equal to the WIDGET drawing (WIDGEDIT=WIDGET). After you load the file, your screen should look like the Setting Up for Editing illustration.

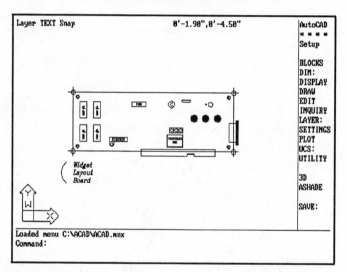

Setting Up for Editing

Setup for Editing the WIDGEDIT Drawing

   Enter selection: **1**   Begin a NEW drawing called WIDGEDIT=CHAP-06.

   Enter selection: **1**   Begin a NEW drawing called WIDGEDIT=WIDGET.

Confirm the settings shown in the Setup for Editing table below.

AXIS	COORDS	GRID	SNAP	UCSICON
Off	On	.5	.1	OR

UNITS	Engineering, 2 decimal points, 2 fractional places for angles, default all other settings.
LIMITS	0,0 to 11,8.5
ZOOM	Zoom All.
VPORTS	3 viewports saved as 3VIEW.
VIEW	Saved as Resistor.

Layer name	State	Color	Linetype
0	On	7 (white)	CONTINUOUS
BOARD	On	2 (yellow)	CONTINUOUS
TEXT	CURRENT	3 (green)	CONTINUOUS
HIDDEN	On	1 (red)	HIDDEN
PARTS	On	4 (cyan)	CONTINUOUS

Setup for Editing the Widget Drawing

You should have a full screen view of the widget. The following exercises do not make use of the viewports stored with the widget drawing, but you can use viewports in the exercises if you want to. Your current layer should be TEXT, but the current layer is not important to the exercises. Editing commands work on any layer!

Practice on a Scratch Layer

If you want additional practice using individual editing commands, make a new SCRATCH layer and set it current. Create some new entities to practice on, and practice the editing command. When you are done, undo, erase, or freeze the SCRATCH layer and take up again where you left off.

MOVE — Some Quick Moves with AutoCAD

Making a move is quite simple. You *grab* what you want, and move it where you want it. Get to the [MOVE] menu by selecting the [EDIT] screen menu, or select from the [Modify] pull-down menu. Then, try moving the solid donuts using a Window selection. Use the following screen shots as a guide. When you are prompted for a *base point* or *displacement,* pick a base point. After you pick this point, the selection set images will drag with your pointer. Pick your second displacement point, using the coordinate values in the exercise as a guide.

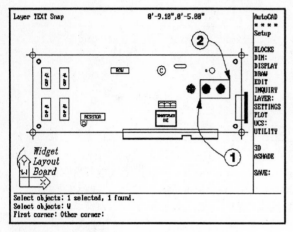

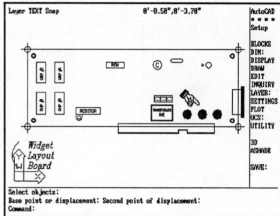

Selecting Donuts With Window for MOVE   ☞ Moved Donuts

Selecting and Windowing Donuts to Move

Command: **ZOOM**   Magnify layout board for a better view.

Command: **MOVE**   Crosshairs change to a pick box.
Select objects: **?**   Any wrong input gives you a full prompt.
Invalid selection
Expects a point or Window/Last/Crossing/BOX/Add/Remove/Multiple/
Previous/Undo/AUto/SIngle
Select objects: Pick the far left donut.
1 selected, 1 found.
Select objects: **W**   Put Window around the two right donuts.
First corner: Pick first corner at ①.
Other corner: Pick second corner at ②.
2 found.   All the donuts are highlighted.
Select objects: **<RETURN>**   This tells AutoCAD you are through selecting.
Base point or displacement: Pick any point near the donuts.
Second point of displacement: Pick polar point @1.00<270.00 and the
                                           move takes place.

When you finish, your screen should look like the Moved Donuts
illustration. As you can see, moving is easy. In the default select objects
mode, the crosshairs cursor changes to a small square pick box. A
selection window is similar to a zoom window. After you collect your
donuts with a window, they are highlighted. You tell AutoCAD you're
through collecting by hitting a <RETURN> in response to the select
objects prompt. When you are through selecting, pick your displacement
points and your donuts are moved.

➤ *TIP: You can change the pick box size with the SETVAR command and the system variable PICKBOX.*

Displacement and Drag

When you change the location of objects that you have collected in a selection set, you use a displacement. You could enter an absolute X,Y displacement at the base point or displacement prompt and then enter a <RETURN> to default to it at the second point prompt, but often you want to show a displacement by entering two points. Think of the first point (base point) as a *handle* on your selection set. The second point is where you are going to put the handle of the set down. The displacement is an imaginary line from the base point to the second point. AutoCAD calculates the X and Y differences between the base and second points. The new location of the object(s) is determined by adding this X,Y displacement to its current location.

AutoCAD does not actually draw a displacement line, it gets the information it needs from the displacement points. When you pick displacement points on the screen, AutoCAD shows you a temporary rubber band line trailing behind the crosshairs from the first point to the second.

As you just saw when you moved the donuts, an image of the selection set also follows the crosshairs. This is called *dragging*. It provides a visual aid to help you pick your second displacement point. Without dragging, it sometimes can be difficult to see if the selection set will fit where you want it.

When you set up a selection set handle for drag, try to pick a base point that is easy to visualize (and remember). If the base point is not in, on, or near the contents of the selection set, it will appear that you are carrying the selection set around magically without touching it. Sometimes you will osnap the points to a different but related object. Otherwise, it's a good idea to make this drag anchor (base displacement point) a reference point, like an attachment point on one of the objects.

Adding and Removing Modes for the Selection Set

Sometimes you put too many objects into a selection set and you need to take some out. AutoCAD has two modes for handling selection set contents, the default add mode and a remove mode. In add mode, you get the select objects default prompt. Picking individual objects or using any other object selection modes, such as **W** (Window) or **L** (Last), puts the objects into the selection set.

You also can type **R** for Remove in response to the normal add mode prompt. You will get the remove objects prompt. Remove objects from the selection set by using any type of object selection in the Remove mode. Type **A** to return to add mode.

Using a Crossing Window

There is a second type of window object selection called a Crossing Window. Crossing selects everything that either falls within your selection window or crosses the boundary of the window. You will find Crossing handy when you want to select objects in a crowded drawing. AutoCAD also knows the difference between objects within the window and objects crossing the window. Some advanced editing commands, like the STRETCH command, treat selected objects in the window differently from those crossing the window boundary.

Use the next example to combine a Crossing Window and the Remove mode to move the ROM chip in the drawing. Select the capacitor and the ROM chip together. The *capacitor* is the circle with a C in it. Use the displacement point values as a guide for your move pick points.

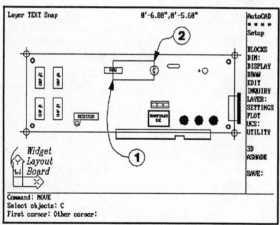

Using a Crossing Window to Move Objects

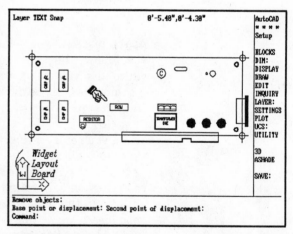

☞ ROM Chip Is Moved

Using Crossing, Add and Remove Selection Set Modes

```
Command: MOVE
Select objects: C          Select ROM chip and capacitor.
First corner:              Pick first corner point at ①.
Other corner:              Pick second corner point at ②.
4 found.                   Highlighting indicates they are selected.
Select objects: R          Remove mode.
```

```
Remove objects:                          Select the circle.
1 selected, 1 found, 1 removed           The circle is removed from the Selection Set.
Remove objects:                          Select the character C.
1 selected, 1 found, 1 removed           The C is removed from the Selection Set.
Remove objects: <RETURN>
Base point or displacement:              Pick lower left corner of ROM chip.
Second point of displacement:            Pick polar point @1.10<270.
```

When you are done your screen should look similar to the ROM Chip Is Moved illustration.

What's in the Selection Set?

By now you have noticed AutoCAD searching through the drawing file for entities that qualify for the selection set. Every time you select more objects for the selection set, AutoCAD lets you know how many you selected and how many it actually found. These numbers are not always the same for two reasons. First, you can select objects that do not qualify for editing. Second, you may have already selected that entity. In the latter case, AutoCAD lets you know it found a duplicate. In all cases, except multiple mode selections, AutoCAD uses the highlighting feature to show you what is currently in the selection set.

Using the Single Option for Object Selection

You will encounter cases where you want to select exactly one object. In this situation, use the single option to precede your object selection. As soon as an object (or group of objects) is selected, object selection ends without your having to enter a <RETURN>. Try moving the diode in the center of the widget down about an inch. Recall the diode was made with a polyline so it moves as a single entity. Use the exercise sequence and illustration as a guide.

Using the Single Option for Object Selection

```
Command: MOVE
Select objects: SI                       SI for Single.
Select objects:                          Pick any point on Diode.
1 selected, 1 found.
Base point of displacement:              Pick absolute point 7.30,5.40.
Second point of displacement:            Pick absolute point 6.70,4.50.
```

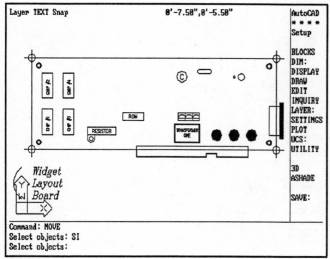

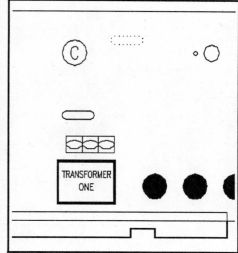

Before Diode Move   *Detail After Diode Move*

When you are done, your screen should look like the Completed Diode Move illustration. You can precede any of the object selection modes with **SI** for single. It is designed for use in menu macros.

➡ *NOTE: There are a number of editing commands, such as FILLET (which you will see later in this chapter), and TRIM and EXTEND (next chapter), that require individual entity selection. To invoke these commands, you must select your objects by picking points using the default selection process.*

Previous Selection Set Options

You will find the previous selection option helpful when you cancel an editing command or use several commands on the same selection set. Previous object selection reselects the object(s) that you selected in your selection set in the previous editing command.

Previous lets you edit the previous set without having to select them individually again. Previous is different from the Last option, which selects the last created object visible on the screen. Previous does not work with some editing commands (like STRETCH or TRIM) where a window, crossing, or point selection is specifically required.

Using DRAGMODE

When you edit very large selection sets, you may wish to control dragging. You can turn drag on or off using the DRAGMODE command. The default for DRAGMODE is Auto, which causes AutoCAD to drag everything that makes sense. If you want to be selective about what you drag, you can turn DRAGMODE on. If DRAGMODE is on and you want to drag in the middle of a command, type DRAG <RETURN> before picking the point that you wish to drag. Off turns dragmode off entirely and ignores a typed DRAG <RETURN>.

Tired of moving? Let's take a look at copying.

The COPY Command

The basic COPY command is similar to the MOVE command. The only difference between a copy and a move is that COPY leaves the original objects in place.

Try copying the widget's transformer, using a BOX selection. BOX combines a window and a crossing window. If you make your box left to right, it acts like a window. Right to left acts like a crossing window. Use the illustrations to guide your copy.

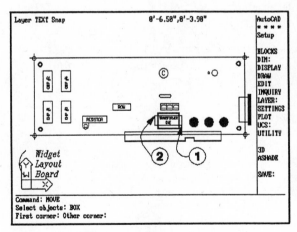

Copy of Transformer in Progress

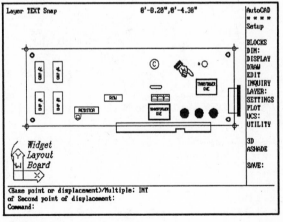

☞ Copied Transformer

Using the COPY Command and BOX Mode

```
Command: COPY
Select objects: BOX              Enclose transformer and text.
First corner:                    Pick first corner at ①.
Other corner:                    Pick second corner at ②.
```

```
3 found.
Select objects: <RETURN>
<Base point or displacement>/Multiple: INT          Intersection.
of                                         Pick lower left corner of transformer.
Second point of displacement:              Pick absolute point 8.20,4.30.
```

When you've completed the exercise, your screen should look like the Copied Transformer illustration. Remember, you can always use osnap and snap functions as modifiers to help you get an exact displacement location, or to help select objects for the selection set.

COPY Options

The COPY command options are similar to the MOVE options. They include displacement points identification, object selection options, and a new one — Multiple.

Copy Multiple Option

Selecting the Multiple option of the COPY command lets you copy the contents of your selection set several times without having to respecify the selection set. If you respond with **M** to the base point prompt, AutoCAD will reprompt for base point, then repeatedly prompt you for multiple <Second point of displacement> points. A simple <RETURN> response gets you out of the multiple loop.

Try making multiple copies of the capacitor. Put three copies next to the original capacitor. Put one copy between the transformers. Finally, put two more copies next to the resistor on the bottom of the board.

Using COPY Multiple to Make Copies of the Capacitor

```
Command: COPY
Select objects: W                          Put a Window around the capacitor.
First corner:                              Pick first corner point.
Other corner:                              Pick second corner point.
2 found.
Select objects: <RETURN>
<Base point or displacement>/Multiple: M
Base point:                                Pick center of capacitor.
Second point of displacement:              Pick polar point @0.40<270.00.
Second point of displacement:              Pick polar point @0.50<0.00.
Second point of displacement:              Pick polar point @0.64<321.34.
Second point of displacement:              Pick polar point @2.26<225.00.
Second point of displacement:              Pick polar point @1.94<235.49.
Second point of displacement:              Pick polar point @1.41<315.00.
Second point of displacement: <RETURN>
```

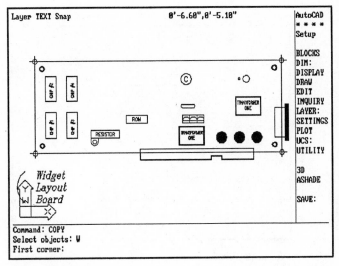

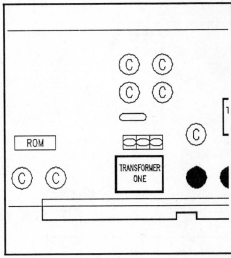

Before Multiple Copy   *Completed Multiple Copy*

Let's look at making arrays.

ARRAY — Making Multiple Copies in a Pattern

Often, you want to make multiple copies of an object or group of objects. For example, suppose you have a rectangle that represents a table in a cafeteria. It would be useful if AutoCAD had some way of placing that table repeatedly every 9 feet in the X direction and every 14 feet in the Y direction to make — say 5 rows by 8 columns of tables.

The ARRAY command works like the COPY command. However, instead of making one copy of the selection set, ARRAY makes a regular pattern of entities. You determine the number of copies and the repetition pattern. The two basic patterns are rectangular and polar.

Rectangular Arrays

Make a rectangular array by specifying the number of rows and columns that you want and an *offset* distance. You can have a single row with multiple columns, a single column with multiple rows, or multiple rows and columns.

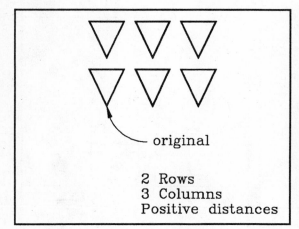

2 Rows
3 Columns
Positive distances

Positive Array Offsets

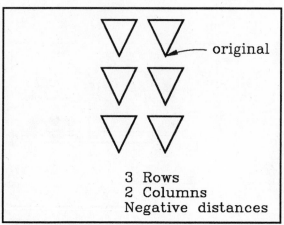

3 Rows
2 Columns
Negative distances

Negative Array Offsets

You can show the displacement between rows or columns by picking two points at the distance between rows prompt. Or you can specify the offsets by using positive or negative offset distances. The offset distance is the X and Y direction from the original set.

```
+ X gives columns to the right.
- X gives columns to the left.
+ Y gives rows up.
- Y gives rows down.
```

Try making a rectangular array using the ROM chip. The target drawing is shown in the Completed Rectangular Array illustration.

Using ARRAY to Make a Rectangular Array

```
Command: ARRAY
Select objects:                              Pick the ROM chip with text.
2 selected, 2 found.
Select objects: <RETURN>
Rectangular/Polar array (R/P): R
Number of rows (---) <1>: 4
Number of columns (||||) <1>: 2
Distance between rows (---): 0.40
Distance between columns (||||): 0.80
```

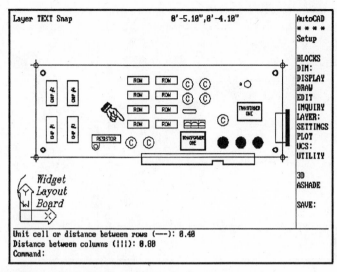

☞ *Completed Rectangular Array*

If you set up a big array (many rows and columns), AutoCAD will ask you if you really want to repeat the selection set so many times. If it gets out of hand, you can stop it with a <^C> and then reverse it with a **U** for Undo.

➥   *TIP: ARRAY is useful even if you want to make only one row or column of entities. It is quicker than copy multiple.*

Try making a set of logo arcs next to the widget layout text at the bottom left of your drawing. This is a single column array of arcs shown in the Completed Column Array illustration.

Using ARRAY to Make a Single Column Array

```
Command: ARRAY
Select objects:                          Pick the logo arc.
1 selected, 1 found.
Select objects: <RETURN>
Rectangular/Polar array  (R/P): R
Number of rows (---) <1>: <RETURN>
Number of columns (| | |) <1>: 6
Distance between columns (| | |): 0.05
```

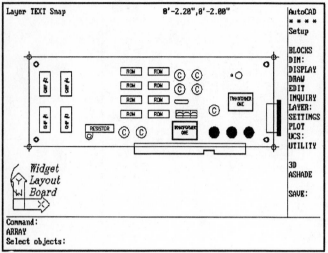

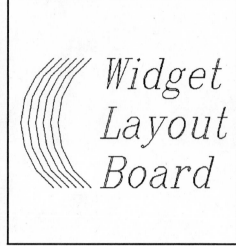

Logo Before Column Array   *Detail of Logo After Array*

Polar Arrays

In polar arrays, you place the entities in the selection set around the circumference of a specified circle or arc. Polar arrays are useful for creating mechanical parts like gear teeth, or a repeating circular hole pattern. Examples of regular and rotated circular arrays are shown in the Polar Array illustrations below.

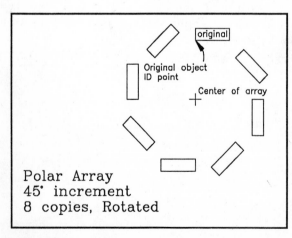

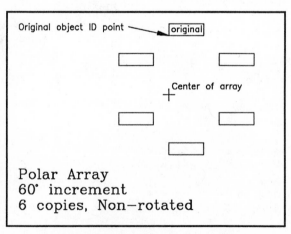

Polar ARRAY Rotated   *Polar ARRAY Non-Rotated*

When you form a polar array, you specify the number of items you want in the array, the angle you want to fill, and whether you want the items rotated. One item is one copy of the selection set to be arrayed. When you count your items, remember to include the original. You can array around a full circle or part of a circle.

The following exercise shows how to array around part of a circle, arraying the small circle (connector) left of the switch on the right side of the widget.

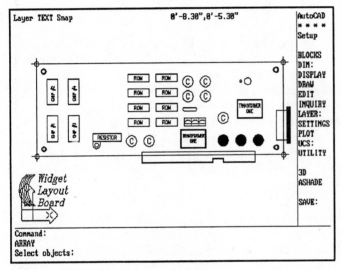

Before Polar Array of Switch Connectors

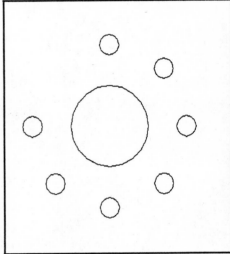

Detail View After Array

Using Polar Array on Switch Connectors

```
Command: ARRAY
Select objects:                                    Select small circle to the left of the switch.
1 selected, 1 found.
Select objects: <RETURN>
Rectangular or Polar array (R/P): P
Center point of array:                             Pick absolute point 8.50,5.30.
Number of items: 7
Angle to fill (+=ccw, -=cw) <360>: 270
Rotate objects as they are copied? Y <RETURN>
```

When you are done your screen will look similar to the Polar Array of Switch Connectors illustration.

➡️ *TIP: Polar arraying a line twice around its midpoint or four times around its endpoint will create a cross. A large number of items will create a sunburst.*

If you can rotate the items in an array, you obviously must be able to rotate other entities.

The ROTATE Command

The ROTATE command lets you turn existing entities at precise angles. Like MOVE, you specify a first point as a base point. This is the rotation base point. The rotation base point doesn't need to be on the object that you are rotating. You can put it anywhere and AutoCAD will turn your selected entities relative to the base point. But be careful, it is easy to become confused with rotation base points (like bad drag handles) that are not on the entities you intend to rotate. After you specify the base point, give a rotation angle. Negative angles produce clockwise rotation, positive angles produce counterclockwise rotation (with the normal direction setting in Units).

As an alternative to specifying an angle, you can use a reference angle. You can change the angle of an entity by giving AutoCAD a reference angle that should be set equal to a new angle. In effect you say, "Put a handle on 237 (for example) and turn it to 165." This is often easier than calculating the difference (72 degrees clockwise) and typing that number at the prompt. You need not even know the actual angles; you can pick points to indicate angles.

Try two rotations. First, use ROTATE to re-position the jumper. The jumper is the rectangular thing with three ellipses in it. It is just above the transformer. Reposition the jumper vertically to the left of the transformer. Second, combine a COPY command and a ROTATE command to place another connector on top of the resistor. Use the base point and displacement values given in the exercise.

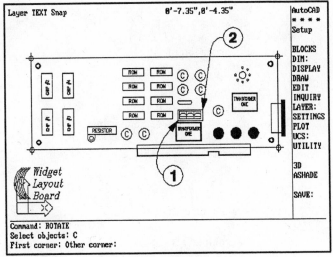

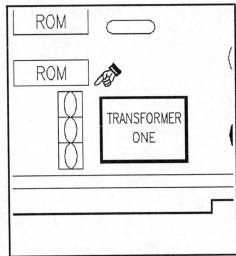

Selecting Jumper With Crossing Window   ☞ *Jumper After Rotate*

Using the ROTATE Command

```
Command: ROTATE
Select objects: C
First corner:
Other corner:
9 found.
Select objects: <RETURN>
Base point:
<Rotation angle>/Reference: -90
```

Place box around jumper.
Pick first corner point at ①.
Pick second corner point at ②.

Pick absolute point 6.45,4.30.

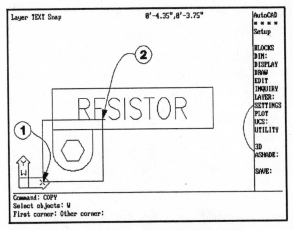

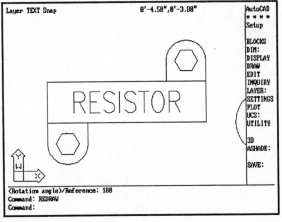

Selecting Resistor Connector With Window   *Connector After Copy and Rotate*

```
Command: VIEW                              Restore view Resistor.

Command: COPY
Select object: C                           Select the connector of the resistor.
First corner:                              Pick first corner point at ①.
Other corner:                              Pick second corner point at ②.
4 found.
Select objects: <RETURN>
<Base point or displacement>/Multiple:     Pick absolute point 4.50,3.80.
Second point of displacement: @            Copies entities on top of themselves.

Command: ROTATE                            Rotate connector to opposite corner of resistor.
Select objects: P                          Reselect entities.
4 found.
Base point: @
<Rotation angle>/Reference: 180            Rotation takes place again.

Command: REDRAW                            Shows the complete resistor.
```

This exercise shows how handy COPY and ROTATE can be in avoiding redrawing entities in new positions.

MIRROR — Imaging Through the Looking Glass

Mirror creates a mirror image of objects. Using the MIRROR command, you can mirror the contents of a selection set at any angle. MIRROR prompts you to identify a selection set in the usual manner. Then comes the mirror twist. AutoCAD prompts you for the beginning and endpoint of a mirror line. The line can be any direction. If you want a straight 180-degree flip, use ortho to help you get a straight mirror line. If you want mirroring at a precise angle, use relative polar coordinates, @8<60 for example, or use a rotated snap.

Finally, AutoCAD asks if you want to keep the original entities in place or to delete them. Think of this as either copying or moving the contents of the selection set through the mirror.

If you have text in your selection set (as our example does), you need to consider whether you want to pass the text through the mirror. If you do not want text mirrored, you can set the MIRRTEXT System Variable, allowing mirror-inverted graphics, but letting text come out reading the way it goes in.

Mirror the resistor you have been working on. Set MIRRTEXT to 0 so text is not mirrored. Mirror the resistor by *flipping* it 180 degrees. Keep the original in place. The target drawing is shown in the Completed Mirror illustration.

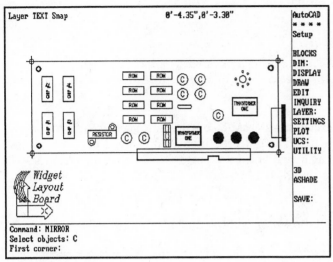

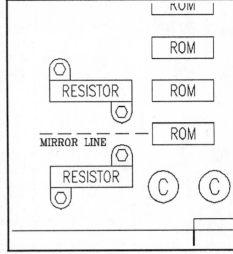

Before Mirror   *Detail After Mirror*

Using MIRROR to Mirror the Resistor

```
Command: SETVAR
Variable name or ?: MIRRTEXT
New value for MIRRTEXT <1>: 0
```

```
Command: ZOOM              Zoom previous to see the layout board.
```

```
Command: MIRROR
Select objects: C                    Place box around resistor.
First corner:                        Pick first point at 4.05,3.45.
Other corner:                        Pick second point at 4.95,4.15.
13 found.
Select objects: <RETURN>
First point of mirror line:          Pick absolute point 5.00,4.20.
Second point:                        Pick a point for a horizontal mirror line.
Delete old objects? <N> <RETURN>
```

Stopping Point

This is a good stopping point. If you need to take a break, save your drawing. So far, the editing commands that you have worked with are variations on a theme — moving or copying single entities, or making multiple copies of entities. The next group of editing commands involves deleting portions of entities, or, in the case of ERASE, deleting entire entities. If you took a break, your screen should look like the Completed Mirror illustration when you resume with ERASE.

ERASE and Its Sidekick, OOPS

Like a hammer, ERASE can be a constructive tool. But, like a hammer, watch out! The ERASE command has been the scourge of many a good drawing file.

The following exercise uses ERASE, but adds a good friend, the OOPS command. You will find OOPS prominently displayed on the [ERASE] screen menu (and also available by typing). OOPS asks no questions — it just goes about its business of restoring whatever you just obliterated with ERASE.

Get rid of the original resistor and the diode with an ERASE.

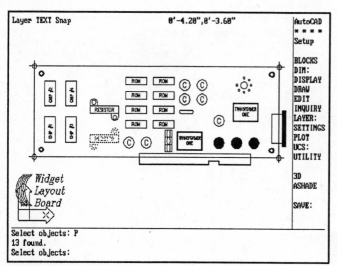

Layout Board Before Erase

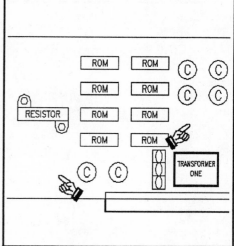

☞ Completed Erase

ERASE Example

```
Command: ERASE
Select objects: P        Previous reselects the Resistor.
13 found.
Select objects:          Pick the diode.
1 found.
Select objects: <RETURN> The deletion takes place.
```

Your screen should look like the Completed Erase illustration. Every time you execute an erase, AutoCAD keeps a copy of what you erased in case you want to oops it back into the file. But only the most recent erase is kept oops-ready!

Try an OOPS now to get your objects back.

Using OOPS on Your Last Erase

Command: **OOPS**   Here come the resistor and diode.

OOPS lets you do the unthinkable. After you have mistakenly deleted an entity from your drawing, you can recover the last deletion (under most circumstances) with OOPS. The OOPS command won't recover after you plot or end and then resume a drawing.

Using BREAK to Cut Objects

Break cuts existing objects and erases portions of objects. To use the BREAK command, you have to let AutoCAD know which entity you want to break, where you want to break it, and how big a chunk you want to break off.

Use any of the standard selection set techniques to let AutoCAD know which entity you want to break. Picking is the safest way to get the object you want. AutoCAD uses the first pick point as the start of the break and prompts you for another point. The second point is the end of the break segment. If you pick the same point again, AutoCAD breaks your object at the selected point, but does not delete any of it.

You have to think ahead about breaking at complicated intersections. AutoCAD can be confused if you select an intersection as a first break point. The way to approach the problem is to first pick the object to be broken, then specify two break points. To do this, don't select the object by a point pick or enter an **F** at the initial second point prompt. The **F** causes AutoCAD to reprompt you for the first point.

Here's the prompt sequence for breaking out the line at the port on the right side of the widget. Use the Before BREAK and After BREAK illustrations as your guides to the break.

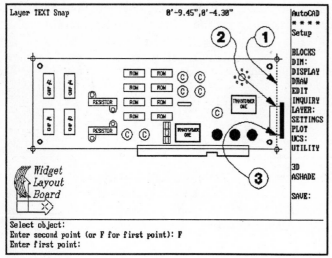

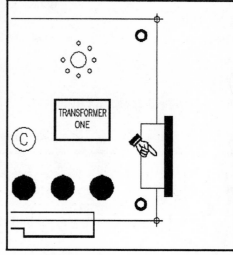

Before BREAK   ☞ *After BREAK*

Using BREAK to Break a Line

```
Command: BREAK
Select object:                                   Pick line of widget board at ①.
Enter second point (or F for first point): F     Reprompt for first point.
Enter first point:                               Use OSNAP INT to pick first point at ②.
Enter second point:                              Use OSNAP INT to pick second point at ③.
```

➡ *NOTE: BREAK works on lines, arcs, circles, polylines, polygons, donuts and traces. Take care to select the first and second points in counterclockwise order when breaking circles. Closed polylines need a little experimentation. BREAK'S effects will depend on the location of the polyline's first vertex. The break cannot extend across this vertex.*

The FILLET Command

A fillet is a tangent arc swung between two lines to create a round corner. The FILLET command is simple; AutoCAD asks you to identify the two lines that you would like joined. You identify the lines by picking them. AutoCAD then creates a new arc for the fillet corner.

Specify the radius of the arc to create the fillet corner. The default radius is <0>. It shows in the fillet prompt sequence when you select radius. The fillet radius you set becomes the new default. The most common use for fillet is to round corners, but using a fillet with radius = 0 (the original default) is good for cleaning up under- or overlapping lines at corners.

FILLET creates a corner, but does not create a new entity. See the Fillet Examples illustration below.

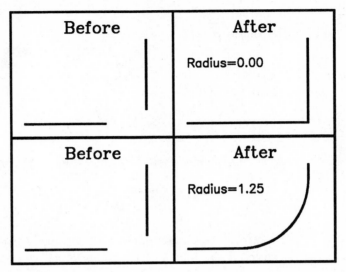

Fillet Examples

FILLET only works on two non-parallel lines, a single polyline, or lines and curves. Try filleting each of the four corners of the layout board.

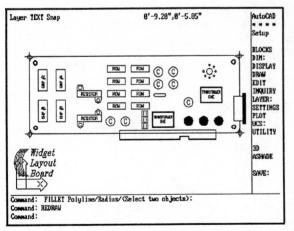

Filleted Corners of Layout Board

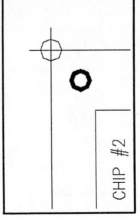

Before Fillet

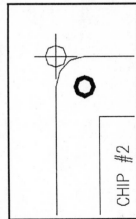

After Fillet

Using FILLET to Round Board Corners

```
Command: FILLET
Polyline/Radius/<Select two objects>: R
Enter fillet radius <0'-0.00">:.2
Command: FILLET                          Fillet a corner of the layout board.
Polyline/Radius/<Select two objects>:    Pick the two lines that make up the corner.
```

Repeat the FILLET command for the remaining corners.

```
Command: REDRAW            Refresh the screen.
```

Your screen should look like the Filleted Corners of Layout Board illustration.

➡ *TIP: When you are faced with a task where the fillets have the same radius arc (like the exercise above), you can speed up the edit by using the MULTIPLE command to make multiple fillets, MULTIPLE FILLET. To speed selection of intersections, double pick the intersection.*

The CHAMFER Command

A chamfer is a beveled edge. Adding a chamfer is easy. As you might expect, the CHAMFER command works like FILLET. To get the chamfer, you supply a chamfer distance along each line that you want to join, rather than an arc radius. The distance that you supply is the distance *from* the intersection of the lines (or arcs). Look at the Chamfer Examples illustration below, then move on to the exercise.

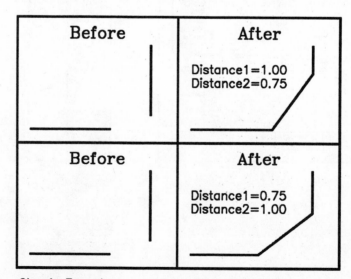

Chamfer Examples

Try two sets of chamfers. Chamfer the corners of the second transformer with a 45-degree chamfer (equal distances). Then chamfer two corners on the right side port.

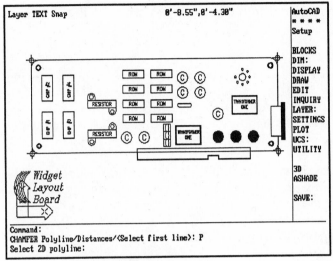

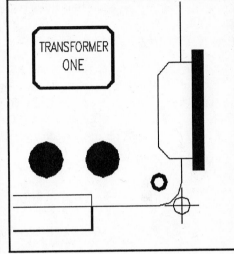

Transformer and Port Before Chamfers

Detail After Chamfers

Using Chamfer on the Layout Board

```
Command: CHAMFER
Polyline/Distances/<Select first line>: D
Enter first chamfer distance <0'-0.00">: .05
Enter second chamfer distance <0'-0.05">: <RETURN>


Command: <RETURN>
CHAMFER Polyline/Distances/<Select first line>: P     Pick Transformer Two polyline.
Select 2D polyline:
4 lines were chamfered


Command: <RETURN>
CHAMFER Polyline/Distances/<Select first line>: D
Enter first chamfer distance <0'-0.05">: .1
Enter second chamfer distance <0'-0.05">: <RETURN>


Command: <RETURN>
CHAMFER Polyline/Distances/<Select first line>:     Pick top horizontal port line.
Select second line:                                 Pick vertical port line.


Command: <RETURN>
CHAMFER Polyline/Distances/<Select first line>:     Pick bottom horizontal port line.
Select second line:                                 Pick vertical port line.
```

As you can see from the exercise, it is easy to chamfer polylines. All four corners were modified at the same time. Your screen should look something like the Port After Chamfer screen shot.

Lets look at two more commands that modify existing entities.

The CHANGE Command

CHANGE can selectively edit one or more parameters that give a drawing entity its identity, location, and appearance in the drawing file. We recommend that you use CHANGE to modify entity points in a 2D drawing file, and use a second command, called CHPROP (see below), to modify appearance. CHPROP works in both 2D and 3D.

When you select objects to change, AutoCAD prompts you for the points and parameters that are changeable for the entities that you select. Change points vary with the type of entity.

How CHANGE Affects Different Entities

- Lines. Change point makes several noncoincident endpoints come together with one change command by picking many lines but only one change point.

- Circles. Change point forces the circumference of an existing circle to pass through a new point, keeping the same center point.

- Text. Changes location, rotation angle, height, style, and/or text string. Change acts as a second chance to re-set all your text parameters.

Use CHANGE to change the text of the second transformer from "ONE" to "TWO." Then, change the diameter of the switch circle on the right side of the board.

Using CHANGE to Modify the Layout Board

```
Command: CHANGE                              Change text in second transformer.
Select objects:                              Select ONE text string.
1 selected, 1 found.
Select objects: <RETURN>
Properties/<Change point>: <RETURN>
Enter text insertion point:<RETURN>
Text style: STANDARD
New style or RETURN for no change: <RETURN>
New height <0'-0.08">: <RETURN>
New rotation angle <0.00>: <RETURN>
New text <ONE>: TWO                          Change ONE to TWO.
```

```
Command: CHANGE
Select objects:
1 selected, 1 found.
Select objects: <RETURN>
Properties/<Change point>:
```

Change diameter of transistor.
Pick the switch circle.

Pick absolute point 8.20,5.30 as the new
circumference point.

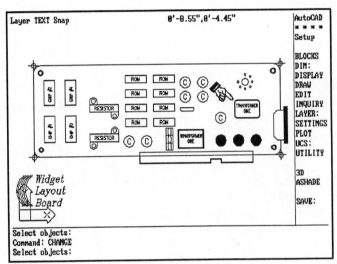

Text and Circle Before Changes

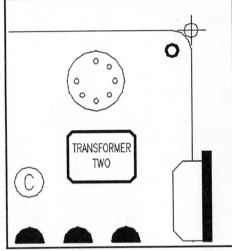

Detail After Changes

You also can use CHANGE to modify the properties of entities. Using
CHANGE to modify properties in 2D drawings works fine, but it may not
always work in 3D drawings. That is why AutoCAD has the CHPROP
command, which always works.

➡ *TIP: When you redefine a text style with STYLE, only changes to the
font and vertical orientation affect existing text. Use the CHANGE
command to force existing text to reflect modifications to width,
height, obliquing angle, etc. Entering a style name at the new style
prompt will update all text parameters, even if the style name entered
is the same as the currently defined style. Entering a <RETURN>
leaves all parameters unchanged.*

Using CHPROP to Change Properties

CHPROP changes properties in a 2D or 3D drawing. So far you have
changed the location, size, or shape of entities already in place.

Entity Properties

If you recall our early discussion on entities (chapter 2), all entities have five properties that you can edit. These are:

- Color

- Elevation

- Layer

- Linetype

- Thickness

When you created the lines in your widget drawing, you gave them a color and linetype. You might not have thought about it at the time. It may seem like a lot of edits ago! You created the individual widget parts on the layer PARTS with both entity color and linetype by layer (PARTS has a cyan (4) default color and a continuous default linetype). When you created the parts, these entities picked up their appearance characteristics by layer. While you were editing these lines, they retained their by layer color and linetype. (At this point the widget's entities have 0 elevation and thickness. These properties apply to 3D drawings. You will learn about them in Part Two which covers 3D drawing and editing.)

Using CHPROP is the best way to change the properties of entities that you have *already* drawn. Use CHPROP to change the interior connector line's layer property to the HIDDEN layer. Once you select the objects, you will get a prompt for the property that you want to change. Use the Before and After screen shots as your guides for the exercise.

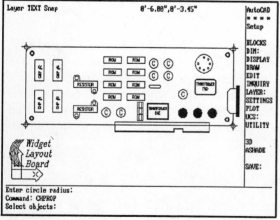

Before Layer Change

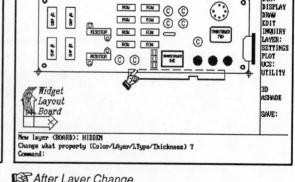

☞ *After Layer Change*

Using CHPROP to Change Layers

```
Command: CHPROP                                    Change lines to the HIDDEN layer.
Select objects:                                    Select the connector lines.
Change what property (Color/LAyer/LType/Thickness) ? LA
New layer <BOARD>: HIDDEN
Change what property (Color/LAyer/LType/Thickness) ? <RETURN>
```

Your drawing should show a red hidden connector line. The linetype and color properties are still by layer.

Entity color and linetype properties can be independent of layer. In fact, an entity can have any color or linetype. Try using CHPROP to change the color of the solid donuts.

Using CHPROP to Change the Color of Donuts

```
Command: CHPROP                                    Change the entity color of the solid donuts.
Select objects:                                    Select the three solid donuts.
Change what property (Color/LAyer/LType/Thickness) ? C
New color <BYLAYER>: 6                              Change color to magenta.
Change what property (Color/LAyer/LType/Thickness) ? <RETURN>
```

Now the donuts are magenta, overriding the cyan PARTS layer default.

CHPROP provides an easy method for changing entity properties. But for organized controlled drawings, it is usually best to deal with color and linetype by layer settings. Instead of changing color and linetype properties, try expanding and redefining the layers you set up in your drawings.

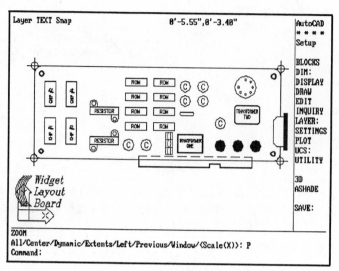

The Completed Widgedit Drawing

Take one last look at your Widget layout drawing with all its edits. As we promised, this is a full four-color widget layout board. Save this drawing, you can use it later when we take up plotting in Part Two.

Ending the Widget Editing Session

Command: **ZOOM**   All to get a full view.
Command: **END**

Exit AutoCAD

Summing Up With Tips on Editing

Now, you can see how important editing is in constructing a drawing. In the beginning of the chapter on graphic entities, we said that drawings are dynamic. With a first course in editing under your belt, you can see just how *dynamic* a drawing can be.

Are you ready for the next Engineering Change Order? Here's an Editor's Guide to Editing to keep you prepared.

Editor's Guide to Editing

Plan ahead for editing. When you first set up a drawing, think about how you are going to use your layers. Everything on one layer complicates editing. Plan to use multiple layers. Think about repetitive features. Draw it once, copy it forever. Think about your building blocks. Start by defining your basic components and building your drawing up from there.

You should not have a favorite edit command. Use them all. Use snap, ortho, and osnaps to set up your MOVE and COPY displacements. MIRROR and ARRAY can help you complete a repetitive drawing in a hurry. Be careful with ERASE. To avoid disasters, there's always OOPS and Undo.

Learn to use all of the object selection options including the Remove option. All the selection set options have their roles. Last and Previous are used all the time when you realize that AutoCAD did what you said, not what you meant. The object picking method is best for detail work, especially with osnap. Window is powerful, but it doesn't do it all. Remember what you see in the window is what goes into the selection set. You can use Crossing like a knife to slice out a selection set. BOX and SIngle are best for menu macros, as we shall see when we get to customization. AUto is a good habit. You can use it like Window, a Crossing or just to select an object. Previous saves time in repetitive editing. Don't forget, a **U** undoes the last object selection operation.

Think ahead about individual edits. Use display control to keep your field of view small and your concentration level high. Don't get caught setting up the base point of a displacement only to find that the second point is off the screen (cancel, zoom, and try again). Don't underestimate the power of CHANGE. It really is an effective tool. Changing an endpoint is easier than erasing and adding a new line segment. Changing text is almost always easier than retyping text. AutoCAD prompts you for every change. CHPROP allows you to change the layer, color, and linetype properties of existing entities.

Stay informed about what AutoCAD is up to. Watch the current layer name on the status line. Create entities on the layers you want them on. Watch the prompt line for edit prompts — it is easy to start creating a selection set window while the prompt line is waiting for you to enter **W** to initiate the Window selection. Use <FLIP SCREEN> to see what's going on.

On to More Editing

So far you have looked at some of AutoCAD's basic editing commands. Let's move on to more advanced editing commands and see how you can combine editing commands with some electronic drafting techniques to get more productivity out of editing your drawings.

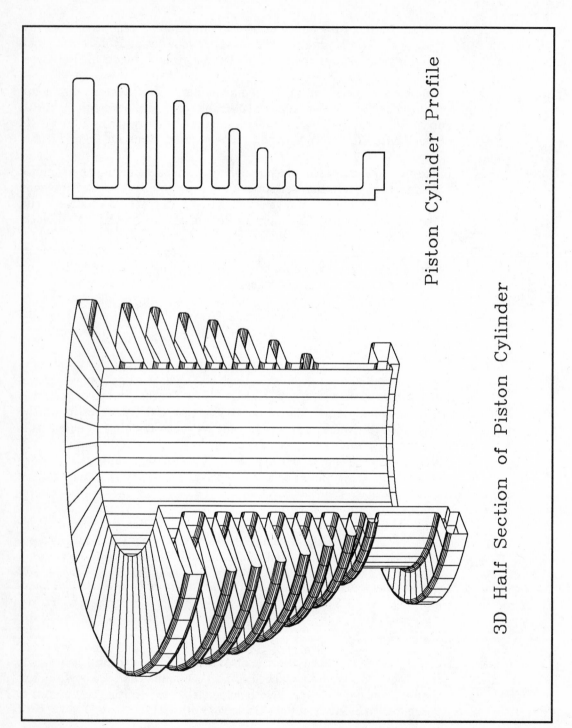

Piston Cylinder Profile

3D Half Section of Piston Cylinder

3D Piston Cylinder and Profile

CHAPTER 7

More Editing

PRELUDE TO 3D EDITING

Putting Drawings Together — CAD Style

To take full advantage of AutoCAD's power, you need to combine AutoCAD's editing commands with CAD drafting techniques. While the editing commands you learned in the last chapter will help you speed up your drafting, the editing commands and techniques you learn in this chapter will change the way you create your drawings. The advanced editing commands that you will use, like EXTEND, STRETCH, TRIM and OFFSET, go beyond copying and moving entities. They build on AutoCAD's knowledge of the geometry of the entities in your drawing. By combining these commands with construction techniques, setting up construction lines, parallel rules, and construction layers, you can *rough out* a drawing quickly, then finish it perfectly.

Plines and Pedits Are Stepping Stones to 3D

Besides construction techniques, we want to emphasize how to get *continuity* in your 2D drawings by using polylines and by editing with PEDIT. Polylines are important to AutoCAD's full 3D. Polylines provide continuity when you form 3D faces and meshes. If your 2D drawing has breaks in its line profile, you will not be able to form a complete 3D surface. The facing page illustration shows the effect of taking a continuous polyline and forming a 3D mesh.

Drawing polylines and modifying them with PEDIT, or converting or joining existing entities into new polylines with PEDIT, are basic 2D skills that you want to master to work in 3D. The exercises in this chapter will show you how to use PEDIT and the other advanced editing commands, combining entity creation and CAD construction techniques into a single drawing process.

Advanced Editing Tools

The editing commands covered in this chapter's exercises are found on the [EDIT] screen menus, and the [Modify] pull-down menu. These commands include EXTEND, OFFSET, SCALE, STRETCH, TRIM, and PEDIT. PEDIT, as you will discover, has an extensive set of options for global PEDITs, and options to edit individual vertices of polylines. The trick to using these advanced editing commands is to plan ahead. The operations of commands like EXTEND, STRETCH, and TRIM can involve a number of entities. PEDIT requires continuity to join lines and arcs. These commands require more setup and more planning for how you are going to use them.

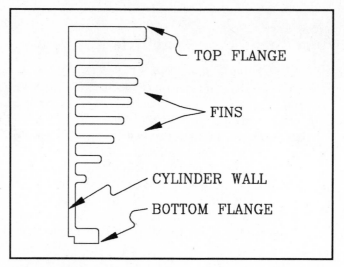

Cylinder Profile Target Drawing

Setting Up the Cylinder Drawing

The drawing that you will create in this chapter's exercises is the Piston Cylinder Profile. The cylinder is approximately 10 inches high by 14.60 inches wide. Here are our sample calculations for estimating a drawing scale factor and setting a sheet size.

```
Finned Piston Cylinder Wall              14.60" x 10.00".
Plot sheet size                          11" x 8 1/2".
Test 1/2" = 1" scale is a scale factor of 2.
    11" x 2 = 22" and 8 1/2" x 2 = 17"    22" x 17" limits.
```

Create a new drawing called CYLINDER. Use Engineering Units, and set your limits at 22" x 17". Use the table settings below to help you complete your setup. If you are using the IA DISK, begin your CYLINDER drawing by setting it equal to CHAP-07.

Setup for CYLINDER Drawing

 Enter selection: **1**   Begin a NEW drawing called CYLINDER=CHAP-07.

Enter selection: **1**   Begin a NEW drawing called CYLINDER.

Complete or verify your setup as shown in the Cylinder Drawing Settings table. Set the 2D layer current.

AXIS	COORDS	GRID	SNAP	ORTHO
Off	On	1	.1	ON

UNITS	Engineering, 2 decimal points, default all other settings.	
LIMITS	0,0 to 22,17	
ZOOM	Zoom All.	

Layer name	State	Color	Linetype
0	On	7 (white)	CONTINUOUS
2D	CURRENT	1 (red)	CONTINUOUS
3D	On	3 (green)	CONTINUOUS

Cylinder Drawing Settings

You can make a layer named SCRATCH to practice individual editing commands. The exercises move sequentially through each editing command to complete the target drawing. If you want to practice a command, say the STRETCH command, switch to layer SCRATCH, create some entities to stretch, and try out some editing variations. When you finish with your doodles, freeze your scratch layer and pick up again where you left off with the exercise sequences.

Using Lines and Polylines to Rough In a Drawing

Let's start by roughing in the section profile of the cylinder. First, use a polyline to draw the top, side, and bottom of the cylinder. Use one line and an array to form the construction lines for what will later become the cylinder fins. Finally, draw an arc on the right side as a construction line to help form the ends of the fins. Get your pick points from the exercise sequence below. Your current layer is 2D.

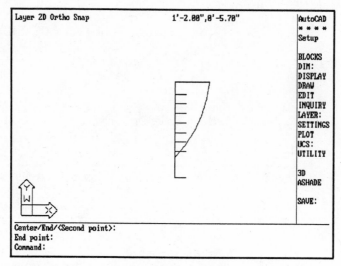

```
Layer 2D Ortho Snap              1'-2.00",0'-5.78"        AutoCAD
                                                         * * * *
                                                         Setup

                                                         BLOCKS
                                                         DIM:
                                                         DISPLAY
                                                         DRAW
                                                         EDIT
                                                         INQUIRY
                                                         LAYER:
                                                         SETTINGS
                                                         PLOT
                                                         UCS:
                                                         UTILITY

                                                         3D
                                                         ASHADE

                                                         SAVE:



 Center/End/<Second point>:
 End point:
 Command:
```

Rough Construction Lines of Cylinder Wall

Using PLINE, LINE and ARC to Rough In the Cylinder Wall

```
Command: PLINE              Draw a profile of the cylinder wall and flanges.
From point:                 Pick absolute point 1'5,1'.
Current line-width is 0'-0.00"
Arc/Close/Halfwidth/Length/Undo/Width/<Endpoint of line>:    Pick 1'2.00",1'0.00".
Arc/Close/Halfwidth/Length/Undo/Width/<Endpoint of line>:    Pick 1'2.00",0'4.00".
Arc/Close/Halfwidth/Length/Undo/Width/<Endpoint of line>:    Pick 1'3.00",0'4.00".
Arc/Close/Halfwidth/Length/Undo/Width/<Endpoint of line>: <RETURN>

Command: LINE               Draw a line from 1'2.00,0'11.00" to 1'3.00",0'11.00".

Command: ARRAY              Array the fin lines from the line.
Select objects: L           L selects the last entity (LINE).
1 selected, 1 found.
Select objects: <RETURN>
Rectangular or Polar array (R/P): R
Number of rows (---) <1>: 7
Number of columns (||||) <1>: <RETURN>
Unit cell or distance between rows (---): -.8

Command: ARC                Draw a three-point arc from 1'5.00",1'0.00" to
                            1'4.10", 0'8.70" to 1'2.00",0'5.70".
```

When you are done your screen should look like the Rough Construction
Lines of Cylinder Wall illustration (above). Your arc should extend down
from the polyline endpoint on the top right, intersect the first line that

you drew, and intersect the polyline on the left a little above halfway between the bottom and the intersected line. This arc will act as a construction line boundary to form the cylinder fins. The fin lines will be formed by extending them to the arc.

EXTENDing Entities

If we want to extend the lines to the arc, it will come as no surprise that the first command we turn to is the EXTEND command. You use EXTEND to extend lines, polylines, and arcs. The command is straightforward. Pick the boundary edge that you want to extend to, then pick the objects you want to extend. The main thing to remember is that you have to individually select each object to extend by picking it. You cannot use other modes to fill a selection set full of objects that you want extended, and then extend them all at once. You can, however, use other selection modes to select your boundary entities. The boundary edge can be lines, polylines, arcs, and circles. Objects to extend are ignored unless EXTEND can project them to intersect a boundary object.

Think about using EXTEND when you are faced with the problem of not knowing (or not wanting to calculate) drawing intersection points. In these cases (and in the current exercise), it is easier to use a construction line, and extend your entities. There are a few constraints on using extend; you cannot extend closed polylines and you cannot use EXTEND to shorten objects.

Try using EXTEND to lengthen the fin lines until they meet the construction arc.

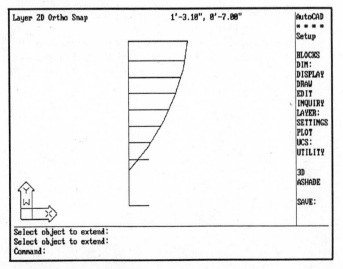

Extending Lines to the Arc

Using EXTEND to Extend Lines to an Arc

```
Command: ZOOM                         Get into a closer working area.

Command: EXTEND
Select boundary edges(s)...
Select objects:                       Pick the arc.
1 selected, 1 found.
Select objects: <RETURN>
Select object to extend:              Pick each of the upper six arrayed lines.
```

The OFFSET Command

Each of the cylinder fins as well as the cylinder wall itself is made up of parallel lines. The command you use to duplicate parallel drawing lines is OFFSET. OFFSET only works on one entity at a time. You have to pick each individual entity that you want to offset. To offset, you have to provide an offset distance and you have to indicate the side where you want the offset to go. You can input values or pick a point to show the offset distances, but you *must* use a pick to show the side for placement. Offset distances cannot be negative.

There are some types of entities that you cannot offset. The legal offset list is line, arc, circle, and polyline. Polyline includes donuts, ellipses, and polygons. Offset actually creates new entities. When you offset an entity, the new entity will have the same linetype, color, and layer settings as the entity that it was copied from. Polylines also will have the same width and curves.

Use OFFSET to create the cylinder wall and the lines that will form the fins. Then add lines to connect the endpoints of the wall and fins. Use the next two illustrations as your drawing guides. The offset distance value is given in the exercise sequence.

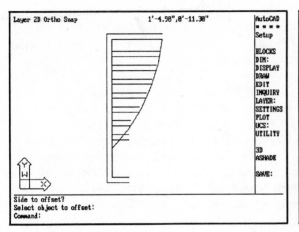

Cylinder After Offset

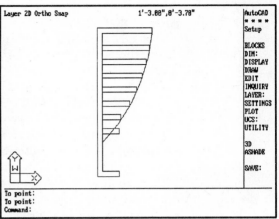

Cylinder With Connecting Lines

Using OFFSET to Create Wall and Fin Lines

```
Command: OFFSET
Offset distance or through <Through>: .3
Select object to offset:        Pick the polyline on left.
Side to offset?                 Pick any point to the left of the polyline.
Select object to offset:        Continue to offset the fin lines, placing
                                each offset line above the selected line.

Command: OSNAP    Set running osnap to endpoint.
Command: LINE     Draw lines between endpoints of the offset lines.
Command: OSNAP    Set running osnap to none.
```

While this exercise has shown how to offset lines and polylines, don't forget that you also can use OFFSET to form concentric circles.

➥ *NOTE: OFFSET forms a new entity by drawing the entity parallel to the original entity. OFFSET will fail to form a new entity inside an arc or circle if the offset distance exceeds the original radius. (You can't create a negative radius.) Donuts, polygons, and arc segments in other polylines are treated similarly. OFFSET also makes a logical attempt at small zig-zag segments and loops in polylines, but you may get confused results. Use PEDIT to clean the offset up if you don't like the results.*

Using STRETCH for Power Drawing

The STRETCH command lets you move *and* stretch entities. You can not only stretch entities in the sense of lengthening them, you can also shorten them and alter their shapes.

The key to learning to use STRETCH is knowing how to use a crossing window. The STRETCH command is built around the crossing window selection set. After you select your objects with a crossing window, you show AutoCAD where to stretch your objects with a base point and a new point. Then, everything inside the window you selected is moved, and everything crossing the window is stretched. Everything inside the window means that all of an object's endpoints or vertex points are within the window. If a point lies outside the crossing window, then the object gets stretched. There is one other constraint on stretch; you cannot stretch text but you can move it.

Try your hand at using STRETCH to widen the top and bottom of the cylinder. Then, use STRETCH again to shorten the fin lines that extend beyond the construction arc on the right. Use the illustrations to help you with your crossing windows, and use the exercise sequences to get your displacement picks.

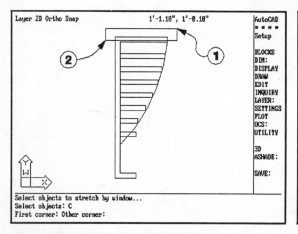

Crossing Window to Stretch Top Flange

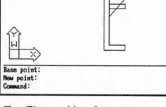

Top Flange After Stretch

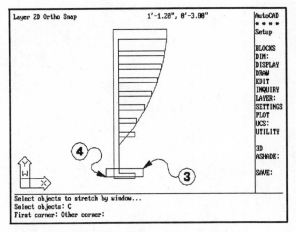

Crossing Window to Stretch Bottom Flange

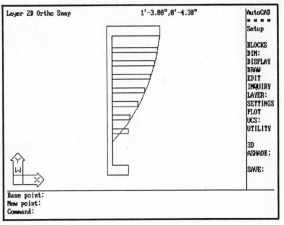

Bottom Flange After Stretch

Using STRETCH to Widen the Flanges

```
Command: STRETCH                          Stretch the top flange.
Select objects to stretch by window       Use Crossing.
Select objects: C
First corner:                             Pick upper right corner at ①.
Other corner:                             Pick lower left corner at ②.
2 found
Select objects: <RETURN>
Base point:                               Pick any point on the screen.
New point:                                Pick a point .3" at 90 degrees.

Command: STRETCH                          Stretch the bottom flange.
Select objects to stretch by window       Use Crossing.
Select objects: C
First corner:                             Pick upper right corner at ③.
Other corner:                             Pick lower left corner at ④.
2 found
Select objects: <RETURN>
Base point:                               Pick any point on the screen.
New point:                                Pick a point .3" at 90 degrees.
```

Use STRETCH again to bring the bottom fin in line with the other fins on the arc.

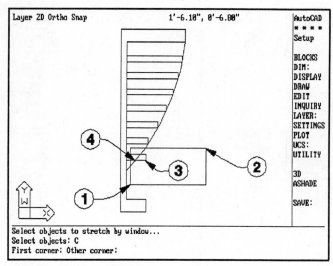

Crossing Window for Stretching the Fin

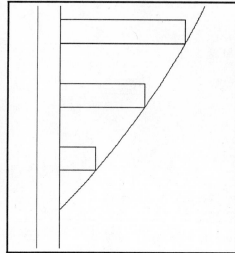

Detail of Stretched Fin

Using STRETCH to Shorten the Fin

```
Command: STRETCH
Select objects to stretch by window...
Select objects: C                      Pick corner points between ① and ②.
4 found.
Select objects: <RETURN>
Base point:                            Pick corner of fin at ③.
New point:                             Pick intersection of the arc and line at ④.
```

As you worked through these stretches, you may have noticed that the construction arc was highlighted by the crossing window but was not changed by the stretch. The arc was not moved or stretched because its endpoints were not enclosed in the window.

➡ *NOTE: STRETCH won't accept absolute displacements, like MOVE and COPY. Recall that an X, Y value at the first prompt becomes an absolute displacement if you <RETURN> at the second point prompt in MOVE and COPY. Picking any point for the base point and then typing relative coordinates, such as @0,-7.5 is equivalent to an absolute displacement.*

We encourage you to play around with STRETCH to discover some of its quirks. Polylines, arcs, and circles act differently depending on what segment, endpoint, or center point rests inside or outside the crossing window. Once you get used to these little idiosyncrasies, STRETCH will do what you expect.

Using TRIM in Quick Construction

Frequently, you are faced with the drawing problem of trimming existing lines. When you are working with a large number of entities, going in and breaking individual entities is tiresome and cumbersome. You can get the same results faster using TRIM. Like EXTEND, TRIM makes use of boundary entities. Also like EXTEND, TRIM's boundary may include lines, arcs, circles, and polylines. The entities that you select as your boundary edge become your *cutting edge*. Once you select your cutting edge, you pick the individual entities that you want to trim. You can trim lines, arcs, circles, and polylines. Other objects to trim are ignored.

Use TRIM to cut the interior lines of the cylinder fins, using the illustrations and sequence below as guides.

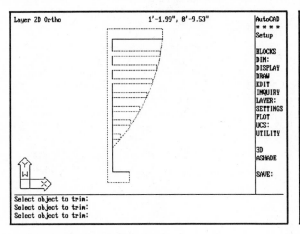

Cylinder With 3 Fins Trimmed

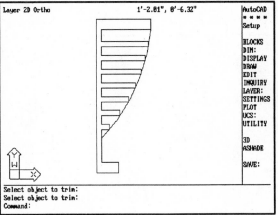

Cylinder After Trim

Using TRIM to Cut Fin Lines

```
Command: TRIM
Select cutting edge(s)...
Select objects:                  Use Window to select all the entities in the drawing.
26 selected, 26 found
Select objects: <RETURN>
Select object to trim:           Pick a point on the cylinder wall between fin lines.
Select object to trim:           Continue picking until all cylinder wall fin lines are trimmed.
Select object to trim:           End the trim command with a <RETURN>.
```

➡ *NOTE: The same entity can be in the cutting edge boundary and be cut as an object to trim.*

The SCALE Command

While we don't like to admit it, occasionally we get our drawing symbol and text scale wrong, or we have to change an object's size in mid-drawing. SCALE lets you shrink or enlarge objects that you have already placed in your drawing. When you re-scale drawing objects, you use a scale factor to change the size of entities around a given base point. The base point you choose remains constant in space; everything around it grows or shrinks by your scale factor. You can enter an explicit scale factor, pick two points to show a distance as a factor, or tell SCALE you want to use a reference length.

The piston cylinder is supposed to be 10 inches high. Use SCALE with the reference option to change the cylinder profile to make it exactly 10 inches. When you are done, erase the construction arc and save your drawing.

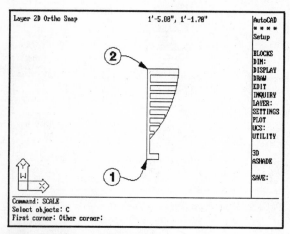

Cylinder Profile Before Scale

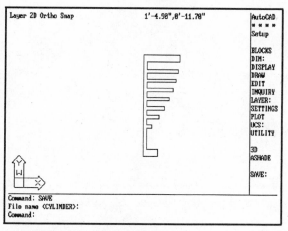

Cylinder Profile After Scale

Using SCALE to Enlarge the Cylinder

```
Command: ZOOM
```
Zoom all.

```
Command: SCALE
Select objects: C
First corner:
Other corner:
33 found.
```
Select every entity with a crossing window.
Pick the first corner point.
Pick the second corner point.

```
Select objects: R                    Select the remove objects option.
Remove objects:                      Pick the construction arc.
1 selected, 1 found, 1 removed.
Remove objects: <RETURN>
Base point:                          Pick corner of wall at ①.
<Scale factor>/Reference: R          Type the reference option.
Reference length <1>:                Pick corner of wall at ①.
Second point:                        Pick corner of wall at ②.
New length: 10                       Enter a new 10 inch length.

Command: ERASE                       Erase the construction arc.

Command: SAVE                        Save to the default file.
```

At this point your drawing should look like the Cylinder Profile After Scale illustration and it should be exactly 10 inches high.

➡ *TIP: The scale base point is also the base point of the new length in the reference options. If you want to show the length on another object by picking, place your base point there, scale the selection, then adjust its location with MOVE Previous.*

This drawing is a mixture of polylines and lines. Let's turn our attention to polyline editing. In the next section you will do some simple polyline edits, like changing polyline width, and you will form a new polyline by joining the individual entities which make up the cylinder profile.

PEDIT Gives Ultimate Control Over Polylines

Since polylines can be complex continuous line and arc segments, AutoCAD provides a command called PEDIT just for editing polylines. As you think about polyline properties you are probably already imagining the list of PEDIT subcommands. To manage the list, AutoCAD divides PEDIT into two groups of editing functions. One group of functions works on the whole pline you are editing. The second group works on vertices connecting segments within the polyline.

There are more restrictions on using the PEDIT command when you edit 3D polylines, as you will see in Part Two on 3D. For now, we will concentrate on editing 2D polylines. However, we will show you how to revolve the final cylinder drawing at the end of this chapter to demonstrate how a 3D polyline mesh image is formed from 2D polylines.

Here are the PEDIT options.

PEDIT Options

Close/Open — Close will add a segment (if needed) and join the first and last vertices to create a continuous polyline. PEDIT toggles between open and closed. When the polyline is open, the prompt shows Close; when closed, the prompt shows Open.

Join — Lets you add arcs, lines, and other polylines to an existing polyline.

Width — Sets a single width for all segments of a polyline, overriding any individual widths already stored.

Edit vertex —Presents a set of options for editing vertices.

Fit curve — Creates a smooth curve through the polyline vertices.

Spline curve — Creates a curve using polyline vertices as control points. The curve usually will not pass through the polyline vertex points.

Decurve — Undoes a Fit or Spline curve back to its original definition.

Undo — Undoes the most recent editing function.

eXit — As you might imagine, the default <X> gets you out of PEDIT and returns you to the command prompt.

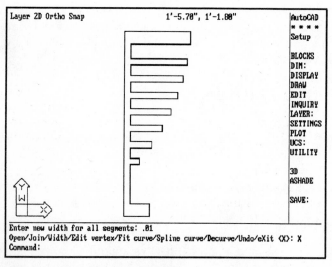

Joined Polyline With Changed Width

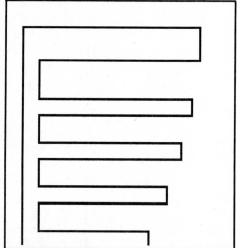

Detail of Wide Polyline

Using PEDIT Join to Create a Polyline

Use PEDIT to join the cylinder lines into a single closed polyline. Use a window to select all the entities that you want to join. After you have created the polyline, increase its width to .01 inch. Then, exit the PEDIT command and use FILLET to fillet all the corners in the polyline profile. Use the illustrations and the exercise sequence to help you.

Using PEDIT to Join and Change a Pline

```
Command: PEDIT
Select polyline:                Select the top line of the top flange.
Close/Join/Width/Edit vertex/Fit curve/Spline curve/Decurve/Undo/eXit <X>: J
Select objects: W              Enclose all the entities in a window.
First corner:                  Pick first corner.
Other corner:                  Pick second corner.
32 found.
Select objects: <RETURN>
32 segments added to polyline
Close/Join/Width/Edit vertex/Fit curve/Spline curve/Decurve/Undo/eXit <X>: W
Enter new width for all segments: .01
Open/Join/Width/Edit vertex/Fit curve/Spline curve/Decurve/Undo/eXit <X>: X
```

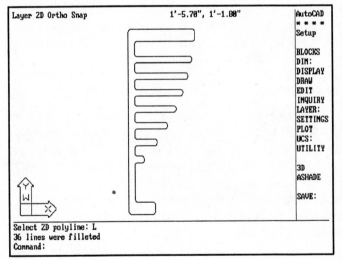

Polyline After Fillet

Detail of Filleted Polyline

```
Command: FILLET
Polyline/Radius/<Select two objects>: R
Enter fillet radius <0'-0.00">: .13
Command: <RETURN>
FILLET Polyline/Radius/<Select two objects>: P
Select 2D polyline:            Pick polyline.
36 lines were filleted
```

➤ *NOTE: Like LTSCALE, polyline width is set for a good plot appearance. The width may look irregular or not show up at some zoom levels or display resolutions.*

Joining polylines and changing their width properties are two common edits that you will use frequently. Later we will show you how to use the curve fit options.

➤ *TIP: Joining becomes tricky and may fail if the endpoints of the entities that you want to join do not coincide exactly. Not using snap and osnaps, and occasional round-off discrepancies can all cause problems. Edit or replace stubborn entities, osnapping to the adjacent endpoints, and PEDIT again.*

Right now, let's look at how you edit individual segments or vertices within a polyline. Selecting the edit vertex option gets you into a separate set of edit vertex subcommands. As soon as you get into this option set, the first vertex of the polyline is marked with an **X**. This **X** shows you what vertex you are editing. Move the **X** until you get the vertex you want to edit. Edit options include moving the vertex, inserting a new vertex, or straightening the segment. Here are the options.

PEDIT Edit Vertex Options

Next/Previous — Next/Previous gets you from one vertex to another by moving the **X** marker to a new current vertex. Next is the default.

Break — Splits or removes segments of a polyline. The first break point is the vertex where you invoke the Break option. You use Next/Previous to get to another break point. Go performs the break. (Using the BREAK command is usually more efficient than using a PEDIT Break unless curve or spline fitting is involved.)

Insert — Adds a vertex at a point you specify after the vertex currently marked with an **X**. This can be combined with Break to break between existing vertices.

Move — Changes the location of the current (X-marked) vertex to a point you specify.

Regen — Forces a regeneration of the polyline so you can see the effects (like width changes) of your vertex editing.

Straighten — Removes all intervening vertices from between the two vertices you select, replacing them with one straight segment. It also uses the Next/Previous and Go options.

Tangent — Lets you specify a tangent direction at each vertex to control curve fitting. The tangent is shown at the vertex with an arrow, and can be dragged or entered from the keyboard.

Width — Controls the starting and ending width of an individual polyline segment.

eXit — Gets you out of vertex editing and back to the main PEDIT command.

Using PEDIT Vertex Options

Once you have formed a polyline, you may need to move a vertex or straighten a line segment. Try exercising these two editing functions by removing two fillets. Remove one at the top left of the cylinder profile and another on the bottom flange. After you get into the PEDIT Vertex option, you need to move the **X** to get the right segment. Use the illustrations below as a guide to locate the **X** and move the vertex. Then, use the Straighten option to make a 90-degree corner.

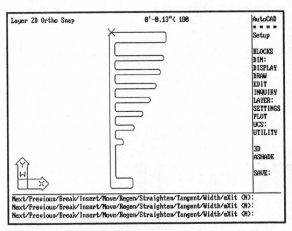

Location of Edit X Before Move

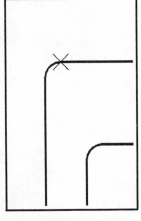

Before Move

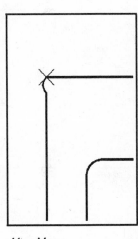

After Move

Using PEDIT Vertex Editing to Remove Fillets

```
Command: PEDIT
Select polyline:           Select the polyline.
Close/Join/Width/Edit vertex/Fit curve/Spline curve/Decurve/Undo/eXit <X>: E
```

An X appears on the polyline. Press <RETURN> until Next moves the X to match the Location of Edit X Before Move illustration.

```
Next/Previous/Break/Insert/Move/Regen/Straighten/Tangent/Width/eXit <N>: <RETURN>
Next/Previous/Break/Insert/Move/Regen/Straighten/Tangent/Width/eXit <N>: M
Enter new location:        Pick polar point @0.13<180
Next/Previous/Break/Insert/Move/Regen/Straighten/Tangent/Width/eXit <N>: S
```

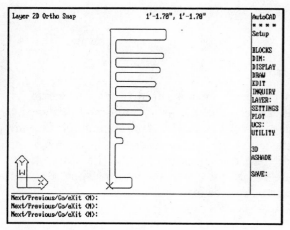

Location of Edit X Before Straightening

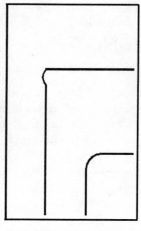

Before Straightening

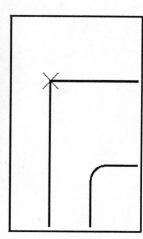

After Straightening

Press <RETURN> until Next moves the X to match Location of Edit X Before Straighting illustration.

```
Next/Previous/Go/eXit <N>: <RETURN>
Next/Previous/Go/eXit <N>: G                Go straightens the line.
```

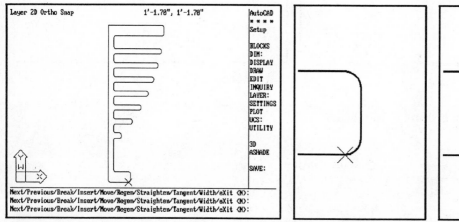

Location of Edit X Before Second Move

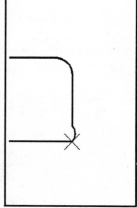

Before Move

After Move

Press <RETURN> until Next moves the X to match Location of Edit X Before Second Move illustration.

```
Next/Previous/Break/Insert/Move/Regen/Straighten/Tangent/Width/eXit <N>: <RETURN>
Next/Previous/Break/Insert/Move/Regen/Straighten/Tangent/Width/eXit <N>: M
Enter new location: @0.13<0                    Type in point coordinate.
Next/Previous/Break/Insert/Move/Regen/Straighten/Tangent/Width/eXit <N>: S
```

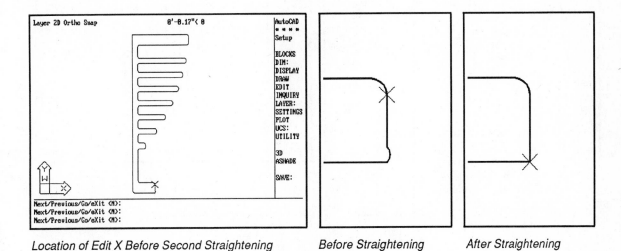

Location of Edit X Before Second Straightening   Before Straightening   After Straightening

Press <RETURN> until Next moves the X to match the Location of
Edit X Before Straightening illustration.

```
Next/Previous/Go/eXit <N>: <RETURN>
Next/Previous/Go/eXit <N>: G                    Go straightens the line.
Next/Previous/Break/Insert/Move/Regen/Straighten/Tangent/Width/eXit <N>:
```

Stay in the command for the next exercise.

You can add a vertex to an existing polyline. Try adding a notch to the
lower left corner of the cylinder profile. This editing sequence uses the
Insert and Move vertex options. Use the next four illustrations to guide
you through the sequence. The new vertex coordinate value is given in
the exercise below.

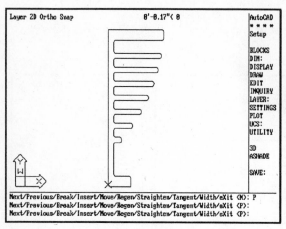
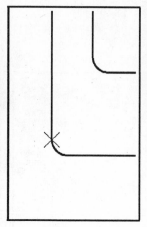
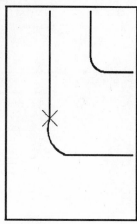

Location of Edit X Before Move   *Before Move*   *After Move*

Using PEDIT to Add a Notch

```
Next/Previous/Break/Insert/Move/Regen/Straighten/Tangent/Width/eXit <N>: P
```

Press <RETURN> until Previous moves the X to match the Location of Edit X Before Move illustration.

```
Next/Previous/Break/Insert/Move/Regen/Straighten/Tangent/Width/eXit <P>: <RETURN>
Next/Previous/Break/Insert/Move/Regen/Straighten/Tangent/Width/eXit <P>: M
Enter new location:              Pick polar point @0.17<90
```

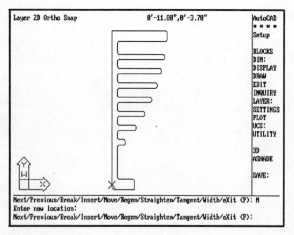
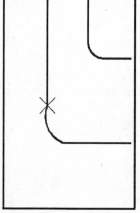
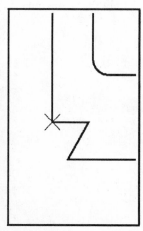

Location of Edit X Before Insert   *Before Insert*   *After Insert*

```
Next/Previous/Break/Insert/Move/Regen/Straighten/Tangent/Width/eXit <P>: I
Enter location of new vertex:          Pick polar point @0.30<0
Next/Previous/Break/Insert/Move/Regen/Straighten/Tangent/Width/eXit <P>: N
Next/Previous/Break/Insert/Move/Regen/Straighten/Tangent/Width/eXit <N>:
<RETURN>
```

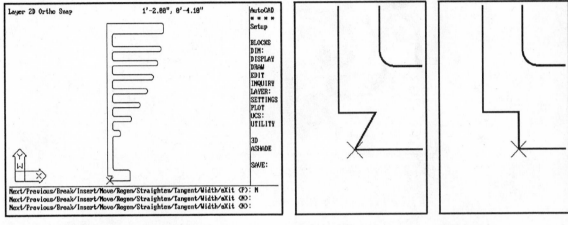

Location of Edit X Before Second Move   Before Move   After Move

```
Next/Previous/Break/Insert/Move/Regen/Straighten/Tangent/Width/eXit <N>: M
Enter new location:                    Pick polar point @0.17<0
Next/Previous/Break/Insert/Move/Regen/Straighten/Tangent/Width/eXit <N>: X
Close/Join/Width/Edit vertex/Fit curve/Spline curve/Decurve/Undo/eXit <X>: X
```

Using EXPLODE on Polylines

If you are faced with extensive edits on polylines, it is difficult to determine whether it is easier to edit the vertices or to explode the polyline into individual segments, do your edits, then re-join the segments. EXPLODE is the command you use to break a polyline into its individual segments. There are drawbacks to exploding polylines. They lose their width and tangent information. EXPLODE locks in curves and splines by converting the polyline to many arcs or small straight lines. Polylines come out of an explosion looking like shaved poodles with only their center lines showing. If you were to explode the cylinder's polyline, you would get 72 entities.

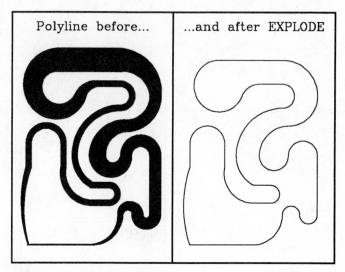

Polyline Before and After Explosion

PEDIT Fit and Spline Curves

The PEDIT command provides two options for making polyline curves through control points: a fit curve and a spline curve. One reason we chose the cylinder profile to demonstrate pedits is that this profile dramatically shows the different results between fit curves and spline curves. A fit curve passes through your control points. Fit curves consist of two arc segments between each pair of vertices. A spline curve interpolates between your control points but doesn't necessarily pass through the control points.

PEDIT spline curves create either arcs or short line segments approximating the curve of the arc. To help you visualize your spline curve, AutoCAD provides a system variable called SPLFRAME. You can set SPLFRAME on **1** to show you the reference frame and vertex points for a spline curve. The fineness of the approximation and type of segment is controlled by the SPLINESEGS system variable. The numeric value controls the number of segments. A positive value generates line segments while a negative value creates arc segments. Arcs are more precise, but slower. The default is **8**.

Try both fit and spline curves using the cylinder fins as your control points. After you have generated the spline curve, turn SPLFRAME on to see the reference frame for the curve. The exercise sequence will show you how to regenerate the drawing within the PEDIT command to make the frame visible. When you are done, use the Undo option to restore the original cylinder profile. If you use the Decurve option, you will remove the fillets in the drawing. Be careful with the Decurve option. If you try it, Undo to recover. When you have the original image back, save the drawing.

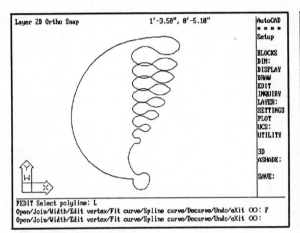

Piston Cylinder After Fit Curve

Piston Cylinder After Spline Curve

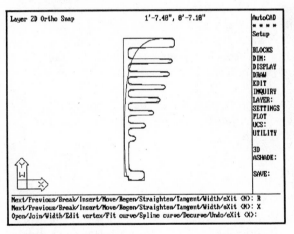

Spline Curve With Frame

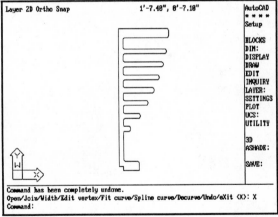

Original Cylinder After Undo

Using PEDIT to Make a Fit and a Spline Curve

```
Command: PEDIT
Select polyline: L
Open/Join/Width/Edit vertex/Fit curve/Spline curve/Decurve/Undo/eXit <X>: F
Open/Join/Width/Edit vertex/Fit curve/Spline curve/Decurve/Undo/eXit <X>: S
Open/Join/Width/Edit vertex/Fit curve/Spline curve/Decurve/Undo/eXit <X>: 'SETVAR
>Variable name or ?:
```

```
>New value for SPLFRAME <0>: 1
Resuming PEDIT command.
Open/Join/Width/Edit vertex/Fit curve/Spline curve/Decurve/Undo/eXit <X>: E
Next/Previous/Break/Insert/Move/Regen/Straighten/Tangent/Width/eXit <N>: R
Next/Previous/Break/Insert/Move/Regen/Straighten/Tangent/Width/eXit <N>: X
Open/Join/Width/Edit vertex/Fit curve/Spline curve/Decurve/Undo/eXit <X>: U
Open/Join/Width/Edit vertex/Fit curve/Spline curve/Decurve/Undo/eXit <X>: U
Open/Join/Width/Edit vertex/Fit curve/Spline curve/Decurve/Undo/eXit <X>: U
Open/Join/Width/Edit vertex/Fit curve/Spline curve/Decurve/Undo/eXit <X>: X
```

Command: **SAVE**   Save to default name.

When you displayed the reference frame for spline curves, it showed the original cylinder profile and points. If you are editing a spline curve and you need to know where your control points are located, use the SPLFRAME system variable to get your frame of reference back.

After undoing your curve fitting your screen should look like the Original Cylinder After Undo illustration. While you have moved, stretched, curved, and pummeled the poor polyline, it is still a *continuous* polyline.

➡ *NOTE: The BREAK and TRIM commands make curve and spline fitting permanent. The PEDIT Break option and EXTEND command allow subsequent PEDITs to decurve and refit curves or splines. Curve and spline fit polylines get complex. See the AutoCAD Reference Manual for quirks and interactions with other editing commands.*

➡ *NOTE: You can generate spline curves two ways, controlled by the SPLINETYPE system variable. The types are a quadratic b-spline (type 5) or a cubic b-spline (type 6).*

Using REVSURF to Create a 3D Solid

Use your cylinder profile to get a 3D solid. The following exercise sequence will guide you through a quick 3D setup, giving you a 3D viewpoint that looks down at the cylinder so that you can see the solid as it is formed. You will use a 3D entity command called REVSURF to form the solid. REVSURF forms a polyline surface mesh from the 2D polyline making up the cylinder profile.

Don't worry about the commands or the sequence used to create the 3D cylinder. Just try the exercise to see how easily a complex 3D part is created. If the results whet your appetite, you will be pleased that there is much more to come in Part Two on 3D. When you are done, save your drawing as 3DCYLIND.

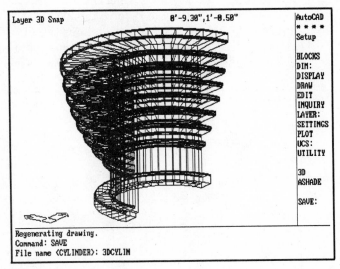

3D Half Section of Cylinder

Using REVSURF to Make a Quick 3D Mesh

Command: **GRID**	Turn grid off.
Command: **ZOOM**	Zoom all.
Command: **LINE**	Draw from absolute point 10,1'3 to polar point @1'1.0<270. This is a rotation line.
Command: **LAYER**	Set layer 3D current.
Command: **SETVAR**	Set vertical mesh value, SURFTAB1, to 24.
Command: **SETVAR**	Set horizontal mesh value, SURFTAB2, to 4.
Command: **SETVAR**	Set WORLDVIEW to 0 for viewpoint change.

Command: **REVSURF**   Create 3D half section of piston cylinder.
Select path curve: Pick the polyline.
Select axis of revolution: Pick the rotation line near the Bottom.
Start angle <0>: **<RETURN>**
Included angle (+=ccw, -=cw) <Full circle>: **180**

Command: **LAYER**   Freeze layer 2D.
Command: **UCS**   Rotate the X axis -90 degrees.
Origin/ZAxis/3point/Entity/View/X/Y/Z/Prev/Restore/Save/Del/?/<World>: **X**
Rotation angle about X axis <0.0>: **-90**

Command: **VPOINT**   Move to a better view point.
Rotate/<View point> <0'-0.00",0'-1.00",0'-0.00">: **R**
Enter angle in X-Y plane from X axis <270>: **215**
Enter angle from X-Y plane <-0>: **17**

Command: **SAVE**   Save as 3DCYLIN.

To cut down on computing time, the exercise only created a half section of the cylinder. You could revolve the 2D polyline 360 degrees to get the full cylinder. If you have about an hour to kill (and some patience), you can do a HIDE to let AutoCAD sort through all those lines and generate a more realistic image by getting rid of the hidden lines.

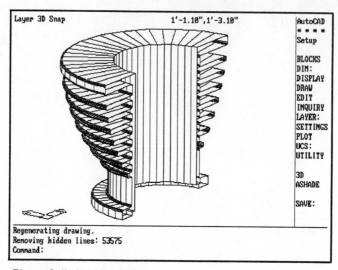

Piston Cylinder After HIDE

Using HIDE to Get a Not-So-Quick Hide

Command: **HIDE**   Start your timer!

You can get some sense of how powerful 3D editing commands are by how easy it is to create the complex cylinder solid from your 2D profile. This 2D cylinder profile is a continuous polyline. We mentioned how important continuity becomes in 3D. To show the effect of discontinuity, we have gone back and *nicked* the cylinder polyline in two places. Then, we revolved the cylinder again with REVSURF to get a 3D solid.

The nicked profile is shown in the Broken 2D Polyline illustration. The two **X**s mark the places where we broke the polyline. The resulting 3D image is shown in the accompanying illustration, 3D Half Cylinder With Nicked Polyline. As you can see, the 3D mesh formation halts at the break points. The nicked 2D profile looks the same as your original profile, but it gives vastly different results when you form a 3D surface image.

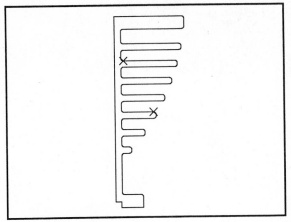

Broken 2D Polyline

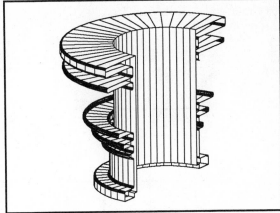

3D Half Cylinder With Nicked Polyline

Summing Up

In the last chapter on editing, we said that when you start editing, your drawings become dynamic. Now, with a second course in editing under your belt, you may sense that the drawing process itself can give you added power and control. The editing commands, EXTEND, OFFSET, STRETCH, TRIM, SCALE, and PEDIT, are *new* tools. They don't have exact counterparts in the manual world. All of these editing commands operate on multiple entities. When you combine these advanced editing tools with the electronic equivalent of construction lines, you can create fast, accurate drawings.

The trick to using these commands is to plan ahead. Don't get trapped into traditional thinking. It would have been a laborious process to draw the cylinder profile line by line and point by point. Plan on using EXTEND, OFFSET, STRETCH, and TRIM to rough in your drawing. Then, get the details that you want using PEDIT.

The second trick to using these new editing commands is to think about *how* the drawing is constructed. As you work with the more complex commands, the behind-the-scenes construction is almost as important as the appearance of the final 2D drawing. You saw how two little nicks in a 2D polyline could have a drastic effect on a 3D image.

There are two more editing techniques that we want to show you in the next chapter. These are using XYZ point filters as super fast invisible construction lines, and undo marks, a way to mark your drawing file so that you can backtrack and try different editing paths in your drawing.

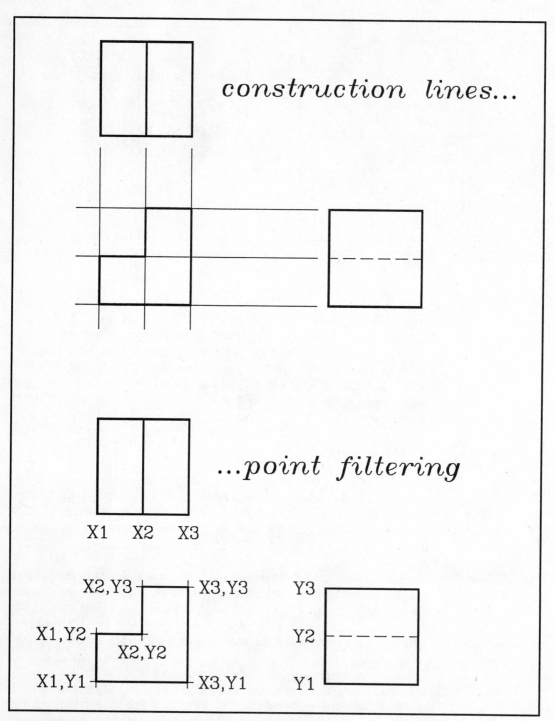

Construction Lines and Point Filter Techniques

CHAPTER 8

Advanced Editing Techniques
QUICK WAYS TO BUILD WHOLE DRAWINGS

Advanced Editing Techniques

This chapter on editing is a methodology chapter. It will focus on two extremely powerful drawing and editing techniques: point filters and editing marks. You will learn how to use these techniques by combining them with the editing commands that you have covered in the two previous chapters.

Point Filters

Point filters are construction tools. The best way to visualize point filters is to think of them as invisible construction lines. The facing page illustration compares a construction line and a point filter. When you use a construction line to help draw an entity, you are really looking for the coordinate values of an intersection point, say an X value and a Y value. When you use point filters, you indicate the coordinate values that will give you the intersection point, eliminating the need to actually draw a construction line. Once you get the hang of using point filters, they will increase your drawing productivity. They are a fast on-the-fly technique.

Editing Marks

As you use more powerful editing commands like ARRAY, EXTEND, STRETCH, and TRIM, you must be aware that you can botch up your entire drawing with a single command that deposits hundreds of entities into your drawing file, or worse still, deletes pieces of entities in the file.

"If I could just back up three commands and try that again," is a familiar refrain that we all find ourselves thinking at one time or another. But, what if you could place a *mark* in your drawing session so that you could backtrack to that editing point? Well, you can. Think of using editing marks as placing editing checkpoints in your drawing. By placing a mark, you can try an editing sequence, then go back to your mark if it doesn't work and try an alternate sequence.

This marking process is available to you through AutoCAD's UNDO command. Each time you start an editing session AutoCAD keeps track of every command you execute by writing it to a temporary file on disk. This temporary file records all your moves whenever you are in the drawing editor. You won't find this file on disk when you're done with an editing session because it is a hidden file. At the end of a session, AutoCAD wipes it out and cleans up the disk. However, while you are in an editing session, you can play back this sequence, undoing each command, or if you undo too much, you can redo parts of your past command sequence.

After you master this chapter, don't expect AutoCAD to do all the work for you. However, you can look forward to a better division of drafting labor — you can do the thinking and setting up, and let AutoCAD do the bulk of the carrying out.

Advanced Editing Tools

The tools that you will use are on the [EDIT] screen menus and the [Modify] and [Tools] pull-down menus. [FILTERS...] is on [Tools] along with all the osnaps.UNDO is on the second [EDIT] screen menu page.

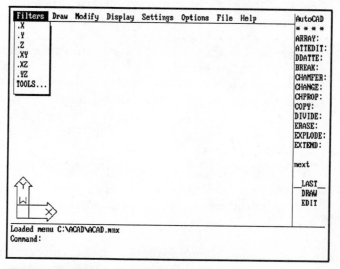

Editing and Construction Tools Menus

This chapter's editing exercises also use the OFFSET, ARRAY, TRIM, FILLET, CHAMFER, CHANGE, CHPROP, and PEDIT commands. If you need to review these commands, refer to the two previous editing chapters.

➡ *TIP: If you have a printer hooked up to your system, you can get a hard copy of all your command prompt lines by typing Control-Q <^Q> to start your printer printing, or select the PRINTER TOGL on the tablet menu. It will print everything that scrolls by on the text screen. Another <^Q> turns off printing.*

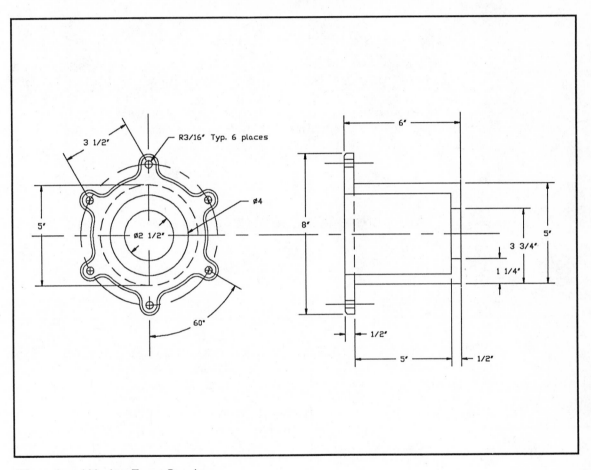

Dimensioned Mockup Target Drawing

Setup for the Mockup Drawing

To get a handle on using drawing construction techniques, you will build a new drawing called Mockup. The dimensions needed to create the drawing are shown in the Mockup Target Drawing illustration.

The Mockup is actually a plan and section drawing of a flange. Like the now-familiar widget drawing, you don't have to know or care about flanges to get something out of this drawing. You will learn the basic concepts of editing marks, construction lines, and point filters.

Set up the Mockup drawing with fractional units, and set your drawing limits to 34 inches by 22 inches. The scale factor is 1:2 for a 17" x 11" final drawing.

Alternate Start for Point Filters

If you are using the IA DISK, you have the Mockup drawing setup stored as the CHAP-08A drawing. A second drawing on the disk, CHAP-08B, has the completed left view of the flange. XYZ point filters are used to help construct the section view on the right. If you want to go directly to practicing with point filters, proceed to the section on point filters and use the CHAP-08B drawing as your starting drawing.

Setting Up the Mockup Drawing

   `Enter selection: 1`   Begin a NEW drawing called MOCKUP=CHAP-08A.

   `Enter selection: 1`   Begin a NEW drawing called MOCKUP.

Check or set up your drawing settings to match the Mockup Drawing Settings table.

COORDS	GRID	LTSCALE	ORTHO	SNAP
On	1	1	ON	.5

UNITS	Set UNITS to 5. Fractional, 64ths denominator. Default the other Units settings.
LIMITS	Set LIMITS from 0,0 to 34,22.
ZOOM	Zoom All.
VIEW	Save view as A.

Layer name	State	Color	Linetype
0	On	7 (white)	CONTINUOUS
CENTER	CURRENT	1 (red)	CENTER
DIMS	On	2 (yellow)	CONTINUOUS
HIDDEN	On	4 (cyan)	HIDDEN
PARTS	On	3 (green)	CONTINUOUS

Mockup Drawing Settings

When you are done setting up, the CENTER layer (with a center linetype) should be your current layer.

Using a Construction Layer and Lines

The first step in making the Mockup is to rough in some construction lines. Take a quick look at the target drawing. Notice that there are two center lines and a circle center line. Create these lines by using your CENTER layer as a background layer to help you lay in the two major sections of the drawing. Then, you can use the PARTS layer to draw the flange and its section view.

Use OFFSET to help draw the construction lines. Follow the illustrations and the exercise sequence below.

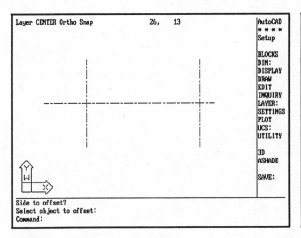

Offset on a Line

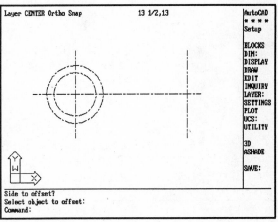

Offset on a Circle

Using OFFSET to Create Construction Center Lines

```
Command: LINE                      From absolute point 4,13 to polar point @24<0.
Command: LINE                      From absolute point 10,7 to polar point @12<90.

Command: OFFSET
Offset distance or through <Through>: 16
Select object to offset:            Pick vertical line.
Side to offset?                     Pick any point to the right of line.
Select object to offset: <RETURN>

Command: CIRCLE                    Draw a 3" radius circle at absolute point 10,13.
```

```
Command: OFFSET                   Create a 4" radius circle.
Offset distance or through <16>: 1
Select object to offset:          Pick the circle.
Side to offset?                   Pick any point outside the circle.
Select object to offset: <RETURN>
```

The two circles on your screen are temporary construction lines to help you form the complex image that makes up the perimeter of the flange.

Placing an UNDO Mark

Look at the Mockup Target Drawing again. The perimeter of the top flange is a polyline with six things (lugs) sticking out. It would be difficult to draw this entire perimeter as a single polyline. The next three exercises will show you how to create one-sixth of the perimeter, array this sixth to get the basic perimeter, then form a polyline by joining the arrayed entities.

Since you will be creating several entities to represent the top flange and you also will be using several different editing commands, this is a good place to put an undo mark in your drawing file. If you botch the next three sequences, you can easily come back to this point.

Use UNDO to place a mark in your drawing, then resume construction of the lug that sticks out from the top of the flange perimeter. Construct the lug on your PARTS layer. Use the following illustration and exercise sequence to help you pick your points.

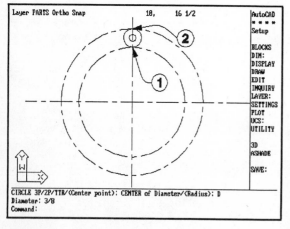

Lug Construction After Circles

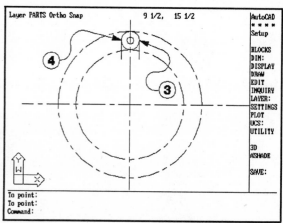

Lug Construction After Lines

Using Construction Entities to Draw a Lug

```
Command: UNDO                                 Set a mark.
Auto/Back/Control/End/Group/Mark/<number>: M


Command: ZOOM                                 Position window around circles for a better view.
Command: LAYER                                Set layer PARTS current.


Command: CIRCLE                               Use 2P to draw a 1" diameter circle.
3P/2P/TTR/<Center point>: 2P
First point on diameter:                      Use osnap INTersection to pick first point at ①.
Second point on diameter:                     Use osnap INTersection to pick second point at ②.


Command: <RETURN>
CIRCLE 3P/2P/TTR/<Center point>:              Draw a 3/8" diameter circle
                                              centered on the last circle.


Command: LINE                                 Osnap QUAdrant to add the lines of the flange cut.
From point: QUA
of                                            Pick a point on the circle at ③.
To point:                                     Pick any point below the circle at 270 degrees.
To point: <RETURN>


Command: <RETURN>
LINE From point: QUA
of                                            Pick a point on the circle at ④.
To point:                                     Pick any point below the circle at 270 degrees.
 To point: <RETURN>
```

Your screen should resemble the Lug Construction After Lines illustration. Let's set some time aside and look at undoing and redoing command sequences.

Controlling AutoCAD's UNDO

There are three basic commands that control undos in your draw and edit sequences. These are U, UNDO, and REDO.

You may be thinking, "I already know how to delete the last entity that I drew using the ERASE Last command. If I make an erase mistake, I can even OOPS to restore the last item erased. And I already know how to use U."

However, erasing the last item you drew is only part of going back through your drawing file. When you decide to go back, it is usually not just to erase or undo the last item, but to undo a whole sequence of draw and edit commands. Here is where the UNDO set of commands comes in handy.

The U Command

The U command backs up by one step or command. Whatever you did immediately before issuing the U command will be undone when you type U. But, unlike the OOPS command, U works any number of times, stepping back through each previous *last* command, one by one. In this sense, U is similar to the Undo option within LINE or PLINE which gets rid of line or pline segments by going back one segment at a time. You can U an OOPS or U an ERASE.

The UNDO Command

The UNDO command offers more control than U. You can UNDO <number>, where <number> equals the number of steps you want to return. Or you can group a series of commands together and then, if what you are working on doesn't work out, you can undo the whole group at once. UNDO lets you step back through a number of recently entered commands, undoing their effects (in reverse order) and restoring the drawing to its previous condition. It extends the U feature, giving you complete control over stepping back through your past commands one at a time or in groups.

REDO Gives an Extra Measure of Safety

Say you undid more than you planned. If you issue a REDO immediately after one of the undo commands (U, UNDO Back, or UNDO <number>), the REDO will undo the UNDO. This means you can be daring if you are not sure how far back you want to go. You can do something drastic like UNDO 20, then recover with a REDO. When you are teaching someone else, you can *play back* your drawing sequences with an UNDO and REDO to show how it is done.

Use the following illustrations and exercise sequence to test the U, UNDO and REDO commands. When the test is complete, your drawing should look the same as it does now.

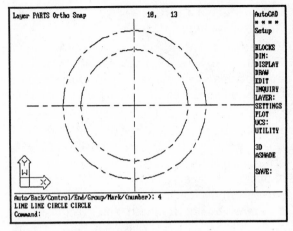

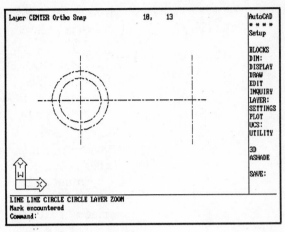

Mockup After an UNDO 4   Mockup After an UNDO Back

Using U, UNDO and REDO on an Editing Sequence

Command: **U**	A simple U undoes the last command.
LINE	AutoCAD shows the last command it undid.
Command: **REDO**	Reverses the U command and returns the line.
Command: **UNDO**	Undo the last 4 commands.
Auto/Back/Control/End/Group/Mark/<number>: **4**	
LINE LINE CIRCLE CIRCLE	
Command: **REDO**	Reverse the UNDO command.
Command: **UNDO**	Undo back to the mark set at the beginning of the exercise.
Auto/Back/Control/End/Group/Mark/<number>: **B**	
LINE LINE CIRCLE CIRCLE LAYER ZOOM	
Mark encountered	
Command: **REDO**	Reverse the UNDO command.

The UNDO Back that you used is only one of six options that control UNDO. Here is the complete list.

UNDO Options

<number> — If you type a number here, AutoCAD will step back through the temporary file by that many steps.

Auto — requires an On/Off answer. Auto affects menu items only. You can set UNDO Auto On or Off at any time. Sometimes a single menu item creates or edits many entities. Everything done by one command is one step back in UNDO. Auto On causes an entire menu item to be treated as a single step.

Back and **Mark** — An UNDO Back will make AutoCAD step back through the temporary file, undoing along the way, until it comes to the beginning of the editing session (or a mark) in the temporary file. Back cannot go back to anything before a PLOT or PRPLOT command because they re-initialize the undo file as if beginning the editing session at that point. If no mark has been placed, you get a warning, "This will undo everything. OK <Y>". You say Yes or No. Leave a mark simply by executing the UNDO command with the Mark option. You may mark as many times as you like, each time setting a stop for the next UNDO Back.

Control — Creating a temporary file and storing all the command sequences take a lot of disk space. Control lets you specify how active the temporary file will be with three options — All/None/One.

Group and **End** — are advanced control features. Like Mark and Back, Group and End put boundaries on series of commands in the temporary file so that you can undo the series in one sweep. Unlike Back, however, you can begin a group with the Group option, end the group with the End option, and continue doing work. Later you step back with U or UNDO <number>. When the backstep gets to an End, the next UNDO step will wipe out everything between the End and Group markers as a single step.

UNDO Control Options

All — is the default.

None — Turns UNDO off.

One — Limits UNDO to just going back one step by keeping only the last step in the file. When Control is set to One, none of the other UNDO options are available. All restores Control to its full function.

Watch out for undoing more than you want. Any settings in a command, including toggles (such as snap) or transparent commands, will be undone along with the main command. UNDO has the power to wipe out your entire drawing in one step, but if you catch it immediately with REDO, you can save it.

You can't undo some things. You can't undo a SAVE or any other disk operation. A PLOT or PRPLOT also wipes out the temporary editing session file; you can't step back beyond a PLOT or PRPLOT. And you can't UNDO past the beginning of the current editing session.

As you construct the flange in the following exercises, try placing your own editing marks to give you additional check points in the editing session.

Using Array Techniques to Construct the Flange Perimeter

Let's resume with the flange. First, finish the lug using the TRIM command. This is easier than trying to calculate the exact arc and line lengths that make up the lug. It also insures that all the endpoints of each entity match. The trim cutting edges are shown in the following illustration.

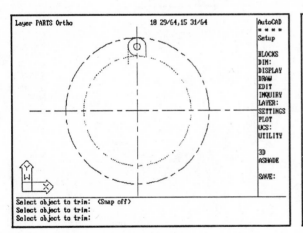

Lug After First Circle and Line Trim   Completed Lug After Trim

Using TRIM to Draw First Lug of Flange

```
Command: TRIM
Select cutting edge(s)...
Select objects:                    Pick the 3" diameter circle on the Center layer.
1 selected, 1 found.
Select objects:                    Pick the first lug line.
1 selected, 1 found.
Select objects:                    Pick the second lug line.
1 selected, 1 found.
Select objects: <RETURN>
Select object to trim:             Pick the bottom right half of 1" diameter circle.
```

```
Select object to trim:              Pick bottom left end of right lug line.
Select object to trim:              Pick the bottom half of 1" diameter circle again.
Select object to trim:              Pick bottom end of left lug line.
Select object to trim: <RETURN>
```

The first lug is complete. The perimeter in the target drawing shows the lug in six places. You could array the lug now and draw the remaining entities between the arrayed lugs, but it is more efficient to create one-sixth of the perimeter and then do the array.

Completing One-Sixth of the Top Flange

Here we will rely on AutoCAD's editing commands to do the calculation and construction. Use the ROTATE command to set up a one-sixth segment of the circle. Then, use the ARC and FILLET commands to complete the segment.

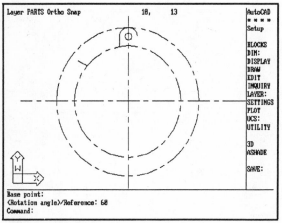

Rotated Lug Line

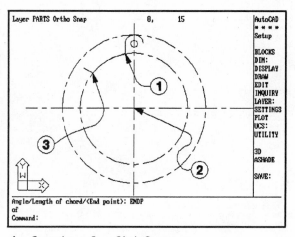

Arc Completes One-Sixth Segment

Using ROTATE and ARC to Construct a Perimeter Segment

```
Command: ROTATE
Select objects:                     Select short lug line on the right.
1 selected, 1 found.
Select objects: <RETURN>
Base point:                         Pick center of circles at absolute point 10,13.
<Rotation angle>/Reference: 60
```

```
Command: ARC
Center/<Start point>: ENDP
of                                              Pick endpoint of left lug line ①.
Center/End/<Second point>: C
Center: INT
of                                              Pick intersection of center lines ②.
Angle/Length of chord/<End point>: ENDP
of                                              Pick endpoint of rotated lug line ③.
```

Now, fillet the perimeter segment.

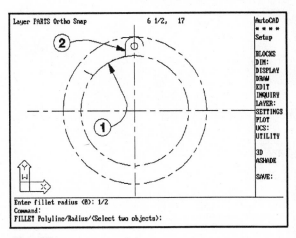

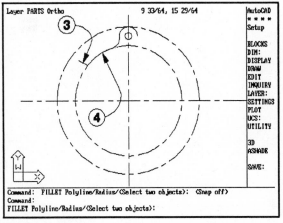

First Fillet   *Second Fillet*

Using FILLET to Complete the Perimeter Segment

```
Command: FILLET                                 Set fillet radius to 1/2 inch.
Polyline/Radius/<Select two objects>: R
Enter fillet radius <0>: 1/2


Command: FILLET
Polyline/Radius/<Select two objects>:           Pick arc at ① and line at ②.


Command: FILLET
Polyline/Radius/<Select two objects>:           Pick arc at ③ and line at ④.
```

Now, you are ready to create the perimeter by arraying the one-sixth segment. If you followed the construction sequence, all the entity points will line up. Notice that you have made only one trivial calculation: dividing the circle into sixths (60 degrees). By using osnaps and editing commands, you have let AutoCAD do all the hard calculations and locations.

Using ARRAY and PEDIT to Create the Perimeter

Use a polar array to replicate the one-sixth segment to complete the perimeter of the flange. Then, use PEDIT Join to group the entity segments into a single polyline. After you have joined the segments, create two circles in the interior of the flange. Use the following illustrations and exercise sequence to guide you.

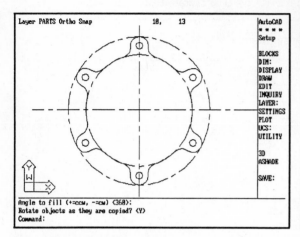

Top Flange After Array

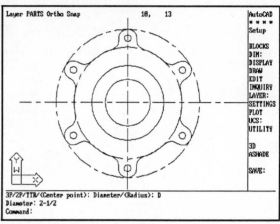

Circles Complete the Top Flange

Using ARRAY and PEDIT to Complete the Flange

```
Command: ARRAY
Select objects: W
First corner:
Other corner:                  Put window around all flange entities on the PARTS layer.
7 found.
Select objects: <RETURN>
Rectangular or Polar array (R/P): P
Center point of array: INT
of                             Pick intersection of center lines at absolute point 10,13.
Number of items: 6
Angle to fill (+=ccw, -=cw) <360>: <RETURN>
Rotate objects as they are copied? <Y> <RETURN>

Command: PEDIT
Select polyline:               Pick first arc created on top flange.
Entity selected is not a polyline
Do you want to turn it into one? <Y> <RETURN>
Close/Join/Width/Edit vertex/Fit curve/Spline curve/Decurve/Undo/eXit <X>: J
Select objects: W
First corner:                  Make the window as large as you like.
Other corner:                  As long as it includes all the top flange entities,
44 found.                      Join will ignore extra entities.
```

```
Select objects: <RETURN>
35 segments added to polyline
Open/Join/Width/Edit vertex/Fit curve/Spline curve/Decurve/Undo/eXit <X>:
<RETURN>
```

Command: **CIRCLE**   Draw a 4" diameter circle for the inside of the flange.

Command: **CIRCLE**   Draw a 2-1/2" diameter hole in the bottom of the part.

The PEDIT Join requires that each entity endpoint matches the adjacent endpoint exactly. If you did not get a join, undo and try again.

➡ *TIP: You can use a far-off drawing corner or a scratch UCS for background construction, putting together pieces of a drawing that you can later move, copy, or array into place.*

Editing by Recycling Entities

Frequently, you can save a little drawing time by recycling entities rather than creating new ones. Think of this technique as giving you a clean drawing environment. Rather than erasing the now-surplus construction circles, recycle them by changing the inner circle's layer (linetype) and radius, and by changing the outer circle's radius.

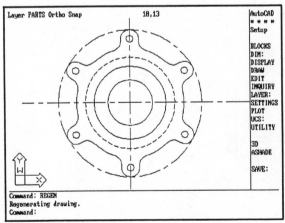

Change Construction Circle Layer and Diameter

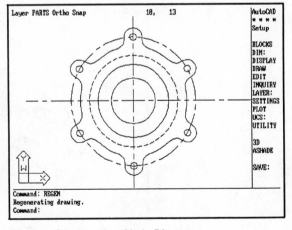

Change Construction Circle Diameter

Using CHPROP and CHANGE to Complete Top View

```
Command: CHPROP
Select objects:          Select inner center line construction circle.
1 selected, 1 found.
```

```
Select objects: <RETURN>
Change what property (Color/Elev/LAyer/LType/Thickness) ? LA
New layer <CENTER>: HIDDEN
Change what property (Color/Elev/LAyer/LType/Thickness) ? <RETURN>

Command: CHANGE
Select objects: P              Previous reselects the circle.
1 found.
Select objects: <RETURN>
Properties/<Change point>: <RETURN>
Enter circle radius: 2.5       Remember you can type decimal entry even in fractional units.

Command: CHANGE              Change the radius of the outside circle to 3-1/2".
Command: REGEN              Regenerate drawing to verify changes.
Command: END              Save as default drawing.
```

The plan view of the flange is finished.

Stopping Point

This is a good stopping point. The next section uses XYZ filters to construct the section view of the flange. If you have other commitments, take a break here and pick up again with the point filters.

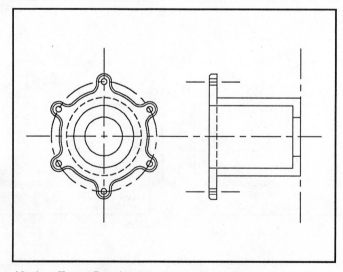

Mockup Target Drawing

Using XYZ Point Filters for Section Construction

If you look at the Mockup Target Drawing (above), you will see that most of the geometry you need to draw the section view on the right already exists in the plan view. You can draw an accurate section quickly by aligning the new section lines with intersections of the lines and entities making up the plan view. However, you cannot draw the lines by simply aligning your cursor crosshairs because many of the intersection points are not on snap increments.

Using XYZ point filters makes this alignment easy. Point filters let you pick X, Y, and Z coordinates independently. Because we are drawing in 2D, we are only concerned with X and Y coordinates. Don't worry about Z filtering.

If you are resuming your drawing, re-check your setup with the table at the front of the chapter. If you are using the IA DISK and jumping in at this point, use the CHAP-08B drawing. This drawing contains the completed plan view of the flange. Your current layer should be PARTS. Restore View A to start the drawing.

Setting Up for XYZ Point Filters

Enter selection: **1**   Begin a NEW drawing called MOCKSECT=CHAP-08B.

Enter selection: **1**   Begin a NEW drawing called MOCKSECT=MOCKUP.

Command: **VIEW**   Restore View A.

Since the flange is symmetrical, you only need to draw half of the section view, then mirror the other half. Use the next exercise sequence with X and Y filters to create the lower half of the section. Precede any point that you pick (or type) with a .X (or .Y) point filter. AutoCAD will then take only the specified coordinate from the following point, and reprompt you for the other coordinate values. When you specify an .X value, you pick an entity that has the X value that you want, then AutoCAD will tell you that you need a Y value. You can pick, type or use an osnap to get your Y value, giving you the X,Y intersection point. Use the following illustrations and sequences to guide your drawing. The exercises will give you the osnaps and coordinate values that you need.

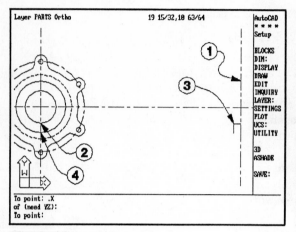

First and Second Lines of Section

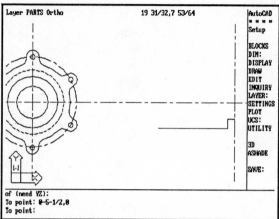

Third Line of Section

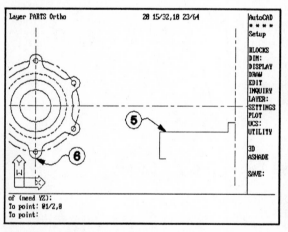

Fourth and Fifth Lines of Section

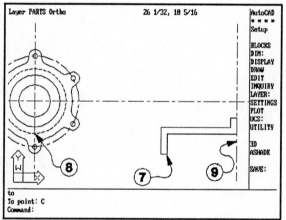

Completed Section

Using XYZ Point Filters to Draw a Section View

Command: **OSNAP**	Set a Running Osnap to INT,END.
Command: **SNAP**	Turn Snap off.
Command: **LINE**	
From point: **.X**	Build the first line.
of	Pick anywhere on vertical base line at ①.
(need YZ):	Pick intersection of hole and vertical center line at ②.
To point: **@-1/2,0**	
To point: **.X**	Build the second line.
of	Pick left side of last line drawn at ③.
(need YZ):	Pick inside of flange circle and vertical center line at ④.
To point: **@-5-1/2,0**	Draw the third line.

```
To point: .X            Build the fourth line.
of                      Pick left side of last line drawn at ⑤.
(need YZ):              Pick intersection of arc and vertical center line at ⑥.
To point: @1/2,0        Draw the fifth line.
To point: .X            Build the sixth line.
of                      Pick right side of last line drawn at ⑦.
(need YZ):              Pick intersection of hidden circle and vertical line at ⑧.
To point: PERP          Use PERP to override running Osnap.
to                      Pick anywhere on vertical base line at ⑨.
To point: C             Close to beginning point.
```

Your screen should now show half a section view of the mockup part. Complete the section half by using XYZ filters to add the lines for the hole in the top flange.

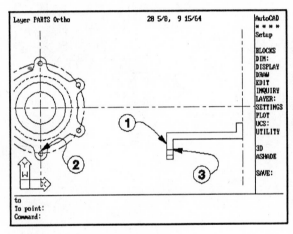

Section View With Hole Lines

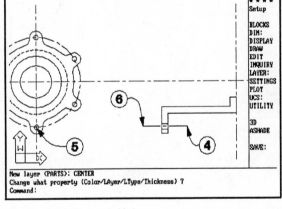

Center Line Through Hole

Using XYZ Filter to Draw a Hole in the Section View

```
Command: LINE
To point: .X            Build first line of hole.
of                      Pick line of top flange in the section view at ①.
(need YZ):              Pick where the drilled hole and center line intersect at ②.
To point: PERP
to                      Pick line in the section view at ③.
To point: <RETURN>
Command: LINE           Repeat the process for second hole line.

Command: LINE
To point: .X            Build center line for hole.
of                      Pick a point 1" to the right of the bottom flange at ④.
(need YZ):              Pick center of lug hole at ⑤.
```

To point:	Pick a point 1" to the left of the top flange at ⑥.
To point: **<RETURN>**	
Command: **CHPROP**	Change last line to the CENTER Layer.

Mirroring the Section View

All you need to do to get the rest of the section view is to mirror the lower half, and add four more lines. Here is the exercise sequence.

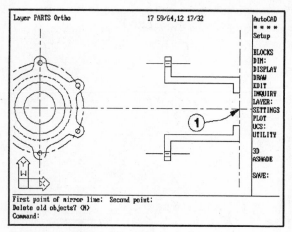

Section After Mirror

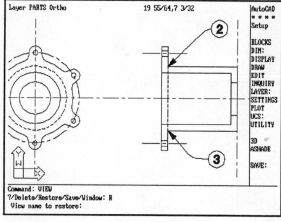

Completed Section

Using **MIRROR** to Complete the Section View

Command: **MIRROR**	
Select objects: **W**	Enclose the entire section image.
First corner:	Pick first corner point.
Other corner:	Pick second corner point.
11 found.	
Select objects: **<RETURN>**	
First point of mirror line:	Pick intersection of center lines at ①.
Second point:	Select any point 180 degrees to the left.
Delete old objects? <N> **<RETURN>**	
Command: **LAYER**	Set HIDDEN layer current.
Command: **LINE**	Draw hidden line from ② to ③.
Command: **LAYER**	Set PARTS layer current.
Command: **LINE**	Draw lines to complete the top and bottom of section.
Command: **VIEW**	Restore View A.
Command: **OSNAP**	Set Ortho to None.
Command: **SAVE**	Save to the default drawing.

The target flange has a chamfer. Take one more moment to chamfer the
section view, then add the chamfer to the plan view by offsetting the
perimeter. Here are two illustrations and a sequence to help you.

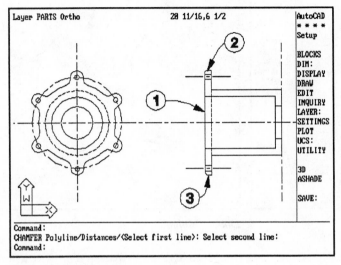

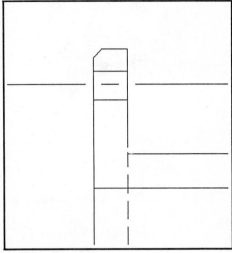

Section After Chamfer   *Detail of Chamfer*

Chamfer Edge of Flange

```
Command: CHAMFER
Polyline/Distances/<Select first line>: D
Enter first chamfer distance <0>: 1/8
Enter second chamfer distance <1/8">: <RETURN>
```

```
Command: <RETURN>
CHAMFER Polyline/Distances/<Select first line>:          Pick top flange line at ①.
Select second line:                                      Pick end flange line at ②.
```

```
Command: <RETURN>
CHAMFER Polyline/Distances/<Select first line>:          Pick top flange line at ①.
Select second line:                                      Pick end flange line at ③.
```

```
Command: OFFSET
Offset distance or Through <1>: 1/8
Select object to offset:   Pick any perimeter point on the top flange in the plan view.
Side to offset?            Pick a point inside the perimeter.
Select object to offset: <RETURN>
```

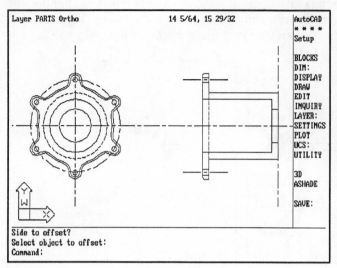

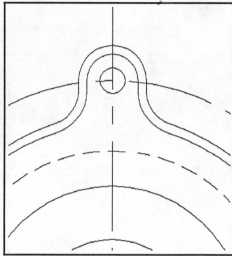

Top View After Offset   *Detail of Offset*

Restore your View A, then save the MOCKSECT drawing. You will use this drawing later when we take up dimensioning.

Saving the Mockup Section Drawing

Command: **END**   Save your work.

Summing Up

AutoCAD's drawing construction tools are as much a frame of mind as a framework of commands and options. In the course of constructing the mockup, you have learned how to drop construction lines, use a construction underlayer, and trace over construction lines. You also have learned how to use point filters, combining them with osnaps to create a section view.

There is never just one way to build an AutoCAD drawing. In fact the opposite is true — there are always many ways to build the same drawing. The trick is to find the methods that work most intuitively and efficiently for you. Planning ahead can save you many unnecessary steps; try to envision the commands you will use well in advance. If you can visualize the construction technique ahead of time, your drawing productivity will increase dramatically.

Use point filters and construction lines to line up entities. Use construction lines for center lines, base lines and lines to align large numbers of points. Use point filters for everyday on-the-fly alignments. Set up one or more layers for your construction lines. Construction lines don't need to be linear — use arcs and circles for angular or curved tracing. A few extra construction lines never hurt and could help make your drawing life easier.

Use point filters (.X .Y .Z .XY .XZ or .YZ) to pick a single coordinate value off an existing entity, then independently pick or enter the other coordinates. For 2D drafting, ignore the Z component. Use osnaps to help you pick filtered points.

Use UNDO control to protect your work sequences. Use REDO for a rescue — but only immediately after a U, UNDO Back, or UNDO <number>. Marks and Groups help control undos and make life going back easier. Watch out for PLOT and PRPLOT when you UNDO! Going back to a mark is no substitute for saving regularly. Saving is still the best way to protect your drawing file.

On to BLOCKS

Talking about saving, wouldn't it be useful if you could save the contents of the selection set and use it as a rubber stamp whenever you need it? It is time to make BLOCKS.

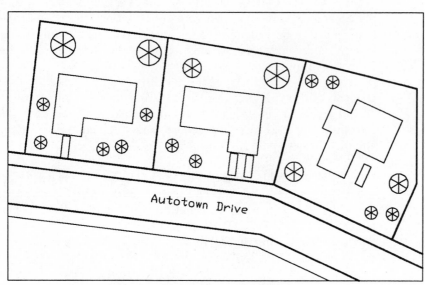

Autotown Drive

Autotown With Simple Blocks

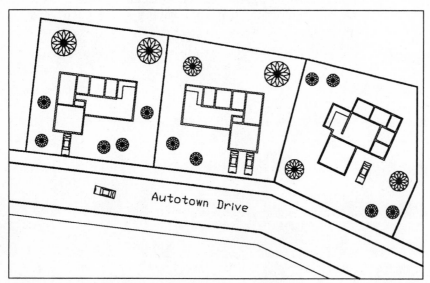

Autotown Drive

Autotown With Complex Blocks

Autotown Drawing With Simple and Complex Blocks

CHAPTER 9

Grouping Entities into Blocks

DRAWING WITH PARTS AND SYMBOLS

The Benefits of Using Blocks

In this chapter, you will learn how to create, store and use blocks. Blocking entities into more formal associations allows them to be used conveniently within one or more drawing files, or made into permanent symbols as parts of a symbol library.

Parts and Symbols vs. Blocks

AutoCAD makes it possible to group individual entities together and treat them as one object. Symbols and drawing parts are typical candidates for such groupings. AutoCAD calls these groups of entities BLOCKS. We consider *parts* to represent real objects, drawn full size or to scale, such as a car or a desk. *Symbols* are symbolic objects, not drawn to scale, such as section bubbles, electrical receptacles and weld symbols.

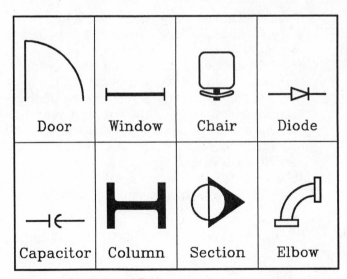

Common Symbols and Parts

If you merely move or copy symbol objects, you can collect the individual drawing entities into a selection set and make the appropriate edits.

However, as drawings become crowded, it becomes more difficult to get the entities that you want into the selection set. It is much easier to group the entities together as a block, give the block a name, save it, and make it available for later use in the drawing or in other drawings.

AutoCAD lets you do just that: group entities, give the group a name, and then operate on the group as a whole. What's the catch? Entities in blocks stick together; move one part of the block and the whole moves. You can, of course, break up a block by exploding it. You'll see how, when, and why.

To BLOCK or not to BLOCK, that is the question.

—Hamlet at his Workstation

Besides their convenience, blocks provide additional editing benefits. When you insert blocks into your drawing file, you can change their scale and rotation. This allows you to build your drawing quickly and easily by modifying simple blocks. Typically, users build up libraries of frequently used blocks to speed up drawing creation. You also can globally replace one block with another, revising an entire drawing with a single insertion command.

Block Efficiency and Storage

If you need further convincing of the value of blocks, consider efficiency. When you draw 100 lines, you add 100 entities to your drawing. When you make a block containing 100 lines, AutoCAD creates a *block definition* containing 100 entities. Block definitions are invisibly stored in the drawing file. When you visibly insert a block in your drawing, you only add one new entity, a reference to the block definition. So if you insert a block containing 100 lines into your drawing in 12 places, you only have 112 entities for AutoCAD to store: 100 lines in the block definition and 12 block references for the visible inserts. On the other hand, if you draw and copy 12 groups of 100 lines without blocks, you add 1200 entities of data to your drawing file. It's easy to see that proper use of blocks can save huge amounts of disk space.

Block Editing Tools

Grouping entities into blocks is really very simple. You use BLOCK to create a block definition, use INSERT to place a block reference in a drawing, and use WBLOCK to store a block's entities permanently as a separate drawing file on disk. You will find these commands located on the BLOCKS screen menu, along with two other block commands, BASE and MINSERT. You will also find the [Insert] command as a menu item on the [Draw] pull-down menu.

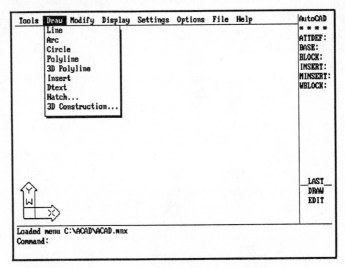

Blocks Screen Menu and Draw Pull-Down Menu

Besides these block commands, we will introduce three additional commands that you can use to edit blocks. These are the EXPLODE, DIVIDE and MEASURE commands. You will find these commands on the [EDIT] screen menus.

➡ *NOTE: AutoCAD has a second type of symbol creation called SHAPES. Text is a special form of the shape feature. To learn more about shapes, see CUSTOMIZING AutoCAD (New Riders Publishing).*

Setup for Blocks

To get going, you have to do some setup. You are going to start a new drawing called Autotown. Autotown is our version of a site plan. It encompasses three building lots along an elegant street, "Autotown Drive."

How the Block Exercises Are Organized

You can use the Autotown drawing and its associated exercises in two ways. First, use the exercises in the early part of the chapter to guide you through the basic block commands, including learning how to write blocks to disk files and how to redefine blocks in a drawing.

Second, use the last exercise, called the Autotown Block Exercise, to create the actual Autotown drawing. This exercise will give you more extensive practice working with blocks and placing them in a drawing. It contains some additional drawing techniques. It will show you, for example, how to use a UCS to locate drawing objects within each building lot in the site plan.

If you are using the IA DISK, you can choose your starting point. The drawing called CHAP-09A will get you started with this first section. The drawing called CHAP-09B has the site plan setup that you will need to create the Autotown drawing in the last exercise. The blocks for the Autotown drawing are also on the IA Disk.

Use the following exercise sequence and the Autotown Settings table to help you set up your drawing. The drawing uses decimal units to represent feet (not inches). Set your drawing limits at 360 feet by 240 feet. The drawing is sized to fit a 36" x 24" D-sized sheet plotted at 1"=10', so one unit represents one foot, not one inch. Notice that the drawing is set up to use Distance<Angle input in Surveyor's angles for the site plan.

Setting Up Autotown for Block Exercises

   Enter selection: **1**   Begin a NEW drawing called AUTOTOWN=CHAP-09A.

   Enter selection: **1**   Begin a NEW drawing called AUTOTOWN.

Make sure you have the layers and settings shown in the Autotown Settings table.

AXIS	COORDS	GRID	SNAP	UCSICON	
Off	ON	10	1	OR	
UNITS	Decimal units, 4 decimal points, decimal angle, 2 fractional places, defaults all other settings.				
LIMITS	0,0 to 360,240				
ZOOM	Zoom All				
VIEW	Save view as All				
Layer name	**State**		**Color**		**Linetype**
0	Current		7 (white)		CONTINUOUS
SITE	On		3 (green)		CONTINUOUS
PLAN	On		5 (blue)		CONTINUOUS

Autotown Drawing Settings

Your current layer should be layer 0. Before you can do anything, you need to draw some objects on layer 0 to make into blocks.

Making Some Objects

Trees and cars can be found in most subdivisions. Draw a car and a tree using the dimensions in the following drawings. (We admit the tree looks a little sparse. We will have a better tree for Autotown later.)

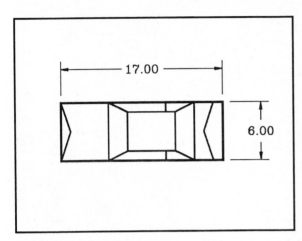

Car for Block Exercise

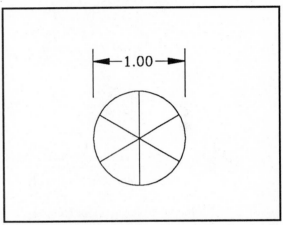

Tree for Block Exercise

Making a Car and Tree Symbol

```
Command: ZOOM                          Zoom to a working area of the screen.
All/Center/Dynamic/Extents/Left/Previous/Window/<Scale(X)>: L
Lower left corner point: 168,110
Magnification or Height <258.9646> : 40
```

Draw the tree and car using the dimensions shown in the illustrations.

When you are done your screen should look like the Car and Tree Symbols screen shot below.

The BLOCK Command

Now, turn the car and tree into blocks. When you execute the BLOCK command, AutoCAD will first ask you for the block name that you want to use. Call the tree TREE1, and the car CAR2. Then, AutoCAD will ask you for an insertion base point. This is the reference point that you will later use to put the block in a new location. After you identify a base point, select the entities forming the blocks with a window. Here is the exercise sequence.

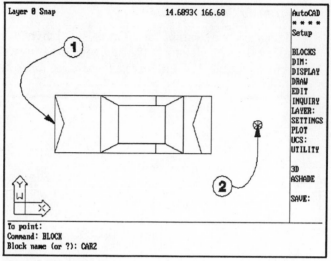

Car and Tree Symbols

Using BLOCK to Create Your First Blocks

```
Command: BLOCK
BLOCK Block name (or ?): CAR2
Insertion base point: MID        Use MIDpoint osnap.
of                               Pick the front of the car at ①.
Select objects: W
First corner:                    Pick first corner point.
Other corner:                    Pick first corner point.
20 found.
Select objects: <RETURN>         And they're erased! (Oops will bring them back.)

Command: BLOCK
BLOCK Block name (or ?): TREE1
Insertion base point:            Pick the center at ②.
Select objects: W
First corner:                    Pick first corner point.
Other corner:                    Pick first corner point.
4 found.
Select objects: <RETURN>
```

Right now you should have a blank screen (unless you oopsed the blocks back). After selecting your entities, all the window contents disappeared. They are not lost. The entities are safely stored away as a block called CAR2, and a block called TREE1.

Where are they? AutoCAD keeps track of all blocks in an invisible part of the drawing file called the BLOCK table. When you used the BLOCK command, it created a definition of the car and the tree and stored the definitions in the block table of the current drawing file. The block definition defines the entities associated with the block name. The BLOCK and INSERT illustration (below) shows how the block storage area is set up and how the block command stored your car symbol.

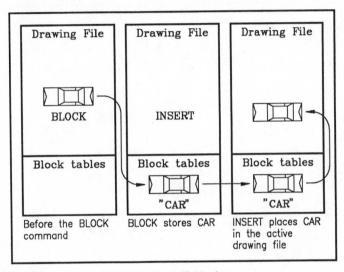

BLOCK and INSERT With Block Table Area

The INSERT Command

We will leave the tree in storage for now. To get the car back, you need to INSERT it from the block table into the active part of the drawing file. First, AutoCAD wants to know which block you want to insert. If you respond with **?**, AutoCAD will give you a list of the names for all defined blocks that are currently in the table area of your drawing. Take a look at the names.

Using INSERT ? to Get Block Names

```
Command: INSERT
Block name (or ?): ?          Screen flips to text mode and displays:
Defined blocks.
CAR2
TREE1
2 user blocks, 0 unnamed blocks.
```

When you've seen the list, do a flip screen.

Now, INSERT your car. After you give the block name, CAR2, you can drag the block to insert it, or you can give coordinates for the insertion point. Drag the car using the illustration below as a guide to place the car. AutoCAD also will ask for scale and rotation factors. Default these factors. After you get the car inserted, copy it in your drawing. Here is the prompt sequence.

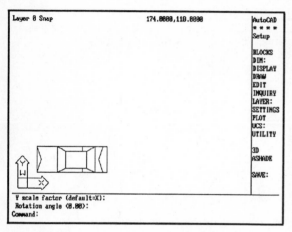

Inserted Car

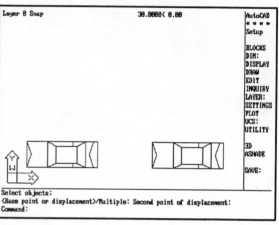

Copied Car

Using INSERT to Insert the Car Block

```
Command: INSERT
Block name (or ?): CAR2
Insertion point:                Pick absolute point 174,118.
X scale factor <1>/Corner/XYZ: <RETURN>
Y scale factor <default=X>: <RETURN>
Rotation angle <0.00>: <RETURN>          Car is inserted.

Command: COPY               Copy car from absolute point 174,118 to polar point @30<0.
```

Your car came back on the screen with the insertion. But this car is not the same as your original car. When you copied the car, you saw that you could select it with a single object pick. Once you have inserted a block in your drawing, you can edit the block as a single entity with your usual arsenal of editing commands. You can move, copy, and array the block.

What took place behind the drawing insertion? Insert did three things: it created a block reference to the block definition; it left the original block definition in the block table area; then it drew an image representing the entities which make up the block definition.

Modifying Block Insertions

Not only does INSERT place a block reference in the active drawing area, but it allows you to modify the block reference as you place it. Instead of defaulting the scale and rotation factors, you can input values and INSERT will place a modified image of the block in the drawing.

Define scale by inputting an X and Y multiplier. AutoCAD will give you the same <default> prompt for the Y factor as the X factor to default your drawing symbol to a 1:1 ratio. You can use different X and Y scales by typing different responses (the XYZ option is for 3D control). You also give an angle of rotation. You type an angle or pick a rotation by dragging the crosshairs.

Try your hand at modifying two car block insertions. First, insert your car using different X and Y scales. Use the values given in the sequence below to give you an elongated car. (We think it looks like a stretch limousine.) Second, do another insertion to angle the car. Use the illustrations and the prompt sequence to help you. If you make a mistake, use Undo or Erase Last to remove the block insertion.

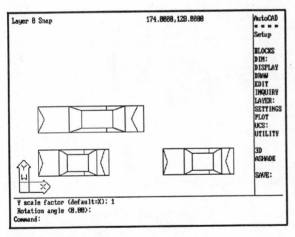

Stretched Limousine

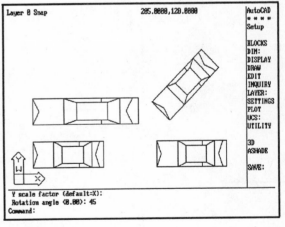

Angled Car

Using INSERT With Scale and Rotation Changes

```
Command: INSERT
Block name (or ?) <CAR2>: <RETURN>
Insertion point:                     Pick absolute point 174,128.
X scale factor <1>/Corner/XYZ: 1.5
Y scale factor <default=X>: 1
Rotation angle <0>: <RETURN>
```

```
Command: INSERT
Block name (or ?) <CAR2>: <RETURN>
Insertion point:                        Pick absolute point 205,128.
X scale factor <1>/Corner/XYZ: <RETURN>
Y scale factor <default=X>: <RETURN>
Rotation angle <0.00>: 45
```

What happened behind the insertion scenes this time? The Car Drawing — Inserted With Changes illustration shows how the scaled insertion was done. Again, INSERT made a reference to the block table, then it placed a modified image of the car in the active drawing.

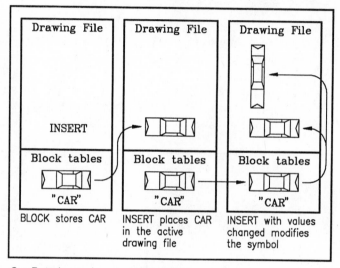

Car Drawing — Inserted With Changes

While you were inputting your scale values, you may also have noticed that you have a second option, called Corner, to input scale factors. If you use the Corner option to input your scale values, the insertion point is the lower left corner of a rubber band rectangle. AutoCAD asks you to drag the upper right corner to determine scale. When you pick the upper right corner, AutoCAD uses the width of the rectangle as X scale and the height as Y scale. The width and height are measured in drawing file units.

You do not need to type a **C** to use corner point scaling. Just picking a point at the scale prompt works exactly the same as typing **C** and then picking a point. The **C** option is used in menus because it limits scaler input to corner point picking and issues an Other corner: prompt.

Be careful with Corner! The dragged scale is relative to one unit square. It works great if your block definition is about one unit in size. But if your block definition is many drawing units in size, even a small rubber band rectangle will give a large scale factor.

When using corner scale input, be sure to use snap or osnap to control accuracy. It is most useful when inserting unit scale blocks.

Using Unit Scale to Make Flexible Blocks

At first you may think that you will use insertion scale and rotation only occasionally. Nothing could be further from the truth! Scaling and rotating blocks during insertion are invaluable tools.

What's the trick? The trick is to create your parts in a 1 x 1 unit cell. Then, when you insert the block, you can stretch or shrink it to fit. The block is good at any scale with any insertion scale factor. For example, you can store a window symbol so that the symbol endpoints are on the left and right edges of the unit cell. Then insert the symbol with appropriate scale factors to fill the area you need. To see how this works, see the Unit Block illustration.

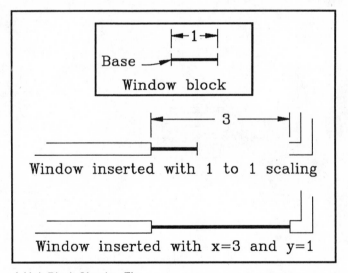

A Unit Block Sized to Fit

➡ *NOTE: Whether you use keyboard entry (or the Corner option), you can specify negative scale factors to mirror the block's insertion or turn it upside-down (or both).*

➡ *TIP: A handy trick for inserting objects that are normally horizontal or vertical is to use your pointer to pick a rotation angle with Ortho <^ O> turned On. This limits the rotation angle to 0, 90, 180, or 270 degrees.*

Using Preset Scales

So far when you have inserted blocks, you have given an insertion point first, then specified scale and angle. This is quick and easy, but you can't see the angle or how big the block is until after you have placed it. This makes it hard to visually drag scaled or rotated blocks into place. Fortunately, you can preset the scale and rotation. When you preset the block's scale and angle, insertion point dragging is suspended until you have completed your preset options. Then, you can you can see the block's scale and angle as you drag it to pick the insertion point.

Try making one more stretch limousine using the preset values given in the following exercise.

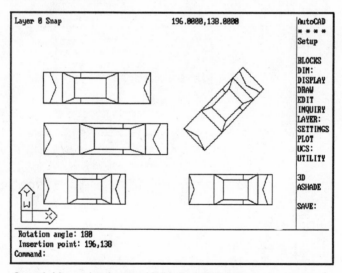

Stretch Limousine Inserted With Preset Scale

Using INSERT With Preset Scales

```
Command: INSERT                          Insert a stretched car rotated 180 degrees.
Block name (or ?) <CAR2>: <RETURN>
Insertion point: X                       Preset the X scale.
X scale factor: 1.3
Insertion point: Y                       Preset the Y scale.
Y scale factor: 1
```

```
Insertion point: R                    Preset the rotation angle.
Rotation angle: 180
Insertion point: 196,138
```

Presets offer several options, but they are not shown in the insert prompt. Here is a complete list.

Preset Scale and Rotation Options

Scale and **PScale** will prompt for Scale factor which will be preset to X, Y, and Z axes.

Xscale and **PXscale** only preset an X scale factor.

Yscale and **PYscale** only preset a Y scale factor.

Zscale and **PZscale** only preset a Z scale factor.

Rotate and **PRotate** preset Rotation angle which you can enter from the keyboard, or by picking two points.

Just type the first one or two characters of the preset option to tell AutoCAD what you want to preset. P stands for preliminary, not preset.

Options prefixed with a P establish a preliminary scale and rotation value to aid in insertion. After the insertion point is selected, the normal prompts are displayed to let you change the preset values.

Preset scale factors have limitations. You cannot mix fixed presets, like Xscale, with preliminary presets, like PYscale. If you try to mix them, the preliminary presets become fixed, and you will not be reprompted for their values.

➡ *NOTE: Preset options work best when you use them in macros in a menu. These macros can transparently apply preset options, making dragging while in the insert command natural and easy to do.*

When is a Block Not a Block?

Use the BLOCK command to collect entities into a single group. When you insert the block in a drawing file, the insertion is a single entity. When you erase a block, the whole block (but not its stored definition) is erased. The same holds for moving and copying blocks.

When is a block not a block? A block is not a block when it is *inserted or exploded.

Using *INSERT

Sometimes you want to be able to individually edit different entities that make up a block after you insert them. In your car, for example, the line entities that make up the car lose their individual identity when they are stored as a block.

What if you want to edit the car to make a sports car after you insert it? To edit individual pieces of a block after insertion, AutoCAD provides an asterisk option (*) for the INSERT command. Placing an * in front of a block name at insertion time tells AutoCAD to break the block back into its individual entities. An *insertion does not insert a block reference; it duplicates the original entities of the block definition. However, unlike duplicating entities with COPY, an *insertion allows you to modify the scale and rotation of the copy.

Here's the prompt sequence for an * insertion. Insert the car to the clear area of your screen.

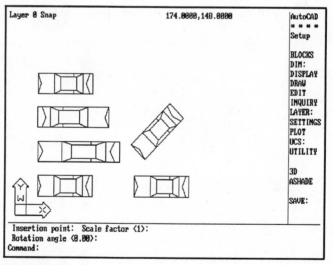

* Inserted Car

Using *INSERT to Break Blocks Into Components

```
Command: ZOOM                              Use the left option for more screen space.
All/Center/Dynamic/Extents/Left/Previous/Window/<Scale(X)>: L
Lower left corner point: 165,107
Magnification or Height <40.0000> : 60
```

```
Command: INSERT
Block name (or ?) <CAR2>: *CAR2
Insertion point:                        Pick absolute point 174,148.
Scale factor <1> <RETURN>
Rotation angle <0.00>: <RETURN>
```

➥ *TIP: If you place a complex *inserted block in the wrong place, use Undo to get rid of all the pieces.*

The newest car is really a collection of separate entities. Don't believe it? Prove it to yourself by changing the car to a sports car. Use some of the editing commands on the *inserted car. Use the exercise below as a guide and create a car as complex as you like, but make sure it looks different from the original. It will be used in a later exercise. We refer to this car as the *sports* car.

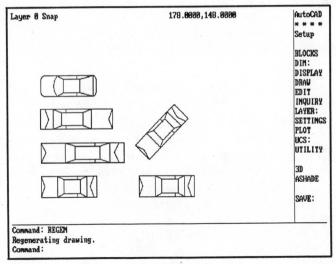

Sports Car

Editing *INSERT Car into a Sports Car

Command: **ERASE**	Erase the windshield line and two lines on the trunk and hood.
Command: **STRETCH**	Stretch the rear glass towards the back.
Command: **STRETCH**	Make the roof smaller.
Command: **ARC**	Draw a new windshield.
Command: **FILLET**	Round the corners of the car.

When you use the * option to insert a block, AutoCAD restricts your flexibility in rescaling the objects as they are placed. You can only specify a single, positive scale factor in the * mode. Negative scale and X not equal to Y are not allowed. You can also rescale your *inserted blocks with STRETCH, SCALE, EXTEND and other editing commands.

The EXPLODE Command

What do you do when you want to edit individual components of a block that is already inserted? You could find out the insertion point, scale and rotation, write them down, delete the block, and re-insert it using *insertion at the same place. That seems like a lot of work. It is easier to just EXPLODE it!

As you might imagine, EXPLODE blows a block back to bits and pieces. Try exploding the first car you inserted on the far bottom left of your drawing.

Using EXPLODE to Explode a Block

```
Command: EXPLODE
Select block reference, polyline, or dimension:      Pick the first inserted car
                                                     in the lower left corner.
```

The block is redrawn as it explodes.

The exploded car pieces left over are identical to the image before the explosion. There may be exceptions where byblock, color, linetype, and layer assignments can come undone when you explode a block. If an exploded block includes nested blocks, only the outer level of nesting is broken up by the explosion. (We will cover nesting and byblock properties a little later in this section's discussion of block properties.)

There are some things that you cannot explode. You can't explode an *inserted block because it already is exploded. You can't explode a minserted block. And, you can't explode a block with differing X and Y (and Z) scale factors or mirrored blocks.

The MINSERT Command

A block is more than a block when it is minserted. Suppose you wanted to put a whole bunch of cars in your drawing (or desks, or printed circuit board drill locations, or any other symbol you might have blocked away). You could insert one copy of the block and then use an array to make several columns and rows.

MINSERT provides another option. Think of MINSERT (multiple insertion) as a single command combining insertion and rectangular arrays (no polar arrays with minsert). However, there is a difference. Every entity that the standard array command generates is an individual entity in the drawing file – it can be edited, deleted, copied or even arrayed individually. Every occurrence of the block that MINSERT generates is part of a single minserted block. You cannot edit the individual component blocks. (You also cannot *minsert blocks.)

Use MINSERT to fill your screen with cars. Pan to the right side of your drawing to get a clear space. After you have minserted the cars, use an ERASE Last to get rid of them. Use the following illustration and the array values in the sequence to get your cars.

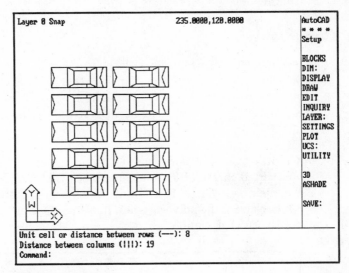

Minserted Cars

Using MINSERT to Insert a Block

Command: **PAN**   Pan from absolute point 240,112 to polar point @60<180.

Command: **MINSERT**
Block name (or ?) <*CAR2>: **CAR2**
Insertion point: Pick absolute point 235,120.
X Scale factor <1>/Corner/XYZ: **<RETURN>**
Y Scale factor <default=X>: **<RETURN>**
Rotation angle <0>: **<RETURN>**
Number of rows (---) <1>: **5**
Number of columns (||||) <1>: **2**
Unit cell or distance between rows (---): **8**
Distance between columns (||||): **19**

Command: **ERASE**   Last to prove that all are tied to one another.

➡ *NOTE: When you specify a rotation in minsert, the array is rotated, as well as the individual blocks within it.*

MINSERT is an efficient way to place multiple copies of a block in a drawing file. In an array, every entity occurrence takes up disk space. In a minsert, the block reference occurs only once along with information about the number of rows, columns, and spacing of elements, saving drawing file disk space.

There are two additional editing commands that you can use to insert multiple copies of a block. These are the DIVIDE and MEASURE commands.

The DIVIDE Command

Frequently, you are faced with the problem of placing blocks in a drawing at some set interval. You can use the DIVIDE command to divide an entity, say a polyline, into equal length parts. Then you can insert a block at the marked division points. DIVIDE does both the marking and the insertions.

Create a new car block from CAR2 in the space where you erased your minserted cars. Call this new car block CAR3. The only change that you are making in CAR3 is to change the insertion point so that the cars will set back from the polyline when they are inserted. Then, create a polyline for the DIVIDE command.

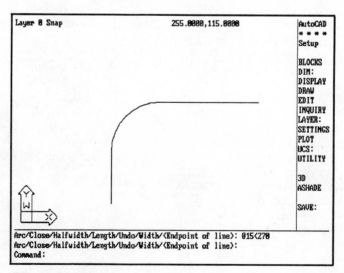

Pline for Divide

Preparing for a Quick Parking Lot

```
Command: INSERT
Block name (or ?) <CAR2>: <RETURN>
Insertion point: 296,137
X scale factor <1> / Corner / XYZ: <RETURN>
Y scale factor (default=X): <RETURN>
Rotation angle <0.00>: -90

Command: BLOCK
Block name (or ?): CAR3
Insertion base point: 269,140         Pick insert point slightly in front of car.
Select objects: L
1 found.
Select objects: <RETURN>

Command: PLINE
From point: 300,145
Current line-width is 0.0000
Arc/Close/Halfwidth/Length/Undo/Width/<Endpoint of line>: @30<180
Arc/Close/Halfwidth/Length/Undo/Width/<Endpoint of line>: A
Angle/CEnter/CLose/Direction/Halfwidth/Line/Radius/Second
pt/Undo/Width/<Endpoint of arc>: CE
Center point: 270,130
Angle/Length/<End point>: @26<180
Angle/CEnter/CLose/Direction/Halfwidth/Line/Radius/Second
pt/Undo/Width/<Endpoint of arc>: L
Arc/Close/Halfwidth/Length/Undo/Width/<Endpoint of line>: @15<270
Arc/Close/Halfwidth/Length/Undo/Width/<Endpoint of line>: <RETURN>
```

Now use DIVIDE to divide the polyline into seven segments and insert the new car block, CAR3.

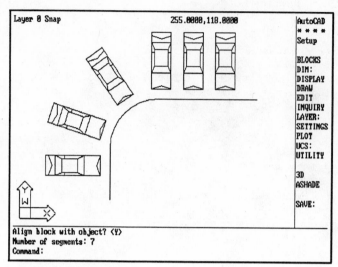

```
Layer 0 Snap                    255.0000,118.0000        AutoCAD
                                                         * * * *
                                                         Setup

                                                         BLOCKS
                                                         DIM:
                                                         DISPLAY
                                                         DRAW
                                                         EDIT
                                                         INQUIRY
                                                         LAYER:
                                                         SETTINGS
                                                         PLOT
                                                         UCS:
                                                         UTILITY

                                                         3D
                                                         ASHADE

                                                         SAVE:

Align block with object? <Y>
Number of segments: 7
Command:
```

Cars Inserted With Divide

Using DIVIDE to Insert a Car Block

```
Command: DIVIDE
Select object to divide:                    Pick the polyline.
<Number of segments>/Block: B
Block name to insert: CAR3
Align block with object? <Y> <RETURN>
Number of segments: 7
```

After you are done, your screen should have six cars. DIVIDE counts the segments between the insertions. Each inserted block is a separate block entity.

You can divide a line or polyline even if you do not use blocks. DIVIDE will insert true points that you can osnap to. You can change their display with PDMODE. When you DIVIDE insert blocks (or points), AutoCAD stores the entities as a Previous selection set. You can get the group again for editing by using the Previous selection set option. There are restrictions on the entities that you can divide. The legal list is lines, arcs, circles, and polylines.

➡ *TIP: You can use a line or polyline as a construction entity for your block insertions, then erase the line after you do your divide (or measure) insert.*

The MEASURE Command

MEASURE works much like DIVIDE. Instead of dividing an entity into equal parts, MEASURE asks you to specify the segment length. Once you specify a segment length, either by inputting a value or by picking two points, AutoCAD marks the entity and asks you for the block name to insert.

Are you getting tired of seeing just cars? Try adding some trees to the parking area by pulling TREE1 out of block storage, and using MEASURE to insert trees along the polyline. Here are an illustration and a prompt sequence to guide you.

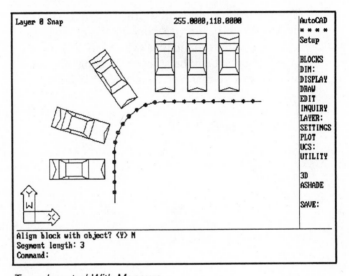

Trees Inserted With Measure

Using MEASURE to Insert a Tree Block

```
Command: MEASURE
Select object to measure:           Pick the polyline.
<Segment length>/Block: B
Block name to insert: TREE1
Align block with object? <Y> N
Segment length: 3                   Place a tree every three feet.
```

The TREE1 was a unit (one foot) block, so the trees came out looking like shrubs. You can make larger trees by creating a larger block and inserting it with MEASURE. A scale of 20 will get you a 20-foot diameter tree. If you do not use blocks, you can measure an entity and insert points.

These points (or blocks) form a Previous selection set that you can use for immediate editing.

WBLOCK — The Write BLOCK Command

So far, the blocks you have created and stored in the block table have been self-contained in the current drawing file. As long as you work in the current drawing file, these block definitions will be there. However, sooner or later you will want to use the blocks created in this drawing file in another drawing file.

Making Permanent Blocks

The WBLOCK command writes a permanent copy of the entities in a block definition as a separate drawing file on disk. In this way, you can call any independently named block file from disk into any drawing file. Any block or selection set can be stored as a separate drawing file, and any drawing on disk can be inserted as a block.

Try storing CAR2 as a separate file on disk called CAR2.DWG, and TREE1 as TREE1.DWG.

Using WBLOCK to Make a Block Drawing File

```
Command: WBLOCK
File name: CAR2          AutoCAD automatically adds the .DWG.
Block name: =            Responding to Block name with = tells AutoCAD the block
                         name equals the file name.

Command: WBLOCK
File name: TREE1         AutoCAD automatically adds the .DWG.
Block name: =
```

➤ *TIP: If a block is really useful, WBLOCK it to a disk file. Periodically group your wblocked symbols into library files and update your lists.*

If you want to insert (or *insert) CAR2.DWG into another drawing file, use the INSERT command and call the file from disk using its disk file name, CAR2. The WBLOCK and INSERT illustration shows WBLOCK and an INSERT operation in a different drawing file.

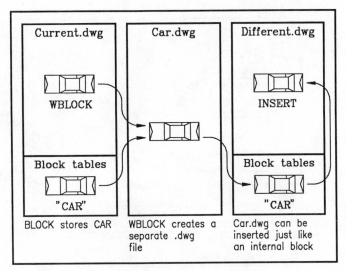

WBLOCK and INSERT

Using Entity Selection to Wblock a File

You can wblock a file without creating a block first. If you enter a
<RETURN> instead of giving an existing block name in response to a block
name prompt, you will be prompted for an insertion base point and object
selection. You can use any of the standard object selection techniques to
select items for wblocking. When you finish selecting with a final
<RETURN>, the entities are copied to the disk file you specified. They are
not defined as a block in the current drawing unless you also insert them
into the current drawing. Any drawing file can be inserted as a block in
any drawing.

The disk file is a normal drawing containing the specified individual
entities and current drawing settings. The entities are not defined as a
block in the new file.

WBLOCK the car (at the top left of your screen) that you made into a
sports car a while back. Call the file name MY-CAR. After you create the
block drawing file, use an Undo or Oops to bring the entities back.

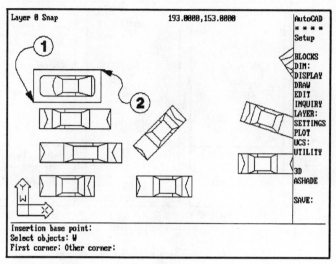

Entities Selected for Block MY-CAR

Creating a Block Drawing File With Entity Selection

Command: **ZOOM**	Zoom previous.
Command: **WBLOCK**	
File name: **MY-CAR**	
Blockname: **<RETURN>**	
Insertion base point:	Pick absolute point 174,148.
Select objects: **W**	Place a window around the sports car.
First corner:	Pick first corner at ①.
Other corner:	Pick second corner at ②.
20 found	
Select objects: **<RETURN>**	
Command: **OOPS**	Return the car to the drawing.

The drawing file created by WBLOCK is just like any other drawing file. WBLOCK doesn't create *any* blocks. It creates a drawing file that contains the entities that you select or that make up an existing block. But since any drawing file can be inserted as a block, you can insert a drawing file created by WBLOCK. Inserting the drawing file creates a block in the current drawing unless you *insert it. *Insertion inserts only individual entities, not blocks.

The BASE Command

The BASE command creates an insertion base point in a drawing file so you can call this whole drawing file into another file. The base point is an insertion handle just like the insertion base point on a regular block. (The base point is not an entity or visible point.) If you make a drawing, store it on disk, and later insert it in another drawing, it defaults to 0,0 as the insertion base point, unless you specify the base point. The following illustration shows how you can use a base point to insert a drawing into another drawing file.

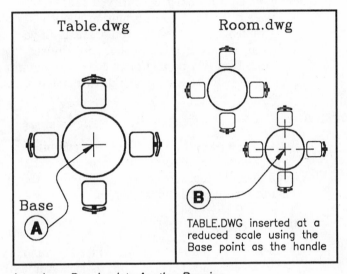

Inserting a Drawing Into Another Drawing

Naming Conventions for Blocks

As your list of blocks and wblocked drawing files grows, you will find that you need some organization and structure in naming your blocks. We recommend that you give your blocks useful names. CAR1 and CAR2 are better than C1 and C2, but not as descriptive as BUG and PORSCHE. If you don't like a defined name, use the RENAME command to rename your block.

Try to keep your block names to less than eight characters, anticipating that you may want to wblock them later (assuming that you have a DOS operating system). You may also want to use common prefixes for similar classes of blocks (and drawings) to make it easy to use DOS file name wildcards. Keep an alphabetical log of block names. Keep the list in a disk text file and print it out as it changes. This way you won't accidently call the wrong block or duplicate block names.

The PURGE Command

As you work with blocks, you can build up extraneous blocks in the block table by inserting them, then later deleting them. Use the PURGE command to remove unused block definitions from the block table of the current drawing file. PURGE can help you keep your storage name list neat and help you keep disk space in check.

PURGE only works in an editing session *before* you make any modifications to your drawing database by either creating a new entity or by editing an existing entity. PURGE is selective and prompts you extensively, giving you information about what blocks are stored in the block table area and asking you explicitly if you want to clean them out. You also can use PURGE to clean out unused layers, views or styles — anything that you named during a drawing editor session. PURGE is a good habit before backing up a drawing on diskettes.

Block Properties

Blocks are a powerful tool. Their use can make your drawing life easier. There are two additional block properties that you should be aware of when you use blocks: blocks can include other blocks, and blocks can include entities on different layers.

Nesting Blocks

A block can be made up of other blocks. This is called nesting. You can place a block inside a block inside a block. AutoCAD does not place a limit on the number of block nesting levels, although editing nested blocks can get confusing if you go more than a few levels deep.

To include a block in another block, you simply select the first block when you BLOCK the second. You can use standard editing commands, like ARRAY, COPY, and MOVE, on nested blocks just as on normal blocks.

Nested blocks further increase the efficiency and control of blocks. In our Nested Block Example illustration, making the chair a nested block allows it to be redefined independently of the outer table block. It also reduces the number of entities in the outer block definition.

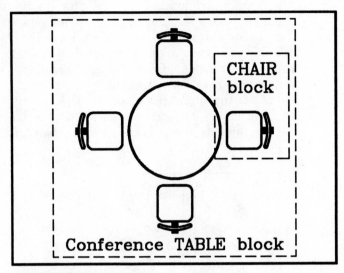

Nested Block Example

Blocks and Layers

When dealing with blocks and layers, we are primarily concerned with what layers the entities in the block definition are on. So far, all the blocks you have used have entities drawn on layer 0. You can, however, create a block with entities on different drawing layers. For example, you can create a block with graphic entities on layer ABC, and text on layer XYZ. When you create the block, AutoCAD will store them inside the block on their appropriate layers.

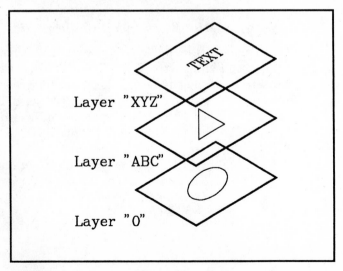

A BLOCK Can Have Entities on Many Layers

When you insert multiple-layer blocks, each entity in the block will display following its rules of color and linetype as they were at the time of the entity's creation. Entities included in the block at the time of block creation can have color or linetype specification set BYLAYER (the default), BYBLOCK, or by explicit color or linetype settings. If the current drawing file does not contain all of the needed block's layers, insertion will create the appropriate layers in the current drawing file. The Color Layer Insertion illustration shows a normal block insertion where the entity retains its original explicit color when it is inserted on a different active layer.

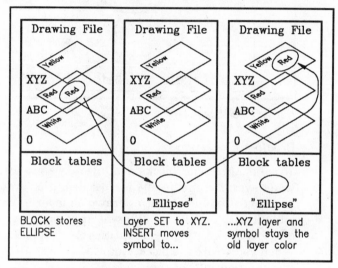

Color Layer Insertion Example

Layer 0's Special Block Insertion Properties

If you create entities on layer 0, store them in a block, and then insert the block on a different active layer, the entities will seem to move to the layer of insertion. If they had explicit color or linetype, they will retain them. However, if they had color and/or linetype set BYLAYER, they will adopt the default layer settings of their layer of insertion. Blocks made from layer 0 BYLAYER entities act like chameleons.

➡ *NOTE: Any entities that were on layer 0 at the time of block creation will go back to layer 0 when you use an *insertion. Exploding blocks will return layer 0 entities to their original layer, color, and linetype.*

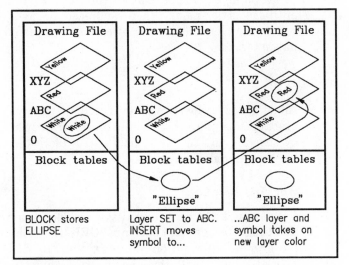

Layer Insertion Example

Using BYBLOCK

You can get a similar effect to layer 0 entities by creating them with the BYBLOCK property (or changing existing entities to BYBLOCK with CHPROP). These BYBLOCK entities will take on the current color and linetype settings of the receiving layer during a block insertion. Unlike blocked layer 0 BYLAYER entities which are predestined to assume the layer default color and/or linetypes of their receiving layer, BYBLOCK entities in blocks are completely flexible. They assume the settings of the receiving layer at the time of insertion, whether explicit (like red), BYLAYER, or even BYBLOCK (for nesting). If you find this confusing, don't be alarmed. BYBLOCK really should be called "BYINSERT," and layer 0 should be called "layer BYINSERT."

Blocks and Frozen Layers

Sooner or later we all have the experience of inserting a block with multiple-layer entities on a layer, freezing the layer, and suddenly have the block disappear from view. How does this happen?

When you give AutoCAD an insertion base point, that invisible reference point is defined in the block at the time of creation. The reference point anchors the block into the drawing file by its insertion point coordinates. When you insert a block, AutoCAD does not actually insert all the information that makes up the block at this point, but only a block reference back to the invisibly stored block definitions. This means that whatever layer you use to insert the block will contain the block reference at this insertion point. When you freeze the layer, you suppress the block reference, even though the block has entities on other layers that you haven't frozen.

Block Redefinition

All of these properties sound good in theory, but what about some practical techniques? We would like to wrap up this first section on blocks by showing you two extremely useful block techniques: using working blocks, and redefining blocks.

Working Blocks

As you insert a block, you can assign a block name by using an equal sign. You use an assignment such as WORK-1=TREE1 to tell AutoCAD to use the graphic information stored in the TREE1.DWG file on disk. The TREE1 symbol will then be inserted in your drawing as the block WORK-1. This provides you with a safety step that makes it difficult to overwrite blocks and makes it easy to redefine blocks in your drawing file. The Autotown Block Exercise will show you how to use both working blocks and block redefinitions.

Redefining Blocks

To see how block redefinition works, try replacing all your CAR2 blocks with MY-CAR blocks. You can use the INSERT command to replace blocks as well as to insert them. The = sign option redefines existing blocks. You do not have to actually complete the insert command. Just cut it short with a <^C> and the redefinition will occur. Here's how it works.

Using INSERT to Redefine Blocks

```
Command: INSERT
Block name (or ?): CAR2=MY-CAR
Block CAR2 redefined
Regenerating drawing.
Insertion point: *Cancel*                Type <^C> to cancel command.
```

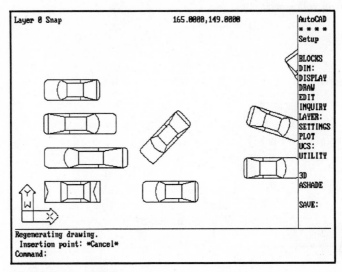

Redefined Car Blocks

You should have sports cars all over the place. Replacing a few cars with a few different cars may seem like a trivial exercise. But, if you have a minor revision to make on a block that occurs several hundred times in a drawing, it is no trivial matter! You can *globally* replace all your blocks with a revised block in a single insertion redefinition.

➡ *TIP: If you are satisfied with a part of a drawing (or a part on a layer) and you won't be working on that part for a while, block it and replace it with a simple block to improve redraw speed and reduce screen clutter. When you are ready, you can insert it with an = to put the drawing back together again.*

Stopping Point

On that global note, let's call this a stopping (or starting point). Save your Autotown drawing. If you have other things to do, take a break. If you want to get more block practice in, move on to the real Autotown.

Saving the Autotown Drawing

 Command: **END**   End your drawing to start fresh.

Command: **SAVE**   Save to the default drawing.

The next Autotown exercise makes use of the BLOCK, INSERT, and WBLOCK commands that you learned in this chapter's first section. The exercise is built around using a set of simple blocks to place houses and trees on the three lots in the Autotown site plan, then replacing those symbols with more complex symbols to create the final drawing. The two target drawings are shown in the Autotown With Simple Symbols and Autotown With Complex Symbols illustrations.

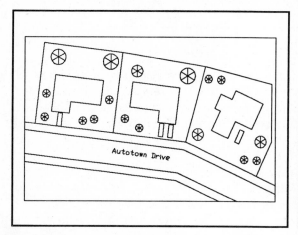

Autotown With Simple Symbols

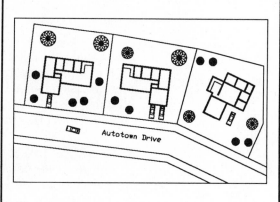

Autotown With Complex Symbols

Autotown Block Exercise

If you have the IA DISK, you can load the CHAP-09B drawing file and proceed directly to block insertions for the first set of simple floor plans. The CHAP-09B drawing has the subdivision layout and the nine blocks that you need. If you do not have the disk, you need to create the subdivision and the blocks. Use the following sequence to set up for the Autotown exercise.

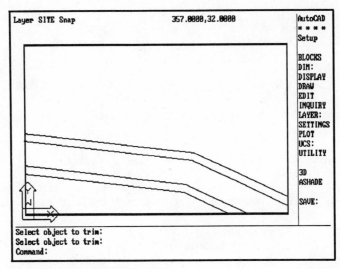

Layer SITE Snap   357.0000,32.0000   AutoCAD
                                                                             * * * *
                                                                             Setup

                                                                             BLOCKS
                                                                             DIM:
                                                                             DISPLAY
                                                                             DRAW
                                                                             EDIT
                                                                             INQUIRY
                                                                             LAYER:
                                                                             SETTINGS
                                                                             PLOT
                                                                             UCS:
                                                                             UTILITY

                                                                             3D
                                                                             ASHADE

                                                                             SAVE:

Select object to trim:
Select object to trim:
Command:

Autotown With Border and Drive

Setting Up Autotown Drive and Lots

Enter selection: **1**

Begin a NEW drawing called AUTOTOWN=CHAP-09B. Then just read the following plan and site exercises.

Continue with this exercise.

Check your setup against the original setup at the start of the chapter.

```
Command: VIEW                   Restore view All.
Command: ERASE                  Erase all entities on layer 0.
Command: LAYER                  Set Layer SITE current.

Command: PLINE                  Draw the border.
From point: 12.5,15
Current line-width is 0.0000
Arc/Close/Halfwidth/Length/Undo/Width/<Endpoint of line>: W
Starting width <0.0000>: 1
Ending width <1.0000>: <RETURN>
Arc/Close/Halfwidth/Length/Undo/Width/<Endpoint of line>: 347.5,15
Arc/Close/Halfwidth/Length/Undo/Width/<Endpoint of line>: 347.5,225
Arc/Close/Halfwidth/Length/Undo/Width/<Endpoint of line>: 12.5,225
Arc/Close/Halfwidth/Length/Undo/Width/<Endpoint of line>: C
```

```
Command: PLINE                              Draw Autotown drive.
From point: 12.5,115
Current line-width is 0.0000
Arc/Close/Halfwidth/Length/Undo/Width/<Endpoint of line>: W
Starting width <1.0000>: 0
Ending width <0.0000>: <RETURN>
Arc/Close/Halfwidth/Length/Undo/Width/<Endpoint of line>: 227.8,90.2
Arc/Close/Halfwidth/Length/Undo/Width/<Endpoint of line>: 359.1,30.4
Arc/Close/Halfwidth/Length/Undo/Width/<Endpoint of line>: <RETURN>


Command: OFFSET
Offset distance or Through <Through>: 50
Select object to offset:                    Pick the last pline.
Side to offset?                             Pick point below last pline.
Select object to offset: <RETURN>           You will trim the extended line later.


Command: OFFSET
Offset distance or Through <50.0000>: 10
Select object to offset:                    Pick the top road pline.
Side to offset?                             Pick point inside the road.
Select object to offset:                    Pick the bottom road pline.
Side to offset?                             Pick point inside the road.
Select object to offset: <RETURN>


Command: TRIM
Select cutting edge(s)...
Select objects:                             Select the border.
Select objects: <RETURN>
Select object to trim:                      Trim all the lines extending beyond the border.
```

Using Surveyor's Angles

Autotown's setup contains Surveyor's angles. AutoCAD will still accept normal decimal angle input for surveyor's angles, but you can enter a simple N, S, E or W for 90-, 270-, 0- and 180-degree angles. Use surveyor's angles to draw the lot lines for the three lots. Use the osnap interrupts shown below when you pick your drawing points.

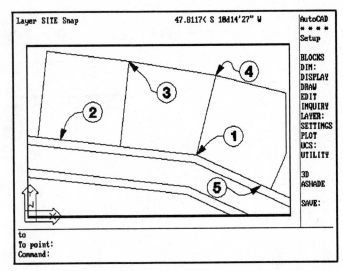

Autotown With Lot Lines

Using Surveyor's Angles to Draw Autotown's Lot Lines

Command: **UNITS**   Set angles to surveyor's units and default the rest of the settings.

Command: **LINE**
From point: **INT**   Use intersection osnap.
of   Pick bend in the road at ①.
To point: **@100.20<N14d52'E**
To point: **@112.46<N80d47'W**
To point: **PER**   Use perpendicular osnap.
to   Pick north side of road at ②.
To point: **<RETURN>**

Command: **LINE**
From point: **INT**   Use intersection osnap.
of   Pick NW corner of center lot at ③.
To point: **@105.00<N82d57'W**
To point: **PER**   Use perpendicular osnap.
to   Pick north side of road at ②.
To point: **<RETURN>**

Command: **LINE**
From point: **INT**   Use intersection osnap.
of   Pick NE corner of center lot at ④.
To point: **@91.67<S76d7'E**
To point: **@74.00<S**
To point: **PER**   Use perpendicular osnap.
to   Pick north side of road at ⑤.
To point: **<RETURN>**

Next, label the road with DTEXT. Use an INTersection osnap interrupt to align the text, then pick the real location to put "Autotown Drive."

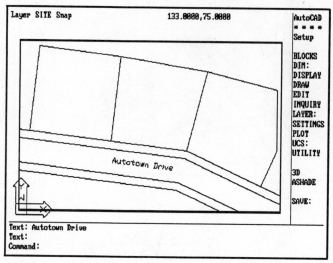

Completed Autotown Drive and Lots

Using DTEXT to Label the Road

```
Command: DTEXT
Start point or Align/Center/Fit/Middle/Right/Style: INT
of                              Pick SW corner of center lot.
Height <0.2000>: 6
Rotation angle <E>: INT
of                              Pick SE corner of center lot.
Text:                           Pick absolute point 133,75 for the real location.
Text: Autotown Drive
Text: <RETURN>
```

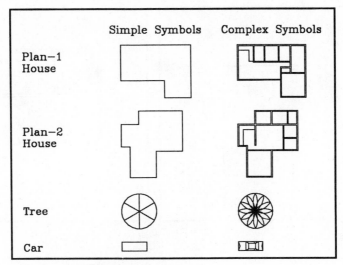

Simple and Complex Blocks

Preparing Autotown's Blocks

All that is left to set up are the blocks. The IA DISK already has them. If you don't have the disk, you need to create seven blocks. (You already have two, CAR2 and TREE1.)

Preparing Blocks for the Autotown Exercise

 Read this exercise. Make sure that you have the following blocks on your disk.

 Continue with this exercise.

Command: **UNITS**	Set angles to decimals units and default the rest of the settings.
Command: **LAYER**	Set Layer 0 current.
Command: **ZOOM**	Zoom in on one of the lots as a construction area.

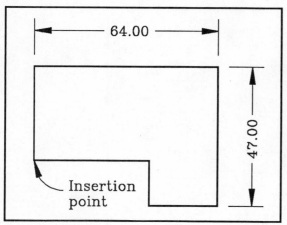

Floor Plan SIMPLE1

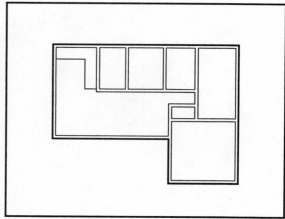

Floor Plan COMPLEX1

Draw the SIMPLE1 floor plan with the dimensions shown.

Command: **WBLOCK**   Wblock the floor plan as SIMPLE1.
Command: **OOPS**   Oops the floor plan back.

Draw the COMPLEX1 floor plan using the SIMPLE1 floor plan. Make the floor plan as complex as you like.

Command: **WBLOCK**   Wblock the floor plan as COMPLEX1.

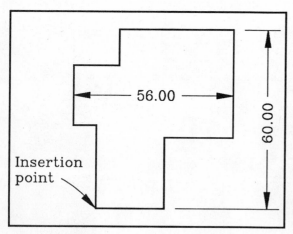

Floor Plan SIMPLE2

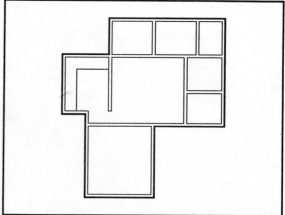

Floor Plan COMPLEX2

Draw the SIMPLE2 floor plan with the dimensions shown.

Command: **WBLOCK**   Wblock the floor plan as SIMPLE2.
Command: **OOPS**   Oops the floor plan back.

Draw the COMPLEX2 floor plan using the SIMPLE2 floor plan. Make the floor plan as complex as you like.

Command: **WBLOCK**   Wblock the floor plan as COMPLEX2.

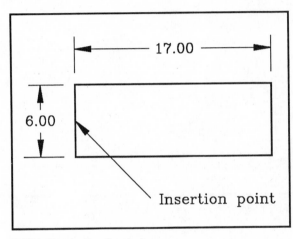

CAR1 Simple Car Symbol

TREE2 Complex Tree Symbol

Draw the CAR1 symbol with the dimensions shown.

Command: **WBLOCK**   Wblock the car symbol as CAR1.

You already have CAR2 and TREE1 from an earlier exercise.

Draw the TREE2 tree symbol with the dimensions shown.

Command: **WBLOCK**   Wblock the tree symbol as TREE2.
Command: **VIEW**   Restore View All.

All the simple symbols should be cleared from the screen. Now it is time to build the subdivision.

Using a UCS to Insert Blocks

To insert the house plans, establish a UCS at the corner of each lot. This will help you align the house plans in relationship to the lot. As you insert each block, use a working block name (such as PLAN-1) within the drawing. You will use an assignment, like PLAN-1=SIMPLE1, to tell AutoCAD to use the SIMPLE1.DWG drawing file on disk when you insert the block.

The exercise sequence below will guide you through setting up a UCS and inserting the floor plans on each lot.

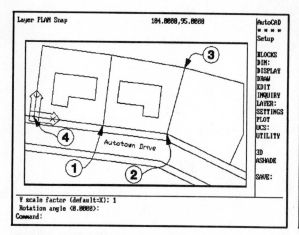

Autotown With First Two Floor Plans

Autotown With Last Floor Plan

Using INSERT to Insert Blocks With An = Sign

    Continue with this exercise.

    Continue with this exercise.

```
Command: LAYER          Set Layer PLAN current.

Command: UCS            Establish a UCS on the center lot.
Origin/ZAxis/3point/Entity/View/X/Y/Z/Prev/Restore/Save/Del/?/<World>: 3
Origin point <0,0,0>:   Pick lower left corner of lot at ①.

Point on positive portion of the X-axis <131.5409,101.3770,0.0000>:
                        Pick lower right corner of lot at ②.

Point on positive-Y portion of the UCS X-Y plane <130.6555,102.3704,0.0000>:
                        Pick upper right corner of lot at ③.
```

```
Command: INSERT                          Insert SIMPLE1 plan on center lot.
Block name (or ?): PLAN-1=SIMPLE1        Make the block name PLAN-1.
Insertion point: 17,36
X scale factor <1> / Corner / XYZ: <RETURN>
Y scale factor (default=X): <RETURN>
Rotation angle <0.0000>: <RETURN>

Command: UCS                             Establish a UCS on the left lot.
Origin/ZAxis/3point/Entity/View/X/Y/Z/Prev/Restore/Save/Del/?/<World>: O
Origin point <0,0,0>:                    Pick lower left corner of lot at ④.

Command: INSERT
Block name (or ?) <PLAN-1>: <RETURN>     Insert a flipped PLAN-1 on west lot.
```

This time you do not have to use the = sign, since the working block PLAN-1 in your drawing's block table already contains SIMPLE1's graphics.

```
Insertion point: 88,36
X scale factor <1> / Corner / XYZ: -1    The -1 flips it.
Y scale factor (default=X): 1
Rotation angle <0.0000>: <RETURN>

Command: UCS                             Establish a UCS on the East lot.
Origin/ZAxis/3point/Entity/View/X/Y/Z/Prev/Restore/Save/Del/?/<World>: O
Origin point <0,0,0>:                    Pick lower left corner of lot at ⑤.

Command: UCS                             Rotate Z axis to make X axis parallel to front lot line.
Origin/ZAxis/3point/Entity/View/X/Y/Z/Prev/Restore/Save/Del/?/<World>: Z
Rotation angle about Z axis <0.0>:       Pick lower left corner of lot at ⑤.
Second point:                            Pick lower right corner of lot at ⑥.

Command: INSERT                          Insert SIMPLE2 on east lot.
Block name (or ?) <PLAN-1>: PLAN-2=SIMPLE2
```

Use an Insertion point of 25.5,28 and Rotation angle of 0.

No subdivision is complete without a few cars scattered around. Insert some cars with CAR (CAR=CAR1). Pick your own insertion points. Use the default scale factor(s) of 1. Use the following exercise and the target drawing to get you started.

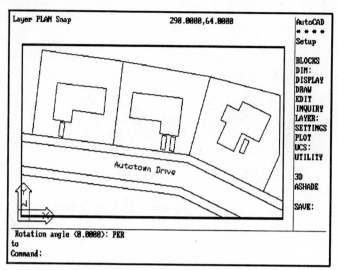

Autotown With Inserted Cars

Using INSERT to Insert Car Blocks

```
Command: UCS              Set UCS to World.
Command: INSERT           Insert CAR=CAR1 for the first car.
Command: INSERT           Insert CAR for the remaining cars.
```

Using Preset Scale Insertions

After you have finished inserting the cars, spruce up the subdivision with a variety of trees using preset scale factors. Since you drew the tree block with a 1 foot diameter, you can supply different scale values to create different diameter trees.

Using Preset Scale to Insert Trees

```
Command: LAYER                              Set Layer SITE current.

Command: INSERT
Block name (or ?) <CAR>: TREE=TREE1
Insertion point: SCALE                      Apply a scale factor before insertion.
Scale factor: 20                            Make a tree 20' in diameter.
Insertion point:                            Pick a point.
Rotation angle <0>: <RETURN>
```

Continue the sequence above to insert more trees with different diameters. Use the Autotown With Trees illustration as a guide.

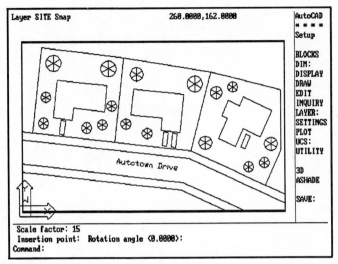

Autotown With Trees

The Autotown with simple symbols is complete. Before you proceed with block redefinitions, take a look at the blocks in your drawing and on your hard drive to get a clearer picture of what you've done.

Displaying Blocks and Drawing Files

Use BLOCK? (INSERT? will also work) and DIR to take a look at your drawing directory files. (The DIR command is defined in AutoCAD's support disk file called ACAD.PGP. ACAD.PGP must be in your AutoCAD directory, or where AutoCAD can find it.) If DIR doesn't work, you can use the FILES command, located as a menu item on the [UTILITY] screen menu.

Using DIR to Display Blocks and Drawing Files

```
Command: DIR                    Display flips to text screen.
File specification: *.DWG

Volume in drive C is YOURDISK
Directory of  C:\IA-ACAD
SIMPLE1   DWG    1998   2-04-89    3:31p
SIMPLE2   DWG    3537   2-04-89    4:14p
AUTOTOWN  DWG    3530   2-04-89   12:24p
COMPLEX1  DWG    2077   2-04-89    3:33p
COMPLEX2  DWG    3952   2-04-89    5:34p
CAR1      DWG    1863   2-04-89    3:29p
CAR2      DWG    2917   2-04-89    5:29p
```

```
MY-CAR   DWG   3313   2-04-89   11:52p
TREE1    DWG   1971   2-04-89    3:34p
TREE2    DWG   3003   2-04-89    5:24p
     ## File(s)   7501824 bytes free
```

Your DIR list will include other files. Your order, volume and directory names, numbers and dates will differ from our list.

```
Command: BLOCK
Block name (or ?): ?

Defined blocks.
  PLAN-1
  PLAN-2
  TREE
  TREE1
  CAR2
  CAR3
  CAR
7 user blocks, 0 unnamed blocks.
```

As you can see above, each working block has two corresponding wblocked drawing files. The working blocks in the current drawing have the simple PLAN-1, PLAN-2, TREE and CAR names because you used an = (equal sign) when inserting them (as in PLAN-1=SIMPLE1). Maintaining the wblocked files separately makes it easy to keep track of both the simple and complex symbols. The BLOCK? listing also tells you that CAR2 is defined in your block tables, although it is not currently inserted anywhere in the active drawing file.

Block Redefinition

Now you can replace the simple blocks with the complex ones. Again, use the = sign option of the INSERT command to redefine the existing blocks. You do not have to actually complete the INSERT command. Just cut it short with a <^C> and the redefinition will occur.

Using INSERT to Redefine Blocks

```
Command: INSERT
Block name (or ?) <TREE>: PLAN-1=COMPLEX1
Block PLAN-1 redefined
Regenerating drawing.
Insertion point: *Cancel*                Hit a <^C>.
```

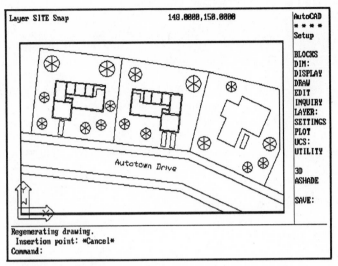

Updated Autotown

The existing Block PLAN-1 was updated. Your drawing should look like
the Updated Autotown illustration.

➡ *TIP: If you have a lot of redefinitions to do, waiting for the
regeneration each time is a nuisance. Turn REGENAUTO Off and use
a single regeneration when you finish.*

Redefine the rest of the working blocks.

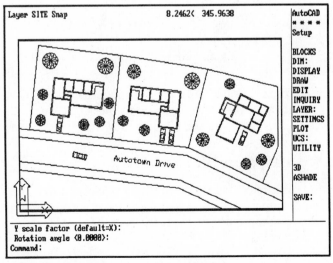

Autotown Redefined With Complex Blocks

Using INSERT to Complete the Block Redefinitions

Command: **INSERT**   Insert PLAN-2=COMPLEX2 and cancel Insert.
Command: **INSERT**   Insert TREE=TREE2 and cancel Insert.
Command: **INSERT**   Insert CAR=CAR2 and cancel Insert.

                             All the blocks are now redefined in the drawing. New insertions will
                             now use the new block definitions.

Command: **LAYER**   Set layer PLAN current.
Command: **INSERT**   Insert a CAR and place it on the road.

Take one last look at Autotown, then do the exercise below to clean and
end your drawing.

Cleaning Up Unused Blocks

The next sequence using WBLOCK * provides an alternative method to
purge unused blocks. You also can use it to delete unused layers,
linetypes, and text styles.

Using WBLOCK* to Clean a Drawing of Unused Blocks

Command: **WBLOCK**   WBLOCK * your drawing, then QUIT.
File name: **AUTOTOWN**
A drawing with this name already exists.
Do you want to replace it? <N> **Y**
Block name: *   It writes the entire drawing to disk.

Command: **QUIT**
Really want to discard all changes to drawing? **Y**

Enter select: **2**   Edit an Existing drawing called AUTOTOWN.

Your finished Autotown drawing has about 250 entities. If you had
created the drawing without blocks, it would have about 1000 entities.
This gives you some idea of how efficient blocks can be.

Summing Up With Tips on Blocks

Without blocks you would not be able to keep track of all the individual
components that make up even a simple drawing. Blocks help you
organize your drawing by grouping useful collections of drawing entities
together.

A well-planned system usually includes a well-organized library of blocks that somebody planned and created. However, don't be afraid to create blocks when you need them. As you form new groups of entities while drawing, use the regular edit commands, like COPY and ARRAY, to manipulate these unblocked entities. If you find that you are copying the same group of unblocked objects all the time, then BLOCK them.

We recommend using drag mode for insertions. Before you dump a block into your drawing file, you will want to know how it's going to look. Use preset scale and rotation to see the block as you drag it. Try to plan ahead to insert as many of the same blocks at the same time as you can. This way you can use AutoCAD's insertion <default prompts> instead of typing block names over and over.

Use MINSERT, MEASURE, and DIVIDE to place many blocks with one command. Use a *INSERT or EXPLODE to convert your blocks back into their individual entities. If you need a new block similar to an existing block, explode the old block, edit it, and block it to a new name.

What can you gain by going through block redefinition? Block replacements can be a big time saver. If you are doing a project which requires that a schematic or simple layout precede a more accurate and detailed drawing, a global replacement can eliminate an entire drawing revision cycle. You can update a drawing by redefining obsolete blocks.

Be careful when you insert from a disk file. Existing named things and their parameters take precedence over incoming named things. When you do an insertion from a disk file, all named things in the outside file get copied into the receiving file. If a layer (or style) already exists in the receiving drawing, it takes precedence. This may change text styles in the newly inserted parts or add to the current drawing file.

Use PURGE or a WBLOCK * QUIT to keep your drawing file clean. PURGE is selective. WBLOCK * QUIT will wipe out all unused blocks.

What About the Artist in You?

Blocks speed production drawing. But what about just sketching and coloring in a few ideas? In the next chapter, we bring out the artist in you.

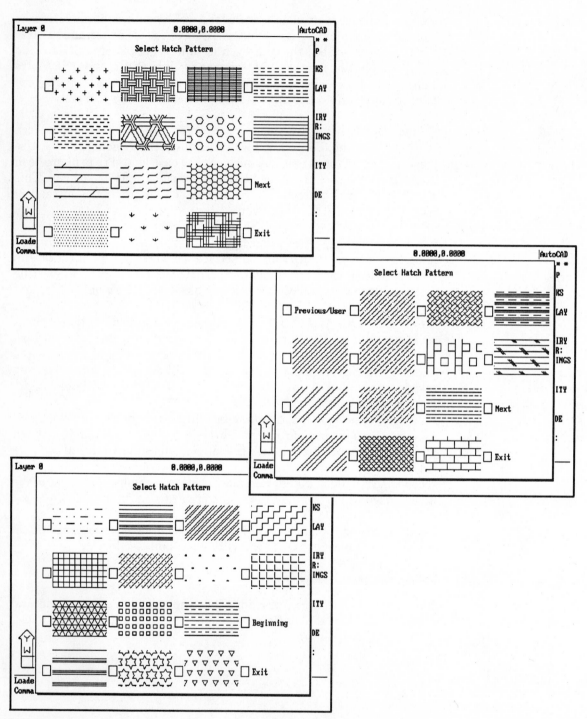

AutoCAD's Hatch Patterns

CHAPTER 10

Drawing Enhancements
MAKING DRAWINGS MORE PRESENTABLE

Making Drawings More Impressive

All the drawings you have tried up to this point have been simple. We wouldn't go so far as to say they are *ugly*. Let's just say they are not very interesting. As a professional, you want to be able to give your drawings design presentation quality.

In this chapter, you will learn how to enhance your drawings with patterns and shading, use sketch lines, use linetype as an enhancement tool, and set up and enhance a title block. In addition, you will learn how to use AutoCAD's inquiry commands to return information about your drawings.

Drawing Inquiry and Enhancement Tools

You will find AutoCAD's inquiry commands on their own [INQUIRY] screen menu. You have already used the ID, HELP, and STATUS commands. We will cover the AREA, DBLIST, DIST, LIST, and TIME commands in this chapter.

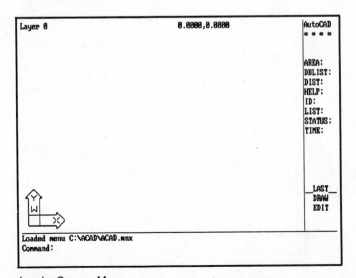

Inquiry Screen Menu

The SKETCH command provides freehand line entry. Both the SKETCH and the HATCH commands are on the [DRAW] screen menu. LINETYPE (and LTSCALE) are on the [SETTINGS] screen menu. [Hatch] also is on the [Draw] pull-down menu. When you pull down the [Hatch] menu, you can access the hatch icon menus shown at the start of the chapter.

Hatches are Blocks

We deferred talking about shading and hatching drawings up to this point because AutoCAD's hatch patterns are really blocks. When you use the HATCH command to place a pattern, say a brick pattern in a walkway area, you are really inserting a block with the brick pattern.

Hatches are specialized blocks. They do not share the efficiency or easy insertion point control of normal AutoCAD blocks, and they require some care in setting up boundaries. Getting good results may take a little practice.

Otherwise, the basic scaling and rotating techniques that you have learned in inserting blocks also apply to placing hatch patterns. AutoCAD's standard hatch patterns (shown on the facing page) are sized as unit blocks. When you insert these patterns in your drawing, you can scale and angle the pattern.

Since you generally will want to fit these patterns within pre-defined areas in your drawing, the focus of the chapter is to give you a set of techniques that will help you define the polygon boundaries that control the insertion of the hatch block.

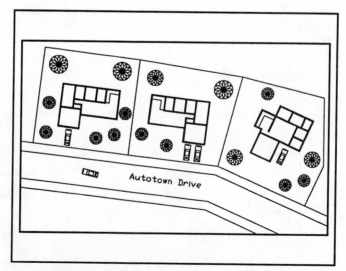

Autotown Drawing

Setting Up for Drawing Enhancements

Consider this chapter's hatching and sketching exercises as sort of a suburban renewal project for Autotown. You are going to pave the road with hatching, hatch some of the lot areas, and enhance the drawing by adding sketched contour lines.

If you are using the IA DISK, start a new drawing called HATCHTWN by setting the drawing equal to the CHAP-10A drawing. Another drawing on the disk, BDR17-11.DWG, contains an enhanced title block for the title block exercise, the last exercise in the chapter.

If you are not using the disk, recycle the AUTOTOWN drawing that you saved at the end of chapter 9 by setting HATCHTWN equal to it. Add two more layers called SCRATCH and HATCH. (See the settings table below.) If you don't have the Autotown drawing, be sure to read the exercise and illustration sequences to learn how hatching works.

Setting Up for Enhancing Autotown

  Enter selection: **1**   Begin a NEW drawing named HATCHTWN=CHAP-10A.

  Enter selection: **1**   Begin a NEW drawing named HATCHTWN=AUTOTOWN.

Make sure your drawing has the settings shown in the Hatchtown Drawing Settings table.

APERTURE	COORDS	GRID	SNAP	UCSICON
5	On	10	1	OR

UNITS	Decimal units, 4 decimal points, decimal angles, 2 fractional places, defaults all other settings.
LIMITS	0,0 to 360,240
ZOOM	Zoom All.
VIEW	View saved as ALL.

Layer name	State	Color	Linetype
0	On	7 (white)	CONTINUOUS
SITE	On	3 (green)	CONTINUOUS
PLAN	On	5 (blue)	CONTINUOUS
HATCH	On	6 (magenta)	CONTINUOUS
SCRATCH	Current	7 (white)	CONTINUOUS

Hatchtown Drawing Settings

Your starting drawing should look similar to the Hatchtown Drawing illustration below.

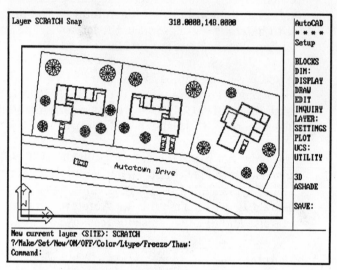

Hatchtown Drawing

Start with the SCRATCH layer current. Hatching often requires building perimeters to control your hatch inserts. Use this SCRATCH layer to build your perimeters, and use it as a pure scratch layer to play with any of the pre-defined hatch patterns that may catch your fancy.

Creating Patterns

Wouldn't Autotown look better if the road looked like a road? The good citizens have been thinking of putting in a brick road. Maybe not a yellow brick road, but at least a brick road. Where do you find the bricks?

Patterns are Stored in ACAD.PAT

AutoCAD comes with at least 41 pre-defined patterns. These are stored in a disk file called ACAD.PAT. You can find the names of these patterns by executing the HATCH command with a **?** response. The text screen will appear, listing pattern names with brief descriptions. You get past the More break by hitting any key. Look for the BRICK listing, then hit the <F1> flip screen key when you are through looking.

Using HATCH ? to Look at Hatch Patterns

```
Command: HATCH
Pattern (? or name/U,style): ?
```

Page through the hatch listings and then <F1> to the drawing screen.

HATCH Icon Menus

Instead of text descriptions of the hatch patterns, you can use the [Hatch...] icon menu which displays the graphic hatch patterns. The icon menu has the advantage of showing your pattern choices when you make your selection. If your video supports the icon menus, take a look at the [Hatch...] icon menu on the [Draw] pull-down menu. You will find the BRICK pattern on the first hatch icon menu page.

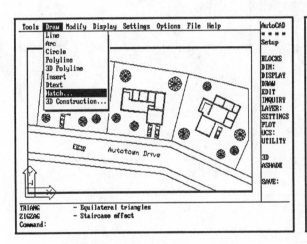

Pull-Down Menu Selecting Hatch

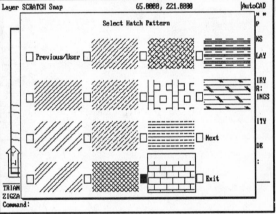

Icon Hatch Menu Showing the Brick Hatch

The HATCH Command

Well, you found the bricks. How do you hatch Autotown drive? The trick to hatching is to define the boundary for the hatch. The HATCH command sees the world as a series of polygons. To use the HATCH command to fill an irregular area, you must completely define the fill area boundaries. You have to watch out for overlaps and gaps at corners and for open-ended polygons.

Tracing over the perimeter of the area that you want to hatch with a polyline is the simplest way to start. Create the boundary on a layer that will not affect the current drawing. When you have the boundary defined, you can use that boundary as the constraint for the fill pattern. This gets around the uncertainty of whether your drawing has any questionable endpoints (like the endpoints where Autotown drive meets the border line), or whether your fill area is open or closed.

Create a boundary for Autotown drive by tracing over the road perimeter with a polyline. Use osnaps to help pick the endpoints. You can select the brick pattern from the [Hatch...] icon menu, or type your input. Use the exercise sequence below to guide you through the hatch.

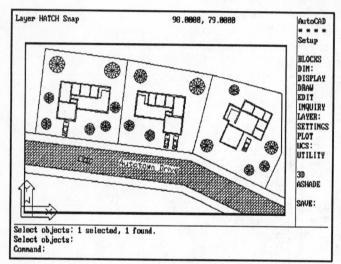

Autotown With Bricked Drive   Detail of Car

Using HATCH to Insert a Brick Pattern

```
Command: LAYER              Make sure SCRATCH is current.
Command: PLINE              Trace the perimeter of the area of the road.
                            Use Osnap and Close to create an accurate closed boundary.

Command: LAYER              Set HATCH current.
Command: HATCH
Pattern (? or name/U, style): BRICK
Scale for pattern <1.0000>: 10       Try the scale factor.
Angle for pattern <0.00>: 45
Select objects: L                    Last finds polyline boundary.
1 selected, 1 found
Select objects:                      Pick the text.
1 selected, 1 found
Select objects:                      Pick the car in the road.
1 selected, 1 found
Select objects: <RETURN>
```

Look closely at your bricked drive. What's wrong with it?

The Hatch Donut and Hole Problem

The brick hatch pattern drew directly over the car in the road. Putting bricks on cars will never do, but it is a classic hatching problem. We call this the donut and hole problem. If you select something as simple as a circle or rectangle, hatch will fill it in, stopping the pattern at the edges. If you want to fill in a more complex boundary, even something as simple as the area around a triangle in a donut, you must explicitly identify the interior boundary area so that the hatch pattern does not flow across it.

Without a little prodding, HATCH cannot recognize the interior boundaries of objects present in the fill area. Hatch normally will decide what is the donut and what is the hole when it is figuring out where to hatch. But you have to tell it what a hole is. In the Autotown Drive case, the text is a hole and the car is a number of holes. AutoCAD normally hatches by starting the pattern at the perimeter boundary and stopping at the next boundary, then starting again at the next boundary. The car is made up of many lines, creating many interior boundaries. That is why the pattern filled over parts of the car. Hatch offers a number of options to help with this problem.

As you work with hatches, you will also need to adjust your scale, angle and style parameters to get the effects that you want. Here is a list of the HATCH command options that you have to work with.

HATCH Options

Pattern — What type of shading do you want to use? Responding with a name from ACAD.PAT calls up that pattern and gets it ready for use. A U lets you define your own simple pattern using angled lines. A **?** gives you a list of the available pattern names stored in ACAD.PAT.

Scale — How big do you want the pattern elements? Pattern insertion is just like block insertion. You can scale the pattern as you insert it. All the standard patterns are scaled to look good in one unit value of space. This means that you almost always will scale the pattern when you bring it into a drawing. If you leave the pattern at the default value (<1.0000>), you will usually find the pattern too dense for your requirements.

Angle — The standard patterns have a horizontal orientation. If you want to slant your patterns, adjust the angle.

Style — There are three styles used to control how hatch patterns see and use boundaries.

■ **Normal** is the default. Normal means that the pattern is drawn alternately from the outside boundary (perimeter) inward. It stops at the first interior line, then turns on at the next interior boundary. It goes off-on until it hits the perimeter boundary again.

■ **Outermost** produces a hatch from the outside boundary to the first interior boundary it encounters. It stays off until it hits the last interior boundary before it hits the perimeter boundary again. You get the outermost effect by appending an **O** after the hatch name, separated by a comma.

■ **Ignore** produces a hatch that ignores any interior boundaries, creating a totally filled polygon. You get the Ignore effect by appending **I** to the hatch name, separated by a comma.

Try the HATCH command with the outermost option to repave the road. The sequence below will get you through this next hatch.

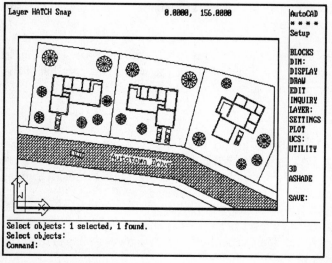

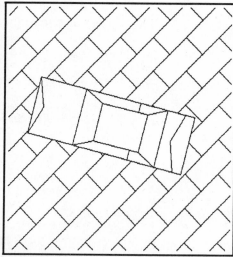

Autotown Drive Properly Bricked   *Detail of Car*

Using HATCH Outermost to Hatch Around an Object

```
Command: ERASE                          Erase Last to get rid of the previous hatching.

Command: HATCH
Pattern (? or name/U, style)<BRICK>: BRICK,0
Scale for pattern <10>: <RETURN>
Angle for pattern <45.00>: <RETURN>
Select objects:                         Reselect the polyline, car and text.
Select objects: <RETURN>
```

Editing Hatch Patterns

You probably noticed that the single Erase Last (above) wiped out the first hatch pattern. The hatch pattern is an *unnamed block*. Any normal editing commands like MOVE, COPY, and ARRAY will operate on the entire pattern just like a block. If you place a pattern that has the wrong scale or angle, you can always Erase Last or U to get rid of it and try again. A <^C> will stop a pattern fill in progress.

➡ *NOTE: If you want to edit individual lines within a pattern, explode it or use the asterisk option, *, before the pattern name when you hatch it. *BRICK, for example works just like an *insertion. An Undo will undo a *HATCH.*

Breaking Existing Entities in a Hatch Boundary

Creating a separate layer for hatching and tracing your boundaries is a good idea. But, in many cases, this may entail more work than is really necessary. You may frequently encounter cases where it is easier to go into your drawing and break (or trim) existing lines to get the boundaries that you need.

In the Autotown drawing, we want to place a grass pattern between the three lot lines and the drawing border. In this case, it is easier to break the four intersections where the border and the outer lot lines meet Autotown Drive than to trace the entire lot and border perimeters.

Try using BREAK to pick the segments as the hatch boundary and fill the area with a grass pattern. The following illustration shows the break points on Autotown Drive's polyline.

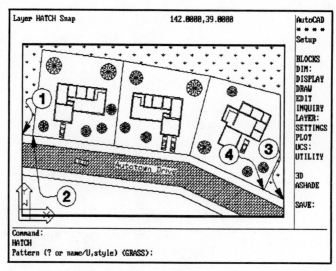

```
Layer HATCH Snap                142.0000,39.0000        AutoCAD
                                                        * * * *
                                                        Setup

                                                        BLOCKS
                                                        DIM:
                                                        DISPLAY
                                                        DRAW
                                                        EDIT
                                                        INQUIRY
                                                        LAYER:
                                                        SETTINGS
                                                        PLOT
                                                        UCS:
                                                        UTILITY

                                                        3D
                                                        ASHADE

                                                        SAVE:


Command:
HATCH
Pattern (? or name/U,style) <GRASS>:
```

Inserted Grass Pattern in Autotown

Using BREAK to Create a Hatch Boundary

Command: **BREAK**	
Select object:	Pick the border near point ①.
Enter second point (or F for first point): **F**	
Enter first point:	Use osnap ENDPoint to pick point ①.
Enter second point: **@**	Repicks the first point.
Command: **BREAK**	
Select object:	Pick the road near point ②.
Enter second point (or F for first point): **F**	
Enter first point:	Use osnap ENDPoint to pick point ②.
Enter second point: **@**	Repicks the first point.
Command: **BREAK**	
Select object:	Pick the border near point ③.
Enter second point (or F for first point): **F**	
Enter first point:	Use osnap ENDPoint to pick point ③.
Enter second point: **@**	Repicks the first point.
Command: **BREAK**	
Select object:	Pick the road near point ④.
Enter second point (or F for first point): **F**	
Enter first point:	Use osnap ENDPoint to pick point ④.
Enter second point: **@**	Repicks the first point.

```
Command: HATCH
Pattern (? or name/U,style) <BRICK,O>: GRASS
Scale for pattern <10.0000>: 13
Angle for pattern <45.00>: 0
Select objects: M              Use multiple to pick the border, road, and lot boundaries.
Select objects:               Pick all nine lines, then <RETURN> to end Multiple.
9 selected, 9 found.
Select objects: <RETURN>
```

Multiple object selection helped avoid AutoCAD's tendency to repeatedly find the same object. That takes care of the grass.

How to Control Hatching Complex Areas

Next, we want to put some mud on the east lot. (It was built too close to the swamp, a common problem in Autotown.) This is a more difficult hatch problem since we want to fill around the house, tree, and car blocks. This lot can only be hatched by tracing boundaries around the objects in the lot.

Using HATCH Outermost Style

```
Command: LAYER                         Make sure SCRATCH is current.

Command: BREAK
Select object:                         Pick the road near point ①.
Enter second point (or F for first point): F
Enter first point:                     Use osnap endpoint to pick point ①.
Enter second point: @                  Repicks the first point.

Command: PLINE                         Trace the perimeter of the house and car.
Command: CIRCLE                        Draw circles around each tree.

Command: LAYER                         Set HATCH current.
Command: COLOR                         Set color to YELLOW.

Command: HATCH
Pattern (? or name/U, style): <GRASS>: MUDST
Scale for pattern <13.0000>: <RETURN>
Angle for pattern <0.0000>: <RETURN>
Select objects:                        Select lot lines and interior boundary lines.
Select objects: <RETURN>

Command: COLOR                         Set color back to BYLAYER.
```

You can see that hatching complex areas can be a lot of work.

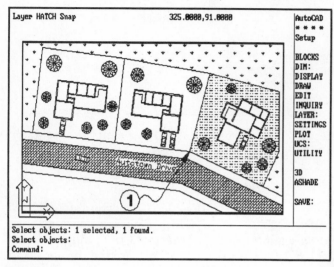

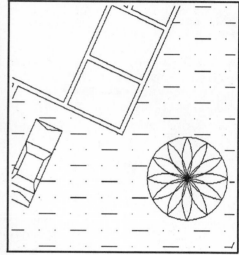

Muddied East Lot   *Detail of Mud Pattern*

➡ *TIP: When creating blocks likely to be hatched around, draw a boundary on a scratch layer before you make them into blocks. When you insert the blocks they will already have boundaries included with them. Turn layers on and off as needed to get just the boundary visible, then hatch.*

➡ *TIP: When creating simple and complex block pairs for redefinition, make sure you have good clean hatch boundaries in the simple blocks. Then you can hatch before you redefine simple blocks with complex blocks.*

So far you have used both the Normal and Outermost hatch styles. The third style option, Ignore, does just that. It ignores any interior boundary. If you want to test Ignore, change to your SCRATCH layer and try it.

Using HATCH U to Shade an Area

Hatch has one more trick up its sleeve. Say that you want to use some simple parallel lines as a shading pattern to fill a boundary. Immediately after you invoke the hatch command, you can screen pick, tablet pick or type U. U stands for *U design it*. This hatch option lets you create parallel lines, or a 90-degree cross pattern.

We want to use U option to show you two hatch features. First, we want to show how to use the option. But, second we want to show some of the constraints that you will face when you edit hatches. Hatches are unnamed blocks, with an insertion point at 0,0. If you hatch multiple areas in a single HATCH command, then try to move them individually, the hatches will move as a group.

➡ *NOTE: The 0,0 insertion point causes a problem with STRETCH. STRETCH ignores hatch patterns, blocks, and text unless the insertion point is included in the selection window. For hatches, you must include 0,0 in your window to get STRETCH to move it.*

The following exercises will take you through hatching the three garages with HATCH U. First, hatch the garage on the left, then hatch the two on the right in a single hatch.

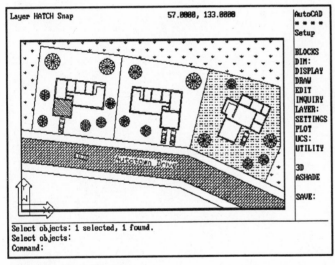

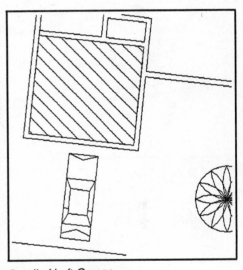

U Hatched Left Garage   *Detail of Left Garage*

Using HATCH U Pattern for the Garage

Command: **LAYER**   Set SCRATCH current.
Command: **PLINE**   Trace a closed boundary in the garages.
Command: **LAYER**   Set HATCH current.

Command: **HATCH**
Pattern (? or name/U,style) <MUDST>: **U**
Angle for crosshatch lines <0.0000>: **-45**
Spacing between lines <1.0000>: **2**
Double hatch area? <N> **<RETURN>**
Select objects: 1 selected, 1 found.
Select objects: **<RETURN>**

```
Command: HATCH                             Double hatch the last two garages.
Pattern (? or name/U,style) <U>: <RETURN>
Angle for crosshatch lines <315.0000>: <RETURN>
Spacing between lines <2.0000>: <RETURN>
Double hatch area? <N> Y
Select objects: 1 selected, 1 found.      Select one garage.
Select objects: 1 selected, 1 found.      Select the other.
Select objects: <RETURN>
```

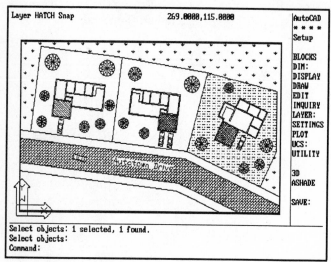

Double Hatched Garages

Detail of Double Hatch

Your screen should show three U hatched garages similar to the screen shot above. Next, we want you to move the hatch on the right (the east lot) to see how the hatched pair move together in an edit move. After you have moved the hatch, try exploding the pair to see what happens.

Using MOVE to Move a Hatch Pattern

```
Command: MOVE
Select objects: 1 selected, 1 found.      Pick a double hatch.
Select objects: <RETURN>
Base point or displacement:               Pick absolute point 230,130.
Second point of displacement:             Pick absolute point @30<270.

Command: EXPLODE
Select block reference, polyline, dimension, or mesh: Pick the double hatch.

Command: UNDO                             Undo the move and explode.
Command: REDRAW
```

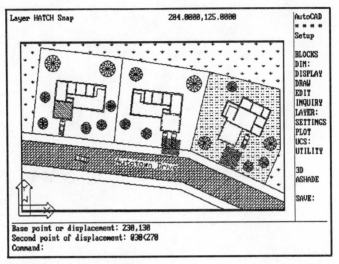

Hatch Pattern After Move

Since the double-hatched area was done as one hatch command, it is treated as a single entity. AutoCAD stores hatches as blocks so they can be exploded like any other block. Frequently, you may find it easier to erase a hatch and rehatch an area rather than move a hatch placement and any underlying objects that you have hatched.

There are several items worth noting in exploding hatches versus hatching with an asterisk (*HATCH). Exploding hatches sends the bits and pieces flying up to layer 0, making it easy to select and modify the entities if you keep layer 0 clean. A *HATCH goes in on the current layer. A normal hatch creates an unnamed block definition containing all the hatch's lines and a block reference. When you explode it, the drawing will temporarily contain twice as much data. You get a new set of individual lines, but the block definition remains until the drawing is ended and reloaded. A *HATCH creates a set of individual lines, but no block definition.

Because HATCH uses blocks simply to group the lines as one entity, every use of the HATCH command creates a unique block definition. Normally, blocks save data storage space through multiple insertions of the same object. But simultaneously hatching multiple areas with the same pattern does not save data space. However, if you copy a hatch, the copy will use the same block definition and save space.

➡ *TIP: When hatching several identical areas, hatch one and copy it several times to save data storage space.*

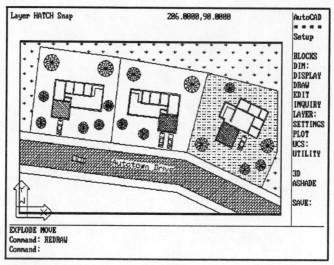

Autotown Restored

If you undid your explode and hatch move, you should have Autotown back in something like the shape of the Autotown Restored illustration.

➡ *TIP: You can use UCS or Snap Rotate to control your hatch insertion point, rather than letting it default to 0,0.*

Using Linetypes and Linetype Scales

All of the hatch patterns that you have used in Autotown are made from simple line entities. Many readers often overlook the opportunity to enhance their drawings by simply altering AutoCAD's standard linetypes, or creating different linetypes.

Every linetype is made up of a pattern of short line segments or dots. You create your own patterns using LINETYPE. Linetype affects only lines, arcs, circles, and polylines. Recall that you can use the LINETYPE command to set different linetypes. You can control the overall length of these patterns with LTSCALE.

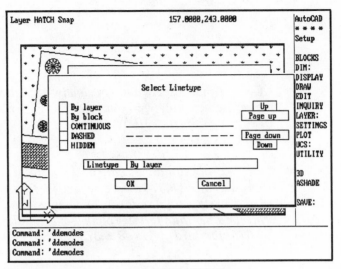

Linetype Dialogue Box From DDEMODES

LTSCALE Controls Line Pattern Spacing

You have used the LTSCALE command to adjust linetype scales. If you can't remember how LTSCALE works, review the examples below, then pick up with the exercise on using LINETYPE to create your own linetypes.

Each standard line pattern is defined to look good in a single unit length at LTSCALE = 1, the default scale. By adjusting LTSCALE, you can condense or stretch the pattern. To change LTSCALE, you simply put in a number other than 1. We recommend using your calculated drawing scale factor as a starting scale. The LTSCALE examples (below) show how several of the standard linetypes look at different LTSCALEs.

LTSCALE Examples

Dashed
1
2
4

Dashdot
1
2
4

```
Divide
1       _  . .  __  . .  __  . .  __  . .  __  . .  __  . .  __  . .  __  .
2       __  . .  ____  . .  ____  . .  ____  . .  ____  . .  ____  . .  __
4       ____      . .      _____      . .      _____      . .
```

➥ *NOTE: If your lines draw very slowly, or if all your lines look solid no matter which linetype you are using, you may need to adjust LTSCALE. Adjustments to LTSCALE do not affect existing entities until you regenerate.*

➥ *TIP: Drafting standards vary and a LTSCALE of 1 may not suit you. Many users find 0.375 a good setting for full size drawings. Whatever setting meets your standards, remember to adjust it for your drawing scale for other than full size plots. For example, a 1/4" = 1'-0" plot with a 0.375 standard yields 48 x .375 = 18 LTSCALE.*

Use LINETYPE to Create Your Own Linetypes

We want to wrap up the Autotown drawing by sketching some contour lines between the road and the lower border. Rather than ask you to use a standard linetype, the next set of exercises will show you how to make your own linetype (called MYLINE), scale it, then use it to sketch the contour lines.

The LINETYPE command lets you define your own dots and dashes pattern and store that pattern away as a linetype. AutoCAD's standard linetypes are stored in a file on your ACAD disk named ACAD.LIN. You can create your own file, like MYLINES.LIN, in this exercise. Here is the sequence for creating a new linetype, MYLINE, and storing it.

Using LINETYPE to Create a Linetype

```
Command: LINETYPE
?/Create/Load/Set: C
Name of linetype to create: MYLINE
File for storage of linetype <ACAD>: MYLINES
Creating new file
Descriptive text: Myline _____ ..... _____ .....
Enter pattern (on next line):
A,.4,-.1,0,-.1,0,-.1,0,-.1,0,-.1,0,-.1
New definition written to file.
?/Create/Load/Set: <RETURN>
```

➥ *TIP: Use a good descriptive name to label any linetype you create so that later you can figure out what it is.*

What is going on in the linetype definition? Here is an explanation of the definition sequence.

Linetype Definitions

Name of linetype to create — This is the name of the linetype you want to create.

File for storage of linetype — This is the name of the disk file where the linetype definition will be stored. Don't use the name ACAD because AutoCAD uses it for the standard linetypes. Think up your own names.

Descriptive text — This is what you will see when you issue a **?** query to list the named linetypes. It is a dot and dash representation of the linetype that shows on a flip (alphanumeric) screen. Just type **underscores___** and **periods . . .** as descriptive text.

Enter pattern (on next line) — Here AutoCAD is asking for the actual definition of the linetype. The pattern includes:

A positive number, like .4, gives the unit length of a pen down stroke. In other words, it is a line length that will appear as the first segment.

A negative number, like -.1, gives the unit length of a pen up stroke. In other words, it is the length of the blank space.

A 0 is a dot.

Separate values with commas.

Once you have stored one or more linetypes in a linetype file, you can load these linetypes for use. After you do a number of drawings, you may find that you build up a library of linetypes in a named .LIN file. You can call these linetypes up for active duty with the Load option of the linetype.

Using LINETYPE to Load a Linetype

```
Command: LINETYPE
?/Create/Load/Set: L
Name of linetype to load: MYLINE
File to search <ACAD>: MYLINES
Linetype MYLINE loaded.
?/Create/Load/Set: S
New entity linetype (or ?) <BYLAYER>: MYLINE
?/Create/Load/Set: <RETURN>
```

Any entities that you create will show the new MYLINE linetype. Try testing and scaling MYLINE in the area where you will be drawing the contour lines.

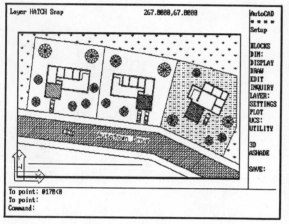

Myline at LTSCALE 1

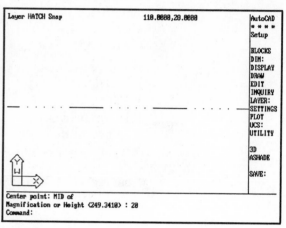

Myline Zoomed

Testing and Scaling a Linetype

Command: **LINE**	
From point:	Pick absolute point 30,35.
To point:	Pick polar point @170<0.
To point: **<RETURN>**	
	The line looks like it is continuous.
Command: **LTSCALE**	Try the drawing scale factor.
New scale factor <1.0000>: **10**	
Regenerating drawing.	
	The linetype is still too small to be sure it's right.
Command: **ZOOM**	Use Center, pick a point on the line and enter 20 for a height.
	Now it looks OK.
Command: **ZOOM**	Use Previous to return to original view.

Just like text, linetypes are not always legible when you are working on your drawing. When you are zoomed way out or in, they may appear continuous. You set LTSCALE for the plotted appearance, not the screen resolution and view. If you need to temporarily set a working LTSCALE for drawing on the screen, remember to reset it before plotting.

Your linetypes will also appear on the linetype dialogue box. Recall that you get to this dialogue box through DDEMODES or by selecting [Entity Creation...] on the [Settings] pull-down menu, then clicking next to [Linetype].

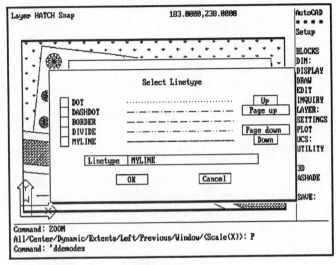

Linetype Dialogue Box With Myline

➡ *NOTE: You can create and store as many linetypes as you desire. If you want to use your linetype as a default layer linetype, you can set the linetype by layer and use the LAYER command to control it, just like you would for any of the standard linetypes.*

➡ *TIP: Like replacement of blocks and styles, loading a new definition of a linetype will cause a regeneration and replace old linetypes with new unless you suppress regeneration with REGENAUTO.*

Creating Hatch Patterns

AutoCAD provides a mechanism for creating your own hatch patterns in a fashion similar to linetype creation. Hatch patterns are more complex. You can find out more about creating hatch patterns in CUSTOMIZING AutoCAD (New Riders Publishing).

Freehand Drawing With SKETCH

The SKETCH command gives you the opportunity to draw lines freehand without being bothered by From points, To points, and other alignment or input parameters. You sketch just like you would doodle or draw on a piece of paper.

How Sketch Works

AutoCAD stores sketches in the drawing file as successive short line segments. Because AutoCAD doesn't know where your sketching may lead you, both you and the program have to take precautions not to let the amount of sketch information get out of hand. Just a few quick passes in the sketch mode can create a huge number of short segments in the drawing file.

To help AutoCAD keep sketch information under control, you have to decide how short a line segment to use to store your sketch data. This is known as the Record Increment. From then on, AutoCAD will store a new segment every time your pointer moves more than the record increment away from the last stored segment endpoint. Try to keep the record increment as large as possible to minimize the number of lines.

The Record Increment is given in current units. For example, if the width of your screen represents 30 inches, and the screen pointing area on your digitizer is 6 inches wide, a **0.5** increment means your sketch segments will be one half-inch, and that AutoCAD will record a new segment every time you move your pointing device about one-tenth-inch (6 inches divided by 30 inches divided by 0.5 inches).

You also have to let AutoCAD know when you consider the sketching pointer **up** (off the paper) or **down** (sketching). AutoCAD keeps all sketch input in a temporary state until you ask that all the sketch lines be entered into the drawing file database. You can **E** (Erase) sketched lines before you **R** (Record) them.

Using SKETCH to Make Contour Polylines

Try making some contour lines with SKETCH. We chose this example because it is a common and extremely useful application of SKETCH. To get good smooth contour curves, you need to sketch with polylines rather than lines (the default). Use a SETVAR called SKPOLY to switch SKETCH from lines to polylines. If SKPOLY is 0, SKETCH will draw lines. If it is 1, it draws polylines.

➡ *NOTE: Polylines can be easily stretched and edited, but their biggest advantage is that you can curve fit polylines and get a smooth curve. When you set SKPOLY to sketch polylines, set your record increment larger than when you sketch with lines. Use an increment one-half the smallest radius or turn that you will sketch. This may seem too large until you curve fit it.*

Try sketching the contour lines. Use the following illustration called Autotown With Contours as a target. It takes a little time to get the hang of sketching. Don't worry if your sketch ends slop over the drive and border lines. You can trim the loose ends in the next exercise. Use the following exercise sequence to help you set up sketch, then sketch and edit the contour polylines.

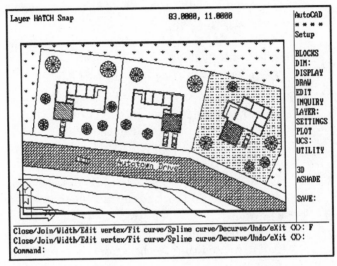

Autotown With Contours

Using SKETCH and SKPOLY to Draw Contour Lines

```
Command: ERASE                          Erase last to remove the test line.

Command: SETVAR                         Set Sketch to draw polylines.
Variable name or ?: SKPOLY
New value for SKPOLY <0>: 1

Command: SKETCH              Draw a contour line. Use Autotown With Contours as a guide.
Record increment <0.1000>: 5
Sketch.    Pen eXit Quit Record Erase Connect.

Command: PEDIT                          Smooth the sketch polyline.
Select polyline: L
Close/Join/Width/Edit vertex/Fit curve/Spline curve/Decurve/Undo/eXit <X>: F
Close/Join/Width/Edit vertex/Fit curve/Spline curve/Decurve/Undo/eXit <X>:
<RETURN>
```

Draw the remaining contours.

When you are in the sketch mode, all other input is ignored except for the sketch mode controls (and toggles like ortho <F8> and snap <F9>). The following modes, entered without a <RETURN>, control SKETCH.

SKETCH Options

Pen — Is a toggle that tells AutoCAD the pointer is up or down. You just type **P**, without a <RETURN>, to change the toggle.

eXit — Stores the sketch segments you have been creating in the drawing file and gets you back to the command prompt. A <SPACE> or <RETURN> will do the same thing.

Quit — Leaves sketch mode without storing the segments you have been creating. A <^C> will do the same thing.

Record — Keeps you in sketch mode, but stores the segments you have been creating so far in the drawing file. It is just like a save, but once you Record, segments that get stored are not available for Erase from within SKETCH.

Erase — Is somewhat like undo but erases any unrecorded segment from a point you pick to the last segment drawn.

Connect — Connects the pen to the end of the last endpoint of an active sketch chain. It is like Continue. You can always use normal AutoCAD editing techniques to connect sketch chains to other elements.

Now, trim any loose sketch ends that you have.

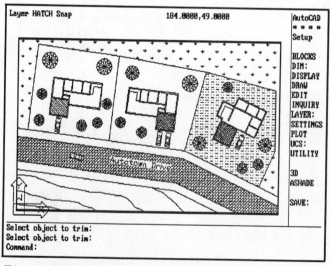

Trimmed Sketch Lines

Using TRIM to Trim Sketch Polylines

```
Command: TRIM
Select cutting edge(s)...
Select objects:                    Select the road and border lines.
Select objects: <RETURN>
Select object to trim:             Select the overlapping ends of the sketch lines.
```

➡ *NOTE: You can use normal toggles, like snap and ortho, when you are in sketch mode.*

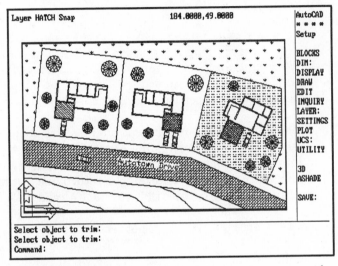

Enhanced Autotown

The added contour lines are the last step in refinishing Autotown. Your drawing should resemble our Enhanced Autotown illustration.

Saving the Hatched Autotown Drawing

 Command: **QUIT**   You have this drawing on disk.

 Command: **END**   Return to the main menu.

Stopping Point

We are not going to edit the Autotown drawing again, but we will use it to look at AutoCAD's inquiry commands. Autotown has a good set of distances and lot areas built into it that makes it easy to use as a practice drawing to retrieve information.

If you need a break, this is a good stopping point. If you are short on time, exit AutoCAD, and pick up with Autotown again by looking at the inquiry commands (below). If you are in a rush, you can read through the next section on inquiry commands and pick up with the last exercise which shows how to create a title block. The following inquiry commands do not require any drawing.

Using Inquiry Commands

Let's turn to look at AutoCAD's inquiry commands. These commands are useful in providing information about Autotown or any other drawing. When lines are placed into a drawing file, they often represent distances and locations with real world relationships. Helping the drawing reader understand these spatial implications is part of creating a good drawing.

Using inquiry commands, you can measure, identify, and generally find out what's in a drawing file. AutoCAD already has much of the spatial intelligence that you may need built into the drawing file. The distance and area commands, for example, return line distances and polygon area values from the entities that you have already placed in the drawing file.

These inquiry exercises do not require any setup. If you are starting after a break, reload your HATCHTWN drawing. If you are jumping in at this point, use any version of the Autotown drawing, as long as it has the lot lines in it.

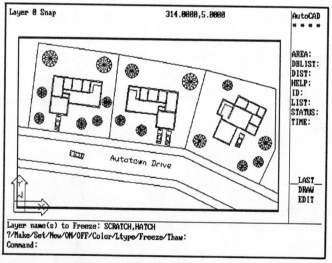

Autotown With Inquiry Menu

Setting Up for Inquiries

  Enter selection: **1**   Begin a NEW drawing called HATCHTWN=CHAP-10B.

  Enter selection: **2**   Edit an EXISTING drawing called HATCHTWN.

Let's start by turning on an elapsed timer built into the TIME command.

Using TIME to Track Your Drawing Time

Unlike the other inquiry commands, TIME is really a management tool. TIME gives you a listing of times and dates about your drawing and editing sessions. These include: the current system time; the date and time a drawing was created; the date and time of the last update; time in the editor; and elapsed time.

Select the TIME command, and set time ON. This will act as an elapsed timer that you can check at the end of these inquiry exercises to measure your time spent in the drawing editor.

Using TIME to Track Your Drawing Time

```
Command: LAYER          Set layer 0 current and freeze the SCRATCH and HATCH layers.

Command: TIME
Current time:           02 Nov 1988 at 13:03:12.930
Drawing created:        02 Nov 1988 at 08:56:36.280
Drawing last updated:   02 Nov 1988 at 11:30:17.500
Time in drawing editor: 0 days 02:25:50.160
Elapsed timer:          0 days 02:25:50.160
Timer on.
Display/ON/OFF/Reset: R
Timer reset.
Display/ON/OFF/Reset: <RETURN>
```

The ID Command

Start your inquiries with the ID command. You have used ID before to locate points. Recall that ID returns the X,Y,Z location of a point. Try locating the surveyor's point at the back corner of the middle and west lots.

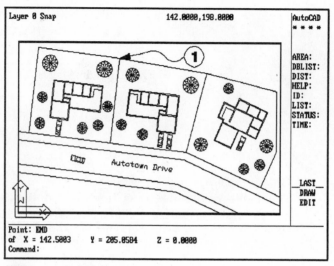

ID Surveyor's Point

Using ID to Get a Survey Point

```
Command: ID
Point:                        Use osnap ENDPoint to pick point at ①.
X = 142.5003   Y = 205.0584   Z = 0.0000     Returns exact location of the point.
```

➡ *TIP: The ID command is useful to reset the last point without drawing anything, so you can use relative coordinates from the reset point. The last point is stored as the system variable, LASTPOINT.*

Using DIST to Get Line Lengths

DIST gives the 3D distance between two points. Say you need to check the length of the lot line between the east lot and the middle lot. DIST will get you this information. Use the osnaps in the exercise sequence to help you pick the lot endpoints. The measured distance is stored as the system variable, DISTANCE.

Using DIST to Get a Lot Length

```
Command: DIST
First point:              Use ENDPoint to pick corner of lot at ①.
Second point:             Use ENDPoint to pick corner of lot at ②.
Distance = 100.2000   Angle in X-Y Plane = 75.1333,   Angle from X-Y Plane = 0.0000
Delta X = 25.7084,   Delta Y = 96.8459,    Delta Z = 0.0000
```

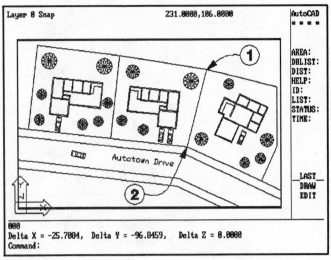

Distance of Lot Lines

Using AREA to Get Area and Perimeter Values

AREA will give you the area surrounded by a straight-sided polygon. The polygon sides are defined by temporary points, and are not saved or displayed. When you select an entity such as a polyline or circle, AREA automatically calculates its area. You can add to or subtract from a running total. If you set the Add or Subtract mode, the AREA command stays active until you exit it with a <RETURN>. Add and Subtract only accumulate in the current command and each use of the AREA command restarts from 0. The area is stored as the system variable, AREA, and the calculated perimeter is stored as the system variable, PERIMETER.

Try getting the area and perimeter for the east lot. Use the following illustration to get your pick points.

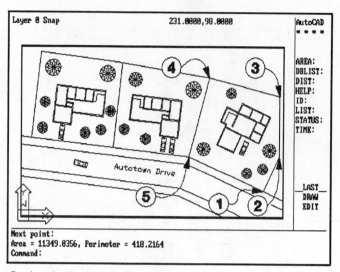

Getting the Area of the East Lot

Using AREA to Calculate a Lot and Perimeter Area

```
Command: OSNAP                        Set running osnap to INT,END.

Command: AREA
<First point>/Entity/Add/Subtract:    Pick corner of the lot at ①.
Next point:                           Pick corner of the lot at ②.
Next point:                           Pick corner of the lot at ③.
Next point:                           Pick corner of the lot at ④.
Next point:                           Pick corner of the lot at ⑤.
Next point: <RETURN>                  RETURN "closes" the boundary.
Area = 11349.0356, Perimeter = 418.2164
```

You also can get an area just be picking an entity. AREA recognizes polylines and circles. Use the entity option when you need the area of a curved boundary. Trace a temporary polyline over your drawing if you need to define the boundary. If you hatched Autotown Drive, try getting the area of the drive by picking the hatch boundary.

Using AREA to Find Area of Autotown Drive

```
Command: OSNAP                        Set OSNAP to NONE.
Command: LAYER                        Thaw layer SCRATCH.

Command: AREA
<First point>/Entity/Add/Subtract: E
Select circle or polyline:            Select polyline hatch boundary.
Area = 9868.6401, Perimeter = 732.5231
```

> ➡ *NOTE: An area is always a closed calculation. AutoCAD assumes a closure line between the first and last pick points of your area boundaries. Likewise, when you select an open polyline, AREA treats it as if it were closed.*

You can access the last calculated area, distance, and perimeter values using the SETVAR command.

Using the AREA and PERIMETER System Variables

```
Command: SETVAR
Variable name or ?: AREA
AREA = 9879.1509 (read only)


Command: SETVAR
Variable name or ? <AREA>: PERIMETER
PERIMETER = 732.5231 (read only)
```

The LIST and DBLIST Inquiry Commands

There are two other inquiry commands that we should mention. These are LIST and DBLIST. LIST gives a complete listing of entities that you select, including where the entities are located. Listing a closed polyline will give its area, including curves.

DBLIST gives a complete data listing on every entity in the drawing file. Once you do a DBLIST, you will never do it again. It scrolls through the entire database. Cancel with <^C> to get out if you get stuck in it.

Using TIME to Get Elapsed Editing Time

Time is coming to an end for this inquiry session. Finish up by looking at TIME again to see how much time you spent in this editor session.

Using TIME to Get Elapsed Drawing Time

```
Command: TIME
Current time:           02 Nov 1988 at 13:15:32.160
Drawing created:        02 Nov 1988 at 08:56:36.280
Drawing last updated:   02 Nov 1988 at 11:30:17.500
Time in drawing editor: 0 days 02:25:50.160
Elapsed timer:          0 days 00:12:19.230
Timer on.
Display/ON/OFF/Reset: <RETURN>
```

When we tested these inquiry exercises, we spent about 12 minutes in the editor.

Saving the Autotown Drawing

Command: **END**

All good things must end, including the time spent in Autotown. End your Autotown drawing so that you can start a new drawing.

Making a Title Block

In the next chapter, you are going to begin dimensioning with the Mockup Drawing. To give the drawing a finished look, you will need a border and a simple title block. This border and title block are sized for a 17" x 11" sheet to accommodate the mockup drawing.

If you have not created a mockup drawing, you can still use the border and title block for any 17" x 11" drawing. The basic principles for creating a border drawing and inserting it into an existing drawing remain the same.

The border target drawing is shown in the next illustration. It does not require any elaborate setup. It is included on the IA DISK as BDR17-11.DWG. Use the following exercise to set up your drawing.

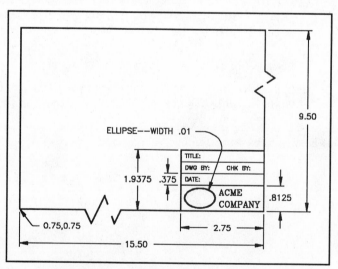

Dimensioned Border Drawing for 17" x 11" Sheet

Setting Up a Border and Title Block Drawing

 Check to see that you have this drawing as BDR17-11 on your disk. Then, just read the exercise.

 Enter selection: **1**   Begin a NEW drawing called BDR17-11.

Make sure your drawing is set up like the Border Drawing Settings table.

AXIS	COORDS	GRID	SNAP		
Off	On	.25	.125		
UNITS	Decimal units, 4 decimal points, decimal angles, 2 fractional places, defaults all other settings.				
LIMITS	0,0 to 17,11				
ZOOM	Zoom All.				
Layer name	**State**		**Color**		**Linetype**
0	On		7 (white)		CONTINUOUS
BORDER	Current		2 (yellow)		CONTINUOUS

Border Drawing Settings

First, draw the border and the basic title block. Then, you can rest your eyes as you search for the magic logo pattern to put in the title. Use the annotated illustration (above) to get your dimensions and pick points.

Making a Title Block

Command: **PLINE**	Draw a .0625 border.
Command: **PLINE**	Draw a .03 title block border.
Command: **LINE**	Draw the title block lines.
Command: **STYLE**	Create a TITLE style with ROMANS.
Command: **COLOR**	Set color to GREEN.
Command: **DTEXT**	Put the title text in.
Command: **STYLE**	Create a LOGO style with ROMANC.
Command: **DTEXT**	Put in logo text.
Command: **COLOR**	Set color to BYLAYER.
Command: **ELLIPSE**	Draw logo ellipse.
Command: **PEDIT**	Change width of ellipse to .03.

When you are done, your drawing will look like the following Border Drawing With Title Block illustration.

➥ *NOTE: This title block is drawn 1:1 to the plot size. When you insert it into a drawing, use your drawing plot scale as the insertion factor. For example, in a drawing intended for 1/4" = 1'-0" plotting (like 1:48), insert it at 48.*

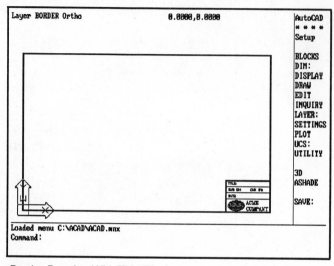

Border Drawing With Title Block

Zoom in on the ellipse area and run some hatch patterns to look for a good logo pattern.

Using HATCH for a Title Block Logo Pattern

Command: **ZOOM**	Place Window around the ellipse.

Command: **HATCH**
Pattern (? or name/U, style): **SQUARE**   Try the square pattern.
Scale for pattern <1.0000>: **.5**
Angle for pattern <0.00>: **0**
Select objects: **L**
1 found.
Select objects: **<RETURN>**

If you are frustrated, try slinging mud on the screen with the MUDST pattern.
If you require a little faith, try the CROSS pattern.
Finish up by using the ESCHER pattern.

Command: **ZOOM**   Zoom all.

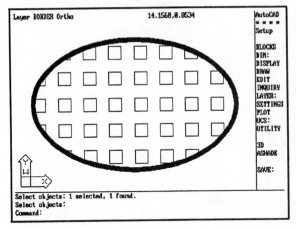

Square Pattern

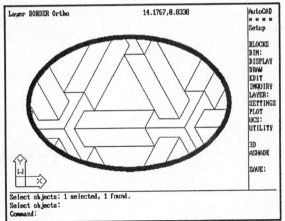

Mudst Pattern

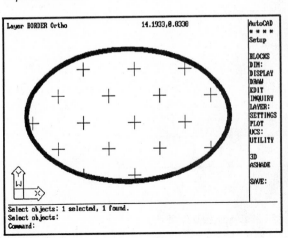

Cross Pattern

Escher Pattern

We chose the ESCHER pattern, but the Acme Company doesn't mind if you choose another pattern. Acme is a liberal company. When you are done, save your drawing. You will use it again when you dimension the mockup drawing. The Mockup With Inserted Border Drawing shows how the inserted drawing will look.

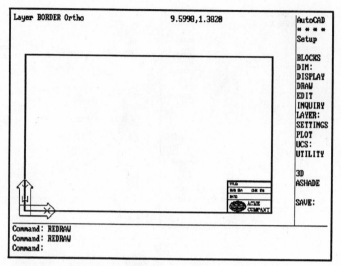

Title Block With Escher Logo

Saving the Border Drawing

Command: **END**

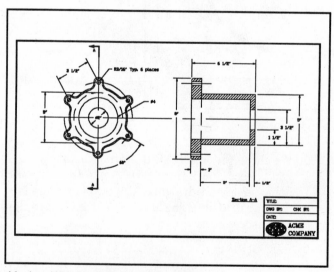

Mockup With Inserted Border Drawing

Summing Up

AutoCAD provides nearly limitless possibilities for enhancing drawings. In this chapter we have tried to cover the essentials that will get you started. In using hatching to improve your drawings, take the time that you need to find the patterns that will work best for your drawings. Don't overlook something as simple (and as easy) as creating your own hatch patterns and linetypes to give your drawings a unique look. Here are some summary reminders on hatching and sketching.

AutoCAD needs a fully closed boundary for hatching. You need to select objects within objects (donuts and holes) when you define the hatch boundary. Use a polyline to create closed continuous boundaries for hatching. If you already have individual lines or polylines bounding an area, join them with PEDIT. Standard AutoCAD patterns are unit scale and usually require further scaling. Use HATCH U when you just want a quick shade. A <^C> will terminate hatching in progress. What you have already drawn will remain in the drawing file. An ERASE Last will get rid of hatch patterns as a block.

Be careful with SKETCH. It's fun to play around with, but before you turn the pointer over to your kids, make sure you understand your disk capacity limitations. Use it with a relatively large increment, set SKPOLY to 1, and Curve Fit with PEDIT for smooth efficient curves.

AutoCAD Dimension Variables

VARIABLE NAME	DEFAULT SETTING	DEFAULT MEANING	DESCRIPTION
DIMALT	0	OFF	Use alternate units ON=1 OFF=0
DIMALTD	2	0.00	Decimal precision of alternate units
DIMALTF	25.4000		Scale factor for alternate units
DIMAPOST	""	NONE	Suffix for alternate dimensions <RO>
DIMASO	1	ON	Associative=1 Line,Arrow,Text=0
DIMASZ	0.1800		Arrow Size=Value (also controls text fit)
DIMBLK	""	NONE	Block name to draw instead of arrow or tick <RO>
DIMBLK1	""	NONE	Block name for 1st end, see DIMSAH <RO>
DIMBLK2	""	NONE	Block name for 2nd end, see DIMSAH <RO>
DIMCEN	0.0900	MARK	Center mark size=Value Add center lines=Negative
DIMDLE	0.0000	NONE	Dimension line extension=Value
DIMDLI	0.3800		Increment between continuing dimension lines
DIMEXE	0.1800		Extension distance for extension lines=Value
DIMEXO	0.0625		Offset distance for extension lines=Value
DIMLFAC	1.0000	NORMAL	Overall linear distance factor=Value
DIMLIM	0	OFF	Add tolerance limits ON=1 OFF=0
DIMPOST	""	NONE	User defined dimension suffix (eg: "mm") <RO>
DIMRND	0.0000	EXACT	Rounding value for linear dimensions
DIMSAH	0	OFF	Allow separate DIMBLKS ON=1 OFF=0
DIMSCALE	1.0000		Overall dimensioning scale factor=Value
DIMSE1	0	OFF	Suppress extension line 1 Omit=1 Draw=0
DIMSE2	0	OFF	Suppress extension line 2 Omit=1 Draw=0
DIMSHO	0	OFF	Show associative dimension while dragging
DIMSOXD	0	OFF	Suppress dim. lines outside ext. lines Omit=1 Draw=0
DIMTAD	0	OFF	Text above dim. line ON=1 OFF(in line)=0
DIMTIH	1	ON	Text inside horizontal ON=1 OFF(aligned)=0
DIMTIX	0	OFF	Force text inside extension lines ON=1 OFF=0
DIMTM	0.0000	NONE	Minus tolerance=Value
DIMTOFL	0	OFF	Draw dim. line even if text outside ext. lines
DIMTOH	1	ON	Text outside horizontal ON=1 OFF(aligned)=0
DIMTOL	0	OFF	Append tolerance ON=1 OFF=2
DIMTP	0.0000	NONE	Plus tolerance=Value
DIMTSZ	0.0000	ARROWS	Tick size=Value Draw arrows=0
DIMTVP	0.0000		Text vertical position
DIMTXT	0.1800		Text size=Value
DIMZIN	0		Controls leading zero (see AutoCAD manual)

<RO> indicates read only in SETVAR command

Dimension Variables Table

CHAPTER 11

Dimensioning

ADDING "SMARTS" TO YOUR DRAWING

Drawing Intelligence

As a communication medium, your drawing may need to represent more information than isolated lines, arcs, symbols, and text can depict. AutoCAD files can store and provide both spatial relationships and non-spatial information to further communicate your design ideas. That is what we mean by adding *smarts* to the drawing.

Spatial vs. Non-Spatial Information

Tools for working with spatial information fall into the category of dimensioning. This chapter will show you how to dimension your drawings in AutoCAD. When you place lines into a drawing file, you often represent distances and locations with real world relationships. Helping your drawing reader understand these spatial implications by measuring the distance between two points or the curve of an arc, for example, and showing these values with dimension lines is part of creating a good drawing.

You also can use non-spatial information to make your drawing communicate. Attaching text tags, like "Phone number 1234," or "W8 x 31 Steel Beam," to graphic entities are examples of using non-spatial information. This type of entity text tagging is called an attribute. The next chapter on attributes will show you how to add non-spatial information and extract it from an AutoCAD drawing file.

How Dimensioning Works

Talking about spatial information sounds very theoretical. In practice, if you can draw it, you can measure it. If you can measure it, you can dimension it. AutoCAD provides dozens of features to measure and draw dimension lines. You have complete control over the way the dimension graphics look. You can set many variables, called dimension variables, to get the dimensioning effect that you want. They can be set with SETVAR or by entering their names like commands in dimensioning mode. (A complete list of the dimension variables is shown in the table on the facing page of this chapter.) You can control:

■ How big and what your dimension arrows look like (or what to use instead of arrows).

■ How big and what style the text will be.

■ What, if any, tolerance ranges will be included with the text.

■ Where the dimension text will go.

After you tell AutoCAD how you want to draw dimensions, you identify what you want to measure. You usually pick endpoints, arcs, or other points of existing entities. Then, you show AutoCAD where you want the dimension line and text located. Finally, you either accept AutoCAD's measurements as dimension text, or type in your own text.

Dimensioning Tools

Take a look at the dimensioning tools available within AutoCAD. You will find the complete set of dimensioning commands, options, and variables available from the [DIM:] screen menu. In all, AutoCAD has six screen menu pages devoted to dimensioning. (You also will find the dimensioning commands located at the lower left of your tablet menu.)

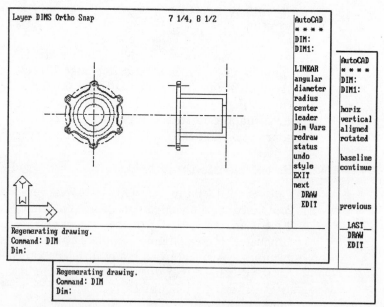

DIM Screen Menus

Because dimensioning is so flexible and has so many command options, AutoCAD sets up a new command mode for dimensioning.

The Dim: Prompt

When you enter dimensioning, you'll see a new prompt, Dim:, instead of the usual AutoCAD command prompt. When you are in Dim:, you can't execute the regular AutoCAD commands. Once you are in the dimensioning mode, you can place extension lines, arrows, and text labels automatically. After you are done, you exit the dimensioning mode and return to the regular command prompt.

AutoCAD lets you abbreviate commands in Dim: mode. Just enter the first three characters of any dimensioning command, like HOR for Horizontal.

Dimensioning has a vocabulary all its own. If you are not familiar with dimensioning, the following section will provide you with a quick primer. If you are familiar with dimensioning terms, give the primer a quick glance and move on to the next section on setting up for the dimensioning exercises.

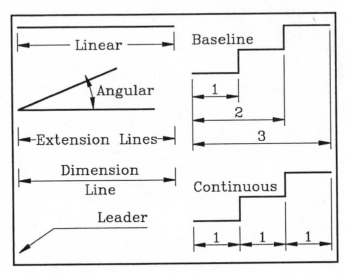

Primer Examples

Dimension Vocabulary Primer

Linear — A set of dimension lines, extension lines, arrows, and text that measures distance between two (or more) points in a straight line.

Angular — A set of dimension lines, extension lines, arrows and text that measures the angle encompassed by an arc, circle, or two joining lines.

Extension Lines — also called witness lines — Short line segments that show the drawing reader what is measured by dimension lines.

Leader — A special single dimension line that joins dimension text with an element being dimensioned or annotated.

Dimension Line — A line that shows what distance or angle is measured by the dimension process. It usually has arrows at the ends.

Baseline Dimensions — A series of dimension lines, starting at the same extension line, that measure successive linear distances.

Continuing Dimensions — A series of dimension lines that follow one another along successive linear distances.

Associative Dimensions — A dimension created as a single entity instead of individual lines, arrows (solids), arcs, and text. Associative dimensions can be moved, scaled and stretched along with the entities being dimensioned, and the dimension text will adjust automatically. This is the default dimensioning mode.

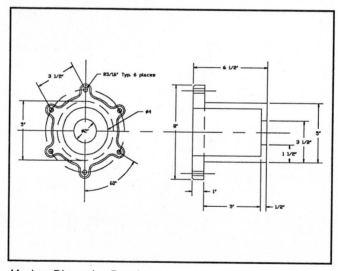

Mockup Dimension Drawing

Dimensioning Setup

In this chapter we are going to re-use the Mockup Drawing that you created in chapter 8. The target drawing for the dimensioning exercises is shown as the Mockup Dimension Drawing illustration.

If you are using the IA DISK, the undimensioned drawing is
CHAP-11A.DWG. To get started, simply set a new drawing, called
MOCKDIM, equal to CHAP-11A.DWG.

If you are not using the disk, you can start by creating a new drawing,
MOCKDIM, and setting it equal to the MOCKUP drawing that you saved
in chapter 8.

If you are starting fresh in this chapter and do not have either the disk
or a saved mockup drawing, you need to create a new drawing with the
settings shown in the Mockup Drawing Settings table. You can follow the
exercises by creating entities that resemble the basic elements, then
dimensioning them.

Setting Up for Dimensioning

 Enter selection: **1**   Begin a NEW drawing called MOCKDIM=CHAP-11A.

 Enter selection: **1**   Begin a NEW drawing called MOCKDIM=MOCKUP.

Check to see that your drawing has the settings shown in the Mockdim Drawing Settings table.

COORDS	GRID	LTSCALE	ORTHO	SNAP
On	1	1	On	.25

UNITS	Set UNITS to 5. Fractional, 64ths denominator. Default the other Units settings.
LIMITS	Set LIMITS from 0,0 to 34,22.
ZOOM	Zoom All.
VIEW	View saved as A.

Layer name	State	Color	Linetype
0	On	7 (white)	CONTINUOUS
CENTER	On	1 (red)	CENTER
DIMS	Current	2 (yellow)	CONTINUOUS
HIDDEN	On	4 (cyan)	HIDDEN
PARTS	On	3 (green)	CONTINUOUS

Mockdim Drawing Settings

Set your current layer to DIMS. You will spend most, if not all, of your
dimensioning time on this layer. Your drawing scale factor is 2, to plot on
a 17" x 11" sheet.

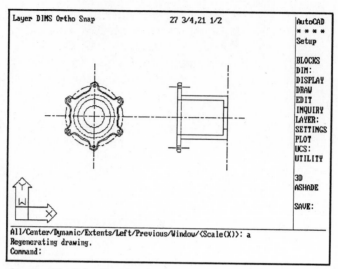

Starting Mockdim Drawing

How the Dimensioning Exercises Are Organized

The dimensioning exercises are organized around three basic levels. The first section shows the basics of how to use the dimensioning commands by placing center, radius, diameter, angular, and linear dimensions. If you are just starting with dimensions, you want to work your way through these exercises.

The second group of exercises shows how to get more complex dimensioning effects by using continuing and baseline dimensions, and by setting dimension variables to tailor dimensions to your needs. In addition, you will learn how to use associative dimensions to update your dimensions as you stretch and alter the scale of a drawing's objects. If you are already familiar with some of AutoCAD's dimensioning features, you may want to start with this second section and move on to the last section.

The third section shows how to finish off your drawing by inserting a border and title block. This last section also provides a discussion of more complex effects that you can get by setting yet more dimension variables using dimension blocks and special text features.

How to Set Up and Scale Dimensions

Setting scale in dimensioning is similar to setting a scale for your basic drawing. AutoCAD makes <default> assumptions about dimension setup parameters, including the scale of your dimension text and arrows. If you are working with a different set of units, or a large limits setting, the default settings may make your dimensions huge or nearly invisible. In a 60-foot by 100-foot facilities planning drawing, for example, the default arrow is 0.18 millimeters — invisible at almost any drawing scale.

You could reset all your dimension variables to get the right size. But, AutoCAD has a better answer called DIMSCALE. Every scalar dimension variable is multiplied by DIMSCALE before it is applied to the drawing. You can use DIMSCALE to change all your dimensioning variables with a scale factor. The default for DIMSCALE is 1.0000.

Set your dimension text scale and arrow size for plotted output. Then set your DIMSCALE to your drawing scale factor. The scale factor for the Mockdim drawing is 2. Select DIM: and set DIMTXT for your text, set DIMASZ for your arrows, then set DIMSCALE to 2, making your dimension scale match your drawing scale. The text and arrow values are given in the exercise sequence.

Setting DIMTXT, DIMASZ, and DIMSCALE to Scale Dimensions

`Command:` **`DIM`**	Puts you in the dimension mode.
`Dim:` **`DIMTXT`** `Current value <3/16> New value:` **`.125`**	Makes text 1/8" high.
`Dim:` **`DIMASZ`** `Current value <3/16> New value:` **`0.14`**	Sets the arrow head size.
`Dim:` **`DIMSCALE`** `Current value <1> New value:` **`2`**	Sets DIMSCALE to 2 (drawing plot scale factor).
	This makes the actual text 0.25 units high (DIMSCALE x DIMTXT = 2 x 0.125 = 0.25 in drawing units), but it will plot 0.125 units high.
`Dim:` **`EXIT`**	Exit to the command prompt with EXIT or <^C>.

Changing your arrow size with DIMASZ keeps your dimension arrow's size in proportion to your text size. The DIMTXT dimension variable controls dimension text.

➡ *TIP: Be careful when you Undo after you exit the dimensioning mode if you have set variables. A command prompt level Undo or U will Undo everything in the preceding dimensioning session as a single Undo step. This makes it easy to accidently undo Dim Vars settings. Make a practice of exiting Dim: immediately after you set your Dim Vars, then reenter. This will protect them from an accidental Undo.*

If you already know the basic dimensioning commands, just skim the following sections on dimensioning the plan view, and pick up with dimensioning the section view.

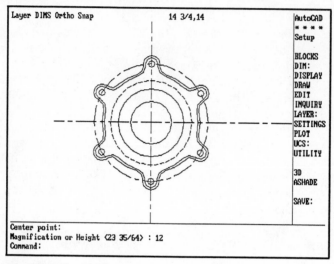

Mockdim Plan View

Dimensioning the Mockdim Plan View

In this first pass through dimensioning, you will work with the plan view (the left side) of the Mockdim drawing. This flange view has enough entity features to test most of the basic dimensioning commands. The Dimension Examples illustration shows the dimensions covered in this first section. We will work through the different dimension types one at a time so that you can see how they're done.

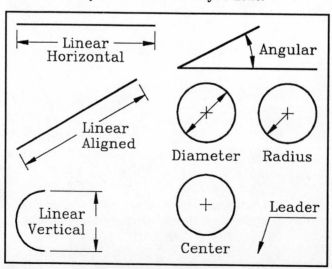

Dimension Examples

Dimensioning With Center Marks

The plan view has a series of small circles in the *lugs* on the flange's edge. Start your dimensioning sequence by placing center marks in these circles with the CENTER command. CENTER puts a cross at the center of an arc or circle.

Make sure you are at the Dim: prompt, then type the command, or select it from the screen or tablet menus. Put the first mark in the circle at the top, then work your way around the flange. Here is the prompt sequence.

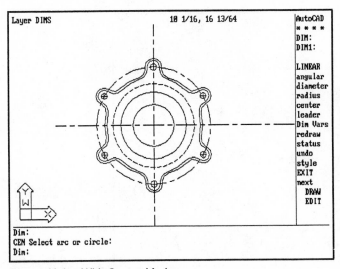

Flange Holes With Center Marks

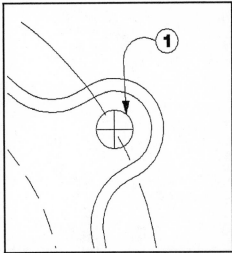

Detail of Center Mark

Using DIM CENTER to Place a Center Mark

Command: **SNAP**	Toggle snap off.
Command: **ZOOM**	Zoom in on top view.
Select: **[DIM:]**	Select [DIM:] from the root menu. Notice the Dim: prompt.
Dim: **CEN** Select arc or circle:	Type CEN or select [center] from the screen menu. Pick a point on the hole's circumference at ①. A center mark appears.
Dim: **<RETURN>** CEN Select arc or circle:	Add center marks to the 5 remaining holes.

➡ *NOTE: The dimension variable called DIMCEN sets the size of the center marker. If you give it a negative value, center lines extending beyond the circumference are added to the center mark.*

Dimensioning a Radius

Next, try placing a radius dimension in the inner flange circle. The radius command measures from an arc or circle center point to a circumference point. In the following example, the dimension text will not fit. Use the exercise input value to offset the dimension line.

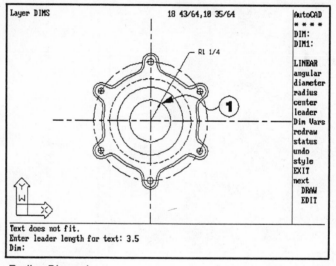

Radius Dimension

Using DIM RADIUS to Place a Radius Dimension

```
Dim: RAD                        Type RAD or pick [radius] from the screen menu.
Select arc or circle:           Select the inner circle at point ① on the circumference.
Dimension text <1 1/4>: <RETURN>
Text does not fit.
Enter leader length for text: 3.5    Type this value.
```

Your screen drawing results should look like the Radius Dimension illustration. AutoCAD measured the radius for you, and offered the correct dimension as default text for drawing the dimension. You can always input your own text to use instead of the <default> dimension text. The dimension lines, arrow, and text wouldn't fit inside the circle, so AutoCAD asked you to decide where the text should go. By entering **3.5** on the keyboard, you set up an offset distance to place the text away from the circle. You are not limited to typed input; you can pick the leader length with your pointer. But the leader angle is determined by the pick used to select the circle.

Using a Pick Point to Place a Dimension

This is all well and good. But what do you do if you want the radius dimension in a different place? You can control the location of the dimension with your pick point. Undo this first radius, and put in another radius dimension. Type **U** or select [undo] from the dimension screen menu to remove all the radius dimension entities — the dimension line, the leader, the arrow, and the text.

Execute the radius command again. This time, select the circle by picking the 85-degree point on the circumference. You should get the drawing shown in Radius Dimension — Second Try.

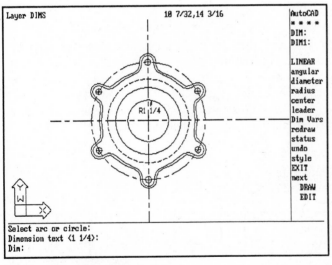

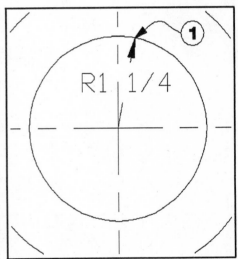

Radius Dimension — Second Try   *Detail of Radius Dimension*

Using DIM RADIUS to Place a Radius Dimension — Second Try

Dim: **U**   Undo the first radius dimension.

Dim: **RAD**   Type RAD or select radius from the screen menu.
Select arc or circle: Pick circle at point ①.

Dimension text <1 1/4>: **<RETURN>**

Notice you got the dimension text within the circle this time. AutoCAD always writes dimension text horizontally, even for angular dimensions, unless you change dimension variables. Text size and your pick point determine whether the dimension will fit in the circle.

➤ *NOTE: You will run into problems if your current text style is vertical when you enter dimensioning. Reset your text to a horizontal style before executing the Dim: commands.*

Using Undo in the DIM Command

Using Dim's Undo is similar to using an undo in the line command, but Dim:'s Undo removes all entities (extension lines, arrows, text, etc.) from the last dimension try. Type **U** to Undo at the Dim: prompt. You can also undo dimensions with the normal Undo commands from the Command: prompt, but one Undo will then wipe out an entire dimensioning session.

Dimensioning a Diameter

Now that you know how the text fits in the inner circle, why not replace the radius with a diameter dimension? Diameter measures between two diametrically opposed points on the circumference of a circle or arc. Placing a diameter is similar to placing a radius. When you select the circle that you want to dimension, diameter uses the point you pick as a diameter endpoint. AutoCAD automatically figures out where the second endpoint goes. (If the text does not fit, a leader will also stem from this first picked point, not the opposite end of the diameter.)

Undo the radius and put in a diameter dimension. Use the following illustration to get your pick point.

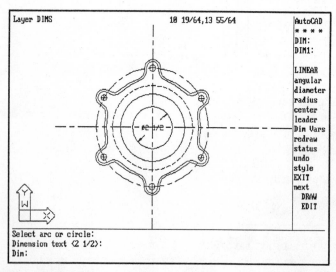

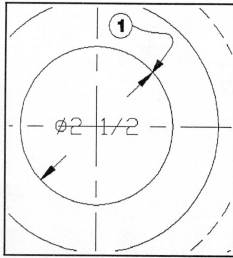

Diameter Dimension   Detail of Diameter Dimension

Using DIM DIAMETER to Place a Diameter Dimension

Dim: **U**   Undo the previous dimension command.

Dim: **DIA**   Type DIA or select diameter from the screen menu.
Select arc or circle: Pick the circle at point ①.
Dimension text <2 1/2>: **<RETURN>**

AutoCAD determines everything and fits and draws the dimension text.

How to Use Spaces to Force a Dimension Location

You may want radius or diameter text to go outside the circle, not inside. But AutoCAD will place the text outside only if it thinks it won't fit inside. You can make it think it won't fit by adding text spaces. Augment the measured dimension text with additional text by typing a pair of angle brackets, <>, to indicate the measurement, followed by about 12 spaces (using the <SPACEBAR>). AutoCAD will count the spaces and put the text outside to the right. (If you were putting it on the left, you would precede the <> with the spaces.) The dimension includes 12 extra spaces, so it won't fit inside. You can use this angle bracket technique to add visible text to the default dimension.

Adding Text to a Dimension

Try adding text to a measured dimension. Return to the lug circle at the top of the flange and place a radius dimension with some added text. Use the following illustration to get your pick points. Use the prompt sequence to get your text input, including the angle brackets, and a leader offset value.

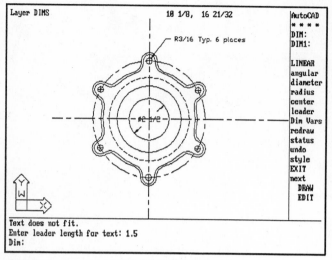

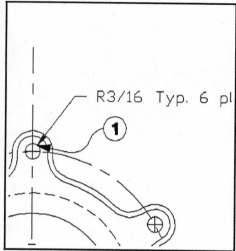

A Radius Dimension With Added Text   *Detail of Radius Dimension*

Adding Text to a Dimension

Dim: **RAD**   Use RADius to dimension the outer flange holes.
Select arc or circle: Pick the top small hole at point ①.
Dimension text <3/16>: **<> Typ. 6 places**   Type the input.
Text does not fit.
Enter leader length for text: **1.5**   Offset value.

Dimensioning With Leader Dimensions

In both the radius and diameter dimensions, you have seen that a leader is used to place text outside the circle (or arc). You can use the LEADER command to create an extended arrow to place text away from the immediate entities you are dimensioning. LEADER is a special version of the line command. It lets you create a *call out* (starting with an arrowhead) to point text to a specific location. You can make a leader line have many continuous segments to snake the leader away from dense drawing parts.

Use a leader to dimension the hole in the flange. AutoCAD will prompt for a starting point for the leader line. Use the illustration to get your leader pick points. Get your text from the prompt sequence.

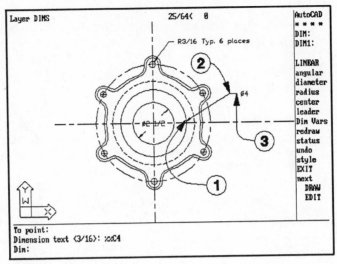

Leader Dimension

Using DIM LEADER to Place a Leader Dimension

Dim: <Ortho off>   Toggle ortho off.

Dim: **LEA**   Type LEA or select leader from the screen menu.
Leader start: Pick right side of the large circle at point ①.
To point: Pick point ②.
To point: Pick point ③.
To point: **<RETURN>**
Dimension text <3/16>: **%%C4**   Input text with %%C for the diameter character.

Dim: **EXIT**   Exit the Dim mode.

If you followed the prompt sequence for the leader (above), you may have noticed that AutoCAD carried the previous dimension as the default. It is possible to use a previous dimension as all or part of the leader text.

How to Put Dimension Text in a Leader

To use a previous dimension, execute any dimension, say a DIAMETER dimension, then execute the LEADER dimension, accepting the default dimension or using angle brackets (<>). After you are done, you can exit dimensioning mode and erase the first dimension text and lines if you don't want them.

Dimensioning Angle Dimensions

Next, measure the typical angle between two of the outer flange holes. This is an ANGULAR dimension. ANGULAR measures the inner or outer (acute or obtuse) angle between two specified nonparallel lines. ANGULAR only works with lines or polylines as take off points for an angle measurement.

Work with the two outer holes at the lower right of the flange. Draw in a reference line for the circle on the right. When you reenter dimensioning, use DIM1 which lets you work with a single command, in this case ANGULAR. When AutoCAD prompts you for an angle decision, pick the small arc (acute angle). The following illustration will help you with the reference line and pick points. After you exit dimensioning, erase the reference line.

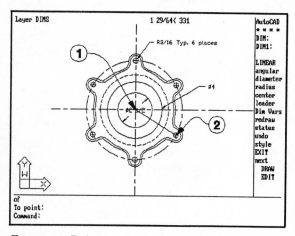

Temporary Reference Line

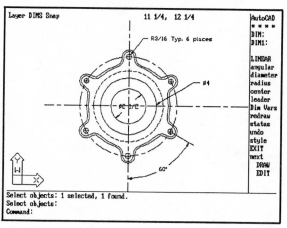

Angular Dimension

Using DIM ANGULAR to Place an Angular Dimension

Command: **LINE**	Draw in a temporary reference line.
From point:	Center of inner hole at ①.
To point:	Center of flange hole at ②.
Command: **DIM1**	Type DIM1 or select [DIM1:] from screen menu.
Dim: **ANG**	Type ANG or select angular from the screen menu.
Select first line:	Pick the temporary reference line.
Second line:	Pick the vertical center line.
Enter dimension line arc location:	Pick absolute point at about 12-3/4,8-3/4.
Dimension text <60>: **<RETURN>**	Accept the default text.
Enter text location: **<RETURN>**	
Command: **ERASE**	Erase the reference line.

If you pick a point in the obtuse angle, you'll get the big arc dimension. If you pick a point in the acute angle, you'll get the small arc dimension (the case above). ANGULAR's dimension arc passes through the pick point. The picked point, 12-3/4,8-3/4, gives a good arc.

Using the DIM1 Command

If you anticipate that you only need to do one dimensioning subcommand, use the DIM1 command. Instead of keeping you in the dimensioning mode, DIM1 returns you to the command prompt after the execution of one dimensioning subcommand.

Dimensioning With Linear Dimensions

Linear is a group of commands (HORIZONTAL, VERTICAL, ALIGNED, BASELINE, and CONTINUE) that measure between two points. The points can be endpoints, intersections, arc chord endpoints, or any two points you can identify.

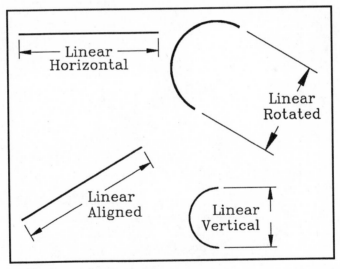

Linear Dimension Examples

The commands do just what their names imply: HORIZONTAL creates horizontal dimension lines; VERTICAL creates vertical dimension lines; ALIGNED creates dimension lines that are aligned to an object or two specified points; and ROTATED creates dimension lines rotated to a specified angle.

Dimensioning a Linear Vertical Dimension

Start your linear dimensions by measuring the overall vertical dimension of the dashed (hidden line) circle. VERTICAL gives you two options for dimensioning: you can pick the origins of the two extension lines that mark the boundaries of the dimension line, or you can select an object (like a line, arc, or circle) and automatically dimension the full length or breadth of that object. Use the second option, selecting the circle, with the circle's top and bottom as starting points for your extension lines.

Once you've selected the circle, AutoCAD will prompt you for the location of the dimension line. Place the dimension line about one unit to the left of the circle. When you are done, your results should look like the Linear Vertical Dimension on a Circle illustration.

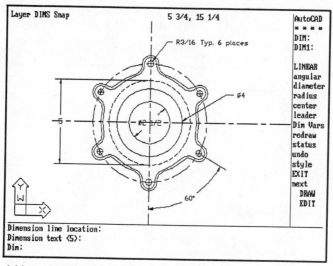

A Linear Vertical Dimension on a Circle

Using Linear VERTICAL to Place a Vertical Dimension

Command: **DIM**	Get back in dimension mode.
Dim: **VER**	Type VER or select [LINEAR] and [vertical].
First extension line origin or RETURN to select: **<RETURN>**	
Select line, arc, or circle:	Pick any point on the hidden circle.
Dimension line location:	Pick absolute point at about 4-1/2,15.
Dimension text <5>: **<RETURN>**	

Aligned Dimensions

Now try measuring a distance that is not horizontal or vertical, such as the distance from the center of one of the outer flange holes to the center of another outer flange hole. This is an aligned dimension. If you used a vertical dimension, you would get the height from the first hole to the second hole. What you want is the actual distance between the two holes. This is what you get from ALIGNED.

ALIGNED works like any linear dimension; you have the option of picking points to locate your dimension lines or of selecting an object. Work with the two holes at the upper left of the flange. Use the Aligned Dimension illustration and prompt sequence to get your pick points and input values.

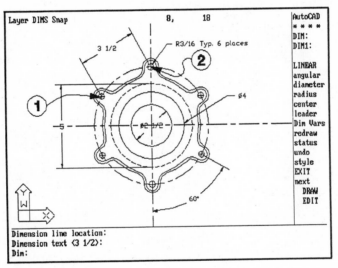

Aligned Dimension

Using Linear ALIGNED to Place an Aligned Dimension

```
Dim: ALI                          Type ALI or select [aligned] from the [LINEAR] screen menu.
First extension line origin or RETURN to select:    Pick the center of hole at ①.
Second extension line origin:     Pick the center of hole at ②.
Dimension line location:          Pick absolute point 8,18.
Dimension text <3 1/2>: <RETURN>  Accept AutoCAD's text prompt.
```

Voila! You've got an aligned dimension. Of course, if your origin points align vertically or horizontally, an aligned dimension produces identical results to vertical or horizontal.

The rotated linear dimension is similar to the other linear options except you must first specify the angle of the dimension. In fact, you can use rotated for vertical and horizontal dimensioning by specifying an angle of 90 or 0 degrees.

Other Dimensioning Commands

There are three other commands on the first dimensioning screen menu page. EXIT (or <^C>) gets you out of Dim: and back to the command prompt. The REDRAW command in dimensioning is the regular REDRAW command. The STATUS command displays all the settings for variable dimension features, like arrow and text size.

Stopping Point

This first pass through dimensioning completes the plan view. This is a good stopping point, a chance to take a break. While the dimensioning commands may seem complex, the basics are quite simple: first, you tell AutoCAD what it is you want to dimension; then, you tell it where to place the dimension entities. Getting the effects you want may take some practice. We haven't exhausted the dimensioning possibilities in the flange. You can use the drawing to try other variations. For now, save the drawing and take a break, then proceed to the next section on working with dimension variables and associative dimensions.

Saving the Mockdim Drawing

Command: **SAVE**   Save to the default drawing name.

Dimensioning the Section View

In the first pass through dimensioning, you didn't change any dimensioning parameters after you set your dimension scale. In this second pass, we will set up different ways to put in dimensions, turning arrows into tick marks, and turning tolerances on. You will see how these parameters affect the dimension process and how you can tailor the dimensioning process to your needs.

Setting Up for Dimensioning the Section View

If you are continuing on from the first section in the chapter, reload your Mockdim drawing. If you have the IA DISK and are jumping in at this point, make a new drawing named MOCKDIM from the CHAP-11B.DWG with the dimension settings shown in the table at the start of this chapter.

Setting Up for Dimensioning the Section View

Enter selection: **1**   Begin a NEW drawing called MOCKDIM=CHAP-11B.

Continue to edit the section view.

Your current drawing layer is DIMS, and your dimension scale (DIMSCALE) is 2.

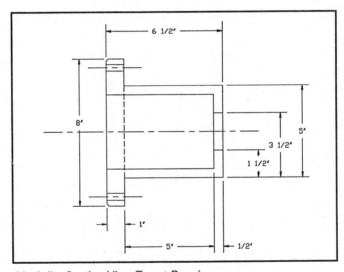

Mockdim Section View Target Drawing

Take a look at the Mockdim Section View Target Drawing. It is made up of linear dimensions. The dimensions along the bottom form a set of continuing dimensions; the dimensions on the right are baseline dimensions.

Dimensioning With Tolerances

To get tolerances, you need to change the Dim Vars parameter settings that control tolerances. It's time to take a closer look at dimension variables. Get into dimensioning mode and select [Dim Vars] from the screen menu. You'll get a list of the dimension variables. There are a lot!

Set DIMTAD, short for dimension text, above the dimension line. Turn DIMTAD on. Next set DIMTOL, dimension tolerance, and turn it on. Set DIMTP for dimension tolerance plus. Give it a value of 1/32. Do the same for DIMTM, dimension tolerance minus. The prompt sequence goes like this:

Setting Dimension Variables

```
Command: ZOOM                    Use dynamic to magnify the section view.
Command: DIM

Dim: DIMTAD                               Set text to go above the dimension line.
Current value <Off> New Value: ON

Dim: DIMTOL                               Set tolerances on.
Current value <Off> New Value: ON

Dim: DIMTP                                Set plus tolerance.
Current value <0> New Value: 1/32

Dim: DIMTM                                Set minus tolerance.
Current value <0> New Value: 1/32
```

Now go to work on the top horizontal dimension.

Using a Linear Horizontal Dimension with Tolerances

Try placing your dimension by selecting the endpoints for the line you want to dimension. The illustration shows the pick points. Put the dimension about 1 inch above the line.

Using Linear HORIZONTAL to Place a Horizontal Dimension

```
Dim: HOR                         Type HOR or pick [LINEAR] and [horizontal] from screen menu.
First extension line origin or RETURN to select:     Pick the first point at ①.
Second extension line origin:                         Pick the second point at ②.
Dimension line location:                              Pick absolute point 23,18-1/2.
Dimension text <6>: <RETURN>
```

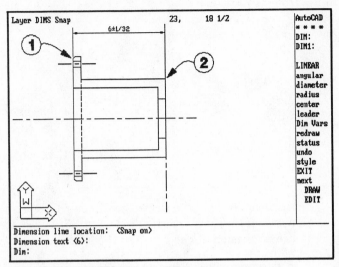

Horizontal Dimension Above Line With Tolerances

If all went well, you got text above the dimension line, tolerance included. AutoCAD combines the plus and minus tolerance symbols as ±1/32 because the plus and minus values are the same. If they were different, AutoCAD would put separate plus and minus text lines adjacent to the 6-inch value.

Dimensioning With Tick Marks

Next, look at the left side of the Mockdim drawing. Here you want to place a vertical dimension using tick marks instead of the normal dimension line arrows. It's back to Dim Vars.

First, you don't want tolerances in this dimension so toggle DIMTOL off. Second, you want the dimension text to break the dimension line, so toggle DIMTAD off as well. Finally, you want this dimension line to end in tick marks, not arrows. As you might guess, there is a Dim Vars for ticks! Select DIMTSZ (dimension tick size), and give it a value of 1/8 as the tick size. Whenever DIMTSZ has a value greater than 0, ticks are drawn instead of arrows. Here is the corresponding prompt sequence.

Using Dim Vars to Set Dimension Ticks

Select Dim Vars to get to the Dim Vars menu.

```
Dim: DIMTOL                                    Turn tolerances off.
Current value <On> New Value: OFF
```

```
Dim: DIMTAD                                    Turn text above dimension line off.
Current value <On> New Value: OFF
```

```
Dim: DIMTSZ                                    Turn on tick marks with a value of 1/8".
Current value <0> New Value: 1/8
```

Now, you're ready to draw the dimension line on the left. Get your pick marks from the Vertical Dimension With Tick Marks illustration. Place the dimension about 1 inch to the left.

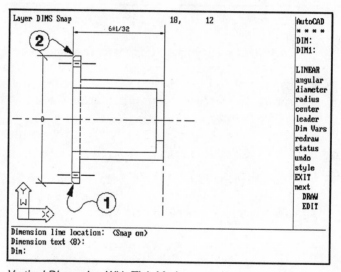

Vertical Dimension With Tick Marks

Using Linear VERTICAL to Dimension With Tick Marks

```
Dim: VER                         Type VER or select [LINEAR] and [vertical].
First extension line origin or RETURN to select:    Pick the lower left corner at ①.
Second extension line origin:        Pick the upper left corner at ②.
Dimension line location:             Pick absolute point 18,12.
Dimension text <8>: <RETURN>         Accept the default text.
```

Dimensioning With Continued Dimensions

Try your hand at placing a continuing horizontal dimension string along the bottom of the section view. Start with Dim Vars again, turning the ticks off, then set the DIMDLI (dimension line increment) variable. DIMDLI controls the spacing increment between successive dimensions. Pick points are shown in the First Continuing Horizontal Dimension illustration.

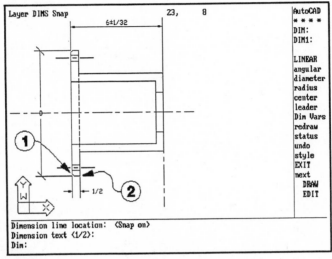

First Continuing Horizontal Dimension

Using Linear CONTINUE Dimensions

Dim: **DIMTSZ**   Set the ticks off.
Current value <1/8> New value: **0**

Dim: **DIMDLI**   Increase dimension line increment for continuing dimensions.
Current value <3/8> New value: **5/8**

Dim: **HOR**   Type HOR or select [LINEAR] and [horizontal].
First extension line origin or RETURN to select: Pick point ①.
Second extension line origin: Pick point ②.
Dimension line location: Pick absolute point 23,8.
Dimension text <1/2>: **<RETURN>**   Accept AutoCAD's text default.

Notice that AutoCAD put the 1/2 outside the extension line because it could not fit into the dimensioned space. If you want the text on the left side, just reverse the order of the two points.

Using the CONTINUE Command

CONTINUE lets you continue dimensioning along successive linear points in the same line. CONTINUE starts a new dimension line where the last dimension line left off, using the old extension line as the first extension line for the new dimension line. Continue by adding new extension lines (to the right).

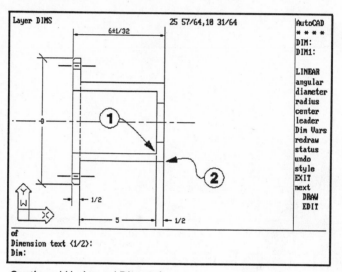

Continued Horizontal Dimensions

Using CONTINUE in Horizontal Dimensions

```
Dim: CON                          Type CON or select [continue] from the screen menu.
Second extension line origin:     Pick the next point dimensioned at ①.
Dimension text <5>: <RETURN>      Accept AutoCAD's text.

Dim: CON
Second extension line origin:     Pick the next point dimensioned at ②.
Dimension text <1/2>: <RETURN>    Accept AutoCAD's text.
```

Notice that AutoCAD automatically put the new dimension lines below the first one. The distance between the two dimension lines is controlled by DIMDLI, which you set to 5/8.

Dimensioning Using Baseline Dimensions

Next, you want to get the overall vertical dimension for the section view. Start by putting in a normal vertical dimension. There is one trick here. You need to set DIMTIX to force AutoCAD to place the dimension text within the dimension lines.

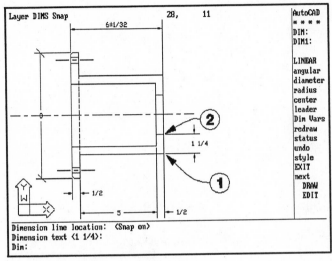

First Vertical Dimension for Baseline

Using Linear VERTICAL to Place a Dimension

```
Dim: DIMTIX                      Force dimension between extension lines.
Current value <Off> New value: ON
```

```
Dim: VER                         Type VER or select [LINEAR] and [vertical].
First extension line origin or RETURN to select:    Pick the corner at ①.
Second extension line origin:                        Pick the corner at ②.
Dimension line location:                             Pick absolute point 28,11.
Dimension text <1-1/4>: <RETURN>                     Accept the default text.
```

Now that the first vertical dimension line is in place, use the BASELINE command to continue the vertical dimensions. BASELINE works like CONTINUE, except it uses the first extension line (base extension line) as the origin for all successive dimension calculations and line placements.

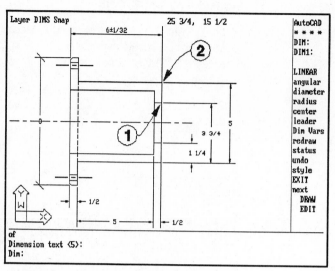

Vertical Dimensions After Baseline

Using Linear BASELINE to Place a Series of Vertical Dimensions

```
Dim: BAS                          Type BAS or select [baseline] from the screen menu.
Second extension line origin:         Pick corner point at ①.
Dimension text <3 3/4>: <RETURN>      Accept the default text.


Dim: <RETURN>
BAS
Second extension line origin:         Pick corner point at ②.
Dimension text <5>: <RETURN>          Accept the default text.


Dim: EXIT                         Return to the command prompt.
Command: SAVE                     Save to default drawing name.
```

Save your drawing because the next set of exercises will stretch, scale, and update it.

Associative Dimensioning

If you're using the Release 9, Release 10, or a later version of AutoCAD, you've probably been creating associative dimensions all along, but didn't know it. Now take a closer look at asodims (associative dimensions) using your dimensioned Mockdim drawing.

How Associative Dimensions Work

An associative dimension is a dimension created as a single entity instead of as individual lines, arrows (solids), arcs, and text. You can move associative dimensions. You can scale and stretch them along with the entities being dimensioned, and the dimension text will adjust automatically. This is the default dimensioning mode. If the dimension variable called DIMASO is on, AutoCAD creates associative dimensions. If DIMASO is off, AutoCAD creates dimensions from several individual entities. If you have not changed the default from on, you have been creating associative dimensions!

When you use associative dimensions, you are creating definition points. Associative dimensions use these defpoints to control the rescaling and updating of asodims. Defpoints are kept on a special layer called DEFPOINTS, which is turned off. But defpoints display no matter what you do to layer DEFPOINTS. They won't plot unless you turn the layer on. You can osnap to these points with osnap NODe. There is also an invisible point at the midpoint of the asodim text. It is not a true defpoint, but osnap NODe will also find it. The subentities of asodims respond to the other osnap modes just like subentities of ordinary blocks.

How to Use Associative Dimensions

Associative dimensions make the task of updating and re-scaling a fully dimensioned drawing much easier. In the following exercises we will show you three ways to use asodims: updating dimension parameters and values, stretching dimensions to relocate dimension text, and stretching and re-scaling drawing entities to get an automatic dimension update.

Using UPDATE to Update Dimensions

If you look closely at your current drawing, you will see that your dimension text does not have any units showing. We are using the multipurpose fractional style of units. You can set an automatic dimension suffix, DIMPOST, to " to get inch tick marks in your dimensions. DIMPOST can append any text character or string to dimensions. Also, while you are setting Dim Vars, re-set DIMEXO to control the offset for extension lines. The default (1/16) is tight for curves. This default makes the extension lines too close to the arc of the flange.

Reset DIMEXO and DIMPOST, then try out UPDATE. UPDATE is the asodim command (you guessed it) that updates asodims. Use the following exercise sequence to guide you through the update.

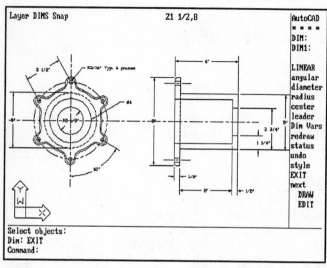

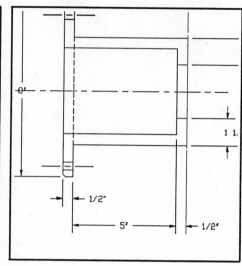

Mockdim After Update   *Detail of Update*

Using UPDATE to Update Dimensions

```
Command: ZOOM              Use dynamic to get all the dimensions on the screen.
Command: DIM

Dim: DIMEXO                Set extension line offset to 1/8".
Dim: DIMPOST
Current value <> New value: "         Set suffix type to ".

Dim: UPD                   Update the dimensions.
Select objects:            Select all the dimensions except the 60-degree angle.
13 found.
Select objects: <RETURN>

Dim: DIMTIX                Set forced inside text to off.
Dim: UPD                   Update the two 1/2" horizontal dimensions.
Dim: EXIT
```

UPDATE redraws any and all selected asodims to the current state of all Dim Vars and to the current text style. When you select your entities with a window, all non-asodim entities are ignored. With DIMEXO on, the arc looks better and your text now has tick marks.

If you look at the tolerance dimensions at the top of the section view, you will see that they were removed and that the dimension text is no longer above the dimension line. The tick marks were also replaced with arrowheads on the 8" vertical dimension on the left. This occurs because the Dim Vars associated with these dimensions are now set *differently*

from when the dimensions themselves were created. This is the way
UPDATE is supposed to work. All current dimension settings, including
text style and placement, apply to selected asodims when they are
updated. There are two other asodim commands besides update. Here are
the three asodim commands.

Associative Dimensioning Commands

HOMETEXT — Restores associative dimension text to its default
(home) position.

UPDATE — Reformats associative dimension(s) to the current
dimensioning settings and text style.

NEWTEXT — Allows editing of associative dimension text, or restores
the default measurement as text.

Stretching Asodims to Relocate Dimension Text

The vertical dimension text (5") on the far left of the flange is located on
top of the flange center line. The 8" vertical texts in the section view is
also on top of the same center line.

Exit the Dim: mode, then use STRETCH to relocate the two dimension
texts to improve their appearance. Use the comments in the exercise
sequence to help you locate your stretch crossing windows. While you are
editing the dimensions, break the center lines going through the inner
circle's 2 1/2" diameter dimension. When you are done, your drawing
results should look something like the Mockdim After Stretching
Dimension Text illustration.

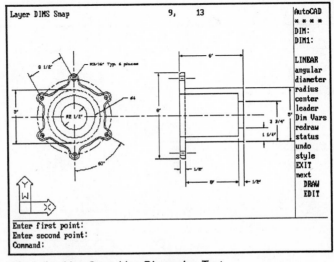

Mockdim After Stretching Dimension Text

Relocating Dimension Text

Command: **STRETCH**	Now adjust your text locations with STRETCH.
Select objects to stretch by window...	
Select objects: **C**	
First corner:	Place the window around the 5" vertical dimension on the left.
Other corner:	The whole dimension will be highlighted.
1 found.	If anything else was caught in the window use **R** to remove it.
Select objects: **<RETURN>**	
Base point:	Pick the midpoint of the text.
New point:	Pick polar point @1/2<90.
Command: **STRETCH**	Stretch the 8" vertical text in the same way as above.
Command: **BREAK**	Break the center lines at the 2 1/2" diameter dimension.

Your drawing should look better. When you stretch the asodim's text out of the dimension line, the line heals itself. The HOMETEXT command makes the asodim text snap back to its default home.

Be careful when you use STRETCH, it does an update. If you had reset dimexo back to 1/16 prior to the stretch, for example, it would have changed the extension line offsets.

Stretching and Scaling Entities and Asodims

You have seen how you can stretch asodims. Now, try your hand at stretching and scaling entities. You will automatically get updated measurements in your asodims in the process. Use STRETCH to double the flange thickness from 1/2" to 1" on the left side of the section view. Get your crossing window from the illustration.

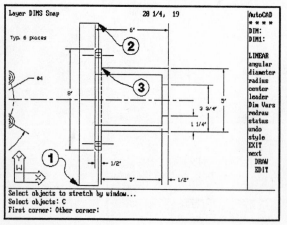

Crossing Window for Changing the Flange

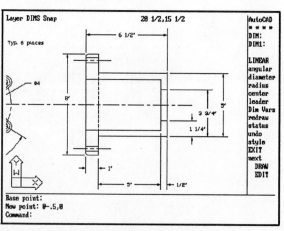

Stretched Flange With Updated Dimensions

Using STRETCH to Stretch an Entity with Asodims

```
Command: STRETCH
Select objects to stretch by window...
Select objects: C          Select the crossing window shown.
First corner:              Pick corner point at ①.
Other corner:              Pick corner point at ②.
1 found.
Select objects: <RETURN>
Base point:                Pick top inside flange corner at ③.
New point: @-.5,0          Increase thickness by 1/2".
```

Now, use SCALE to rescale the inner circle's hole diameter from 2 1/2" to 2" in both the plan view and the section view.

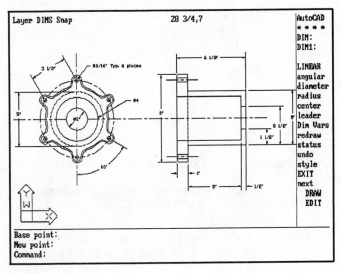

Rescaled Holes

Using SCALE to Rescale Entities with Asodims

```
Command: scale
Select objects:            Pick the 2 1/2" dimension and circle.
Select objects: <RETURN>
Base point:                Pick the exact center of the circle.
<Scale factor>/Reference: R
Reference length <1>: 2.5
New length: 2

Command: STRETCH          Stretch the vertical 3 3/4" dimension to 3 1/2".
Command: STRETCH          Stretch the vertical 1 1/4" dimension to 1 1/2".
```

Stopping Point

This is as far as we go with an introduction to asodims, but we encourage you to play around with them. Try NEWTEXT. It lets you edit any or all selected asodims text. Embedded <> measurements and text are legal. A <RETURN> defaults NEWTEXT back to the measured dimension.

Try using EXPLODE on an asodim. EXPLODE changes an asodim back to an old style dimension. Undo is the only way to restore associativity. If you do an explode, watch out, exploding sends all the dimension parts to layer 0 with color and linetype set BYBLOCK. That is because asodims are really a special form of blocks.

Save your drawing. If you have the time, play around with asodims. Then, quit your drawing. When you resume with the next section, you will add some final touches and insert a border and title block into Mockdim.

Saving Mockdim

Command: **SAVE**   Save to the default drawing name.

Inserting a Border and Title Block Into a Drawing

Throughout this chapter we have worked with bits and pieces of the Mockdim drawing. It would be nice to have at least one finished drawing! This last section will show you how to add some final touches to the Mockdim drawing. More importantly, it will show you how to combine a border and title block drawing with a finished drawing.

Setting Up for the Title Block Insertion

You will need a saved version of the MOCKDIM drawing and the border drawing, called BRD17-11.DWG, that you created in the last chapter. If you are using the IA DISK, you already have this drawing. If you are not using the disk, and you do not have the border drawing, you need to refer to chapter 10 to create it. The illustration below, called Finished Mockdim Drawing, shows the target drawing. The accompanying illustration, Border and Title Block Drawing, shows the drawing that you will insert into Mockdim.

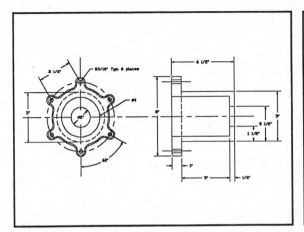

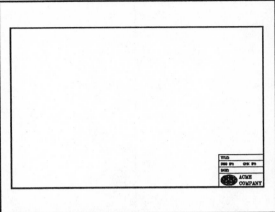

Finished Mockdim Drawing

Border and Title Block Drawing

Setup for Inserting a Border and Title Block

You have the BRD17-11 drawing on the disk.

You need the BRD17-11 drawing from chapter 10.

Your current layer should still be DIMS. The text exercise adds a section line and text to the section view.

Adding a Section Line and Text

The finished drawing has a section line and section text. Use the exercise sequence below to add these to the drawing now.

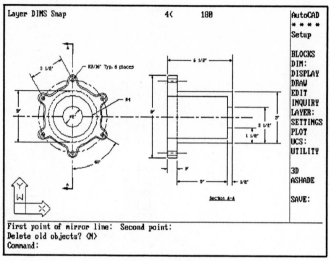

Section Lines and Text Added to Mockdim

Adding Section Lines and Text

Command: **ZOOM**	Zoom All.
Command: **SNAP**	Set snap to 1/4".

Command: **PLINE**   Start by drawing the section line.
From point: Pick absolute point 9,6.
Arc/Close/Halfwidth/Length/Undo/Width/<Endpoint of line>: **W**
Starting width <0>: **<RETURN>**
Ending width <0>: **.25**
Arc/Close/Halfwidth/Length/Undo/Width/<Endpoint of line>:   Pick polar point
                                                            @1/2<0.

Arc/Close/Halfwidth/Length/Undo/Width/<Endpoint of line>: **W**
Starting width <1/4>: **1/16**
Ending width <1/16>: **<RETURN>**
Arc/Close/Halfwidth/Length/Undo/Width/<Endpoint of line>:   Pick polar point
                                                            @1/2<0.

Arc/Close/Halfwidth/Length/Undo/Width/<Endpoint of line>:   Pick polar point
                                                            @1<90.

Arc/Close/Halfwidth/Length/Undo/Width/<Endpoint of line>: **<RETURN>**

Command: **DTEXT**   Now label the polyline and section view.
Start point or Align/Center/Fit/Middle/Right/Style: **C**
Center point: Pick absolute point 9-1/2,6-1/4.
Height <13/64>: **.25**
Rotation angle <0>: **<RETURN>**
Text: **A**
Pick absolute point 25,5.

Text: **%%USection A-A**	The %%U underlines the text.
Text: **<RETURN>**	
Command: **SETVAR**	Set MIRRTEXT to 0.
Command: **MIRROR**	Use mirror to complete the section line.
Select objects:	Select the polyline and text "A."
2 found.	
Select objects: **<RETURN>**	
First point of mirror line:	Pick absolute point 15,13.
Second point:	Pick polar point @4<180.
Delete old objects? <N> **<RETURN>**	

Adding Hatching to Mockdim

If you are a stickler for detail, you can add hatching to the section view. The following screen shot shows the hatched view. We will leave the details to you.

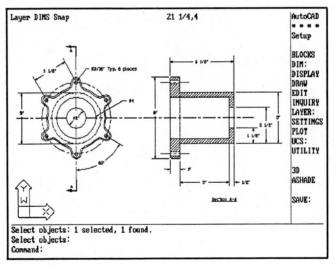

Hatched Section View

Inserting a Border and Title Block Drawing

Both the Mockdim drawing and the Border drawing are scaled for a 17" x 11" sheet when they are output. Combining them is simple. You insert the Border drawing into the Mockdim drawing. Use Mockdim's drawing plot scale of 2 as your insertion scale factor. Here is the sequence.

Inserting a Border and Title Block Into a Drawing

```
Command: INSERT
Block name (or ?): BDR17-11
Insertion point: 0,0
X scale factor <1> / Corner / XYZ: 2
Y scale factor (default=X): <RETURN>
Rotation angle <0>: <RETURN>
```

If all went well, you should have a finished drawing like the one shown below. Save your drawing, you will use it later in Part Two when we take up serious plotting.

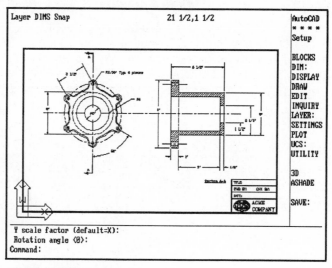

Finished Mockdim Drawing

Saving the Finished Mockdim Drawing

```
Command: END                Save for future use.
```

Since dimensioning occupies six menu pages, we can only point to some of the additional options and controls that you can explore. Use these last few pages as an idea sheet to help you tailor your dimensions to your needs.

Alternative Text for Dimensioning

In the dimensioning exercises, you took advantage of AutoCAD's semi-automatic dimensioning. This means that you let AutoCAD make (fairly good) assumptions about where to put the dimensioning elements. In some cases, you overrode these assumptions and gave AutoCAD more specific, manual locations.

But in most cases, you accepted AutoCAD's measurements as the default values to be put in the text portion of the dimensioning detail. There will be many times when you want numbers or text different from the default. Here are some options to explore.

Dimensioning Text Prefixes and Suffixes

You can override AutoCAD's <default> dimension text either by using the space bar followed by a <RETURN> to put in blank dimensioning text or by typing your own text and a <RETURN>. AutoCAD will use your text in place of the default text.

You can customize the dimension text by adding a suffix, prefix or both, surrounding AutoCAD's <default> dimension text. To do this, you simply type your custom characters before or after a < >, at the dimension measurement text prompt. You also can define an automatic suffix, as you did in the associative dimensioning exercise, setting DIMPOST to any text character(s) you like. Set it to a period . to clear the suffix. You can embellish the default numbers with a suffix or prefix like "cm" or "fathoms," or place your own numbers or text like "3 at 6'-4" = 19'-0"." Here are some alternative text examples.

Alternative Text Examples

When AutoCAD offers:	Type this	To get this
Dimension text <2.5000>:	**<SPACE>**	
Dimension text <2.5000>:	**Not important**	Not important
Dimension text <2.5000>:	**about <>**	about 2.5000
Dimension text <2.5000>:	**roughly <>"**	roughly 2.5000"

Using a Standard Dimension Multiplier

Normally, AutoCAD uses the units settings and actual distances you set up when you draw entities to calculate dimensions. If these units are not the lengths you want shown in dimensioning, you can apply a standard multiplier to alter the default AutoCAD calculations. You might use this to inset a scaled-down or metric detail.

To get AutoCAD to multiply all linear <default> dimensioning measurements by a standard factor, set DIMLFAC in Dim Vars. When DIMLFAC is non-zero, AutoCAD uses the factor as a multiplier before presenting you with a <default> text to use. DIMLFAC has no effect on angular dimensioning. For example, replace the default of <7.05"> with the metric equivalent (17.907cm) by multiplying the default by 2.54. To do this, set DIMLFAC to 2.54, DIMPOST to cm, and set your units to decimal.

Using Two Measurement Systems at the Same Time

To get AutoCAD to display alternative dimension text strings on a dimension line, set DIMALT on. When you do, AutoCAD formats the dimension like "number [alternate number]" on the dimension line.

The first number is the standard dimension measurement (multiplied by DIMLFAC if it is non-zero). The alternate number, shown in [brackets], is the first number multiplied by DIMALTF (dim alternative factor). The alternate number of decimals is set by DIMALTD (dim alternative decimals). The <default> for DIMALTF is 25.4, the number of millimeters in an inch. The <default> for DIMALTD is 2 decimal places.

Use the AutoCAD defaults and an alternate form at the same time. For example, have the text line read 7.05" (17.907cm). To do this, set the Dim Vars, DIMAPOST to cm, set DIMALT on, and set DIMALTF to 2.54.

Customizing Dimension Arrows

If you want larger arrows (and the other dimension variables changed), change the DIMSCALE value. If you change your mind, you can also update any or all asodims to a new DIMSCALE.

➡ *NOTE: If you're working in architectural units with 1/4 inch as the smallest unit, don't be surprised to see DIMASZ (arrow size) displayed at 1/4 inch. The default DIMASZ arrow is really smaller. The 1/4-inch units cut-off overrides the arrow size and the smaller arrow size is rounded up for the units displayed, but the true size is drawn and plotted.*

In addition to controlling the size of AutoCAD's default arrowhead or tick length, you can create your own dimensioning arrowhead. If the Dim Vars called DIMBLK (dimension block) contains the name of a block, AutoCAD will use that block as your dimensioning arrowhead.

You create your custom arrow as a right arrow. AutoCAD will flip it 180 degrees for the left arrow (or rotate it for angular dimensions). Dimension blocks can be any shape you want. A few examples are shown in the DIMBLKS Examples illustration.

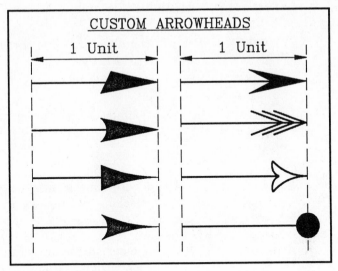

DIMBLKS Examples

➥ *TIP: Make your arrowhead one drawing unit wide. AutoCAD will draw the dimension line or leader up to one unit away from the extension line. If your arrowhead is not one unit wide, there will be a gap between the arrowhead and the dimension line. Point the arrow to the left and make the arrow's tip your block insertion base point. If you do not plan to use a filled arrow, include a line from the arrow tip to where your custom arrow will join the dimension line.*

If there is an effect that you want, it is more than likely that you can find a Dim Vars to do the job. Here are some comments on yet more Dim Vars. You will find the complete list at the start of the chapter.

Other Dimension Variables

DIMSE1 — Suppresses drawing of the first extension line. An On/Off toggle switch. Off means draw the line; On means omit the line.

DIMSE2 — Suppresses drawing of the second extension line.

DIMTIH — When On (Normal), it keeps text inside an extension line horizontal. When Off, the angle of the text takes the angle of the dimension line.

DIMTOH — Same as DIMTIH, but places text above line to keep text from interrupting the dimension line.

DIMLIM — Adds the DIMTP and DIMTM to the text instead of a ± listing.

DIMDLE — Extends the dimension line through tick marks by the DIMDLE amount when ticks are on.

DIMEXE — Sets how far the extension lines extend beyond the dimension line.

DIMRND — Rounds all dimension measurements to this setting.

DIMZIN — Offers several modes of control to suppress leading and trailing zeros in dimensions.

Sometimes when we work with dimensioning we get this mental picture of a multi-levered steam machine that resides inside AutoCAD. You get into dimensioning mode, crank it up, and start pulling Dim Var levers until you get what you want. As you become more proficient, you can make setup files to save dimensioning variables in a prototype drawing which presets the dimension variables before you start a new drawing. Here are some summary tips.

Summing Up With a Few Dimensioning Tips

Put your dimensions on a separate layer with a different color from the main body of your drawing. This way extension lines and dimensions stand out and are not mistaken for actual drawing elements. It helps to set up the dimension variables before you start dimensioning so you don't have to stop and set them in the middle of a Dim: command. Adjusting dimension text to the same height as your annotation text makes text changes and additions easier. Use a text style with a width factor of 0.75 to condense your dimension text into less space. Review your dimension variable settings frequently. It's easy to make changes and forget about them.

Use CONTINUE and BASELINE dimensions to save time by keeping track of extension line locations. Watch for appropriate places to save time with aligned and rotated dimensions. You can use more than one set of units for dimensioning by controlling DIMALT. You can display both metric and English units, for example. If you have created your drawing file in one scale and would like your dimensions to read a different scale, use DIMLFAC to multiply all AutoCAD drawing file units by a standard factor before including them in dimension text.

Attributes Are Next

You have had a chance to look at dimensioning an AutoCAD drawing. Next, you want to look at adding non-graphic intelligence, or as AutoCAD calls them, attributes.

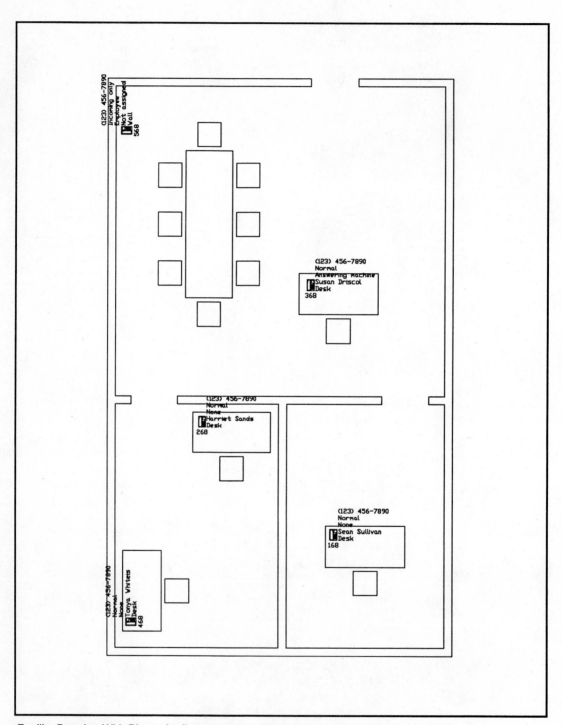

Facility Drawing With Phone Attributes

CHAPTER 12

Attributes and Data Extraction

ASSIGNING INFORMATION TO GRAPHIC ENTITIES IN YOUR DRAWINGS AND GETTING IT OUT AGAIN

Non-Graphic Intelligence

Every drawing example in the book so far has been based on a graphic entity or on a spatial relationship between graphic entities. There's more to creating a full picture than just these graphic entities and their spatial relationships. For example, in the Autotown subdivision map you created a few chapters back, you could have added "House Model Name," "House Size (Sq. Ft.)" and "House Exterior Finish" to each house block to give the drawing reader a little more information about the graphic blocks.

In this chapter, you will learn how to add text *attributes* to drawing entities to give these entities a richer vocabulary in communicating drawing information, and you will learn how to extract this data in report form. Just think of the convenience of tagging entities with attributes. You can extract automatic bills of materials, schedules, and other tabular lists of data, or you can view the information in graphic form. You don't need to clutter your drawing with attribute data you don't want to display. You can store it invisibly in the drawing file along with the graphic entities it describes until you're ready to turn it into a report.

How Attributes Work

You store an attribute, such as a name, in a block much the same way you store graphic entities in a block. Just as you create and carefully lay out graphic entities before inclusion in a block, you define attribute tags prior to creating an attribute-laden block.

An ATTRIBUTE must be part of a BLOCK.

—The Only Attribute Rule

Tagging Graphic Entities with Attributes

AutoCAD provides an attribute definition command called ATTDEF. You use ATTDEF to create attribute tags, defining how the attribute text will be stored. Then, you use the regular BLOCK command to group graphic entities *and* the attribute tags to form a block. In effect, you sweep the attributes into the same block definition.

Frequently, you will want to tag a group of graphic entities that already forms a block. For example, if you design printed circuit boards, you may want to assign labels to an integrated circuit (IC) chip by labeling manufacturer, pin assignment, and clock speed information. If you're a facilities management planner, you may want to label a workstation with an employee's name, title, department, phone number, and desk description. The chances are the employee workstation (or IC chip for the PC board) is already stored as a block. In such cases, you form a new (nested) block by including the attribute tags and the original block in a new block definition.

After you form an attribute block, you insert it into your drawing using the standard INSERT command. You control attribute display and attribute editing with three additional commands: ATTDISP controls visibility of attribute text in the drawing; ATTEDIT lets you change attribute text once it has been inserted in your drawing; and ATTEXT extracts attribute text and block information that can be formed into a report. In addition, there is a dialogue box, DDATTE, that you can access to edit attributes.

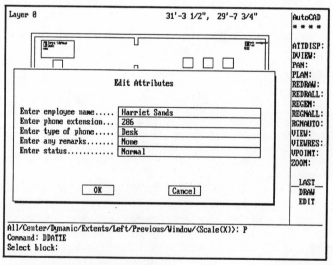

Attribute Dialogue Box DDATTE

The Attribute Toolkit

You will find the attribute commands scattered throughout different screen menus. ATTDEF is on the [BLOCKS] screen menu, ATTDISP is on the [DISPLAY] menu, ATTEDIT and DDATTE are on the [EDIT] menu, and ATTEXT is on the [UTILITY] menu. These commands are easy to find because they are usually the first or second item on the menu page.

Setup for Attributes

Facility management drawings commonly employ attributes. In this chapter, imagine that you are working in an office complex of the Acme Tool Co. One of your job responsibilities is to maintain drawings and produce reports on the equipment in the office. This equipment includes phones, copiers, fax machines, and computers. Each piece of equipment in the office has information, like an identification number and name assignment, that is stored in a drawing with attributes. Your drawing-for-the-day is to show the phone equipment for a small section of the office complex, and to extract a phone report. Here is the type of information that you will store and extract.

Target Phone Report for Acme Tool Co.

Name	Number	Ext	Type	Status	Remarks
Not Assigned	(123) 456-7890	586	Wall	In only	Employee
Tonya Whiteis	(123) 456-7890	486	Desk	Normal	None
Susan Driscoll	(123) 456-7890	386	Desk	Normal	Ans.Mach.
Harriet Sands	(123) 456-7890	286	Desk	Normal	None
Shawn Sullivan	(123) 456-7890	186	Desk	Normal	None

In this chapter, you will be more concerned with manipulating the attribute text associated with the graphics than with manipulating the graphic entities. But you still need a drawing. Create a new drawing called OFFICE. This drawing uses architectural units. The drawing scale factor is 24 for a scale of 1/2" = 1'-0", sized to plot on a 36" x 24" sheet.

If you are using the IA DISK, set OFFICE.DWG equal to CHAP-12.DWG to begin your drawing. Your disk drawing contains the basic office layout drawing. You also will find a graphic block drawing called PHN-BLK.DWG, and a text file called PHONE.TXT that you will use in the data report. After you load your office drawing, check your drawing settings against the table shown below.

If you are not using the disk, you need to create the office drawing, including drawing the simple floor plan. You also need to create the phone icon block, PHN-BLK, before you begin your attribute definitions.

Setting Up the Office Drawing

       Enter selection: **1**   Begin a NEW drawing called OFFICE=CHAP-12.

       Enter selection: **1**   Begin a NEW drawing called OFFICE.

Check to see that your drawing settings are the same as those shown in the settings table below.

COORDS	GRID	FILL	ORTHO	SNAP	UCSICON
ON	12	Off	ON	.25	OR

UNITS	Set UNITS to 4 Architectural.		
	Default the other Units settings.		
LIMITS	Set LIMITS from 0,0 to 72',48'		
ZOOM	Zoom All.		
VIEW	Save view as A.		

Layer name	State	Color	Linetype
0	Current	7 (white)	CONTINUOUS
PLAN	On	3 (green)	CONTINUOUS
DATA	On	7 (white)	CONTINUOUS

Office Drawing Settings

Your current layer is layer 0. If you have the disk drawing, your screen will show the following floor plan drawing.

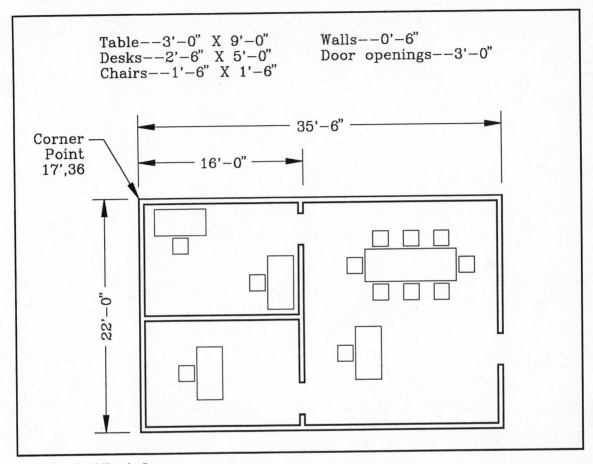

Table--3'-0" X 9'-0"   Walls--0'-6"
Desks--2'-6" X 5'-0"   Door openings--3'-0"
Chairs--1'-6" X 1'-6"

35'-6"

Corner
Point
17',36

16'-0"

22'-0"

Floor Plan for Office Attributes

If you need to create the drawing, change your layer to PLAN, and use the dimensions given in the illustration to draw the plan.

Creating the Office Floor Plan

 You already have the floor plan. Continue reading exercise.

 Complete the floor plan in this exercise.

Command: **LAYER**   Set layer PLAN current.
Command: **PLINE**   Draw walls with polylines.
Command: **SOLID**   Draw table and chair symbols.

If you don't have the phone icon, you need to create it. If you are using the disk, insert *PHN-BLK. After you have the phone icon, set your UCS at the lower left corner. This will be your block insertion base point.

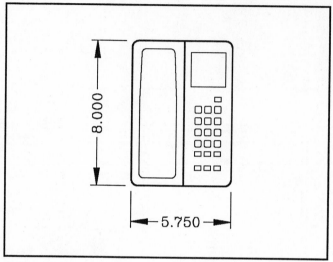

Phone Icon

Creating the Phone Block

Command: **LAYER**   Set layer 0 current, turn layer PLAN off.
Command: **ZOOM**   Zoom center with a height of 32".

    Insert ***PHN-BLK**

    Draw phone as shown in phone illustration.

Command: **UCS**   Use Origin to put origin at lower left corner of phone.

Your screen should look like the following Phone Icon screen shot. You are ready for attributes.

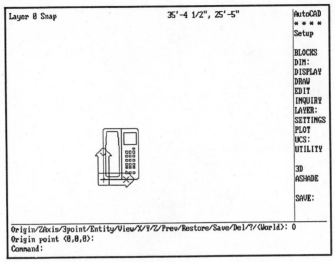

```
Layer 0 Snap                    35'-4 1/2", 25'-5"          AutoCAD
                                                            * * * *
                                                            Setup

                                                            BLOCKS
                                                            DIM:
                                                            DISPLAY
                                                            DRAW
                                                            EDIT
                                                            INQUIRY
                                                            LAYER:
                                                            SETTINGS
                                                            PLOT
                                                            UCS:
                                                            UTILITY

                                                            3D
                                                            ASHADE

                                                            SAVE:


Origin/ZAxis/3point/Entity/View/X/Y/Z/Prev/Restore/Save/Del/?/<World>: 0
Origin point <0,0,0>:
Command:
```

Phone Icon Ready for Attributes

How the Attribute Exercises Are Organized

The attribute exercises are straightforward. In sequence, we will show you how to define the phone attributes, how to block and insert the phone-with-attributes, and how to display and edit the attributes once they are in the drawing. Finally, we will show you how to extract the data in a text report.

Using the ATTDEF Command to Define Attributes

To create an attribute, you use the ATTDEF command. Attributes have several definition modes. Start your definitions by defining the EXTENSION attribute for the phone. We have made the EXTENSION attribute a variable attribute. Variable simply means that the attribute value is just a set of *blanks* waiting for text. This is the normal (default) mode.

Variable Attributes

In a variable attribute, you can define a text value to be offered as a default when you later insert the phone block into the drawing file. In addition, you need to set text parameters to show how the attribute will appear on the screen (and in the drawing file). All of this sounds more complicated than it really is. Type the responses shown in the exercise. Then, look at the modes discussion following the exercise.

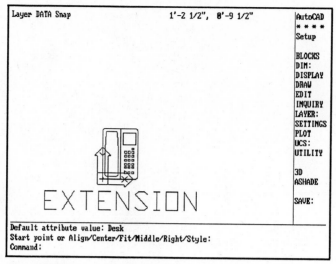

```
Layer DATA Snap                    1'-2 1/2",  0'-9 1/2"        AutoCAD
                                                               * * * *
                                                               Setup

                                                               BLOCKS
                                                               DIM:
                                                               DISPLAY
                                                               DRAW
                                                               EDIT
                                                                INQUIRY
                                                               LAYER:
                                                               SETTINGS
                                                               PLOT
                                                               UCS:
                                                               UTILITY

                                                               3D
                                                               ASHADE

                                                               SAVE:

       EXTENSION

Default attribute value: Desk
Start point or Align/Center/Fit/Middle/Right/Style:
Command:
```

Phone With Extension Attribute

Using ATTDEF to Define a Variable

```
Command: ATTDEF                           The extension attribute is to be Verified.
Attribute modes -- Invisible:N  Constant:N  Verify:N  Preset:N
Enter (ICVP) to change, RETURN when done: V          Turn Verify on.
Attribute modes -- Invisible:N  Constant:N  Verify:Y  Preset:N
Enter (ICVP) to change, RETURN when done: <RETURN>
Attribute tag: EXTENSION
Attribute prompt: Enter phone extension...
Default attribute value: <RETURN>
Start point or Align/Center/Fit/Middle/Right/Style: C
Center point: 2.875,-5                    Centered under the phone.
Height <0'-0 3/16">: 3                    This will create 1/8" high text at 1/2"=1'-0".
Rotation angle <0>: <RETURN>
```

Your screen should show the extension attribute tag centered under the phone.

Before AutoCAD asks how you want to control the appearance of the attribute text, it prompts you for several attribute modes. These modes control attribute visibility and treatment on block insertion.

Attribute Modes

Invisible — turns attribute visibility off. Invisible mode is useful when you want to store a lot of data in the drawing, but you don't want to display or plot all the data.

Constant — creates attributes with a fixed text value. Constant mode is helpful when you want to write boilerplate notes with attribute text. You can't edit a constant attribute once it is inserted as a block without redefining the block.

Verify — lets you check variable attribute text before inserting it into the drawing file. If an attribute has the Verify mode, AutoCAD will display the attribute text on the prompt line after you type it. AutoCAD will wait for a <RETURN> before inserting the text. You can see what you've typed, check for errors, and correct them before the attribute is inserted.

Preset — lets you create attributes that automatically accept their default text value. When the block is inserted, preset attribute values are not requested. Preset values are entered like constant attributes. However, you can edit preset attributes with the ATTEDIT command.

Attributes can be Constant, Invisible, Preset or Verified at the same time, or in any combination. To change one of the ATTDEF modes, you simply type **I**, **C**, **V**, or **P** followed by a <RETURN>. AutoCAD will redisplay the mode's prompt with a Y (for Yes!) next to the item. Their last settings will be saved as new default modes for ATTDEF.

How to Create Attribute Tags

You define your attribute by giving it a tag name, an optional prompt, and an optional default text value. The default text value is what goes in the drawing, unless you change the value when you insert the attribute block. After you define the default value, you set the text location, style, alignment, height, and angle.

Attribute Tag — No Blanks Allowed

Each attribute has a tag. "Name," "Employee-No.," "Extension," and "Part-Numbers" are all valid tags. Think of the tag as the name of the text that you want to insert as an attribute (like block names). The only restriction on tag names is that they cannot include blanks. Use a hyphen in place of a blank (like Employee-No.) to separate the name tag elements. AutoCAD translates all tags into upper case letters whether you type CAPS or not.

Attribute Prompt

In addition to naming the attribute tag, you can assign an instructional prompt to the tag. You use this prompt at insertion time. For example, you might assign the "Enter the Part Number of this widget here" to the tag name, "Part-Numbers."

You can use anything you want for prompts. "Gimme the number now, Dummy" is as valid as "Would you please enter the number here...." If you feel that the attribute tag name says it all, you don't need to enter the added prompt. The attribute tag name is the <default> prompt, if you do not enter another prompt. Enter a <RETURN> to default the attribute prompt.

Default Attribute Values

When you insert the attribute block in the drawing, you enter the attribute text value that will appear in the drawing. When you define the attribute, AutoCAD asks you for a default text value for what the attribute will say. Useful <defaults> for variable attributes are "Not Yet Filled In" or "XXX.NN". Remember, these will show up in the drawing if you accept the <default> with a <RETURN> instead of filling in the attribute at the time of insertion. Constant and preset attributes insert automatically, without showing you their default values.

Attributes Display Just Like Text

After assigning the attribute value, AutoCAD prompts you for information about how to display attribute text and store it in the drawing file. This series of AutoCAD prompts is identical to the standard text prompts. Once you've set all the text parameters, AutoCAD will display the attribute tag on the screen just like it does with text.

Creating a Block With Many Attributes

You have defined the extension attribute as a variable attribute. Before you build the complete phone block, you need to analyze the other attribute data types that you will include in your phone report. Here's another look at the Phone Report as a guide to the attribute definitions that follow.

Target Phone Report

Name	Number	Ext	Type	Status	Remarks
Not Assigned	(123) 456-7890	586	Wall	In only	Employee
Tonya Whiteis	(123) 456-7890	486	Desk	Normal	None
Susan Driscoll	(123) 456-7890	386	Desk	Normal	Ans.Mach.
Harriet Sands	(123) 456-7890	286	Desk	Normal	None
Shawn Sullivan	(123) 456-7890	186	Desk	Normal	None

Since all of the phones have the same number, the number attribute is an obvious pick as a Constant attribute with the value "(123) 456-7890." The rest of the attribute tags have different values, so make them Variable. The status and remarks attributes are likely to change infrequently so define them as Preset to accept their defaults and avoid the prompt on insertion.

The extension, phone type, and the name of the employee seem important, so keep them visible. But the phone number, status and remarks do not seem important enough to display in the drawing. Define them as Invisible and just use the data for reports.

Creating the Rest of the Attributes

Create the rest of the attributes in the following exercise. Change your layer to DATA. This will give you the option of displaying or plotting the drawings with only the extension (on the layer of insertion) visible, or of including the type and name on layer DATA.

Look for the different attribute modes, tags, and <defaults> in the exercise sequence. Notice that you can restart ATTDEF to get a second line of text just below the first. Answer all the attribute-specific prompts first. When the Start point . . .: prompt appears, AutoCAD will highlight the last attribute-defined line on the screen. If you simply hit a <RETURN>, the current ATTDEF will go immediately under the old one.

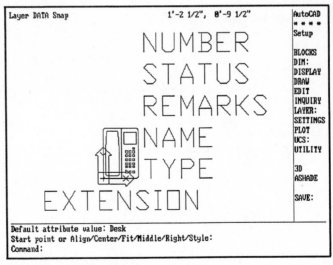

Phone With All Attributes

Using ATTDEF to Define Invisible, Constant, Verify, and Preset Attributes

```
Command: LAYER              Set layer DATA current.

Command: ATTDEF             The NUMBER attribute is Constant and Invisible.
Attribute modes -- Invisible:N  Constant:N  Verify:Y  Preset:N
Enter (ICVP) to change, RETURN when done: V         Turn Verify off.
Attribute modes -- Invisible:N  Constant:N  Verify:N  Preset:N
Enter (ICVP) to change, RETURN when done: I         Turn Invisible on.
Attribute modes -- Invisible:Y  Constant:N  Verify:N  Preset:N
Enter (ICVP) to change, RETURN when done: C         Turn Constant on.
Attribute modes -- Invisible:Y  Constant:Y  Verify:N  Preset:N
Enter (ICVP) to change, RETURN when done: <RETURN>
Attribute tag: NUMBER
Attribute value: (123) 456-7890
Start point or Align/Center/Fit/Middle/Right/Style: 6.75,20
Height <0'-3">: <RETURN>
Rotation angle <0>: <RETURN>

Command: <RETURN>
ATTDEF                      The STATUS attribute is Invisible and Preset.
Attribute modes -- Invisible:Y  Constant:Y  Verify:N  Preset:N
Enter (ICVP) to change, RETURN when done: C         Turn Constant off.
Attribute modes -- Invisible:Y  Constant:N  Verify:N  Preset:N
Enter (ICVP) to change, RETURN when done: P         Turn Preset on.
Attribute modes -- Invisible:Y  Constant:N  Verify:N  Preset:Y
Enter (ICVP) to change, RETURN when done: <RETURN>
Attribute tag: STATUS
Attribute prompt: Enter status...
Default attribute value: Normal
Start point or Align/Center/Fit/Middle/Right/Style: <RETURN>

Command: <RETURN>
ATTDEF                      The REMARKS attribute is also Invisible and Preset.
Attribute modes -- Invisible:Y  Constant:N  Verify:N  Preset:Y
Enter (ICVP) to change, RETURN when done: <RETURN>
Attribute tag: REMARKS
Attribute prompt: Enter any remarks...
Default attribute value: None
Start point or Align/Center/Fit/Middle/Right/Style: <RETURN>

Command: <RETURN>
ATTDEF                      The NAME attribute is normal.
Attribute modes -- Invisible:Y  Constant:N  Verify:N  Preset:Y
Enter (ICVP) to change, RETURN when done: I         Turn Invisible off.
Attribute modes -- Invisible:N  Constant:N  Verify:N  Preset:Y
Enter (ICVP) to change, RETURN when done: P         Turn Preset off.
Attribute modes -- Invisible:N  Constant:N  Verify:N  Preset:N
Enter (ICVP) to change, RETURN when done: <RETURN>
```

```
Attribute tag: NAME
Attribute prompt: Enter employee name...
Default attribute value: Not assigned
Start point or Align/Center/Fit/Middle/Right/Style: <RETURN>

Command: <RETURN>
ATTDEF                      The TYPE attribute is normal.
Attribute modes -- Invisible:N  Constant:N  Verify:N  Preset:N
Enter (ICVP) to change, RETURN when done: <RETURN>
Attribute tag: TYPE
Attribute prompt: Enter type of phone...
Default attribute value: Desk
Start point or Align/Center/Fit/Middle/Right/Style: <RETURN>

Command: ZOOM                Zoom extents in order to see everything.
```

Your screen should now show all six attribute tags even though some attributes will be Invisible when you block the phone.

Using BLOCK to Group Graphics and Attributes Into a Block

The next step is to group all the graphic (phone) and nongraphic (defined attributes) entities together using the BLOCK command. Once the attributes are blocked, you cannot edit the definitions without a block redefinition. Right now you can edit the attribute definitions with the CHANGE command, just as you would strings of text on the screen. You also can erase and redefine the attributes with ATTDEF if you need to make major changes.

Block your phone, using the lower left corner as an insertion base point. The order by which you select attributes is *important* because the selection order controls the prompting order when you insert the block. Call the block PHONE. Here is the exercise sequence.

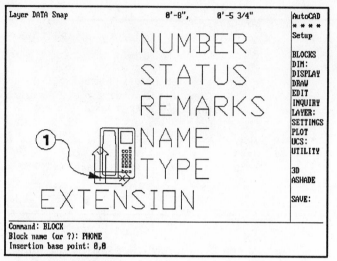

Insert Point for Phone

Using BLOCK to Group Graphics and Attributes Into a Block

```
Command: BLOCK
Block name: PHONE
Insertion base point: 0,0          Pick the UCS point of origin at ①.
Select objects:                    Pick the NAME attribute first.
Select objects:                    Pick the EXTENSION attribute.
Select objects:                    Pick the TYPE attribute.
Select objects:                    Pick the NUMBER attribute.
Select objects:                    Pick the STATUS attribute.
Select objects:                    Pick the REMARKS attribute.
Select objects:                    Pick entities for the Phone.
Select objects: <RETURN>
147 found                          All the graphic elements and attributes tags disappear just
                                   as in normal block creation.

Command: ZOOM                      Zoom All.
```

Congratulations! You have just formatted your first attribute-laden block! There is nothing special about attribute block creation, other than remembering to order your attribute pick sequence the way you want it. You can BLOCK, INSERT, WBLOCK, and redefine an attribute block the same way you would a normal block.

Using INSERT to Insert Attribute Blocks

Put the phones in the offices by inserting them at the appropriate locations in the floor plan. Start by inserting the employee phone on the wall in the conference room on the right.

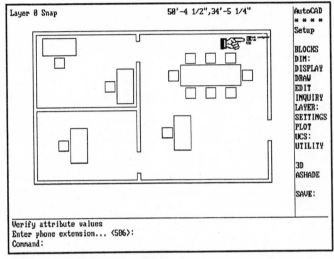

 Inserted Employee Phone   *Detail of Phone*

Using INSERT to Insert Attribute Blocks

```
Command: LAYER                  Set layer 0 current, turn layer PLAN on.
Command: UCS                    Set UCS to world.
Command: UCSICON                Turn icon off.

Command: INSERT                           Start by inserting the employee phone.
Block name: <Offices>: PHONE
Insertion point:                          Upper right corner of conference room.
X scale factor <1> / Corner / XYZ: <RETURN>
Y scale factor <default=X>: <RETURN>
Rotation angle <0>: <RETURN>
Enter Attribute values
Enter employee name...<Not assigned>: <RETURN>
Enter phone extension...: 586
Enter type of phone...<Desk>: Wall
Verify attribute values
Enter phone extension...<586>: <RETURN>
```

The PHONE block will appear on the screen with all the attributes in their correct positions. The NUMBER, STATUS and REMARKS attributes will remain Invisible. They are stored in the correct position, but not displayed. If you turn layer DATA off, you will see that only the phone icon and the extension attribute are visible.

Repeat the insertion process for the next three phones using the following data and the illustration for phone location and rotation.

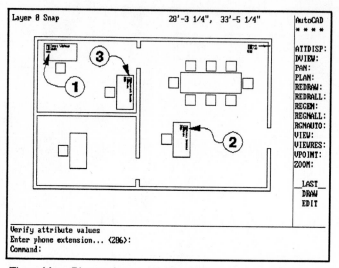

Three More Phones Inserted in the Office

Using INSERT to Insert Three More Attribute Phones

		Name	Ext	Type
Command: **INSERT** at ①		Tonya Whiteis	486	Desk
Command: **INSERT** at ②		Susan Driscoll	386	Desk
Command: **INSERT** at ③		Harriet Sands	286	Desk

Using the Attribute Dialogue Box

If your display supports the AUI, you can take advantage of the DDATTE dialogue box to do your inserts. Using the dialogue box has the advantage that you can edit or change the defaults in any order that you want, including the preset attributes. The dialogue box will display all attribute prompts and defaults except those defined as Constant.

Try inserting the last phone (Shawn Sullivan) using the attribute dialogue box. His phone goes on the desk in the lower left office. Use a system variable called ATTDIA to enable automatic use of the dialogue box. Set this variable to 0. After you insert the block, toggle the dialogue box back off. If your display does not support the AUI, insert the last phone the same way you did in the previous exercise.

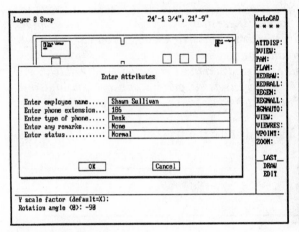

The DDATTE Dialogue Box

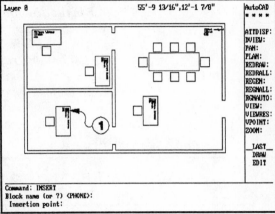

Phone Inserted With Dialogue Box

Using the Attribute Dialogue Box to Insert an Attribute Block

```
Command: SETVAR
Variable name or ?: ATTDIA
New value for ATTDIA <0>: 1
```

Command: **INSERT**   Insert the PHONE block at ①.

The dialog box automatically displays to accept attribute values.

Type in the following data and select [**OK**]:
       Name: **Shawn Sullivan**
       Ext: **186**
       Type: **Desk**

Command: **SETVAR**   Set ATTDIA off by setting the value back to 0.

Using the dialogue box is easier than using the standard insertion prompts. Later, we will show you how to use the dialogue box to change the preset values of an inserted attribute.

➥ *TIP: You also can suppress attribute prompting by setting the ATTREQ system variable to 0. This will force block insertion to accept all the attribute defaults, but will allow normal attribute editing at a later time. This makes block insertions act like all attributes are Preset.*

➥ *TIP: If you use the DDATTE dialogue box, keep your attribute prompts to less than 24 characters to avoid truncating them.*

➥ *TIP: It is possible to form an attribute block that has no graphic entities in it. You simply create a block with attributes and insert the block in the drawing file. For these non-graphic attribute blocks, place the attribute data directly at the insertion point. You can use these non-graphic blocks to automate drawing text entry, and to associate invisible or non-graphic information in a drawing. Be sure at least one attribute has a value when inserted, or you can get an invisible, unselectable block of attributes containing only spaces.*

At this point, your screen should show the floor plan with all five phone locations.

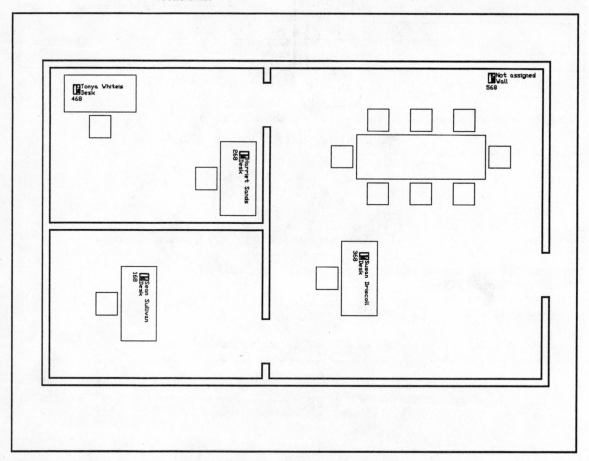

Floor Plan Showing Five Phone Locations

Using ATTDISP to Control Attribute Display Visibility

You can control an attribute's visibility by using the ATTDISP (ATTribute DISPlay) command. ATTDISP temporarily reverses visibility, turning Invisible attributes on, or Visible attributes off. To return to the default condition that was set by the ATTDEF command, set ATTDISP to **N** for normal.

Use ATTDISP to turn all the attributes off, back to normal, then on. On will force all the attributes to display. When the screen is regenerated, you'll see how you have stored the status, remarks and data attributes.

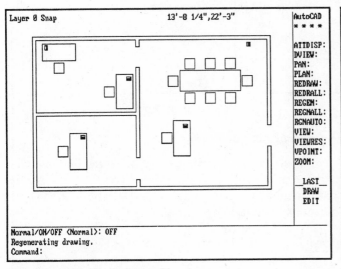

Floor Plan With No Attributes Showing

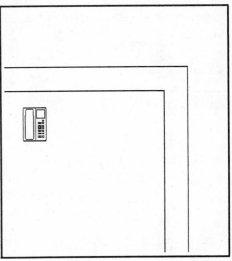

Detail of Wall Phone

Using ATTDISP to Control Attribute Visibility

```
Command: ATTDISP
Normal/ON/OFF <Normal>: OFF
Regenerating drawing.
```
Screen regens, turning off all attributes.

```
Command: <RETURN>
ATTDISP Normal/ON/OFF <Off>: N
Regenerating drawing.
```
Now set it back to Normal.

Back to normal display.

```
Command: <RETURN>
ATTDISP Normal/ON/OFF <Normal>: ON
Regenerating drawing.
```
Now set it to On.

Screen regens, showing all invisible attributes.

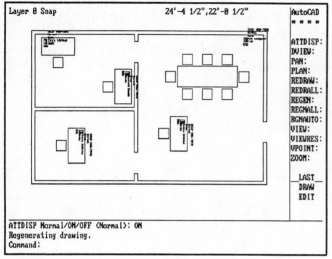

Floor Plan With All Attributes Showing

Detail of Wall Phone

Using Layers to Control Attribute Display

You can extend your control of attribute visibility by putting your attribute data on different layers, then using your normal layer visibility controls to turn data on and off. Insert or define the attribute on the layer that you would normally keep it on.

Attribute Editing With ATTEDIT

Well as sure as the sun rises, you can bet there will be changes in the old phone layout. No sooner is the layout complete, when you find out that Shawn really spells his name Sean. What's needed is a new drawing. What do you do? Edit the attribute, of course!

The ATTEDIT (ATTribute EDIT) command is the change command for attributes. Using ATTEDIT, you form a selection set for editing the attributes. ATTEDIT provides additional filters to help you select attributes. (We will explore these in more detail.) For now, try a simple pick selection to take care of Sean.

An attribute must be displayed in order to be edited. It can be set back to normal as soon as all the editing has been completed.

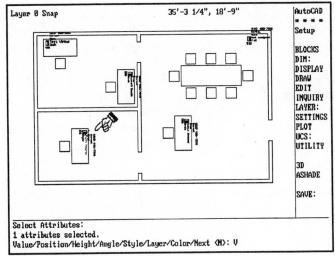

☞ *Selected Attribute With X*

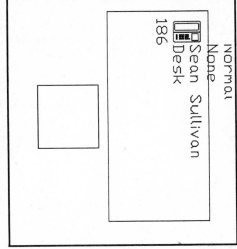

Detail of Corrected Attribute

Using ATTEDIT to Edit Individual Attributes

```
Command: ATTEDIT
Edit attributes one at a time? <Y>: <RETURN>
Block name specification <*>: <RETURN>
Attribute tag specification <*>: <RETURN>
Attribute value specification <*>: <RETURN>
Select Attributes:                          Pick the text string Shawn Sullivan
1 attributes selected.
Val/Pos/Hgt/Ang/Style/Lay/Clr/Nxt <N>: V
Change or Replace? <R>: C
String to change: Shawn
New string: Sean
Val/Pos/Hgt/Ang/Style/Lay/Clr/Nxt <N>: <RETURN>
```

Notice two nice features. First, an **X** appears on the screen adjacent to the attribute to be edited. Second, AutoCAD asks if you want to change part of the attribute text string or completely replace it. You changed part.

You can change much more than the text value when you edit attributes individually. Frequently, you will find that you have attributes overlapping graphic objects. For the invisible attributes, this may not be a concern. But the appearance of visible attributes will be important in your final drawing. You can use ATTEDIT to fine tune your attributes' appearance. You can change the text position and angle, or for that matter, text style, height, layer and color.

Making Global Attribute Edits With ATTEDIT

Taking care of Sean was a simple change. But what about changing 86 in all extensions to 68? Or, changing 86 to 68 only on the Employee Phone?

Your drawing of the office plan only has five phones; individually picking each attribute for editing would not be a problem. But a whole office complex could have five hundred phones. Think about editing five hundred phones! You could gather all the tags named EXTENSION and do the replacement in one window. Or could you? You could if you were able to tell AutoCAD exactly which characters in the EXTENSION attribute you wanted to edit. In other words, you need to set up a selection set filled with just the precise group. Regular selection set techniques are just too imprecise for this type of selection.

Using Wildcards to Selectively Edit Attributes

Rather than trying to individually pick attributes from the screen, you can use a combination of wildcard filters and standard selection set options to select your attributes. Here are some common scenarios.

- Select all attributes within blocks with a name you specify, or use * to select all blocks.

- Select all attributes matching a tag name you specify, or use * to select all tag names.

- Select all attributes matching a specified value, or all values using *.

- Further narrow the selection process by picking an individual attribute object, or Window, Last, Crossing, or BOX.

- Any and all combinations of these selections.

You can narrow the field of attributes to edit by narrowing the selection specification from the wildcard everything (*) to some specific value, or use the wildcard (?) to specify a range.

Using Tag Selection to Edit Attributes

Once you have collected your attributes for editing, AutoCAD prompts you to edit them. If you ask for individual editing (the default), AutoCAD prompts for your changes one at a time. As you have seen, you can tell which attribute you are editing by looking for the highlighting or X on the screen.

Try to tap some of AutoCAD's attribute-editing power by changing the wall phone status from "Normal" to "Incoming only." Narrow your selection by specifying the STATUS attribute to edit, then select all five workstations with a window. Watch the screen to know which attribute AutoCAD wants you to edit. Then, use the <N>, (Next default), to skip to the wall phone status. Change the value of the wall phone status. Use the <N> to skip past the rest, or terminate ATTEDIT with a <^C>. The exercise will guide you through the prompt sequence.

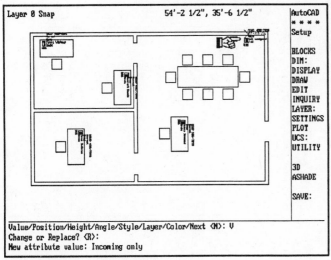

☞ *Editing the Wall Phone by its Tag*   *Detail of Wall Phone*

Using an Attribute Tag to Specify an Attribute Edit

```
Command: ATTEDIT
Edit attributes one at a time? <Y> <RETURN>
Block name specification <*>: <RETURN>
Attribute tag specification <*>: STATUS
Attribute value specification <*>:<RETURN>
Select Attributes: W
First corner:
Other corner:                                      Place window around all phones.
5 attributes selected.
Val/Pos/Hgt/Ang/Style/Lay/Clr/Nxt <N>: N           Use N to get to the wall phone.
Val/Pos/Hgt/Ang/Style/Lay/Clr/Nxt <N>: V
Change or Replace? <R> <RETURN>
New attribute value: Incoming only
Val/Pos/Hgt/Ang/Style/Lay/Clr/Nxt <N>: *cancel*    Terminate command with a <^C>.
```

The editing sequence above is convenient if you are making selective changes to many attributes. But if you have a change that applies to a large group of attributes, you can use a global selection.

Try a division-wide reorganization changing the last two digits in all the phone extensions from "86 " to "68." Use the default <*> wildcard and a window to get all your phone extensions. Here's the prompt sequence.

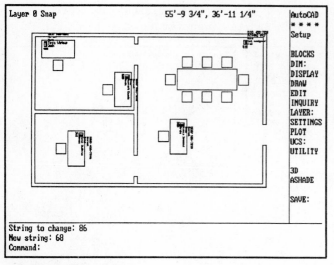

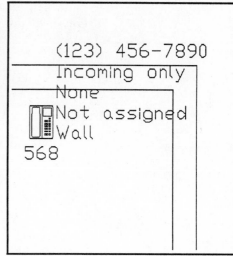

Extensions Edited Globally   *Detail of Wall Phone*

Using ATTEDIT for a Global Edit

```
Command: ATTEDIT
Edit attributes one at a time? <Y> N
Global edit of Attribute values.
Edit only Attributes visible on screen? <Y> <RETURN>
```

All the occurrences are on the screen, but it is nice to know that you have the option!

```
Block name specification <*>: <RETURN>
Attribute tag specification <*>: EXTENSION
Attribute value specification <*>: <RETURN>
Select Attribute: W               Use a window to collect all the phones.
5 attribute selected.            AutoCAD highlights the attributes.
String to change: 86
New string: 68
```

All your extensions should now end in 68. If your editing required adding a prefix to the attribute, you would just <RETURN> at the String to change: prompt, then change the text string.

Using the Attribute Dialogue Box to Edit Attributes

You can use the DDATTE dialogue box to edit attributes. It presents the same dialogue box that you used when you inserted the last phone block. You can only use the dialogue box to edit the text string values and you can only edit one block at a time. Try using the box to edit two Preset REMARKS attributes.

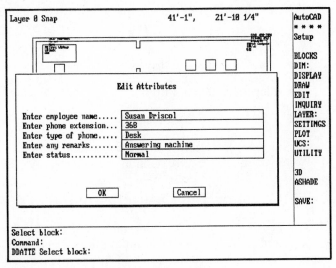

Editing Attributes With the Dialogue Box

Using DDATTE Dialogue Box to Edit Attributes

Command: **DDATTE**	Select the wall phone.
Select:	Change REMARKS from None to **Employee**.
Select: [OK]	
Command: **<RETURN>**	
DDATTE	Select Susan's phone.
Select:	Change REMARKS from None to **Answering machine**.
Select: [OK]	
Command: **ATTDISP**	Set back to Normal.

This is the last attribute editing exercise, so save your drawing. You will need it to extract the attribute data. And we are going to use this drawing later in Part Two on 3D by extruding it into a 3D office drawing.

Save and End the Office Drawing

Command: **END**   Save your work and exit AutoCAD.

Plotting the Office Drawing

If you want to see how attributes plot, try making a quick plot of your office plan. There are four possible ways to plot the drawing data:

■ Turn all the attributes off.

■ Plot the extension number, employee name and phone type (Normal).

■ Plot the extension number only (layer 0).

■ Turn all the attributes on.

The next step is to extract the phone data to format a phone report, something like a simple phone directory or part of an equipment report.

Using the ATTEXT Command to Extract Attributes

You use the ATTEXT command to extract your data. This command sounds like it represents some kind of text operation, but it stands for ATTribute EXTraction. ATTEXT provides a way to extract attribute information from the drawing file and print out that information in a text report.

Setting Up an Attribute Report

In setting up the office drawing, we listed the data for the employee names, status, remarks, type, and extension for each of the five phones in a simple tabular form. While our example shows a phone report, similar kinds of tables form the basis for bills of materials (BOM), listings, schedules, and specifications that regularly accompany professional drawings. These tables organize the attribute value data scattered around the drawing file.

AutoCAD currently provides three ways to extract attribute text from a drawing file and format it in a disk file. You can print these lists or operate on the data in other programs, like dBASE III or IV, Lotus 1-2-3, or your favorite word processor. You also can put the list into a table and bring it back into your drawing. The formats are templates that define how the data will be formatted.

ATTEXT Formats

CDF (Comma Delimited Format) — CDF is easy to use with BASIC programs or with dBASE's "APPEND FROM . . . DELIMITED" operation. (See the example below.)

SDF (Standard Data Format) — for FORTRAN, programs that read a dBASE "COPY . . . SDF" file, or a dBASE "APPEND FROM . . . SDF" operation. (See the example below.)

DXF (Drawing Interchange File) — a subset of AutoCAD's full Drawing Interchange File format that is used by many third party programs.

You can extract data in whatever format is suitable for your application. Many users (and vendors of third party software) now have applications built around AutoCAD using one or more of these data extraction interfaces.

Extracting Attribute Data with CDF or SDF

CDF creates a file that has commas separating the data fields in the attribute extraction. A simple example is.

```
CDF Format
    'Name1', 'Type1', 'Extension1'
    'Name2', 'Type2', 'Extension2'
     . . .
     . . .
     . . .
    'Name9', 'Type9', 'Extension9'
    'Name10', 'Type10', 'Extension10'
```

Formatting extract files gets down to the nitty-gritty placement of alphanumeric characters, commas, spaces, and other bits and bytes. In the CDF format, each data field is separated by a comma, and the spacing of the data field is dependent on the data width within the field. Name10 (in the example above) will take up more room than Name9.

The SDF format creates a file similar to CDF, but without commas and with a standard field length and spacing.

```
SDF Format
    Name1          Type1          Extension1
    Name2          Type2          Extension2
    . . .          . . .          . . .
    . . .          . . .          . . .
    Name9          Type9          Extension9
    Name10         Type10         Extension10
```

Here the data field length is standardized. It is pre-formatted to a standard value, regardless of the data value length. If the data exceeds the length, the data is truncated.

How to Create an Attribute Report Template File

Before you can extract attributes, AutoCAD needs a template file in order to create the SDF or CDF file. The template file is a format instruction list telling AutoCAD where to put what in the extract data file. The IA DISK contains a template file called PHONE.TXT. This file provides an SDF template for the phone data.

If you are using the disk, you can use this file to create the phone report. If you are not using the disk, you can create the file as an ASCII text file using a line editor or word processor. ATTEXT is touchy. Make sure you end the last line of your file with a <RETURN>. Also, make sure you do not have any extra spaces at the end of lines, or extra <RETURN>s after the last line of text.

If you don't feel like making the file, just read through the next two exercises and you will get the sense of how a report is formed.

Here is the PHONE.TXT file format for your example phone data. The template assumes that NAME comes first, TYPE second, and EXTENSION third. The NUMBER, STATUS, and REMARKS will not be included in the report.

Creating an SDF Template File

 Copy PHONE.TXT file from the disk and examine it.

 Use a text editor or word processor to create a plain ASCII file named PHONE.TXT with the following lines. Make sure you end the last line with a <RETURN>.

```
BL:NAME          C011000              Type BL:NAME, not the actual block name.
BL:X             N006002
DUMMY1           C002000
BL:Y             N006002
DUMMY2           C002000
NAME             C015000
TYPE             C008000
EXTENSION        N005000
```

If you look at the right column, you will easily recognize the formatting information. The first C or N says this is character or numeric information. The next three digits (011 in the BL:NAME line) tell how much room to leave for the data. The final three digits specify the number of decimal places for numeric data. The BL:X and BL:Y mean that you can extract the X,Y coordinate values for the block.

DUMMY1 and DUMMY2 only appear in the template file. They are not blocks or attribute definitions; they are used to provide space in the report. The dummy lines force a two-space blank between the X,Y coordinates (BL:X,BL:Y) and a two-space blank between the Y coordinate and the NAME, making the output easier to read.

Extracting the Data File

Once you have the template file, you can extract data for all the attributes, or just for selected attributes. If you have the PHONE.TXT file, get back into AutoCAD. Load your office drawing, and extract the attribute data into a file called PHN-DATA.

Using ATTEXT to Create an SDF Data File

Load AutoCAD to see the Main Menu.

```
Enter selection: 2        Edit an EXISTING drawing called OFFICE.


Command: ATTEXT
CDF, SDF, or DXF Attribute extract (or Entities) <C>: S
Template file: PHONE
Extract file name <OFFICE>: PHN-DATA
```

AutoCAD produced a PHN-DATA.TXT file on disk. If you had entered an E for entities, AutoCAD would have prompted for object selection to extract specific blocks and then reprompted for CDF, SDF, or DXF. The extracted SDF report file is shown in the SDF Report Example (below). You can examine the file by exiting AutoCAD, and opening the file with your text editor or word processor. Take a look at your data text file.

SDF Report Example

```
PHONE    588.00    414.00    Not Assigned     Wall    568
PHONE    226.00    409.75    Tonya Whiteis    Desk    468
PHONE    473.50    279.00    Susan Driscoll   Desk    368
PHONE    372.75    361.75    Harriet Sands    Desk    268
PHONE    289.75    261.00    Sean Sullivan    Desk    168
```

Notice the extracted data gives useful spatial information about this drawing as well as the attribute data. The X and Y data fields give the X and Y insertion points of each phone block. Your X,Y fields will vary from ours, depending on where you inserted the blocks. The PHONE column is set up to *dump* the name of the block acting as the attribute data source. The PHONE has character data (see the C in the template), and an 11-character print width.

The next two columns give the X and Y location of the block insertion point in numeric form (see N in the template). (Your data will vary from the example.) The X and Y data have 2 decimal places and the decimal point in a six-character print width. The other extracted attribute fields are in the last two columns, a character field and a numeric field. If an employee had an unusually long name, you can see that it would be truncated by the print width.

DXF, DXB and IGES Drawing Data

AutoCAD provides additional facilities for extracting spatial and graphic data from the drawing file. Block layers and block levels (for nested blocks, block rotation and scale) are extractable. These spatial attributes are useful for handing data off to engineering programs where the block orientation or relationship among drawing entities is as critical as the text or numeric data associated with the block.

DXF, AutoCAD's Drawing Interchange Format, is used in many third party enhancements and for drawing file exchange. You use the DXFOUT command to extract the DXF file from a drawing. An ATTEXT DXF includes block reference and attribute information only, but the DXFOUT command exports either the full drawing file or selected entities. A full DXFOUT creates a complete ASCII text description of the drawing.

Another command, DXFIN, imports a DXF file. A full DXFIN requires a totally new drawing file, created by starting a new drawing equal to nothing, like NAME = <RETURN>. You can use DXFIN to import to a used drawing, but you will get the message "Not a new drawing — only ENTITIES section will be input." Block definitions and layer information won't be imported. DXFIN behaves like an insert, where the current drawing definitions will override the imported definitions.

The IGES format is another drawing exchange format. You get data in and out by using the IGESIN and IGESOUT commands. IGES is not perfect and editing of the resulting drawing is typically required. IGESOUT loses attribute definitions and solid fills, and 3D data may be represented differently. When you register your AutoCAD, you will receive a detailed IGES Interface Specifications document.

DXB is another file format used by AutoCAD. This is a binary drawing file format. DXBIN imports binary drawing files. You can create a limited (everything converted to straight line segments) DXB format file by configuring your plotter. We will show how to get a DXB file in Part Two on 3D drawing and editing. To learn more about attributes, DXF and other types of file processing with AutoCAD, see CUSTOMIZING AutoCAD (New Riders Publishing).

If you are in your office drawing file, end the session. This is the last of the attributes. It is time to move on to the land of 3D. If you want a quick peek at your office in 3D, take a look at the same office drawing extruded into 3D (below). Then, look at the summary tips on attributes that readers have given us.

Ending Your Office Drawing

Command: **END**   Keep this drawing for use in a later chapter.

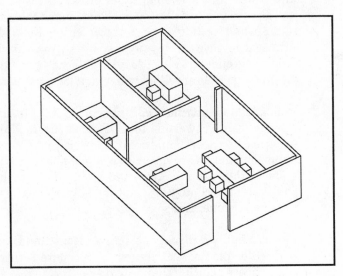

Office Drawing in 3D

Summing Up With Attribute Tips

Attributes provide flexibility in annotating your drawings and producing reports. When you use attributes, you make AutoCAD manage both graphic and non-graphic information. Here are some information management tips for organizing attributes.

Set up report formats before you do attribute definition. Good layout and design of your attribute fields is a critical element in creating a useful attribute file. Do it before you define attributes. Do not give your extract file the same name as your template. It will overwrite the template file.

Scratch out a rough table and make your .TXT extract template first. This will help you plan ahead for field name, size, and prompting. Test your report extraction procedure before you fill up your drawing with information in a format you can't use.

INSERT prompts for attributes in the order of selection. A window selection finds entities in the reverse order of their creation. Select attribute definitions one by one in your desired order when making a block.

Place your attributes on different layers or create them with different colors to distinguish them from regular text. The names you use for tags are important, so keep them brief but explanatory. The tag name is the <default prompt> when no other prompt is given. Tag names are used as handles for your attribute text. This means that you have to type the tag name when setting up reports or edits. Keep the names as brief as practical to save on keystrokes. Break your attribute data into useful fields. Use enough fields to capture all the variable information you need. Avoid fields that are filled with extra long strings of output.

Plan ahead for attribute editing with ATTEDIT. ATTEDIT is an extremely flexible and powerful tool. Novice users (or even unsuspecting experienced ones) should treat it with care. You may need Undo to repair damage if you create havoc in a single pass. Group common edits by the tools available to save time and typing. You can have AutoCAD prompt you for all the changes if you take advantage of grouping edits by layer, tag name, value, and so on.

Use attributes in place of normal text for standardized boilerplate entries and title blocks. Attributes offer more control, automation, and sophisticated editing than text does.

This is the End of Part One

Are you ready to create your own drawing files, attributes and reports? You now have the tools, you just need some practice. In Part One, you have gone from drawing set-up to assigning attributes and extracting data in 2D. If you took the time, you may have turned the polyline cylinder profile into a 3D half-section by revolving the cylinder with a 3D mesh command.

It is time for 3D. Turn to Part Two to learn about full 3D, including how to draw and edit in 3D, how to do dynamic views, and how to shade your images in AutoShade.

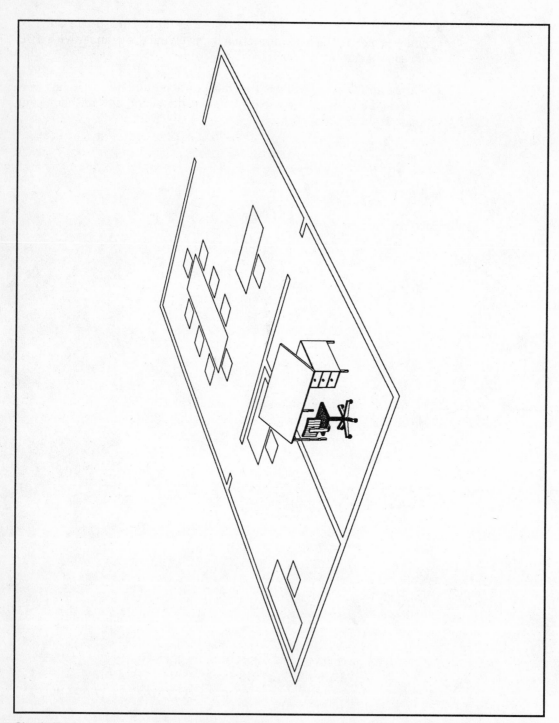

Simple Table and Chair Perspective Drawing

AutoCAD and the 3D Drawing

Making the Transition From 2D to 3D

3D is not for everybody. Clearly some drafting operations are anchored to the plane of the paper and will never need to consider a third spatial dimension. Yet isn't it ironic that while we spend our everyday working life in 3D, we have been forced to work out our 3D expressions using a 2D paper surface?

You have already seen that AutoCAD can take formerly static, two dimensional images and rework, recreate, and annotate them in an *automated* fashion. Using editing commands like ARRAY, OFFSET, TRIM, EXTEND, and STRETCH is a dynamic process. Now, consider going beyond the replacement of 2D drafting functions with the addition of 3D tools. Three dimensional drawing conventions and techniques have been developed to overcome the limitations of the 2D paper plane. What are the drawing conventions that you use with 3D? Where do you start?

The Concept of a 3D Model Image

You can start by using a combination of plan and elevation views to simulate 3D space just like you may do now on the drafting board. But making the jump to 3D gives you the option to set aside these conventions and work with a *model* image of the design that you are creating.

Begin thinking about building a 3D model image by visualizing a tabletop construction project made from an erector set and building blocks. Mentally, picture yourself snapping pieces together to complete your model, some linear, some solid. AutoCAD's 3D drawing entities are equivalent to the erector set and building block components.

As you build your model, you will certainly find yourself moving around the table to get at the *other side* of your model. Occasionally, you will step back to take in the whole view, sometimes you will get down at table level to get your perspective. If you think about it, you need a way to look at the model from all sides (including underneath) as well as a way to see perspective so that you can give a presentation of your model. AutoCAD's 3D viewing tools help you visualize your model-in-progress by splitting your screen into multiple viewports, and placing different 3D views in each port. In effect, you do your walking around (or crawling under) on the screen.

How Part Two Is Organized

Part Two is organized to take you step by step through AutoCAD's 3D drawing and viewing tools. Part Two is broken up into five parts that will take you progressively from getting started in 3D to rendering a 3D image in AutoShade.

Chapter 13, Getting Started with 3D, will introduce you to using 2D drawing and editing commands in 3D. In addition, parts of this chapter will take you behind the scenes to give you the basic idea for using your familiar 2D drawing and editing tools in 3D. AutoCAD has created a new drawing concept called a user coordinate system, UCS, that lets you work intuitively with 2D tools in 3D space. Using a UCS, you can create and place a 2D drawing *plane* anywhere in a 3D drawing, then you can draw and edit on this plane as you are used to doing. We will show you how to place and move a UCS to make your drawing life easy. In addition, this chapter will show you how to control multiple viewports as you navigate through 3D space.

Chapter 14, Using 3D Entities, will introduce you to a new set of 3D drawing entities, including 3D polylines, 3D faces, and 3D meshes. We use an office chair drawing as the chapter exercise, blocking 3D parts and inserting the blocks to assemble the chair. Like its predecessor drawing, the 2D widget, the 3D chair exercise will walk you through your first use of the entities introduced in the chapter. After you have created this chair with its polyline mesh seat, we will show you how to remove hidden lines to generate a wireframe image.

In Chapter 15, Using 3D Perspective Displays, we will show you how to get perspective views of 3D drawings. One of the first 3D benefits that you may gain from AutoCAD is making 3D presentations of your drawings using AutoCAD's dynamic viewing tools. We will show you how to put together a drawing presentation by setting up and recording a series of perspective views of a simple 3D office drawing. You will learn how to set camera and target positions to control your perspective views. You can use these same techniques to *walk through* an architectural drawing or to rotate a 3D part in space.

Chapter 16, Using AutoShade, will take you through the same perspective process, this time using AutoShade as a rendering program to create surface-shaded images. We will show you how to pass AutoCAD images into AutoShade, then set camera, target, lights, and surface textures to produce realistic shaded images.

Chapter 17, Plotting, will show you how to plot regular 2D images and how to convert 3D images for 2D plotting. Paper is still the final drawing medium! There are a few tricks to getting a 3D plotted image onto paper, and we will pass these on to you.

When to Use 3D

One of our goals in this next section on 3D is to help you assess and evaluate what 3D takes in drawing and editing time. Many drafting projects just don't require 3D. Simple plans, diagrams, and flow charts are common examples. Even many spatially oriented projects do not require full 3D drawings to represent the design.

On the other hand, much of what you design and build has a 3D orientation. With AutoCAD, you can create 3D images that represent a 3D model of your design. You will not model many aspects of your 3D design, but you can use AutoCAD to visualize and document images that represent it. To help you evaluate the drawing and editing processes, take a close look at the exercises spread over the next five chapters. You will be able to get a feel for the drawing time (and the processing time) involved in working with 3D. The chapters will take you from simply extending your 2D drawing and editing commands to working with true 3D drawing entities.

Using 3D is an important part of communicating with the drawing community. You can achieve impressive presentations by simply souping up your 2D drawings and presenting them in dynamic views. Alternatively, you may find that you can gain a competitive edge by taking the time to build full 3D drawings. Whether you extrude your 2D drawings or build full 3D images, you will find that once you have created the image, AutoCAD generates accurate 3D views faster than you ever dreamed of doing by hand.

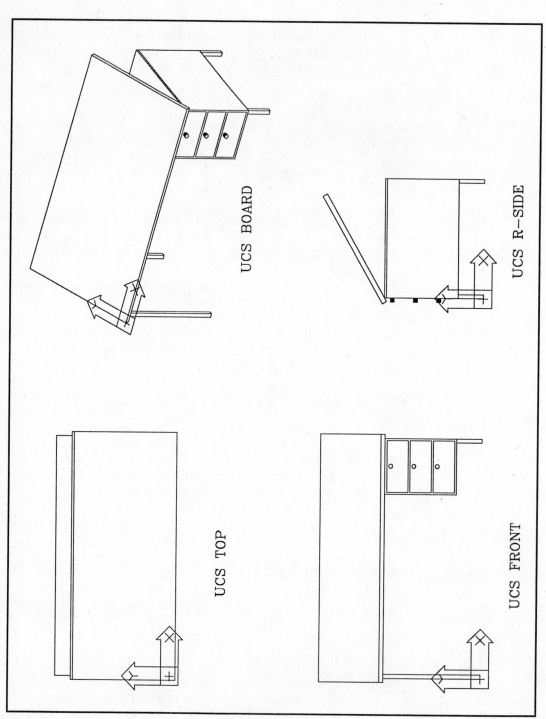

UCS BOARD

UCS R–SIDE

UCS TOP

UCS FRONT

Table Drawing With UCS Icons

CHAPTER 13

Getting Started With 3D

Working in a 3D World

In the 2D work you have done so far with AutoCAD, what you see is what you get. The graphic and non-graphic images you have collected on the screen constitute the drawing as it will be printed or plotted. With 3D work this is not necessarily true. In 3D, what you see is just one of many possible views of the 3D model you have created and stored inside AutoCAD. The distinction between model and view-of-model is important. AutoCAD has certain tools devoted to building 3D models and other tools devoted to viewing them. Before we turn to look at the tools, let's look at the key concept behind the tools, the UCS (User Coordinate System).

The UCS Concept — User Coordinate System

You've been working in a UCS all along. The normal AutoCAD coordinate system is called the WCS (World Coordinate System). The WCS is the default UCS, but you can create as many UCSs as you want, at any angle and location in 3D space.

The UCS lets you work in 3D space with your 2D drawing and editing tools. Look at the four views of the table drawing on the facing page. The four views are of a single table drawn in 3D. Each view has an associated UCS that lets you work on a different plane as if it were a 2D X,Y plane. In the course of this chapter, you will create and edit this table using 2D drawing entities and editing commands! Learning how to locate your UCS in your drawing is the key to learning 3D.

You can draw 2D entities in any UCS X,Y plane, and extrude them in their Z axis. The drawing board, for example, is drawn at a 30-degree angle to the table top. It was drawn by first placing the UCS on the table top, then rotating the UCS X axis angle 30 degrees to the top of the table. The board is given a thickness by extruding it in the Z plane. All 2D drawing and editing commands work for drawing and editing on, or parallel to, the X,Y plane in any UCS in 3D space. Learning how to locate and use your UCS gives you an immediate leg up on 3D because it lets you use everything you already know about 2D drawing and editing.

What This Chapter Covers

This chapter will give you the basics for working in 3D. The type of drawing that you will create is called a wireframe drawing. Sequentially, the chapter will take you through:

■ Learning to set and use VPOINT.

■ Learning to set and use VPORTS.

■ Locating and moving your UCS.

■ Drawing and editing in 3D with 2D commands.

■ Using HIDE to remove hidden lines from your drawing to get a more realistic 3D image.

■ Blocking and inserting blocks into your drawing.

■ Assembling and saving multiple 3D views of your drawing.

The chapter focuses on learning to use the UCS. AutoCAD has additional 3D entities, including 3D surface meshes. We will cover these 3D entities in the next chapter (chapter 14) to create more realistic surfaces. AutoCAD also has dynamic viewing, DVIEW, that lets you quickly create orthographic and perspective views of your drawings. We will cover dynamic viewing in chapter 15.

Finding Your 3D Tools

Working in a 3D world is a mix of drawing and editing, and setting up views and viewports to display what you are doing and what you have done. AutoCAD has tools for all of these activities. You can find all the 3D commands in each of AutoCAD's three standard menu areas: the screen menu, pull-down menus, or tablet menu. Here is a quick list of where to find your main display and UCS controls on the screen and pull-down menus.

Viewpoint and Viewport Are on Display Menus

You will find the VPOINT command on the [DISPLAY] screen menu. The VPORTS command is on the [SETTINGS] menu. VPOINT sets your viewing position in 3D space. VPORTS controls the configuration of your screen display viewports. You can access customized versions of both commands from the [Display] pull-down menu. The [Vpoint 3D...] calls a viewpoint icon menu; [Set Viewports] also calls an icon menu. In addition, you will find another command called PLAN on both the pull-down and screen display menus. The PLAN view will return you to a top-down view (sitting on the

Z axis looking down at the X,Y plane) in whatever coordinate system you specify.

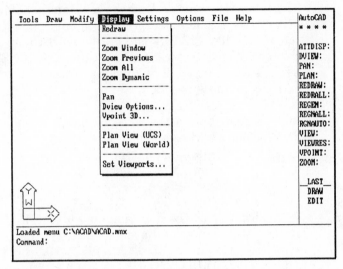

Display Screen and Pull-Down Menus

UCS Is on Settings Menus

You will find the UCS command and the UCSICON command, which controls the icon display, on the [SETTINGS] screen menu. You can set and control the UCS through a series of menu items, [UCS Dialogue...], [UCS Options...], and [UCS Previous], on the [Settings] pull-down menu.

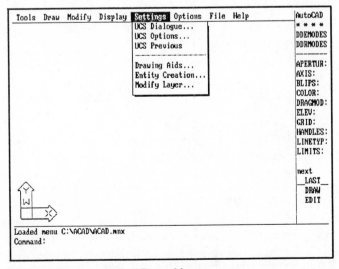

Settings Screen and Pull-Down Menus

Drawing and Editing Commands

You will find your drawing tools on the [DRAW] screen menus and the [Draw] pull-down menu. Look for your familiar editing commands on the [EDIT] screen menus and the [Modify] pull-down menu. You will use some commands, like CHPROP and PEDIT, more than you have in the past to change an entity's thickness or Z value. THICKNESS is not a command, but a system variable setting that controls the thickness of entities extruded in the Z direction.

In some cases, finding the 3D commands is not immediately obvious. The more advanced 3D commands that you will use in the next chapter are called from the [3D] menu item on the screen's root menu (and [DRAW] menu), and from the [3D Construction...] menu item on the [Draw] pull-down menu.

Take a little time to become familiar with the 3D commands in the menu system. Make a note of the menu pathways that you feel comfortable in using to get you to the 3D display and settings commands. Of course, in a pinch you can always type the command name at the command prompt. The chapter's exercises will always give you the command name at the command prompt.

Setting Up for a 3D Drawing

In this chapter, you will draw a drafting table in 3D. At first you will draw a few simple 3D entities and move around them to get familiar with setting a viewpoint in 3D space. Begin by setting up a new drawing called TABLE using default units and settings from the following table. If you are using the IA DISK, set TABLE equal to the CHAP-13A drawing from your disk. The table is drawn at full scale. It is 42 inches high, 62 inches long, and 31.5 inches deep.

COORDS	FILL	GRID	ORTHO	SNAP	UCSICON
ON	OFF	2	ON	.25	OR

UNITS	Use defaults for all Unit settings.			
LIMITS	Set LIMITS from 0,0 to 68,44.			
ZOOM	Zoom All.			

Layer name	State	Color	Linetype
0	On	7 (white)	CONTINUOUS
SCRATCH	Current	7 (white)	CONTINUOUS
TABLE	On	7 (white)	CONTINUOUS

Table Drawing Settings

Setting Up the 3D Table Drawing

Enter selection: 1   Begin a NEW drawing called TABLE=CHAP-13A.

Enter selection: 1   Begin a NEW drawing called TABLE.

Verify the settings shown in the Table Drawing Settings table.

When your drawing is set up, make SCRATCH your current layer.

Getting Around Simple 3D Drawings

So far in AutoCAD, every entity you have created has been in the world coordinate system. The X and Y values of the entities have been in a flat plane and the Z value for all of these entities has been 0. But just as you have control over X and Y locations for entities, AutoCAD gives you control of the Z value for creating 3D objects.

You can draw some entities directly in 3D. There is no reason a point or line has to lie flat on the X,Y plane. Adding a Z coordinate any time AutoCAD requests a pick point is the simplest way to give 3D life to these familiar entities. Other 2D entity commands accept a Z coordinate for their first point, but they are created parallel to the current X,Y plane. The fully 3D entity commands, 3DPOLY, 3DFACE, 3DMESH, and several surfacing commands, accept Z input for any point. While many 3D objects look complex, they are easy to input. Try a simple exercise to put lines in 3D space using all three coordinates, X, Y, and Z. Zoom Center your drawing at 0,0.

Using LINE to Make 3D Lines

Command: **ZOOM**	Zoom Center, 0,0 for center point and 3" for height.
Command: **COLOR**	Set color to red.
Command: **LINE**	Draw line along Y axis.
From point: **0,0,0**	Start at the corner of the drawing.
To point: **0,1,0**	To a point 1" in the Y direction.
To point: **\<RETURN\>**	
Command: **COLOR**	Set color to yellow.

```
Command: LINE            Draw line along X axis.
From point: 0,0,0        Start at the corner of the drawing.
To point: 1,0,0          To a point 1" in the X direction.
To point: <RETURN>


Command: COLOR           Set color to green.


Command: LINE            Draw line along Z axis.
From point: 0,0,0        Start at the corner of the drawing.
To point: 0,0,1          To a point 1" in the Z direction.
To point: <RETURN>
```

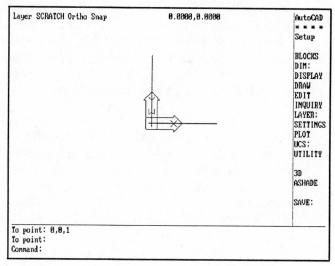

Three Lines in 3D Space

Notice that you used three values for coordinate entry. The third value is for the Z axis. While the first two lines did not actually require a Z value, we added the Z coordinate to clarify the exercise.

Take a look at your screen. You will see two lines and the UCS icon. You are probably wondering where the third (green) line is. Although you drew three lines, only the two lines in the X,Y plane are clearly visible. From your current viewing direction, you cannot see the third line because you are looking directly down at its endpoint. It is as if the line is coming directly out of the screen at you, so you see it as a single point. What you need is a way to view 3D drawings from a better angle. Fortunately, AutoCAD gives you that ability with the VPOINT command.

Using VPOINT to Get Around

Until now you have used your screen to represent the X,Y plane only. Your vantage point in front of the screen is actually some distance away from the X,Y plane in the Z direction. If the plane of the screen represents flat ground, you are looking at that flat ground from a perch atop a flagpole.

In AutoCAD, the direction from which you view your drawing or model is called the viewpoint. AutoCAD's VPOINT command controls this direction in relation to the drawing. The default VPOINT is 0,0,1 implying your viewpoint is over the X,Y plane origin. For VPOINT determination, AutoCAD considers your *entire drawing* to be viewed *through* point 0,0,0. The viewpoint 0,0,1 is directly above the drawing looking down. This is called the *plan view*. So long as you are directly above your drawing (sitting on the Z axis) looking down, everything you create looks flat.

In order to see 3D, you have to get off of this Z axis and look from the side. In VPOINT terms, you must have a non-zero X or Y, or both. For example, a 1,1,1 setting gives you a 45-degree angle looking back at 0,0,0 where your image is located. You can set VPOINT to any X,Y, and Z location you please. The best way to understand VPOINT and become comfortable with it is to try to develop a sense for where your eye is in relation to 0,0,0. Everyone has a different perception of 3D space. For this reason AutoCAD provides three different ways to select a viewpoint. Try using the following VPOINT setting tools to see which is most comfortable for you.

Using the VPOINT Prompt Screen

You can use the viewpoint screen globe icon to select your viewpoint. You can get this globe up on your screen in several ways: selecting [VPOINT] from the [DISPLAY] screen menu, then selecting [axes]; selecting the tablet viewpoint globe icon (concentric circle diagram in the 3D section of the tablet menu), or selecting [Vpoint 3D...] from the [Display] pull-down menu, then selecting the globe icon from the icon menu; or typing VPOINT and hitting a <RETURN>. A second <RETURN> executes the command.

Here's how to use the VPOINT screen icon. Consider your drawing to be located at the center of the earth. The concentric circles on the screen represent the earth, the center point equals the north pole and the outer circle equals the south pole. When you move the cursor around, you move around the outside of the earth's sphere. If the cursor is in the inner circle, you are looking from the northern hemisphere. If the cursor is in the outer circle, you are looking from *under* your drawing, or from the southern hemisphere. The horizontal and vertical lines represent the X and Y axes, dividing the world into four quadrants, just as the screen X and Y axes divide your drawing world.

The dynamically moving X, Y, and Z axes which show on your screen reflect the position of your viewpoint. For some people, this is an intuitive way to select a viewpoint. Get the VPOINT globe on screen, use the following illustrations and exercise to position your cursor in the concentric circles, then pick your viewpoint. Your drawing will regenerate to reflect your VPOINT position.

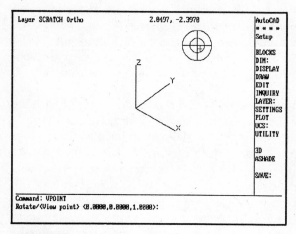

VPOINT Screen Icon

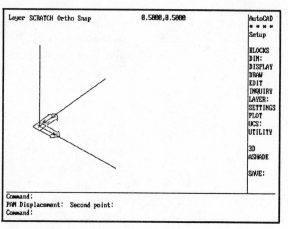

Lines After VPOINT

Using VPOINT Screen Icon

```
Command: VPOINT
Rotate/<View point> <0.0000,0.0000,1.0000>: <RETURN>
```
Move your pointing device until it matches
the illustration above and press the pick button.
```
Command: PAN            Pan to a clear view of axis lines.
```

Your drawing should match the axes of the screen icon.

➡ *TIP: The VPOINT command always causes a regeneration and displays the image as a zoom extents. You can cancel the regeneration as soon as you see how the drawing will be displayed and zoom in to the desired view. For frequently used viewpoints, save and restore named views with the VIEW command.*

Using the VPOINT Tablet and Icon Menus to Select a Viewpoint

The second tool that AutoCAD provides for selecting viewpoints is a series of menu boxes with VPOINT *calculators* built into the commands behind those boxes. Select [Display] and [Vpoint 3D...] from the pull-down menu, or use the 3D section on your tablet menu.

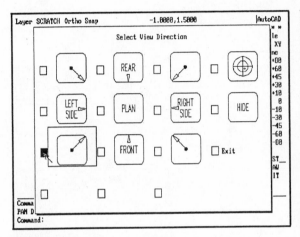

VPOINT Icon Menu

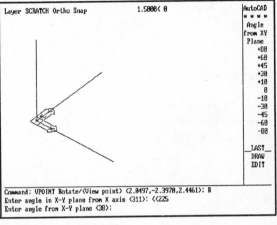

VPOINT Screen Menu

Selecting the globe icon gets you the VPOINT screen icon. Now look at the nine boxes. The PLAN box sets VPOINT to 0,0,1, the plan view. The other eight boxes position you away from your drawing at the sides noted. As soon as you pick a side to look from, you get a screen menu that asks you to select an angle from which to view your drawing. After you select a side and angle, AutoCAD calculates the VPOINT from your selections and regenerates the drawing.

Using Polar Angles to Select a VPOINT

If you looked at the VPOINT prompt on the command line, you saw a Rotate option. You also can set VPOINT by inputting two angles. The first angle determines the rotation in the X,Y plane from the X axis (X axis equals 0 angle) and the second angle determines the Z angle (inclination) from the X,Y plane. This approach seems more natural to many users. Use the following exercise to experiment with the VPOINT options to see which you like.

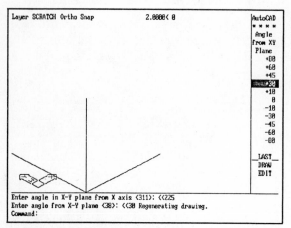

View Established With Icon Menu

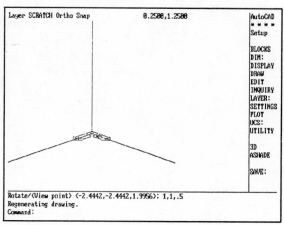

View Established With Coordinate Values

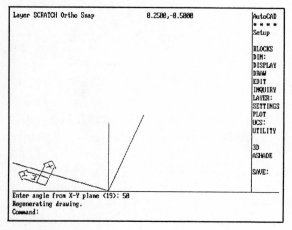

View Established With Rotate Values

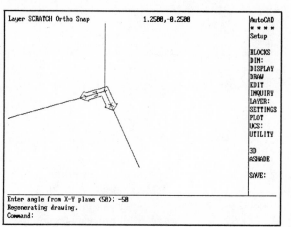

Bottom View Using Rotate Option

Using VPOINT to See All Three Lines

```
Select [Display] [Vpoint 3D...]        Try using the icon menu.
Select                                 Select icon with arrow pointing to upper right.
Select [     +30]                      Select 30 degrees from the screen menu.
Regenerating drawing.
```

```
Command: VPOINT                        Try using coordinate values.
Rotate/<View point> <2.4442,-2.4442,1.9956>: 1,1,.5
Regenerating drawing.
```

```
Command: VPOINT                             Try using the Rotate option.
Rotate/<View point> <1.0000,1.0000,0.5000>: R
Enter angle in X,Y plane from X axis <45>: 200
Enter angle from X,Y plane <19>: 50
Regenerating drawing.

Command: VPOINT                             Use Rotate to view from the bottom.
Rotate/<View point> <-0.9060,-0.3298,1.1491>: R
Enter angle in X,Y plane from X axis <200>: <RETURN>
Enter angle from X,Y plane <50>: -50
Regenerating drawing.
```

Practice with VPOINT for a few minutes to get an understanding of how it works. VPOINT will make sense if you remember that you are always looking through the specified VPOINT towards 0,0,0. You move around the drawing, not the other way around.

As you try the different options, you will find that the XYZ axis icon matches your three lines. The lines' three colors should help you identify your vantage point and see that the intersection of the three lines is at 0,0,0. Notice that the UCS icon also helps you orient your vantage point to the origin plane of the drawing model. If you happen to select a viewpoint at 90 degrees or 180 degrees that is *edge on* to your X,Y plane, you will see the UCS icon turn into a *broken pencil* icon. This means point selection on the screen may be meaningless (more about UCS icons soon).

➡ *TIP: If you are having trouble picking a viewpoint, try to pinpoint the X,Y angle first and then adjust the viewpoint.*

WORLDVIEW and TARGET System Variables

So far, we have been setting viewpoints in the default WCS (world coordinate system). As you begin to work with a UCS, two system variables control your viewpoint. VPOINT defaults to accept and prompt for coordinates in WCS values regardless of your current UCS. This is controlled by the WORLDVIEW system variable (default 1 = WCS). If WORLDVIEW is set to 0, coordinates are accepted and prompted for in current UCS values. When customizing, use the system variable TARGET (read only) to store the (view through) point for the coordinate system. When you change your UCS, TARGET stores the WCS origin point in the current UCS values. In practice, we recommend working with the default WORLDVIEW (1). It provides a constant viewpoint reference to the world coordinate system, and makes it easier not to get lost in space. Regardless of WORLDVIEW setting or current UCS, you are always looking through your drawing at the WCS origin.

Using the PLAN Command

What do you do if you get lost in space? Use the PLAN command to take you home. If you get lost in outer space, you can always return to your plan view by selecting [PLAN] or [Plan View]. PLAN is a fail safe option for reorienting lost viewers. It automatically resets the viewpoint to 0,0,1. The PLAN command can return you to three possible plan views:

- The current UCS (default).

- The world coordinate system (WCS).

- A saved user coordinate system.

Try a quick PLAN.

Using PLAN to Return to a Plan View

Command: **PLAN**	Select or type.
<Current UCS>/Ucs/World: **<RETURN>**	The current UCS is the WCS.
Regenerating drawing.	
Command: **ZOOM**	Zoom Center at 0,0,0 with a height of 2.

Drawing 2D Entities in 3D Space

The simple exercise you just did showed that you can use AutoCAD's basic LINE command in 3D space. With few exceptions, you can draw AutoCAD's basic 2D entities with a Z coordinate value. But 2D entities such as polylines, circles, arcs, and solids are constrained to a parallel plane. The Z value is accepted only for the first coordinate to set the elevation from the current plane.

When entering pick coordinates for entities, AutoCAD assumes a Z value of 0 if none is entered. This is equivalent to drawing all entities on the X,Y plane — the same way you were drawing until you began this 3D section of the book. However, picking coordinates off the X,Y plane is as easy as adding a Z value when AutoCAD asks for a point, where a Z value is allowed. Here are a few tips for making 3D objects from familiar entities.

- Circles are best for closed cylinders. Donuts make good open-ended cylinders, with desired wall thickness.

- Solids are good and quick for rectilinear closed objects. Keep FILL turned off to speed up regenerations.

- Lines and polylines make good open rectilinear objects. Polylines show their width.

- Lines can approximate any object in wireframe, but can't hide anything.

- Solids, wide polylines, and traces fill only in plan view, and do not plot filled in other views.

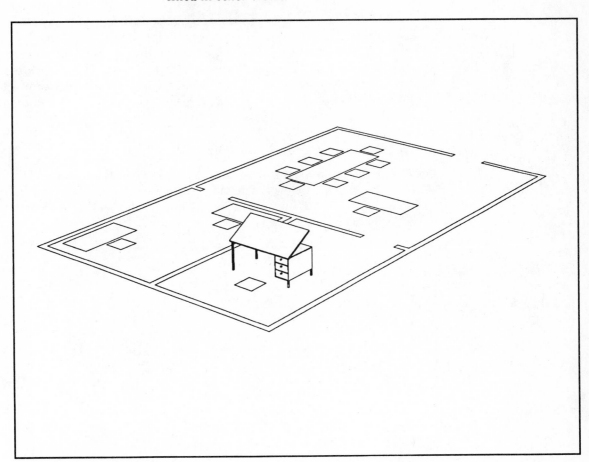

Growing a 3D Drawing From 2D Entities

Three Dimensional Thickness

So far, all of the entities you have drawn are displayed in the X,Y plane or in 3D space defined by X, Y, and Z coordinates. In addition, lines, polylines, arcs, circles, and solids can have a thickness *extruded* from the entities themselves in their Z direction. Think of thickness as a wall rising from an entity in its Z direction. For example, if you draw a line on the X,Y plane, its thickness will appear as a wall stretching from the line itself to the height of the THICKNESS variable setting.

All entities created when the THICKNESS setting is non-zero will carry that thickness. You can edit the thickness of an existing entity using the CHPROP editing command. Use the SETVAR command to globally change THICKNESS for future entities.

➡ *NOTE: Thickness can be positive (up in the Z direction) or negative (down in the Z direction). Thickness is relative to the Z axis of 2D entities, not the current UCS. 3D entities that can accept thickness, such as points and lines, will appear oblique if they do not lie in or parallel to the current UCS. If thickness is added to a line drawn directly in the Z direction, it will appear that the line extends the positive or negative thickness.*

Using THICKNESS to Draw Table Legs

Let's draw the table. Begin by setting the layer TABLE current and by setting a thickness which will determine the extruded height of the legs. Draw one table leg with lines and a second with a polygon, then copy both to create the table's other two legs.

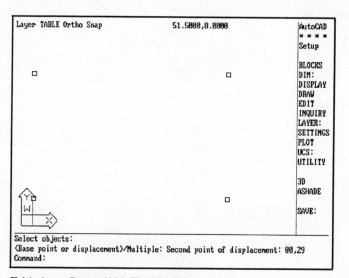

Table Legs Drawn With THICKNESS

Using a THICKNESS Setting to Extrude a 2D Entity

| Command: **LAYER** | Set TABLE current and SCRATCH off. |
| Command: **ZOOM** | Zoom All. |

```
Command: SETVAR
Variable name or ?: THICKNESS
New value for THICKNESS <0.0000>: 25
```

Command: **COLOR**   Set color to yellow.
Command: **LINE**   Draw a 1" square with the lower left corner at 4,7.5.
Command: **POLYGON**   Draw a 4 sided polygon at 51.5,8.
                          circumscribed about a .5 radius circle.
Command: **COPY**   Copy the 2 legs up 29".

You have what appears to be four squares for table legs. You need to view the legs from a different viewpoint to see the thickness. The recurring problem of drawing in 3D is that you can't see what you've done without changing your viewpoint. You need multiple views of your drawing in order to work effectively in 3D.

Using VPORTs to Control Screen Display and 3D Viewing

AutoCAD provides a facility to set up several different viewpoints of your drawing model and to show these views simultaneously. VPORTS is the command that creates and controls viewpoints in multiple viewports. Each viewport can have different snap, grid, and zoom settings.

Using VPORTS in 3D

You have already used VPORTS to set up and control 2D drawing viewports in chapter 4. The command options are listed below the next exercise. Recall that VPORTS divides the AutoCAD graphics screen into two, three, or four rectangular drawing areas. You still retain your screen menu area on the right, and your command prompts at the bottom of the screen.

Remember that you can work in only one viewport at a time, the current viewport. You make the viewport current by clicking on it with your pointer. When you work within a viewport, you can use all your normal zoom display controls just as if you were working with a single screen. The key point for 3D, however, is that as you draw or edit in one viewport, your drawing is updated in all viewports.

You can select [VPORTS:] from the [SETTINGS] screen menu or use the [Set Viewports...] item from the [Display] pull-down menu. When you select [Set Viewports...], you will get the following icon menu.

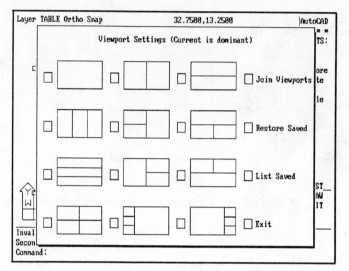

VPORTS Icon Menu

The same VPORTS command options that controlled your 2D view also control your 3D views. You set up your screen display by adding, deleting and joining rectangles, then saving and naming the group. A group of viewports is a *configuration*.

When you work in 3D, we recommend setting up three viewports as a starting configuration. Set up one viewport for your plan view. Use a second as a viewport for *building* your 3D drawing. Use the third viewport to hold a WCS view of your drawing or to provide a second 3D view of your drawing.

Using VPORTS to View 3D Table Construction

Set up three VPORTS so you can see the 3D table construction as you draw it. Split the screen into a large top view for construction and two smaller views below to give you different views. The lower left viewport looks down on the table. The lower right viewport looks up from under the table. The top view is your plan view. The table you are building will appear in each viewport. Use the following illustration and exercise to help you set up the viewports. When you're done, save the configuration as TABLE.

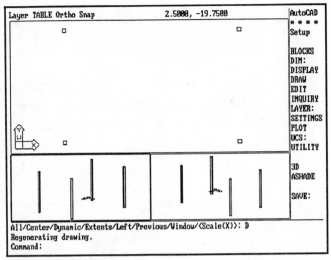

Table Shown in Three Viewports

Using VPORTS to Set Three Viewports

Command: **VPORTS**
Save/Restore/Delete/Join/Off/?/2/<3>/4: **3**
Horizontal/Vertical/Above/Below/Left/<Right>: **H**

Command: **VPORTS**
Save/Restore/Delete/Join/Off/?/2/<3>/4: **J**
Select dominant viewport <current>: **<RETURN>**
Select viewport to join: Pick any point in the center viewport.

Click in the bottom viewport to make it active.
Command: **VPORTS**
Save/Restore/Delete/Join/Off/?/2/<3>/4: **2**
Horizontal/<Vertical> **<RETURN>**

Command: **VPOINT**   Set VPOINT to -1,-1,-.4.

Click in the bottom left viewport to make it active.
Command: **VPOINT**   Set VPOINT to 1,1,.3.
Command: **ZOOM**   Magnify each view as much as possible.
Command: **VPORTS**   Save viewports as TABLE.

After you make the viewports, the table legs will be visible in all three viewports. Their thickness makes them 25 inches long. (See the Table Shown in Three Viewports illustration above.)

VPORTS Command Options

Here is a listing of the VPORTS command options for your review.

Save — Stores the current viewport configuration under a name that you supply.

Restore — Displays a saved viewport configuration.

Delete — Removes a named viewport configuration.

Join — Combines two adjoining viewports into a single viewport.

SIngle — Restores a single screen viewport.

? — Displays a detailed description of the current viewport in the drawing.

2 — Divides the current viewport in half vertically or horizontally.

<3> — Divides the current viewport into three viewports. You can choose from several configuration options.

4 — Divides the current viewport into quarters.

You can name, save and restore viewports the same way you save named views with VIEW. In the DOS and OS/2 operating system environments, AutoCAD limits each viewport configuration to a maximum of four viewports. You should preset, name, and save a few standard VPORTS configurations that help you quickly (and easily) see the 3D model you are creating.

➥ *NOTE: When you are using multiple viewports and you want to redraw or regenerate all the ports, use the REDRAWALL or REGENALL commands. The standard REDRAW and REGEN commands only affect the current viewport.*

Using SOLID to Make a 3D Object

Now we are ready to put a top on the table. We want the table top to show as a solid surface, so we will make it a SOLID entity. The top is 0.5 inches thick; we can extrude the top by assigning a thickness to it. The only constraint on using SOLID in 3D is that all the extruded Z points must lie in a plane parallel to the X,Y plane.

Using XYZ Filters in 3D

How do you get the table top up on top of the legs? You have two choices. You can assign a thickness of 0.5 inches for your table top, then begin your solid at the Z height of 25 inches above the current UCS X,Y plane, or you can set a new UCS 25 inches above the current one so that Z=0 is the top of the legs, beginning your solid from there.

The following exercise shows you how to start the solid at the right Z height using XYZ filters. Start by changing your thickness setting with SETVAR to 0.5 inches. Then, use SOLID to create the table top. Get your X,Y pick points from the following illustration, input the Z value by typing in the value (25) given in the exercise. When you are done, your screen should look like the Table Top Added With SOLID illustration.

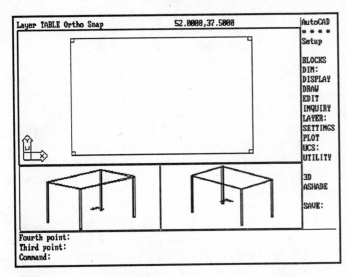

Table Top Added With Solid

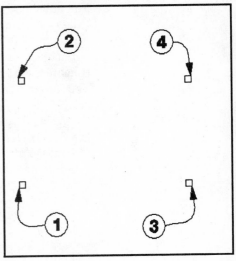

Detail of Pick Points

Using SOLID and XYZ Filters to Make 3D Table Top

Click in the top viewport to make it active.

Command: **SETVAR**	Set THICKNESS to .5
Command: **OSNAP**	Set to ENDPoint.
Command: **SOLID**	
First point: **.XY**	Use XYZ filters for first point.
of	Pick corner of leg at ①.
(need Z): **25**	Type in Z value.
Second point:	Pick corner of leg at ②.
Third point:	Pick corner of leg at ③.
Fourth point:	Pick corner of leg at ④.
Third point: **<RETURN>**	
Command: **OSNAP**	Set to None.

Note that after you entered the Z value for the first coordinate point, AutoCAD assumed the same Z value for the three remaining points. The SOLID command assumes that all other Z values lie parallel to the X,Y plane.

➡ *TIP: Using XYZ point filters is an efficient way to create entities at various Z elevations without having to change your UCS. You can osnap the XY point to an existing object without needing to know its coordinates, then type in a Z value, or osnap Z in a different viewport.*

How to Keep an Eye on Z Values and Thickness

You have made a simple 3D table by extruding the legs and top, assigning thickness values, and drawing the entities at the Z height that you want. When you work with 3D, you have to remember that setting thickness is not a part of an entity command prompt. You can find the current thickness setting by using SETVAR thickness to see the current default. You also can find the Z value and thickness of an existing entity by doing a LIST, and picking the entity on the screen. You will get both the beginning Z value and the thickness for the entity. If you want to change the thickness of an existing entity, use the CHPROP command. You select the entity, respond with thickness as the property you want to edit, then input a new value. The current thickness is given as the <current default> prompt value.

➡ *NOTE: There is another (older) command called ELEV that can assign a thickness value, but this command is destined for the command scrap heap. We recommend using SETVAR to set your thickness. ELEV can also set a default ELEVATION variable, but we do not recommend its use because it confuses Z coordinate entry.*

➡ *TIP: Text ignores the thickness setting when created. If you want text with a 3D thickness, use the CHPROP command to set a thickness after creating the text.*

Some congratulations are in order. You have created a good-looking 3D drawing of a table! Before we move on to more 3D drawing and editing, take a minute to check your 3D table drawing by removing hidden lines.

Using HIDE for Hidden Line Removal

The different views of the table in the bottom viewports are *wireframe* representations. All of those wire edges help you visualize just how the table appears in 3D space. When AutoCAD generates a wireframe image, it does not stop to think whether a piece of the frame would be visible from your viewpoint if the objects on the screen were solid. Instead AutoCAD shows it as if it were transparent or constructed of wires. This is the quickest way the program can get the image on the screen.

Once you get an image that you like on the screen, you can remove lines that should be hidden using the HIDE command. HIDE gives you a 3D image that appears to jump out at you from the flat 2D screen. While the HIDE command is simple to use (all you do is type HIDE), calculating a hidden line removal can take AutoCAD a very long time. AutoCAD tells you that it is processing hidden lines with a number count. Don't despair, eventually you will get your hidden line view. Try hiding the table.

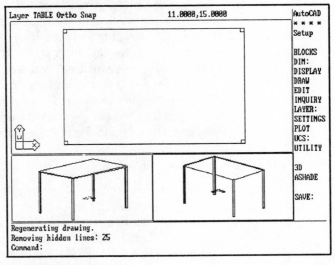

Table After a HIDE

Using HIDE to Remove Hidden Lines in the Table

Click in the bottom left viewport to make it active.
Command: **HIDE**
Regenerating drawing.
Removing hidden lines: 25

Make the bottom right viewport active.
Command: **HIDE**
Regenerating drawing.
Removing hidden lines: 25

When you are done, your screen should look like the Table After a HIDE illustration. Don't let the lower right view fool you. It should look the way it does. Did you remember that the bottom right viewport looks up from under the table? Since a wireframe image sees through the whole drawing, you can't distinguish front from back or top from bottom without doing a HIDE or checking your viewpoint values.

What Gets Hidden With HIDE?

Here's a way to think about hidden lines. If you were to cover your view of a 3D wireframe model with a tight-fitting piece of cloth, you would only see the sides of the cloth facing you, and nothing behind the cloth. In effect, AutoCAD attempts to hide all wireframe edges from view that would be on the backside of the image.

It helps to know how AutoCAD treats various entity surfaces when it calculates hidden line removal. AutoCAD puts an opaque cap on the bottom and top of most graphic entities that surround an area. For example, circles or solids have top and bottom surfaces that hide lines enclosed within or behind the surface. (You saw the effect of the solid table top in your table view.) A polyline (or trace) only hides what is behind its thickness extrusion or concealed by its width. Areas *enclosed* by closed polylines are not hidden because they have no top or bottom. Remember, polygons, ellipses and donuts are really polylines.

Using Hidden Layers to See Hidden Lines

What happens to all those hidden lines? When you generate a HIDE view, AutoCAD removes the vectors that are hidden. Let's say you build your plan view 3D model entities on a layer called STUFF. If you also create a layer called HIDDENSTUFFf, all hidden line vectors will get put on the HIDDENSTUFF layer when you use HIDE to generate a hidden line view. Any layer in your drawing file can have a hidden line counterpart, even layer 0 (HIDDEN0). To create a hidden layer, just create a layer with the same name as your drawing layer, using HIDDEN as a prefix.

You can control hidden layers just as you would any drawing layer. You can turn them on and off, and give them colors (a hidden layer ignores its layer linetype setting for hide). These hidden vectors are not real entities. You cannot edit them. A popular use for hidden layers is to construct a 3D view, hide it, and plot it or look at the screen view of the drawing with the hidden lines in a different color. Try creating a hidden layer for the table. Make it any color you like. Then try another HIDE.

Using HIDE With a Hidden Layer

Make the bottom left viewport active.

Command: **LAYER**   Create a new layer named HIDDENTABLE with
                            color of your choice, but don't set it current.

Command: **HIDE**   Hidden lines are removed and drawing is regenerated.
Command: **END**

➡️ *TIP: All normal editing commands work on 3D-generated images, but a regeneration will unhide the drawing. When you edit a hidden image, turn REGENAUTO off to avoid accidentally regenerating the drawing.*

➡️ *TIP: Freeze layers that contain extra information before doing a HIDE. Don't have AutoCAD spend time removing hidden lines unnecessarily.*

➡️ *TIP: If you have created top and bottom objects from entities that do not hide lines behind them, try solidifying the surface boundaries with circles, solids, or wide polylines.*

Stopping Point

This is a good break point. If you have other demands on your time, take a break by ending your drawing. Then, pick up with the next section of the table drawing. While THICKNESS and Z coordinate values are useful tools for constructing 3D drawings, they cannot handle all the 3D construction tasks that you will encounter. In the next set of exercises, you will make some last additions to the table by adding a cabinet, drawers, and a drawing board at a 30-degree slant on top of the table. Think about how you would draw these additions with the tools you have used so far. You may have figured out how to draw the cabinet and drawers, but we bet you will be stumped on the drawing board.

Establishing a User Coordinate System in 3D

If you took a break, welcome back. Let's start this section by taking a look at the UCS command and the UCS icon. So far, you have been using AutoCAD's world coordinate system (WCS), the default coordinate system. You can create you own coordinate system using the UCS and UCSICON commands. These commands were developed for 3D to let you work with 2D entities and editing commands by locating your coordinate system anywhere in 3D space. In chapter 3, you created and used a UCS to move your 2D X,Y drawing plane and rotate it 90 degrees. (If you don't remember the UCS command, you may want to briefly review its use in chapter 3. The UCS command options are listed below.)

You can establish or modify a UCS with the [Settings] screen menu or with several items in the [Settings] pull-down menu. The [UCS Dialogue...] pull-down selection uses the DDUCS command with its two UCS dialogue boxes.

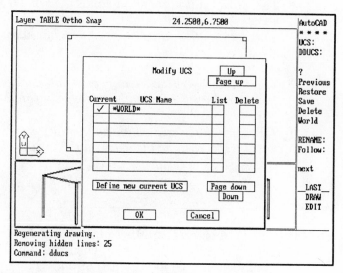

Modify UCS Dialogue Box

As you can see by looking at the dialogue boxes (or at the command prompt line), the UCS command has several options. However, there are just four basic ways to establish a new UCS in 3D.

- Specify a new origin, a new X,Y plane, or a new Z axis.

- Copy the orientation of an existing entity.

- Align the new UCS to your current view.

- Rotate the current UCS around any one, or all X/Y/Z axes.

You can establish your new UCS by using any one of these methods, or you can combine them by executing the UCS command several times in succession. In fact, if you anticipate a complex UCS move, you may want to break up your move sequence so that you can undo it easily. You can define any number of UCSs, naming and saving them. However, only one UCS can be current at any one time. The current UCS defines all coordinate input. If you are using multiple viewports, they all share the current UCS.

As we construct the rest of the table, we will show you how to use most of the command options to define, name, and save UCSs. Here is a complete list of the options. We will give you more details when we work with the individual options.

➥ *NOTE: The X,Y plane of the current UCS is also known as the current construction plane unless the ELEV command has set a non-zero elevation. A non-zero elevation creates a current construction plane above or below the UCS X,Y plane and makes drawing in 3D very confusing. That is why the ELEV command will be discontinued and we do not recommend setting elevations. For the sake of simplicity, we use the term UCS in lieu of construction plane.*

UCS Command Options for Existing 3D Applications

Origin — Establishes the X and Y axes at a new point of origin.

ZAxis — Provides the option specifying a new Z axis direction and point of origin.

3point — Specifies a new origin and a new X,Y plane. You input or pick three points: the origin, a point on the positive X axis, and a point in the new X,Y plane. This is the most flexible method for defining a new UCS.

Entity — Provides for specifying a new UCS by selecting an existing entity. The entity type determines the origin and the direction of the X,Y plane. The X,Y plane will lie parallel to the existing entity's plane.

View — Defines a new UCS with the X,Y plane perpendicular to your view direction (parallel to the screen). The origin is unchanged.

X/Y/Z — Provides the option of rotating the current UCS around the axis that you specify. You pick the angle with two points, or input the value.

Prev — Lets you step back, up to ten previous coordinate systems.

Restore — Sets the coordinate system to a previously saved named UCS.

Save — Stores a coordinate system under a user-specified name.

Del — Removes a saved coordinate system.

? — Displays a list of saved coordinate systems by name, point of origin and orientation.

<World> — Sets the UCS to the world coordinate system.

Establishing and Saving a New UCS

Let's get back to the drafting table, and define and save a new UCS to work from the top of the table. During the next set of exercises, we are going to use a single viewport so that you can easily see the UCS icon as you construct the rest of the table. Use the following exercise to define a UCS at the top left corner of the table. (Make sure UCSICON is on.) Use the coordinate values given in the exercise sequence to set a new viewpoint, and save your VIEW as 3D. Define your UCS by osnapping ENDPoint at the top left corner of the table. Name your new coordinate system TOP.

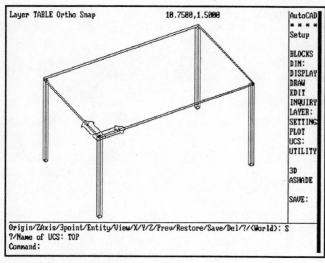

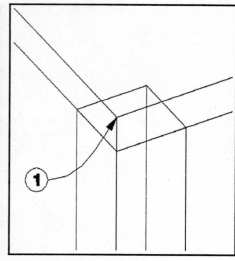

UCS on the Table Top   *Detail of Table Corner*

Defining and Saving a UCS at the Table Top

Make top viewport active.

Command: **VPORTS**	Set viewports to SIngle.

Command: **UCSICON**
ON/OFF/All/Noorigin/ORigin <ON>:**OR**   Make sure UCSICON is set to origin.
Set UCS icon to origin.

Command: **VPOINT**
Rotate/<View point> <0.0000,0.0000,1.0000>: **R**
Enter angle in X,Y plane from X axis <270>: **240**
Enter angle from X,Y plane <90>: **35**

Command: **ZOOM**	Zoom at a value of .75X.
Command: **VIEW**	Save view as 3D.

Command: **UCS**   Type or select UCS.
Origin/ZAxis/3point/Entity/View/X/Y/Z/Prev/Restore/Save/Del/?/<World>: **O**
Origin point <0,0,0>:   Use ENDPoint to pick the corner of the table at ①.
Command: **UCS**   Save UCS as TOP.
Origin/ZAxis/3point/Entity/View/X/Y/Z/Prev/Restore/Save/Del/?/<World>: **S**
?/Name of UCS: **TOP**

Your screen should show a new UCS at the top left corner of the table as in the illustration above. Notice that the new UCS lies in an X,Y plane on the top of the table. Also notice that it does not change your view of the drawing.

When you define a new UCS by specifying a new origin (as you did in the example above), you are only shifting the origin point. The Z axis direction of the new UCS is the same as in its previous UCS, and its X,Y planes are parallel and aligned. If you want to change the X,Y plane or change the Z axis, you need to use one or more of the other options.

Using SOLID With the TOP UCS to Draw a Cabinet

Try using the new TOP UCS to construct a cabinet on the table's right side. Later, we will add drawers. Use SOLID to draw the cabinet, but extrude the solid downward in the Z direction with a negative thickness. Set a new color to help you distinguish the cabinet from the table. (We used cyan.) The following detailed illustrations will help you locate your pick points. The exercise shows how you can mix XY filtering and an osnap (NEAr) to work in the X,Y plane, using the same techniques that you used in 2D.

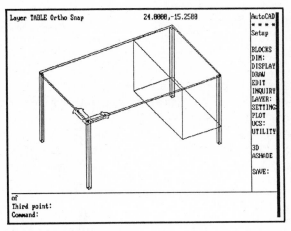

Table With Cabinet

Detail of Pick Points

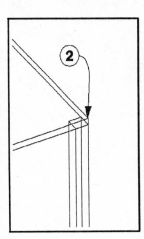

Detail of Pick Point

Drawing the Cabinet

Command: **SETVAR**	Set a negative THICKNESS to -18.5.
Command: **COLOR**	Set color to cyan.
Command: **SOLID**	
First point: **34,0,-.5**	Establishes the upper left front corner of cabinet.
Second point: **.X**	Use point filters to pick the left back corner.
of **@**	Use the X value of the last point.
(need Y): **NEA**	Use NEAr to pick a point on the back of the table.
to	Pick any point on line at ①.
Third point: **ENDP**	Use ENDPoint to select the right front corner of the table.
of	Pick any point on line at ②.
Fourth point: **ENDP**	Use ENDPoint to select the right rear corner of the table.
of	Pick any point on line at ③.
Third point: **<RETURN>**	

If all went well, you should have a good solid cabinet mounted under the right side of the table.

Using the UCSICON to Get UCS Information

As you begin to work in 3D by defining UCSs, you will come to rely heavily on the UCS icon as a reminder of your X,Y plane orientation, or to confirm that you have defined your UCS the way you want it.

Looking closely at your screen, you will see that the icon's X and Y axes point along the axes of the table. The + on the icon means that it is located at the origin of the current UCS. The **W** on the Y axis is missing, indicating that your current coordinate system is not the WCS. The box at the icon's base means you are viewing the UCS from above (a positive Z direction). No box means that you are looking at the icon from below (a negative Z direction). The following illustration shows a collection of icon views that you will encounter. Try reading the icons to make sure you understand your view relative to the UCS. If you see the *broken pencil* icon in your viewport, your view is within one degree of parallel (edge on) to the current UCS.

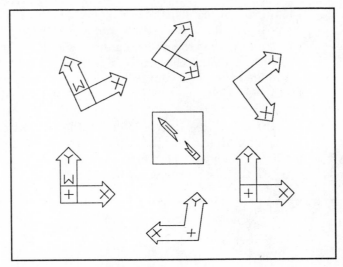

Different UCS Icon Views

As a reminder, the following list reviews the UCSICON command options available to control the display of the UCS icon.

UCSICON Options

ON — Makes the UCS icon visible.

OFF — Removes the UCS icon.

All — Displays the UCS icon in all viewports.

Noorigin — Displays the UCS icon in the lower left corner of viewport.

ORigin — Displays the UCS icon at the point of origin (0,0,0) or lower left corner if origin is not visible.

As you may have noticed when you were working with three viewports, you can display the UCS icon in each viewport. If more than one viewport is present, you also can set different display settings for the icon in each viewport. The system variable UCSICON controls the current icon setting.

Using 3Point Option to Define a UCS

Let's establish two more UCS planes, one at the front of the table, and a second on the right side. Start with the front UCS. Here we will use the 3point option. You can use this option to establish *any* possible UCS. If you don't pick up all the options immediately, this is the one option we recommend learning first. To execute the option, you pick (or input) three coordinate points. The first point defines the origin, the second point defines the positive X axis from the new origin point (first picked point), the third point defines the X,Y plane. The third point need not be on the Y axis, but its Y coordinate defines the positive Y axis. The only constraint is that the points cannot lie in a straight line. If you default any of the prompts, the new UCS will default to the current UCS for that point. For example, if your default is the origin, it will use the same origin for the new UCS.

Use the following exercise to define the UCS at the base of the table's lower left front leg. Pick the first origin point on the front lower left corner of the leg. (The pick points are shown in the detailed illustration.) After you pick the points, save the UCS as FRONT.

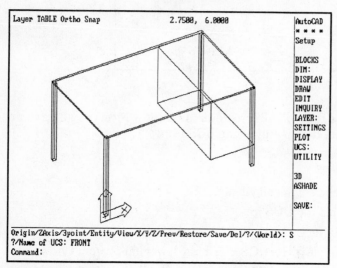

Table With UCS at the Front

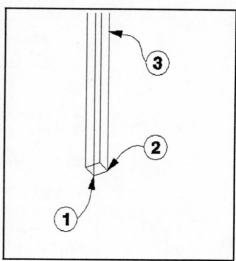

Detail of Pick Points

Using 3point to Create a Front UCS

```
Command: UCS                                Create the front UCS with 3point.
Origin/ZAxis/3point/Entity/View/X/Y/Z/Prev/Restore/Save/Del/?/<World>: 3P
Origin point <0,0,0>:                       Use Osnap INTersection to pick point ①.
Point on positive portion of the X-axis <1.0000,0.0000,-25.5000>:
                                            Use Osnap INTersection to pick point ②.
Point on positive-Y portion of the UCS X,Y plane <0.0000,1.0000,25.5000>:
                                            Use Osnap NEAr to pick point ③.

Command: UCS                                Save UCS as FRONT.
```

When you are done, your UCS icon should be on the front of the left leg with the X axis pointing towards the right leg and the Y axis pointing vertically up the left leg towards the top.

Using the ZAxis Option to Define a UCS

While we are at it, let's define the second UCS on the right side. We want to move our UCS to the right leg with the X,Y plane on the table's right side. Here, we want to use the ZAxis option. This option lets you specify a new positive Z axis, and the UCS rotates the X,Y plane based on your new Z axis. Again, this is a quick and easy option to use. You pick a first point for the origin and a second point for the Z direction.

Use the following illustrations and exercise sequence to help you define the UCS. The new Z direction faces outward from the right side of the table. After you pick your origin point, pick a relative polar second point at 0 degrees. Save the new UCS as R-SIDE.

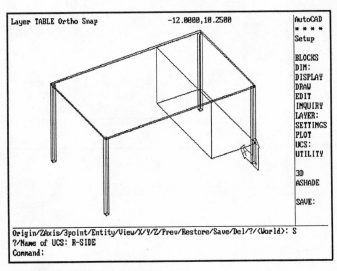

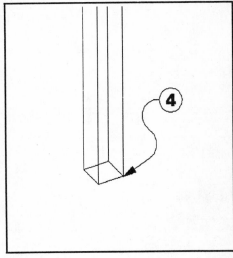

Table With UCS at the Right Side   Detail of Pick Points

Using ZAxis to Create Right Side UCS

```
Command: UCS                            Create the right side UCS with ZAxis.
Origin/ZAxis/3point/Entity/View/X/Y/Z/Prev/Restore/Save/Del/?/<World>: ZA
Origin point <0,0,0>:                   Use INTersection to pick ④ at the right front leg.
Point on positive portion of Z-axis <48.0000,0.0000,1.0000>:
                                        Pick any point at exactly 0 degrees (@1<0).

Command: UCS                            Save the UCS as R-SIDE.
```

Your screen should show the new UCS icon on the right front leg with the Z axis pointing toward the rear right leg.

Using the Front UCS to Construct Drawers

After you have defined a UCS, you can always work in plan view if it is easier to find your pick points that way. Use the following exercise to get a plan view of the FRONT UCS, then move the UCS onto the cabinet front to help you construct the drawers. Invoke the UCS command to help draw the first (lower) drawer on the cabinet with a 2D polyline, then use COPY multiple on the first drawer to add the next two drawers. When you are done, restore your 3D view.

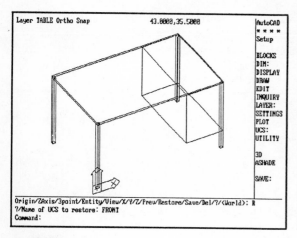

Table With UCS at FRONT

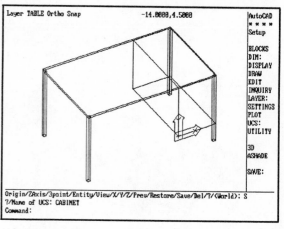

Table With UCS at CABINET

Using UCS to Add Drawers to the Table

Command:	COLOR	Set color to red.
Command:	UCS	Restore the FRONT UCS.
Command:	UCS	Move the UCS to the lower left corner of cabinet with Origin.
Command:	UCS	Save the UCS as CABINET.
Command:	SETVAR	Set THICKNESS to 0.
Command:	PLAN	View the front of the desk in plan to the cabinet UCS.
Command:	PAN	Move to a better view.

```
Command: PLINE
From point:                    Pick absolute point .5,.5.
Current line-width is 0.0000
Arc/Close/Halfwidth/Length/Undo/Width/<Endpoint of line>: Pick polar point @13<0.
Arc/Close/Halfwidth/Length/Undo/Width/<Endpoint of line>: Pick polar point @5.5<90
Arc/Close/Halfwidth/Length/Undo/Width/<Endpoint of line>: Pick polar point @13<180
Arc/Close/Halfwidth/Length/Undo/Width/<Endpoint of line>: C
```

```
Command: COPY                      Do a copy multiple to place two drawers above the original.
Select objects:                    Select the drawer polyline.
1 selected, 1 found.
Select objects: <RETURN>
<Base point or displacement>/Multiple: M
Base point:                        Pick absolute point 0,0.
Second point of displacement:      Pick polar point @6<90.
Second point of displacement:      Pick polar point @12<90.

Command: VIEW                      Restore view 3D.
```

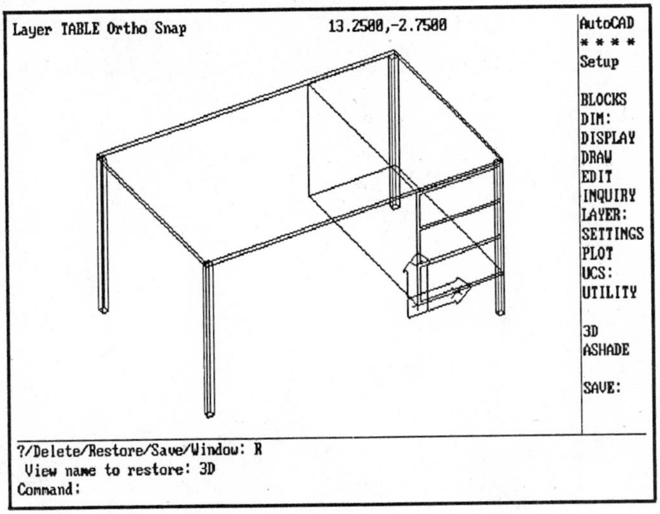

```
Layer TABLE Ortho Snap             13.2500,-2.7500          AutoCAD
                                                            * * * *
                                                            Setup

                                                            BLOCKS
                                                            DIM:
                                                            DISPLAY
                                                            DRAW
                                                            EDIT
                                                            INQUIRY
                                                            LAYER:
                                                            SETTINGS
                                                            PLOT
                                                            UCS:
                                                            UTILITY

                                                            3D
                                                            ASHADE

                                                            SAVE:

?/Delete/Restore/Save/Window: R
  View name to restore: 3D
Command:
```

Table With Drawers Added

When you restore your 3D view, your screen should look like the Table
With Drawers Added illustration above.

MOVE and COPY in 3D Space

In the exercise above, you used COPY to duplicate the drawers in the Z
axis of the WCS, but since the current UCS was already oriented in the
plane of the drawer faces, it was just a normal 2D copy. But if you need
to move or copy entities in the Z axis of the current UCS, it's still easy.
MOVE and COPY are fully 3D compatible. Just enter Z values for the base
point and/or second point coordinates and you can move any entity
anywhere in 3D space without reorienting your UCS. XYZ point filters
are useful in establishing your 3D MOVE and COPY coordinates.

Using the X/Y/Z Options to Establish a UCS

Besides the 3point and ZAxis options that you have used so far, the UCS has two other basic options to help you establish a new UCS. The X/Y/Z options are straightforward. They let you rotate the current UCS around the X or Y or Z axis. The angle you specify is relative to the X axis of the current UCS if you apply the right-hand rule of rotation to the specified axis. The right-hand rule of rotation is that if you close your right fist and extend your thumb to point in the positive direction of the specified axis, your curled fingers point in the direction of positive rotation angle. The Rotation Angles illustration (below) shows the direction of angle rotations. If you want to rotate more than one axis, you simple re-execute the UCS command to rotate the second (or third) axis. (You will use the X/Y/Z options once or twice in the remaining exercises.)

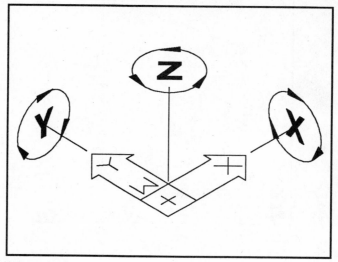

Rotation Angles

Using Entity Selection to Establish a UCS

You also can define a new UCS by selecting an existing entity. We are going to use entity selection in the next set of exercises when we create and insert a block to form the drawing board. If you select an entity, the entity type and your pick point determine the new UCS X,Y plane. There are two entity types you can't use: 3D polylines and 3D meshes. (You will see these two entities in the next chapter.) Here is the official list of how the entities specify a new UCS.

ARC — The arc's center is the new origin point, and the X axis goes through the endpoint nearest your pick point.

CIRCLE — The center is the new origin point, and the X axis passes through your pick point.

LINE — The endpoint nearest your pick point is the new origin, and the second endpoint determines the X axis. (The Y coordinate is 0.)

POINT — The point is the new origin point.

2DPOLY — The polyline's start point is the new origin point, the X axis lies along the line to the first vertex point. (The first vertex Y coordinate is 0.)

SOLID — The first point is the new origin point, and the X axis lies along the line between the first two points.

TRACE — The first point of the trace is the new origin point, and the X axis lies along the trace's center line.

3DFACE — The first point determines the new origin point, the X axis lies along the first and second points, and the positive Y axis is determined by the first and fourth points.

DIMENSION — The new origin is the middle of the dimension text, and the X axis is parallel to the X axis in effect when the dimension text was drawn.

TEXT, ATTRIBUTE, INSERT — The new origin is the entity's insertion point. The X axis is defined by the entity's rotation about the extrusion direction (Z axis). In effect, the entity that you select will have a 0 rotation angle in the new UCS.

Since each entity type behaves differently, you have to play with each type to see how it is going to behave when you use it to establish a new UCS. Use your SCRATCH layer to draw any type that catches your fancy, then use it to define a new UCS. When you are done, resume with the next exercise on blocks.

Using BLOCK and INSERT to Insert Blocks in 3D

Well, you have a drafting table with a decent set of drawers. The last item to add to the drafting table is the drawing board. The drawing board is 1.25 inches thick and overlaps the table top on all sides by 1 inch. The next two exercises will show you how to make the drawing board and insert it as block, slanting it at a 30-degree angle.

You can build and insert 3D blocks into a drawing just like you build and insert 2D blocks. The standard INSERT command accepts a 3D insertion point and gives you the option of X-scaling, Y-scaling, *and* Z-scaling the block's entities. The current UCS defines the X,Y plane for the block when it is created.

Using BLOCK to Create a Unit 3D Block

As the first step in making the board, use SOLID to build a 1x1x1 block and name it CUBE. Extrude the solid in the Z direction by setting your thickness to 1. Build the block with the TOP UCS. The insertion point is shown in the accompanying illustration.

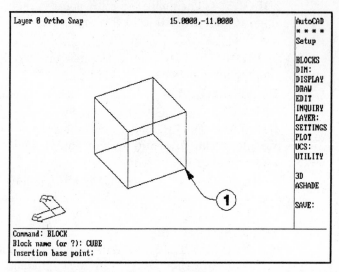

A 1x1x1 Building Block With Insert Point

Making a Solid Building Block

```
Command: UCS                           Use Entity selection to see how it works.
Origin/ZAxis/3point/Entity/View/X/Y/Z/Prev/Restore/Save/Del/?/<World>: E
Select object to align UCS:            Select the table top solid anywhere.

Command: COLOR                         Set color to BYLAYER.
Command: ZOOM                          Zoom to a clear area in the drawing.
Command: LAYER                         Set layer to 0 so CUBE will take on properties of the
                                       inserted layer.
Command: SETVAR                        Set THICKNESS to 1.
Command: SOLID                         Draw a 1" square.

Command: BLOCK                         Block solid as CUBE.
Block name (or ?): CUBE
Insertion base point:                  Pick point ①.
Select objects:                        Select the Solid.
1 selected, 1 found.
Select objects: <RETURN>

Command: SETVAR                        Set thickness back to 0.
Command: ZOOM                          Zoom Previous.
```

The cube is now safely defined and tucked away in your drawing.

Using INSERT to Insert a 3D Block

Use the INSERT command to insert the cube into the drawing. The TOP UCS is the current UCS. When you insert a 3D block, the block's X,Y plane is aligned *parallel* to the current UCS. To get the slanted 30-degree surface of the drafting board, use the X option to rotate the TOP UCS 30 degrees about the X axis. Offset the insertion by one inch to provide the overlap. Use the exercise sequence to get your X, Y, and Z scale values. The X/Y/Z scale option tells INSERT to prompt for all three scale factors. If you do not provide a Z scale value, INSERT will default the Z scale to the X scale. We have purposely made the board longer than the table so your X scale value will extend the board 12 inches beyond the right side of the table. (We will come back to the table later and edit it to make it fit.)

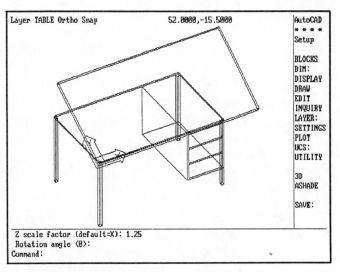

Table With Drawing Board

Using INSERT to Insert a 3D Block to Create Drawing Board

Command: **COLOR**	Set color to green.
Command: **LAYER**	Set layer TABLE current.
Command: **UCS**	Restore TOP UCS.

```
Command: UCS
Origin/ZAxis/3point/Entity/View/X/Y/Z/Prev/Restore/Save/Del/?/<World>: X
Rotation angle about X axis <0.0>: 30
```

```
Command: UCS                           Save UCS as BOARD.

Command: INSERT
Block name (or ?): CUBE
Insertion point: -1,-1                 Start point is 1" from 0,0 to get 1" overlap.
X scale factor <1> / Corner / XYZ: XYZ
X scale factor <1> / Corner: 62        Drawing board length.
Y scale factor (default=X): 31         Drawing board width.
Z scale factor (default=X): 1.25       Drawing board thickness.
Rotation angle <0>: <RETURN>
```

When you finish, your screen should look like the Table With Drawing Board illustration above. The board should lie in the same X,Y plane as your X-rotated UCS. The UCS icon should appear to lie just under the drawing board at the lower left corner of the table. The Z scale value of 1.25 scaled the board's thickness in the positive Z direction from the rotated UCS icon. While we did not use the option in the current insertion, you can orient the insertion by specifying a rotation angle when you insert the block. When you provide an angle, you rotate the block in the current X,Y plane around a Z axis at the insertion point.

Building a Library of 3D Blocks

As you begin to work in 3D, build a library of useful blocks like a cube, a wedge, a pyramid, or whatever shapes you need that you can insert and scale easily in your drawings. These shapes are common elements that you will use in many 3D constructions. Having a library of shapes will help you create drawings quickly. Using the same blocks many times also helps reduce the size of your drawing files.

AutoCAD provides a set of AutoLISP routines that create a set of primitive shapes (however, these are not blocks). If you have accessed the [3D Construction...] icon menu from the [Draw] pull-down menu, you have seen them. The routines form unit shapes that provide a start in building a library set. If you use them repeatedly, BLOCK them for greater efficiency. The curved primitives are formed using 3D meshes. You will get a chance to make and use 3D meshes in the next chapter.

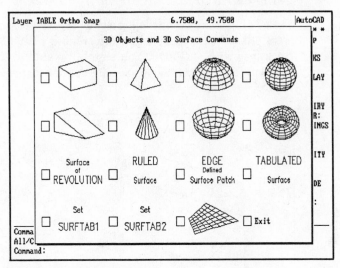

3D Construction Icon Menu

Editing in 3D Space

Meanwhile back at the table, the drawing looks a bit funny. The board overhangs on the right, and the two legs on the right extend up through the cabinet. It must be time — you guessed it — for 3D editing.

Editing in 3D is always an adventure. It pays to take a conservative approach. There are several things that you can do to cut down on getting lost in 3D space, or mis-picking the entities that you want to edit. First, you can use color extensively to help keep track of your entities. (You may have noticed that we have been adding colored components to the table as we have been working.) Second, you need to keep track of the UCS that you use when you create an entity so that you know when you are viewing an entity at an oblique angle. Most of the problems that you may encounter in editing result from picking objects at an oblique viewing angle when some (not all) of the 2D editing commands only work at a non-oblique viewing angle relative to the current X,Y plane. In these cases, you need to adjust your UCS. Keep track of your THICKNESS setting, and remember to reset it to 0 after use. In addition, there are some editing commands, like FILLET and CHAMFER, where adjusting your coordinate system may still not be enough to get you the edit you want. These commands are best performed in plan view *even* if you have the correct coordinate system. (The complete list of these exceptions is given below.) If you have any doubts about the outcome of your edits, work in plan view.

Using CHPROP to Edit an Entity's Thickness

Try getting some decent legs on the table. First, set your UCS back to the WCS. (Recall that these legs were created with a WCS.) Then change the thickness with CHPROP. You should be able to select the entities using your current 3D view. The exercise sequence gives you the new thickness value.

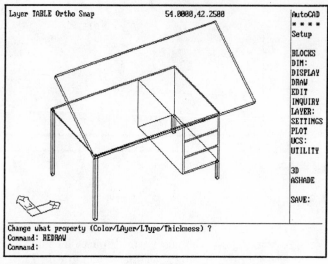

Edited Table Legs

Using CHPROP to Edit Entity Thickness in 3D

```
Command: UCS                                    Set the UCS to world.
Command: ZOOM                                   Zoom Extents.

Command: CHPROP                                 Type or select.
Select objects:                                 Select the two right legs at the cabinet.
Select objects: <RETURN>
Change what property (Color/LAyer/LType/Thickness) ? T          Thickness.
New thickness <25.0000>: 6.5                    New value.
Change what property (Color/LAyer/LType/Thickness) ? <RETURN>

Command: REDRAW                                 Clean up the display.
```

That takes care of the legs.

Using STRETCH to Edit 3D Entities

Now, stretch the table to fit the drawing board. Use your familiar STRETCH command and a crossing window to select the table entities.

The pick points for the crossing window and the completed stretch are shown in the following illustrations.

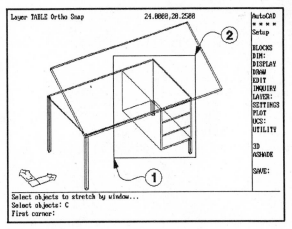

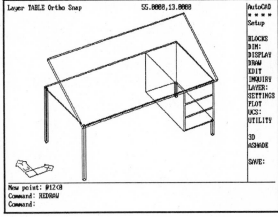

Crossing Window for STRETCH

Table After STRETCH

Making the Table Longer With STRETCH

```
Command: STRETCH                          Type or select.
Select objects to stretch by window...
Select objects: C                         Crossing.
First corner:                             Pick first corner point at ①.
Other corner:                             Pick second corner point at ②.
8 found.
Select objects:<RETURN>
Base point:                               Pick any point.
New point: @12<0                          Moves 12 inches.

Command: REDRAW                           Clean up the display.
```

While CHPROP and STRETCH act as you would expect, the editing commands in the list below will require some care and attention in 3D.

2D Editing Commands Requiring Special Attention

The following editing commands work correctly only in the X,Y plane (or a plane parallel to the entity's coordinate system).

BREAK — Projects the entity and break points to the current UCS.

TRIM — Projects the trim edge and entities to the current UCS.

EXTEND — Projects the extend edge and entities to the current UCS.

FILLET and CHAMFER — All objects being filleted or chamfered must lie in a plane parallel to the current UCS (extrusion thickness parallel to current Z axis).

OFFSET — is performed relative to the current UCS.

You may find it easiest to just work in plan view when you encounter these commands.

Using FILLET to Edit in 3D

To see how FILLET behaves, try filleting the 2D polylines that make up the cabinet drawers using a radius value of 0.5. Follow the next exercise sequence to see the type of error messages that you will encounter before you change your UCS.

Trying to Use FILLET in 3D to Fillet Drawers

```
Command: FILLET                                        Set radius to .5".
View is not plan to UCS. Command results may not be obvious.
Polyline/Radius/<Select two objects>: R
Enter fillet radius <0.0000>: .5

Command: FILLET
View is not plan to UCS. Command results may not be obvious.
Polyline/Radius/<Select two objects>: P        Drawers are polylines.
Select 2D polyline:                            Pick a drawer.
Entity not parallel with UCS.                  An error message is displayed.
Select 2D polyline: *Cancel*                   Use <^C> to cancel fillet.
```

Now, try it again after you restore the CABINET coordinate system that you used when you created the drawers.

Using FILLET to Fillet Drawers in 3D

```
Command: UCS           Restore CABINET.
Command: FILLET        Fillet the first (lower) drawer.
Command: FILLET        Fillet the second drawer.
Command: FILLET        Fillet the last drawer.
```

Your screen should look like the Table With Filleted Drawers illustration. If you are wondering why your CABINET UCS icon seems to be floating in space, remember that you stretched the table 12 inches to the right.

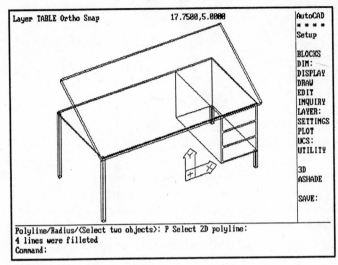

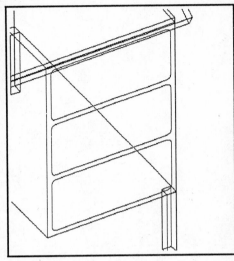

Table With Filleted Drawers   Detail of Filleted Drawers

➡ *TIP: While regular VPOINT 3D views are editable, lines that have been hidden may lose their hidden properties. If you have to edit a hidden view, execute HIDE, when you are through, to regenerate the hidden view.*

Using HATCH to Add Hatches in 3D

The HATCH command projects the hatch boundaries onto the X,Y plane of the current UCS when the hatch itself is drawn. Change your current UCS back to the WCS. Then create four boundary lines on layer 0 and try to hatch the board.

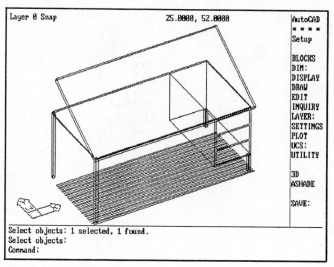

```
Layer 0 Snap                      25.0000, 52.0000        AutoCAD
                                                          * * * *
                                                          Setup

                                                          BLOCKS
                                                          DIM:
                                                          DISPLAY
                                                          DRAW
                                                          EDIT
                                                          INQUIRY
                                                          LAYER:
                                                          SETTINGS
                                                          PLOT
                                                          UCS:
                                                          UTILITY

                                                          3D
                                                          ASHADE

                                                          SAVE:

Select objects: 1 selected, 1 found.
Select objects:
Command:
```

Table With Incorrect Hatch

Trying to Hatch the Drawing Board

Command: **UCS**	Set UCS back to World.
Command: **LAYER**	Set layer 0 current.
Command: **COLOR**	Set color to BYLAYER.
Command: **LINE**	Use osnap INTersection to draw 4 boundary lines around the top of the drawing board.

```
Command: HATCH
Pattern (? or name/U,style): LINE
Scale for pattern <1.0000>: 6
Angle for pattern <0>: <RETURN>
Select objects:          Select the 4 boundary lines
4 selected.
Select objects: <RETURN>
```

The hatch was projected to the current UCS. To get the right hatch, you need to locate the UCS on the same plane as the (projected) hatch surface. Erase your first hatch, restore your BOARD UCS and try again. Use the following detailed illustration to help you get the pick point to move the UCS origin to the top of the board.

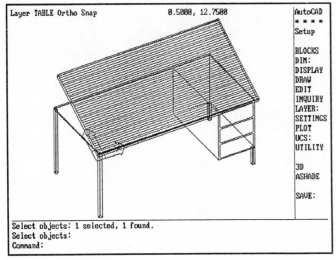

```
Layer TABLE Ortho Snap          0.5000, 12.7500        AutoCAD
                                                       * * * *
                                                       Setup

                                                       BLOCKS
                                                       DIM:
                                                       DISPLAY
                                                       DRAW
                                                       EDIT
                                                       INQUIRY
                                                       LAYER:
                                                       SETTINGS
                                                       PLOT
                                                       UCS:
                                                       UTILITY

                                                       3D
                                                       ASHADE

                                                       SAVE:

Select objects: 1 selected, 1 found.
Select objects:
Command:
```

Table With Correct Hatch

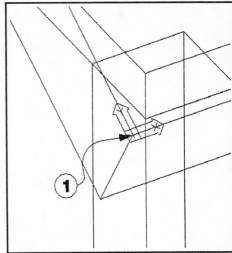

UCS Icon After Move

Hatching the Drawing Board

Command: **ERASE**	Erase the previous hatch.
Command: **UCS**	Restore BOARD UCS.
Command: **UCS**	Use origin to move UCS to the top of the board.
Command: **HATCH**	Repeat the hatch sequence in the previous exercise.

Your table should have a hatch on the plane of the drawing board. You will find that both the TRIM and EXTEND commands behave similarly to HATCH, taking their boundary edges and entities and projecting them onto the plan view of the current UCS. However, the trimmed or extended entities remain in their own planes after modification.

➡ *NOTE: As you edit in 3D, you will find that it usually pays to name and save your UCS. If you forget what you have, you can always get a listing with the first UCS dialogue box.*

➡ *TIP: Spruce up your 3D images by using surface boundaries as edges for hatching.*

Using BASE to Define Base Point for Inserts

We are going to insert this drawing later into another drawing. Clean up the drawing by erasing the last hatch and boundary lines. Reset UCS to World, then use the BASE command to define an insertion point at the lower front corner of the left front leg. Get your pick point from the illustration below.

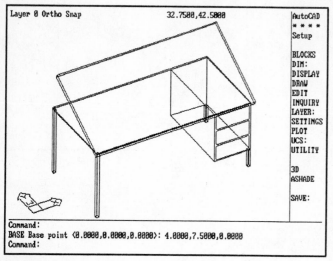

Completed Table

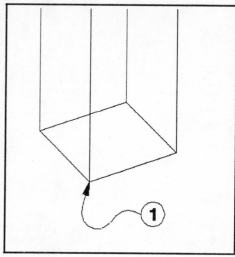

Detail of Pick Point

Setting Up the Drawing as a Block

Command: **ERASE**   Erase the hatch and boundary lines on layer 0.
Command: **UCS**   Set the UCS to World.

Command: **BASE**
Base point <0.0000,0.0000,0.0000>:   Pick lower left corner of left front leg at ①.

Using the System Variable UCSFOLLOW

Before we put the table to rest, take a moment to review its construction by looking at the plan view in the different UCSs you saved. Viewing each saved UCS in plan view will show the top, front and right side. AutoCAD provides a system variable called UCSFOLLOW that will generate a plan view each time you change coordinate systems. Set UCSFOLLOW to 1, and look at your drawing's UCS planes. Your starting screen should look like the Original View illustration.

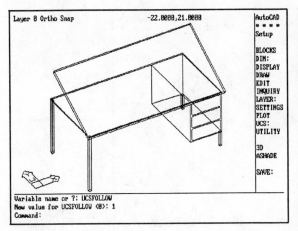

Original View

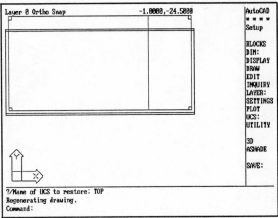

Plan View of Top

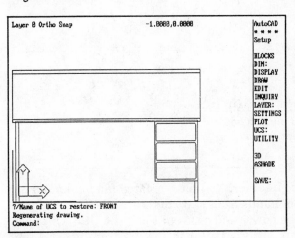

Plan View of Front

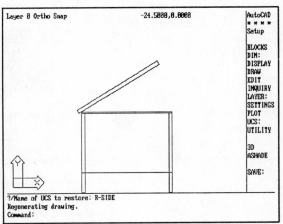

Plan View of Right Side

Using UCSFOLLOW to View Saved UCS Planes in Plan

```
Command: SETVAR
Variable name or ?: UCSFOLLOW
New value for UCSFOLLOW <0>: 1
```

Command: **UCS**	Restore TOP UCS.
Command: **UCS**	Restore FRONT UCS.
Command: **UCS**	Restore R-SIDE UCS.

After you have reviewed your drawing, restore your 3D view and HIDE the table. Then, END the drawing.

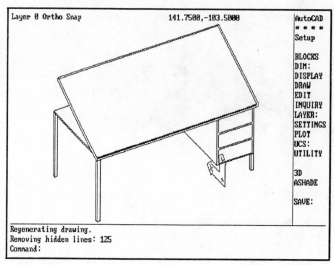

```
Layer 0 Ortho Snap                      141.7500,-103.5000    AutoCAD
                                                              * * * *
                                                              Setup

                                                              BLOCKS
                                                              DIM:
                                                              DISPLAY
                                                              DRAW
                                                              EDIT
                                                              INQUIRY
                                                              LAYER:
                                                              SETTINGS
                                                              PLOT
                                                              UCS:
                                                              UTILITY

                                                              3D
                                                              ASHADE

                                                              SAVE:

Regenerating drawing.
Removing hidden lines: 125
Command:
```

Hidden Table

Using HIDE to View Hidden Table

Command: **VIEW**	Restore 3D View.
Command: **LAYER**	Turn off layer HIDDENTABLE.
Command: **HIDE**	Take a look at a hidden view.
Command: **UCS**	Set UCS to World.
Command: **END**	

More congratulations are in order. You have created (and edited) a 3D table using 2D entity commands from start to finish! We hope we have given you some feel for the power and ease built into the UCS. Once you get the hang of it, using a UCS is still just like 2D drafting. The only difference is that you can climb all over your drawing. Think of it as fly-on-the-wall drafting. Take a break now; you deserve it.

Stopping Point

As soon as you start working in 3D, you will want to create assembly drawings in some form. You will also run into the need to update your 3D drawings. The next section shows how to assemble a multiview drawing, and how to update your 3D drawing using block redefinitions.

Creating 3D Assembly Drawings

Once you have a basic 3D drawing, like the table, it is easy to create a multiview drawing. The next set of exercises will take you through a series of multiple inserts where you insert the TABLE drawing, then use the UCS, the ROTATE and the BLOCK commands to get a plan, top, right side, and 3D view in the same drawing.

Setup for Multiview Drawing

To get started, create a new drawing and call it MULTVTBL. If you are using the IA DISK, set MULTVTBL=CHAP-13B. The following table provides the starting settings for the drawing. Since we are inserting the TABLE drawing, it will carry the TABLE layer (and any other layers you made) into the new drawing. Use the exercise as a guide to help you get set up.

COORDS	FILL	GRID	ORTHO	SNAP	UCSICON
ON	OFF	2	ON	.5	OR

UNITS	Use defaults for all Unit settings.
LIMITS	Set LIMITS from 0,0 to 204,132.
ZOOM	Zoom All.

Layer name	State	Color	Linetype
0	On	7 (white)	CONTINUOUS

Multvtbl Drawing Settings

Setting Up the Multvtbl Drawing

Enter selection: **1**   Begin a NEW drawing called MULTVTBL=CHAP-13B.

Enter selection: **1**   Begin a NEW drawing called MULTVTBL.

Check your drawing settings with the Multvtbl Drawing Settings table.

Command: **SETVAR**   Set UCSFOLLOW to 1 to automatically generate plan views.

Your new drawing will bring you up in plan view in the WCS.

Using INSERT and BLOCK to Create a Front View

Start the drawing by inserting the TABLE drawing. Recall that the table drawing was constructed with its legs *sitting* on the WCS. When you INSERT the table, it will align to the current WCS and insert in plan view.

To get the front view in the current drawing, you need to rotate the table 90 degrees, flipping it on its back side. This is a two-step process. First, you need to rotate the UCS 90 degrees about the Y axis; *then* you rotate the table block with the ROTATE command. (ROTATE will only rotate about the Z axis, perpendicular to the X,Y plane of rotation.) After you rotate the table, BLOCK it out as FRONT. Use the exercise sequence to take you through the process. Your screen should look like the Front View of Table when you block the table.

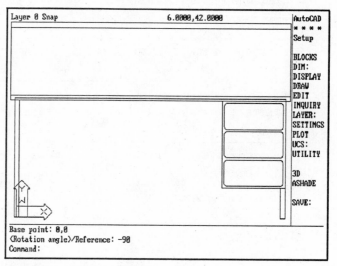

Front View of Table

Using BLOCK to Make the Table's Front View

```
Command: ZOOM            Zoom Center at 0,0,0 and 100 height.
Command: INSERT          Insert TABLE at 0,0,0 default scale factors and angle.

Command: UCS             Use Y option to rotate 90 degrees about Y axis.
Origin/ZAxis/3point/Entity/View/X/Y/Z/Prev/Restore/Save/Del/?/<World>: Y
Rotation angle about Y axis <0.0>: 90

Command: ROTATE          Rotate -90 degrees at base point 0,0,0.
Command: UCS             Set UCS to World.
Command: BLOCK           Block table to FRONT at insert point 0,0,0.
```

You now have the FRONT block tucked away in the drawing. This is a nested block. We will come back and use its nesting properties later. For now, let's move on and create the remaining blocks.

Using INSERT and BLOCK to Create Right Side View

Create the right side view by inserting the FRONT block. Use the same two-step process to flip the table 90 degrees about the X axis. Your screen should look like the following illustration when you block the table.

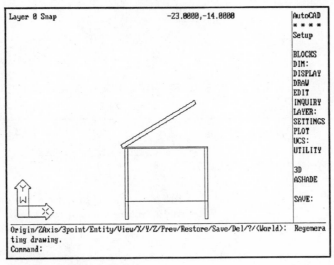

Right Side View of Table

Using BLOCK to Make the Table's Right Side View

Command: **INSERT**	Insert FRONT at 0,0,0 default scale factors and angle.
Command: **UCS**	Use X option to rotate 90 degrees about X axis.
Command: **ROTATE**	Rotate 90 degrees at base point 0,0,0.
Command: **UCS**	Set UCS to World.
Command: **BLOCK**	Block table to R-SIDE at insert point 0,0,0.

You need one more view, the 3D view.

Using INSERT and BLOCK to Create 3D View

Start with an insert of the TABLE drawing. To get a view similar to the 3D view in the original table drawing, you need to follow the same two-step process of changing your UCS and then rotating the block. Make your insert with an angle of -30 degrees, following the exercise sequence to get the rest of the rotation values. Call the block 3D.

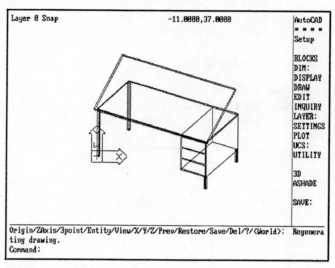

3D View of Table

Using BLOCK to Make 3D View of Table

Command: **INSERT**	Insert TABLE at 0,0,0 default scale factors and an angle of -30.
Command: **UCS**	Use Y option to rotate 90 degrees about Y axis.
Command: **ROTATE**	Rotate -60 degrees at base point 0,0,0.
Command: **UCS**	Set UCS to World.
Command: **BLOCK**	Block table to 3D at insert point 0,0,0.

You have four blocks with four views of the table, each created in the WCS.

Using INSERT to Assemble the Multiple View Drawing

Four simple inserts create the multiple view drawing. Make the table insertion for the plan view an *insertion (*TABLE). You will use this *inserted block to update the drawing. Each view's insertion point values are given in the following exercise sequence.

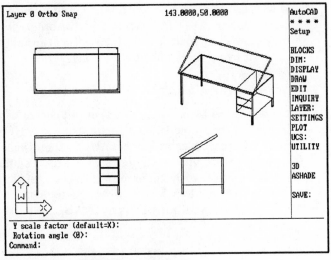

Drawing With Multiple Views of Table

Using INSERT to Create a Multiview Drawing

Command: **ZOOM**	Zoom All.
Command: **INSERT**	Insert *TABLE at 20,91,0 default scale factors and angle.
Command: **INSERT**	Insert FRONT at 20,18,0 default scale factors and angle.
Command: **INSERT**	Insert R-SIDE at 125,18,0 default scale factors and angle.
Command: **INSERT**	Insert 3D at 125,81,0 default scale factors and angle.

If all went well, you should have a drawing with multiple views of the table like the one shown above. When you want to assemble a multiview drawing, two key things to remember are to construct your blocks in the same UCS (we used the WCS), and to *manually* rotate the entities to get the view that you want. This involves changing your UCS because of the Z constraint on the 2D ROTATE command.

Using Block Redefinition to Update a 3D Drawing

Now, it's time for some frosting on the cake. Why go though all the trouble of creating a multiview drawing if you have to reassemble the drawing to make a change? You don't have to! You can use the same block redefinition techniques you used to update your drawings in 2D.

We anticipated the revisions by using an *insertion for the table plan view block. You can revise the drawing by modifying the original table block. Once you revise this block, all the other views will be updated since they are nested blocks, referencing the original table block. Prove this to yourself by adding knobs to the drawers.

Revising the Multiview Table Drawing

The *inserted block is in the upper left corner of your screen. In order to work on this view you need to establish a new UCS to work on the cabinet front. When you establish this UCS, the other views, particularly the lower left front view, will get in your way. Temporarily BLOCK all three views together, with the name VIEWS, to get some working room. Then, create your drawer knobs with one-inch thick circles; redefine your TABLE block; and *insert your VIEWS. You will have an instant updated drawing.

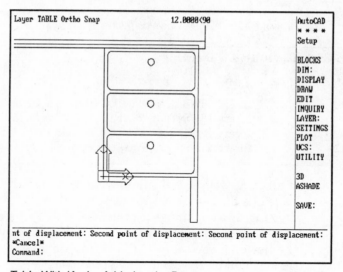

Table With Knobs Added to the Drawers

Using Block Redefinition to Revise a 3D Drawing

Command: **BLOCK**	Block the FRONT, R-SIDE, and 3D with the name VIEWS and insert point at 0,0,0. This will provide room to edit the table.
Command: **UCS**	Rotate the X axis 90 degrees.
Command: **UCS**	Move the Origin to the corner of the cabinet.
Command: **LAYER**	Set layer TABLE current.
Command: **COLOR**	Set color to blue.
Command: **SETVAR**	Set THICKNESS to 1.
Command: **CIRCLE**	Draw a 1" circle at 7,4.5.
Command: **COPY**	Copy multiple the circle to other drawers.
Command: **UCS**	Set UCS to World.
Command: **BLOCK**	Redefine TABLE block with insert point at 20,91.
Command: **OOPS**	Bring the table back.
Command: **INSERT**	Insert *VIEWS at 0,0,0.
Command: **ZOOM**	Zoom All.
Command: **END**	

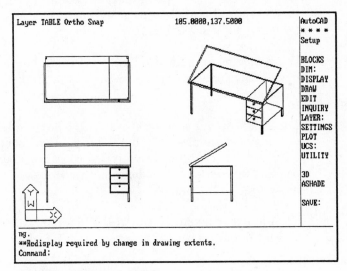

Completed Multiview Drawing

When you are done, END your drawing.

Summary of Getting Started in 3D

Good layer and color management can greatly ease and speed 3D work. Colors help clarify an overlaid mass of wireframe images. Layers allow you to turn objects off to ease picking points in heavy traffic, and to freeze unneeded layers to speed up regenerations and hidden line removal.

It is sometimes hard to select objects and pick points in a single viewport, particularly when osnapping to an existing object. Remember that you can use XYZ point filters, and even switch viewports midstream. For example, you can select your objects in one or more viewports, pick your XY point in another viewport, and then switch to a third viewport to osnap the Z value.

A standard set of named UCSs, viewports and viewpoints makes jumping around in 3D a snap. Don't forget, each viewport can have its own set of snap and grid settings.

Use the UCS entity option for quick edits to existing entities, or to add new entities parallel to existing ones. The XY orientation may look unusual, but it seldom matters.

When moving around with UCS or VPOINT, be careful your image is not upside down or backwards from where you think it is. It's hard to tell with wireframes.

For 2D entities that are constrained to be parallel to the current UCS, you need not change UCS just to place them above or below the current UCS. A Z value entered for their first coordinate point will establish their position in 3D space. And don't confuse things by setting ELEVATION or using the ELEV command.

Don't forget that you can COPY and MOVE any entity up and down in the current Z axis, as well as around in the X,Y plane.

Remember to use blocks when you have repeated 3D objects, or multiple views of identical objects in the same drawing. 3D allows you to generate a lot of drawing data while blocks help keep your drawing file compact. Temporary blocks are also a good way to get complex objects out of your way.

Save your settings in a 3D prototype drawing.

3D Entities

There is more to come. The next chapter shows you how to work with 3D entities. If you have a drafting table, you need a chair — a real 3D chair.

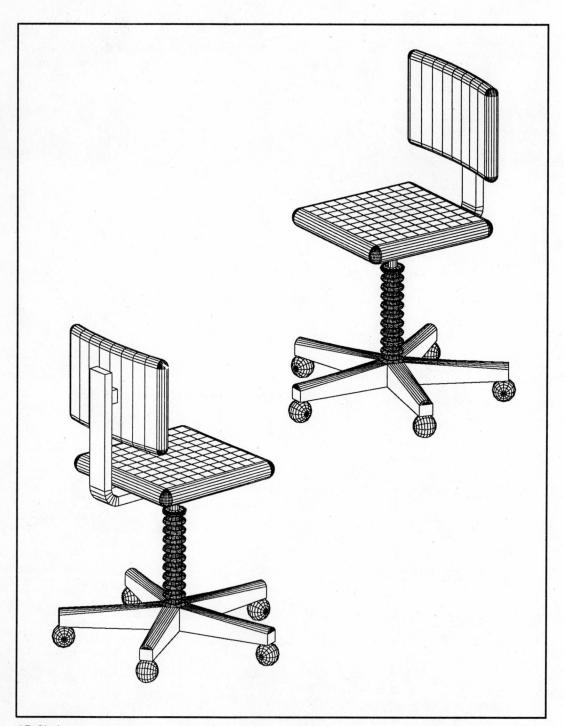

3D Chair

Chapter 14

Using 3D Entities

Lay of the Land — 3D Graphic Entities

You have built a table in 3D space using simple surfaces. In this chapter, you will learn how to draw and edit objects with more complex mesh surfaces. AutoCAD provides a series of 3D entities to construct polyline meshes. You can use these 3D entities to construct complex shapes, creating meshes on flat and curved surfaces. You also can construct blocks of your 3D entities and insert them to build a drawing.

Since you have a table, you need a comfortable chair to sit in while you watch your AutoCAD screen do all this 3D work. The facing page shows the chair that you will create using the chapter's exercises. This chair uses all of AutoCAD's 3D entities. The casters, legs, pedestal, seat, and back are all built as blocks and then the chair is assembled from the 3D *component* parts.

Faces vs. Meshes

The new 3D entities that you will work with in this chapter let you construct *faceted* surfaces. A 3D face is an entity that is a three- or four-sided section of a plane. If you look at the chapter's chair illustration on the facing page, the sides of the legs are constructed as 3D faces.

The chair's seat, back, and pedestal have multiple faces. While you could build these surfaces using individual faces, AutoCAD provides a series of 3D mesh commands that automatically generate a surface mesh. These meshes let you work in 3D with both planar and curved surfaces, like the pedestal and corners of the chair.

Mesh Concepts

AutoCAD makes automatic mesh generation quite easy. Think of the mesh as a *blanket* that you can put on or wrap around a surface. To make a circular mesh, you simply specify a *path profile* and an axis of rotation. The path profile is the profile of the surface that you want. If you rotate the surface 360 degrees, you will get a circular or cylindrical surface, like the chair's pedestal, depending on the complexity of your path profile. You also can generate a mesh by creating a path profile and projecting the surface with a *direction vector*. The surface of the chair's backrest is made by projecting an elongated arc which profiles the top edge, making the surface the height of the backrest. You also can control the fineness of these meshes with system variable settings called SURFTABS. That's all there is to meshes: path profiles, a direction vector or rotation axis, and some surface settings.

3D Entity Tools

You will find the 3D entity commands on the [3D] screen menu. These commands include 3DFACE, 3DPOLY, 3DMESH, and the SURF commands, EDGESURF, REVSURF, RULESURF, and TABSURF. The [3D OBJECTS] menu item on the 3D screen menu calls a submenu of pre-built geometric objects like sphere, cone, and torus, that are built from the surface commands. These same pre-built objects are available on an icon menu called by [3D Construction ...] on the [Draw] pull-down menu. You also will find [3D Polyline] on the [Draw] pull-down menu.

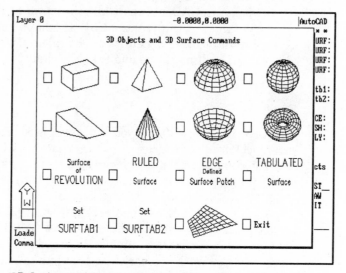

3D Screen and Construction Icon Menus

Goals for Modeling the 3D Chair

The goals for this chapter are two-fold. The first goal is to show you how to use each of the 3D entity commands. In sequence, we will take you through each command to build a part of the chair. The illustration (below) shows the individual 3D entities that you will use to construct the chair. As you make these entities, we will give you some helpful practice (and tips) on placing your UCS to draw and edit entities in 3D space.

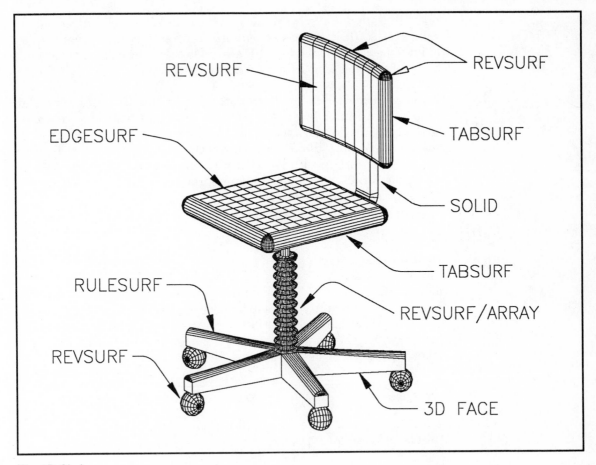

The 3D Chair

The second goal is to show you how to make and insert 3D blocks. You construct the chair by blocking out each component with an insertion base point: inserting the casters on the legs, the legs on the pedestal, the pedestal on the seat, and so on. Using 3D blocks is not a separate command, but an application of the standard BLOCK and INSERT commands. After you have constructed the chair, we will show you how you can go back and edit some of the chair's meshes with PEDIT. Standard editing commands such as PEDIT and CHPROP take on new meaning when dealing with entities like 3DPOLYs and surface meshes.

How to Use the Chair Exercises

Since the chair is built from parts, you can work your way through the exercises block by block, or you can pick and choose the entity commands that you want to learn by working on a particular component. If you are using the IA DISK, the component blocks are on the disk so that you can build some components, but still assemble the chair using the pre-built blocks if you choose not draw all the component parts.

If you want to spend more time working with any 3D entity command, practice on a scratch layer. We have set up the chair's drawing viewports so that you can use the upper right viewport as a scratch viewport while you are working in the chair drawing. Use your scratch layer and this viewport to practice with the 3D entity commands. When you are done using the scratch layer, set the appropriate CHAIR layer current and freeze your scratch layer.

Setup for Using 3D Entities

To do the chair exercises, you need to begin a new drawing called CHAIR. The drawing uses two layers, CHAIR and BUILD, and it uses AutoCAD's default drawing units. The chair is 35" high and about 25" wide at the base, with varied entity colors to help your viewing in 3D. It is drawn as a block for insertion into other drawings, therefore scale is not a factor in this drawing. The limits are set large enough to contain the chair. The following table provides the settings for the drawing.

COORDS	FILL	GRID	SNAP	UCSICON
ON	OFF	Off	.25	OR & ON

UNITS	Use defaults for all Unit settings.
LIMITS	0,0 to 68,44

Layer name	State	Color	Linetype
0	On	7 (white)	CONTINUOUS
CHAIR	Current	7 (white)	CONTINUOUS
BUILD	On	1 (red)	CONTINUOUS

3D Chair Drawing Settings

If you are using the IA DISK, you have the basic drawing setup in the CHAP-14.DWG file. To get started, begin a new drawing by setting your CHAIR drawing equal to it. Then, set up your viewports. The initial setup will give you three viewports: a full-height port on the left where you will spend most of your time building the chair; a lower right port with a plan view of the chair; and an upper right viewport to use as a scratch port. This last port is set with a default world UCS. Use the input values in the exercise to get your view points, and to set your UCS.

If you are not using the IA DISK, you need to create the drawing and adjust the settings before you create the viewports.

Setting Up for 3D Entities

    Enter selection: **1**   Begin a NEW drawing named CHAIR=CHAP-14.

    Enter selection: **1**   Begin a NEW drawing named CHAIR.

Make or verify the settings shown in the Chair Drawing Settings table.

Command: **VPOINT**   Enter a view point -1.0,-1.0,0.5.
Command: **ZOOM**   Zoom Center at 0,0 and a height of 20.
Command: **VIEW**   Save view as CHAIR.
Command: **UCS**   Set origin at 0,88,0.
Command: **ZOOM**   Zoom Center at 0,0 and a height of 20.
Command: **VIEW**   Save view as BUILD.

Command: **VPORTS**   Create 3 viewports.
Save/Restore/Delete/Join/SIngle/?/2/<3>/4: **3**
Horizontal/Vertical/Above/Below/Left/<Right>: **L**

Make upper right viewport active.
Command: **UCSICON**   Turn icon off.
Command: **VIEW**   Restore view CHAIR.

Make lower right viewport active.
Command: **PLAN**   Go to plan view of current UCS.
Command: **ZOOM**   Zoom Center at 0,0 and a height of 20.
Command: **VPORTS**   Save Vports as BUILD.

When you are done, your screen should look like the Viewports for Chair illustration (below). Layer CHAIR should be current and the UCS icon should be in the center of two viewports with the BUILD view. The lower right viewport should be active.

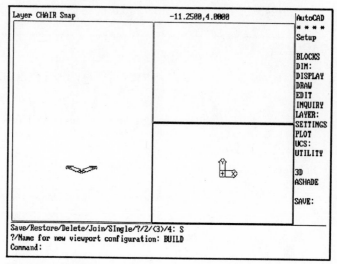

Viewports for Chair

Working in 3D requires more preparation to create entities. Drawings can become complex and difficult to visualize. Your ability to visualize and select entities easily will depend on your display resolution. The following exercises will specify zooms, snap, ortho, and osnaps, but you should also use these commands freely if you need to get better display resolution. Use the illustrations as guides for your zooms.

Extruding a 2D Polyline

To start, we are going to extrude a 2D polyline to create the chair's hub. The hub is a pentagon, a polyline constructed with the POLYGON command. It becomes three dimensional when a thickness is assigned to it in the Z plane.

Using a 2D Polygon to Construct the Chair's Hub

Create the hub of the chair using the POLYGON command. After you make the polygon, assign a thickness with CHPROP. A negative thickness will extrude the hub in the Z plane below the UCS. Work in plan view in the lower right viewport. When you extrude the hub, you will see the extruded hub in your left viewport, extending below the UCS icon. Your screen will look like the Hub of Chair illustration below. Your polygon radius and thickness values are in the exercise.

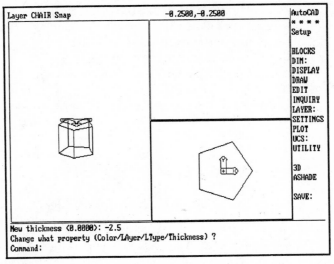

```
Layer CHAIR Snap                          -0.2500,-0.2500        AutoCAD
                                                                 * * * *
                                                                 Setup

                                                                 BLOCKS
                                                                 DIM:
                                                                 DISPLAY
                                                                 DRAW
                                                                 EDIT
                                                                 INQUIRY
                                                                 LAYER:
                                                                 SETTINGS
                                                                 PLOT
                                                                 UCS:
                                                                 UTILITY

                                                                 3D
                                                                 ASHADE

                                                                 SAVE:


New thickness <0.0000>: -2.5
Change what property (Color/LAyer/LType/Thickness) ?
Command:
```

Hub of Chair

Using CHPROP to Extrude a 2D Polyline

Command: **COLOR**   Set color to yellow.

Command: **POLYGON**   Create the center base in lower right viewport.
Number of sides: **5**
Edge/<Center of polygon>: **0,0**
Inscribed in circle/Circumscribed about circle (I/C): **C**
Radius of circle: **@-1.25,0**   Entering only 1.25 won't align the polygon at the correct angle.

Command: **CHPROP**   Extrude polygon to a thickness of 2.5.
Select objects: **L**
1 found.
Select objects: **<RETURN>**
Change what property (Color/LAyer/LType/Thickness) ? **T**
New thickness <0.0000>: **-2.5**   UCS is at top of polygon so thickness is negative.
Change what property (Color/LAyer/LType/Thickness) ? **<RETURN>**

You should have a plan view of the hub polygon in your right viewport, and a 3D view of the extruded hub in your left viewport.

Using the 3DFACE Command

Next, we are going to create the chair's leg with 3DFACE entities. 3DFACEs are true 3D entities, defined by three or four edges and points. A SOLID is confined to a single plane (in any UCS), but the edges and points of a 3DFACE can be anywhere in space. The 3DFACE prompts are similar to those for a 2D SOLID, but the pick point order is more natural. You can pick clockwise or counter clockwise instead of in a crisscross bow tie. An unextruded 2D solid and a 3D face may look the same if they both lie in the same plane, but they will have different edge and transparency properties. If all points and edges of a 3DFACE lie in a single plane, HIDE treats it as opaque. If it is not planar, it is transparent and won't hide. Unlike a solid, you can't extrude a 3DFACE, and it always has 0 thickness.

Use 3DFACEs when you want to draw simple three- or four-point planar faces. This is the case presented by the chair's leg, where we want to create an end cap, an underside, and two simple planar sides.

Using 3DFACEs to Create Chair's Leg

Create the leg by constructing a four-sided 3DFACE as the leg's end cap. Create the face in the left viewport. The X,Y,Z coordinates are given in the exercise for the cap. As you build the cap, you will see rubber band lines forming the cap to the left of the hub. You will notice that you pick a rectangle to get a rectangle. (You don't have to pick a bow tie to get a rectangle, as you do with a 2D solid!) After you create the end cap, you can create the bottom and the two sides by osnapping to endpoints on the cap and the hub.

Use the exercise to get your cap coordinates. Then, use the exercise and illustration as guides to get your pick point sequences for creating the remaining three faces.

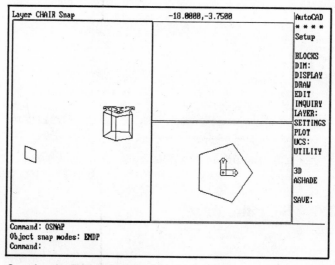

Creating the End Cap of the Leg

Using 3DFACE to Make First Leg

Make left viewport active.

Command: **3DFACE**	Create end cap of leg.
First point: **–12.5,.75,–2**	
Second point: **–12.5,–.75,–2**	
Third point: **–12.5,–.75,–.75**	
Fourth point: **–12.5,.75,–.75**	
Third point: **<RETURN>**	
Command: **OSNAP**	Set Object snap mode ENDP to draw the leg.
Command: **3DFACE**	Draw the legs left face first, then the remaining faces clockwise.
First point:	Upper left corner of polygon face at ①.
Second point:	Upper left corner of leg cap at ②.
Third point:	Lower left corner of leg cap at ③.
Fourth point:	Lower left corner of polygon face at ④.
Third point:	Lower right corner of polygon face at ⑤.
Fourth point:	Lower right corner of leg cap at ⑥.
Third point:	Upper right corner of leg cap at ⑦.
Fourth point:	Upper right corner of polygon face at ⑧.
Third point: **<RETURN>**	
Command: OSNAP	Set OSNAP back to NONe.
Command: SAVE	Save the drawing.

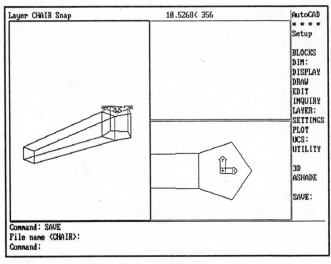

Chair Leg Constructed With 3DFACEs

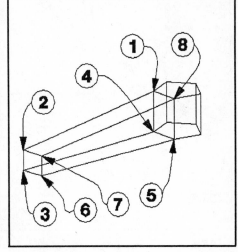

Detail of Leg

You should have a drawing in your left viewport that looks like the Chair Leg Constructed With 3DFACEs (above). The two sides will appear as lines extending from the plan view in your right viewport.

How to Use Invisible Edges

You can enhance the faces of your images by using invisible edges. Invisible edges are a property of 3DFACEs. Using invisible edges, you can create a solid surface face, then turn off the display of the lines which make up the face so that you get a solid face in a wireframe display. The SPLFRAME system variable controls the invisible edge display. This is the same variable that you used to control the framing points for a curve fit polyline in 2D.

Using 3DFACE to Cap the Chair Hub

We want the top of the chair hub to look like one piece. We can use invisible edges to get this effect. Use the SPLFRAME system variable to temporarily make invisible edges visible. Then, use the 3DFACE command and pick the two end points of the top surface leg connection and the center of the hub. Precede each pick with an I, indicating an invisible edge. This will create a triangular solid that you can array with the leg later to complete the chair base. Use the following illustration and exercise as guides.

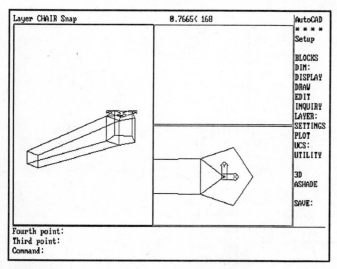

3DFACE With Invisible Edges Shown

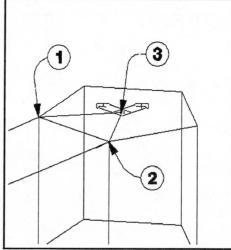

Detail of Edges

Using 3DFACE With Invisible Edges

Command: **SETVAR**	Set SPLFRAME to 1.
Command: **3DFACE**	Remember to precede all picks with I.
First point: I	Pick first corner of Polygon at ①.
Second point: I	Pick second corner of Polygon at ②.
Third point: I	Pick center of Polygon at ③ or type 0,0.
Fourth point: **\<RETURN\>**	
Third point: **\<RETURN\>**	
Command: **SETVAR**	Set SPLFRAME to 0.
Command: **REGEN**	Regen to verify edges are invisible.
Command: **SETVAR**	Set SPLFRAME to 1.

After you have turned SPLFRAME back on and regenerated your drawing, leave the frame on.

➡ *TIP: If you create a 3DFACE with all edges invisible and SPLFRAME is off (0), AutoCAD will not be able to see it. This means that selecting with Window or Last will overlook the 3DFACE. Leave SPLFRAME on (1) until you perform a hide or end the drawing.*

So far, you have manually constructed the chair base using simple flat 3D entities or extruded 2D entities. The rest of the chair construction involves curves and contours. Let's look at the mesh tools that AutoCAD provides to make 3D surface constructions more manageable. Then, we will come back to the chair leg and put a *ruled* surface on top of it.

3D Polygon Meshes

There is only one 3D mesh entity, but AutoCAD provides five commands to create 3D meshes. The basic mesh command is 3DMESH. The other four commands also generate various 3D meshes. While 3DMESH generates a mesh directly, point by point, the other commands rely on existing entities to establish the edges, directions, paths, and profiles of the resulting surface. Here is a listing of the commands. Examples of the entities are shown in the illustration below.

■ 3DMESH is a wireframe rectilinear *blanket* composed of *m* column lines by *n* row lines passing through a matrix of *m* x *n* 3D points in space. You have complete control over *m*, *n*, and the coordinate location of each of the 3D points.

■ RULESURF lets you stretch and bend a ladder in 3D space. You select the lines, 3DPOLYs or curves that make up the rails, AutoCAD fills in the ladder rungs.

- TABSURF is short for tabulated surface. AutoCAD extrudes any curve through space along a direction vector you select. For example, if you extrude a circle through a straight line, you create a cylinder.

- REVSURF is short for Surface of Revolution. AutoCAD sweeps any curve you select about an axis of revolution. For example, if you sweep a 90-degree arc about the Z axis, you create a bowl shape.

- EDGESURF is the *flying carpet* of 3D entities. You select four rectilinear boundaries, and AutoCAD fills in m x n column and row lines to define the surface.

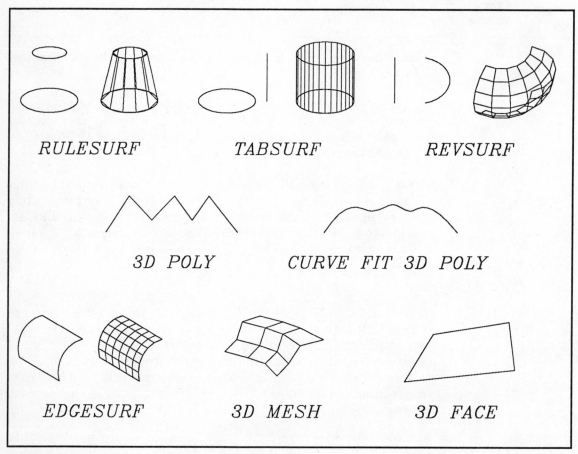

Mesh Entity Primitives

The 3DMESH Command

You will rarely use the 3DMESH command unless you are using AutoLISP to automatically generate mesh points. 3DMESH is made up of rows and columns, where m and n are indices specifying the number or rows and columns that make up the mesh. These indices determine the number of vertices required in the mesh. Once you set m and n, you input the vertices as X,Y,Z points. Meshes can be open or closed depending on whether the mesh joins in either the m or n direction, or both. The following illustration gives an example of a 3D mesh, showing the m and n directions. This is an open mesh. A donut mesh would be an example of a mesh closed in both directions. Later when we look at editing meshes, we will identify the vertices in a mesh so that you can see how the mesh vertex information is displayed.

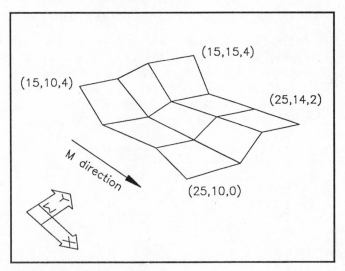

3D Mesh Example

In most of your constructions, you generally will not know your surface points. Instead, you will find yourself using the four SURF commands to generate your 3D surfaces based on boundary and direction information.

System Variables Used in Mesh Construction

Although you probably will not use the 3DMESH command, you still need to set the system variables that control the m and n indices. These are set by the SURFTAB1 and SURFTAB2 system variables. SURFTAB1 sets the m index, and SURFTAB2 sets the n index. While you can use values up to 256 for either index, we recommend working with low values (8 to 12). Dense meshes will significantly increase your drawing processing time. If you don't like the mesh that you get, you can't respecify these variables for an *existing* mesh. You have to erase the mesh, reset your surftab values, and create a *new* mesh.

The RULESURF Command

Use RULESURF to create a ruled surface between two irregular boundaries. RULESURF creates a polygon mesh between two curves. The entities that define the edges of the surface can be points, lines, arcs, circles, 2D polylines or 3D polylines. (If you use a point, only one edge can be a point.) Since you are making a ruled surface, you only need to set one system variable, SURFTAB1. This will control the intervals for the rules. After setting SURFTAB1, execute the command by picking the edge entities.

Using RULESURF to Create the Leg's Top

Use RULESURF to finish the leg's top surface. This surface will run as a ruled surface from an arc (that you will make) on the end cap to the line at the hub's top. The same arc will act as an edge to finish off the end cap surface. To create the arc, you need to set a new UCS in the plane of the end cap. Work in your left viewport. Use the following annotated illustrations and exercise to locate the UCS and make the arc.

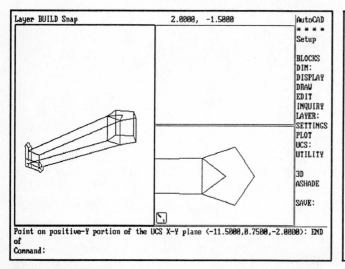

Setting a New UCS

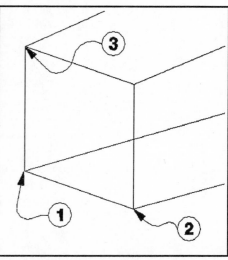

Detail of UCS

Preparing for RULESURF

Command: **LAYER**	Set layer to BUILD.
Command: **COLOR**	Set color to BYLAYER.
Command: **UCS**	Use the 3 point option and set the UCS on the leg cap, picking ①,②, and ③.

Command: **LINE**	Draw a line from ④ to ⑤.
Command: **SETVAR**	Set PDMODE to 66 to make points visible.
Command: **POINT**	Draw a point at ⑥.
Command: **ARC**	Draw an arc beginning at ⑦, ending at ⑧, and an included angle of 135 degrees.

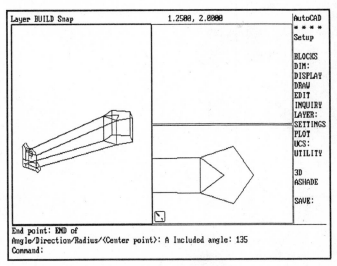

Creating the RULESURF Defining Curves

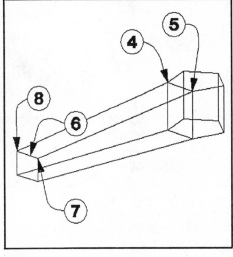

Detail of Curves

Once you have the defined curves for RULESURF, you can begin the surfacing. The arc defines a curve for the top of the leg, *and* it closes the space at the end cap. In order to use the arc for both surfaces, you will need to temporarily move one mesh to reselect the arc. The current viewport settings were set up to anticipate this type of condition. The following exercise will demonstrate how to make the top ruled mesh, then move the top mesh to the WCS so that you can make the second mesh on the end cap arc.

This second ruled mesh goes between the point and arc on the leg's end cap. After you have made the second mesh, you can move the top mesh back in place. Use the annotated illustrations and the exercise to get your pick points and values. The input value of *0,0 gives the displacement point for moving the top mesh surface to the WCS in the upper right viewport. Prefixing any coordinate value with an asterisk makes AutoCAD interpret the coordinate value in the world coordinate system. You will see the ruled surface in your upper right viewport (set as the WCS viewport) when you move the surface.

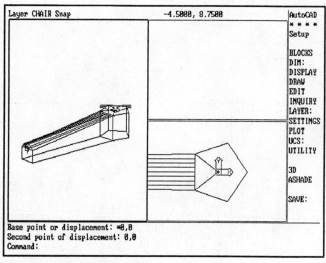

Top of Leg After RULESURF

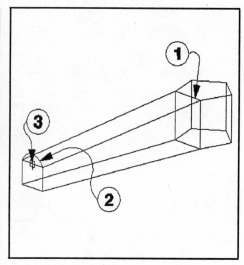

Detail of RULESURF

Using RULESURF to Complete the Leg

Command: **LAYER**	Set layer CHAIR current.
Command: **COLOR**	Set color to yellow.
Command: **UCS**	Change UCS to Previous.
Command: **SETVAR**	Set SURFTAB1 to 8.

```
Command: RULESURF
Select first defining curve:        Select line at ①.
Select second defining curve:       Select arc at ②.

Command: MOVE                       Temporarily move the Rulesurf to the WCS.
Select objects: L                   Selects the Rulesurf entity.
1 found.
Select objects: <RETURN>
Base point or displacement: 0,0     Origin of current UCS.
Second point of displacement: *0,0  Origin of WCS.

Command: RULESURF
Select first defining curve:        Select the Point at ③ with NODe osnap.
Select second defining curve:       Select Arc at ②.

Command: MOVE                 Move the rulesurf in the WCS back to the UCS.
Select objects:              Selects the Rulesurf entity in the upper right viewport.
1 found.
Select objects: <RETURN>
Base point or displacement: *0,0    Origin of WCS.
Second point of displacement: 0,0   Origin of current UCS.
```

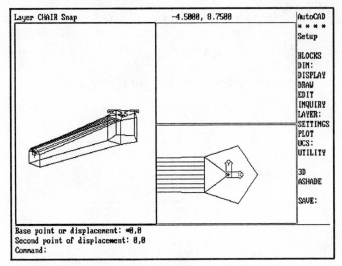

Layer CHAIR Snap   -4.5000, 8.7500   AutoCAD
                                                            * * * *
                                                            Setup

                                                            BLOCKS
                                                            DIM:
                                                            DISPLAY
                                                            DRAW
                                                            EDIT
                                                            INQUIRY
                                                            LAYER:
                                                            SETTINGS
                                                            PLOT
                                                            UCS:
                                                            UTILITY

                                                            3D
                                                            ASHADE

                                                            SAVE:

Base point or displacement: *0,0
Second point of displacement: 0,0
Command:

Completed Leg Surface

When you work with RULESURF, your pick points can be important. If your edge curves are open, the rule is built from the endpoint nearest your pick point on each entity. The ruled surface can twist if you don't pick the nearest endpoints on the edge entities. You also can get a twist with closed entities. The mesh is generated from the 0 degree point of circles and from the starting vector of closed polylines. If you are generating a mesh between two circles, make sure that your 0 points are aligned to avoid a twist in the mesh.

➤ *TIP: You may often want to RULESURF between a circle and a polyline ellipse. It is almost impossible to align the 0 point on the circle with the starting vector of the ellipse. The easiest method to control RULESURF alignment is to use the ELLIPSE command to create both entities.*

The mesh commands require that you pick the entities that you are going to use to create the ruled surface. If you are going to create meshes that have a common entity as a boundary, then you need to move one mesh to pick the entity to form the second mesh. If you don't move the first mesh to a SCRATCH or BUILD work area, it is almost impossible to pick the profile entity for the second surface. Putting your profiles on a different layer also helps you control the selection of profile entities.

➥ *TIP: Two other methods for temporarily removing a mesh at a common boundary is to block the mesh to a temporary name and *insert it after the other meshes are created, or erase the mesh and oops it back after the other meshes are created.*

Arraying the Legs for the Chair Base

Now, one leg is complete. We can array the leg to make the chair's base, then block the base as a finished component. Use the standard ARRAY command to array the leg and BLOCK to create the block called BASE. The following illustrations show how the base looks before and after the array.

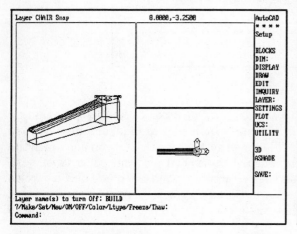

Completed Leg Before Array

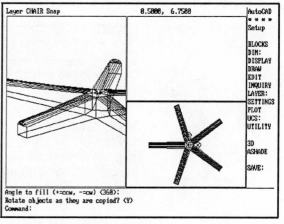

Completed Base After Array

Arraying the Legs to Complete the Base

Make the lower right viewport active.

Command: **LAYER**	Turn layer BUILD off.
Command: ARRAY	Array leg and cap of hub 5 places in 360 degrees with center point at 0,0.
Command: BLOCK	Block to BASE with the insert point at 0,0.

The block called BASE is stored in your current CHAIR drawing. If you are using the IA DISK, you will also have the block stored on disk as BASE.DWG.

Using 3D Constructions

You will frequently encounter cases where you can take advantage of predefined geometric shapes. AutoCAD has created primitive 3D shape routines using the mesh surface commands. These objects include a sphere, a cone, a torus, and a pyramid. The objects are generated by predefined AutoLISP routines that are executed when you select the object from the screen or icon menu. They automate the creation of the defining entities, such as edges and axes, that the mesh commands require. The spheres that we will use to make the casters for the chair are generated by an AutoLISP routine that uses the REVSURF command.

Using a 3D Sphere to Construct the Chair's Casters

Select Sphere from either the screen [3D Objects] menu item or the [3D Construction ...] menu item. You will be prompted for the sphere's vertical axis line and its diameter. Make the diameter 2.5 inches. You will see the AutoLISP code scroll by at the command line as the sphere is built. The routine will automatically clean up after it is done, erasing the arc and axis line. When you have the sphere, BLOCK it to a block named CASTER. Get your insert point from the exercise. The following illustration shows the completed sphere.

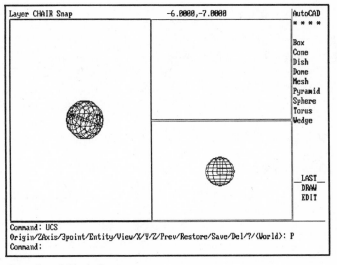

Completed Chair Caster

Using a Pre-Built 3D Sphere to Make a Simple Caster

Make the left viewport active.

Command: **UCS**	Rotate the X axis 90 degrees.
Command: **COLOR**	Set color to red.

Select **[Sphere]**	Select sphere from the screen or icon menu.
Please wait... Loading 3D Objects. nil	

Command: Sphere	The sphere command is started.
Center of sphere: **0,0**	
Diameter/<radius>: **1.25**	
Number of longitudinal segments <16>: **12**	
Number of latitudinal segments <16>: **12**	

Command: **UCS**	Restore the previous UCS.
Command: **BLOCK**	Block sphere, selecting as last, to CASTER with insert point at top of sphere (0,0,1.25).
Command: **SAVE**	Save drawing.

Before you block the caster, it should look like the Completed Chair Caster illustration (above).

The REVSURF Command

REVSURF creates a surface by revolving a path curve around an axis of revolution. You select the path curve and the axis of rotation. The path curve can be a line, arc, circle, or 2D or 3D polyline. You can specify the axis of rotation with a line or open polyline. After you specify the path profile and axis, you give the angle that you want the surface rotated. You also can specify a start angle as an offset from a 0 start angle. You have seen REVSURF in action generating the sphere.

Using REVSURF to Construct the Pedestal

Let's look at using REVSURF to create a more complex surface, the chair's pedestal. The chair's pedestal is, of course, pneumatic! The pedestal mesh is made up of two different revolved shapes. You first create the bottom and top 3D-revolved surface entities with REVSURF. Then array the bottom entity vertically to create the final pedestal.

In the following exercise, we will set up a UCS and create a vertical axis line of revolution, a polyline path profile for the bottom entity, and a path curve for the top entity. We will use PEDIT to edit the bottom path profile to get a curve fit. The following illustration and exercise sequence will guide you through the preparation steps.

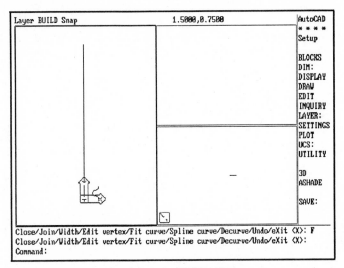

Bottom Path Curve and Axis for REVSURF

Preparing Axis and Bottom Path Curve for REVSURF

Command:	**LAYER**	Set layer BUILD current.
Command:	**COLOR**	Set color to BYLAYER.
Command:	**ERASE**	Erase any remaining build entities.
Command:	**UCS**	Rotate the X axis 90 degrees.
Command:	**LINE**	From 0,0 to 0,13 for axis of revolution.
Command:	**PLAN**	Default to current plan view.
Command:	**PLINE**	From 1.25,0 to .75,.5 to 1.25,1.

```
Command: Command: PEDIT
Select polyline: L
Close/Join/Width/Edit vertex/Fit curve/Spline curve/Decurve/Undo/eXit <X>: E
Next/Previous/Break/Insert/Move/Regen/Straighten/Tangent/Width/eXit <N>: T
Direction of tangent: 90
Next/Previous/Break/Insert/Move/Regen/Straighten/Tangent/Width/eXit <N>: N
Next/Previous/Break/Insert/Move/Regen/Straighten/Tangent/Width/eXit <N>: N
Next/Previous/Break/Insert/Move/Regen/Straighten/Tangent/Width/eXit <N>: T
Direction of tangent: 90
Next/Previous/Break/Insert/Move/Regen/Straighten/Tangent/Width/eXit <N>: X
Close/Join/Width/Edit vertex/Fit curve/Spline curve/Decurve/Undo/eXit <X>: F
Close/Join/Width/Edit vertex/Fit curve/Spline curve/Decurve/Undo/eXit <X>: X
```

The top of the pedestal will terminate with a shaft. Draw the second path curve to establish the top shaft profile. This shaft profile combines polyline arc and line segments. The point values are in the exercise.

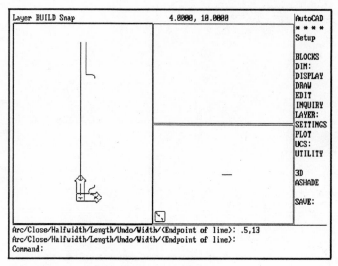

Top Path Curve for the Pedestal Shaft Top

Creating Top Path Curve for the Shaft Top

```
Command: PLINE
From point: 1.25,10
Current line-width is 0.0000
Arc/Close/Halfwidth/Length/Undo/Width/<Endpoint of line>: A
Angle/CEnter/CLose/Direction/Halfwidth/Line/Radius/Second pt/Undo/Width/
<Endpoint of arc>: D
Direction from start point:            Pick any point at 90 degrees.
End point: 1,10.25
Angle/CEnter/CLose/Direction/Halfwidth/Line/Radius/Second pt/Undo/Width/
<Endpoint of arc>: L
Arc/Close/Halfwidth/Length/Undo/Width/<Endpoint of line>: .5,10.25
Arc/Close/Halfwidth/Length/Undo/Width/<Endpoint of line>: .5,13
Arc/Close/Halfwidth/Length/Undo/Width/<Endpoint of line>: <RETURN>
```

Now, complete the shaft with REVSURF. Set your SURFTAB1 and SURFTAB2 settings. When you execute REVSURF, pick your profile entity, then the axis line. Default the start angle and the included angle. The default is a full circle. After you have revolved the bottom, do the same with the top path profile. Finish the pedestal by using a rectangular ARRAY to create 9 copies (10 rows, 1 column) of the bottom surface entity. When you are done, reset your UCS and block the PEDESTAL.

The following illustrations and the exercise will help you get your pick points and input values.

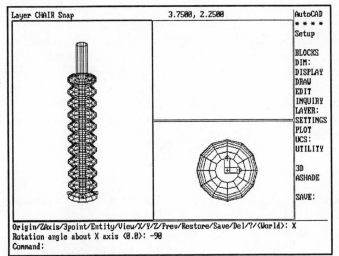

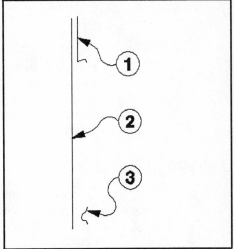

Completed Pedestal   *Detail of REVSURF*

Using REVSURF to Make the Pedestal Surface

Command: **VPORTS**	Restore Build viewport.
Command: **LAYER**	Set layer CHAIR current.
Command: **COLOR**	Set color to cyan.
Command: **SETVAR**	Set SURFTAB1 to 12.
Command: **SETVAR**	Set SURFTAB2 to 4.
Command: **REVSURF**	Revolve bottom pedestal segment.
Select path curve:	Select first path ③.
Select axis of revolution:	Select axis ②.
Start angle <0>: **<RETURN>**	
Included angle (+=ccw, -=cw) <Full circle>: **<RETURN>**	
Command: **REVSURF**	Revolve top pedestal shaft.
Select path curve:	Select second path ①.
Select axis of revolution:	Select axis ②.
Start angle <0>: **<RETURN>**	
Included angle (+=ccw, -=cw) <Full circle>: **<RETURN>**	

Now, use a rectangular array to complete the pedestal.

Command: **ARRAY**	Array the pedestal segment with 10 rows at 1" and 1 column.

Change your UCS to set up for block.

Command: **UCS**	Rotate the X axis -90 degrees.
Command: **LAYER**	Turn layer BUILD off.
Command: **BLOCK**	Block to PEDESTAL with insert point at 0,0.

Your drawing should look like the Completed Pedestal (above) before you block it.

The pedestal used the default (full circle) rotation. If you select a rotation less than 360 degrees, the direction of surface rotation is determined by your pick point on the axis of rotation. If you align your right thumb on the axis, pointing along the axis away from the pick point, your curled fingers will indicate the direction of rotation. The start angle (0) also is measured in this direction. Assigning a non-zero start angle will offset the rotated segment.

Combining 3D Entities to Create Complex Parts

So far we have used mesh entities to create simple geometric shapes. Many 3D objects are made by combining different 3D entities. Even building something as simple as the chair's seat and back support requires more than one entity type. The following exercises will take you through building the seat and back support using a solid, a 3D polyline, and a 90-degree REVSURF.

Extruding a SOLID to Create Seat Support

First, create the seat and back supports by extruding a 2D SOLID. In many cases, it is easier to extrude a 2D solid into a box shape than to create one from 3D faces. This is often the case where you have the 2D dimensions that will determine your construction points. The following exercise will help you set a UCS and create the solids for the seat and back supports. The construction points are given in the exercise.

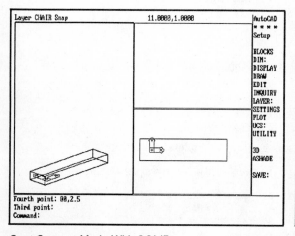

Seat Support Made With SOLID

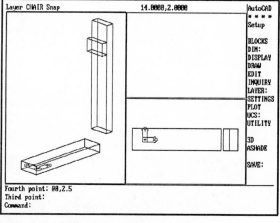

Back Support Made With SOLID

Combining Entities to Create Seat and Back Support

> The left viewport should still be active and layer CHAIR should be current.

Command: **SETVAR**   Set THICKNESS to 1.
Command: COLOR   Set color to green.

Command: **SOLID**   Use SOLID to create seat support base.
First point: **-1.5,-1.25**
Enter points @0,2.5 and @10.5,-2.5 and @0,2.5 then <RETURN> to end.

> Note that the 3rd and 4th points are reversed from 3DFACE, which uses a clockwise/counterclockwise order.

Command: **SETVAR**   Set THICKNESS to 13.

Command: SOLID   Create the back support upright.
First point: **10,-1.25,2**
Enter points @0,2.5 and @1,- 2.5 and @0,2.5 then <RETURN>.

Command: **SETVAR**   Set THICKNESS to 1.5.

Command: **SOLID**   Create back support block.
First point: **9.25,-1.25,11.5**
Enter points @0,2.5 and @.75,-2.5 and @0,2.5 then <RETURN>.

> Your screen should show a completed seat and back support. (See illustrations above.)

Using 3D Polylines

3DPOLY is a polyline with independent X,Y, and Z axis coordinates. While 2D polylines can exist in any 3D plane, 3D polylines are not bound to a single plane. Unlike 2D polylines, 3D polylines have no thickness and you can only create straight line segments. (You can spline curve fit 3D polylines with PEDIT, but the curve fit will still be made up of short, straight segments.) Use 3D polylines when you need to traverse a 3D space in multiple planes.

Editing a 3D polyline with PEDIT is similar to editing a 2D polyline. The prompt looks like this:

```
Close/Edit vertex/Spline curve/Decurve/Undo/eXit <X>
```

3D polylines cannot be joined, curve fit with arc segments or given a width. Except for the Tangent and Width options, editing vertexes allows the same options as 2D polylines.

In the following exercise, we are going to use a 3D polyline to create a rectangular path line for a revsurf to connect the two extruded blocks. The 3D polyline allows you to draw the path curve without adjusting the UCS. The following illustration shows the polyline, and the line that will act as the axis of rotation. Create the axis line and the path polyline.

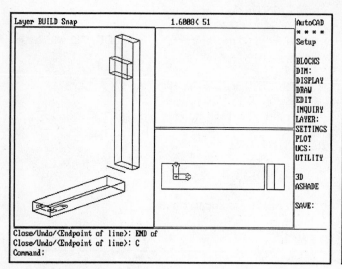
Axis and 3D Polyline Path Curve

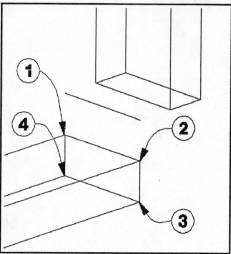
Detail of 3DPOLY

Creating the Axis and Path Curve for REVSURF

Command:	**SETVAR**	Set THICKNESS to 0.
Command:	**LAYER**	Set layer BUILD current.
Command:	**COLOR**	Set color BYLAYER.
Command:	**ERASE**	Erase all entities on the BUILD layer.
Command:	**LINE**	Draw line from 9,1.25,2 to 9,-1.25,2 for revolution axis.

```
Command: 3DPOLY                          Osnap a rectangle around end of seat support.
From point:                              Pick ENDPoint at ①.
Close/Undo/<Endpoint of line>:           Pick ENDPoint at ②.
Close/Undo/<Endpoint of line>:           Pick ENDPoint at ③.
Close/Undo/<Endpoint of line>:           Pick ENDPoint at ④.
Close/Undo/<Endpoint of line>: C         Close completes the rectangle.
```

Now that you have the polyline path profile, connect the two segments using REVSURF.

Using REVSURF to Connect Back and Seat

Revolve the 3DPOLY profile through a 90-degree arc to get a 90-degree section connecting the two solids. The following illustration shows the REVSURF connection. When you get the supports connected, BLOCK the solids and REVSURF mesh as a block called SUPPORT.

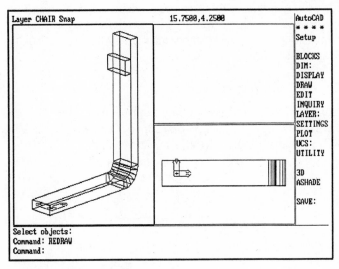

Support After REVSURF

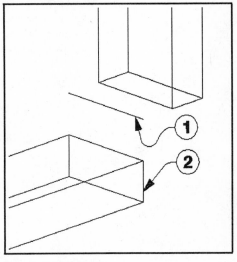

Detail of REVSURF

Using REVSURF to Make 90-Degree Section

Command: **SETVAR**	Set Surftab1 to 6.
Command: **LAYER**	Set layer CHAIR current.
Command: **COLOR**	Set color green.

Command: **REVSURF**
Select path curve: Select rectangle on near side edge at ②.
Select axis of revolution: Select axis line at ①.
Start angle <0>: **<RETURN>**
Included angle (+=ccw, -=cw) <Full circle>: **-90**

Command: **ERASE**   Erase all path curves and axis lines.
Command: **BLOCK**   Block as SUPPORT with insert point at 0,0.

The seat and back support construction involved simple surfaces. You frequently will encounter curved surfaces and corners that require using more complex meshes.

Methods for Complex Mesh Construction

Let's look at how to generate a curved back cushion with curved corners. First, we'll create the defining arc, polyline, and axis. Then we're going to use TABSURF and REVSURF to create the backrest surfaces. When you deal with many mesh entities, you will frequently encounter cases where the edges coincide. This is the case that you encountered adding the surface mesh to the top of the chair's leg. The following exercises incorporate the same technique you used previously for temporarily moving meshes to build the component part.

Using Arcs to Create the Backrest Top

Begin your backrest construction by creating a set of arcs, then joining them to form a continuous polyline for the top profile of the backrest. This polyline profile will provide the path profile for the following TABSURF. Build the back in plan view in your lower right viewport. Create a line to indicate the direction vector. The following exercise will provide you with input values.

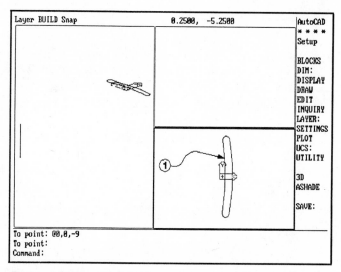

Backrest Profile and Axis Line

Creating a Pline Path Curve of Back Cushion

Make the lower right viewport active.

Command: **LAYER**	Set layer BUILD current.
Command: **COLOR**	Set color BYLAYER.

```
Command: ARC
Center/<Start point>: 0,-7
Center/End/<Second point>: E
End point: 0,7
Angle/Direction/Radius/<Center point>: A
Included angle: 20
```

```
Command: OFFSET                        Offset arc 1.5 to the right.
```

```
Command: ARC                           Connect ends of arc with another arc.
Center/<Start point>: ENDP
of                                     Pick top end of right arc.
Center/End/<Second point>: E
End point: ENDP
of                                     Pick top end of right arc.
Angle/Direction/Radius/<Center point>: A
Included angle: 180
```

```
Command: ARC                           Repeat arc command for other end of backrest.
Command: PEDIT                         Join all the arcs into a single polyline.
```

```
Command: LINE                          Draw a line for a direction vector and rotation axis.
From point: CEN
of:                                    Pick the arc at ① to get the center point.
To point: @0,0,-9                      Draw a 9" line in the Z direction.
To point: <RETURN>
```

The chair back has rounded edges; we are going to use a 90-degree
REVSURF to get the rounded corners. Use the following exercise and
illustration to generate an arc that will act as the path curve for the
corner and top REVSURFs. The exercise will help you locate your UCS to
define the arc.

Creating One Path Curve for Two Meshes

Make left viewport active.

```
Command: ZOOM                          Zoom dynamic to corner of chair.
Command: LINE                          Connect the endpoints of the small arc at ① and ②.
```

```
Command: UCS                           Move UCS to upper left seat corner.
Origin/ZAxis/3point/Entity/View/X/Y/Z/Prev/Restore/Save/Del/?/<World>: 3
Origin point <0,0,0>: ENDP
of                                     Pick front end of line at ①.
Point on positive portion of the X-axis <1.0000,7.0000,0.0000>: ENDP
of                                     Pick back end of line at ②.
Point on positive-Y portion of the UCS X-Y plane <-0.1736,7.9848,0.0000>: @0,0,1
```

```
Command: ARC
Center/<Start point>: ENDP
of                           Far end of short line at ②.
Center/End/<Second point>: E
End point: ENDP
of                           Near end of short line at ①.
Angle/Direction/Radius/<Center point>: A
Included angle: 180

Command: ZOOM            Zoom dynamic to enclose chair back and axis line of
                         first pline arc.
```

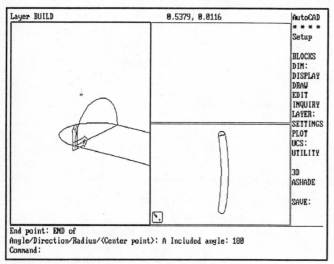

Axis and Path Curve for Rounded Edges

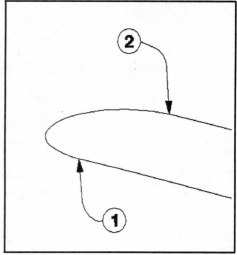

Detail of Arc

Now you are ready to create the three basic mesh entities for the backrest.

The TABSURF Command

TABSURF creates a *tabular* surface using a path curve and a direction vector. Like RULESURF, you only need to set SURFTAB1. TABSURF uses the usual set of entities for the path curve: line, arc, circle, 2D or 3D polyline. After you select the entity you are using for the path curve, you select your direction vector. The tabsurf is drawn from the point that you pick on the path curve to the direction vector pick point. In effect, TABSURF is extruding your path profile along the direction vector. The surface lines it creates are parallel to the direction vector.

Using TABSURF (and REVSURF) to Create the Chair's Back

First, use REVSURF to create the top edge of the chair, then use TABSURF to create the main part of the chair's back. Finally, use REVSURF again to create the first rounded corner. The following illustrations and exercise will help you locate your pick points, and move the first two meshes out of the way so that you can create the corner mesh.

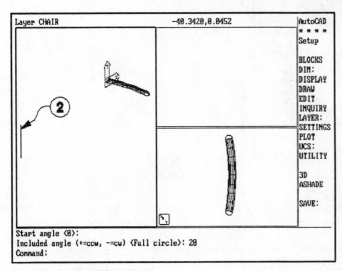

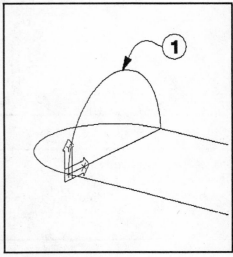

Surface the Top Edge Backrest   *Detail of Top Edge*

Using REVSURF to Surface the Top Edge Backrest

Command: **LAYER**	Set layer CHAIR current.
Command: **COLOR**	Set color magenta.
Command: **SETVAR**	Set Surftab1 to 8.
Command: **SETVAR**	Set Surftab2 to 8.

Command: **REVSURF**   Create top edge of chair back.
Select path curve: Select the last arc drawn at ①.
Select axis of revolution: Pick the axis line at ②.
Start angle <0>: **<RETURN>**
Included angle (+=ccw, -=cw) <Full circle>: **20**   20 degrees matches the angle
                                                          of the profile.

Command: **TABSURF**   Draw the main surface of the chair.
Select path curve: Pick the joined pline at ③.
Select direction vector: Pick the top of the same line at ②.

Command: **MOVE**   Move the two meshes from 0,0 to *0,0.

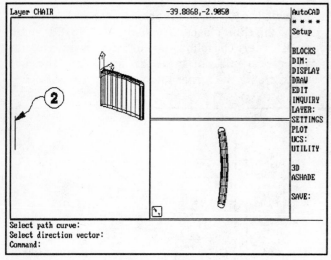

Surface the Center Backrest

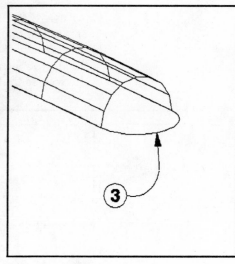

Detail of Polyline

Moving the two meshes to the upper right viewport allows you to select the arc to create the corners.

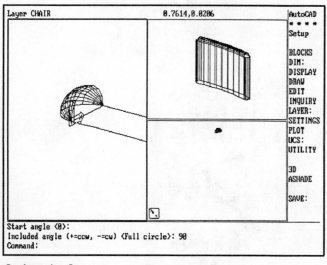

Surface the Corners

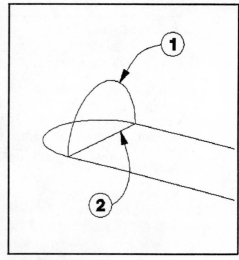

Detail of REVSURF

Using REVSURF to Create the Backrest Corner

```
Command: REVSURF                          Make the first corner of the backrest.
Select path curve:                        Pick the arc at ①.
Select axis of revolution:                Pick the short line connecting arc ends at ②.
Start angle <0>: <RETURN>
Included angle (+=ccw, -=cw) <Full circle>: 90

Command: MOVE           Move the meshes in upper right vport from *0,0 back to 0,0.
```

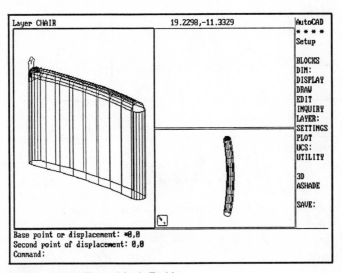

Backrest With Three Mesh Entities

You have created all the entities you need to complete the backrest. You could work your way around the backrest creating the remaining edges and corners the same way, but it is much easier to MIRROR the existing entities. Before you MIRROR the entities, change the UCS plane back to the center of the backrest to make the mirroring easy.

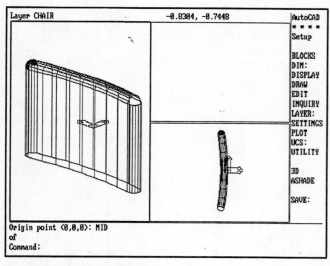

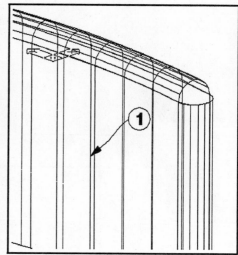

Locating a UCS for Mirroring   *Detail of Midpoint*

Locating a UCS for Mirroring

Command: **UCS**   Previous returns the UCS to the center of the backrest.

Command: **UCS**

Origin/ZAxis/3point/Entity/View/X/Y/Z/Prev/Restore/Save/Del/?/<World>: **O**

Origin point <0,0,0>: **MIDP**

of   Pick the back midpoint of the center segment of the
                                    tabsurf mesh at ① (2.1124,0,-4.5).

                                    This places the UCS at the correct orientation and origin point to
                                    create the backrest block.

Command: **UCS**   Save UCS as BACK-CENTER.

Command: **UCS**   Change the UCS to do the mirrors.

Origin/ZAxis/3point/Entity/View/X/Y/Z/Prev/Restore/Save/Del/?/<World>: **Z**

Rotation angle about Z axis <0.0>: **-90**

Command: **<RETURN>**

UCS

Origin/ZAxis/3point/Entity/View/X/Y/Z/Prev/Restore/Save/Del/?/<World>: **X**

Rotation angle about X axis <0.0>: **90**

Now you can complete the backrest with two MIRRORs; then, BLOCK the
resulting entities to BACK. Work in your plan view to do the MIRRORs.
Get your pick points from the illustration and the exercise.

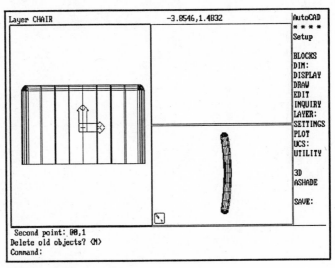

Mirror of Backrest Corner

Using MIRROR to Complete the Backrest

```
Command: PLAN                              Go to a plan view.
<Current UCS>/UCS/World: <RETURN>


Command: MIRROR                            Mirror corner mesh to other side.
Select objects:                            Pick corner mesh.
1 selected, 1 found.
Select objects: <RETURN>
First point of mirror line: 0,0
Second point: @0,1
Delete old objects? <N> <RETURN>


Command: <RETURN>
MIRROR
Select objects:                            Pick the top edge and both corners.
3 selected, 3 found.
Select objects: <RETURN>
First point of mirror line: 0,0
Second point: @1,0
Delete old objects? <N> <RETURN>


Command: UCS                               Restore BACK-CENTER
Command: LAYER                             Turn layer BUILD off.
Command: BLOCK                             Block to BACK with insert point at 0,0.
```

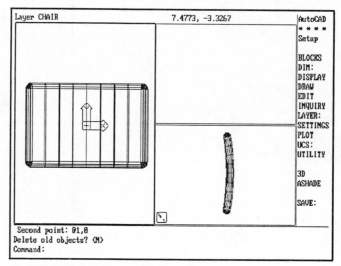

Completed Backrest

Stopping Point

This is a good stopping point if you want to take a break. You have all the chair components but the seat itself. If you take a break, END your drawing, then resume with the same drawing in the next exercise.

In the next section, we will create the chair's seat using the EDGESURF command and spend a little time showing you how you can use PEDIT to change the surface contours of the seat by changing vertices in the mesh and curve fitting the changed mesh points. Finally, we will assemble the chair by inserting the blocks that make up the component parts.

The EDGESURF Command

EDGESURF creates a polygon mesh from four adjoining edges. The edges can be lines, arcs, or open 2D or 3D polylines, but the four edges must touch at their endpoints. A polyline is a single edge no matter how many vertices it has. You need to set SURFTAB1 and SURFTAB2 to specify your mesh. Executing the command is quite simple; you select the entities making up four edges. The first pick determines the SURFTAB1 mesh direction.

Using EDGESURF to Create Seat Surface

In the following exercise, create four lines to define the planar edges for the seat, then use the EDGESURF command to add 10 x 10 mesh for the top surface of the seat cushion. With this same mesh, you can use PEDIT to add contours to the seat cushion by changing the Z value at various vertex points. Later, we will finish the seat construction by using a 3DFACE for the seat bottom, and by using REVSURF and TABSURF to create rounded edges and corners.

The cushion is 2 inches thick, so begin by drawing the line edges with a 2-inch elevation. The exercise provides the coordinate values. Get your pick points for EDGESURF from the illustration.

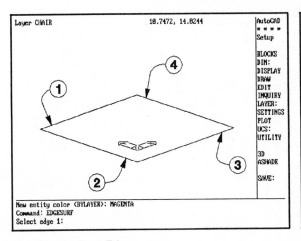

Creating the Seat Edges

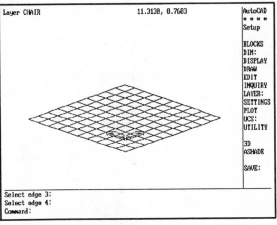

The EDGESURF Mesh

Using EDGESURF to Create the Top Surface of the Seat Cushion

Command: **ZOOM**	Zoom Previous.
Command: **VPORTS**	Set left viewport to single.
command: **ZOOM**	Zoom Center at 0,0 with 36" height.
Command: **SETVAR**	Set Surftab1 to 10.
Command: **SETVAR**	Set Surftab2 to 10.
Command: **LAYER**	Set layer BUILD current.
Command: **COLOR**	Set color BYLAYER.
Command: **LINE**	Draw lines for EDGESURF command.
From point: **7,7,2**	
To point: **7,-7,2**	
To point: **-7,-7,2**	
To point: **-7,7,2**	
To point: **C**	

```
Command: LAYER                      Set layer CHAIR current.
Command: COLOR                      Set color magenta.

Command: EDGESURF                   Create a 10 x 10 mesh 2" above seat bottom.
Select edge 1:                      Pick line at point ①.
Select edge 2:                      Pick line at point ②.
Select edge 3:                      Pick line at point ③.
Select edge 4:                      Pick line at point ④.
```

When you are done, your screen should look like the EDGESURF Mesh illustration above.

You can change the surface contours of a 3DMESH by editing the 3D vertex points with PEDIT.

Using PEDIT to Edit 3D Meshes

PEDIT is an intelligent command. When you select PEDIT to edit a mesh, it will provide you with the prompt options that you have available to edit the mesh. (The editing options also change with editing a 2D or 3D polyline.) You can use PEDIT to move a vertex point by identifying the vertex point and by providing a new 3D coordinate point. You also can Smooth and Desmooth the line fit vertex mesh point. You control the type of curve fit by setting the SURFTYPE system variable. Two other system variables, SURFU and SURFV, control the fineness of the fit in the m and n mesh directions. Finally, you also can use the SPLFRAME system variable to display the control points when you curve fit a mesh.

To get a feel for curve fitting the mesh, try the following exercise. It exaggerates the movement of the vertex points so that you can see the effects of different curve fits.

Using PEDIT to Edit Mesh Vertex Points

```
Command: PEDIT
Select polyline:          Pick mesh.
Edit vertex/Smooth surface/Desmooth/Mclose/Nclose/Undo/eXit <X>: E
Vertex (0,0). Next/Previous/Left/Right/Up/Down/Move/REgen/eXit <N>: N
                          Try all the vertex direction options to move about the mesh.
                          After you finish experimenting, stop at vertex (3,3).
```

```
Vertex (3,3). Next/Previous/Left/Right/Up/Down/Move/REgen/eXit <U>: M
Enter new location: @0,0,3            Move vertex 3" in the Z direction.
Vertex (3,4). Next/Previous/Left/Right/Up/Down/Move/REgen/eXit <U>: M
Enter new location: @0,0,2            Move vertex 2" in the Z direction.
Vertex (4,4). Next/Previous/Left/Right/Up/Down/Move/REgen/eXit <U>: M
Enter new location: @0,0,2            Move vertex 2" in the Z direction.
Vertex (4,3). Next/Previous/Left/Right/Up/Down/Move/REgen/eXit <U>: M
Enter new location: @0,0,2            Move vertex 2" in the Z direction.
Vertex (7,4). Next/Previous/Left/Right/Up/Down/Move/REgen/eXit <U>: M
Enter new location: @0,1,9            Move vertex 9" in the Z direction and 1"
                                      in the Y direction.
Vertex (8,5). Next/Previous/Left/Right/Up/Down/Move/REgen/eXit <U>: M
Enter new location: @0,0,-5           Move vertex -5" in the Z direction.
Vertex (8,5). Next/Previous/Left/Right/Up/Down/Move/REgen/eXit <U>: X
Edit vertex/Smooth surface/Desmooth/Mclose/Nclose/Undo/eXit <X>: X
```

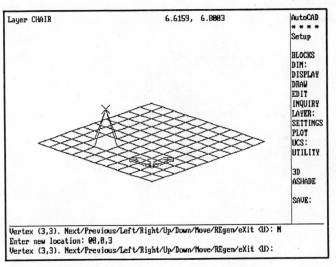

Top of Seat During Editing

The smooth surface option allows three types of spline curve fitting. Each type produces a different blended smooth surface based on formulas that produce a surface passing near the vertex points.

Smooth Surface Options

- Cubic B-spline curve — SURFTYPE 6 (AutoCAD's default).

- Quadratic B-spline curve — SURFTYPE 5.

- Bezier curve — SURFTYPE 8.

Try all the smoothing options on the mesh to see the effect each has. Use the exercise to get your SURFU, SURFV, and SURFTYPE settings.

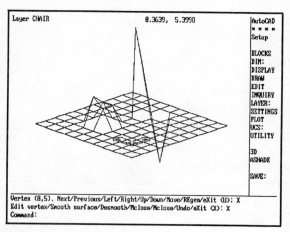

Surface Before Smooth

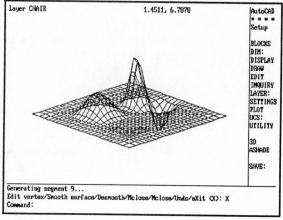

SURFTYPE 5 Smoothing

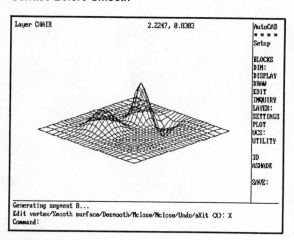

SURFTYPE 6 Smoothing

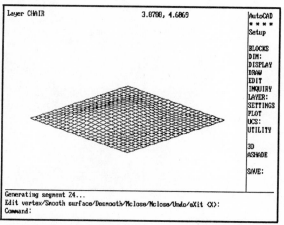

SURFTYPE 8 Smoothing

Using PEDIT to Smooth Mesh Surface Fitting

Command: **SETVAR**	Set SURFU to 24.
Command: **SETVAR**	Set SURFV to 24.
Command: **SETVAR**	Set SURFTYPE to 5.
Command: **SETVAR**	Set SPLFRAME to 0.

```
Command: PEDIT                                    Try quadratic B-spline surface.
Select polyline:                                  Select mesh.
Edit vertex/Smooth surface/Desmooth/Mclose/Nclose/Undo/eXit <X>: S
Edit vertex/Smooth surface/Desmooth/Mclose/Nclose/Undo/eXit <X>: X

Command: SETVAR                                   Set SURFTYPE to 6.

Command: PEDIT                                    Try cubic B-spline surface.
Select polyline:                                  Select mesh.
Edit vertex/Smooth surface/Desmooth/Mclose/Nclose/Undo/eXit <X>: S
Edit vertex/Smooth surface/Desmooth/Mclose/Nclose/Undo/eXit <X>: X

Command: SETVAR                                   Set SURFTYPE to 8.

Command: PEDIT                                    Try Bezier surface.
Select polyline:                                  Select mesh.
Edit vertex/Smooth surface/Desmooth/Mclose/Nclose/Undo/eXit <X>: S
Edit vertex/Smooth surface/Desmooth/Mclose/Nclose/Undo/eXit <X>: X
```

Undo or Pedit mesh back to a flat mesh surface.

When you are done, you should have a mesh similar to the starting mesh.

Other PEDIT Mesh Options

The Mclose and Nclose options control whether a mesh connects the first vertex to the last vertex of the mesh. A mesh in the shape of a dish (half a sphere) is closed in the M direction and open in the N direction. If you were to open the dish in the M direction by selecting Mclose, the dish would be redrawn with a wedge segment missing. Likewise if you closed the dish in the N direction, the dish would be redrawn with a mesh going from the edge to the center of the dish, creating a cone inside the dish. The M and N options will display the close or open prompt depending on the current status of the mesh being edited.

You should now have a good understanding of the PEDIT options available for a mesh. If you like, you can try your hand at adding a realistic contour to the mesh seat cushion, or just proceed with the completion of the seat cushion exercise.

Let's turn now to finishing the seat. First, create a seat bottom using a 3DFACE. Then locate your UCS on the front edge of the seat cushion. This will let you create the arcs defining the path for the seat's edges and corners using the same REVSURF and TABSURF techniques that you used to build the backrest. Use the following exercise to guide you through making the 3DFACE and creating the corner arc.

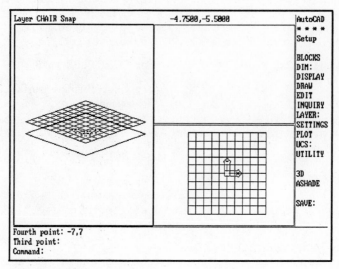

```
Layer CHAIR Snap                    -4.7500,-5.5000          AutoCAD
                                                             * * * *
                                                             Setup

                                                             BLOCKS
                                                             DIM:
                                                             DISPLAY
                                                             DRAW
                                                             EDIT
                                                             INQUIRY
                                                             LAYER:
                                                             SETTINGS
                                                             PLOT
                                                             UCS:
                                                             UTILITY

                                                             3D
                                                             ASHADE

                                                             SAVE:


Fourth point: -7,7
Third point:
Command:
```

Seat With Bottom

Using 3DFACE and Setting a UCS for Seat's Edges

Command: **VPORTS**	Restore BUILD.
Make left viewport active.	
Command: **3DFACE**	Draw bottom of seat.
First point: **7,7**	
Second point: **7,-7**	
Third point: **-7,-7**	
Fourth point: **-7,7**	
Third point: **<RETURN>**	
Command: **LAYER**	Set layer BUILD current.
Command: **COLOR**	Set color BYLAYER.
Command: **LINE**	Draw line connecting top and bottom corners of seat at ③ and ①.

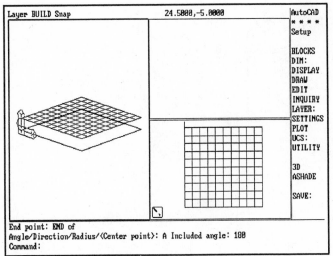

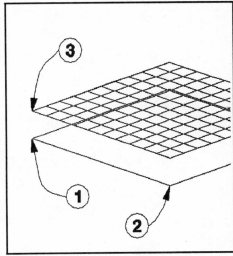

UCS for Creating the Seat's Edges   *Detail of Seat*

Command: **UCS**   Place UCS on front edge of seat cushion.
Origin/ZAxis/3point/Entity/View/X/Y/Z/Prev/Restore/Save/Del/?/<World>: **3**
Origin point <0,0,0>: **ENDP**
of   Pick lower left front corner of seat at ①.
Point on positive portion of the X-axis <-6.0000,7.0000,0.0000>: **ENDP**
of   Pick lower right front corner of seat at ②.
Point on positive-Y portion of the UCS X-Y plane <-6.0000,7.0000,0.0000>: **ENDP**
of   Pick upper left front corner of seat at ③.

Command: **ARC**   Create arc for seat corners.
Center/<Start point>: **ENDP**
of   Pick point ③.
Center/End/<Second point>: **E**
End point: **ENDP**
of   Pick point ①.
Angle/Direction/Radius/<Center point>: **A**
Included angle: 180

Now, use REVSURF and TABSURF to create the first corner and edge. Then, use a polar ARRAY to complete the seat cushion. This array takes advantage of the fact that the seat is symmetrical. It will save the steps of mirroring the edges and corners, or of individually creating each corner mesh and each edge. The illustration and the exercise will help you with the pick points.

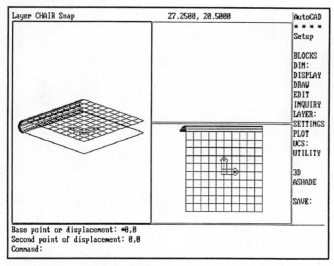

Seat Cushion After Meshes

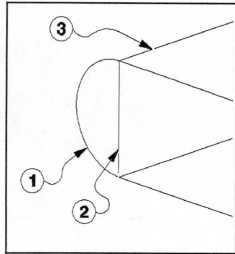

Detail of Corner

Using REVSURF, TABSURF, and ARRAY to Complete the Seat

```
Command: LAYER              Set layer CHAIR current.
Command: COLOR              Set color green.

Command: REVSURF                    Revolve arc to fill corner.
Select path curve:                  Pick arc at ①.
Select axis of revolution:          Pick line at ②.
Start angle <0>: <RETURN>
Included angle (+=ccw, -=cw) <Full circle>: 90

Command: UCS                Set UCS back to previous.
Command: MOVE               Move corner and top mesh from 0,0 to *0,0.
Command: REDRAW

Command: TABSURF                    Create edge of seat cushion.
Select path curve:                  Pick arc at ①.
Select direction vector:            Pick line at ③.

Command: MOVE               Move meshes in upper right viewport from *0,0 to 0,0.

Command: ARRAY             Array edge and corner mesh to 3 remaining sides.
Select objects:           Pick edge mesh.
1 selected, 1 found.
Select objects:           Pick corner mesh.
1 selected, 1 found.
Select objects: <RETURN>
Rectangular or Polar array (R/P): P
```

```
Center point of array: 0,0
Number of items: 4
Angle to fill (+=ccw, -=cw) <360>: <RETURN>
Rotate objects as they are copied? <Y> <RETURN>
```

Command: **LAYER**	Turn layer BUILD off.
Command: **BLOCK**	Block as SEAT with insert point at 0,0.
Command: **SAVE**	Save to default drawing.

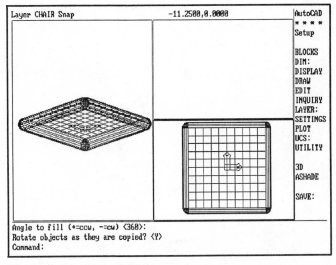

The Completed Seat Cushion

Congratulations! You now have all your component seat parts tucked away in your drawing as blocks.

Inserting 3D Blocks

In 3D, building complex parts as a series of smaller blocked parts offers productivity benefits. First, you only have to deal with a limited number of entities on the screen for a particular part. This makes construction and editing less confusing because other parts will not get in your way. You will also find that you save redraw and regeneration time. Another benefit is that you can redefine the component parts quite easily. You could, for example, have a variety of seat cushions and backs, casters, and pedestals. Using block redefinition, you could quickly build a new chair from different parts. The important thing to remember is that you need to maintain your insertion points when you assemble your drawing. The following table provides the insertion points to assemble the chair.

Block Name	Insertion Point
CASTER	-12,0,2.5
BASE	0,0,4.5
PEDESTAL	0,0,4.5
SUPPORT	0,0,17.5
SEAT	0,0,18.5
BACK	9.25,0,29.75

Use the INSERT command to construct the chair. When you are done, set a base point at the center of the chair at floor level so that you can insert it later into other drawings.

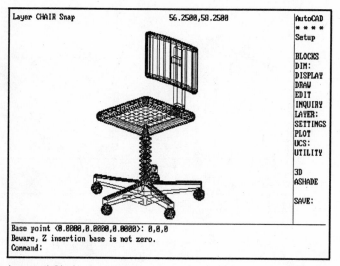

Inserted Chair

Using INSERT to Assemble the 3D Chair

Command: **UCS**	Set Origin to 30,22,0.
Command: **VPORTS**	Set left viewport to single.
Command: **ZOOM**	Zoom Center at 37,25,0 with a height of 43.
Command: **INSERT**	Insert CASTER at -12,0,2.5 with default scale and rotation.
Command: **ARRAY**	Polar array the caster 5 times in 360 degrees about 0,0.
Command: **INSERT**	Insert BASE at 0,0,4.5 with default scale and rotation.
Command: **INSERT**	Insert PEDESTAL at 0,0,4.5 with default scale and rotation.

Command: **INSERT**	Insert SUPPORT at 0,0,17.5 with default scale and rotation.
Command: **INSERT**	Insert SEAT at 0,0,18.5 with default scale and rotation.
Command: **INSERT**	Insert BACK at 9.25,0,29.75 with default scale and rotation.
Command: **BASE**	Set base point at UCS origin for future insert.
Base point: **0,0,0**	

Sit back and take a look at your chair from all sides. When you get a view you like, try the HIDE command to clean up hidden lines. But, set aside some time, the HIDE can take one to two hours. The following illustration shows our favorite view. When you're through, END your drawing.

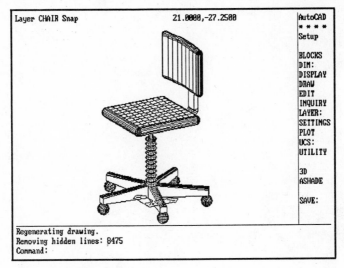

Our Favorite Chair View

Using HIDE to Remove

Command: **VPOINT**	Rotate view to 240 in the XY direction and 19 in the Z.
Command: **HIDE**	This may take 1 to 2 hours.
Command: **END**	Put your chair away.

Table and Chair in Office Drawing

Summary on 3D Entities

When you construct a 3D drawing, use the entities and commands that fit your purpose. Use a mix of 2D extruded entities and 3D entities. If you are building a complex drawing, we recommend using the approach taken in this chapter. Build your drawing from component parts using the standard BLOCK and INSERT commands. Don't use surface meshes if you don't need to. If you do use meshes, set a reasonable surface mesh density with SURFTAB1 and SURFTAB2. Don't forget to look at these settings. Remember, if you forget to set them with the values you want, you have to erase your mesh and create a new one. Keep your mesh profile entities on a separate layer. If you have meshes with a common edge, you will have to move one mesh out of the way to pick the edge entity for the second mesh. If you really want to control your meshes, look at some AutoLISP routines in INSIDE AutoLISP (New Riders Publishing).

In the next chapter, we will take a walk through an office complex. You will be able to get a dynamic view of your table and chair inserted in the office drawing.

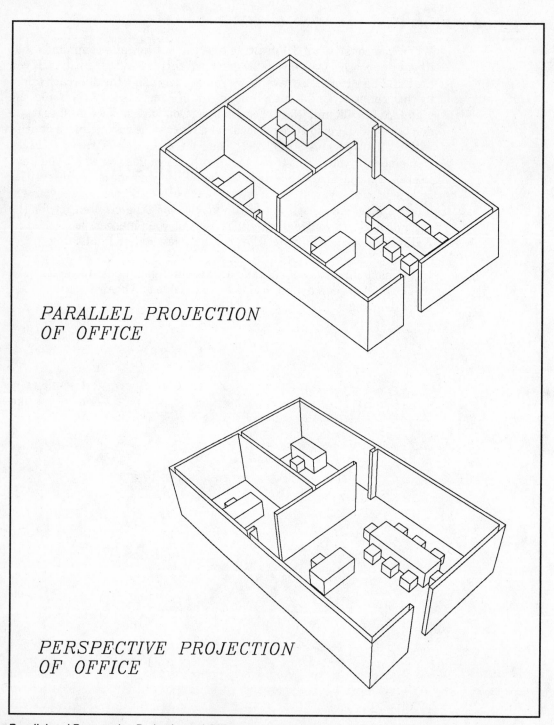

PARALLEL PROJECTION
OF OFFICE

PERSPECTIVE PROJECTION
OF OFFICE

Parallel and Perspective Projections of Office

CHAPTER 15

Controlling Dynamic 3D Displays

HOW TO DISPLAY AND PRESENT 3D DRAWINGS

Lay of the Land — Dynamic Viewing

So far, you have been working in 3D to create and edit drawings. What do you do after you have created your 3D drawing? You display it, and the odds are good that you also will build a design presentation with it, offering different views in 3D space. Even something as simple as our chair looks impressive when it is revolved in 3D space. This chapter will show you how to use AutoCAD's dynamic viewing to get enhanced 3D perspective views of your drawings. We will also show you how to create slides of these views and how to run a slide show using a script file.

DVIEW vs. VPOINT Commands

The command that you use to generate and control dynamic views is called DVIEW. Think of DVIEW as an enhanced VPOINT command. Unlike VPOINT, DVIEW can provide either parallel (orthographic) or perspective views to visualize your drawing. The illustration on the facing page shows a parallel (orthographic) and a perspective view of an office. Both views were created with DVIEW. The perspective view shows a vanishing point as lines recede from your view. In the parallel view, the lines always remain parallel. This is the only type of view that you get with VPOINT. If you find VPOINT frustrating, it stems from the parallel projection. Your eyes are accustomed to lines converging at a vanishing point. You might say parallel projection is unnatural.

➡ *NOTE: VPOINT always zooms to the entire drawing extents but DVIEW gives you full control over the zoomed display of your view. You may find VPOINT to be outdated by DVIEW.*

DVIEW utilizes a camera and target metaphor to control your drawing view. To select a view, you *point* the camera at a target in your drawing. Think of the line from the camera to the target as a line of sight. You can move the camera and target to get different views. The camera metaphor is carried further to let you change your field of view by changing the *lens* length. You also can get cut-away sections of your drawing by *clipping* the front or back plane of your view. This is helpful when you want to look at an office interior in a building plan, or create a section view of a part.

All these DVIEW enhancements give you more control over generating views of your drawing, but the most important point is they are done *dynamically*. DVIEW works with a selection set. You can select and *drag* the drawing entities that will make up your view, adjust your camera and target settings, and see a *screen preview* of your view. As you change and drag the image, DVIEW rapidly and dynamically updates the display. Unlike VPOINT, which requires a lot of trial and error, DVIEW lets you home in on your view faster. You will find the whole viewing process more intuitive; it is like the point and shoot viewing process that you *do* use with a camera.

What You Can Get From the Chapter's Examples

Our goal in this chapter is to take you from start to finish in preparing 3D views of a drawing for a presentation. Most of the chapter is devoted to using the DVIEW command. The focus of the chapter's drawing examples is to show you the *types* of viewing enhancements that you can get with DVIEW for display and presentations. In sequence, the chapter will take you through:

- Setting up dynamic views.

- Locating camera and target points.

- Panning a camera.

- Getting perspective and hidden views, including clipped views.

- Creating and scripting a slide show.

- Editing a perspective view using viewports.

- Preparing a 3D view for rendering.

Often a good 3D view can save you time and money. If you systematically revolve a drawing in 3D space, it may reveal a design condition that wasn't anticipated, say something like the clearance between machinery and a wall in a factory plan. Often, a good presentation is the margin between winning and losing projects. Learning to use tools like dynamic viewing and AutoShade (which we will cover in the next chapter) will help you improve your drawing presentations. Inserting a 3D perspective view into a 2D drawing is an important, but obscure, technique (using a DXB file) that is useful if you need to add 2D annotations to a 3D image. As you work through the chapter's examples, look for types of viewing enhancements that you can adapt for your own presentations.

Dynamic Display, Slide, and Script Tools

Where do find DVIEW? It is on the [DISPLAY] screen menu. You also can access and control the command settings via the [Dview Options...] icon menu on the [Display] pull-down menu.

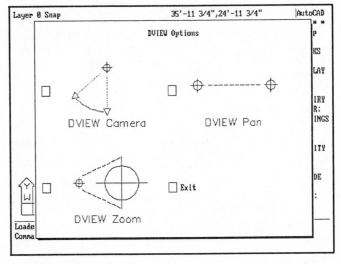

DVIEW Options Icon Menu

In addition to DVIEW, you also will use the SCRIPT, MSLIDE, and VSLIDE commands. These commands are on the [UTILITY] screen menu. MSLIDE and VSLIDE are commands for making and viewing slides. You access these commands by selecting the [SLIDES] menu item on the [UTILITY] screen menu. To use the chapter's slide script, you will need a text editor to create or modify the script text file. We will show you what you need when we get to the section on scripting slides.

Setting Up for DVIEW

This chapter uses the office plan drawing from chapter 12 that you saved as OFFICE. We chose this drawing because you can get different perspective views from different rooms and, since it is a simple drawing, it will regenerate quickly in the exercises. To use the drawing in 3D, you need to extrude the drawing in the Z direction to give the walls, tables, and chairs some height. Use the following setup information to help you get the drawing ready. If you have any attributes showing, freeze the data layer or erase the attributes. You only need the floor plan for this chapter's exercises.

If you do not have a copy of the OFFICE drawing, you need to create the drawing, but you don't need any attributes. You just need the floor plan (shown below) from chapter 12.

If you are using the IA DISK, your starting drawing, called CHAP-15, is already extruded and ready for the first DVIEW exercise. Just set OFFICE3D=CHAP-15 and verify the drawing's settings with the following table.

COORDS	GRID	ORTHO	FILL	SNAP	UCSICON
ON	12	ON	OFF	.25	ON

UNITS	Set UNITS to 4 Architectural,
	Default the other Units settings.
LIMITS	Set LIMITS from 0,0 to 72',48'.
ZOOM	Zoom All.
VIEW	Save view as A.

Layer name	State	Color	Linetype
0	Current	7 (white)	CONTINUOUS
PLAN	On	3 (green)	CONTINUOUS
DATA	Off	7 (white)	CONTINUOUS

Dynamic View Office Drawing Settings

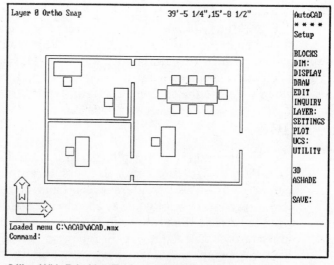

Office With Primitive Tables and Chairs

Setting Up the Dynamic View Office Drawing

`Enter selection: `**1**   Begin a NEW drawing named OFFICE3D=CHAP-15.
Just check the drawing settings.

`Enter selection: `**1**   Begin a NEW drawing named OFFICE3D=OFFICE.

Verify the drawing settings in the Dynamic View Office Drawing Settings table.

`Command: `**ERASE**   Erase the phone blocks from chapter 12.

`Command: `**CHPROP**   Change thickness of all walls to 8'.
`Command: `**CHPROP**   Change thickness of all tables to 30".
`Command: `**CHPROP**   Change thickness of all chairs to 18".
`Command: `**ZOOM**   Window to 16',13' and 34',26'.

After you zoom to the values given, your screen should show a room with a primitive chair and table in the center of the room. This is the lower left room in the floor plan, shown in plan view. You should be in the WCS with the UCS icon showing in the lower left corner of your screen. You will see the effect of the extrusions in your first dynamic view.

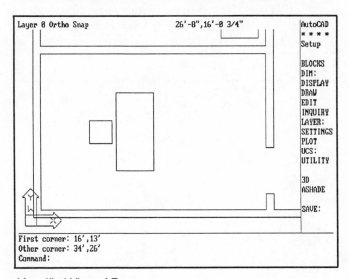

Magnified View of Room

The DVIEW Command

DVIEW is a complex command with twelve options, but it is easy to use. After you enter the command, DVIEW asks for a selection set. Once you select the objects you want, you can establish your point of view (camera) and the focus (target) point of view by picking points. Or you can set these points explicitly with a POints option. You can then add some refinements, like zooming or hiding the view. When you have established the view you want, exit DVIEW with the eXit option. DVIEW regenerates the drawing with the viewpoint established when you exited the drawing. When you enter DVIEW, the default view is parallel projection. Perspective is set with the Distance option (as you will see a little later). All normal and transparent drawing and editing commands are unavailable when you are within the command.

Using Points Option to Set a Realistic View

Try setting your first DVIEW with the POints option. Using points, locate the camera and target with X,Y,Z coordinates. Locate the target point first, then the camera point. After you locate the target point, you will see a rubber band line drawn from the target point to the camera point as a line of sight to help you establish the view.

In the following example, select the desk as your viewing object, then use POints to establish a camera position in the upper left corner of the room at approximately eye level, looking at a target point on the center of the table top. Use the point values given in the exercise. The first screen shot (below) will show you what you should see on your screen after you input the points. The second shot shows what you should see when you exit DVIEW.

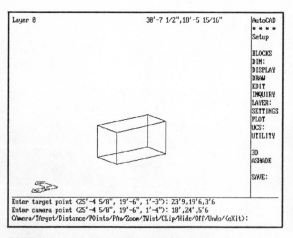

DVIEW Screen After Point Selection

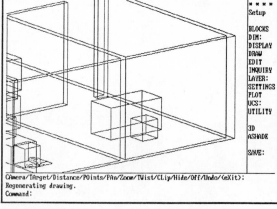

Office Viewed From the Corner of the Room

Using Points to Place the DVIEW Camera

```
Command: DVIEW                                          Select or type.
Select objects:                                         Pick the table.
1 selected, 1 found.
Select objects: <RETURN>
CAmera/TArget/Distance/POints/PAn/Zoom/TWist/CLip/Hide/Off/Undo/<eXit>: PO
Enter target point <25'-4 5/8", 19'-6", 1'-3">: 23'9,19'6,3'6
                                                        Middle of the table top.
Enter camera point <25'-4 5/8", 19'-6", 1'-4">: 18',24',5'6
                                                        Upper left corner of the room.
CAmera/TArget/Distance/POints/PAn/Zoom/TWist/CLip/Hide/Off/Undo/<eXit>: X
```

Your screen should regenerate after you exit DVIEW, showing a view of the table with the office doorway in the left background as in the illustration above. The table and chairs are primitive, but you get the idea. (Some of our local office wags refer to this drawing as Fred Flintstone's office.) If you do not specify target and camera points, AutoCAD will provide default points. These points are aligned with the X,Y plane of your current UCS.

The DVIEW House Icon

If you give a <RETURN> response to the DVIEW select objects prompt, you will get a *house* icon on the screen. It, like the VPOINT icon, helps you locate your viewing points. When you change your DVIEW settings, the house icon is updated. When you exit DVIEW, your drawing regenerates with the same viewpoint as the icon. You can customize your own icon by defining a block named "DVIEWBLOCK." If you do, create the block as a 1 x 1 x 1 unit block with an origin point at the lower left corner. Using an icon instead of selecting complex objects makes DVIEW quick and efficient.

➡ *TIP: Create a DVIEW block that is easily recognizable in your application. Remember to create the block with a unique top, bottom, left, right, front, and back side to help your visual orientation. Also, keep the block simple so it will drag efficiently in DVIEW.*

Using Camera Option to Change Camera's Location

Next, try the CAmera option to rotate your point of view. When you select CAmera, you will get two angle prompts in sequence. The first prompt asks for the angle from the X,Y plane. This angle rotates the camera up and down. The second prompt asks for the angle from the X axis (in the X,Y plane). This angle moves the camera from side to side. You can input the angles from the keyboard or pick the values from the slider bars that will appear at the right, then the top of your screen (in the X,Y plane). This option is like the VPOINT Rotate option, except the order of the angle prompts is reversed.

➤ *NOTE: A camera angle of 0 from the X,Y plane is looking edge on to the current UCS.*

Use the next exercise sequence to guide you through the CAmera option. Keep your first camera angle at the current setting, but change the angle of the X axis so the view will be from the lower left corner of the room looking back at the table. The office doorway will appear on the right. Again, our two screen shots will show you what you will see during the CAmera option and after you exit DVIEW.

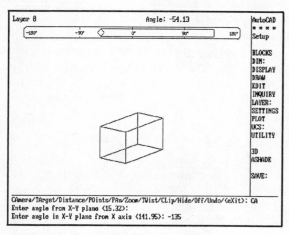

DVIEW Screen During Camera Selection

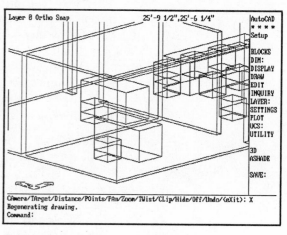

Camera Moved to Lower Left Corner

Using Camera Option to Locate DVIEW Camera

```
Command: DVIEW
Select objects:                                   Pick the table.
1 selected, 1 found.
Select objects: <RETURN>
CAmera/TArget/Distance/POints/PAn/Zoom/TWist/CLip/Hide/Off/Undo/<eXit>: CA
Enter angle from X,Y plane <15.32>: <RETURN>    Keep the current camera angle.
Enter angle in X,Y plane from X axis <141.95>: -135  Type or select approximate angle
                                                     from slider bar.
CAmera/TArget/Distance/POints/PAn/Zoom/TWist/CLip/Hide/Off/Undo/<eXit>: X
```

As you move the slider bar, AutoCAD shows the updated angle in place of the status line coordinates display.

How to Use Slider Bars

While typed input is good for accuracy, the slider bars are better for getting the image by dynamic trial and error. The slider bar on the right goes between 90 degrees (plan view) and -90 degrees. The top slider bar goes from -180 degrees (on the left) through 0 degrees to 180 degrees. At 0 degrees, you are looking along the X axis. To pick from the bar, move your cursor along it until you get the angle (and view) that you want. Then press your pick button. As you move your cursor along the bar, you will see a rubber band track and diamond (the pending setting). AutoCAD updates the angle and image as you move your cursor. If you want to play with the slider bar, try moving the camera around the X axis. When you are done, return the camera to the angle value (-135) in the exercise. The disadvantage to slider bars is that precise values are hard to pick.

➡ *TIP: For precise angles, use the sliders to approximate the angle, then type in an exact value.*

➡ *TIP: DVIEW automatically turns snap off, but you can toggle it back on with <F9> or <^B>. The angle slider bar moves in a snap increment of the snap setting times 180 degrees. A snap of 0.1 moves it in 18-degree increments. The maximum increment is 45 degrees, regardless of setting.*

Using the Distance Option to Get Perspective Views

How do you switch from parallel to perspective view? Easy. You turn distance on with the Distance option. AutoCAD will prompt you for a new camera/target distance, the distance from the camera to the target. It gives your current distance as the default prompt. You also will get a slider bar with values ranging from 0X (on the left) to 16X (on the right). 1X is your current distance factor. Moving to the right will get you farther away from the target, 2X is twice the distance. You will see a continuous update of your distance on the status line. Keep in mind that the prompt and status show the distance, but the slider is a multiplication factor, not a distance. When you select the Distance option, you will also see your UCS icon replaced with a perspective icon (a small cube) in the lower left corner of your screen. This is a reminder that you are *in* perspective. If you want to turn perspective off, select the Off option.

Try getting a perspective view and changing your camera/target distance. The current distance is about seven feet; increase the distance to nineteen feet (about 2.7X). Again, select the table. Default the distance prompt the first time to see the desk in perspective at seven feet. Then, change your distance. When you are done, set an undo mark so that you can return to this view later in the chapter. The next two illustrations show the different perspective views.

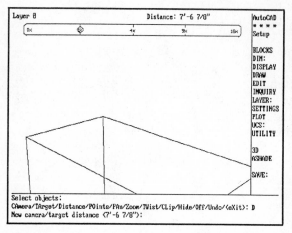

Table at a Distance of 7'-6 7/8"

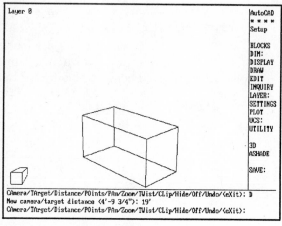

Table at a Distance of 19'-0"

Using Distance Option to Create a Perspective View

```
Command: DVIEW
Select objects: P              Previous selects the table.
1 selected, 1 found.
Select objects: <RETURN>
CAmera/TArget/Distance/POints/PAn/Zoom/TWist/CLip/Hide/Off/Undo/<eXit>: D
New camera/target distance <7'-6 7/8">: <RETURN>
CAmera/TArget/Distance/POints/PAn/Zoom/TWist/CLip/Hide/Off/Undo/<eXit>: D
New camera/target distance <7'-6 7/8">: 19'   Type or select approximate distance.
CAmera/TArget/Distance/POints/PAn/Zoom/TWist/CLip/Hide/Off/Undo/<eXit>: X

Command: UNDO
Auto/Back/Control/End/Group/Mark/<number>: M
```

Working with distance values is like setting a camera magnification. You can also magnify an image with the Zoom option without changing distance. Zoom acts like a lens swap.

Let's leave perspective on and change the target.

Using the Target Option to Get a New Viewpoint

One of the frustrating constraints imposed by VPOINT is that it always looks at the WCS origin point. DVIEW's target point and TArget option allow you to move the target point. When you select the TArget option, you get two angle prompts in sequence, similar to the camera prompts. The first prompts for a new angle from the X,Y plane, the second for a new angle in the X,Y plane from the X axis. Here you are changing the target's angles relative to your vantage point (camera point). If you keep the X,Y angle the same, the effect is like turning your head to look around the room.

Use the TArget option to change the point of view to the office door on the right. When you select your viewing objects, select the table and the wall on the right behind the table. Keep your current angle from the X,Y plane by defaulting the first prompt. Change your X,Y target angle to get a new view with the doorway near the center of your screen. You will see more tables and chairs in the office beyond the one you are looking at.

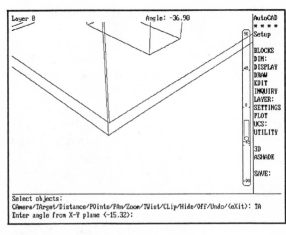

DVIEW of Target Options

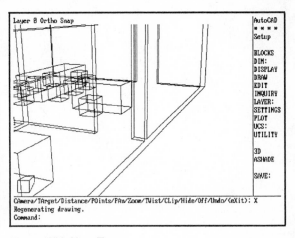

Room With New Target

Using Target Option to Get a Viewpoint of Door

```
Command: DVIEW
Select objects:          Pick the same table and the wall behind the table.
2 found.
Select objects: <RETURN>
CAmera/TArget/Distance/POints/PAn/Zoom/TWist/CLip/Hide/Off/Undo/<eXit>: TA
Enter angle from X,Y plane <-15.32>: <RETURN>
Enter angle in X,Y plane from X axis <45.00>: 22      Type or select.
CAmera/TArget/Distance/POints/PAn/Zoom/TWist/CLip/Hide/Off/Undo/<eXit>: X
```

Your screen should look something like the Room With New Target illustration (above).

Selection Sets and Dragging in DVIEW

As you formed these perspective images, you got some sense of your workstation's performance in updating DVIEW's preview image. Selecting many entities will slow the responsiveness. If your entities are extremely complex (with 3Dmeshes), you may not get a fully formed preview image. When you select the entities that you want to view, pick just what you need to establish the view. Try to avoid selecting any unnecessary entities. Remember the whole drawing will be regenerated with the view when you exit the command.

Using the PAn Option to Center the Room View

DVIEW provides another option for changing your view without changing your viewing distance. The PAn option lets you change your view by moving the camera side to side and up and down relative to the plane of your current view. The target and camera points change but their distance doesn't. If you are in perspective mode (like you are now), you must pick a first (base point) and second point to show camera displacement. AutoCAD dynamically drags the image as you drag the camera point. Use PAn when you want to reposition the image.

➤ *NOTE: Panning repositions your camera and target by the panned distance. In parallel projection, this will have no effect on the image but in perspective projection, new positions will be reflected.*

Try centering the desk in your current view of the room. Select the table and the wall with the door.

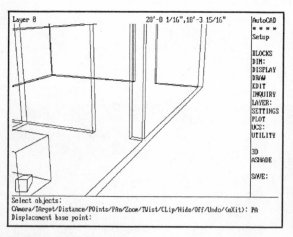

DVIEW of Pan Option

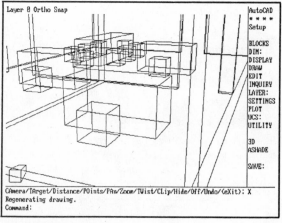

Panned to the Center of the Room

Centering the Room With Pan

```
Command: DVIEW
Select objects: P                          Selects table and wall.
7 found.
Select objects: <RETURN>
CAmera/TArget/Distance/POints/PAn/Zoom/TWist/CLip/Hide/Off/Undo/<eXit>: PA
Displacement base point:                   Pick any point near the table.
Second point:                              Drag table to center of screen.
CAmera/TArget/Distance/POints/PAn/Zoom/TWist/CLip/Hide/Off/Undo/<eXit>: X
```

You should have a perspective view with the table in the center of the room.

➡ *NOTE: It may be impossible to get the centered perspective view you want and have it fill the screen. For example, using DVIEW's house icon, try to look down on the roof while maintaining parallel vertical walls. To get this, you must set the camera angle from the X,Y plane to 0 and pan up several times until you are above the house. Despite your efforts, the house will be small and at the bottom of your screen.*

Using DVIEW's Undo Option

Like AutoCAD's other complex commands, DVIEW provides an Undo option to step back through your setting and point location changes made in the current DVIEW command. DVIEW's Undo goes back one step at a time.

If you have exited DVIEW (as we have), you can use the UNDO command to undo an entire DVIEW operation. We are going to try some clipping operations next, using the original perspective view that you established with the table as a target at a distance of 19 feet. Go back to your marked view by Undoing back at the command prompt. If you get lost, just repeat the initial DVIEW sequence to get the perspective view. Your screen should look like the Office After Undo illustration (below). Check to see that you are still in perspective mode.

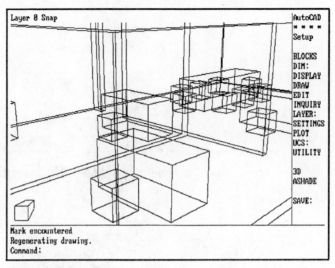

```
Layer 0 Snap                                              AutoCAD
                                                          * * * *
                                                          Setup

                                                          BLOCKS
                                                          DIM:
                                                          DISPLAY
                                                          DRAW
                                                          EDIT
                                                          INQUIRY
                                                          LAYER:
                                                          SETTINGS
                                                          PLOT
                                                          UCS:
                                                          UTILITY

                                                          3D
                                                          ASHADE

                                                          SAVE:

Mark encountered
Regenerating drawing.
Command:
```

Office After Undo

Undoing Dynamic Views

```
Command: UNDO                    Undo back to view for clipping.
Auto/Back/Control/End/Group/Mark/<number>: B
DVIEW DVIEW
Mark encountered
Regenerating drawing
```

Using the Clip Option to Clip Away Obstructions

If you were to hide your current view of the office, the two walls forming
the corner would obstruct your view. As you develop your views
anticipating hidden line removal, you need a way to get foreground
objects (like the walls) out of the way, or remove background objects that
clutter the image that you want. The CLip option lets you place a front
and a back clipping plane (or both) in your view to get these effects. Place
these clipping planes by specifying their distances from the target. The
back plane obscures everything behind it; the front plane obscures
everything in front of it. A third option, Off, turns both clipping planes
off. (You also can turn the back plane on and off.)

If you select the back plane, a positive distance puts the plane between
the target and the camera; a negative distance puts the plane beyond the
target. The plane is perpendicular to the line of sight between the camera
and the target. If you select the front clipping plane, you must also specify

a distance to the target or put the plane at the camera by selecting the Eye option.

If you looked closely at the perspective views you have generated so far, you may have already seen the front plane clipping effect. When you switch perspective mode on, it turns the front clip on and defaults to the current camera position (the Eye option).

Try clipping the front left corner of the room. Put your clipping plane at about two and a half feet from the target.

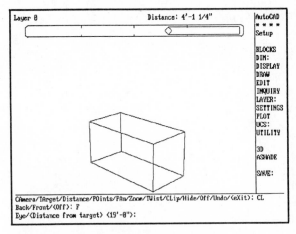

DVIEW During Clip Option

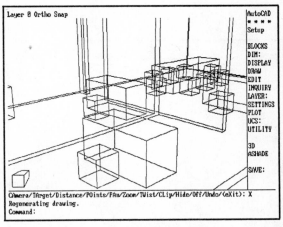

Lower Left Corner Clipped From Room

Using the Clip Option to Clip a View

```
Command: DVIEW
Select objects:                     Select the table.
1 selected, 1 found.
Select objects: <RETURN>
CAmera/TArget/Distance/POints/PAn/Zoom/TWist/CLip/Hide/Off/Undo/<eXit>: CL
Back/Front/<Off>: F
Eye/<Distance from target> <19'-0">: 2'6
CAmera/TArget/Distance/POints/PAn/Zoom/TWist/CLip/Hide/Off/Undo/<eXit>: X
```

Now when you execute HIDE (in the next exercise), you will have an unobstructed view of Flintstone's table and chair.

➡ *NOTE: Watch your clipping values! When you exit DVIEW, clipping values remain in effect. If you think that you have suddenly lost portions of your drawing after working with a clipped view, you probably left some clipping settings on. Go back and turn CLip off.*

Using Hide Option to Get Hidden View

A DVIEW hide works like a standard HIDE, except you can see perspective. However DVIEW hide is temporary and affects only the selected entities. Exiting DVIEW regenerates the drawing. To rehide it, use the HIDE command. When you have the dynamic view you want, select the Hide option. Set the front clip back to Eye and try a hide. The following illustrations show the clipping effect on the hidden view.

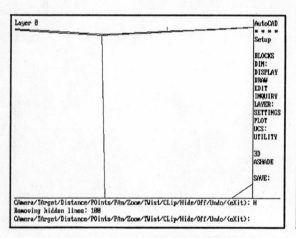

Hide Without Clipped Corner

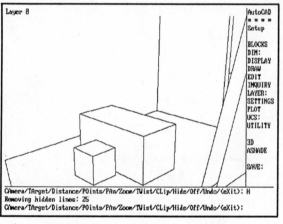

Hide With Clipped Corner

Using DVIEW's Hide

```
Command: DVIEW
Select objects:            Select the table, chair and wall.
1 selected, 1 found.
Select objects: <RETURN>
CAmera/TArget/Distance/POints/PAn/Zoom/TWist/CLip/Hide/Off/Undo/<eXit>: CL
Back/Front/<Off>: F
Eye/<Distance from target> <2'-6">: E
CAmera/TArget/Distance/POints/PAn/Zoom/TWist/CLip/Hide/Off/Undo/<eXit>: H
CAmera/TArget/Distance/POints/PAn/Zoom/TWist/CLip/Hide/Off/Undo/<eXit>: CL
Back/Front/<Off>: F
Eye/<Distance from target> <19'-0">: 2'6
CAmera/TArget/Distance/POints/PAn/Zoom/TWist/CLip/Hide/Off/Undo/<eXit>: H
CAmera/TArget/Distance/POints/PAn/Zoom/TWist/CLip/Hide/Off/Undo/<eXit>: X
```

If you are curious about the effect of a back clip, let's try one. Then, cancel it.

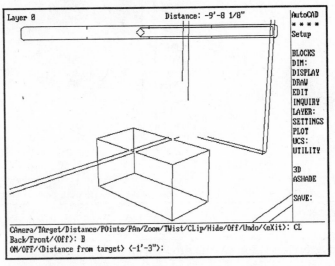

DVIEW of Office With Back Clipping

Using Clip Option to Clip Back of Office

```
Command: DVIEW
Select objects:                           Pick the table and wall.
2 found.
Select objects: <RETURN>
CAmera/TArget/Distance/POints/PAn/Zoom/TWist/CLip/Hide/Off/Undo/<eXit>: CL
Back/Front/<Off>: B
Eye/<Distance from target> <1'-3">: <^C>   Move slider bar to see the clipping,
                                           then cancel.
CAmera/TArget/Distance/POints/PAn/Zoom/TWist/CLip/Hide/Off/Undo/<eXit>: X
```

We mentioned earlier that you can change your field of view by changing the lens length in DVIEW.

Using Zoom Option to Change Camera Lens

Zoom is the option that lets you change lenses. Once you have set your camera and target distance, changing your lens lets you include more (or less) of your image in your view. The default lens is 50mm. Increasing your lens length (105mm in the next example) has a telephoto effect. Decreasing the lens (35mm) gives a wide angle effect. Use your current view and try switching lenses.

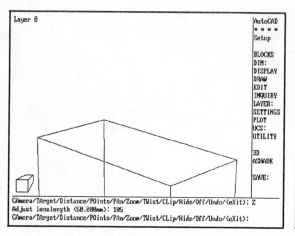

View With 105mm Lens

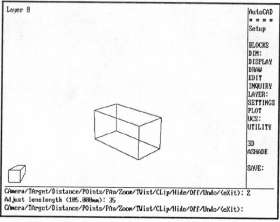

View With 35mm Lens

Using Zoom Option to View Room With Different Lenses

```
Command: DVIEW
Select objects:                        Pick the table.
1 selected, 1 found.
Select objects: <RETURN>
CAmera/TArget/Distance/POints/PAn/Zoom/TWist/CLip/Hide/Off/Undo/<eXit>: Z
Adjust lens length <50.000mm>: 105      Try a telephoto lens.
CAmera/TArget/Distance/POints/PAn/Zoom/TWist/CLip/Hide/Off/Undo/<eXit>: Z
Adjust lens length <105.000mm>: 35      Try a wide angle lens.
CAmera/TArget/Distance/POints/PAn/Zoom/TWist/CLip/Hide/Off/Undo/<eXit>: X
```

The 35mm lens is a good choice for interior room views because the wider angle encompasses more of the room.

Contrary to popular belief, the lens length does not affect perspective. Only the distance and angle from camera to target determines perspective. The lens length only determines the width of the view. Many people think lens length affects perspective because wide angle (short) lenses coincidentally tend to be used for close distances and telephoto (long) lenses are used for distant subjects. Unlike real lenses (especially very short fish-eyes), AutoCAD's lenses are perfect with no distortion. They always yield a geometrically true perspective.

➡ *NOTE: Using Zoom on parallel projection acts just like AutoCAD's standard zoom. It just increases or decreases magnification.*

Twist, the Other Option

DVIEW has one more option, called TWist. As its name implies, TWist lets you rotate your view *around* your line of sight by specifying a (counterclockwise) angle. If you try a twist, you can see how easy it is to turn the room upside down. Undo to the current view if you do.

Organizing Your Views

After all the trouble of setting up perfect perspectives, it would be nice if you could save and later restore them. You can, with the VIEW command. VIEW can name and save perspective views just like normal views. VIEW Save stores all of the current DVIEW settings so you can go about your work and later use VIEW Restore to return to your perspective.

Since VPORTS saves all of the display parameters for each of its viewports, you can also save perspectives by saving and restoring named viewports.

Making and Displaying Slides

As you develop a set of views, you will want to capture these images either for presentation or for your own files. Slides have been the mainstay for drawing presentations since their early use in computer shows. When you make a slide, you save a screen image that AutoCAD can quickly recreate on the screen.

Using MSLIDE to Make a Slide

The MSLIDE (Make SLIDE) command creates a disk file with the extension .SLD. AutoCAD does not store all its drawing file information in the .SLD file. It only stores the display vector list needed to paint the screen quickly. AutoCAD cannot edit slides. If you want to change a slide, you must first edit the drawing file that was used to create the slide, then create a new one.

Make a slide of your current office view. You must be outside DVIEW and use HIDE at the command prompt to get a hidden view. Then use MSLIDE to make the slide. Call this first slide VIEW-1.

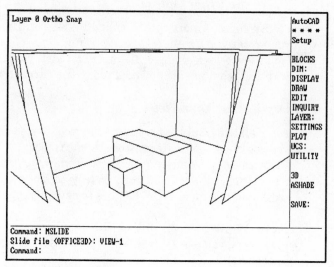

View of Office for Slide

Using MSLIDE to Create a Slide of the Office

Command: **HIDE**   Hide before creating the slide.

Command: **MSLIDE**
Slide file <OFFICE3D>: **VIEW-1**

Your image is stored on disk as VIEW-1.SLD.

Using VSLIDE to Display a Slide

The VSLIDE (View SLIDE) command displays the slide image. This command recalls the display image file from the disk and paints the screen with it. When you display a slide, it temporarily takes over the screen, leaving whatever drawing file you were working on intact and active.

To see how this works, put a plan view (WCS) of the office back on your screen, then show the VIEW-1 slide.

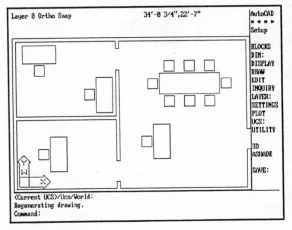

Office in Plan View

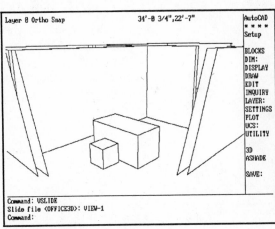

Viewing the Slide

Using VSLIDE to View the Slide

Command: **PLAN**   Go to the WCS plan view.

Command: **VSLIDE**
Slide file <OFFICE3D>: **VIEW-1**

Command: **REDRAW**   Redraw removes the slide.

After you show the slide, you should be back in plan view.

➡ *NOTE: Slides appear over your actual drawing. Any attempt at drawing or editing the slide will actually wind up on the drawing which is obscured by the slide.*

➡ *TIP: Use viewports to display slides. The slide will fill the current viewport, allowing you to work in the remaining viewports and use the slide for reference.*

Making Slides for a Slide Show

Next, we want to show you how to script a slide show. But to do this, we need at least three more slides. (A slide show with one slide isn't enough, even for the Flintstones!)

Create three more perspective views, and make a slide of each. Use the following table to get your camera and target points. These next three views will take you around the office plan. VIEW-2 and VIEW-3 provide two views of the large room on the right. VIEW-4 gives a view of the office with two tables in the upper left. Default the distance option to get perspective views. Try to follow our viewpoints because we will provide you with a companion AutoShaded set of these views in the next chapter. You can use the two sets to compare DVIEW and AutoShade effects.

SLIDE NAME	TARGET	CAMERA	LENS
VIEW-2	33'0,33'0,2'0	51'6,21'6,5'6	35
VIEW-3	52'0,35'6,0'0	33'0,14'6,6'0	35
VIEW-4	38'0,33'6,0'0	17'6,25'0.6'0	35

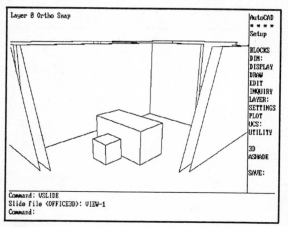

Slide VIEW-1

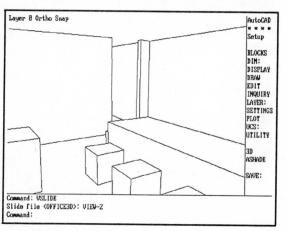

Slide VIEW-2

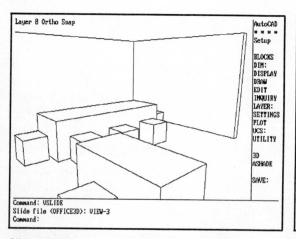

Slide VIEW-3

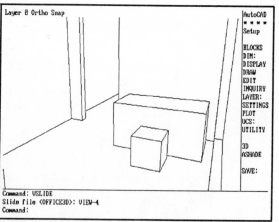

Slide VIEW-4

Using MSLIDE to Create Three More Slides

Command: **DVIEW**   Turn clipping off.

Create three slides using the table above and the following sequence.

Command: **DVIEW**   Create view with the VIEW-2 data above.
Use the POints option to set target and camera points.
Use the Distance option and default the distance to turn on perspective.
Use the Zoom option to set lens to 35mm, then exit.

Command: **HIDE**   Remove hidden lines.
Command: **MSLIDE**   Make slide with name VIEW-2.

Repeat the sequence for the remaining views.

After you have created the slides, end your drawing. To work with script files you need to exit to the operating system and set up a text editor.

Ending the OFFICE3D Drawing

Command: **PLAN**   Return to plan view of office.
Command: **ZOOM**   Zoom All.
Command: **END**   End drawing and exit AutoCAD to create script.

SCRIPT Files

You have the slides. Now, how to get a script? A SCRIPT is a utility for hands-free operation. It is a listing of commands, input, and responses that is stored in a text file and *played* character for character exactly as if it was typed directly at the keyboard. Like slides, scripts were designed for self-running demonstrations of AutoCAD at presentations and shows.

Making a Script File for Slide Presentations

You create script files as ASCII text files. In order to create or modify a script, you need to have a text editor that creates ASCII text files. If you are using the IA DISK, we have provided a script file called SLIDSHO.SCR to run the four slides. To look at this script, you need to place a copy of a text editor in the IA-ACAD directory. If you need help setting up the text editor, look at the setup sequence in the first chapter on customization (chapter 18.) If you don't want to look at the script, you can still use it to run the slide show.

If you do not have the IA DISK, you can create the script with a text editor. Type it in exactly as it is shown in the next exercise. If you don't create the script, read along.

Scripts were designed to control VSLIDE (View SLIDE) shows. They use a DELAY command to control display time. Scripts also can use a preloading feature of VSLIDE to load the next slide while the current one displays. Prefacing a slide name with an asterisk * preloads it to speed up the time gap between slides. There is also a RSCRIPT command which repeats a script.

All script files have the extension .SCR. The SLIDSHO.SCR (below) controls the display of the slides, VIEW-1 through VIEW-4, by stringing a series of VSLIDE and DELAY commands. The delays are in milliseconds (2000 is 2 seconds). The final RSCRIPT command loops the script to start over. After you create the file, or look at it, move on to the next exercise to run it.

Using a Script to Make a Slide Show

 You have SLIDSHO.SCR. Look at it, then test it.

 Create the SLIDSHO.SCR text file, then test it. Or just look at it.

C:\IA-ACAD>**NE SLIDSHO.SCR**   Starts our editor, NE.
                                                Use *your* editor to create or look at SLIDSHO.SCR.

Don't use tabs or invisible trailing spaces.
Use a <RETURN> to end the last line.

```
vslide view-1
vslide *view-2
delay 2000
vslide
vslide *view-3
delay 2000
vslide
vslide *view-4
delay 2000
vslide
delay 2000
rscript
```

Save SLIDSHO.SCR and exit your editor.

Using SCRIPT to Run a Slide Show

You now have a script that you can run with AutoCAD's SCRIPT command. Get back into AutoCAD and into the drawing editor. Load your OFFICE3D drawing (or any drawing). Run the script, sit back, and enjoy your slide show. The slides will show on the screen, cycling through in sequence and repeating until you cancel the script with a <^C>.

Using SCRIPT to Run the Slide Show

```
Enter selection: 2          Edit existing drawing named OFFICE3D.

Command: SCRIPT
Script file <OFFICE3D>: SLIDSHO
Command: vslide
Slide file <OFFICE3D>: view-1
Command: delay Delay time in milliseconds: 2000
```

The script command and slides appear on the screen.

```
Command: rscript            Rscript repeats the script sequence.
Command: vslide
Slide file <OFFICE3D>: view-1
Command: vslide
Slide file <OFFICE3D>: *view-2
Command: delay Delay time in milliseconds: 2000
Command: vslide
Command:                    Type <^C> to exit script.

Command: QUIT               Quit to discard any changes you may have made.
```

If a script has an error, it will not run to completion. Instead, AutoCAD will stop when it encounters the error and return control to you at the command prompt. You then can correct the script by going back into the text editor. Look for the error where the script returned control to the command prompt. When you are done, QUIT your drawing.

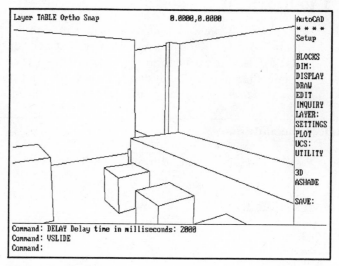

Slide of VIEW-2

Stopping Scripts

You can stop a running script by hitting the <BACKSPACE> key or a
<^C>. This causes the script to finish the command it is working on and
return you to the command prompt. You can do some work and then pick
up where you stopped the script by using the RESUME command.

➥ *NOTE: Any command that forces a redraw or regen will cause
AutoCAD to leave the slide mode and return to the normal underlying
screen, but the script will continue running. A RESUME will start a
script that was stopped by a keystroke.*

After you run the slide show, you can go back and adjust the delay or slide
name sequence to alter the show. If you want to show slides of your own,
substitute your own names and extend the script by repeating the *vslide,
delay, vslide pattern. You also can organize your slides in a slide library
file.

Slide Library Files

Although slides were originally designed for giving slide show
presentations, they now have the additional important use of storing
images for icon menus. To avoid cluttering your disk with dozens of slide
files, you can group and store slides in name.SLB (Slide LiBrary) files.

To display a slide from a library, use the format *libraryname(slidename)* in your script. The slide name is placed inside the parentheses after the library name. To display a slide stored as an individual .SLD file, give the slide file name. When you display an icon menu, you are displaying slides from a named slide library file. The standard slide library file is ACAD.SLB.

Making a Slide Library File

Slide libraries are created by AutoCAD's SLIDELIB.EXE program. You can create your own slide library files using this same program. Creating a slide library is a three-step process.

- Make all the needed slides.

- Create an ASCII text file (as an example call it SLDLIST.TXT), listing each slide name (not name.SLB) on a separate line. Do not include any extra <RETURN>s or <SPACE>s. Make sure that you <RETURN> after the last name.

- Run the SLIDELIB.EXE program. (You can run it via the SHELL command from within the drawing editor.) Running the SLIDELIB program will create the SLDLIST.SLB file from your SLDLST.TXT file and the named slides.

   Assuming that a slide list file named SLDLIST.TXT is in your current IA-ACAD directory, and that the SLIDELIB.EXE program is in the ACAD directory, the command line format to create a slide library named IA-LIB.SLB is:

```
C:\IA-ACAD> \ACAD\SLIDELIB IA-LIB <SLDLIST.TXT
```

AutoFlix

If you like showing slides, you should look into AutoFlix, another Autodesk program. AutoFlix can take AutoCAD and AutoShade slides, and combine them with text files and even music to create a *movie*. AutoFlix includes AutoLISP programs to automate the production of slides and shaded images. It can even follow animation sequences. You can make the movies self-running or interactive. Interactive movies can prompt the user for a choice and then branch to various movie subsections or even run external programs. AutoFlix movies require an EGA standard video card. The AutoFlix program is *shareware*, meaning that you can copy and distribute it freely. But if you find AutoFlix useful, you are required to pay ($35 to Autodesk) for it.

Other Uses for Scripts

Scripts can do other things besides run slide shows. Scripts offer two unique advantages. First, you can run them outside the drawing editor. While they can be started from inside a drawing or from the DOS command prompt, they can end a drawing, run through the Main Menu, the Configuration Menu, the plot or printer plot dialogues, and go back into a drawing. The second advantage is that scripts can loop indefinitely. We will show you how to create a script to run plots in the chapter on plotting (chapter 17).

Stopping Point

This is a stopping point in the chapter's script. Put your slides to rest, take a break. Then come back and take a look at editing with dynamic views and at getting a 3D view into a 2D drawing file that you can enhance and annotate.

How to Work With Perspective Drawings

How do you edit perspective drawings created with DVIEWs? If you are in perspective mode, PAN, ZOOM and SKETCH commands are not allowed. You will get a prompt and AutoCAD will cancel the command:

```
This command may not be invoked in a perspective view
```

Instead of PAN and ZOOM, you can use DVIEW's pan and zoom options. The big limitation in perspective views is that you cannot pick points. You will get a message at the command line telling you that:

```
Pointing in perspective view is not allowed here
```

However, you can still enter points from the keyboard. Normal object selection still works, including entity picking with some exceptions. Several commands (BREAK, FILLET, CHAMFER, TRIM, EXTEND, the UCS Entity option, and DIM by entity picking) *require* picking by point, which is not allowed. You can still use these commands by typing coordinates.

Rather than trying to work directly with a perspective view, we recommend taking advantage of viewports to enter points and select objects. Any command that you execute in another, normal viewport is reflected in the perspective viewport.

Using VPORTS to Work With Perspective Views

You can set dynamic views in viewports. By setting up at least two viewports, you can retain one view for DVIEW displays and use your second viewport for plan view editing. (You can also edit in a parallel projected 3D view.) As you modify your drawing, you will get automatic updates in your perspective view.

Setting Up VPORTS for Perspective Editing

Let's go back to the office drawing. We are going to edit the lower left office by inserting our 3D drafting table (from chapter 13) and our chair (from chapter 14) in place of the Flintstone furniture that is in the office now. If for some reason you don't have the TABLE and CHAIR drawings handy, you can use any 3D block that you want by creating it on layer 0 and inserting it. (If you use a unit block, you will need to scale the block when you insert it.) We are not as interested in the office's graphics as in showing you a simple setup that lets you take advantage of dynamic views while making your editing life easier.

After you load the OFFICE3D drawing, create a plan view (in WCS) of the drawing. Set up two horizontal viewports. Create a dynamic perspective view of the office.

Use the exercise and the Screen Prepared for Editing illustration to help you get your starting dynamic view. After you have your dynamic view, make the lower viewport active and zoom to the lower left corner office.

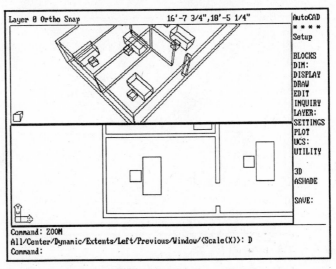

Screen Prepared for Editing

Using VPORTS to Create a Perspective and Plan View

Enter selection: **2**   Edit existing drawing named OFFICE3D.

Command: **VPORTS**   Make 2 horizontal viewports.

Make the top viewport active.

Command: **DVIEW**   Create a perspective view of office.
                                        Use the POints option to set target to 26',22'6,0'.
                                        Use the POints option to set camera to 11'6,3',46'.
                                        Use the Distance option to create a perspective view.
                                        Use the Zoom option to set lens to 35mm.
                                        Continue to adjust the values and image location to get
                                        an image similar to illustration above.

Make the bottom viewport active.

Command: **ZOOM**   Dynamic zoom to lower left office.

You should have a perspective view in the top viewport, and a zoomed plan view of the office in your current lower viewport.

Editing to Update a Perspective View

Next, erase the simple table and chair blocks from the lower left room. After you erase the blocks, insert the TABLE and CHAIR drawings (or your blocks if you had to create some surrogates) into the office. Get your insertion scale and rotation values from the exercise sequence.

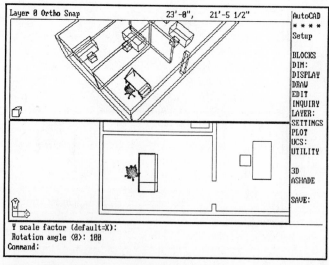

Office With Real Chair and Table

Using INSERT to Insert 3D Chair and Table

```
Command: ERASE                    Erase the primitive chair and table in the lower left office only.

Command: INSERT
Block name (or ?): TABLE
Insertion point: 22'6,22',0
X scale factor <1> / Corner / XYZ: <RETURN>
Y scale factor (default=X): <RETURN>
Rotation angle <0>: 270

Command: INSERT
Block name (or ?) <TABLE>: CHAIR
Insertion point: 21'6,19'6,0
X scale factor <1> / Corner / XYZ: <RETURN>
Y scale factor (default=X): <RETURN>
Rotation angle <0>: 100
```

As you insert the table and chair, your dynamic view in the upper viewport is updated with the new table and chair.

Saving the Perspective Drawing

After you have admired your update, save the drawing in plan view as FURNISHD. (This drawing is an optional drawing that you can use in the next chapter when we look at AutoShaded images.) Then, quit the drawing.

Saving the Drawing as FURNISHD

```
Command: VPORTS          Make bottom viewport single.
Command: VIEW            Restore view A.
Command: SAVE            Save the drawing as FURNISHD.
Command: QUIT            We will use the simple office drawing in the last exercise.
```

Sooner or later you will want to enhance or annotate a 3D perspective image. How do you do it? As you have learned, adding title text or drawing a border around a perspective view is practically impossible. If you wanted to place trees and shrubs around the exterior of a perspective building you would need 3D trees. It's not very easy or practical to create 3D trees. The best solution is to create the desired perspective view and turn it into a 2D drawing. Then you can use all of AutoCAD's commands to enhance the drawing. You can make a 3D image into a 2D image by plotting to a DXB file.

Using DXB to Make a 2D Drawing From a 3D Perspective Drawing

DXB (Drawing Interchange Binary) is an AutoCAD file format that you can create by using the "ADI" plotter driver. Once you have made a DXB file, you can import the DXB file back into a drawing using the DXBIN command. The imported DXB image is totally converted to a collection of lines. Think of a DXB file as pure *spaghetti*. Arcs, circles, and polylines are all made up of tiny line segments. However, when you create a 2D drawing with the imported DXB image, you can *enhance* the drawing by adding text, a border, or by drawing around the image.

Making a DXB File

To get a DXB file, you need to plot to a file. The process is simple. All you need to do is establish the view of the office you want and plot it out. Instead of a hard copy, however, you will plot a 2D drawing of that view in a file with the extension .DXB. Once the DXB file is created, you create a 2D drawing of the office by importing the disk file.

To get a DXB file, you need to configure AutoCAD to plot DXB files. Use the following exercise to help you reconfigure AutoCAD. Start at the Main Menu.

➡ *NOTE: Before you do this exercise, MAKE SURE that you know how to restore your current plotter configuration after you finish the exercise. If you are not sure, save a backup of your current configuration. Exit AutoCAD and, in your IA-ACAD directory, copy ACAD.CFG to the name ACADCFG.BAK and copy ACADPL.OVL to ACADPL.BAK. Then when you finish the exercise, exit and copy the two files back to their original names.*

Configuring AutoCAD to Plot DXB Files

```
Enter selection: 5          It displays your current AutoCAD configuration.
Press RETURN to continue.  <RETURN>

Enter selection <0>: 5      Configure plotter.

Do you want to select a different one? <N> Y
```

Display shows a list of plotters.

```
Select device number or ? to repeat list <#>: 2     Select ADI plotter.
Select output format:
```

```
0.  ASCII file
1.  Binary file
2.  AutoCAD DXB file
3.  Installed ADI driver
```

Output format, 0 to 3 <0>: **2**
Maximum horizontal (X) plot size in drawing units <0'-11"> **18**
Plotter steps per drawing unit <83'-4">: **100**
Maximum vertical (Y) plot size in drawing units <0'-8 1/2">: **12**

Do you want to change pens while plotting? <N> **<RETURN>**

If you have previously measured the lengths of a horizontal
and a vertical line that were plotted to a specific scale,
you may use these measurements to calibrate your plotter.

Would you like to calibrate your plotter? <N> **<RETURN>**

Size units (Inches or Millimeters) <I>: **<RETURN>**
Plot origin in Inches <0.00,0.00>: **<RETURN>**

Standard values for plotting size

```
Size    Width    Height
A       10.50     8.00
B       16.00    10.00
C       21.00    16.00
MAX     32.00    32.00
```

Enter the Size or Width,Height (in Inches) <MAX>: **<RETURN>**
Rotate 2D plots 90 degrees clockwise? <N> **<RETURN>**
Pen width <0.010>: **<RETURN>**
Adjust area fill boundaries for pen width? <N> **<RETURN>**
Remove hidden lines? <N> **Y**

Specify scale by entering:
Plotted Inches=Drawing Units or Fit or ? <F>: **<RETURN>**

Command: Enter selection: **0**   Exit to Main Menu.

If you answer N to the following question, all configuration
changes you have just made will be discarded.

Keep configuration changes? <Y> **Y**   Returns to Main Menu.

You are ready to output a DXB file.

Plotting to a DXB File

Get back into the drawing editor by calling up your OFFICE3D drawing. Use the next exercise to help you create a DVIEW of the office. Our view is shown in the 3D Perspective of Office illustration below.

When you have the view you want, plot it using the PLOT command from within the drawing editor. (We will go into plotting in more detail in chapter 17.) After you complete the plot, end the drawing.

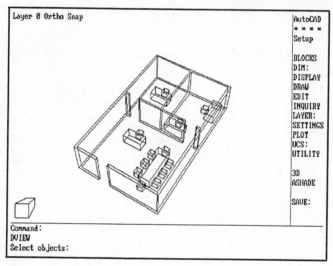

3D Perspective of Office

Creating a 2D Drawing From a Perspective Drawing

Enter selection: **2**	Edit existing drawing OFFICE3D.
Command: **DVIEW**	Create a view as shown above. Use the POints option to set target to 34'6,20'6,4'6. Use the POints option to set camera to 70'0,45'0,46'0. Use the Distance option to create a perspective view. Use the Zoom option to set lens to 35mm. Continue to adjust the values and image location to get an image similar to illustration above.

```
Command: PLOT
What to plot -- Display, Extents, Limits, View, or Window <D>: <RETURN>
Plot will be written to a selected file
Sizes are in Inches
Plot origin is at (0.00,0.00)
Plotting area is 32.00 wide by 32.00 high (MAX size)
Plot is NOT rotated 90 degrees
```

```
Pen width is 0.010
Area fill will NOT be adjusted for pen width
Hidden lines will be removed
Scale is Fit.

Do you want to change anything? <N> <RETURN>
Effective plotting area: 32.0 wide by 31.20 high

Enter file name for plot <OFFICE3D>: <RETURN>
Removing hidden lines: xx            AutoCAD cycles through drawing.
Plotting vectors: xx                 AutoCAD cycles through drawing.
Command: END
```

You should have an OFFICE3D.DXB file on your disk. The next step is to import that file back into a new drawing. Create a drawing called OFFICE2D, and import the drawing with the DXBIN command.

After you load the drawing, your screen should show something like the following 2D Perspective of Office screen shot. If you want to, edit the drawing by adding some notes or a title block. Editing the perspective image itself is possible but tedious because the curves are made up of lots of little lines. End the drawing when you are done.

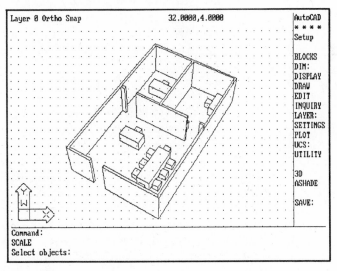

2D Perspective of Office

Using DXBIN to Create a 2D Perspective Drawing.

```
Enter selection: 1          Begin a NEW drawing called OFFICE2D.

Command: DXBIN
DXB file: OFFICE3D

Command: GRID              Set grid to 1".
Command: LIMITS            Set limits to 36" x 24".
Command: ZOOM             Zoom All.
Command: SCALE            Scale the office to fit within limits.
```

Do any editing to the drawing, like adding a border or notes.

```
Command: END
```

You now have a 2D drawing with a 3D image that you can plot. If you want to see how to plot this drawing, it is the first plot sequence in chapter 17.

Reset Your Plotter Configuration

Before you exit AutoCAD, you need to go back to the configuration menu and restore your original plotter configuration. Or, if you made backup files, exit AutoCAD and copy them back to their original names. You will need your standard plotter configuration for plotting in chapter 17.

Dynamic Viewing Summary

For speed and efficiency in DVIEW, remember three techniques. You can use the DVIEW house icon (or your own custom icon) instead of selecting complex entities. You can select a representative subset of entities to use in DVIEW. And you can use block redefinition, substituting simple blocks for complex ones until you get it right, then swapping them back.

If you know where you want to look from (camera point) and what you want to look at (target point), then establish these points ahead of time instead of using trial and error in DVIEW. You can use the ID command to get points, with osnaps and XYZ point filters to align them with known geometry.

Use sliders for dynamic image adjustment, then type in exact values if you need precision in your views.

Remember, you can use named viewports and named views to save and restore your perspective DVIEWs after you get them right.

When importing a DXB image, block it. Blocking and inserting makes it easier to position and scale, and protects entities from accidental editing.

AutoShade Is Next

You have created a series of 3D perspective hidden views, but they don't represent the most realistic images that you can present of your drawings. Take one step further and create images with surface shading and lighting effects. The next chapter on AutoShade will step you through creating a companion set of shaded images, rendering the same simple (and now familiar) office that you used in this chapter.

3D Shaded Chair

CHAPTER 16

Inside AutoShade
ENHANCING 3D WITH SHADED RENDERINGS

Real 3D

In AutoCAD, 3D is represented by wireframe images. Although you can add meshes to represent surfaces and remove hidden lines, many design applications require more realistic representations of objects, including shaded surfaces and perspectives.

The AutoShade program renders AutoCAD 3D drawings, letting you light and shade your images to achieve more realistic 3D effects. Using AutoShade's tools, you can adjust camera angles and set multiple light sources to give life to your 3D surfaces. Think of AutoShade as a 35mm camera for your AutoCAD drawings!

Scenes and Filmroll File

AutoShade runs as a separate program from AutoCAD. After you create your 3D drawings in AutoCAD, you pass the drawings to AutoShade via a filmroll file that you create with AutoCAD. AutoCAD provides the film file, and AutoShade processes, displays, and prints the film.

The *scene* is the key element in the filmroll file. When you make a filmroll file, you *shoot* scenes in AutoCAD. A scene is made up of a 3D drawing, a camera, and one or more light sources. Making a scene is not too distant from stop frame animation. In fact, the scene icon is a miniature clapper board just like you find on the movie set. When you create your scene in AutoCAD you set your camera position, distance, angle, and lighting, then you execute the SCENE command. Think of a scene as an individual frame of film. You can create as many scenes as you like before developing your filmroll.

The Benefits of Using AutoShade

Besides the pleasure that you get from seeing your drawing shaded, there are several benefits to using AutoShade. First, you get more realistic representations of your drawings. Rendered images shown in color on a good display screen are absolutely impressive. You can get an immediate gain in the quality of your design presentations by using

AutoShade-rendered images. Second, 3D rendered drawings can show errors and interferences that are not seen in wireframe representations. Under- and overlapping faces, or discontinuities in 3D surfaces, are visible in AutoShade. Third, AutoShade produces both rendered and wireframe images in perspective.

Assumptions About AutoShade

This chapter is designed to show you the interface between AutoShade and AutoCAD and to give you a feel for AutoShade's capabilities. The exercises are written as if you had AutoShade. However, if you don't have AutoShade yet, the exercises provide enough information so that you can follow along easily. The rendered drawings speak for themselves!

The emphasis in the chapter is on the AutoCAD side of the AutoCAD-to-AutoShade interface. Since you don't create your 3D drawings in AutoShade, how you prepare your drawings in AutoCAD can have a large impact on your AutoShade renderings. Seemingly slight differences between 2D or 3D commands, extruded 2D or 3D entities, and the order of entity creation in AutoCAD can make big differences in the results you get in AutoShade. How you prepare your drawing for AutoShade also affects AutoShade's efficiency in rendering the drawing. For example, you set your cameras and lighting *within* AutoCAD before you pass the drawings to AutoShade. Using the 3D tools provided within AutoCAD and working out good lighting schemes are keys to creating efficient AutoShade-bound 3D drawings in AutoCAD.

AutoShade Tools in AutoCAD

You will find the AutoShade tools that you need through the [ASHADE] menu item on the root screen menu. [ASHADE] loads a set of AutoLISP functions and calls a page of AutoShade menu items. They are [LIGHTS:], [CAMERA:], [ACTION], and [CAMVIEW:]. The [ACTION] menu item calls a menu with the [SCENE:] and [FLMROLL:] menu items. You can access the same set of tools through the [Options] pull-down menu where [Ashade...] calls an AutoShade icon menu. Of these tools, only FILMROLL is an AutoCAD command. The rest of the AutoShade *commands* (SCENE, LIGHT, CAMVIEW, and CAMERA) are defined in AutoLISP. They are loaded by the [ASHADE] menu item, and can't be typed as commands until loaded.

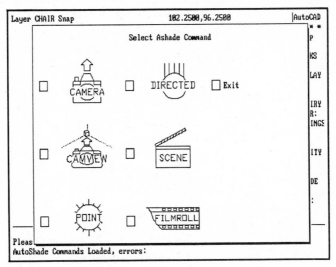

AutoShade Icon Menu

Setting Up for AutoShade

If you are using AutoShade, we assume that AutoShade and its supporting files are loaded in your AutoCAD directory. These supporting files include ASHADE.LSP, the CAMERA.DWG camera block, the OVERHEAD.DWG and DIRECT.DWG light blocks, and the CLAPPER.DWG and SHOT.DWG scene (clapper) blocks. We also assume you have gone through the AutoShade User Guide tutorial and can find your way around the AutoShade commands and menus. The exercises will not show every little step in AutoShade, but they do emphasize the major points. Key sequences are captured and shown in screen shots.

Creating a Filmroll File

Before you can use AutoShade, you must have a filmroll file to shade. The exercises in this chapter use the handy chair that you created in chapter 14, and the handy (but humble) office that you worked with to get some dynamic views in chapter 15.

Let's start with the chair and do a fast shade. To take a quick look at your chair in AutoShade, you need to get into AutoCAD and create a filmroll file to pass into AutoShade. Load your drawing called CHAIR. (If you do not have the CHAIR drawing, you need to assemble the chair drawing in chapter 14. Or, you can read along and start with the next exercise which uses the office drawing from chapter 15. The starting office drawing is provided on the IA DISK.) After you load your chair drawing, set your

VPOINT using the values given in the exercise sequence. Then, type FILMROLL and create the chair filmroll file.

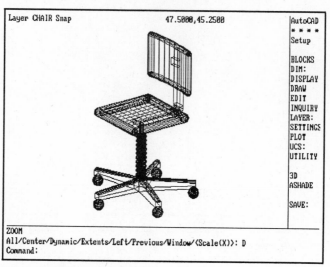

```
Layer CHAIR Snap                      47.5000,45.2500        AutoCAD
                                                             * * * *
                                                             Setup

                                                             BLOCKS
                                                             DIM:
                                                             DISPLAY
                                                             DRAW
                                                             EDIT
                                                             INQUIRY
                                                             LAYER:
                                                             SETTINGS
                                                             PLOT
                                                             UCS:
                                                             UTILITY

                                                             3D
                                                             ASHADE

                                                             SAVE:



ZOOM
All/Center/Dynamic/Extents/Left/Previous/Window/<Scale(X)>: D
Command:
```

View of Chair for AutoShade

Using FILMROLL to Create a Film

Use the IA batch file to get into AutoCAD.

Enter Selection: **2**	Edit an EXISTING drawing named CHAIR.
Command: **VPOINT**	Set VPOINT to -.75,-1,.5.
Command: **ZOOM**	Zoom Dynamic to fill screen.
Command: **FILMROLL**	Make CHAIR.FLM.
Enter filmroll file name <CHAIR>: **<RETURN>**	
Creating the filmroll file	
Processing face: 257	AutoCAD processes the filmroll.
Filmroll file created	
Command: **END**	END drawing and exit AutoCAD.

AutoCAD creates a filmroll file of all the objects in the drawing. AutoShade processes this file into rendered images. A filmroll can contain many different viewpoints, called scenes. Each scene gets rendered individually. This first chair example does not have any defined scenes, so your current AutoCAD viewpoint for the 3D drawing becomes the default viewpoint for the scene. You can use this approach to get a quick rendering of a 3D drawing to see how it is going to look before you commit to a full-blown filmroll with different camera positions and multiple light settings in several scenes.

Now you want to get into AutoShade and use the Fast Shade option. We assume AutoShade is in the ACAD directory. After you select the Fast Shade option, it should take about 30 to 90 minutes for AutoShade to process the chair drawing.

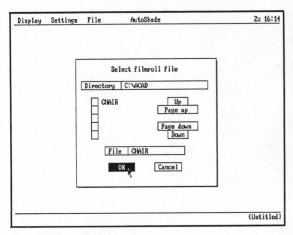

Filmroll File Dialogue Box

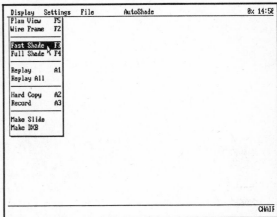

Fast Shade on the Display Pull-Down Menu

Using Fast Shade

`C:\IA-ACAD>`**CD \ACAD**	Change to the ACAD directory.
`C:\ACAD>`**SHADE**	Get into AutoShade by typing SHADE.
Pull down **[File]**	Pull down file menu.
Select **[Open]**	AutoShade opens a Filmroll dialogue box displaying the current directory and filmroll files.

Highlight box next to Directory
and change to IA-ACAD directory.

Select **[DIRECTORY]**	
Select **[CHAIR]**	Highlight box next to CHAIR and CHAIR is displayed in the File Box.
Select **[OK]**	Highlight the OK box or simply press <RETURN>.
Pull down **[Display]**	Pull down Display menu.
Select **[Fast Shade]**	AutoShade processes the rendering. Before the image is displayed, AutoShade displays a percentage of completion of each task it performs as it processes the rendering.
Pull down **[File]**	Pull down file menu.
Select **[QUIT]**	

Your screen should show the First Chair Rendering.

The First Chair Rendering

Fast Shade gives a quick preview of the chair, showing the effects of the default (ambient) light and shading. Fast Shade performs a rendering, but it does not check for overlapping faces. If you look closely at the screen image, you will see overlapping faces that give unusual shaded patches to the chair. The casters are showing through some of the legs and the back support appears to come out of the seat. The chair may also appear quite dark. This darkness is due to default lighting conditions assumed by AutoShade and the colors the chair was drawn in. Despite these limitations, Fast Shade gives you a quick check rendering to preview a drawing. A Fast Shade is much quicker than a Full Shade (which we will explore a little later). A Full Shade checks for overlapping faces and will give a correct rendering, but it takes much longer to process.

> ➡ *TIP: When it becomes necessary to overlap or nest entities, small changes in Z values or thickness can control the final order and appearance of your image.*

Preparing 3D Drawings for AutoShade

AutoCAD displays 3D images as wireframes. This means any of AutoCAD's entities can create a 3D image drawing. However, AutoShade ignores all entities without surfaces or thickness. It only recognizes the following entities.

- Circles, solids, traces, donuts, and wide polylines.

- 3DFaces and 3D polyline meshes.

- Extruded entities.

> ➡ *TIP: Be careful when you construct 3DFaces. In AutoShade, front faces obscure back faces. Faces constructed in a clockwise order are considered front faces, while counterclockwise faces are considered back faces. You can set UCS to Entity to check an existing face. If the Z axis points toward the camera, it's a front face. The MIRROR command will flip a face. The wrong order can create a rendering where the back faces obscure the front faces. The [Back norm is neg] check box will reverse the order of the rendering if you get the wrong order.*

If your shaded images have missing areas, they may have been created as wireframe lines, which AutoShade does not recognize. You need to go back and reconstruct your 3D drawing to show the area as solid or mesh surfaces. When you create drawings for AutoShade, it helps to think of your drawing objects as having solid surfaces. If you build your objects this way in AutoCAD from the start, it will save you from having to come back later to edit your drawings.

Sprucing Up the Drawn Image

AutoShade renders each surface with a single shade of color, which may cause a large surface to look incorrect when it is rendered. For example, a long wall receding away from your point of view should normally become darker as it recedes. However, since AutoShade applies a single shade of color, you can only get this shading effect by making the wall's surface out of many smaller faces. Try to anticipate the need for mesh surfaces where you want complex or graduated surface effects. You can control the number of faces on curved surfaces by adjusting VIEWRES and the surface system variables SURFTAB1, SURFTAB2, SURFU, and SURFV.

➧ *TIP: You can use hatches to add texture to 3D drawings. The hatch must be exploded and given a small thickness. You can apply a small thickness to other entities so they will be recognized by AutoShade.*

Creating AutoShade-bound drawings usually will require more work and more entities to define objects with solid surfaces. The more solid faces you use in constructing your drawing, the better your AutoShade rendering will look. However, there is a trade off. The more solid faces you have, the larger the drawing will be and both AutoCAD's and AutoShade's processing time will increase. For example, a Full Shade rendering of the chair drawing takes from one to three hours, depending on your computer.

Using Perspective in AutoShade

AutoShade renders in perspective by default. Smaller objects may not display the perspective well. You can enhance perspective views and relative scale by adding foreground and background objects in AutoCAD. In architectural scenes, these objects could be walls, trees, and vehicles. You can enhance mechanical drawings by adding contrasting surfaces in the background of the view. You will find that AutoShade's perspective works the same way as DVIEW within AutoCAD. In fact, the perspective tools for setting a target distance, camera, camera angle, and clipping were released in AutoShade before they were released in AutoCAD. AutoShade has a few more tools that AutoCAD lacks, such as side, top, and bottom clipping.

The rendered chair looks good, although it is floating in space. Let's move on to work with the office drawing that you developed in chapter 15. The remainder of the exercises will use the office drawing to show you how to control cameras and lighting in making shaded scenes. We will also show you how to prepare a presentation by running a series of AutoShade renderings with a script file. These perspective renderings will form an exact parallel to the perspective view slides that you created with DVIEW.

Lights, Camera and Action

Before you can get anything from a roll of film, you need a camera and lights. You shoot a scene as you would with a camera. AutoShade provides a camera block, two types of light blocks, and an AutoLISP program (in the ASHADE.LSP file) to establish scenes in your drawing. You place the camera and light blocks and name them with unique (attribute) names in your drawing. Once you have placed the camera and lights, you can create a scene, or multiple scenes, by creating a scene block(s). When you make your filmroll, all these scenes will be recorded for rendering in AutoShade. All the AutoShade blocks are automatically placed on a layer named ASHADE to help with your drawing organization.

Options for Making Scenes of the Office Drawing

We want to provide you with two options for working with the office drawing. You can either work with the simple block drawing that you saved as OFFICE3D (chapter 15), or work with the drawing called FURNISHD (chapter 15) which has the table and chair inserted in the corner office of the office drawing. The table and the chair in FURNISHD contain a number of solid faces that will require substantial processing time in AutoShade. If you don't want to tie up your workstation processing complex AutoShade images, we recommend that you use the simple OFFICE3D drawing to do the following exercises. Then, if you want to shade the more complex images, you can come back and use the FURNISHD drawing. The exercise illustrations will show both the simple and complex block drawings, but the exercise sequence uses the simple drawing names.

If you are using the IA DISK, the OFFICE3D drawing is provided as CHAP-16A, and the FURNISHD drawing is provided as CHAP-16B.

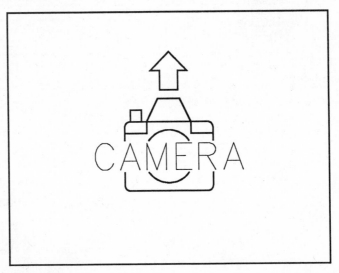

Camera Icon

Using CAMERA to Place Cameras

The following exercise shows how to create two scenes of the floor plan by placing two cameras in the drawing. To use the camera you need to select an image or target point, locate the camera point, and give the camera a name. (You need to name the camera because you can have more than one camera in the drawing.) The first camera is targeted at the office chair and is set at about eye level. The second camera is targeted at the right corner of the room. It also is set at eye level. Use the placement values given in the exercise sequence. Make sure AutoCAD can find ASHADE.LSP and that the AutoShade blocks are in your ACAD directory.

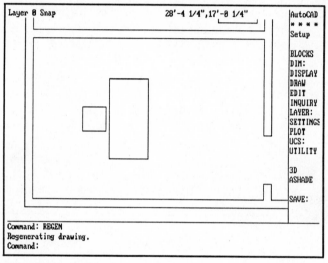

Office Room for Shading

Using CAMERA to Locate a Camera for AutoShade

Get into AutoCAD.

	Enter selection: **1**	Begin a NEW drawing named OFIC-SHD=CHAP-16A.
	Enter selection: **1**	Begin a NEW drawing named OFIC-SHD=OFFICE3D.
Command: **ZOOM**		Magnify the office with the chair and table.
Select **[ASHADE]**		Select from the screen menu.

```
Command:  Please wait...  Loading ashade          AutoCAD tells you it's loading.
AutoShade Commands Loaded, errors: nil            Loading is complete, no errors.

Command: CAMERA                                   Select or type Camera.
Enter camera name: CAMERA1                        Your first camera.
Enter target point: 21'6,19'6,1'6                 Center of the chair seat.
Enter camera location: 17'6,14'6,5'6              Lower left corner of the room.

Command: CAMERA                                   Your second camera.
Enter camera name: CAMERA2                        Lower right corner of the room.
Enter target point: 32'6,14'6,0                   Upper left corner of the room.
Enter camera location: 17'6,24'6,5'6
```

When you finish selecting your target and camera locations, a camera icon with your assigned name appears at each picked location, pointing at the target icon. The 5'-6" dimension in the Z axis places the camera at approximately eye level.

Using CAMVIEW to Preview a Camera View

The icons are shown in plan view, but you can't really tell what you will see through the lens. The ASHADE.LSP file has another command called CAMVIEW that you can use to see what the camera will see in AutoShade. CAMVIEW is an AutoLISP-defined command that uses DVIEW to show you a wireframe view of what the camera will see. While you are still in AutoCAD, select the camera you want to look through at the CAMVIEW prompt. Try the CAMVIEW command on CAMERA1.

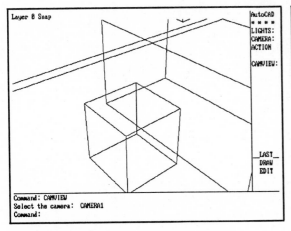

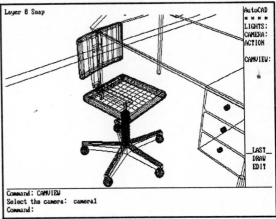

Simple View Through the Lens of CAMERA1   Complex View Through the Lens of CAMERA1

Using CAMVIEW to Preview a Camera View

Command: **CAMVIEW**	Select or just type.
Select the camera: camera1	Select camera one.
Command: **U**	Undo back to the plan view.
GROUP Regenerating drawing.	

If you didn't like the view, you could erase the camera and put in a new one. Alternatively, you could wait and position it in AutoShade, but we recommend using CAMVIEW to get a good starting view. Camera settings in AutoCAD are saved in the drawing and rendering files, but camera changes in AutoShade are temporary and not saved.

Using LIGHT to Set Lights

You still need to establish your lighting. AutoShade provides two types of light sources: point sources and directed lights. A point source is a light that radiates in all directions. A bare light bulb or overhead lights are good examples of point sources. A directed light provides parallel rays in a given direction. Think of directed light as light from a spotlight, a flashlight, or direct sunlight through a window. The sun is a point source in the scale of the solar system, but to objects on earth, it is directed.

Lighting Icons

Place lights the same way you place cameras. A light requires a location and name. A direct source also needs a target or aim point. Place four lights in the drawing to represent an overhead light (point); a light from a window (directed); and a flash (directed) aimed from each camera towards the camera's target. Again, use the location values given in the exercise sequence.

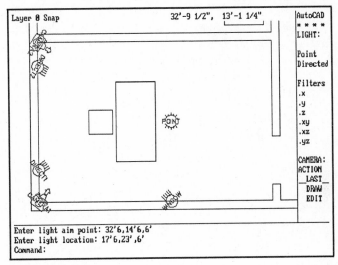

Office With Lights

Using LIGHT to Locate Lighting Types

```
Command: LIGHT                              Type or select LIGHT from menu.
Enter light name: POINT
Point source or Directed <P>: <RETURN>
Enter light location: 26'0,19'6,10'0        A ceiling light in the middle of the room.


Command: LIGHT
Enter light name: WINDOW
Point source or Directed <P>: D
Enter light aim point: 21'6,19'6,1'6        Middle of the chair seat.
Enter light location: 26'0,14'6,6'0         A window in the wall.


Command: LIGHT
Enter light name: DIRECT1                    One flash.
Point source or Directed <P>: D
Enter light aim point: 21'6,19'6,1'6        Middle of the chair seat.
Enter light location: 17'6,16'6,6'0         Near Camera1.


Command: LIGHT
Enter light name: DIRECT2                    The other flash.
Point source or Directed <P>: D
Enter light aim point: 32'6,14'6,6'0        Lower right corner of the room.
Enter light location: 17'6,23'0,6'0         Near Camera2.
```

After you place the lights, the light icons appear with their names. Each direct light source is pointing at its aim point. When you get into more detailed lighting setups, you can use XYZ filtering to help you with your camera and light placement.

➡ *TIP: You can construct complex lights, like linear and fluorescent lights, by using many small lights. In AutoShade, you can adjust the intensity of each light.*

Action!

All that remains is to group your cameras and lights into a scene. A scene consists of one camera and as many lights as you want. Try creating two scenes using the window and ceiling lights in both, and each camera's flash in its scene. When you pick a point to locate the scene's clapper icon block, pick a convenient point in your drawing. The location of the scene block is not critical.

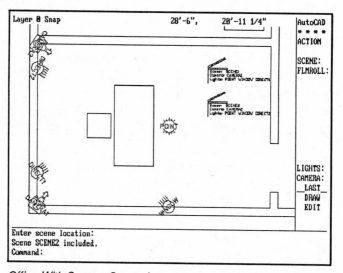

Office With Scenes Created

Using SCENE to Set a Scene

Command: **SCENE**	Type or select SCENE from a menu.
Enter scene name: **SCENE1**	
Select the camera:	Pick the CAMERA1 icon.
Select a light:	Pick the POINT light source.
Select a light:	Pick the WINDOW light source.
Select a light:	Pick the DIRECT1 light source.
Select a light: **<RETURN>**	

```
Enter scene location:               Pick a point in the left corner.
Scene SCENE1 included

Command: SCENE                      Type or select SCENE from a menu.
Enter scene name: SCENE2
Select the camera:                  Pick the CAMERA2 icon.
Select a light:                     Pick the POINT light source.
Select a light:                     Pick the WINDOW light source.
Select a light:                     Pick the DIRECT2 light source.
Select a light: <RETURN>
Enter scene location:               Pick a point below SCENE1.
Scene SCENE2 included
```

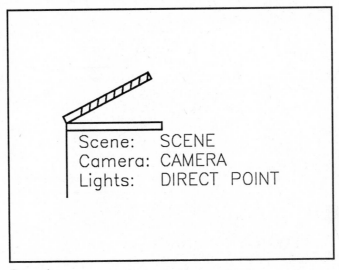

Scene Icon

The scene blocks are shown to indicate how many scenes the drawing contains and what cameras and lights go with each scene. Once you have established all the scenes, you make the filmroll.

Roll 'em

```
Command: FILMROLL                   Make OFFICE.FLM.
Enter filmroll file name <OFIC-SHD>: OFFICE
Creating the filmroll file
Processing face: 257                AutoCAD processes filmroll.
Filmroll file created

Command: END                        END drawing and exit AutoCAD.
```

Your filmroll now contains SCENE1 and SCENE2. You are ready to render these scenes in AutoShade.

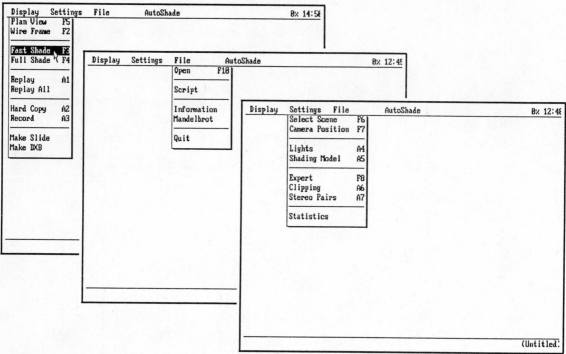

AutoShade Pull-Down Menus

AutoShade's Display and Pull-Down Menus

You have already made one quick pass through AutoShade to get a Fast Shade of the chair. Let's take a second look at the screen display and menu system. The first display you see in AutoShade is an interactive screen which displays wireframe images. The top line contains the menu bar with three pull-down menu headers, an area to display the amount of memory that has been used, and a digital clock. The illustration above shows the three pull-down menus.

The bottom line displays messages indicating the current activity and the name of the current filmroll file. The center of the screen is where the pull-down menus and dialogue boxes are displayed along with your wireframe images. You use your pointing device to control the arrow pointer, to highlight selections, and to make your menu choices.

Most of the selections you make from the menus will present you with a dialogue box. Dialogue boxes are your primary means of control in AutoShade. The dialogue boxes let you set values and toggles for the program. After highlighting your selections, leave the dialogue box by selecting [OK] or [CANCEL] at the bottom of the dialogue box.

Using Full Shade to Render the Office Scenes

Return to AutoShade to examine your scenes of the office. Load your office filmroll, then select the [Full Shade] option to render the two scenes.

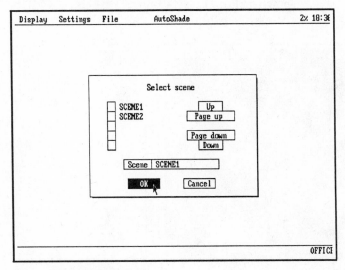

Select Scene Dialogue Box

Using Full Shade to Render a Scene

Change to the ACAD directory and get into AutoShade.

Pull down **[File]**   Pull down file menu.

AutoShade opens a Filmroll dialogue box displaying the current directory and filmroll files.

Change to the IA-ACAD directory.

Select **[OFFICE] [OK]**   Highlight box next to OFFICE and load filmroll.

A Select scene dialogue box is presented showing SCENE1 and SCENE2 for selection.

Select **[SCENE1] [OK]**   Select SCENE1 and OK.

Pull down **[Display]**   Pull down Display menu.
Select **[Full Shade]**   AutoShade processes the rendering.

Before the image is displayed, AutoShade displays a percentage of
completion of each task it performs as it processes the rendering.

Examine the rendering and repeat the process for SCENE2.

Your scenes should look like the SCENE1 and SCENE2 illustrations
shown below. Each scene is displayed with the lighting and camera
angles you established in AutoCAD.

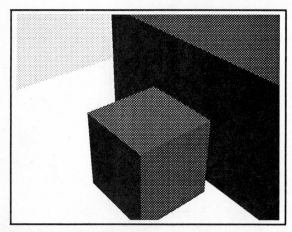

Simple Rendering of SCENE1

Complex Rendering of SCENE1

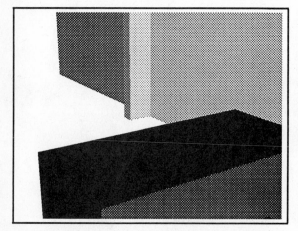

Simple Rendering of SCENE2

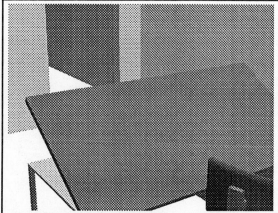

Complex Rendering of SCENE2

The rendering in SCENE1 is fine although the camera has cut off the top of the table. Let's focus on your current SCENE2, where there is relatively little contrast between the table top and the walls behind it. Also, it may be possible to get a better camera angle. AutoShade gives you a set of tools to adjust your lighting and camera settings.

➡ *TIP: You can give 3D meshes and faces the appearance of different colors on each side of the face by duplicating the face with an extremely small distance separating the face and the duplicated face. Use the COPY and SCALE commands.*

Using Lighting and Shading to Enhance Images

You can adjust your lighting while in AutoShade. The [Settings] pull-down menu provides two dialogue boxes for adjusting the lighting appearance.

The Set Light Intensity dialogue box shows all the lights available for the current scene. The display shows the light's name, type, and intensity. You can make a scene's lights brighter or dimmer by increasing or decreasing the intensity value. A value of 0 is the same as turning the light off. In fact, a negative value can actually subtract light (like a black hole).

AutoShade does not let you add lights or adjust the type and location of existing lights. If you need to change or add lighting you must return to your drawing in AutoCAD, make the lighting adjustments, and create a new filmroll. We recommend providing more lights than you think you will need when you create your scenes in AutoCAD. This approach is similar to lighting a stage where you try to anticipate a variety of light schemes. Setting up a variety of lighting situations lets you try different lighting effects in AutoShade without having to return to AutoCAD.

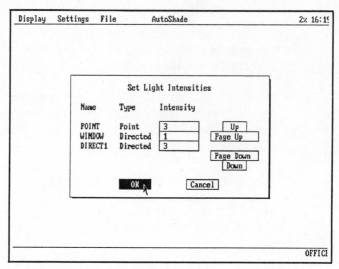

Set Light Intensity Dialogue Box

In real life, objects appear to get darker as their distance from you increases. AutoShade cannot depict shading differences relative to distance from a light source unless it has been told to do so. The Shading Model dialogue box offers a number of ways to adjust your lighting. These settings adjust how the light will reflect from the objects in your drawing. The settings affect the look and texture of the rendering. Changing the settings can give surfaces a shiny or a matte-like finish. You also can control visual depth by having AutoShade make objects with the same color brighter in the foreground than in the background. You can choose other options to set a background color, preview B&W (black and white) output according to NTSC standards, and create B&W or color separations.

The factors we will adjust in the exercise include the ambient factor (controlling overall background light level), and the diffuse and specular factors (controlling reflectivity). The [Ambient factor] setting uniformly controls the brightness of background light (such as is bounced off walls, ceilings and all objects in the real world) versus your defined light sources. An ambient setting of 0 contributes no background light (unrealistic) and a maximum setting of 1.0 ignores all light sources, lighting all surfaces equally. While the ambient factor controls *how much* and *from what sources* light hits the surfaces, other factors control how it is then reflected.

The [Diffuse factor] controls (from 0 to 1.0) the diffuse reflection of all surfaces. Diffuse reflection is light reflected equally in all directions, relative to the *amount* of light striking the surface, regardless of the direction of the source. The specular settings control directional reflections.

The [Specular factor] controls (from 0 to 1.0) the amount of shiny surface reflection versus diffuse reflection. Specular reflection is *directional relative to the light source* (the angle of reflection equals the angle of incidence). The [Specular exponent] controls how perfect the shine is. (While a setting from 3 to 20 is recommended for the specular exponent, it is recommended that the sum of the ambient, diffuse and specular factors equal 1.0.) A perfect mirror receiving a perfect parallel beam would reflect a perfect parallel beam. In reality, shiny surfaces reflect an imperfect cone of light. A low specular exponent, such as 3, reflects a wide cone. A high value, such as 20, reflects a narrow beam. If the cone is too narrow, none of the specular light from angled surfaces will reach the camera.

Shading Model Dialogue Box

Try enhancing the room in SCENE2 with some lighting and shading model adjustments. Use the recommended values in the following exercise as a guide. The comments will tell you what the adjustments do. You will also turn stretch contrast off in the shading model. Leaving stretch contrast on renders the image as if it were a picture taken with automatic exposure. If stretch contrast is on, AutoShade will automatically adjust lighting based only on the ambient factor and ignore all light intensity settings.

Using Lights and Shading Settings to Enhance Contrast

Pull down **[Settings]**	Pull down Settings menu.
Select **[Lights]**	Opens Set Light Intensity dialogue box.
Select Direct1 **[Intensity]**	Set value to 3 to increase intensity.
Select **Point [Intensity]**	Set value to 3 to increase intensity.
Select **Window [Intensity]**	Leave value at 1.
Select **[OK]**	Close dialogue box.
Pull down **[Settings]**	Pull down Settings menu.
Select **[Shading model]**	Opens Shading Model dialogue box.
Select **[Ambient factor]**	Set value to 0.2 to decrease background light.
Select **[Diffuse factor]**	Set value to 0.8 to increase the reflectivity of drawing.
Select **[Specular exponent]**	Set to 12 to adjust reflection from shiny surfaces.
Select **[Stretch contrast]**	Set to OFF so the shades are computed at absolute intensities.
Select **[OK]**	Close dialogue box.
Pull down **[Display]**	Pull down Display menu.
Select **[Full Shade]**	AutoShade processes the rendering.

When you are done, your screen should show an image with differing contrasts like the following illustrations of SCENE2.

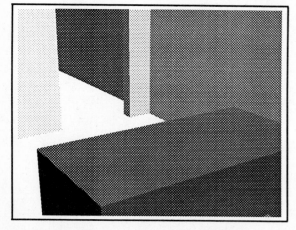

Simple SCENE2 Rendered With New Settings

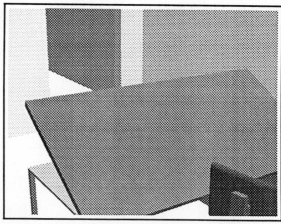

Complex SCENE2 Rendered With New Settings

The new light and shading model settings show AutoShade's flexibility. With practice, you can make settings to simulate actual lighting situations. Take a look at SCENE1 to see the effect of the light changes. Experiment with different settings. Try your own hand at using a wide variety of values to see new effects. The best way to understand lighting is to experiment.

Shading Model Distance Factors

Several factors adjust the shading of surfaces relative to their distance from light sources or from the camera. [Inverse square] causes light intensity to decrease as the square of the distance from the light source to the object face. [Linear lighting] causes light intensity to decrease linearly from the light source to the object face. Linear lighting does not produce distance shades of color as dark as Inverse square. [Inverse contrast] is used in conjunction with linear lighting to produce an effect similar to fluorescent lighting. [Z Shading] produces a rendering with the foreground brighter than the background. Light placements, intensities and shading factors, except stretch contrast, are ignored. This is adequate for most quick studies, and easier than setting linear and inverse factors.

Compare the next two illustrations to see the effect of inverse square.

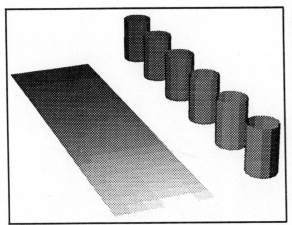

Shading With Inverse Square

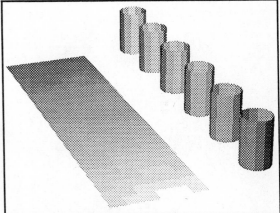

Shading Without Inverse Square

Using Camera Position Settings to Improve an Image

You have seen how lighting can affect the appearance of a rendering, now try some other camera positions to get a new perspective. AutoShade gives you a lot of flexibility in setting a camera's position and target point. However, any changes you make to the camera are only set for AutoShade. If you want to permanently set a new camera setting, you need to record the values and change your values in your AutoCAD drawing.

Setting New Camera Positions

The Camera Specifications dialogue box provides three types of settings: you can adjust the camera angle from X in the X,Y plane, and up from the X,Y plane; you can change the camera distance from the target; and you can change the camera's lens length. AutoShade treats the camera as if it were a normal 35mm camera with a 50mm lens (standard on most cameras). You can change the lens in the same manner as a regular camera, with the same results. Changing to a 35mm lens will give you a wide angle view, whereas changing to a 135mm lens will act like a telephoto lens producing a zoomed-in view of the target.

Return to SCENE2, keeping the lighting changes you made in the previous exercise. Use the following exercise to help you change the camera settings to get a birds-eye view of the office.

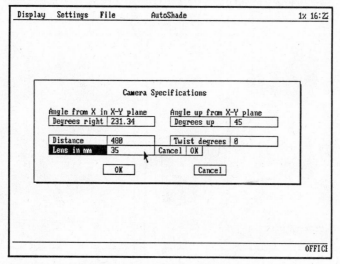

Camera Specifications Dialogue Box

Using Camera Position to Set a New Camera View

Pull down **[Settings]**	Pull down Settings menu.
Select **[Camera position]**	Opens Camera Specifications dialogue box.
Select **[Distance]**	Set value to 480, moving the camera 40' away from the target.
Select **[Lens in mm]**	Change to a 35mm lens for a wide angle view.
Select **[Degrees up]**	Set degrees to 45 to get a view looking down on the office.
Select **[OK]**	Close dialogue box.
Pull down **[Display]**	Pull down Display menu.
Select **[Full Shade]**	AutoShade processes the rendering.

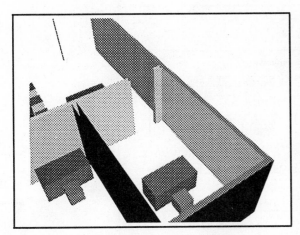

Simple SCENE2 With New Camera Settings

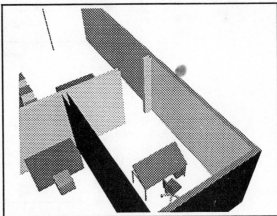

Complex SCENE2 With New Camera Settings

Your new view of SCENE2 should look much different from the original scene. You are looking down on the office. The perspective should be more evident. See chapter 15 on AutoCAD's DVIEW for a more complete discussion of perspective.

Using Expert and Clipping Controls

Your drawings may require more than camera and lighting adjustments to get a good rendering. AutoShade's Expert and Clipping Specifications dialogue boxes offer you more sophisticated controls over your renderings.

The Expert dialogue box gives you additional control over camera placements. You can adjust the camera's target position as well as the camera's position. These positions are shown as X,Y,Z values. You should record these values so you can match the changes you make in AutoShade when you go back to your drawing in AutoCAD. If your drawing contains faces that intersect, you will have to turn [Intersections] on to get a correct rendering. [Intersections] is off by default because intersection checking takes a lot of time. A number of other settings are available for the more advanced user to control depth, intersections, and rendering order.

The [Perspective] setting lets you override perspective rendering. With perspective off, AutoShade will use a parallel projection to create an orthographic wireframe and rendering, like the views you get with AutoCAD's VPOINT command.

Display	Settings	File	AutoShade		2% 16:2%

Expert Specifications

Target X	258		Camera X	45.971
Target Y	300		Camera Y	−31.036
Target Z	18		Camera Z	357.41

Film diagonal	42		Intersection	
mm/dwg unit	25.4		Perspective	✓
Screen percent	100			

Sort roundoff	0.0001		Discard back faces	
Chop roundoff	0.0001		Back norm is neg	✓

OK   Cancel

OFFICE

Expert Specifications Dialogue Box

The current view of SCENE2 focuses on one office. Use the Expert setting to move the camera's target to get a better view of all three offices. Change the Target Y value to move the camera from the lower left corner of the current office to the lower left corner of the office with two tables. The values in the dialogue box are shown in inches, so we will enter a value of 300 to move the camera's target 25 feet in the Y direction.

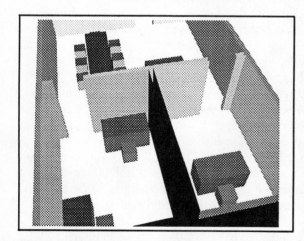

Simple Office Viewed With New Target

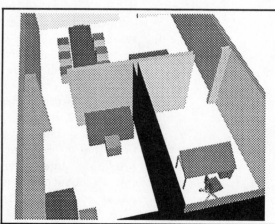

Complex Office Viewed With New Target

Using the Expert Box to Change Camera Positions

Pull down **[Settings]**	Pull down Settings menu.
Select **[Expert]**	Opens Expert specifications dialogue box.
Select **[Target Y]**	Set value to 300 to move target to lower right corner of upper office.
Select **[OK]**	Close [Target Y] dialogue box.
Select **[OK]**	Close dialogue box.
Pull down **[Display]**	Pull down Display menu.
Select **[Full Shade]**	AutoShade processes the rendering.

You are through with SCENE2. Return to SCENE1 and set up for clipping. The following exercise will recreate the office clipping view that you created using DVIEW in the previous chapter (chapter 15). Start by moving the camera 19 feet (228 inches) from the center of the chair. Use a 35mm lens. When you get into SCENE1, all of the settings will remain from SCENE2 except those involving camera position and light intensities.

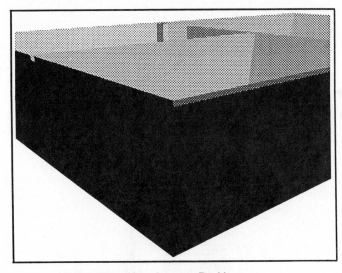

Shade of Office From New Camera Position

Positioning the Camera for Clipping

Pull down **[Settings]**	Pull down Settings menu.
Select **[Select Scene]**	Select SCENE1.
Select **[OK]**	Close dialogue box.

Pull down **[Settings]**	Pull down Settings menu.
Select **[Lights]**	Opens Set Light Intensity dialogue box.
Select **Direct1 [Intensity]**	Set value to 3 to increase intensity.
Select **Point [Intensity]**	Set value to 3 to increase intensity.
Select **Window [Intensity]**	Leave value at 1.
Select **[OK]**	Close dialogue box.
Pull down **[Settings]**	Pull down Settings menu.
Select **[Camera position]**	Opens Camera Specifications dialogue box.
Select **[Distance]**	Set value to 228, moving the camera 19' away from the target.
Select **[Lens in mm]**	Make sure lens is set to 35mm.
Select **[OK]**	Close dialogue box.
Pull down **[Display]**	Pull down Display menu.
Select **[Full Shade]**	AutoShade processes the rendering.

Your rendering will show only the outside corner of the office drawing. AutoShade defaults to clipping at the camera, which you moved outside the office. You need to adjust clipping so that the corner of the room is clipped, allowing a view into the office.

Clipping the View

The camera sees everything in your drawing, but you may not want to render everything. You can determine how much of the drawing you want rendered by adjusting values in the Clipping dialogue box. Settings are provided to clip background and foreground images perpendicular to your line of sight. You also can determine the size and shape of your viewing frame by adjusting the top, bottom, left, and right clipping values.

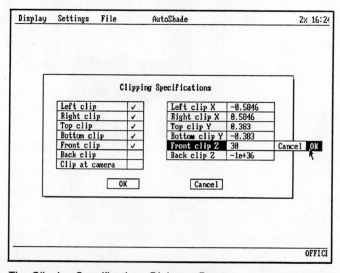

The Clipping Specifications Dialogue Box

The following exercise will guide you through setting clipping values to open up the office. Use our values to get the view shown in the Office With Clipping illustration.

Simple Office With Clipping   *Complex Office With Clipping*

Using Clipping to Enhance the Office Image

Pull down **[Settings]**	Pull down Settings menu.
Select **[Clipping]**	Opens Clipping Specifications dialogue box.
Select **[Clip at camera]**	Turn clip at camera off.
Select **[Front clip Z]**	Set front clip to 30".
Select **[OK]**	Close dialogue box.
Pull down **[Display]**	Pull down Display menu.
Select **[Full Shade]**	AutoShade processes the rendering.

Your screen should show the corner of the wall clipped perpendicular to your view, revealing the office with table and chair. This view is the shaded equivalent of the clipped office view that you made in the last chapter with DVIEW. You will find that AutoShade's clipping tools work the same as those in DVIEW except you have more clipping options. The left, right, top, and bottom clips can be thought of as cropping values.

Unlike DVIEW, where your desired perspective may force the image to be small and off-center, you can crop your AutoShade display. AutoShade always adjusts its display to fill the screen with the current image. But remember, like front and back clipping, the cropping is perpendicular to your line of sight. If you want to experiment, try some more clipping values.

If you were to quit AutoShade now, all the changes you made to SCENE2 would be lost. Before we leave AutoShade, let's look at what AutoShade offers in the way of saving your finished scenes.

Saving and Printing AutoShade Renderings

If you have a PostScript printer or AutoShade ADI device installed and configured, you can make a printed copy by opening the Display pull-down menu and selecting [Hard Copy]. Then, do a Full Shade. Rather than producing a rendering on the screen, AutoShade will prompt you for a PostScript print file name. After the file is created (with the file extension .PS), you can send it to your printer by using the DOS print command. If you were wondering how we produced the shaded images in this chapter, they were output as PostScript files and printed on a standard 300 dpi PostScript printer.

➡ *NOTE: AutoShade 1.1 directly creates Encapsulated PostScript formatted files. Earlier versions require slight modification to the print file by an ASCII text editor if you need an Encapsulated PostScript file. You must change the first line to read* **%!PS-Adobe-2.0EPSF-1.2** *to change the version. You must move the* **%%BoundingBox** *line from the end of the file and insert it as the second line. Then insert a new line that reads* **%%EndComments** *directly after the last comments line (usually the %%Pages line). All comments begin with %%.*

The most common method for saving scenes is to select [Record] from the Display pull-down menu. AutoShade will then prompt for a rendering file name each time a shade rendering is made. The rendering is written to a file as well as displayed on the screen. Rendering files have an extension of .RND. You can view them in AutoShade at any time by selecting [Replay All] or [Replay] and the file name. These renderings are displayed much faster than the original shade because they do not require reprocessing. In this chapter's last set of exercises, we will show you how to create rendering files and run them with a script.

➡ *NOTE: Rendering files are display device specific. Files created with one type of video configuration cannot be displayed on any other type of video.*

AutoShade Scripts

You can display renderings using the [Script] selection from the File pull-down menu. Create scripts with an ASCII text editor, the same way you create them for AutoCAD. You can use scripts to view renderings and for demonstrations. You also can use them to automate AutoShade processing. As you may have noticed, rendering a drawing can take a long time. If you have many scenes to process, you can create a script to do the tedious processing, stepping through each scene, adjusting camera settings and recording the rendering. If you run the script at night, your renderings will be ready for viewing in the morning!

Making and Saving Wireframe Images

The last two methods for saving scenes are the [Make Slide] and [Make DXB] selections on the Display pull-down menu. If you make a slide, you can view it in AutoCAD. You can also import a DXB file into AutoCAD with DXBIN. Both the slide and DXB files are created as wireframe images of the current view. These images will look like the perspective wireframe images that you obtain with DVIEW in AutoCAD, however you have AutoShade's cropping advantage.

The following sequence shows how to get a quick wireframe image of the current view and a plan view to verify camera and light placement.

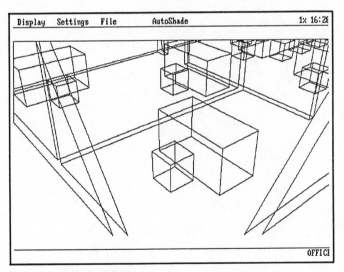

Wireframe View of Office

Getting a Wireframe Image in AutoShade

Pull down **[Display]**   Open Display pull-down menu.
Select **[Wire Frame]**   Produces a wireframe image of the current scene.

This is a good way to preview the shaded image.

Select **[Plan View]**	Produces a wire frame plan view of the current scene.
Pull down **[File]**	Open File pull-down menu.
Select **[Quit]**	Exit AutoShade.

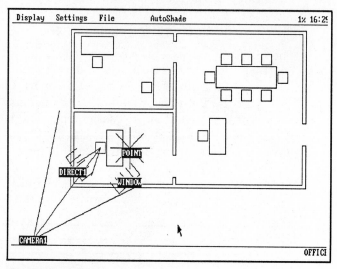

Plan View of Office

Selecting [Wire Frame] is the quickest way to verify a new camera location before doing a shade. The [Plan View] selection also provides a quick wireframe view of the current scene. In addition to the drawing, the current scene locations of camera and lights are shown to refresh your memory.

Use [Plan View] to refresh your memory if you have done many camera and target moves.

Stopping Point

If you are running short on time, this is a good stopping point. Quit AutoShade, and take a break. In the next section we will go back to AutoCAD and set up four final scenes to create renderings of the office plan. These renderings will correspond to the same perspective views that you developed with DVIEW. The exercise set will give you the starting tools that you need to develop renderings for scripted presentations.

Developing Scenes for a Scripted Show

So far you have explored AutoShade's camera and lighting settings to get a desired rendering. The office with the chair and table are small objects and you can control their renderings easily. Larger and more complex drawings require more control in AutoShade, and more thought when you create your camera, lights, and scenes in AutoCAD.

Return to AutoCAD and the simple office drawing. This time you will recreate the camera positions from the DVIEW exercise in chapter 15. You will create a set of renderings which will be replayed the same as the slide show in chapter 15. The difference this time is that each image will be fully shaded.

Make a new drawing named RENDER from the simple office plan and prepare it for a filmroll.

Creating a Drawing for a Rendering Show

 Enter selection: **1**   Begin a NEW drawing named RENDER=CHAP-16A.

 Enter selection: **1**   Begin a NEW drawing named RENDER=OFFICE3D.

Command: **ZOOM**   Zoom 0.7x.

Select **[ASHADE]**   Select from the screen menu.

Command: Please wait... Loading ashade   AutoCAD tells you it's loading.
AutoShade Commands Loaded, errors: nil   Loading is complete.

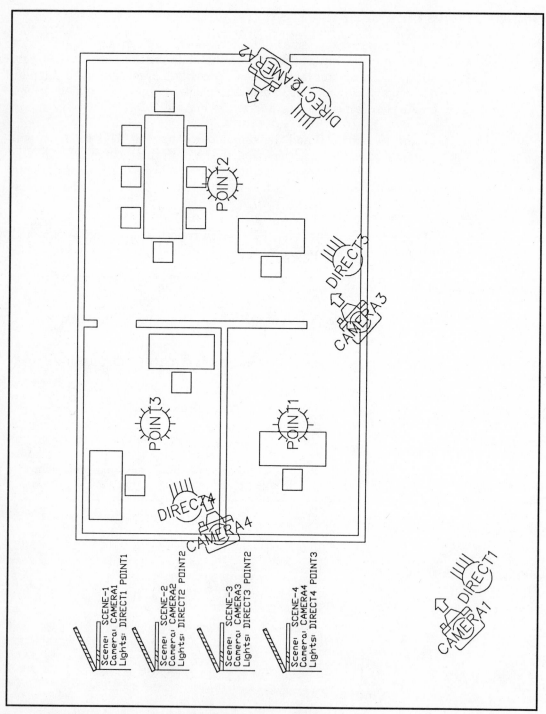

The RENDER Drawing Ready for FILMROLL

Use the full page RENDER Drawing Ready for FILMROLL illustration and the table below to create the four scenes for the filmroll.

SCENE-1		Target Location	Icon Location
CAMERA1		23'9,19'6,3'6	10'9,6'6,8'6
POINT1	(point)		25'6,19'6,10'0
DIRECT1	(direct)	23'9,19'6,3'6	14'6,5'6,8'6
SCENE-2		Target Location	Icon Location
CAMERA2		33'0,33'0,2'0	51'6,21'6,5'6
POINT2	(point)		43'0,25'0,10'0
DIRECT2	(direct)	33'0,33'0,2'0	49'0,18'0,5'6
SCENE-3		Target Location	Icon Location
CAMERA3		52'0,35'6,0'0	33'0,14'6,6'0
POINT2	(same as above)		43'0,25'0,10'0
DIRECT3	(direct)	52'0,35'6,0'0	37'6,15'6,6'0
SCENE-4		Target Location	Icon Location
CAMERA4		38'0,33'6,0'0	17'6,25'0,6'0
POINT3	(point)		25'6,30'0,10'0
DIRECT4	(direct)	38'0,33'6,0'0	19'6,27'6,6'0

Creating Four Scenes for a Filmroll

Use the table above to place the cameras and lights, and to create the scenes.

```
Command: FILMROLL                         Make RENDER.FLM.
Enter filmroll file name <RENDER>: <RETURN>
Creating the filmroll file
Processing face: 257                      AutoCAD processes the filmroll.
Filmroll file created

Command: END                              End the drawing and exit AutoCAD.
```

Now that you have the four scenes safely stored in the filmroll file, return to AutoShade and create a render file for each scene.

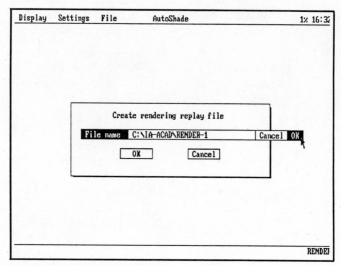

Create Render Replay File Box

Rendering the Four Scenes

Change to the ACAD directory and get into AutoShade.

Pull down **[File]**	Pull down file menu.
Select **[Open]**	AutoShade opens a Filmroll dialogue box displaying the current directory and filmroll files.
Select **[RENDER] [OK]**	Highlight box next to RENDER and select [OK].
Select **[SCENE1]**	Start with scene one.

Set lens to 35mm and front clip Z to 30.

Select **[Display]**	Pull down display menu.
Select **[Record]**	Select record.
Select **[Display]**	Pull down display menu, there's a check mark next to [Record].
Select **[Full Shade]**	Open dialogue for file name.
Select **[File name]**	Create a file named C:\IA-ACAD\RENDER-1.

Repeat the record sequence above for the remaining
3 scenes. Leave clipping set at camera and set the
lens to 35mm for each scene.
Name each rendering C:\IA-ACAD\RENDER-2 thru 4.

Once you have all the rendering files created, you can replay them individually or by directory. [Replay All] displays all .RND files found in the currently selected directory. Use the replay function to see all of the renderings.

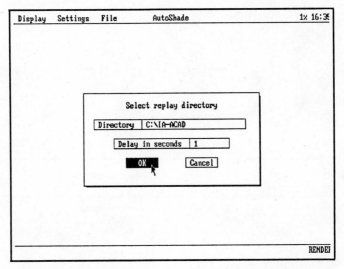

Select Replay Directory Box

Replaying the Rendering Files

Select **[Display]**	Pull down display menu.
Select **[Replay All]**	Select replay all.
Select **[OK]**	Select OK to accept default settings.
	Renderings are displayed on the screen.

The renderings are displayed in sequence, with a one second delay between each.

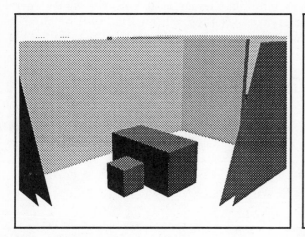

Rendering Of Scene 1

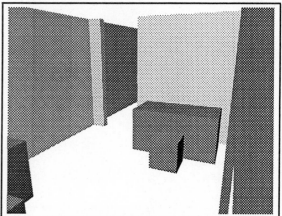

Rendering Of Scene 2

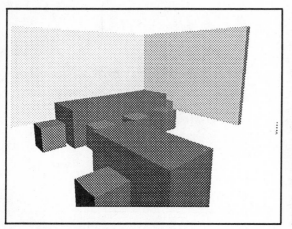

Rendering Of Scene 3

Rendering Of Scene 4

The following script file would produce the same display as the replay all did, except the delay would be 15 seconds.

```
replay render-1
delay 15
replay render-2
delay 15
replay render-3
delay 15
replay render-4
delay 15
rewind
```

The advantage of the script is that it can control which renderings to display, the order of display, and give different delays as needed. A script can also be started at the DOS prompt

AutoFlix and AutoShade Automation

AutoFlix, as mentioned in chapter 15, can include AutoShade slide and rendering file images in its *movies*. Movies require a lot of images, so the complete AutoFlix package includes a set of AutoLISP commands and functions to automate the process. AutoFlix requires an EGA standard display. Even if you don't need movies, or don't have EGA, AutoFlix is worth investigating. The AutoLISP functions supplied with it automate the creation of batches of filmroll files and AutoShade scripts to create rendering files.

Additional AutoShade Features

Fractals! Yes, AutoShade has fractals and a few more interesting and entertaining features. You will find fractals (and an information box) on the File pull-down menu.

- **[Mandelbrot]** displays a dialogue box of settings to create displays of the mandelbrot set (fractals).

- **[Information]** displays a box with the AutoShade version number.

You will also find a facility for creating stereo pairs, and a statistics box on the [Settings] pull-down menu.

- **[Stereo Pairs]** presents a dialogue box to generate two separate images side by side for stereoscopic viewing.

- **[Statistics]** displays a box of information to inform you about the size of the rendering in faces and triangles, and the extents of the rendering. This information can be used to calculate the amount of memory required for a rendering.

AutoShade can produce quality shaded images but requires some patience and a good understanding of how lighting, reflection, and shading is calculated. Trial and error will set you through the settings you will use most of the time, but experimenting with the more obscure settings will help you get a better understanding of AutoShade and produce better renderings.

Quitting AutoShade

Pull down **[File]**   Pull down file menu.
Select **[QUIT]**

➡ *TIP: Exit AutoShade in an emergency or apparent lock-up by holding
down the <ALT> key and typing CRASH. But don't assume it's locked
up just because a complex drawing takes many hours to process.*

Summing Up With Tips

What you see on screen isn't necessarily what you get in hard copy,
particularly on B&W (black and white) printers. You may need to adjust
your colors in AutoCAD to get the effects you want. We had to set all
colors to white to get the first [Fast Shade] CHAIR illustration to look right
in print.

Use AutoShade's command line options from the DOS command prompt
to start up AutoShade and to bypass AutoShade's screen and menus. Use
the following for single shot preset renderings, or to start scripts:

SHADE -S*<filename>* — Runs a script file after loading AutoShade.

SHADE -B -S*<filename>* — Runs a script file without loading
AutoShade screen and menus.

SHADE -R — Reconfigures AutoShade.

SHADE -? — Prints the command line options.

For impressive presentations, animate your drawings with AutoFlix
movies. With its AutoLISP tools, it may not take much of your time
(although it may tie up your system all weekend). And the results will be
worth it.

On to Plotting

Sooner or later you need to get plotted output of your drawings. The next
chapter will show you how to get your 2D and 3D images out on paper.

CHAPTER 17

Drawing Output

As you create a drawing file, AutoCAD stores your drawing information in a compact form. A line is stored as two endpoints; a circle is a center point and radius. When it is time to make a picture, AutoCAD translates this cryptic code into visible images. Each time AutoCAD makes a plot, it takes the drawing information out of its database, turns it into plot instructions, and scales the drawing to fit the specified plotting area. In this chapter, we want to take you through the plotting basics. Plotting setups vary substantially from plotter to plotter, particularly with newer plotters where you can control most of your plot parameters through the plotter rather than through AutoCAD. We have focused this chapter on using AutoCAD to fit and scale your drawing for output, rather than on any detailed controls for color, pen width, and pen speed.

The Steps From Disk to Plotter

A lot of *getting ready* occurs well before a plotter begins to draw an image on paper. You have to compose what will go into the final image. You have to make sure the plot parameters are correctly set. You have to physically get the plotter ready for action. When you install AutoCAD on your computer, you automatically set up the flow shown in the Plot Flow Diagram (below). You set 90 percent of AutoCAD's plot flow controls when you configure your system and tell AutoCAD what type of plotter you have. If you have not already configured AutoCAD for your plotter, you should do so now.

Checking Your Default Plotter Setup

You have made one or two quick plots up to this point in the book, but we assume that this chapter is the first time your AutoCAD installation and configuration will be used for extensive plotting. This means we assume certain default settings for plotter pen assignment, pen speed, and plotter linetypes. The plot sizes shown in the chapter's exercises may vary slightly based on the type of plotter you are using.

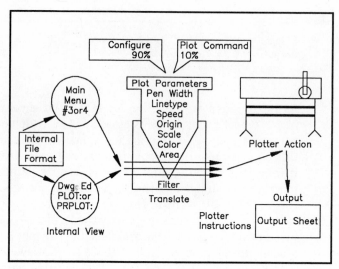

Plot Flow Diagram

If your AutoCAD installation has been used for plotting before, there is a good chance that some of the default settings shown in this chapter will be different from your own. Our examples are based on a generic D-size (34x22) plotter and a generic wide carriage printer plotter. If you are uncertain about your plotter settings, you can reconfigure your plotting parameters. Use AutoCAD's Main Menu Task 5, and specify that you want a new plotter configuration. Then reselect your same plotter and take all the defaults for prompts. Your sheet size, pen speed, linetypes and other settings may differ, but these settings will not affect the exercises.

AutoCAD can also produce drawings on printer plotters, like dot matrix and laser printers. Most discussion in this chapter is generic for all plotting device types, printer plotters or pen plotters. You use virtually the same setup and run features to get images from the drawing file to a pen plotter or to a printer plotter. If you do not have a pen plotter, wherever you see a pen PLOT command sequence, you can substitute an equivalent printer plotter PRPLOT sequence and adjust your scale accordingly. If you want to make sure that you have a default setup for your printer plotter, use the same Main Menu Task 5 procedure to specify a new printer plotter configuration, taking the defaults.

Plotting Tools

You can either plot from the Main Menu, or you can plot from within the drawing editor by accessing the plotting prompt screen with the [PLOT] menu item on the screen menu. You also can [Plot] and [Print] by selecting these items from the [File] pull-down menu.

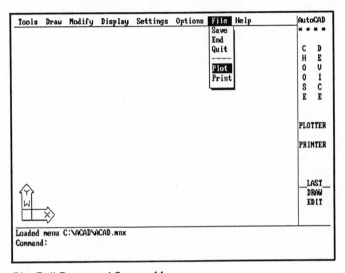

Plot Pull-Down and Screen Menus

At the end of the chapter, we will show you how to use a script file to run a plot. You will find the SCRIPT command on the [UTILITY] screen menu.

Setting Up for Plotting

You get ready for plotting in two stages: readying the plotter for action; and readying your drawing file within AutoCAD. Readying the plotter requires a one-time internal plotter setup and a once-a-plot setup of the paper and pen.

Getting Ready Checklist

Here's a checklist for getting the plotter ready:

First time check

❑ Is the plotter plugged in and turned on?
❑ Is the plotter data cable plugged into the computer port?
❑ Are the internal plotter settings correct?
❑ Run the plotter self-test. Does the example drawing look okay? Any pen skips? Paper misalignments?

Every plot check

❑ Is the paper movement path clear? No obstructions?
❑ Are the pens in the pen holder? Do you have the right pen widths and colors? Have you tested the pens lately to make sure they are not clogged?
❑ Is the paper loaded properly? Is the paper aligned?
❑ Is the plotter set for the correct paper size?
❑ If you use a single communication port computer, is the data cable coming from the computer switched from the digitizer (or other input device) to the plotter?

The PLOT and PRPLOT Commands

AutoCAD's PLOT or PRPLOT commands allow you to set your drawing scale and other drawing parameters. You can use the commands by selecting options **3** or **4** from the Main Menu or you can plot from within the drawing editor, whichever method you prefer.

Plotting a Drawing to Fit

Let's start by plotting the 2D Perspective Office Drawing that you created in chapter 15. Recall that you created this image from the DXB file that you saved on disk as OFFICE2D. If you didn't save the file, you can use any drawing that you think will work, following along with the text explanations and examples. (The remainder of the exercises will use the MOCKDIM drawing from chapter 11.) The exercises show the complete command prompt sequences so you can see how different types of plots work even if you don't actually do the plots.

This first plot lets AutoCAD determine the best fit for the drawing on the maximum plotting area for the limits that you select. This is the quickest way to get a plot since you are using AutoCAD's default settings. It will also ensure plotting of the entire drawing limits at the largest scale your plotter can accommodate. Try this first plot from the main menu. The perspective drawing is shown in the following illustration.

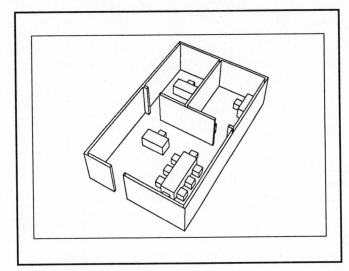

Perspective Office Fit Plot

Plotting With Fit Scale

Use the IA batch file to get into AutoCAD.

Enter selection: **3**   Select Option 3, Plot a drawing.

Enter NAME of drawing: **OFFICE2D**
Specify the part of the drawing to be plotted by entering:
Display, Extents, Limits, View, or Window <D>: **L**

Plot will NOT be written to a selected file
Sizes are in Inches
Plot origin is at (0.00,0.00)
Plotting area is 33.00 wide by 21.00 (MAX size)
Plot is NOT rotated 90 degrees
Pen width is 0.010
Area fill will NOT be adjusted for pen width
Hidden lines will NOT be removed
Plot will be scaled to fit available area

Do you want to change anything? <N> **<RETURN>**
Effective plotting area: 31.50 wide by 21.00 high
Press RETURN to continue or S to Stop for hardware setup   **<RETURN>**

Make sure your sheet of paper and plotter are ready, then hit <RETURN>.

Processing vector: nn   Cycles through all vectors.
                          Plotting takes place.
Plot complete.
Press RETURN to continue: **<RETURN>**   Main Menu reappears.

➥ *NOTE: If you use a single pen plotter, AutoCAD prompts you for pen changes when you plot a multiple pen plot.*

If this is your first plot, take it out of the plotter and show it off. You should have a 3D image plotted in 2D! When you are done parading around the office, reset the plotter and put in another sheet of paper for the next example.

The Logic Behind Plotting

In the plot you just completed, AutoCAD used all default plotter parameters to set up the plotter, viewing area, and scale. These defaults were set up at the time AutoCAD was configured. Here are the key steps you have to go through every time you set up a plot:

■ **Ready the Plotter.** You have already done this: turning the plotter on, checking the cable (and any switches), aligning the paper, and checking the pen(s).

■ **Size the Plotting Area.** Pick the size of the paper area for the plot. This can be any size you specify, making use of part or all of the plotting paper. The lower left corner of the plot will be placed at the plot origin.

■ **Pick the Part of the Drawing to Plot.** You can pick all or part of the drawing you want to plot by specifying just the screen display (whatever magnification), drawing extents or limits, a named view, or a window. (In the first example, you used limits.)

■ **Set Up the Plot Scale.** You can set up the scale relation between your drawing view and your plotting area. Using fit, the default, fills the plotting area with the largest view that fits inside the area. Or you can specify scale by setting the *Number of plotting units = Number of drawing units*. (Don't use fit if you want scaled drawings.)

When you configure the plotter for use with AutoCAD, you set up default plotting parameters for plotting area, view, and scale, as well as physical plotting parameters like pen speed. Occasionally, you may want to change these physical settings. The short list of parameters you can change includes plot origin, plot rotation, plotter pen width, pen speed, and linetype.

Default Plot Settings

Unless you specifically change the settings for the plotter, AutoCAD's setup parameters default to those set by the most recent plot or configuration setup. The defaults for your plotter were given in the prompt sequence after you selected limits in the fit plot (above). AutoCAD stores these plotting parameters in a file created at configuration. You have the option of changing any of these parameters by answering **Y** to the plot change prompt:

```
Do you want to change anything? <N>:
```

AutoCAD provides this prompt for each plot. If you make changes, AutoCAD will store your new settings as defaults in the configuration file for your next plot.

Plotting Exercises

Plotting requires some trial and error until you arrive at plot settings that fulfill your needs. In the rest of the chapter, we will set out some plotting examples to show you how to tailor the parameters to get different types of plots. All of these examples use the dimensioned mockup drawing (MOCKDIM) that you saved in chapter 11. If you are using the IA DISK, this drawing is provided as CHAP-17.

The three examples that we will use are:

❏ Plotting MOCKDIM.DWG at 1 plotted inch = 2 drawing units (inch).
❏ Printer plot a window of the MOCKDIM drawing at 1 plotted inch = 1 drawing unit (inch).
❏ Change plotter parameters to use colors and linetypes to create a colored plot.

Setting the Plotting Scale

In your first plot, you used the default fit to plot the entire drawing in the default MAXimum plotting area (plotter extents). When you plot to fit, AutoCAD calculates the maximum X scale that will fill the selected plotting size with the X coordinates of the specified area to plot. It repeats this for the Y scale, and then uses the smaller of the two scales. The plot menu displays the calculated X and Y effective plotting area. One will always be exactly equal to its corresponding maximum (or selected) plot size. The other will leave some extra space in its axis, but fit will always include everything you specify, at the maximum scale possible.

We placed the office perspective drawing on a 36" x 24" sheet by setting the limits to 36,24. The effective plotting area of the plot was 31.50" x 21.00" which means our plot to fit is close, but less than an accurate 1=1 scale. For perspectives, scale is irrelevant, but for other work, close often isn't good enough. If your plotter's maximum plotting area is much different from ours, your fit plot will be noticeably different.

Plotting to Scale

While plot to fit may be OK for quick checks, most plotting work requires an exact scale. Recall in a chapter long ago (chapter 2), we showed how to calculate drawing limits by a scale factor to match your expected plotted sheet size. (If you have forgotten how to prepare your drawing scale, refer back to chapter 2.)

When you drew the mockup part at full scale and dimensioned it, you anticipated using a 17" x 11" sheet for the plot. The part was too large to fit on a 17" x 11" inch sheet, so a scale factor was applied at 1=2 to determine dimensions, text, limits and the border. (The limits were set at 0,0 and 34,22.) When the drawing was dimensioned, dimensioning text was placed in the drawing at a height of 1/4 inch, anticipating a plotted text height of 1/8 inch.

To set your own scale for plotting, don't let AutoCAD go through its MAX Fit default calculations. Instead, set the scale function in response to AutoCAD's prompts:

```
Specify scale by entering:
Plotted units = Drawing units or Fit or ? <Fit>:
```

To specify scale, simply enter the number of output (plotter) units you want equal to one drawing file unit. By setting your plotting scale at 1=2 on a 17" x 11" sheet of paper, you will get the final mockup plot at the right scale. Each plotted inch equals two drawing inches, so all values in the drawing are reduced by two during plotting.

Plot Origin vs. Drawing Origin

A plotter's starting pen position (plot origin) is critical when you plot to scale. On a pen plotter (such as our generic plotter), home is usually at or near the lower left corner of the paper. For a printer plotter, the home position is the upper left corner. The plotter pen begins its plot at the lower left point of the area that you specify in the plot command, using display, extents, limits, view, or window.

We standardized the book's drawings to set limits to the sheet size (in drawing units). If your plotter can plot the full sheet from edge to edge, you can plot limits at the default plot origin (home position at the lower left corner of the sheet). But most plotters grip a portion of the paper during the plot. This means the lower left corner of the paper is not at the home position of the pen, so you can't plot limits. You still can get an accurate scaled plot by doing a window plot, using the offset distance of your plotter (from the lower left corner of the sheet to the home position).

The plot window option requires two points describing the rectangular area to be plotted. The lower left coordinate is the home position offset converted to drawing units (offset times scale factor). The second corner can be any point value slightly larger than the drawing limits. We assume that the actual drawing does not extend beyond this window, or it will be clipped.

To see how this works, try plotting MOCKDIM at 1 plotting inch = 2 drawing units (1=2), using the following exercise to guide you though the plot prompts. Plot from the Main Menu using the window option. Assume that from the lower left corner of the paper to the home position (plot origin) is 1/2 inch in both the X and Y directions. This makes your offset one inch (1/2 inch times a scale factor of two). This aligns the drawing limits with the plotting sheet. When you complete the plot, the part itself will be half size (1/2 inch = 1 inch) on the plotted sheet.

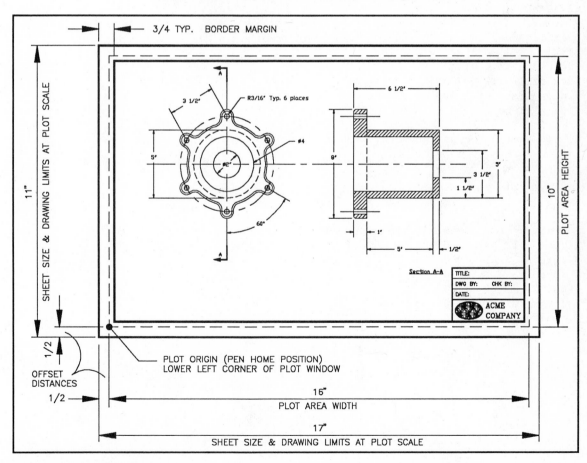

Plot Offset for MOCKDIM at 1:2 Scale

Window Plotting the Mockup Drawing at 1:2 Scale

    Copy CHAP-17.DWG to MOCKDIM.DWG.

    Make sure you have the MOCKDIM.DWG.

```
Enter selection: 3          Plot a drawing named MOCKDIM.
Specify the part of the drawing to be plotted by entering:
Display, Extents, Limits, View, or Window <L>: W

First corner: 1,1           Offset of the paper times the drawing scale. Use your value.
Other corner: 40,30         Any point greater than the upper limits of the drawing will do.

Plot will NOT be written to a selected file
Sizes are in Inches
Plot origin is at (0.00,0.00)
Plotting area is 33.00 wide by 21.00 (MAX size)
Plot is NOT rotated 90 degrees
Pen width is 0.010
Area fill will NOT be adjusted for pen width
Hidden lines will NOT be removed
Plot will be scaled to fit available area

Do you want to change anything? <N> Y
```

AutoCAD displays the current settings for plot parameters:

Entity Color	Pen No.	Line Type	Pen Speed	Layer Color	Pen No.	Line Type	Pen Speed
1 (red)	1	0	16	9	1	0	16
2 (yellow)	1	0	16	10	1	0	16
3 (green)	1	0	16	11	1	0	16
4 (cyan)	1	0	16	12	1	0	16
5 (blue)	1	0	16	13	1	0	16
6 (magenta)	1	0	16	14	1	0	16
7 (white)	1	0	16	15	1	0	16
8	1	0	16				

```
Line types: 0 = continuous line        Pen speed codes:
            1 = ..................
            2 = . . . . . . . . . .    Inches/Second:
            3 = -------------------      1, 2, 4, 8, 16
            4 = - - - - - - - - - -
            5 = -- -- -- -- -- -- -    Cm/Second:
            6 = --- --- --- --- ---      3, 5, 10, 20, 40,
            7 = -- - -- - -- - -- -
            8 = __ -- __ -- __ -- _
```

```
Enter line types, pen speed codes
blank=go to next, Cn=go to Color n, S=show current choices, X=Exit
Do you want to change any of the above parameters? <N> <RETURN>
```

If your colors are not set to pen 1 and linetype 0, enter **Y** and change them before proceeding.

```
Write the plot to a file? <N> <RETURN>
Size units (Inches or Millimeters) <I>: <RETURN>
Plot origin in Inches <0.00,0.00>: <RETURN>

Standard values for plotting size

Size         Width          Height

A            10.50            8.00
B            16.00           10.00
C            21.00           16.00
MAX          33.00           21.00

Enter the Size or Width,Height (in Inches) <MAX>: B

Rotate 2D plots 90 degrees clockwise ? <N> <RETURN>
Pen width <0.010>: <RETURN>
Adjust area fill boundaries for pen width ? <N> <RETURN>
Remove hidden lines ? <N> <RETURN>

Specify scale by entering:
Plotted Inches = Drawing Units or Fit or ? <F>: 1=2    Don't enter ft/in tick marks.

Effective plotting area: 16.00 wide by 10.00 high
Position paper in plotter.
Press RETURN to continue or S to Stop for hardware setup S
Do hardware setup now.
Press RETURN to continue:
```

Check plotter readiness and hit <RETURN>.

```
Processing vector: nn       AutoCAD cycles through whole drawing.

                            Plotting takes place.

Plot complete.
Press RETURN to continue: <RETURN>      To get back to the Main Menu.
```

The plot will draw the lower left corner of the border in the MOCKDIM drawing 1/4 inch in the X and Y directions from the plotter pen's home position. The MOCKDIM border allowed only a 3/4 inch margin. If your plotter cannot accommodate this border, experiment to determine how much margin is required for your plotter to grip the paper, how big an area your plotter can use, and what the offset distance is from the pen's home position and the corner of the paper. Once you have that information, create your borders with margins that work for your plotter and create a standard view named PLOT, with the lower left corner equal to the offset of the paper times the scale factor. Then, all you need to do is to plot the view named PLOT and provide the correct scale factor.

Besides using the window and view options, you can get the same results by plotting with extents, if you are sure your drawing does not have any loose entities outside the border. If your plotter lets you position the pen's home position at the corner of the paper, you can plot with limits.

➡ *NOTE: If you plot using the display option and have multiple viewports set, you get a plot of whatever is displayed in the current (active) viewport.*

➡ *TIP: Organize layers to set up efficient plotting for separate colors. If you have not organized specific parts of the drawing by entity or layer color, use the CHPROP command to regroup. Remember that colors are for pen line weights too, not just pen colors.*

➡ *TIP: Think ahead about leaving room for a border and a title block. Make your limits your paper size, sizing and positioning your title block and border margins to compensate for the area the plotter needs to grasp the paper.*

Plotting a Specific Area

In the previous example, you may have noticed that one of the parameters you can change is the plotting area. You can select how big you want your final drawing to be, independent of its view size or scale. By plotting a window or named view, you can use your plot to clip, or exclude, everything beyond the defined limits of the view. Plotting this way is like using electronic scissors to cut out and plot a piece of a drawing.

When you plot to a selected plotting area, anything that will not fit within the area at the specified scale will also be clipped. Unfortunately this happens without warning, so you can lose a part of the plot that you *did* want. To avoid this accidental clipping, you need to coordinate the size of your selected view with your scale and the plotting area. Use the next exercise (with a printer plotter) as a guide to see how to set up a view for creating and plotting a full scale plot.

Using Printer Plots

You can plot with a printer by using the PRPLOT from within the drawing editor, or by using option **4** on the Main Menu. Since the printer is a simpler device, you have fewer prompts to work through. PRPLOT a view of the MOCKDIM drawing.

Load the MOCKDIM drawing into the editor and make a named view around the top flange. This plot view is set up for an 11" x 9" area that is just large enough to enclose the top flange, creating a full-sized template when you plot at 1:1 scale. (Recall that the part was drawn full size.) The example assumes you are using a wide carriage printer. If you have a narrow carriage printer, part of the drawing will be cut off. The exercise provides the window coordinate points to get the view. See the illustration below to see what the window should look like.

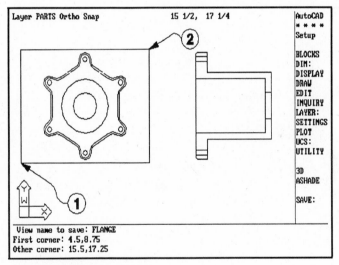

MOCKDIM With View Window

Printer Plotting MOCKDIM With a Window

Enter selection: **2**   Edit an EXISTING drawing named MOCKDIM.

Command: **CHPROP**   Change the hatch color to magenta.
Command: **LAYER**   Turn off all layers except for PARTS.

```
Command: VIEW                  Create a view named FLANGE.
?/Delete/Restore/Save/Window: W
View name to save: FLANGE
First corner: 4.5,8.75      Locate at ①.
Other corner: 15.5,17.25    Locate at ②.


Command: PRPLOT
What to plot -- Display, Extents, Limits, View, or Window <D>: V
View name: FLANGE

Plot will NOT be written to a selected file
Sizes are in Inches
Plot origin is at (0.00,0.00)
Plotting area is 13.59 wide by 11.00 high (MAX size)
2D Plots are rotated 90 degrees clockwise
Hidden lines will NOT be removed
Plot will be scaled to fit available area

Do you want to change anything? <N> Y
Write the plot to a file? <N> <RETURN>
Size units (Inches or Millimeters) <I>: <RETURN>
Plot origin in Inches <0.00,0.00>: <RETURN>


Standard values for plotting size

Size    Width    Height
A       10.50     8.00
MAX     13.59    11.00


Enter the Size or Width,Height (in Inches) <MAX>: <RETURN>
Rotate 2D plots 90 degrees clockwise? <Y> <RETURN>
Remove hidden lines? <N> <RETURN>


Specify scale by entering:
Plotted Inches=Drawing Units or Fit or ? <F>: 1=1
Effective plotting area:  9.00 wide by 11.00 high
Position paper in printer.
Press RETURN to continue: <RETURN>
Processing vector: nn      AutoCAD cycles through the drawing.


Printer Plot Complete.
Press RETURN to continue <RETURN>


Command: LAYER               Turn on all the layers.
Command: END                 End to save named view.
```

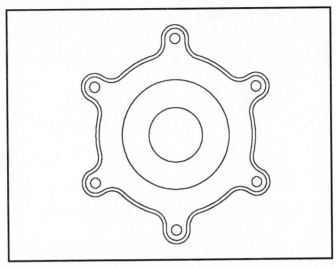

Full Scale Plot of Top Flange

➡ *TIP: Take advantage of your printer plotter. Use the printer plotter for easy and inexpensive check plots. It also is useful for 11" x 8 1/2" detail prints.*

Using Drawing Colors in Your Plots

So far, the plots you have created have ignored the layer and entity colors originally set up in the drawing file. When the mockup drawing was put together, for example, the border lines were drawn in blue on a layer named BORDER. You can do two things with layer and entity colors when you plot. You can assign a pen number to that color to plot a different color (or a different line weight), and you can assign a plotter linetype to that color. In the following exercise, we will show you how to use a different color pen for each layer color, a different pen for the object lines (green), and how to change the hatch lines (magenta) to a dot linetype using a plotter linetype.

➡ *NOTE: Do not confuse plotter linetypes with AutoCAD's drawing layer or entity linetype. A plotter linetype is a line pattern created by the plotter. Many plotters support several different linetypes. So far, you have simply assigned all layer colors to pens with a linetype = CONTINUOUS.*

Whether you have a single pen plotter or a multiple pen plotter, AutoCAD will select the correct pen. With a multiple pen plotter, AutoCAD switches pens automatically. With a single pen plotter, AutoCAD plots one pen color first, pauses and prompts you to change the pen, and then continues plotting in the next color. The following exercise shows the sequence for a single pen plotter.

Try a color plot, using the same scaled (1=2) plot that you used for your first MOCKDIM plot. The linetype effect will show up in the drawing, changing the hatch lines (magenta) from continuous to dots, and the green object lines will be wider than the other lines. This example assumes the plotter is using a 0.3mm pen for all colors except green which is 0.5mm. When you are done, compare this with your first plot.

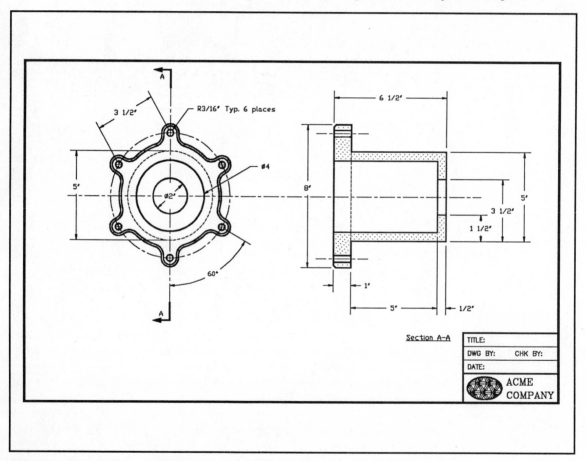

Plot With a Different Color, Linetype, and Line Weight

Plotting Using Color to Control Linetype and Line Weight

```
Enter Selection: 3
Enter NAME of drawing <MOCKDIM>: <RETURN>
```

Specify the part of the drawing to be plotted by entering:
Display, Extents, Limits, View, or Window <W>: **<RETURN>**
First corner: **1,1**
Other corner: **40,30**

Plot will NOT be written to a selected file
Sizes are in Inches
Plot origin is at (0.00,0.00)
Plotting area is 16.00 wide by 10.00 (B size)
Plot is NOT rotated 90 degrees
Pen width is 0.010
Area fill will NOT be adjusted for pen width
Hidden lines will NOT be removed
Plot will be scaled to fit available area

Do you want to change anything? <N> **Y**

> AutoCAD displays the current settings for plot parameters.

Layer Color	Pen No.	Line Type	Pen Speed	Layer Color	Pen No.	Line Type	Pen Speed
1 (red)	1	0	16	9	1	0	16
2 (yellow)	1	0	16	10	1	0	16
3 (green)	1	0	16	11	1	0	16
4 (cyan)	1	0	16	12	1	0	16
5 (blue)	1	5	16	13	1	0	16
6 (magenta)	1	0	16	14	1	0	16
7 (white)	1	0	16	15	1	0	16
8	1	0	16				

Line types: 0 = continuous line   Pen speed codes:
            1 = ...
            2 = ...   Inches/Second:
            3 = --------------------   1, 2, 4, 8, 16
            4 = - - - - - - - - - -
            5 = -- -- -- -- -- -- -   Cm/Second:
            6 = --- --- --- --- ---   3, 5, 10, 20, 40
            7 = -- - -- - -- - -- -
            8 = __ -- __ -- __ -- _

Enter line types, pen speed codes
  blank=go to next, Cn=go to Color n, S=Show current choices, X=Exit
Do you want to change any of the above parameters? <N> **Y**

Layer Color	Pen No.	Line Type	Pen Speed	
1 (red)	1	0	16	Pen number <1>: **<RETURN>**
1 (red)	1	0	16	Line type <0>: **<RETURN>**
1 (red)	1	0	16	Pen speed <16>: **<RETURN>**
2 (yellow)	1	0	16	Pen number <1>: **2**
2 (yellow)	2	0	16	Line type <0>: **<RETURN>**
2 (yellow)	2	0	16	Pen speed <1>: **<RETURN>**
3 (green)	1	0	16	Pen number <1>: **3**
3 (green)	3	0	16	Line type <0>: **<RETURN>**
3 (green)	3	0	16	Pen speed <16>: **<RETURN>**
4 (cyan)	1	0	16	Pen number <1>: **4**
4 (cyan)	4	0	16	Line type <0>: **<RETURN>**
4 (cyan)	4	0	16	Pen speed <16>: **<RETURN>**
5 (blue)	1	0	16	Pen number <1>: **5**
5 (blue)	5	0	16	Line type <0>: **<RETURN>**
5 (blue)	5	0	16	Pen speed <16>: **<RETURN>**
6 (magenta)	1	0	16	Pen number <1>: **6**
6 (magenta)	6	0	16	Line type <0>: **1**
6 (magenta)	6	1	16	Pen speed <16>: **<RETURN>**
7 (white)	1	0	16	Pen number <1>: **7**
7 (white)	7	0	16	Line type <1>: **<RETURN>**
7 (white)	7	0	16	Pen speed <16>: **<RETURN>**
8	1	0	16	Pen number <1>: **X**

Write the plot to a file? <N> **<RETURN>**
Size units (Inches or Millimeters) <I>: **<RETURN>**
Plot origin in Inches <0.00,0.00>: **<RETURN>**

Standard values for plotting size

Size	Width	Height
A	10.50	8.00
B	16.00	10.00
C	21.00	16.00
MAX	33.00	21.00

Enter the Size or Width,Height (in Inches) <B>:**<RETURN>**

Rotate 2D plots 90 degrees clockwise? <N>: **<RETURN>**
Pen width <0.010>: **<RETURN>**
Adjust area fill boundaries for pen width? <N> **<RETURN>**
Remove hidden lines? <N> **<RETURN>**

Specify scale by entering:
Plotted Inches = Drawing Units or Fit or ? <F>: **1=2**

Effective plotting area: 16.00 wide by 10.00 high
Position paper in plotter.
Press RETURN to continue or S to Stop for hardware setup **S**
Do hardware setup now.

```
Press RETURN to continue: <RETURN>        Check plotter readiness and hit <RETURN>.

Processing vector: nn        AutoCAD cycles through whole drawing.
```

Unless you have a multiple pen plotter, when AutoCAD is through with the first pen it will prompt for a new pen number and color. Change pens and proceed with the plot.

```
Install pen number 3, color 3 (green)
Press RETURN to continue: <RETURN>
Processing vector: nn        AutoCAD cycles through green color.

Install pen number 2, color 2 (yellow)
Press RETURN to continue: <RETURN>
Processing vector: nn        AutoCAD cycles through yellow color.

                             Prompts for the remaining pens continue.

Install pen number 5, color 5 (blue)
Press RETURN to continue: <RETURN>
Processing vector: nn        AutoCAD cycles through blue color.


Plot complete.
Press RETURN to continue: <RETURN>        Drawing editor appears.
```

When you assign a plotter linetype to a drawing color, everything in that color will plot with the linetype, regardless of scale or entity type. If you plot an AutoCAD layer or entity linetype with a plotter linetype, you will get an odd combination of the two. Use the plotter's continuous linetype for all of AutoCAD's broken linetypes. The last exercise showed how plotter linetypes work. We generally recommend that you use AutoCAD's software linetypes, but only lines, circles, arcs, and 2D polylines accept software linetypes. AutoCAD linetypes intelligently adjust to balance between endpoints. But that means spline and curve fit polylines generally plot continuous, because the distance between vertex endpoints is usually too short to break the line. Plotter linetypes solve this problem. Consider using plotter linetypes when you need curved polyline linetypes, or a special effect like applying a linetype to 3D meshes or even text. If you use a plotter linetype, make sure your entities are drawn in a unique color for that linetype only.

Losing Fills

If you are plotting and you don't get solid fills where you expect them, you need to turn fill on in the drawing editor prior to plotting. If you still don't get fills, check your viewpoint. If the drawing entities that require fills, like solids and 2D polylines with widths, are not parallel to the plotted viewpoint, you *won't* get fills in your plots. Finally, if you plot with hidden line removal, all fills are ignored. This includes AutoCAD's standard dimension arrow heads. The pen width setting controls the line spacing for fills. Too small a setting overlaps and wastes time. Too large a setting leaves gaps.

Plotter settings allow for only 15 colors; if your drawing displays more than 15 colors, any pen over 15 will default to pen 15. If you type an asterisk in front of the pen value when you adjust your plot pen parameters, AutoCAD will change the current pen and all the following pens to that value. For example, a quick way to change all of the pen speeds to 10 inches per second is to type *10 at the pen speed prompt for pen 1 and then exit.

➡ *TIP: If you plot multiple colors with a single pen plotter, it's important not to move, remove, or alter the paper's position in the plotter. The layers will not line up (register) if you move the paper.*

➡ *TIP: If you get skips in a long plot, WBLOCK the affected portion of the drawing to a new file and plot it with the same settings on the same sheet.*

➡ *TIP: If plotted text shows partial skips in characters, or characters run together, check your pen width plot setting. Too large a value causes these symptoms.*

Sticky Plotting Default Settings

During your last pass through the plot prompts, you may have noticed that AutoCAD presented you with several default settings that were not the same as the original defaults in your first plot at the start of the chapter. For both the PLOT and PRPLOT routines, AutoCAD maintains your most recent plot parameters from plot to plot and from one AutoCAD use session to the next. This saving of defaults is advantageous, but it can also cause problems.

The advantage of saving settings is apparent whenever it takes several attempts to get your plot correct. The first time through, you can set your plot parameters and try out the plot. Then, if you have to make a few changes to the plot parameters, you do not have to go back to ground zero and set all the parameters over again.

A problem may arise, however, when you do not use the plotting routines for a while (like a few days) and you forget what the parameter settings were. In this case, you do not have a standard set of defaults to work from. Instead, what you have is whatever you set last time. The best solution is to standardize your plotting as much as possible. You also can set AutoCAD to save and use several sets of defaults, using configuration subdirectories. And you always have the option of viewing all the defaults or current parameter settings, making whatever changes are necessary. Just keep an eye on them!

➡ *TIP: Use scripts to store and execute standard plot setups.*

➡ *TIP: Sometimes your digitizer configuration or screen can get disturbed when you are drawing. This can happen when you use memory resident (TSR) programs or use AutoCAD's SHELL command to access other programs from AutoCAD. Rather than end your drawing, you can start a PLOT command, then <^C> to cancel as soon as the plot prompt screen appears. This resets all devices and redraws the screen. (It also clears Undo and reloads the menu.)*

Changing Pen Speed

Besides pen color and linetype, you can also adjust pen speed. As you test your pens, you will learn which ones require plotting at a slower speed. AutoCAD can control the speed of the pen. From trial and error (and advice from friends), you will eventually determine the best plotting speed for different pen combinations and media. The default plotting speed in our examples is 16 inches per second. We have found that too fast for the .35 mm (0.010") ink pens. We use 6 inches per second.

➡ *TIP: You can optimize your plotting speed. This takes a little practice, but you will soon learn the maximum speed for plotting without pen skipping. Ask your supplier what pens work best with which speed / ink / media combinations — it is a three-way balance.*

➡ *TIP: Continuous lines improve plot speed. If you can minimize the amount of running around the plotter does with the pen up, then you will speed up your plots. Drawing with plines, or creating them with pedit, helps continuity.*

Using Script Files to Help Plotting

You have used a script (or at least looked at our script in chapter 15) for running a slide show. We want to pass on one other useful script. Readers often overlook the fact that scripts can start and run plots. Scripts have the unique property that they can run outside the drawing editor. You can use a script, for example, to load a drawing, create some entities, then end the drawing. You can use any input for scripts that you can use in your drawings or in AutoCAD's Main and Configuration Menus. You can end the drawing and start another, edit it, end it and so on. If you have a specific set of operations to run on a group of drawings, use a script file to batch process the drawings.

How to Use Scripts to Run Plots

You also can run a script from inside a drawing file. Say that you have four standard plotting sequences, each requiring resetting parameters in the plot dialogue. You can simply create four standard scripts, one for each setup. If you set up a standard view to plot named PLOT, your script might look like the following script. This script is provided on the IA DISK as DPLOT.SCR. It plots to a D size sheet at a 1=1 scale. (The right-hand comments are not part of the script file.)

A Standard PLOT Script

```
PLOT        The Plot command.
V           View.
PLOT        PLOT name.
Y           Yes change some parameters.
N           No, don't change pen/color/linetypes.
N           No, don't plot to file.
I           Inches.
0,0         Origin.
D           Size.
N           No, don't rotate.
0.01        Pen width.
N           No, don't adjust for pen width.
N           No, don't Hide.
1=1         Scale.
            And a blank line to start the plotter.
            And a blank line to return to the drawing.
```

If you named the above script, DPLOT.SCR, running it from the command prompt would look like:

```
Command: SCRIPT
Script file <SCRTEST>: DPLOT
```

AutoCAD would run through the plot dialogue, plot the drawing, and return to the drawing editor after the plot is complete. If you have the IA DISK, examine (and modify) the script to adapt it to your own use. If you don't have the disk, you can create the script with your text editor. If you do, don't input the comments on the right in the example.

➡ *TIP: AutoCAD can plot to file. With some plotters, you can plot files with the DOS Print command or with a third party plot spooling program.*

Ending Your Drawing

If you are still in the drawing editor, end your drawing. This is the end of the plotting examples. Here is a collection of comments and tips on plotting from readers.

Summing Up Plotting

Think ahead about plotting. Plan ahead for scale, pen types and colors. When you set up your drawing file, you should have an idea about how it eventually will be plotted out. We don't recommend plotting scale to fit for final drawings. Set a standard plot = drawing scale.

For high speed plotting, try cross-grooved tungsten or jeweled pen points. For good no-fuss plots, use disposable liquid ink pens. For everyday check plots, use disposable fiber or roller ball pens. Remember, even tungsten and jeweled points wear out, especially on mylar.

Plotter maintenance is essential. Pen plotters are mechanical beasts. Keep your paper and pen supplies stored in the right humidity. It really helps! Your paper and pen supplier should be able to recommend storage requirements. A dust free environment helps keep pens from clogging.

Keep the paper path clean. Brush the paper or mylar before plotting. Finger prints can cause skips. Rubbing alcohol removes finger prints. Cap pens when not in use, they dry out quickly. Worse, they can get partially clogged and skip in the last minute of a one hour plot. Disposables may pay for themselves by lessening trouble. If your plot skews and the paper slips, adjust or replace worn rollers. On adjustable width plotters, slippage may occur if the rollers are not set at the wider settings. For final copies, it pays to slow the plotter way down to improve line definition. Once slow is better than twice fast.

Above all, plotting is an art. Experiment and learn what works best for you.

End of Part Two

This is the end of Part Two. We hope you have enjoyed our office tour in 3D space, and that you got some enjoyment from your 3D chair. Now, if you are looking for some productivity gains, or if you just want to know how AutoCAD's menu system really works, turn to Part Three on Customizing AutoCAD.

Customizing AutoCAD

Increasing Your Productivity

Creating a Custom Environment

For most of the book, you have been on a guided tour through AutoCAD land. By now you have covered a lot of territory, learned many commands, and explored many screen menus. The standard tour is over. The next three chapters will help you customize AutoCAD to make it your own.

Why Customize AutoCAD?

Most CAD drawings are repetitive. There are many kinds of repetition, ranging from using the same symbols and parts over and over to creating drawings from standard details with countless variations on a design. CAD thrives on repetition, yet if you just run AutoCAD by typing and picking from the standard AutoCAD menu, you are starving AutoCAD.

AutoCAD's standard menu is a good starting tool, but it becomes cumbersome as you gain experience. You probably use 20 percent of the commands 80 percent of the time. If you stop at the standard menu, you are not taking full advantage of AutoCAD's efficiency. The trick to improving your productivity is to capture the repetition in your drawing, to recognize patterns in what you do, then customize AutoCAD to automate the repetition. If you can see a method in what you do, you can customize AutoCAD by creating your own drawing environment, menus, and even AutoLISP programs. Your ultimate benefits are finding ways to type less and do more.

How Part Three is Organized

Part Three is broken up into three chapters on customizing AutoCAD.

- Shaping your AutoCAD working environment by creating simple menus and macros.

- Shifting more of the work to AutoCAD through more complex menus and macros.

- Using AutoLISP to create new commands.

Chapter 18 will show you how to create your own environment within the AutoCAD environment. Because drafting and design frequently lack universal standards, you often need to adapt AutoCAD to fit your particular standards. Customizing at this level involves:

- Getting to know all the default settings in the prototype drawing and changing them to your normal settings.

- Learning to write macros.

- Understanding how screen, tablet, and pointing device menus work, and tailoring them to your liking.

- Setting up your own standard drawings and symbol libraries.

- Setting the system variables that work behind the scenes in the AutoCAD program.

Chapter 19 explores a second level of customization. Here, you can go beyond the standard AutoCAD working environment. This customization involves:

- Creating screen and tablet menu macros that ask for information and then execute commands based on the input.

- Grouping pages of macros to fit the flow of your work.

- Capturing complex sequences and turning them into simple commands on a menu.

Chapter 20 will introduce you to AutoLISP. You can use AutoLISP to create new commands. AutoLISP can do calculations and run programs to execute commands, draw pictures, and create reports and databases. This last chapter will give you a hands-on look at working with menu macros and AutoLISP.

Learn by Doing

Customization is easy when you get into it. Like magic, it just seems intimidating until you see the real tricks. The funny part about customizing AutoCAD is that you already know how to do a lot of it. The most important tools you will use in customization are the commands and sequences you already have used, and what you know about your unique application. A prototype drawing is just another drawing. When you write macros and set up custom menus, you just type commands and options that you have been using all along, adding a few special characters. When you create symbol libraries, you will call on old friends like WBLOCK and

INSERT. AutoLISP . . . well, that's not until the last chapter anyway — wait and see!

If you're not sure that customization can make your AutoCAD life better, these three chapters will give you a convincing overview. If you are already convinced, you may want to just skim these chapters and go into more detail with the books CUSTOMIZING AutoCAD and INSIDE AutoLISP (New Riders Publishing). These books give you a thorough step-by-step approach to customization with comprehensive explanations.

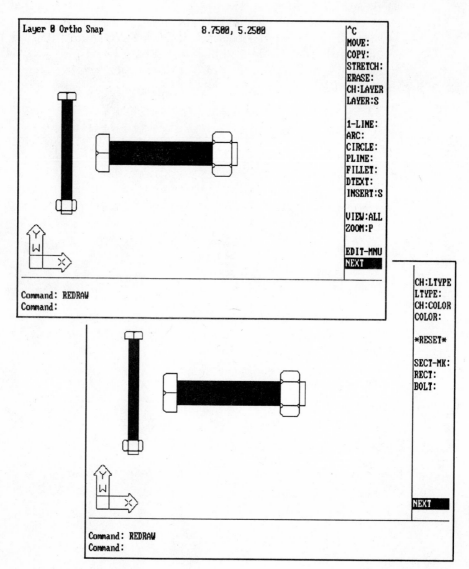

Custom Menu Macros

CHAPTER 18

Customizing Macros and Menus

AutoCAD YOUR WAY

Tailoring AutoCAD to Your Needs

This chapter will show you how to begin tailoring AutoCAD to meet your special needs by standardizing your default settings in a prototype drawing and by creating simple menu macros. Customizing AutoCAD does not require any elaborate effort. The chapter's focus is to show you the *types* of things that you can do to automate your drawing procedures. Simple things, such as setting drawing parameters in your prototype drawing or making a macro to automatically scale a block that you use frequently, often pay the largest dividends in time saved.

What Is a Macro? And What Is a Menu?

Macro is shorthand for macro-command, meaning a large or long command. In this chapter (and the next two chapters), we use macro to mean a series of one or more AutoCAD commands and parameters strung together to perform a drafting or design task. You can make macros that pause for user input and execute any of AutoCAD's commands, or even automatically repeat commands. Here is a simple macro that executes three Control-Cs:

[^C] ^C^C^C

If you placed this macro in a screen menu and selected the [^C] item, it would execute three ^Cs. The Control-Cs would execute just as if you had typed them from the keyboard. You build macros by writing keyboard command sequences in a text file.

You group macros into menu files. A menu is a text file listing each menu item or macro for every box on the screen, tablet, button, pop-up, and icon menu. AutoCAD's standard menu text file is ACAD.MNU. (The compiled menu file is ACAD.MNX.) You can make items in a menu very short, even a single character, or very complex involving many commands. You also can use AutoLISP in menu items. We will refer to any menu item as a macro. When you create your own commands using menu macros, you automate your drawing command sequences.

What Are Some Common Menu Macro Tasks?

There is a common set of tasks that any custom menu performs. As you start to think about what procedures you can automate, use the following list as a take-off point. A custom menu system can help you:

- Standardize.

- Set up, format and fill in data for title sheets.

- Place text on the drawing.

- Locate, draw and insert components, assemblies and materials.

- Dimension and annotate components.

You will find these tasks in most drawing applications. Any or all of these tasks are candidates for creating custom menu macros.

How to Use Menu Macro Examples

After we show you how to tailor your prototype drawing, we will show you how to build a simple menu with some seventeen macros. (If you have the IA DISK, you already have the menu.) These macros provide *examples* of the control that you exercise over AutoCAD commands. You can do anything in a macro that you can do with AutoCAD commands. You can, for example, preset command parameters by hard coding values, or you can make a macro pause for input. You can control object selection in a macro by limiting the type of selection input, or you can open your macro to accept different types of input. As you work with these examples, look for the *types* of macros that will help you.

After you have worked with these macros, we will show how to write more complex macros by using special characters that are recognized by AutoCAD's menu interpreter. Finally, we will show you how to automate your macros by creating two macros that are driven by input data, saving and recalling coordinate input points. The last example is called a *parametric macro*, a macro that is driven by input values. You can use these examples as models for automating your own drawing macros.

Menu and Macro Tools

You will use two commands, SHELL and MENU, that are on the [UTILITY] screen menu. MENU, as its name implies, lets you load a menu file from within the drawing editor. SHELL is one of the [External Commands] on the [UTILITY] screen menu. It lets you exit AutoCAD from within the drawing editor, execute another program or DOS level command, then resume your drawing in the drawing editor.

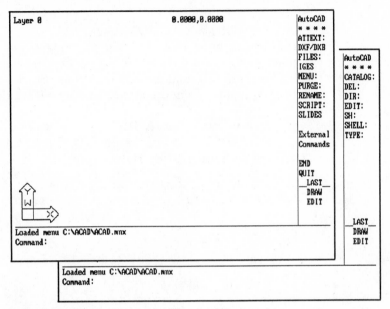

Utility Screen Menu Pages

Mastering the Prototype Drawing

Many readers overlook customizing their drawing setup through modifying the prototype drawing. This is a simple task that can save time-wasting setups. You don't need a text editor to modify the prototype drawing; it can be modified from within the AutoCAD drawing editor.

A long time ago in chapter 1, we talked about how AutoCAD establishes a default working environment for units, grid, and snap settings by loading a prototype drawing called ACAD.DWG. The ACAD.DWG file comes with the AutoCAD program. (All the ACAD.DWG variables and their default values are listed in the System Variables table in Appendix C.)

You can create your own prototype drawing and use it to initialize your drawings. After you create this drawing with the defaults (and any standard graphics like a title block) that you want, you can save it on disk with a name that you choose. Then, you can either load the drawing as an option, or set up AutoCAD to load it automatically. We will show you how to do it both ways.

Use the following exercise as a guide to creating a prototype drawing file with your own default settings and standard graphics. Our example is called IA-PROTO.

For simplicity, our IA-PROTO uses an 11" x 8 1/2" setup at full scale with engineering units. Use our settings as suggestions of parameters that you may want to set. If you are using a different scale factor and sheet size, adjust your text and dimension scales. Start your drawing with the factory defaults from the Main Menu by setting IA-PROTO=.

If you are using the IA DISK, you already have the drawing. Use CHAP-18.DWG to create IA-PROTO. Then, follow the exercise to see what is set in the IA-PROTO drawing.

APERTURE	AXIS	COORDS	GRID	LTSCALE	SNAP	ORTHO
6	.25	ON	.5	.375	.0625	ON

UNITS	Engineering units, default all other settings.
LIMITS	0,0 to 11,8.5
ZOOM	Scale of .75X
VIEW	Save view ALL

Layer name	State	Color	Linetype
0	On	7 (white)	CONTINUOUS
TITLE	On	2 (yellow)	CONTINUOUS
DIM	On	2 (yellow)	CONTINUOUS
TEXT	On	4 (cyan)	CONTINUOUS
HATCH	On	1 (red)	CONTINUOUS
CENTER	On	3 (green)	CENTER
HIDDEN	On	5 (blue)	HIDDEN
DASHED	On	2 (yellow)	DASHED
NO-PLOT	On	6 (magenta)	CONTINUOUS
OBJECTS	Current	3 (green)	CONTINUOUS

IA-PROTO Drawing Settings

Customizing a Prototype Drawing

 Enter selection: **1**   Begin a NEW drawing named IA-PROTO=CHAP-18, verify the settings shown in the IA-PROTO Drawing Settings table, and END.

 Enter selection: **1**   Begin a NEW drawing named IA-PROTO= and perform exercise.

Make the layers and settings shown in the IA-PROTO Drawing Settings table.

```
Command: STYLE
Text style name (or ?) <STANDARD>: STD   A quick, short name.
New style.
Font file <txt>: ROMANS              The font for the STD style.
Height <0'-0.0000">: <RETURN>
Width factor <1.00>: <RETURN>
Obliquing angle <0>: <RETURN>
Backwards? <N> <RETURN>
Upside-down? <N> <RETURN>
Vertical? <N> <RETURN>
STD is now the current text style.

Command: SETVAR
Variable name or ?: TEXTSIZE
New value for TEXTSIZE <0'-0.2000">: .125
```

```
Command: DIM            Set the following dimension variables.
Dim: DIMDLI            Set to 0.375.
Dim: DIMTXT            Set to 0.125.
Dim: DIMASZ            Set to 0.1875.
Dim: DIMEXE            Set to 0.1875.
Dim: DIMCEN            Set to 0.0625.
Dim: DIMEXO            Set to 0.9375.
Dim: EXIT

Command: END           END to save IA-PROTO for use.
```

How to Optionally Load a Prototype Drawing

Now that you have preserved IA-PROTO, you can call IA-PROTO as an option by setting any new drawing equal to it. This is a technique that you've used throughout the book. Check IA-PROTO.

Testing a Prototype Drawing

```
Enter selection: 1                    Begin a NEW drawing.
Enter NAME of drawing: TEST=IA-PROTO
```

                                 AutoCAD puts you into the drawing editor and starts a new drawing identical to IA-PROTO.

```
Command: QUIT                         If it is identical to IA-PROTO, it's OK.
```

How to Automate Loading a Prototype Drawing

You can set up AutoCAD to automatically use IA-PROTO for your new drawing in two ways. One is to copy IA-PROTO.DWG to the name ACAD.DWG, replacing the original default ACAD.DWG. (You should find ACAD.DWG in the same directory as your AutoCAD program files.) If you do this and you want to restore the standard ACAD.DWG prototype drawing, you just begin a new drawing named ACAD= and then END it.

The other way to automate IA-PROTO is to set it as the default prototype drawing in AutoCAD's Configuration Menu. Here are the steps to automating a prototype drawing by reconfiguring AutoCAD.

Automation Steps Using a Prototype Drawing

■ From the Main Menu, select: 5. Configure AutoCAD.

■ From the Configuration Menu, select: 8. Configure operating parameters.

■ Select the operating parameter: 2. Initial drawing setup.

■ Enter name of default prototype file for new drawings: IA-PROTO.

■ <RETURN> three times to save the changes and exit to the Main Menu.

Now all new drawings started in this configuration (set up by the IA.BAT startup file) will start up with IA-PROTO's defaults. Your normal AutoCAD configuration should be unaffected. Let's turn our attention to macros.

Creating Menu Macros

To develop a good menu, you need working macros and working symbols. Of course, good working macros (and symbols) don't appear under a pillow overnight. You get them by reading and using examples, like those you will find in this chapter, and by writing down the commands, options and input parameters that you use when you are drawing. Your own repetitive drawing sequences are the raw material for macros. If you think you have a candidate sequence, write it down. You can then make a test macro to see if it will help you. The key to efficient AutoCAD use is customizing your menu macros for your own drawing application.

How to Think About Macros

Take a look at the following First Screen Menu illustration. This is the first target set of menu macros that you will write (or use pre-built if you have the IA DISK). All of these menu items are macros that extend common AutoCAD commands. At the top of the menu, [MOVE:] and [COPY:] automatically repeat the MOVE and COPY commands. At the bottom of the menu, [ZOOM:P] transparently executes a ZOOM Previous command, and [VIEW:ALL] transparently restores a view named ALL.

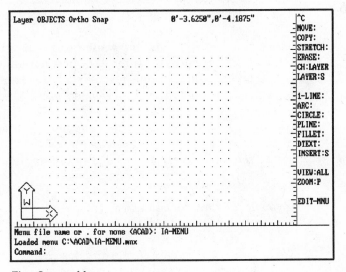

First Screen Menu

Each of these target macros automates an AutoCAD command by extending it with one or two new features. Say you need a line command that will draw just *one* line segment. Try the [1-LINE:] macro. It draws one segment. When you start to consider making macros, think about that one- (or two-) step addition to a command sequence that will save you a lot of time and effort. As these macros show, it doesn't have to be an elaborate drawing sequence. Just think about the things that annoy you, or think about the times that you have said, "If only AutoCAD could do this!" When a drawing sequence seems tedious and annoying, that sequence is a candidate for a macro.

Since the IA DISK has a pre-built set of the menu macros in the IA-MENU.MNU file, we recommend that you use the disk's macros. This will save you the trouble of typing in the macros, and let you concentrate on seeing the macros work and looking at *how* they work. Whether you just read the menu files or create them yourself, you should have a text editor.

Getting Started With Your Editor

To write a menu macro, you must have a text editor or word processor that is able to create standard ASCII text files. We recommend installing a copy of your text editor in the IA-ACAD directory, where you are creating the drawings for this book. Or, your editor and system may be configured so that you can start your editor from the current directory and create files in the current directory. Either way allows you to use it interactively via the SHELL command. You can even automate editing and reloading menu files with a menu macro.

Otherwise, or if you do not want to set up your text editor to work interactively, simply end AutoCAD when you edit the menu files. You can end AutoCAD and load your text editor to read and modify the menu text files, then exit your editor, and reload AutoCAD to use the modified files.

If you are not sure of your editor and need information on choosing and testing a suitable editor, or need further directions on setting up your text editor, see Appendix B. You need a suitable editor to work with the menu files.

If you do not have an editor, you can read the exercise sequences to learn how the macros work. All the macros are annotated.

We assume that you are in the directory called IA-ACAD, and your text editor is installed in the same directory.

The following exercise provides you with a test to see whether you can SHELL to your text editor from within AutoCAD.

Using SHELL to Run Programs From Inside AutoCAD

Enter selection: **1**	Begin a NEW drawing named MENUTEST=IA-PROTO.
Command: **SHELL** DOS Command:	Executes the ACAD.PGP SHELL command. Here you can enter any valid operating system command or program.

If you got the DOS command prompt, proceed with the next exercise to edit the IA-MENU.MNU file.

➡ *NOTE: On other operating systems, such as UNIX, SHELL may show a different prompt.*

If you didn't get the DOS command prompt, your ACAD.PGP file isn't where AutoCAD can find it, or your system is set up incompatibly. Find the ACAD.PGP file on your original or master backup AutoCAD diskettes and copy it to your AutoCAD program directory, or get help from your support source. (See Appendix B for more information on setting up your system environment, including AutoCAD's PGP file.)

Otherwise, if this or the next exercise step won't work for you, end AutoCAD and edit the menu file, or just read the text editor sections. If you end AutoCAD and start your editor in your normal manner, be sure that the file gets created in or copied to the IA-ACAD directory.

Use the next exercise step to edit or examine the IA-MENU.MNU file. If you are using the IA DISK, load the IA-MENU.MNU file into your text editor. If you are not using the disk, start up your editor and create the IA-MENU.MNU. Either way, start your editor exactly as you would if you were creating a plain ASCII text file from the DOS C:> (or other operating system) prompt. In the following exercises, we use NE (Norton's Editor) for our editor. Use the name that you normally use to start *your* editor.

Starting a Text Editor in SHELL

 Just examine the finished menu from the IA DISK.

 Create the IA-MENU.MNU file with your editor.

DOS Command: **NE IA-MENU.MNU**   NE is our editor's name. You use yours.

If everything is set up right, you're now in your text editor.

Using the IA DISK IA-MENU.MNU File

Your text editor should automatically load the IA-MENU.MNU file if you are using the IA DISK file. Use the next exercise as a guide to read the file with your editor. You don't have to type in any input. You'll see the complete menu file, which includes more lines than the next exercise sequence shows. When you exit your editor to return to AutoCAD, quit instead of saving to avoid changing the file. Even if you have the disk, going through the editor exercises will teach you the process for creating and modifying your own menus.

Creating the IA-MENU.MNU File

If you are not using the IA DISK file, your text editor should start a new IA-MENU.MNU file in the IA-ACAD directory. Some editors can't automatically load files. If your editor does not automatically load files, you will need to load them manually in your editor. We will assume that your editor loads the file automatically.

Create the following menu macros. Type the characters that you input exactly as the book shows them. Don't use tabs or invisible trailing spaces. Don't put in any blank lines. End each line with a <RETURN>, including the last line.

Here is the menu sequence for IA.MENU.MNU.

Creating or Examining the IA-MENU.MNU

 Examine these menu items in the file, then quit your editor.

 Type these 20 lines into the IA-MENU.MNU file.

```
[^C] ^C^C^C
[MOVE:     ]*^C^C^CMOVE AUTO
[COPY:     ]*^C^C^CCOPY AUTO
[STRETCH: ]*^C^C^CSTRETCH C
[ERASE:    ]*^C^C^CERASE AUTO
[CH:LAYER ]^C^C^CSELECT AU \CHPROP P ;LAYER (getvar "CLAYER") LAYER \;
[LAYER:S  ]^C^C^CLAYER S \;
[]
[1-LINE:  ]*^C^C^CLINE \\;
[ARC:     ]^C^C^CMULTIPLE ARC
[CIRCLE:  ]*^C^C^CCIRCLE
[PLINE:   ]*^C^C^CPLINE \W 0 ;
[FILLET:  ]^C^C^CFILLET R 0 MULTIPLE FILLET
[DTEXT:   ]^C^C^CDTEXT
[INSERT:S ]*^C^C^CINSERT \SCALE
[]
[VIEW:ALL ]'VIEW R ALL
[ZOOM:P   ]'ZOOM P
[]
[EDIT-MNU ]^C^C^CSHELL \MENU ;
```

Save the file in ASCII mode and exit your editor.

You should be back in AutoCAD and have an IA-MENU.MNU file in the current directory. If you ended AutoCAD to run your text editor, get back into AutoCAD.

To use your new-found menu, you must load it.

How to Load Menus

AutoCAD provides two methods for loading your .MNU files and making them active within the AutoCAD drawing editor. Once in the drawing editor, you can use the MENU command, or select [MENU] from the [UTILITY] screen menu. This command simply asks you for the name of the .MNU file and loads it. If you load any .MNU file in your prototype drawing instead of the default ACAD.MNU, it will automatically load in new drawings. You can also integrate your menu macros into another menu, even into the standard ACAD.MNU. We will show you how to load your menu with the MENU command. It will replace the standard AutoCAD menu, so you will have to do without tablet and pull-down menus for a while. Later, in the next chapter we will show you how to integrate macros into the standard ACAD.MNU menu.

Generally, you want to load and test your menu before you do any menu integration. Try loading your new menu with the MENU command. Use the following exercise sequence as a guide to help you test the menu. Use the comments to help you test each menu item.

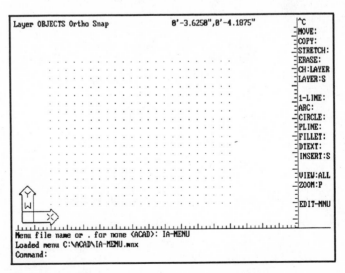

First Screen Menu

Using MENU to Load the IA-MENU.MNU for Testing

```
Command: MENU
Menu file name or . for none <ACAD>: IA-MENU
Compiling menu IA-MENU.MNU...
```
[^C] appears at top of menu,
[EDIT-MNU] at bottom.
Now, test the menu.

```
Command: ZOOM
```
Make a 6" high working area with Zoom Center.

```
Select [DTEXT: ]
```
It's an ordinary DTEXT command, preceded by three <^C>s to cancel anything that might be pending.

```
Command: DTEXT Start point or Align/Center/Fit/Middle/Right/Style: Use it or <^C>.
```

```
Select [CIRCLE: ]                           Acts like an ordinary CIRCLE.
Command: CIRCLE 3P/2P/TTR/<Center point>:   Pick point.
Diameter/<Radius>:                          Enter a radius.
Command: CIRCLE 3P/2P/TTR/<Center point>:   Except it repeats.
Diameter/<Radius>:
Command: CIRCLE 3P/2P/TTR/<Center point>: <^C>   Until you <^C> to cancel it.
```

```
Select [ARC: ]                              A MULTIPLE ARC command.
Command: MULTIPLE ARC Center/<Start point>: Pick point.
Center/End/<Second point>:                  Pick point.
End point:                                   Pick point.
ARC Center/<Start point>: <^C>               It also repeats until cancelled.
```

```
Select [1-LINE: ]      It issues LINE and draws only one segment.
Command: LINE From point: Pick point (the first backslash).
```

```
Select [VIEW:ALL ]     It transparently zooms to the view ALL.
```

```
To point:              Pick point (the second backslash).
To point:              The semicolon ends the LINE and * repeats the macro.
Command: LINE From point: Pick point.
```

```
Select [ZOOM:P]        It transparently Zooms Previous.
```

```
To point:              Pick point.
To point: <^C>         Until cancelled.
```

```
Select [EDIT-MNU ]     Access your text editor.
```

```
Command: SHELL                  It issues the SHELL command.
DOS Command: NE IA-MENU.MNU     Type the command that starts your text editor.
```
Make any necessary corrections, save and end the editor, then SHELL returns you to AutoCAD.

Where the [EDIT-MNU] continues with the menu command:

```
Command: MENU Menu file name or . for none <IA-MENU>:
Compiling menu C:\IA-ACAD\IA-MENU.MNU...
```
Which reloads the modified menu.

➥ *NOTE: If you end AutoCAD to edit your menu, just use the MENU command to manually reload the menu each time you change it.*

If all went well, your screen showed the IA-MENU menu screen in the First Screen illustration above, and you were able to execute the menu macros. Spend some time trying the macros. Use Undo if you crash a menu macro. Any error in a menu item crashes the rest of the item, but Undo cleans it up. If your drawing accumulates clutter, just erase what you don't need.

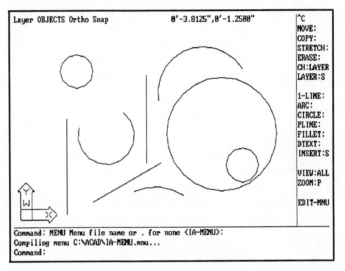

First Screen With Test Drawing

➥ *NOTE: If you are examining the IA DISK's IA-MENU, your screen may show eight more menu macros. These are more advanced macros that we cover later in the chapter. They may appear on a second menu page, accessible with a [NEXT] item, depending on your video display.*

➥ *NOTE: The [INSERT:S] macro requires a scale block to work. We will cover this macro later in the chapter.*

Executing the last menu item [EDIT-MNU] should SHELL you out to your text editor after you enter your editor's name and the IA-MENU.MNU file name. When you exit your editor, you should come back into AutoCAD, and the menu should automatically compile. If it doesn't work, try ending AutoCAD when you need to edit your menu. If it all works, you can automate the editor.

Automating Menu Editing

If you want to automate menu editing, you can add to the [EDIT-MNU] macro. You simply need to insert the exact character sequence you typed to load your editor at the DOS command prompt (above). For example, our line for Norton's Editor becomes:

```
[EDIT-MNU ]^C^C^CSHELL NE +IA-MENU.MNU;MENU ;
```

Or, if your editor is EDLIN, the last line would be:

```
[EDIT-MNU ]^C^C^CSHELL EDLIN IA-MENU.MNU;MENU ;
```

Go ahead and change [EDIT-MNU] now if you want to automate it. But the exercises assume you'll just continue entering your editor and file name whenever you need to edit the menu.

How to Construct Menu Macros

Now, let's take the macros apart to show you how they are constructed. There are really just two basic parts: AutoCAD commands and parameters; and a group of special character codes used by the AutoCAD menu (and command) interpreter. As you read through the following sections, try out the macros again by picking the menu items from the screen. Then look at the macro text in our explanations.

Labeling Macro Commands

If you look at the first menu item, [^C], the first special character that you encounter is a pair of the brackets.

```
[^C]^C^C^C
```

The square brackets act as labels for the menu interpreter. You control what is displayed on the screen by putting a macro label in square brackets [ ]. The characters after the right-hand bracket are the macro. Only eight characters display on the screen menu label, but you can make labels longer for documentation. Labels can include letters, numbers, and any displayable character. Control and extended ASCII characters are simply ignored. The square brackets identify the label to AutoCAD's menu interpreter. You can use a pair of brackets [ ] to make a blank menu item.

The INSert key can make quick selections from the screen menu. Whenever you type input to AutoCAD, if the characters typed match a screen menu label, the label will highlight. When a label is highlighted, hitting the <INS> key executes its macro. If you begin each of your screen page macro labels with one or two unique characters, it makes it easy to select and execute items with <INS>.

Using <^C> to Cancel

If you look at the macros, you will see that they all start with two or three <^C>s. Control-C is a special code in a menu that cancels a command just like cancelling from the keyboard.

```
[LAYER:S  ]^C^C^CLAYER S \;
[]
[1-LINE:  ]*^C^C^CLINE \\;
[ARC:     ]^C^C^CMULTIPLE ARC
```

Since you want any macro to have a clean slate to execute, starting a macro with three <^C>s insures that all previous commands are cancelled. Why three? There are some dim recesses in AutoCAD that require three <^C>s to get you back to the command prompt. If you look at how the macros are constructed, you see that the AutoCAD command in the macro comes after the Control-Cs. In effect, you cancel everything, then start your macro.

To put a <^C> in a macro, type a caret ^ (the shifted character above the 6 on your keyboard) followed by a **C**. This caret-character format allows menus to include codes for any control character without interfering with the meaning that a real control character might have to your text editor.

Subcommands and Parameters

If you are using subcommands or parameters within a macro command, use the same characters that you would normally type at the keyboard. For example, you use S for the Set option in the LAYER command in the [LAYER:S] macro (below).

Using Semicolons vs. Spaces in Macros

If we look again at the macros, you will see that they have some spaces and semicolons in them.

```
[LAYER:S  ]^C^C^CLAYER S \;
[]
[1-LINE:  ]*^C^C^CLINE \\;
```

The semicolon is the special character for a <RETURN>. In macros, spaces act like the <SPACE> and semicolons act like the <RETURN> keys from the keyboard. You usually can use semicolons and spaces interchangeably in macros. However, if you need a semicolon or space at the end of a macro, use a semicolon that you can see. Don't use an *invisible* trailing space. The semicolons in the two examples above act as <RETURN>s to end the macros.

Repeating Commands and Macros

AutoCAD Release 9, 10, or later versions allow you to repeat macros indefinitely by placing an asterisk as the first character of the macro. If you use a screen [LABEL], put the asterisk immediately after the closing right bracket.

```
[MOVE:    ]*^C^C^CMOVE AUTO
[COPY:    ]*^C^C^CCOPY AUTO
[STRETCH: ]*^C^C^CSTRETCH C
[ERASE:   ]*^C^C^CERASE AUTO
```

The asterisk triggers the menu interpreter to repeat the macro in its entirety. The * must be followed by at least one <^C> (or <^X>). Otherwise, it is interpreted as a character and part of the following command or input. AutoCAD would see *MOVE, for example, not recognize it, and cause an error.

With Release 9, 10, and later versions, you can repeat single commands without an asterisk by using the MULTIPLE command. The MULTIPLE command modifier causes AutoCAD to repeat one command until you hit a <^C> to cancel it. MULTIPLE only repeats the command, ignoring any options or parameters used in the first execution.

```
[ARC:     ]^C^C^CMULTIPLE ARC
[CIRCLE:  ]*^C^C^CCIRCLE
[PLINE:   ]*^C^C^CPLINE \W 0 ;
[FILLET:  ]^C^C^CFILLET R 0 MULTIPLE FILLET
```

MULTIPLE works for simple menu items, or you can use it to repeat the last command in a macro. However, if you tried to make TEXT automatically repeat a mode, like M for Middle, it would use the mode the first time, then ignore the mode on repeats. MULTIPLE is intended primarily for on-the-fly keyboard use or for single commands. We find the asterisk method works better for most macros.

Pausing for Automation

Several of the macros in this first set pause for input. The backslash \ is the special character that makes a macro pause. Macros need automation. The pause makes automation possible, pausing for input from the user, then resuming execution with more commands or options. The pause lets you string together multiple commands and input.

```
[1-LINE:  ]*^C^C^CLINE \\;
[ARC:     ]^C^C^CMULTIPLE ARC
[CIRCLE:  ]*^C^C^CCIRCLE
[PLINE:   ]*^C^C^CPLINE \W 0 ;
[FILLET:  ]^C^C^CFILLET R 0 MULTIPLE FILLET
[DTEXT:   ]^C^C^CDTEXT
[INSERT:S ]*^C^C^CINSERT \SCALE
```

A single backslash tells AutoCAD to wait for a single piece of input. In the [INSERT:S] macro example, the macro pauses for the insert point. Without a backslash, AutoCAD would continue taking its input from the macro and would pass the next item along to the command processor. It would read the SCALE and cause an error. You must supply one backslash for each point that you want for input. The [1-LINE:] macro above pauses for two inputs, the From point and the To point.

➥ *NOTE: If you use directory path names in your macros, use forward slashes /, not the backslashes \ that you are used to using in the DOS operating system. AutoCAD recognizes either kind of slash, but backslashes make menus pause! Also, some operating systems, such as UNIX, use forward slashes for paths.*

Transparent Commands

Transparent operations such as 'ZOOM P do not *use up* backslashes present in the macro. They work exactly as if typed from the keyboard, and the macro waits for them to finish. When you have a macro pausing for point input with a backslash, like the [INSERT:S] macro, you can use a transparent command and the macro will continue to pause. You can type the transparent command, or use a transparent macro like [VIEW:ALL] or [ZOOM:P].

```
[INSERT:S ]*^C^C^CINSERT \SCALE
[]
[VIEW:ALL ]'VIEW R ALL
[ZOOM:P   ]'ZOOM P
```

Osnaps and XYZ point filters are also transparent. Other common transparent commands are: 'GRAPHSCR, 'HELP, 'RESUME, 'SETVAR, 'TEXTSCR, and 'PAN. You make these commands transparent by preceding the command with an apostrophe '. You can enter transparent commands and filters in the middle of other AutoCAD commands in your menu macros. The AutoCAD menu observes the same command suspension rules as the AutoCAD command processor. AutoCAD applies filtering modes and commands, like osnaps, point filters, or 'SETVAR, to the current command when paused for input by a backslash in the menu.

It suspends filling the backslash until the transparent operation is completed and the current command receives more input.

Special Characters in Menus

You will use about a dozen special characters in macros. You have already seen the backslash \ for pause, semicolon ; for <RETURN>, brackets [ ] for labels, asterisk * to repeat, and <^C> to clear previous commands. Backslashes, semicolons and spaces are the most frequently used special characters in menus. AutoCAD automatically places a space at the end of a menu line, unless the line ends with a special character. But if AutoCAD encounters a special character at the end of a menu line, it *does not* add an automatic space to the end of the line.

The following table provides a complete list of the special characters used by AutoCAD's menu interpreter. The @ (lastpoint) is not listed as a special character because it does not share in the special treatment by the AutoCAD menu interpreter.

```
                    SPECIAL MENU CHARACTERS

\    Pauses for input              ;    Issues RETURN
+    Continues to next line        []   Encloses Label
*    Autorepeats, or marks page    ^B   Toggles SNAP
     The <SPACE> character         ^M   Issues RETURN
^D   Toggles COORDS                ^E   Toggles ISOPLANE
^G   Toggles GRID                  ^H   Issues BACKSPACE
^C   *Cancel*                      ^O   Toggles ORTHO
^P   Toggles MENUECHO              ^Q   Toggles Echo to Printer
^T   Toggles Tablet                ^X   *Delete* input buffer
^Z   Does "nothing." Put at end of line to suppress
     automatic space
```

If you use control characters, like Control-B in your macros, type them into a menu file as two characters. Use a carat ^ followed by the upper case letter, like ^B.

How to Control Command Parameter Macros

You can do anything in a macro that you can do in an AutoCAD command. You can preset command parameters by hard coding values, or you can pause for input by using backslashes. Take a look at the [STRETCH:], [PLINE:] and [FILLET:] macros.

```
[STRETCH: ]*^C^C^CSTRETCH C
[PLINE:    ]*^C^C^CPLINE \W 0 ;
[FILLET:  ]^C^C^CFILLET R 0 MULTIPLE FILLET
```

Now, try testing the macros again using the following exercise sequence as a guide. Start by drawing some entities to use with the macros. Notice that the [STRETCH:] macro put you in a crossing selection mode. [FILLET:] automatically sets the fillet radius to 0, and [PLINE:] sets the width to 0.

Using Command Parameters in Macros

Select **[STRETCH:]**	Try to stretch some entities.
Command: STRETCH	It issues the command.
Select objects to stretch by window . . .	
Select objects: C	And automatically puts it in Crossing mode.
First corner:	Pick point.
Other corner: 2 found.	Pick point.
Select objects: **<RETURN>**	
Base point:	Pick point.
New point:	Pick point.
Command: STRETCH	It repeats the macro until cancelled.

Select **[FILLET:]**	Try filleting some entities.
Command: FILLET	It issues the command.
Polyline/Radius/<Select two objects>: R	And sets the radius.
Enter fillet radius <0E+00>: 0	Forcing it to a 0 default.
Command: MULTIPLE FILLET	Multiple repeats the command.
Polyline/Radius/<Select two objects>:	

Select **[PLINE:]**	
Command: PLINE	It issues the command.
From point:	Pick point (the backslash).
Current line-width is 0'-0.0000"	
Arc/Close/Halfwidth/Length/Undo/Width/<Endpoint of line>: W	
Starting width <0'-0.0000">: 0	Forces the width to 0.
Ending width <0'-0.0000">:	Semicolon <RETURN> defaults it.
Arc/Close/Halfwidth/Length/Undo/Width/<Endpoint of line>:	Stays in PLINE command.
	And repeats.

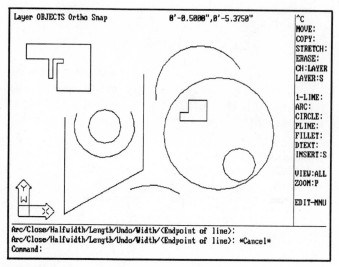

Using Command Parameters

How to Control Object Selection in Macros

You can control object selection in a macro by limiting the type of selection input, or you can open your macro to accept different types of input. The next exercise shows you how you can control object selection in macros. Look at the [COPY:] and [CH:LAYER] macros.

```
[COPY:    ]*^C^C^CCOPY AUTO
[CH:LAYER ]^C^C^CSELECT AU \CHPROP P ;LAYER (getvar "CLAYER") LAYER \;
```

Again, test the two macros to see how they work. Draw some entities to work with. Then try [COPY:]. It puts you in AUTO selection mode. [CH:LAYER] puts you in the SELECT command in AUto mode, issues the CHPROP command with a Previous selection set, then sets the objects that you selected to the current layer. The (getvar "CLAYER") is a bit of AutoLISP. You can ignore it for now. We will explain how the AutoLISP get variable function works in the last chapter.

Using Object Selection in Macros

```
Select [COPY: ]                         Test the copy command.
Command: COPY                           It issues the command.
Select objects: AUTO
Select objects:                         Pick object.
1 selected, 1 found.
Select objects:                         Pick window point.
```

```
1 selected, Other corner: 2 found.        Pick.
Select objects: <RETURN>
<Base point or displacement>/Multiple:
Second point of displacement:
Command: COPY

Select [LAYER:S]                          Set the current layer to 0.

Select [CH:LAYER ]
Command: SELECT                           It issues the SELECT command.
Select objects: AU                        With selection mode AUto.
Select objects: 1 selected, 1 found.      Select several objects.
Select objects: 1 selected, Other corner: 2 found.
Select objects: 1 selected, Other corner: 1 found.
Select objects: <RETURN>    SELECT loops at the backslash until you <RETURN>.
Command: CHPROP                           Then issues the CHPROP command.
Select objects: P 3 found.                Using the Previous selection set.
Select objects:                           The semicolon <RETURN> ends selection.
Change what property (Color/LAyer/LType/Thickness) ? LAYER
New layer <OBJECTS>: (getvar "CLAYER")   It sets them to the current layer.
Change what property (Color/LAyer/LType/Thickness) ? LAYER
New layer <0>:                            Making it the default. You can <RETURN>,
                                          or input another layer (the last backslash).
Change what property (Color/LAyer/LType/Thickness) ? The semicolon <RETURN> exits.
Command:
```

Using Selection Sets With Macros

Selection sets let you control how your macro selects objects. AutoCAD editing commands always ask for a set of entities before any edit tasks begin. This limits your macro writing by allowing only a fixed number of picks. Whether you use Window, Last, or another selection mode, you still need to predefine one \ per pick. AutoCAD's SELECT command is indispensable in macros because it has the unique feature of pausing the macro indefinitely until the entire selection process is complete. It pauses even when other commands follow.

As you saw in the [CH:LAYER] macro, SELECT doesn't do anything except create a selection set of entities, allowing an indefinite number of picks. This is invaluable because you can use a subsequent command, like MOVE, to select that selection set with a P (Previous) selection mode.

AutoCAD has three selection modes that you will find especially useful in macros. These are:

■ **SIngle.** Stays in selection mode until an object or set is successfully picked.

- **BOX**. Acts like either Crossing or Window, depending on the order of the two points picked.

- **AUto**. If the first point finds an object, AUto picks it. Otherwise AUto acts like BOX.

You can use SIngle combined with other modes, like Crossing or AUto. You also can use it with SELECT if you want to force the creation of a Previous set with only a single selection. But, before you assume SIngle solves the problem of a missed pick ruining or aborting a menu macro, read on. Although SIngle ends object selection when an object or set is picked, it doesn't suspend the rest of a macro. SIngle will work for simple macros like:

```
[STRETCH1]*^C^C^CSTRETCH SI C
```

SIngle keeps you from having to <RETURN> to end the selection process. However, if you miss your first selection and additional commands or parameters follow, SI will try to use them as input. For example, this macro changes an entity to yellow (color 2):

```
[C-YELLOW]^C^C^CCHPROP SI \C 2 ;
```

This macro works fine if you don't miss the entity, but if you do miss, SI tries to use PROP as object selection input.

We recommend using SELECT and BOX or AUto for most macros. BOX is clean and simple. Pick left-to-right for a Window and right-to-left for a Crossing. AUto gives the most flexibility, combining picking by point with the BOX mode. If your first point misses, you go into BOX mode, otherwise AUto selects the entity at the first pick point. Like SIngle, this causes a problem if the macro has other parameters following it:

```
[C-YELLOW]^C^C^CCHPROP AU \\; C 2 ;
```

This macro needs two backslashes for crossing/window. It works fine if you use it as window or crossing. However, if your first pick finds something, AUto is satisfied, but the macro is still suspended by the second backslash. Hit the button again at the same point. The macro will find the same object by pointing again. The best solution is to use SELECT to pause indefinitely with AUto:

```
[C-YELLOW]^C^C^CSELECT AU \CHPROP P ;;C 2 ;
```

The SELECT AUto \ builds a Previous selection set before you get into typical editing commands in your macros. Then you use P;; to select Previous to feed the selection to the editing command itself.

Setting Defaults in Macros

The [PLINE:] and [CH:LAYER] macros show two methods for setting defaults in macros.

```
[CH:LAYER ]^C^C^CSELECT AU \CHPROP P ;LAYER (getvar "CLAYER") LAYER \;
[PLINE:   ]*^C^C^CPLINE \W 0 ;
```

[PLINE:] hard codes the polyline width for the macro. Since you can't predict the incoming default pline width, make your pline macros set the width explicitly, as in W 0 ; (above). The [CH:LAYER] macro forces a layer change based on object properties. Both methods offer ways to enforce drawing standards in your macros.

Text Input in Macros

When you enter text in a macro command, all special characters except spaces act exactly the same whether they are in the middle of a text string or not. You can use a semicolon anywhere to issue a <RETURN>. The sacrifice you must make is that the only way to enter a real semicolon in text created by a menu is to use ASCII codes. The AutoCAD menu interpreter doesn't recognize ASCII codes, but the text string does. You are familiar with AutoCAD's underscores in text where the %%u gives an underscore in a text string. The %% is the *escape* character. ASCII 59 is the ASCII code for the semicolon. If you imbed a %%59 in a text string, you get a semicolon. For example, "Word%%59 item, stuff" becomes "Word; item, stuff." This is the text method for special characters and text modes. The %%nn works for any character where nn is the ASCII code number.

Since you must be able to type space characters in the middle of text strings, AutoCAD's menu interpreter treats them as true spaces in your text, not as being equivalent to <RETURN>s as in the AutoCAD program itself. If you want the macro to continue after the text input, you need some way to tell AutoCAD that the string of text is complete. You can't use the automatic space at the end of the menu line for text. Use a semicolon.

Stopping Point

This is a stopping point. If you want to take a break, END your drawing session. You can pick up with the next section later. This last section will show you how to create more complex macros with some built-in intelligence.

Creating Intelligent Macros

So far, the macros that you have worked with have been simple macros. In this last section we want to show you some of the power inherent in making your own macros. As you work with the next eight macros, think of them as models for the types of automation that you can incorporate into AutoCAD.

The first four new macros, [CH:LTYPE], [LTYPE:], [CH:COLOR] and [COLOR:] are similar to [CH:LAYER].

The [*RESET*] is an example of a macro that resets a default drawing environment by running through a series of AutoCAD setup commands. You may find this macro, or some variation that you make from it, useful. Say you have temporarily changed snap, grid and several other settings to draw something. Having a reset macro like [*RESET*] can save you time and trouble re-establishing your normal drawing setup.

The [SECT-MK:] macro is a section block macro that shows how to insert a block into a drawing, presetting scale and automatically sizing the block for insertion. This same macro also controls attribute rotation.

The last two macros, [RECT:] and [BOLT:] show how to get and retain coordinate points. These are examples of intelligent macros. The [RECT:] macro creates a rectangle by using two (diagonal) pick points. The [BOLT:] macro is a parametric command. It draws a bolt, requiring only two input points and a scale factor.

Setting Up for Intelligent Macros

To get started you need to get back into AutoCAD. If you are using the IA DISK you already have the next eight macros in your IA-MENU. Use your text editor to look at the macros.

If you are creating the macros from scratch, you need to get into your text editor to add more lines to IA-MENU.MNU. Add the following macros, starting with the blank label [ ] just after [EDIT-MNU] in the menu file. The bold lines in the exercise are the lines you need to add to your existing menu. After you add the lines, compile and load the new expanded menu with the MENU command. If you are using the [EDIT-MNU] macro in your menu, the macro will do this automatically.

Adding Complex Macros to IA-MENU

 Examine these menu items in the IA-MENU.MNU file, then quit your editor.

 Add these new **(bold)** lines into the IA-MENU.MNU file.

Select **[EDIT-MNU]**   Load IA-MENU into your text editor.

Add the following lines after [EDIT-MNU].

```
[EDIT-MNU ]^C^C^CSHELL \MENU ;
[]
[CH:LTYPE ]^C^C^CSELECT AU \CHPROP P ;LTYPE BYLAYER LTYPE \;
[LTYPE:   ]^C^C^CLINETYPE S BYLAYER S \;
[CH:COLOR ]^C^C^CSELECT AU \CHPROP P ;COLOR BYLAYER COLOR \;
[COLOR:   ]^C^C^CCOLOR BYLAYER ;
[]
[*RESET* ]^C^C^CSETVAR MENUECHO 0 ;COORDS 2 ;ORTHOMODE 1 ;EXPERT 0 ;PICKBOX 3;+
COLOR BYLAYER LINETYPE S BYLAYER ;ELEV 0 0 FILLET R 0 APERTURE 6;+
OSNAP NON SNAP R 0,0 0 ;.0625 GRID .5
[]
+
[SECT-MK: ]INSERT SECT-MK S (getvar "DIMSCALE") \\\ATTEDIT ;;;;L A 0 ;
+
[RECT:    Draw rect by 2 corner pts.]^C^C^C^P+
ORTHO OFF LINE;\\;SETVAR MENUECHO 3 SELECT L;;+
ARC @ C MID,QUI @ A 180 ID END,QUI @ ERASE P ;+
COPY L ;@ CEN,QUI @ ID CEN,QUI @ SCALE P L ;@ 2;+
PLINE @ .X @ CEN,QUI @ ;PEDIT L E I ;^C+
PLINE @ .Y @ CEN,QUI @ ;PEDIT L E I ;^CID CEN,QUI @;+
PLINE @ .X @ CEN,QUI @ ;PEDIT L E I ;^CID CEN,QUI @;+
ERASE P ;PEDIT L J M @ @ ;;C ;ORTHO ON SETVAR MENUECHO 0
+
[BOLT:    Pick 2 endpoints and enter scale to create a bolt.]^C^C^C^P+
LINE;\\;INSERT SCALE S \@ 0 SETVAR MENUECHO 3;+
INSERT NUT S @ CEN,QUI @ @ MID,QUI @;+
ERASE L ;MOVE L ;@ MID,QUI @ OOPS;+
ERASE QUA,QUI @ ;PEDIT MID,QUI @ Y E I ;^C+
OOPS PEDIT END,QUI @ W MID,QUI @ CEN,QUI @;;+
INSERT HEAD S MID,QUI @ CEN,QUI @ @ MID,QUI @ ERASE P ;SETVAR MENUECHO 0
```

Save the file in ASCII mode and exit your editor back to AutoCAD.

`Command: MENU Menu file name or . for none <IA-MENU>:` The menu reloads.
`Compiling menu C:\IA-ACAD\IA-MENU.MNU...`   The menu recompiles.

You may have several of the new items visible. Unless all are visible, you will have [NEXT] at the bottom.

Select **[NEXT]**   To get to the second page.
Select **[NEXT]**   Select it to flip back and forth between the two pages.

The modified menu on your screen should look similar to the illustration, A Full Page of Macros (below).

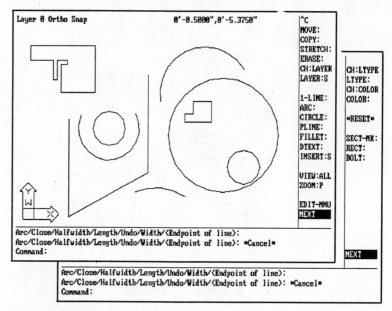

A Full Page of Macros

The first four new macros, [CH:LTYPE], [LTYPE:], [CH:COLOR] and [COLOR:] are similar to [CH:LAYER]. Try them to see how they work.

[NEXT] Paging

You won't see all of the entries immediately if your menu exceeds one page. Most video displays support 20 to 30 items per screen page, but a few video displays support as many as 80 items per screen. Unless your display shows the entire menu, you will see a [NEXT] at the bottom of the screen. AutoCAD automatically pages the screen menu for you, creating [NEXT]. When you select [NEXT], another page of the macros appears. [NEXT] is a continuous loop with any number of pages. When you reach the last page, [NEXT] brings you to the first page.

Using a Macro to Reset a Drawing Setup

Use the following exercise to familiarize yourself with the [*RESET*] macro.

Resetting Defaults in Macros

```
Select [*RESET* ]                          A series of settings scrolls by, beginning with:
Command: SETVAR Variable name or ? <PICKBOX>: MENUECHO
New value for MENUECHO <0>: 0            MENUECHO suppresses prompts.
Command:
SETVAR Variable name or ? <MENUECHO>: COORDS

                                        And several others, ending with GRID.


Command: GRID
Grid spacing(X) or ON/OFF/Snap/Aspect <0'-0.5000">: .5
Command:
```

Long Macros

Menu items can get very long, especially macros that set many parameters or set up layers. You can continue a macro for many lines by ending each line with a plus **+** sign.

Look at the plus signs ending the [*RESET*] macro lines. When AutoCAD sees a **+** at the end of a line, it treats the next line as part of the same item.

```
[*RESET*  ]^C^C^CSETVAR MENUECHO 0 ;COORDS 2 ;ORTHOMODE 1 ;EXPERT 0 ;PICKBOX 3;+
COLOR BYLAYER LINETYPE S BYLAYER ;ELEV 0 0 FILLET R 0 APERTURE 6;+
OSNAP NON SNAP R 0,0 0 ;.0625 GRID .5
```

Adding blank lines containing only a solitary plus sign, like the **+** before [RECT:] tells AutoCAD to continue to the next line. This **+** has no effect on the menu. It makes the file easier to read by providing a visual break. AutoCAD ignores the solitary **+**.

The SETVAR MENUECHO 0 suppresses the command line display as the macro sets drawing defaults. You can see what defaults are set by looking at the macro code (above). To really test the macro, try changing some settings like your aperture, grid, and snap. Then [*RESET*] again.

Using Macros to Control Block Insertions

The [INSERT:S] macro in the first group you created is a simple example of controlling a block insertion with preset scale. To make it work, you need a block to test. If you are using the IA DISK, you already have a block named SCALE. Any block would work with [INSERT:S], but you'll also need this block for a later exercise. Make the block.

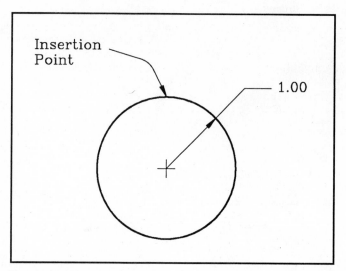

The SCALE Circle Block

Making a Scale Block

  You have SCALE block, skip to the insert test.

  Build the block first, then do the insert test.

Command: **LAYER**	Set Layer 0 current.
Command: **CIRCLE**	Draw a 1-unit radius circle.
Command: **WBLOCK**	Wblock it to name SCALE.
Insertion base point: **QUA,QUI**	Pick point at top of circle.

Now, try the macro.

Controlling Block Insertion Scale With a Macro

```
Select [INSERT:S ]
Command: INSERT Block name (or ?) <default>: SCALE      Enter the block name.
Insertion point: SCALE   Scale factor: 2                It prompts for scale.
Insertion point:                                        Pick point.
Rotation angle <0>: <RETURN>
Command: INSERT Block name (or ) <scale>:               And it repeats.
```

[INSERT:S] is an improvement over the raw INSERT command for most insertions. Presetting scale lets you see your scale when dragging and picking an insertion point. You have only one scale prompt to respond to, instead of X and Y. Here is the macro text.

```
[INSERT:S ]*^C^C^CINSERT \SCALE
```

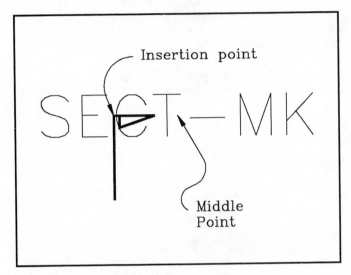

The Section Mark Block

The next macro, [SECT-MK:], shows how preset scale can be automatically sized to the drawing, and how attribute rotation can be controlled in a macro. First, you need to make the block as shown in The Section Mark Block drawing. If you are using the IA DISK, you already have the block.

Making a Section Mark

 You have SECT-MK block, skip to the insert test.

 Build the block first, then do the insert test.

```
Command: PLINE
From point:                                 Pick a point in a clear area.
Current line-width is 0.0000                Set Width to .0125 units.
Arc/Close/Halfwidth/Length/Undo/Width/<Endpoint of line>: @0,0.375
```

Enter points at @0.25,0 and @-.1875,-.0625 and PERP to the horizontal line.

```
Arc/Close/Halfwidth/Length/Undo/Width/<Endpoint of line>: <RETURN>
```

```
Command: ATTDEF
Attribute modes  --  Invisible:N  Constant:N  Verify:N  Preset:N    Set these modes.
Enter (ICVP) to change, RETURN when done: <RETURN>
Attribute tag: SECT-MK
Attribute prompt:Enter letter:
Default attribute value: ?
Start point or Align/Center/Fit/Middle/Right/Style: M
Middle point:                Pick a point .16 units to the right of the section marker point.
Height <0'-0.125">: .25
Rotation angle <0>: <RETURN>

Command: WBLOCK           Wblock both to file name SECT-MK.
                          Insertion base point at upper left corner of the section marker.
```

Now, test the block by inserting it.

Inserting the Section Mark Block

```
Command: INSERT           Insert SECT-MK in a clear area.
Enter attribute values    It prompts for the mark letter.
Enter letter:  <?>: A     Enter a character.
```

The [SECT-MK:] macro is designed to insert this block at the current text height, at any rotation. You don't want the attribute text to be rotated. The macro is designed so that you can use the ATTEDIT command to change the rotation of attribute text after insertion without affecting the block. The macro uses ATTEDIT to adjust the text angle. Try the macro using the following exercise as a guide.

Using a Macro to Control Block Scale and Rotation

```
Command: PAN                               Move to clear area of the screen.
Command: ZOOM                              Zoom Center, to Height 3".
Select [SECT-MK: ]
Command: INSERT Block name (or ?) <SCALE>: SECT-MK
Insertion point: S                         It presets scale to text height,
                                           with the TEXTSIZE System Variable.
Scale factor: (getvar "TEXTSIZE")    Insertion point:  Pick point (the first backslash).
Rotation angle <0>:                        Pick point above first (the second backslash).
Enter attribute values
Enter letter: <?>: B                       Enter character (third backslash).
Command: ATTEDIT                           Then it rotates the text to 0 degrees.
Edit attributes one at a time? <Y>
Block name specification <*>:
Attribute tag specification <*>:
```

```
Attribute value specification <*>:
Select Attributes: L                        The block was Last.
1 attributes selected.
Value/Position/Height/Angle/Style/Layer/Color/Next <N>: A      Angle.
New rotation angle <270>: 0                                    0 degrees.
Value/Position/Height/Angle/Style/Layer/Color/Next <N>:
```

Here is the macro text, if you want to look at it more closely.

```
[SECT-MK: ]INSERT SECT-MK S (getvar "DIMSCALE") \\\ATTEDIT ;;;;L A 0 ;
```

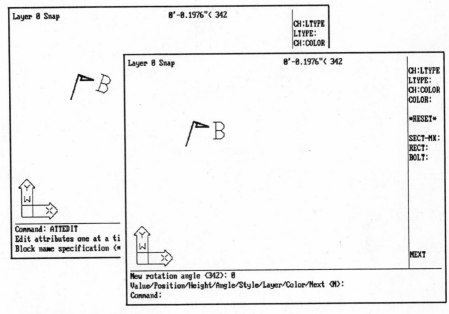

SECT-MK Insert Sequence

You have created a semi-intelligent macro. The next step in automation is controlling points.

How to Automate Macros

You can create your own commands and automated parametric tools using osnap, AutoCAD's editing commands and geometric properties associated with drawing entities. Think of an entity as a graphic representation of geometric data. The next macro, [RECT:], uses arcs as tools to save and recall coordinate points, creating a two-point (LL and UR cornerpoints) rectangle. Try the macro. When you are done, read the annotation that follows the exercise.

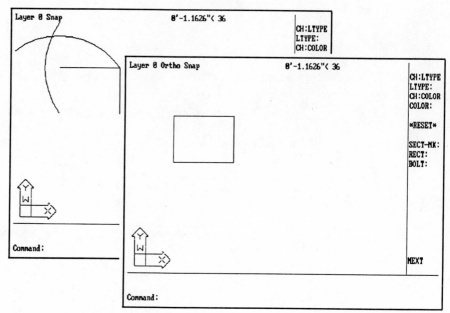

Two-Point Rectangle Sequence

Using a Two-Point Rectangle Macro

Command: **ERASE**   Erase the section mark.

Select **[RECT:]**
Command: ON/OFF <On>:   The Ortho prompt.
Command:
From point: Pick point.
To point: Pick point, diagonally.

It draws a line between the points, then two arcs. It erases the line, then draws three pline segments. Then it erases the arcs, and Pedits to create the pline rectangle. It only shows a few messages, like:

```
Current line-width is 0'-0.0000"
*Cancel*
X = 0'-4.2500"     Y = 0'-3.6875"     Z = 0'-0.0000"
2 segments added to polyline
```

[RECT:] uses ^P and the MENUECHO system variable to suppress the commands, parameters and input generated by the menu macro. It uses osnaps to control point selection, and ID to reset lastpoint, jumping back and forth from the center of one arc to the center of the other. XYZ point filters control the corner points of the polyline rectangle as it is drawn.

[RECT:] also uses PEDIT to reset the lastpoint. A PEDIT Edit vertex operation such as Insert vertex resets the lastpoint to the last vertex, even if the Edit vertex is exited and cancelled without doing anything. See the earlier listing for the complete and correctly formatted menu code — the following merely explains how it *works*.

Annotated [RECT:] Macro

```
[RECT:    Draw rect by 2 corner pts.]
^C^C^C^P+                  ^P toggles LINE off, but shows prompts.
ORTHO OFF                  Always control settings that a macro depends on.
LINE;\\;                   Draws line between two input points.
SETVAR MENUECHO 3          Suppresses everything possible.

SELECT L;;+                Saves the line as Previous selection set.
ARC @                      First point of arc.
C MID,QUI @                Puts center at line's MIDpoint.
A 180                      Draws 180-degree arc.
ID END,QUI @               Resets lastpoint to line's ENDpt.
ERASE P ;+                 Erases line (Previous).
COPY L ;@ CEN,QUI @        Copies arc, offset by distance from corner to center.
ID CEN,QUI @               Resets lastpoint to arc's CENter.
SCALE P L ;@ 2;+           Doubles scale of Last and Previous arcs.
PLINE @                    Draws pline.
.X @ CEN,QUI @ ;           From .X coord of lastpoint to osnapped Y coord of arc's CENter.
PEDIT L E I ;^C+           Reset lastpoint: PEDIT Last, Edit vertex, Insert, ; exits, and ^C.
PLINE @ .Y @ CEN,QUI @ ;        Draws second pline.
PEDIT L E I ;^CID CEN,QUI @;+   Resets lastpoint.
PLINE @ .X @ CEN,QUI @ ;        Draws third pline.
PEDIT L E I ;^CID CEN,QUI @;+   Resets lastpoint.
ERASE P ;                       Erases the arcs.
PEDIT L J M @ @ ;;C ;           Join and Close the plines.
ORTHO ON
SETVAR MENUECHO 0
```

QUIck mode makes the macro find the most recent nearby osnap points instead of the closest qualified point. Since the macro drew entities, you know they will be the most recent. This avoids finding the wrong entities in heavy traffic. QUIck also speeds up osnap.

How to Create a Parametric Macro

A parametric macro is a macro that is driven by input values. The following [BOLT:] macro is a parametric command. It draws a bolt, requiring only two input points and a scale factor. It requires the NUT and HEAD blocks to work, and it uses the SCALE block that you created earlier. First create the NUT and HEAD blocks, then try it. If you are using the IA DISK, you already have the blocks.

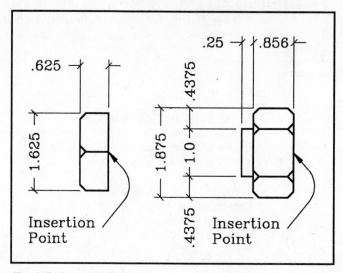

The HEAD and NUT Blocks

Making Blocks for a Parametric Bolt Macro

 You have the NUT and HEAD blocks.

 Draw and Wblock the NUT and HEAD as illustrated.

After you have the blocks, try the macro.

Using a Parametric Macro Called [BOLT:]

```
Command: ERASE                              Erase the rectangle.
Command: ZOOM                               Zoom Center, to Height 5".
Select [BOLT: ]                             ^P and MENUECHO suppress commands, input and prompts.


Command:
From point:                                 Pick one endpoint.
To point:                                   Pick other endpoint.
To point:
Command: Block name (or ?) <default>:    Insertion point:
Scale factor: .5                            Enter a scale. The following scrolls by.
Insertion point:   Rotation angle <0>:
Command:  Variable name or ? <MENUECHO>:
New value for MENUECHO <0>:
Entity selected is not a polyline
*Cancel*                                    It cancels PEDIT and it draws the bolt.
Command:
```

➡ *NOTE: If you cancel the macro, or if the macro's command prompts are strange, use the [*RESET*] macro, or reset MENUECHO.*

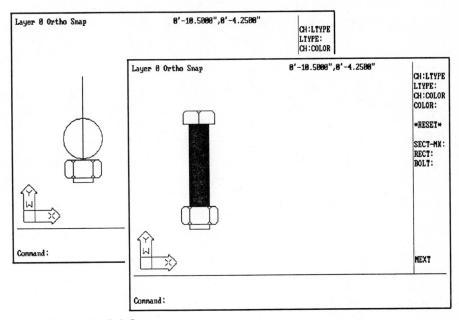

The Parametric Bolt Sequence

[BOLT:] uses the same osnap, <^P>, MENUECHO and lastpoint techniques used in [RECT:], and introduces a few new techniques. It depends on the AutoCAD fact that PEDIT object selection does not alter the contents of the Previous selection. [BOLT:] uses the SCALE block as a way to store a scale value and retrieve it. It moves the block to a location where it can osnap to it, and retrieves the value by osnapping to its CENter point. [BOLT:] uses ERASE and OOPS to temporarily get objects out of the way to avoid finding the wrong objects. Again, the following is not the complete code — it merely shows how the macro works.

Annotated [BOLT:] Macro

```
[BOLT:   Pick 2 endpoints and enter scale to create a bolt.]
^C^C^C^P+                         ^P suppresses commands.
LINE;\\;                          Prompts for the two endpoints.
INSERT SCALE S;\@ 0               Prompts for Scale and Inserts the SCALE block.
SETVAR MENUECHO 3;+               Suppresses everything possible.
INSERT NUT S @ CEN,QUI @          Presets the NUT scale by Osnapping to the SCALE block.
 @ MID,QUI @;+                    Insert point for NUT. Rotates it to the line's MIDpoint.
ERASE L ;                         Gets the NUT out of the way.
MOVE L ;@ MID,QUI @               Moves SCALE to the line's MIDpoint.
OOPS;+                            Restores the NUT.
ERASE QUA,QUI @ ;                 Gets the SCALE out of the way.
PEDIT MID,QUI @ Y E I ;^C+        Turns line into a pline. Resets lastpoint to its start point.
OOPS                                                Restores SCALE.
PEDIT END,QUI @ W MID,QUI @ CEN,QUI @;;+            Changes pline's width,
                                                    Osnapping it to SCALE.
INSERT HEAD S MID,QUI @ CEN,QUI @ @ MID,QUI @       Inserts HEAD like NUT.
ERASE P ;                                           Erases SCALE.
SETVAR MENUECHO 0
```

When you are done with [BOLT:], END your drawing. Ending will save IA-MENU.MNU with your drawing. When we reload the drawing, it will automatically find and load IA-MENU.

Ending Your Drawing and Saving the IA-MENU.MNU.

```
Command: END                      End to save the drawing.
```

Summing Up Menu Macros

The [BOLT:] macro is a working example of how much power you can put into a macro. To develop good macros, you need to carefully work out the drawing sequences that you want to automate. When you write menu macros, your command syntax must be exact. Use your drawing editor interactively as a testbed so that you know what options and input parameters are expected in your macros. Write your sequences down. Make your mistakes in the drawing editor. It is a lot easier to work out the sequences in the drawing editor, *then* type them into your text editor when you think you have them down pat. Here are some notes from users on menu macros.

Make sure you are creating simple ASCII files for your menus and macros. These are sometimes called DOS text files, programmers mode, or nondocument files. Use existing menu items as templates. It is often easier to overtype or copy complex text like commas, control characters and brackets [ ] than to type anew.

Look for tricks that you have picked up using AutoCAD, like the sequence LINE;^C that resets the last point @ to the end of the last line drawn. It is great for inserting blocks at the end of a line.

Start new macros with three ^C^C^Cs to cancel the previous command. Use the MULTIPLE command modifier for simple single or last command repeats. Use an asterisk *^C^C^C at the beginning of macros for automatic repeating. (You also can use *<^X>.) Give all your menu items [LABELS], including blank [ ] lines.

Be careful not to leave any extra spaces at the end of the line; AutoCAD reads spaces the same as <RETURN>s. Watch out for extra blank lines. Never use two spaces in a row. You can't see them to count them. Use one space and then semicolon <RETURN>s for subsequent ones.

Set your defaults. You never know what was used last before your macro. It is good practice to explicitly set defaults, modes and settings, like text styles, if they are important for your macro to function.

Use the SELECT command to automatically pause for a selection set. Use SELECT to make the set and then pass the set to other editing commands via the Previous option. Look for ways to use osnaps as tools in macros, like using rotating block inserts to get correct angles. When you use *intelligent* blocks in macros, give your blocks and macros unique yet explanatory names. DESK1 and [DESK2] don't say much. DeskEXEC and [DeskREG] are more descriptive.

If you want more in-depth information on how to write and organize macros (and want more example macros), we recommend the book CUSTOMIZING AutoCAD (New Riders Publishing).

Next — Behind the Scenes With Menus

After this brief tour of macros, you have two screen menu pages of working macros. The next chapter shows you how menus are structured and how to assign your macros items to other devices, including icon menus and tablet menus.

Chapter 19

Tailoring Your Menu System

ANATOMY OF AutoCAD'S MENU

How a Menu Is Put Together

So far, you have been using a simple automatic [NEXT] paged screen menu for your menu macros. As you add more commands to your menu, you need a way to organize your menu system. This chapter will take you on a behind-the-scenes tour of AutoCAD's ACAD.MNU system. We will show you how AutoCAD controls and assigns menu pages to different devices like the tablet, buttons, icon, and pull-down menus. Then, we will show you how you can add menu macros to ACAD.MNU, not only to the screen menu, but by modifying the tablet menu and the other device menus. We will also show you how to use slides to make icon menus. Finally, we will provide you with a custom menu that expands the previous chapter's menu. We will show you how to control menu paging with your menu macros and how to integrate the custom menu into the ACAD.MNU.

The Benefits of Tailoring Your Menu System

You gain several productivity benefits from modifying AutoCAD's menu system or from tailoring your own menu system. You can save time and effort by simply assigning frequently used macros, like toggling an intersection osnap, to one or two buttons on your pointing device. Or you can use pages of symbols to make inserting symbols into the drawing faster and more accessible. You can improve your productivity by assigning these symbol macros to your tablet (as well as to your screen) menu. By designing your menu pages and assigning them to the appropriate device, you can group your own drawing applications by task instead of AutoCAD functions, making your drawing more straightforward and efficient. If this convincing argument has you excited enough, you may want to jump directly to the book CUSTOMIZING AutoCAD (New Riders Publishing) for the complete story. Or read on for a good introduction to menu structure.

How to Use Menu Device Macro Examples

This chapter, like the previous chapter on menu macros, shows you the different *types* of modifications you can make to your menu system. The macros that we provide are *examples* of the kinds of control that you can exercise over AutoCAD's menu system by assigning macros to menus and by assigning menu pages to different devices. We will show you how to use the special menu codes that control menu paging and menu assignment. Symbol macros are usually more effective for you if they are on your tablet, so try assigning them to your tablet menu instead of the default screen menu. As you work with these examples, look for the type of menu modification that will help you.

After you have worked with these menu assignment examples, we will show how to build a more complex set of screen menu pages and control the menu paging by using special menu paging codes *within* your menu macros. Again, if you are using the IA DISK, these menu macros are provided in the IA-MENU2.MNU file and several .TXT files. The .TXT files are text files you can merge into a copy of the ACAD.MNU file. We encourage you to use these menu macros to see how menu paging works. You can use these examples as models of how to automate your own drawing macros.

Menu System Tools

You can use the same two commands, SHELL and MENU, that you used in the last chapter. Or you can use your [EDIT-MNU] macro to automate menu editing. In addition, you will use the SCRIPT, MSLIDE, and VSLIDE commands. These commands are accessible through the [UTILITY] screen menu. MSLIDE and VSLIDE are commands for making and viewing slides. Select the [SLIDES] menu item on the [UTILITY] screen menu to find them.

Setup for Looking at Menu Systems

For most of the chapter you will be working with IA-ACAD.MNU, a copy of ACAD.MNU. To get started, make sure that you have your trusty text editor set up to be able to SHELL out of the drawing editor to edit or look at the text menu files. Otherwise, you'll have to exit AutoCAD to edit or read the menu text files with your editor. If you are uncertain about your editor setup, see the previous chapter.

In order to protect your standard ACAD.MNU file, make a copy of ACAD.MNU in the \IA-ACAD directory with the name IA-ACAD.MNU. Find your original ACAD.MNU file so you can copy it. We assume it is in your \ACAD directory. If not, ACAD.MNU is supplied in a \SOURCE subdirectory on your original AutoCAD Support Disks. By copying it to IA-ACAD.MNU, you won't modify your original menu file when you modify IA-ACAD.MNU. If you are using the IA DISK, several of the menu macro modifications are already provided as text files. Rather than create the menu macros, you only need to merge them into the IA-ACAD.MNU file, using the exercises as a guide.

Before you start AutoCAD, make a copy of ACAD.MNU and look at it.

Copying and Looking at ACAD.MNU

```
C:> CD \IA-ACAD
C:\IA-ACAD> COPY \ACAD\ACAD.MNU IA-ACAD.MNU          Find and copy your ACAD.MNU.

C:\IA-ACAD> NE IA-ACAD.MNU                    Starts our editor, NE.
                                              Use your editor to look at IA-ACAD.MNU.
```

Use your editor's PAGE-UP, PAGE-DOWN and SEARCH to move around in the menu.
Be careful to NOT alter it yet.

Previously, you looked at (and modified) different menu devices with single menu pages (or single menu items). Single page menus serve simple applications. When you have more than two or three pages, it becomes a nuisance to flip through pages. Most applications need a more extensive, structured menu. While it is a general purpose, not an application-specific menu, the ACAD.MNU provides an example of menu structure. Learn from it, and then go on to develop your own more efficient application-specific menus.

How ACAD.MNU Is Organized

ACAD.MNU is organized by devices and menu pages. Three asterisks precede the device name; ***SCREEN indicates the screen as a device. Two asterisks precede a page name; **LAYER precedes the layer menu page. As you move through the following exercise examples, use your editor to search for the ***DEVICE and **PAGE names.

The standard AutoCAD menu begins with the ***BUTTONS (and identical ***AUX) section, followed by ***POP1 and the other POP-ups. Then come the ***ICON and ***SCREEN sections, followed by ***TABLET1 through ***TABLET4. AutoCAD supports 18 devices in Release 9, Release 10, and later versions. The TABLET is four devices, and POP-ups are up to ten devices. (The ACAD.MNU has eight pop-ups.) Take a look through the menu and see if you can find the different device sections. (It is a long file so don't get discouraged!) The following is a list of AutoCAD's devices.

```
***BUTTONS
***AUX1
***POP1
***POP2
***POP3
***POP4
***POP5
***POP6
***POP7
***POP8
***POP9
***POP10
***ICON
***SCREEN
***TABLET1
***TABLET2
***TABLET3
***TABLET4
```

Menu Devices

The menu devices available to you in AutoCAD are the screen, tablet, buttons, pull-down (or pop-up), icon, and auxiliary devices. If you do not assign a device name in a menu file, AutoCAD assigns the macros to the screen, like the IA-MENU in the previous chapter. The buttons menu assigns macros to mouse or digitizer puck buttons. The tablet menus assign commands to your digitizer tablet. An auxiliary device is another electronic box that plugs into your computer. There are only one or two on the market, and they require an ADI driver. You can define pull-down and icon menus with Release 9, Release 10, and later versions of AutoCAD. They are treated as separate devices from the standard screen menu (device).

The Default Device(s)

We have been treating the screen as if it was the default menu device. The truth is that the screen, tablet and buttons are all active as defaults. Any of these devices can access as many menu items as it has lines, boxes or buttons. For example, when you made your menu macros (in the last chapter), you could have called your menu macros by using a different device. If your digitizing device has more than two active buttons, you could have called a menu macro item just by hitting one of the buttons (other than your pick button). Since we didn't explicitly assign the menu macros to the screen, AutoCAD defaulted them to the screen, but they were also active on other devices.

How Menu Pages Work

A menu structure is created by dividing the menu up into pages. The single page structure that you saw in the previous chapter is the default. AutoCAD automatically creates pages with [NEXT] menu items. But it leaves the division of items between pages up to chance and the number of items your particular video can display. You can control menu page divisions.

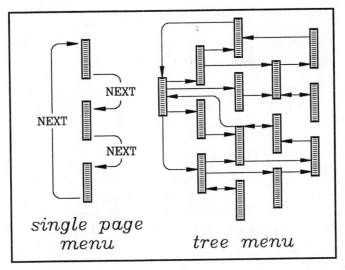

Menu Paging

Naming Menu Pages

You can break menus into named pages of commands and macros by labeling each page with a unique name. You distinguish this page name or label from other lines in a menu by using two leading asterisks **, like **LAYER. The format is **name, where name is any name you like. AutoCAD uses this label to find and activate the menu items as a set. You tell AutoCAD which page to load with the $ menu special character code. Since you are working with a screen menu, you use a $S. The format is $S=pagename.

Assigning Menu Pages to Devices

How do you assign menu pages to different devices? First, you break up your menu into **pages, then you assign a page, or pages, to a device with $= codes. The execution of a $= code is called a *menu call*. Each device has its own code. $S= assigns a menu page to the screen. $B= assigns a menu page to your buttons (pointing device). Here are the menu device assignment codes.

```
CODE                    ACTION
$S=                     Screen menu
$P1= thru $P10=         Pull-down screen menus 1 thru 10
$B=                     Buttons menu
$T1= thru $T4=          Tablet areas 1 thru 4
$I=                     Icon menu
$A1=                    Aux Box 1
```

A name following the device code, like $B=pagename, will send the named page to that device.

➥ *NOTE: Do NOT use a semicolon as a <RETURN> following a page name call. In some cases, like $S=NAME;+, AutoCAD will not recognize it as a <RETURN>. Use a <SPACE>, like $S=NAME +.*

Menu Page Order

The key to menu structure is not where you put **pages, the *key* is which $ codes call what pages. An AutoCAD menu structure is determined by the page structure and what devices you assign those pages to. If you organize your own menu, it is your own organization that will help you keep your page assignments straight. AutoCAD doesn't care!

The order of menu ***devices and **pages is not particularly important. You can place pages in any order you want, but you need to be careful not to duplicate any **page or ***device names in a menu file. AutoCAD will only recognize the first name. *Menu **pages are completely independent of the device section under which they are listed.* The code $S=OSNAPB will load **OSNAPB to the screen as intended, but any menu item can load or restore any page to any device. You can just as easily write $B=OSNAPB to send the **OSNAPB screen to the ***BUTTONS.

Then what are ***device labels for? Device labels are specially reserved names that AutoCAD uses to default load each device with the first page following its device label. When AutoCAD loads a menu, it looks for each device label. AutoCAD loads each device with those items that follow its label, up to the next ***device or **page.

The ***SCREEN Menu

Let's examine the standard AutoCAD ACAD.MNU to see the menu devices and pages and how menu pages are directed to specific devices. If you have been browsing through the menu, return to the ***BUTTONS device section at the top of the menu. Then, find the ***SCREEN section. The *root* page of the screen section is called **S. It has a short simple name because it is referenced in numerous items.

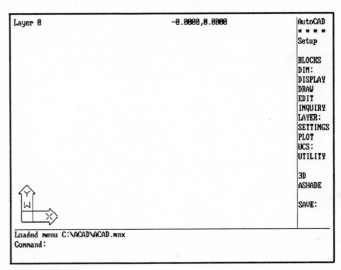

Screen Menu Root Page

Looking at the ***SCREEN Device Menu

The top of your IA-ACAD menu should show the buttons device:

```
***BUTTONS
;
$p1=*
^c^c
^B
^O
^G
^D
^E
^T
```

Search for the characters ***SCREEN to find the screen device and **S page:

```
***SCREEN                   This is the device.
**S                                  This is the default screen page, named S.
[AutoCAD]^C^C$S=X $S=S $P1=POP1 $P3=POP3              Restores **S and **X to screen,
                                                     ***POP1 and ***POP3 to pop-ups.
[* * * *]$S=OSNAPB          Call the **OSNAPB page to the screen.
[Setup]^C^C^P(progn(prompt "Loading setup...   ")(load "setup")) ^P$S=X $S=UNITS
                            Blank line.
```

```
[BLOCKS]$S=X $S=BL
[DIM:]$S=X $S=DIM ^C^CDIM
[DISPLAY]$S=X $S=DS
[DRAW]$S=X $S=DR
[EDIT]$S=X $S=ED
[INQUIRY]$S=X $S=INQ
[LAYER:]$S=X $S=LAYER ^C^CLAYER          Calls **X and **LAYER and executes LAYER.
[SETTINGS]$S=X $S=SET
[PLOT]$S=X $S=PLOT
[UCS:]$S=X $S=UCS1 ^C^CUCS
[UTILITY]$S=X $S=UT
                                         Blank line.
[3D]$S=X $S=3D
[ASHADE]^C^C^P(progn(setq m:err *error*)(prin1))(defun *error* (msg)(princ msg)+
(setq *error* m:err m:err nil)(princ))(cond ((null C:SCENE)(vmon)+
(if (/= nil (findfile "ashade.lsp"))(progn (terpri);+
(prompt "Please wait...  Loading ashade.  ")(load "ashade")+
(menucmd"S=X")(menucmd"S=ASHADE")(setq *error* m:err m:err nil))(progn(terpri);+
(prompt"The file 'Ashade.lsp' was not found in your current search direc-
tories.")+
(terpri)(prompt "Check your AutoShade Manual for installation instructions.");+
(setq *error* m:err m:err nil)(princ))))+
(T (setq *error* m:err m:err nil)(menucmd "S=X")(menucmd "S=ASHADE")(princ))) ^P
                                         Blank line.
[SAVE:]^C^CSAVE
```

The default **S screen menu (sometimes called the *root* menu) consists
mostly of menu page calls. The [DRAW] item is typical. It does nothing but
call the **DS (draw menu) and **X pages. Items that execute a command,
like [LAYER:], are indicated by a colon. This colon is simply part of the
label and is Autodesk's convention for identifying command macros. Let's
look more closely at the [LAYER:] macro. It's obvious that it calls the
**LAYER page that you've been looking at, and that it executes a LAYER
command, but what is the **X page? And how can you call two screen
menu pages at one time?

How Overlaying Pages Work

Did you ever wonder at how the [LAST], [DRAW], and [EDIT] menu items
always appear at the bottom of many screen menu pages? Simple. Look
at the typical [LAYER:] menu item. It can call two screen menus at once
because AutoCAD provides a means to control overlaying menu pages.
Any menu page name, like **X, can include a line number, like **X 3.
This tells AutoCAD to load the menu page at screen menu box (line)
three, leaving the first two items unchanged. Look at **X and **LAYER.

Looking at **LAYER Over **X Over **S in Screen Menus

Find **X and then **LAYER and look at them. First search for **X.

```
**X 3
                              Blank line.
                              Blank line.
                              Blank line.
                              Blank line.
                              Blank line.
                              Blank line.
                              Blank line.
                              Blank line.
                              Blank line.
                              Blank line.
                              Blank line.
                              Blank line.
                              Blank line.
                              Blank line.
                              Blank line.
[__LAST__]$S= $S=
[  DRAW  ]^C^C$S=X $S=DR
[  EDIT  ]^C^C$S=X $S=ED
```

Now search for **LAYER.

```
**LAYER 3
[DDLMODES]'DDLMODES
[LAYER:]^C^CLAYER
[?]? *
                              Blank line.
Make
Set
New
ON
OFF
[Color]COLOR $S=X $S=LACOLOR \$S=X $S=LAYER
[Chroma]^C^CVSLIDE chroma
[ Restore]'REDRAW
[Ltype]LTYPE $S=X $S=LALT \$S=X $S=LAYER
Freeze
Thaw
```

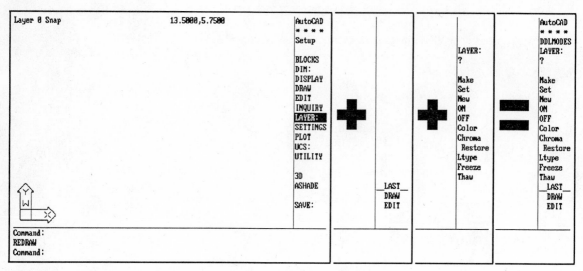

*[LAYER:] **LAYER Over **X Over **S*

The standard AutoCAD screen menu is designed to be 20 items long, but the **X menu has only 18 items. It, like virtually all ACAD.MNU screen menus, is coded with a 3 to load at box three. This leaves the top two items in the **S root screen menu on the screen. [AutoCAD] and [* * * *] items remain on the screen and the **X menu *overlays* the rest of the **S page.

But why is **X mostly just blank lines? **X is frequently called a footer page, and is designed to be typically overlaid by specific pages, such as **LAYER. That is why the **S menu's [LAYER:] item called **X before **LAYER. Notice that **LAYER is a shorter page than **X. That lets **LAYER overlay the blank lines of **X, leaving the [_LAST_], [DRAW] and [EDIT] footer items in place. Almost all AutoCAD screen menu calls include **X or **S.

➥ *NOTE: The standard AutoCAD ACAD.MNU has many unlabeled items and blank lines. We recommend that you label all items in your own menus. It's too easy to accidently add or delete a blank line, and it's hard to differentiate items. Use [ ] for blank lines and [label] all items. Number all your button labels and tablet items. Labeling makes it easier to read and maintain your menus.*

Transient Paging in Macros

It is often convenient to have lists of menu choices such as color, linetype names or a list of settings, but it is a nuisance to have to manually flip through menu pages to find them. Since you can insert page changes at any point in any macro, you can automatically have pages available when you need them.

Let's examine how this menu paging works. In the following menu excerpts, the page codes and labels will be shown in bold type (but you don't need to type in any changes). The ACAD.MNU aperture setting page demonstrates labeling and switching menu pages and automating page choices in macros.

Looking at Transient Paging

Search for **SET (the page called by [SETTINGS] on the root screen menu.
Look at the [APERTUR:] item. It calls **X and **APERTURE.

```
**SET 3
[DDEMODES]'DDEMODES
[DDRMODES]'DDRMODES
[--------]
[APERTUR:]$S=X $S=APERTURE ^C^CAPERTURE
[AXIS:]$S=X $S=AXIS ^C^CAXIS
[BLIPS:]$S=X $S=BLIPMODE ^C^CBLIPMODE
```
                                    The rest of the **SET page follows.

Search for the **APERTURE page and look at it.
```
**APERTURE 3
[APERTUR:]'SETVAR APERTURE
[PICKBOX:]'SETVAR PICKBOX

[1]$S= $S= 1
[2]$S= $S= 2
[3]$S= $S= 3
[4]$S= $S= 4
[5]$S= $S= 5
[6]$S= $S= 6
[7]$S= $S= 7
[8]$S= $S= 8
[9]$S= $S= 9
[10]$S= $S= 10
[15]$S= $S= 15
```
                Quit your editor back to AutoCAD.

The [APERTUR:] item calls both **X and **APERTURE. You've seen how this works, but since it calls two menus, the **APERTURE settings items need to restore two pages to return the screen menu to its previous settings page. The aperture items could each restore **X and **APERTURE.

But AutoCAD offers a better way to get back to any previous menu page. AutoCAD saves the eight last-used menu page names. You can step back through each one by using a $S= without a name, like [Last]$S=. The **APERTURE page uses the $S= last technique in each of the above items with two $S= items. Start up AutoCAD and start a new drawing called MENUTEST. Set it equal to IA-PROTO (the prototype from the last chapter). Let's see how it works.

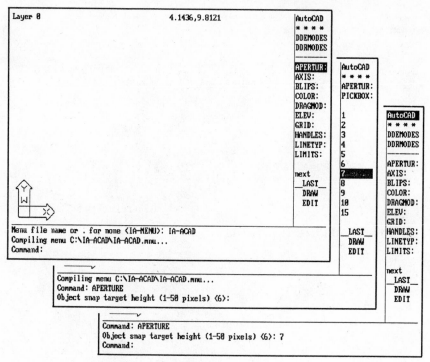

**SET to **APERTURE Page and Back Automatically*

Testing Transient Paging

Quit your text editor to leave your IA-ACAD.MNU unchanged.
Start AutoCAD with the IA.BAT file.

```
Enter selection: 2           Edit an EXISTING drawing named MENUTEST=IA-PROTO.
Loaded menu C:\IA-ACAD\IA-MENU.mnx      Last chapter's menu automatically loads.
```

```
Command: MENU                              Load your newly copied menu.
Menu file name or . for none <ia-menu>: IA-ACAD
Compiling menu C:\IA-ACAD\IA-ACAD.mnu...    The menu recompiles and loads.

Select [Settings]        It flips to the settings **SET page.
Select [APERTUR:]        It flips to the **APERTURE page.
Command: APERTURE        And executes the command.
Object snap target height (1-50 pixels) <6>:    Select [7].
                         It flips back to the settings menu.

              Try it again and reset it to 6.
```

Notice that these items all place the $S= page change code at the beginning. Putting the page change at the beginning insures that the page change will be made even if an error occurs.

Adding Menu Items to ACAD.MNU

Often when you begin tailoring your menu system, it is easiest to add a few items to ACAD.MNU. Later, you can create your own custom menus. You can add your own macros to ACAD.MNU quite easily. In the following exercises, we will show you how to add macros to the different devices in your IA-ACAD.MNU copy of ACAD.MNU.

If you need to add more than a few macros to the standard AutoCAD menu, you should either create your own custom menu or organize your additions as one group of pages at the top or bottom of the ACAD.MNU file. If you simply sprinkle your macros throughout the ACAD.MNU, you will have a tough time merging them into the new ACAD.MNU when you update to the next version of AutoCAD. See CUSTOMIZING AutoCAD (New Riders Publishing) for complete details on integrating your menus.

Adding Menu Items to the Screen Menu

The following exercise shows you how to add your edit macro to the root menu page. Just copy the same [EDIT-MNU] macro that you set up in the previous chapter. (If you set it up to include your editor's name and menu filename, change the filename here to IA-ACAD.MNU.) First quit your text editor; don't save the file. Reload your editor with the unchanged IA-ACAD.MNU copy of ACAD.MNU. This ensures that you're working with a clean copy, and no accidental changes were made in our travels. We show additions to existing menu files in bold text.

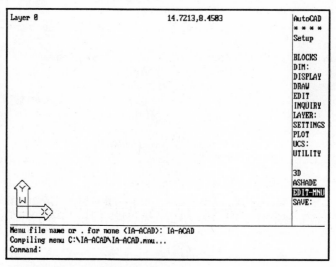

Modified Root Screen Menu Page

Modifying the **S Screen Menu

```
Command: SHELL                    Access your text editor.
DOS Command: NE IA-ACAD.MNU              Starts our editor, NE.
                    Use your editor to edit IA-ACAD.MNU.
```

Search for ***SCREEN to find the **S page.
Add your [EDIT-MNU] macro to the bottom of the page just above [SAVE:]. You'll have:

```
***SCREEN
**S
[AutoCAD]^C^C$S=X $S=S $P1=POP1 $P3=POP3
[* * * *]$S=OSNAPB
[Setup]^C^C^P(progn(prompt "Loading setup...   ")(load "setup")) ^P$S=X $S=UNITS
                    And the rest of the **S page, ending with:
(setq *error* m:err m:err nil)(princ)))+
(T (setq *error* m:err m:err nil)(menucmd "S=X")(menucmd "S=ASHADE")(princ))) ^P
[EDIT-MNU ]^C^C^CSHELL \MENU ;          Add the macro.
[SAVE:]^C^CSAVE
**X 3
```

Save the IA-ACAD.MNU file and exit your editor back to AutoCAD.

Now, load the menu and test it. Select the draw, osnaps and layer items we've looked at to see the **S, **X and other menu pages in action. Then test your [EDIT-MNU] macro.

Testing the Screen Menu [EDIT-MNU] Macro

```
Command: MENU                                  Load your newly modified menu.
Menu file name or . for none <IA-ACAD>: <RETURN>
Compiling menu C:\IA-ACAD\IA-ACAD.mnu...       The menu recompiles and loads.


Select [* * * *]             Calls the **OSNAPB page.
Select [AutoCAD]             Restores the **S root screen.
Select [LAYER:]              Calls the **X and **LAYER pages and LAYER command.
Select [__LAST__]            Uses $S= to restore previous (root) page.


Select [EDIT-MNU ]                   Access your text editor.


Command: SHELL                       It issues the SHELL command.
DOS Command: NE IA-ACAD.MNU          Type the command that starts your text editor.
```

Make any necessary corrections, save and end the editor, then SHELL returns you to AutoCAD.

```
                                  Where the macro continues with the menu command:
Command: MENU Menu file name or . for none <IA-ACAD>:
Compiling menu C:\IA-ACAD\IA-ACAD.MNU...      Reloads the modified menu.


Command: SAVE           Save as IA-PROTO to make IA-ACAD the new default menu.
```

Your screen should look like the Modified Root Screen Menu Page illustration (above). The [EDIT-MNU] item should be second from the bottom of the screen. The rest of the original screen menu pages are unaffected.

The single menu item that you add to the root page could just as easily be a call to a set of custom menu pages added to the screen menu. Such a menu item can call a custom page which may have items branching to other custom pages. Or, the root page item can be a MENU command to load your own custom menu (like the IA-MENU) instead of the ACAD.MNU. Swapping items back and forth between a custom menu and the standard ACAD.MNU is a good alternative to extensive additions to the ACAD.MNU. Later in this chapter we will show you how to add four custom menu pages to the ACAD.MNU screen menu.

➡ *NOTE: If you end AutoCAD to edit your menu file, be sure to save or copy it to the \IA-ACAD directory and use the MENU command to manually reload it each time we edit it in this chapter.*

➡ *TIP: When writing menus, use a standard template page to handle page setups and ensure that they are all the same length. A template is just a blank ** label followed by 18 (or 20 or as many as you need) blank labels [ ].*

➡ *TIP: If you do modify the ACAD.MNU extensively, you don't want to have to update pages scattered throughout ACAD.MNU with each new release of AutoCAD. Duplicate any pages you want to modify and place the copies above the body of the unmodified menu. Then you can delete the body of the ACAD.MNU and append the new one when you get updates. When you add to ACAD.MNU, check for duplicate ***device and **page names. If there are duplicate ***device and **page names, the first occurrence overrides all others.*

The ***TABLET Menu

One of the first customization steps that many users take is to add their own customized macro blocks to their tablet menus. In effect, you can load your symbol library onto your tablet menu. After you have done this, you can modify the standard TABLET.DWG to create your own tablet template with your symbols to overlay your digitizing tablet.

The standard AutoCAD tablet menu sets aside one section, called ***TABLET1, for this type of customization. Since we haven't looked at the tablet menu before, use the following exercises as a guide to look at ***TABLET1 and ***TABLET2 to see what the tablet menu looks like. These next three exercises examine the tablet menu and add a macro to ***TABLET1. They do not require that you have a tablet menu configured on your system, but you do need to be configured for the standard AutoCAD tablet menu to *test* them. (See Appendix C to configure the standard tablet menu.)

Looking at ***TABLET1 in IA-ACAD.MNU

Select **[EDIT-MNU]**   Access your text editor.
Command: SHELL
DOS Command: **NE IA-ACAD.MNU**   Start *your* text editor.

Find ***TABLET1:

```
***TABLET1
[A-1]
[A-2]
[A-3]
[A-4]
```

```
[A-5]
[A-6]
[A-7]
[A-8]
```
And so on, to [A-25].
```
[A-25]
[B-1]
[B-2]
[B-3]
[B-4]
```
And it continues through [H-25], followed by 25 lines of semicolons.

The standard AutoCAD tablet menu starts with 200 wide open, blank but nicely labeled items, inviting your customization efforts. The column numbers (1-25) and row letters (A-H) correspond to the markings on the standard AutoCAD tablet template. The last 25 items (row H) are all semicolon <RETURN>s without numbered labels.

➡ *TIP: If you find the last 15 of these <RETURN> items annoying (we do), replace them with blank, numbered labels. We often accidently hit them when trying to access the pull-down menus.*

Find the ***TABLET2 section. See if you can identify the items where they appear on the AutoCAD Template on your tablet. (If you don't have a template, see appendix C for a tablet illustration.) They start at [J-1] with HIDE and the first row ends at [J-11] with 'REDRAW. We show the first two items.

Looking at ***TABLET2 in IA-ACAD.MNU

Still in your text editor, search for ***TABLET2.

```
;                        The last line of ***TABLET1.
***TABLET2
$S=X $S=HIDE
$S=X $S=VPOINT VPOINT;;
```

As these show, adding tablet macros is like putting macros in a screen menu except you have to keep track of the tablet box numbers. Modifying them can be tricky because unlike the ***TABLET1 section, they lack numbered labels. If you modify them and accidently delete one or add a new line, it will throw the rest of the menu section off by one box.

Adding Macros to the Tablet Menu

Box numbers are numbered sequentially within each ***TABLET section. They lay out on the tablet itself row by row, starting from the top left box of each section. In your fully customized menus, the number of rows and columns in each section is up to you. The standard AutoCAD ACAD.MNU uses arbitrary letters (A-Y) along the left side, and numbers (1-25) across the top to identify the positions on the tablet itself. The following illustration shows the Tablet1 area of the standard tablet template drawing. It shows the [D-12] box where we are going to add a macro.

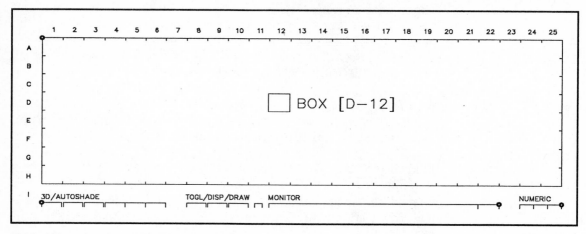

Tablet1 Template Area With Target Macro Box

The SECT-MK Block Macro

The SECT-MK block that you made in the last chapter is a good block macro (symbol) candidate for the tablet menu. Remember that this macro menu item (as a screen menu item) looked like this:

```
[SECT-MK: ]INSERT SECT-MK S (getvar "DIMSCALE") \\\ATTEDIT ;;;;L A 0 ;
```

It uses the SECT-MK block from the previous chapter or from your IA DISK. Make sure that you have the SECT-MK.DWG in your IA-ACAD directory, then add the SECT-MK macro at position [D-12].

Modifying the ***TABLET1 Menu

Still in your text editor, search for D-12.
Edit the ***TABLET1 section as shown below.
The numbered lines not shown are left unchanged.

```
[D-8]
[D-9]
[D-10]
[D-11]
[D-12 SECT-MK: ]INSERT SECT-MK S (getvar "TEXTSIZE") \\\ATTEDIT ;;;;L A 0 ;
[D-13]
[D-14]
```

Save IA-ACAD.MNU and exit your editor back to AutoCAD.

```
Command: MENU Menu file name or . for none <IA-ACAD>:        [EDIT-MNU] continues.
Compiling menu C:\IA-ACAD\IA-ACAD.MNU...              And reloads the modified menu.
```

To test it, you must be configured for tablet area one. If not, see Appendix C for instructions for setting up the standard AutoCAD tablet template. Then try the SECT-MK macro.

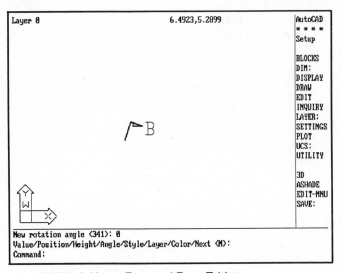

Sect-Mk Block Macro Executed From Tablet

Testing SECT-MK on the Tablet

```
Select [D-12 ]                          Try SECT-MK by picking the twelfth box in the fourth row.
Command: INSERT Block name (or ?) <SCALE>: SECT-MK
                                        The lock insertion scrolls by. Pick insert point and angle, then:
Enter attribute values
Enter letter: <?>: B                    Enter character (third backslash).
Command: ATTEDIT

                                        Attedit scrolls by and rotates the text to 0 degrees.
```

When you execute the SECT-MK block macro from the tablet, it functions just like it did from the screen menu.

You can easily create a mirror image hand block and add another tablet menu item. Whether you add one symbol macro to the tablet or 200, or even design a completely new tablet, the process is the same. The design, layout and symbols are yours. You can have multiple **named pages of tablet items, and change pages or swap parts of pages just like screen menu items.

Adding to the Standard Tablet Template Drawing

After you have implemented your macros in the tablet menu, you can create a template or modify the standard TABLET.DWG by adding the symbol drawings that you want in the appropriate boxes. The standard menu's individual tablet boxes are 0.4 x 0.4. If you want to make your items larger, you can make each tablet menu item two boxes, or four boxes. If you use multiple boxes like this, don't forget to add the macro to the corresponding menu item labels in the tablet menu itself. The attdef, help and change items on the standard menu are examples of this. If you create your own totally custom tablet, you can make the boxes any size you want.

If you haven't looked at the tablet menu, it's TABLET.DWG on your original AutoCAD Bonus/Support disk. You can load and modify it like any drawing. It has two helpful background layers that you can turn on. Layer BOXES provides a box grid and layer NUMBERS identifies the box numbers. (NUMBERS may have an obsolete T1-nn numbering system. If so, ignore it.)

If you have modified your tablet template, you can plot it out. If you are just modifying and using the TABLET1 area, plot it as a window at 1:1 and lay it under the clear area in the standard template. If you are modifying the entire tablet menu, plot the whole thing. Unless you change the size, location or overall pattern of the areas, you don't need to reconfigure your tablet.

Adding Macros to a Buttons Menu

The buttons are always at your fingertips. You can simultaneously execute a macro and pick its first point. Button menus are efficient and dynamic. Many users overlook the advantage of adding a few macros to their cursor buttons.

Buttons are the most personal menu devices. Experiment to find what you like. Choose the menu items that fit your needs. Like screen menus, you can have multiple **named pages of button items but if you have more than a couple of pages, it's hard to keep track of them.

The following exercise shows how to add two macros to your cursor buttons. The specific digitizer (or mouse) buttons used for the menu items depend on your equipment. In the examples, we'll refer to the second button item as [B2]. Button two means the second active button, excluding your normal *pick* button. If your normal pick button is numbered with a 1, then [B2] means the button numbered with a 3! A two-button mouse has no [B2], only a pick button and [B1]. Any items in excess of your available buttons are simply ignored.

The original ***BUTTONS section is near the top of your menu file. You saw it when you looked at the screen menu. Let's modify it by adding two new macro items to the top. The first macro picks an osnap intersection or endpoint. The second macro issues the line command and simultaneously picks a point.

Modifying the ***BUTTONS Menu

```
Select [EDIT-MNU ]                              Access your text editor.
Command: SHELL
DOS Command: NE IA-ACAD.MNU                      Start your text editor.
```

Search for ***BUTTONS. Add the new lines [B1] and [B2] as shown:

```
***BUTTONS
[B1 ]INT,ENDP \                                 Add first macro.
[B2 ]LINE \                                      Add second macro.
;
$p1=*
^c^c
^B
^O
^G
^D
^E
^T
***AUX1
```

Save IA-ACAD.MNU and exit your editor back to AutoCAD.

```
Command: MENU Menu file name or . for none <IA-ACAD>:      [EDIT-MNU] continues.
Compiling menu C:\IA-ACAD\IA-ACAD.MNU...           And reloads the modified menu.
```

```
Select [B2 ]                      It issues a LINE command.
Command: LINE From point:         And picks the first point.
To point:                         Pick a few more points, and make an intersection.
To point:
To point:
To point: INT,ENDP of             Pick an endpoint with [B1]. It Osnaps and picks the point.
To point: INT,ENDP of             Pick an INTersection with [B1]. It Osnaps the point.
To point: <RETURN>
```

Pull-Down Menus — AutoCAD's Special Interface

Pull-down menus (pop-ups) are specially implemented AutoCAD menus that pull down to overlay a portion of your display. They are dynamic in nature. They only appear when they are opened, and disappear as soon as another action is taken. Unlike the screen menu, pull-downs borrow temporary space from the drawing.

Each of the pull-down menu positions are separate devices in the menu file. There are ten positions on the display for pull-downs, so there are ten device names: ***POP1 through ***POP10. Like other devices, the

***labels identify the defaults. You can access any number of **pages, just like screen menus. Like the screen page code $S=, pull-downs are loaded using $P1= through $P10= page codes. The ten positions are shown in the screen shot, Pull-Down Menu Locations.

How Pull-Downs Work

Pull-downs work differently from other devices. They need to be *opened* to be used. Using $P2=NAME loads **NAME to the P2 position, but it does not display it. You must use an asterisk * in combination with a $P code to tell AutoCAD to open a pull-down. $P2=* causes AutoCAD to display whatever is currently loaded to the POP2 device. Menu item toggling also works with pull-downs, but you need to remember to explicitly open them if you want them displayed.

Of course, you also can open a pull-down by moving the pointer up to the status area of the display and picking the pull-down currently loaded to that portion of the status line.

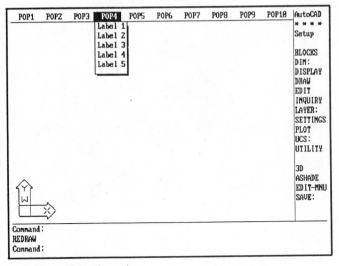

Pull-Down Menu Locations

If your video supports pull-downs, you can customize them. First, find the ***POP4 and ***POP5 device menus and take a look at these menus. They make extensive use of transparent commands to call display commands and to display icon menus and dialogue boxes.

Looking at Transparent Commands in ***POP4 Menu

```
Select [EDIT-MNU ]                          Access your text editor.
Command: SHELL
DOS Command: NE IA-ACAD.MNU                  Start your text editor.
```

Find the ***POP4 and ***POP5 sections:

```
***POP4
[Display]                                   Just a label.
[Redraw]'redraw                             A transparent redraw.
[~---]                                       A greyed-out dashed label.
[Zoom Window]'zoom w
[Zoom Previous]'zoom p
[Zoom All]^C^Czoom a
[Zoom Dynamic]'zoom d
[~---]
[Pan]'pan
[Dview Options...]^C^C$i=dviewi $i=*        Calls and opens the DVIEW icon menu.
[Vpoint 3D...]^C^C$S=X $S=VPOINT3D $i=3dviews $i=*
[~---]
[Plan View (UCS)]^C^Cplan;;
[Plan View (World)]^C^Cplan wo
[~---]
[Set Viewports...]^C^C$S=X $S=vports $i=vporti $i=*   Screen and icon VPORTS menus.
                                            Blank line.
***POP5
[Settings]
[UCS Dialogue...]^C^C$S=X $s=ucs1 dducs     Screen menu and dialogue box.
[UCS Options...]^C^C$S=X $S=ucs1 $i=ucs $i=*
[UCS Previous]^C^CUCS P
[~---]
[Drawing Aids...]'ddrmodes
[Entity Creation...]'ddemodes
[Modify Layer...]'ddlmodes
                                            Blank line.
***POP6
```

Exit your editor back to AutoCAD.

```
Command: MENU Menu file name or . for none <IA-ACAD>:      [EDIT-MNU] continues.
Loading menu C:\IA-ACAD\IA-ACAD.MNU...   And reloads the unmodified menu.
```

Try several of the items from ***POP4 and ***POP5 as you look at the code.

If you look at the use of transparent command macros in these menus, you will see that they do not begin with <^C>s. The <^C> cancels any pending command. If you issue a transparent command like 'ZOOM when no other command is pending, the leading apostrophe causes no problem. 'ZOOM functions as both a transparent and a normal zoom.

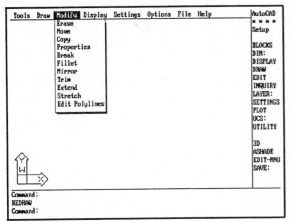

**POP3 Menu*

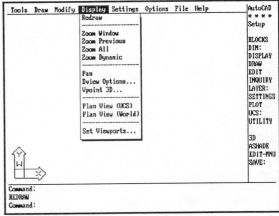

**POP4 Menu*

Notice that each menu page ends with a blank line. This is not required, but a blank line or even a blank [ ] *will* cause a POP menu page to end.

Adding Macros to Pull-Down Menus

Pull-downs are best for single-shot operations and settings, particularly transparent settings, because the menu disappears as soon as it is selected or as soon as any other action is taken.

Try adding a page of transparent settings to create a ***POP9 menu. These macros are all variations on a transparent SETVAR; for example, setting aperture, pickbox, and ortho mode. If you are using the IA DISK, you have these macros already pre-built as POP9.TXT. All you need to do to create a ***POP9 menu is to merge this text just above the ***ICON Menu. If you are not using the disk you need to type in the macros. ['SetVars] is the menu bar label.

Adding Pull-Down Settings to the ***POP9 Menu

Select [EDIT-MNU]   Access your text editor.
Command: SHELL
DOS Command: **NE IA-ACAD.MNU**   Start *your* text editor.

 Merge the POP9.TXT file into the menu as shown.

 Type in the POP9 menu page.

Add the ***POP9 page just above the ***ICON section label.

```
***POP8
[Help]
[Help]'help
```
                                                      Blank line.

```
***POP9
['SetVars]
['REGENAUTO ON ]'SETVAR REGENMODE 1
['REGENAUTO OFF]'SETVAR REGENMODE 0
['APERTURE     ]'SETVAR APERTURE 6 'SETVAR ;
['PICKBOX      ]'SETVAR PICKBOX 2 'SETVAR ;
[~--]
['SNAP ANG/BASE]'SETVAR ORTHOMODE 1 'SETVAR SNAPBASE @ 'SETVAR SNAPANG
['SNAP BASE    ]'SETVAR SNAPBASE @ 'SETVAR ;
['SNAP normal  ]'SETVAR SNAPBASE 0,0 'SETVAR SNAPANG 0
[~--]
['OS INT,ENDP  ]'SETVAR OSMODE 33 I
['OS NONE      ]'SETVAR OSMODE 0
['OS NEAREST   ]'SETVAR OSMODE 512
[--]
[HIGHLIGHT ON ]'SETVAR HIGHLIGHT 1
[HIGHLIGHT OFF ]'SETVAR HIGHLIGHT 0
[DRAGMODE AUTO ]'SETVAR DRAGMODE 2
[DRAGMODE OFF  ]'SETVAR DRAGMODE 0
```
                                                      Blank line.
```
***icon
```

Save IA-ACAD.MNU and exit your editor back to AutoCAD.

Command: MENU Menu file name or . for none <IA-ACAD>:   [EDIT-MNU] continues.
Compiling menu C:\IA-ACAD\IA-ACAD.MNU...   And reloads the modified menu.

Pull-down ['SetVars]   Pull down the menu by moving the cursor up to the status line.
                              The pull-down line labels should appear. Highlight and select
                              ['SetVars].

Try the settings.

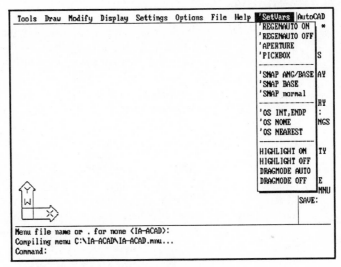

The New Pull-Down 'SetVars Menu

Look at the labels. The settings with a single quotation mark ' in their labels are fully transparent. Notice the difference in the *greyed out* [~--] labels versus the [--] labels.

The [HIGHLIGHT] and [DRAGMODE] items use a transparent SETVAR to avoid disturbing pending commands, but they do not take effect until the next command starts. These macros are useful for dealing with large blocks and large selection sets, which drag poorly and take a long time to highlight. Use these macros to turn drag and highlight off.

The [REGENAUTO OFF] is useful if you are doing a block redefinition that otherwise forces a regeneration. The [REGENAUTO ON] macro turns regenauto back on.

Try the ['APERTURE] and ['PICKBOX] macros during object selection. Their immediate effect is to change the pickbox and aperture size in heavy traffic. The 'OS items let you transparently reset a running osnap. Try the ['APERTURE] and ['OS NEAREST] items while you are in a drawing command to see how they suspend the command. The 'SNAP items are macros that have the advantage of not causing a redraw as they relocate the snap base point to the lastpoint with @, and rotate the snap angle.

Play around with the ['SetVars] menu. If you find any macros that you like and find useful, use them in your own menu. You can use the same procedure that we used to create the ***POP9 menu to create other pull-down menus such as 3D system variables.

SLIDES and ICON Menus

Next, let's look at ICON menus. Icon menus use groups of AutoCAD slides as graphic labels. See the slides exercises in chapter 15 if you need a refresher on slides. Icon menus have the advantage of showing pictures to help you choose menu items. You have seen this type of menu in AutoCAD's use of the hatch and text icon menus. Before we look at icon menus, we need to look at slides.

Icon Menus Are Made From Slide Library Files

Slides were originally designed for giving slide show presentations of AutoCAD drawings. These slide shows were (and are) controlled with SCRIPT files. Now, slides have the important use of storing images for icon menus. To avoid cluttering your disk with the dozens of slide files that a few icon menus would need, slides are grouped and stored in *name*.SLB (Slide LiBrary) files. When you display an icon menu, you are displaying slides from a named slide library file. The standard file is ACAD.SLB. Try using the VSLIDE command to display one of the slides from the hatch icon menu.

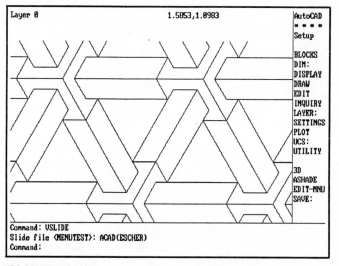

ESCHER Slide

Using VSLIDE to Display a Slide From a Slide Library

```
Command: VSLIDE
Slide file <MENUTEST>: ACAD (ESCHER)          Displays the ESCHER slide from ACAD.SLB.
```

To display a slide from a library, you give the library file name and then the slide name in parentheses. To display a slide stored as an individual .SLD file, give the slide file name.

How to Make a Slide Library File

Icon menus use slide libraries that are created by AutoCAD's SLIDELIB.EXE program. You can create your own slide library files for your icon menus by using this same program.

Steps to Making a Slide Library File

■ Make all the needed slides.

■ Create an ASCII text file (the example is called SLDLIST.TXT) listing each slide *name* (not name.SLD) on a separate line. When you make the file, do not include any extra <RETURN>s or <SPACE>s. Make sure you <RETURN> after the last name.

■ Run the SLIDELIB.EXE program. (You can run via the SHELL command.) Use the following example to see how a library named IA-SLIDE.SLB is created.

```
Command: SHELL

DOS Command: \ACAD\SLIDELIB IA-SLIDE <SLDLIST.TXT
SLIDELIB 1.1  (2/10/88)
(C) Copyright 1987 Autodesk, Inc.
All rights reserved
```

If all went well, you should be able to display the slides from your library file.

➡ *TIP: When you make slides for icon menus, keep your images simple. Simple slides display much faster than complex ones.*

To see how to call a slide library file from an icon menu, let's go back and look at the IA-ACAD.MNU file again.

ICON Menus

An ICON menu is written just like any other pull-down menu except for its labels. You need to load the device with a $I=pagename and then display it with $I=*. However, icons use the label [ ] differently. Icon labels supply AutoCAD with the name of the slide to show in the box. Each label corresponds to one box on the screen. These boxes are automatically arranged in groups of 4, 9, or 16. If the label is in the form *libraryname(slidename)*, then the named slide from the named library is displayed as an icon.

If you put a space as the first character in the label, AutoCAD treats it like an ordinary label. AutoCAD displays any label text in that item's screen box instead of a slide. You can use this label technique to show a MORE to the user, guiding access to additional pages of icons. Try out the hatch icon menu, then examine its code.

Trying the [Hatch] Menu

Pull-down **[DRAW]**	Pull down the [DRAW] menu (POP2).
Select **[Hatch]**	It displays a screen full of hatch icons.
Select **[Next]**	Select [Next] twice and select any pattern:

```
Command: hatch
Pattern (? or name/U,style) <default>: ansi31          We selected ansi31.
Scale for pattern <1.0000>:                            Cancel it. Or use it.
```

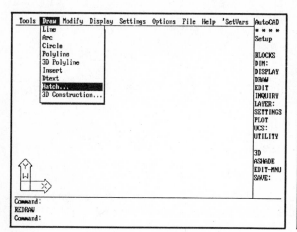

Draw Pops Hatch

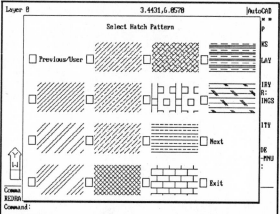

Hatch Pops Hatch1 Icon

The macros following the icon menu labels work just as you would expect them to. The [Next] line is an example of using a text label in an icon screen. The [MORE] macro loads the second menu to the ***ICON device, then displays it.

Looking at the ***ICON **Hatch Menu Code

Select **[EDIT-MNU]**   Access your text editor.
Command: SHELL
DOS Command: **NE IA-ACAD.MNU**   Start *your* text editor.

Find ***POP2 and look at the [Hatch] macro.

```
[Hatch...]^C^C$i=hatch1 $i=*
```

Find ***icon section, then skip to the **hatch1 page.

```
***icon
**poly
[Set Polymesh and Polyline Variables]
[acad(pmq)]'setvar surftype 5
[acad(pmc)]'setvar surftype 6
[acad(pmb)]'setvar surftype 8
```

Skip past the **poly and several other pages to find the **hatch1 page.

```
**hatch1
[Select Hatch Pattern]
[ Previous/User]^c^chatch
[acad(ansi31)]^c^chatch ansi31
[acad(ansi32)]^c^chatch ansi32
[acad(ansi34)]^c^chatch ansi34
[acad(ansi35)]^c^chatch ansi35
[acad(ansi33)]^c^chatch ansi33
[acad(ansi36)]^c^chatch ansi36
[acad(ansi37)]^c^chatch ansi37
[acad(ansi38)]^c^chatch ansi38
[acad(box)]^c^chatch box
[acad(brass)]^c^chatch brass
[acad(brick)]^c^chatch brick
[acad(clay)]^c^chatch clay
[acad(cork)]^c^chatch cork
[ Next]$i=hatch2 $i=*
[ Exit]^c^c
```

Blank line.

```
**hatch2
[Select Hatch Pattern]
[acad(cross)]^c^chatch cross
[acad(dash)]^c^chatch dash
```

Exit your editor back to AutoCAD.

```
Command: MENU Menu file name or . for none <IA-ACAD>:      [EDIT-MNU] continues.
Loading menu C:\IA-ACAD\IA-ACAD.MNU...   And reloads the unmodified menu.
```

The [Hatch] pull-down item is a menu page change. First $i=hatch1 loads the **hatch1 page to the icon device, then the $i=* displays it. Except for their labels, the hatch icon macros themselves are simple hatch commands and pattern names. [Next] is just like [Hatch] except it loads and displays **hatch2. That's all there is to it!

Icon menus are great for symbol libraries. For more details on how to create icon menus, see CUSTOMIZING AutoCAD (New Riders Publishing).

Integrating Menus Into the ACAD.MNU

You can integrate your own custom menu, such as the previous chapter's IA-MENU.MNU, into ACAD.MNU, IA-ACAD.MNU or any menu. We have just a few recommendations. Make each page only 18 items long so it will be easy to merge into the ACAD.MNU. Then add the number 3 to each of your **page labels, like ACAD.MNU. This allows the [AutoCAD] and [* * * *] items to always stay at the top of the screen menu area.

Organize your custom pages with one main page that accesses each of the other pages directly or through other pages. This gives your custom menu a single point of entry. Then you can access your custom pages with a single item added to the **S (root) page of the ACAD.MNU. You can replace the **S screen page [EDIT-MNU] (just above [SAVE:]) with a call to **IA-MENU and merge the whole IA-MENU2.MNU into the end of IA-ACAD.MNU.

➡ *TIP: Design your page footers to always get back to the main menu and restore settings.*

➡ *TIP: Use menu page switch macros as control points to make settings and enforce defaults for your application program.*

This is our last pass through menus and menu devices. You have traversed the entire ACAD.MNU, adding a macro here and a macro there. We hope that we have given you an idea of the range of options and the types of additions you can make to the standard AutoCAD menu to adapt it for your own use. Whether you ended or quit your drawing, you saved your working menu files with your text editor. All AutoCAD needs to use a menu is the compiled .MNX file. But if you want to adapt and modify a menu for your own use, be sure to save its .MNU ASCII files. You never changed your original ACAD.MNU (you copied it) and it's still the default menu loaded by the default ACAD.DWG prototype. Your IA-ACAD menu is the default loaded by your IA-PROTO prototype.

Summing Up Menus

As you start to consider modifying and adding to AutoCAD's standard menu, think about the type of modifications that will save you time and money. Two areas that many users start with are customizing their set-up procedures and adding their own standard symbols to their tablet menus. But any drawing task that will save you time is a candidate for some tailoring. You can standardize; set up, format and fill in data for title sheets; place text in your drawing; locate, draw and insert components, assemblies and materials; automate dimension components; and annotate components. All these tasks are common to most drawing applications.

To develop a good menu, you need working macros and working symbols. Use your text editor interactively to develop and test your working macros and symbols. Your menu layout depends on what you want to achieve in your application. If you are uncertain about layout, use a simple paging structure. Use different pages for different operations. How you set up and use your pages and devices are the keys to developing a successful menu. For complete details on developing and integrating menus, see CUSTOMIZING AutoCAD (New Riders Publishing).

When you write complex menu items, test your command syntax extensively. Use your drawing editor as a testbed so that you know what options and input parameters are expected in your macros. Write your sequences down. Make your mistakes in the drawing editor, not in your text editor. If you think your macros are getting too complex, take a look at the next chapter on AutoLISP.

On to AutoLISP

If you followed the menu macros closely, you may have noticed that we made use of getvar, an AutoLISP function, in some of the menu items. The next chapter provides a closer look at AutoLISP, AutoCAD's built-in programming language. There are some commands that you can do in AutoLISP that you can't do with simple macros, and there are many macros that you can make simpler and more straightforward by using a few AutoLISP functions. It's on to AutoLISP!

CHAPTER 20

Using AutoLISP for Drawing Automation

What Is AutoLISP?

AutoLISP is a dialect of the LISP language that was derived from XLISP. AutoLISP coexists with AutoCAD itself within the AutoCAD program. Every programming language, including AutoLISP, provides some general programming tools. These include ways to structure the flow of a program, tools to manipulate program data, and means to input and output data to computer devices.

In addition to these general tools, AutoLISP has AutoCAD-specific tools. These tools let it access and update AutoCAD's drawing entity data, access AutoCAD's tables for blocks, layer, views, styles and linetypes, and control AutoCAD's graphics screen and device input.

Although the macros you created in the last two chapters were powerful and complex, they were just sequences of standard AutoCAD commands. Adding AutoLISP to your macros and writing AutoLISP programs lets you create custom commands which can prompt, instruct, and provide choices and defaults just like AutoCAD's standard commands.

The Benefits of Using AutoLISP

What are the benefits of using AutoLISP?

AutoLISP is your direct pipeline to AutoCAD. With it, you have access to AutoCAD drawing entities, reference tables, and to passing files in and out of AutoCAD.

Using AutoLISP in Macros

By using AutoLISP in your menu macros, you can save data in variables, process that data, and send it back to AutoCAD. Points, distances, and other values can be stored, calculated, compared, and used to draw with. You can control your drawing environment through AutoCAD system variables by storing the system variables, prompting with drawing status, and changing and restoring the settings. You can change system settings transparently during commands for more responsiveness. You can access and extract entity data, use the data in programs, and even modify entities transparently.

What You Can Get From This Chapter

This chapter will give you an idea of the types of things that you can do to enhance your menu macros with AutoLISP. You can't learn AutoLISP in one chapter. In fact, there is a whole book, INSIDE AutoLISP (New Riders Publishing) to teach it to you. This chapter will give you a few simple tools and techniques. But its main purpose is to give you a feel for what's involved and to encourage you to go on and learn to customize your system with AutoLISP.

The first focus of the chapter is to show you the power that just a few AutoLISP functions, like the GET functions, setq, getvar and setvar, can add to your macros. There are some menu macros that are impossible to write without these AutoLISP functions. We will show you how to get and set variables in menu macros, and we will provide you with a drawing setup that partially automates setting drawing scale in a series of menu macros.

The second focus of the chapter is to create some working examples of AutoLISP programs. As you write macros using AutoCAD's menu and command syntax, you reach a trade-off point where it is often easier to use AutoLISP to write your programs than to use the standard commands. To show you how to do this, we will use AutoLISP to re-work the [RECT:] and [BOLT:] menu macros that you used in the earlier chapters. Notice that AutoLISP gives you direct access to drawing variables and data. It is easier, for example, to just get the drawing corner points for the rectangle macro using AutoLISP than to try to coax them out of the AutoCAD ARC used in the original macro.

Finally, we will show you some of the math, logic, and conditional functions built into AutoLISP that can extend the power and capabilities of your drawing macros. These functions will be rolled up into a type of AutoLISP function that acts like an AutoCAD command. You'll learn to create your own custom commands.

AutoLISP Tools

You need only one tool to work with AutoLISP: your trusty text editor. Your text editor should be set up as in the previous two chapters; see chapter 18 if you need setup information. Use SHELL, as you have done previously, to take you from AutoCAD to your text editor where you can create and edit AutoLISP menu macros and AutoLISP program files.

Setup for Looking at AutoLISP

If you are using the IA DISK, the AutoLISP menu macros and AutoLISP files are already provided as text files. Rather than create the menu macros and commands, you only need to load the files to look at them with your editor, and use them within AutoCAD to see how they work.

The examples work with Release 9 or 10. If you have problems, are uncertain about your version of AutoLISP, or need information on setting up for AutoLISP, see Appendix B.

Let's move on to the first exercise. It shows you how to enter AutoLISP variables and expressions by typing them directly into the drawing editor, and it explains our format for interpreting the AutoLISP responses that you see at the command line.

Creating an AutoLISP Command

Let's start by looking at a little AutoLISP. You are going to make a new AutoLISP command, called HOLE, by typing two lines of input at the command line. This AutoLISP command will automate the standard CIRCLE command to draw repeating holes using your specified diameters and center points.

In the exercise sequence, you will see the words *Lisp returns:*. We use this line to show AutoLISP's backtalk. You won't see those same words on your screen, but you should see the line or lines that follow it on your screen.

Start a new drawing called LISPTEST. Type the input shown in bold. Don't panic if AutoLISP returns a 1> during the input. This is just AutoLISP telling you that you need another right parenthesis. Keep typing the input as shown. After you get the C:HOLE response, try the command by typing in the command name HOLE.

Making an AutoLISP Command Called HOLE

Enter selection: **1**   Begin a NEW drawing named LISPTEST.

Command: **(defun C:HOLE () (setq rad (/ (getdist "\nDiameter: ") 2))**   Type in.
1> **(while T (command "CIRCLE" pause rad)))**   Continue typing.
Lisp returns: C:HOLE

Command: **HOLE**   Test the command.
Diameter: **1**   Enter a diameter.

```
CIRCLE 3P/2P/TTR/<Center point>:              Pick a point.
Diameter/<Radius>: 0.500000000000000         AutoLISP returns the radius.
Command: CIRCLE 3P/2P/TTR/<Center point>: <^C>   It repeats until cancelled.
```

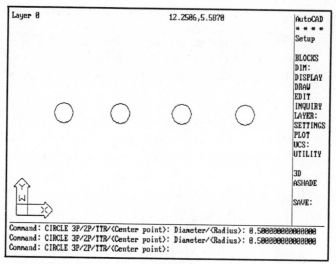

Holes Drawn With AutoLISP Command

If all went well, you should have one or more holes on your screen, depending on how many times you repeated the command.

If you keep getting a 1>, type a) and a <RETURN>, then hit a <^C> and try inputting the AutoLISP variables and expressions again.

In AutoLISP, opening parentheses in expressions must have matching closing parentheses. Failure to close a parenthesis will give you a prompt like 1> or 2>. The AutoLISP error prompt form is n> where *n* indicates how many closing parentheses are missing.

Any AutoLISP opening quotation marks must have matching closing quotation marks. If you get an n> error prompt and adding additional parentheses doesn't help, then you left out a quotation mark. Type a single " and then type as many)) as you need. The hardest part of AutoLISP is getting matching pairs of parentheses and quotation marks!

If you have any other problems, see Appendix B.

The new HOLE command you made will remain available until you quit or end this drawing. We will explain the AutoLISP syntax used in the command and explain how it works. Later in the chapter, you will learn how to store an AutoLISP-made command.

AutoLISP Variables and Expressions

When AutoLISP was first introduced into the AutoCAD program, it wasn't even called AutoLISP. It was just called "Variables and Expressions" for building macros. Don't let AutoLISP intimidate you. It is often easier to think about AutoLISP as it was originally introduced, providing variables and expressions that you can use in your macros.

Variables

A *variable* is a label used to refer to a changeable value. You use variables every day. The current interest rate on your credit card is multiplied by the outstanding balance every month to see what finance charge will be added to your account. Rate and balance are variables. In AutoLISP, you can attach a value to a variable name and use it in a command or within AutoLISP expressions to perform calculations and make logical decisions.

In the HOLE example that you typed in and tested, rad (for radius) is a variable. It gets a value from the expression that divides the diameter distance in half. This value is passed to the CIRCLE command as the rad (radius) value.

```
(defun C:HOLE () (setq rad (/ (getdist "\nDiameter: ") 2))
(while T (command "CIRCLE" pause rad)))
```

AutoCAD's System Variables

When you change the settings or values of snap, osnap, ortho or when you just pick a point, AutoCAD saves the newly set condition, value or point as a system variable. You have used the SETVAR command to set system variables. You can see all of the current system variable settings with the SETVAR command and a question mark.

Using SETVAR to Look at System Variables

```
Command: SETVAR
Variable name or ?: ?      Gives a listing.
```

```
ACADPREFIX    "C:\ACAD\"                      (read only)
ACADVER       "10"                            (read only)
AFLAGS        0
ANGBASE       0
ANGDIR        0
APERTURE      6
AREA          0.0000                          (read only)
ATTDIA        0
ATTMODE       1
ATTREQ        1
AUNITS        0
AUPREC        0
AXISMODE      0
AXISUNIT      0.0000,0.0000
BACKZ         0.0000                          (read only)
BLIPMODE      0
CDATE         19881128.092910741             (read only)
CECOLOR       "BYLAYER"                       (read only)
CELTYPE       "BYLAYER"                       (read only)
CHAMFERA      0.0000
CHAMFERB      0.0000
-- Press RETURN for more --
```

The SETVAR Display

See the system variables table in Appendix C for a complete listing, along with descriptive comments on the variables.

Variable Types

You can access these system variables and create new variables with names of your own with AutoLISP. If you look closely at the list of system variables in Appendix C, you will see three types of variables: string, integer, and real. (Points are lists of variables.) System variables and any AutoLISP variables that you may create are one of these three types.

- STRING variables have text values placed in quotes to identify the value as a string. For example, the system variable ACADPREFIX is currently "C:\ACAD\". The values "3.1", "FLOOR-3", "-1234", and "The quick brown fox . . ." are all strings.

- INTEGERs are positive or negative whole numbers, without fractions, decimal places or decimal points. AutoCAD often uses values of 0 and 1 to indicate whether a system variable toggle, like SNAPMODE and ORTHOMODE, is turned off (0) or on (1). Integers must be between -32768 and +32767. The values 1, 3234, and -12134 are valid integers.

- REALs are positive or negative numbers with decimal points. In AutoLISP, you cannot begin or end a real with a decimal. If the value is less than 1.0, you must put a 0 before the decimal point (0.123) or you will get "error: invalid dotted pair." Examples of real system variables are FILLETRAD, LTSCALE and AREA. Unlike integers, you can make reals very large or very small. AutoLISP formats reals in scientific notation when the values are very large or very small. Valid reals look like 1.0, 3.75218437615, -71213.7358 and 1.234568E+17.

- POINTs are really AutoLISP LIST variables. A list is one or more values of any variable type grouped within parentheses. The LASTPOINT system variable is a point list with a value such as: (6.500000 1.500000).

Using system variables, you can control many AutoCAD drawing editor settings. You have changed these system settings with the SETVAR command, and you have used the transparent 'SETVAR command to change settings in the middle of another AutoCAD command. You can change some, but not all, of the system variable settings. Certain variables are indicated as *read only* meaning you can only extract, not update, their values.

How to Use AutoLISP to Get and Set System Variables

You can also access AutoCAD's system variables with AutoLISP's getvar and setvar functions. Getvar is a function, not a command. Setvar is the name of an AutoLISP function and also the name of the AutoCAD command. In the last two chapters, you used and set several system variables in macros. The flaw in those macros was that settings were left changed, with their original settings not restored.

With getvar and setvar, you can write macros that get, save, and restore your drawing settings. You already used getvar in the change layer menu macro, [CH:LAYER] that you built.

```
[CH:LAYER ]^C^C^CSELECT AU \CHPROP P ;LAYER (getvar "CLAYER") LAYER \;
```

This [CH:LAYER] macro uses the getvar CLAYER to get and enter the current layer name as a default to the CHPROP command. Look at the macro above. Try some getvar and setvar functions by typing the input shown in the following exercise.

Using Getvar and Setvar Functions to Get and Set System Variables

Continue in your LISPTEST drawing.

Command: **LAYER**	Make a layer named OBJECTS. Leave it current.
Command: **(getvar "CLAYER")** *Lisp returns:* "OBJECTS"	Get the current layer value. The value, the layer name.

```
Command: (setvar "ORTHOMODE" 1)          Reset the ortho value.
Lisp returns: 1

Command: (setvar "CLAYER" "0")           Try to reset layer.
error: AutoCAD rejected function         You can't. It's read only.
Lisp returns: (SETVAR "CLAYER" "0")      The offending AutoLISP function.
```

Expressions

An AutoLISP expression begins with an opening parenthesis and ends with a closing parenthesis. AutoLISP expressions can contain other AutoLISP expressions. You must nest each expression in its own pair of parentheses.

A typical AutoLISP expression has this syntax:

```
(function argument )
```

Here are the rules for the expression game:

- Every expression has opening and closing parentheses.

- Every expression has a function name. The name must immediately follow the opening parenthesis.

- Every expression gets evaluated (executed) and returns a result. The result may be nil, or the last evaluated value.

- Everything in AutoLISP is either True or nil. If something has no value, it's nil. If it has a value, it's True (non-nil).

Functions and Arguments

A *function* is a subroutine that tells AutoLISP what task to perform. Tasks include addition, subtraction, multiplication or division. A function may have any number of arguments or no arguments.

An *argument* provides data to the function. Arguments may be variables, constants, or other functions. Some arguments are flags that alter the action of the function. If you define a function to take an argument, you must provide the function with a value for the argument.

How AutoCAD and AutoLISP Communicate

The opening and closing parentheses allow AutoCAD to distinguish between AutoCAD commands and AutoLISP expressions. Each time AutoCAD detects an opening parenthesis, it passes the entire expression to AutoLISP. AutoLISP evaluates the expression and returns the result to AutoCAD. AutoCAD uses the result and continues.

AutoCAD can cause a problem within AutoLISP when AutoCAD wants a literal text string. There are two places where AutoCAD wants a literal text string: when prompting for text, or prompting for an attribute. A system variable called TEXTEVAL controls the situation. Setting TEXTEVAL to 1 (On) forces AutoCAD to send the expression to AutoLISP for evaluation and print the results (instead of the expression itself).

Using Math Functions in AutoLISP

AutoLISP has several built-in math functions. In the initial HOLE command that you typed, you used a divide function in the expression:

```
(defun C:HOLE () (setq rad (/ (getdist "\nDiameter: ") 2))
(while T (command "CIRCLE" pause rad)))
```

This expression divides the diameter distance that you get by 2 to give you the radius value.

When you talk about AutoLISP functions you say (+ 1 2) evaluates to 3, for example. In algebra, you say 1 + 2 equals 3. This addition example has two arguments, both constants. Arguments are the data for the function. Some AutoLISP math functions, like + - * and /, can have any number of arguments. Some functions require a specific number of arguments, while others require specific arguments, but also take optional parameters. Here is a list of built-in functions that you can use in your macros:

```
(/ arg1 arg2 arg3 ... )     ARG1 divided by ARG2
                              divided by ARG3 ...
(* arg1 arg2 arg3 ... )     ARG1 times ARG2 times ARG3 ...
(+ arg1 arg2 arg3 ... )     ARG1 plus ARG2 plus ARG3 ...
(- arg1 arg2 arg3 ... )     ARG1 minus ARG2 minus ARG3 ...
(1+ arg)                    ARG plus 1
(1- arg)                    ARG minus 1
(abs arg)                   Absolute value of ARG
(exp arg)                   e to the ARG power
(expt base power)           BASE to the POWER
(gcd arg1 arg2)             Greatest Common Denominator
                              of ARG1 and ARG2
```

```
(log arg)                         Natural log of ARG
(max arg1 arg2 arg3 ... )         Maximum of arguments
(min arg1 arg2 arg3 ... )         Minimum of arguments
(rem arg1 arg2 arg3)              The remainder only of ARG1,
                                     divided by ARG2 ...
(sqrt arg)                        SQuare RooT of ARG
```

How AutoLISP Evaluates Expressions

AutoLISP evaluates expressions at the same nesting level, left to right. When a nested expression is encountered, the entire nested expression is evaluated before the next expression on the right. One good thing about having all these parentheses is that you never write a formula that evaluates in a different order than you expect. If all the arguments are integers, the results will be an integer and any fractional part will be dropped. If any argument is a real, the result will be a real. Try some math functions and look at nesting. Type the functions in at the command line.

Using AutoLISP Math Functions

Command: **(+ 1 2.0)**   Returns a real.
Lisp returns: 3.0

Command: **(/ 3 2)**   Drops the .5 remainder.
Lisp returns: 1

Command: **(* 5 (- 7 2))**   The (- 7 2) expression is nested.
Lisp returns: 25

Command: **(setq a 1)**   Assigns the value 1 to a variable.
Lisp returns: 1

Command: **(+ (setq a (* a 3)) (+ a 2))** Assigns variable before second expression.
Lisp returns: 8

Command: **(+ (+ a 2) (setq a (* a 3)))** Uses variable, then reassigns it.
Lisp returns: 14

Making Your Own Variables and Expressions

You create variables by giving a value to a symbol. In the HOLE command, you gave a distance to the symbol rad (for radius) with the expression (setq rad (getdist ...).

AutoLISP automatically assigns data type when you create a variable. AutoLISP variables are completely independent of AutoCAD system variables and their names may duplicate AutoCAD system variable names. Each time you use the variable name or refer to the variable name in a macro, program or expression, the program replaces the variable name with the most recent value assigned to that name.

Variables can be any printable combination of letters and numbers except those reserved because of their special meanings in AutoLISP. There also are some ill-advised characters that may confuse or interfere with AutoLISP when you use them in menu macros. Avoid using the following characters:

```
RESERVED AND ILLEGAL CHARACTERS:    . ' " ; ( ) or <SPACE>
AutoLISP FUNCTIONS:    ~ * = > < + - /
ILL-ADVISED CHARACTERS:    ? ` ! \ ^ or any control character.
```

The Atomlist

There are also AutoLISP function names that you should not use as variable names. The ATOMLIST is an AutoLISP variable that stores all defined functions and variable names. You can see these functions by looking at AutoLISP's Atomlist.

```
Command: !ATOMLIST
(C:RHAND C:LHAND C:WIN LTSCALE C:CROS C:CRSH C:APER C:ICON S1 C:BUBBLE PT3 PT2 P
T1 SCL C:ANT INTERS GRREAD GRTEXT GRDRAW GRCLEAR VPORTS TRANS HANDENT TBLSEARCH
TBLNEXT ENTUPD ENTMOD ENTSEL ENTLAST ENTNEXT ENTDEL ENTGET S'MEMB SSDEL SSADD SS
LENGTH SSNAME SSGET ANGTOS RTOS COMMAND OSNAP REDRAW GRAPHSCF TEXTSCR POLAR DIST
ANCE ANGLE INITGET GETKWORD GETCORNER GETINT GETSTRING GETORIENT GETANGLE GETREA
L GETDIST GETPOINT MENUCMD PROMPT FINDFILE GETENV SETVAR GETVAR  TERPRI PRINC PR
IN1 PRINT WRITE-LINE READ-LINE WRITE-CHAR READ-CHAR CLOSE OPEN STRCASE ITOA ATOF
 ATOI CHR ASCII SUBSTR STRCAT STRLEN PAUSE PI MINUSP ZEROP NUMBERP FLOAT FIX SQR
T SIN LOG EXPT EXP COS ATAN 1- 1+ ABS MAX MIN NOT OR AND > >= /= = <= < ~ GCD BO
OLE LSH LOGIOR LOGAND REM * - + ASSOC MEMBER SUBST LENGTH REVERSE LAST APPEND CD
DDDR CDDDAR CDDADR CDDAAR CDADDR CDADAR CDAADR CDAAAR CADDDR CADDAR CADADR CADAA
R CAADDR CAADAR CAAADR CAAAAR CDDDR CDDAR CDADR CDAAR CADDR CADAR CAADR CAAAR CD
DR CDAR CADR CAAR CDR CAR CONS COND LISTP TYPE NULL EQUAL EQ BOUNDP ATOM NTH PAG
ETB PICKSET ENAME REAL FILE STR INT SYM LIST SUBR T MAPCAR APPLY LAMBDA EVAL *ER
ROR* / QUIT EXIT _VER VER IF UNTRACE TRACE DEFUN FOREACH REPEAT WHILE PROGN FUNC
TION QUOTE READ LOAD SETQ SET MEM VMON ALLOC EXPAND GC ATOMLIST)

Command:
```

The ATOMLIST

AutoLISP will list all user-defined variables and functions and their function names if you type **!ATOMLIST**. The exclamation point tells AutoCAD to return the value of the AutoLISP variable that follows it.

Looking at the Atomlist

Command: **<F1>**	Flip to the text screen.
Command: **!ATOMLIST**	You will see the ATOMLIST display.

A few of these functions are used exclusively by the AutoLISP evaluator and are not intended for users. The rest of the functions are documented in the AutoLISP Programmer's Reference, and most are used in examples in the book, INSIDE AutoLISP (New Riders Publishing).

When you type your variable names, upper or lower case makes no difference. Try to keep your names under six characters since names over six characters require more memory. Don't begin a variable name with a number.

```
INVALID VARIABLE NAMES:                           VALID NAMES:
123 (represents an integer number)                PT1
10.5 (represents a constant real value of 10.5)   txt
ANGLE (redefines the AutoLISP function ANGLE)     ANGL
A(1) (contains invalid characters)                A-1
OLD SUM (contains space)                          OLD_SUM
```

How to Assign Values to Variables

Setq binds a stored value to a variable name. In algebra, you write y=3, but in AutoLISP you enter **(setq y 3)**. Both the = of the algebraic expression and the setq of the AutoLISP expression are functions. Each function binds (sets) the value 3 to the variable y. The opening (left) and closing (right) parentheses form the expression.

After binding a value to a variable name, you can use an exclamation point to supply that value to AutoCAD. The exclamation point identifies the word that follows as an AutoLISP symbol, usually a variable name. When AutoCAD sees the ! character, it passes the variable name to AutoLISP. AutoLISP interprets it and passes its value back to the AutoCAD command processor. You can also use the new variables in other AutoLISP expressions.

Using Setq to Set and ! to Use AutoLISP Variables

Command: **(setq y 2)**   Set variable Y to the integer value 2.
Lisp returns: 2

Command: **!Y**   Send Y's value to AutoCAD.
Lisp returns: 2

Command: **(setq x 3)**
Lisp returns: 3

Command: **(+ x y)**   Use the values in an addition expression.
Lisp returns: 5

Well, you can create variables, assign values to them, and use the values in functions. How do you use these simple variables and expressions to improve and enhance your macros?

Automating a Drawing Setup With AutoLISP

Let's look again at automating drawing setups. The prototype drawing, IA-PROTO, that you created at the start of Part Two took care of most aspects of setup, but several settings are scale-dependent. Some simple variables and expressions can automate scale factors in your drawing setup. The following menu covers the basics of automating a drawing setup using AutoLISP. Use the following macros as a model for macros that you can add to your own setup menus.

The default ACAD.DWG prototype's settings are set for a 12 x 9 sheet for plotting at 1:1 scale. The following menu lets you select your sheet size and scale, then the menu macro computes the correct limits. In this sense, the menu is similar to AutoCAD's setup menu, but it has some enhancements, like setting dimensioning scale (dimscale). The menu uses the dimscale value as a global scale value.

If you are using the IA DISK, you already have this menu on the disk as IA-SETUP.MNU. Just copy the menu to your IA-ACAD directory and examine it with your text editor. If you are not using the disk, read the exercise to see how the menu works. If you want to create the menu with your text editor, it's simpler than it looks. The third and fourth lines of the [**GO**] are copied from the IA-MENU's [*RESET*] macro. Most of the other items are repetitive, so you can just type, copy and edit.

Creating an IA-SETUP Menu With AutoLISP

Continue in your LISPTEST drawing, or start a new drawing named LISPTEST.

Command: **SHELL**   Start your text editor with IA-SETUP.MNU.
DOS Command: **NE IA-SETUP.MNU**   Starts our editor, NE.
                                            Use *your* editor to create or look at IA-SETUP.MNU.

 Just look at the menu.

 Enter these two screen menu pages.

```
***SCREEN
[ SET-UP ]
[  MENU  ]
[=======]
[ Select ]
[ Sheet  ]
[ Size   ]
[=======]
[]
[11 x 17 ](setq x 17.0) (setq y 11.0);$S=SCALE
[]
[22 x 34 ](setq x 34.0) (setq y 22.0);$S=SCALE
[]
[24 x 36 ](setq x 36.0) (setq y 24.0);$S=SCALE
[]
[]
[]
[]
[]
[]
[]
**SCALE
[ Select ]
[ Plot   ]
[ Scale  ]
[=======]
[ 1"=10' ](setq dscale 120.0) SNAP 12 (prompt "Select [**GO**]...^M");
[]
[.25"=1' ](setq dscale 48.0) SNAP 6 (prompt "Select [**GO**]...^M");
[]
[ .5"=1' ](setq dscale 24.0) SNAP 3 (prompt "Select [**GO**]...^M");
[]
[ 1"=1' ](setq dscale 12.0) SNAP 1 (prompt "Select [**GO**]...^M");
[]
[QUARTER ](setq dscale 4.0) SNAP .5 (prompt "Select [**GO**]...^M");
```

```
[]
[  HALF  ](setq dscale 2.0) SNAP .25 (prompt "Select [**GO**]...^M");
[]
[  FULL  ](setq dscale 1.0) SNAP .125 (prompt "Select [**GO**]...^M");
[--------]
[ **GO** ]^c^c^cGRID !dscale ^GAXIS (/ dscale 2) AXIS OFF;+
(setvar "DIMSCALE" dscale) (setvar "TEXTSIZE" (* 0.125 dscale));+
SETVAR COORDS 2 ;ORTHOMODE 1 ;EXPERT 0 ;PICKBOX 3 COLOR BYLAYER;+
LINETYPE S BYLAYER ;ELEV 0 0 FILLET R 0 APERTURE 6 OSNAP NON SNAP R 0,0 0;+
LIMITS 0,0 (list (* x dscale) (* y dscale));+
REGENAUTO ON ZOOM W 0,0 (getvar "LIMMAX") ZOOM .75X REGENAUTO OFF;+
VIEW S ALL LTSCALE (* 0.375 dscale) MENU IA-ACAD ^GAXIS ON
[--------]
```

Save IA-SETUP.MNU and exit to AutoCAD.

Look at the menu before you test it. The first page is simple. Whichever macro you select saves the appropriate sheet dimensions as the variables X and Y, using the AutoLISP setq function. The macros then flip to the **SCALE page. The top part of **SCALE is similar, with a series of scale macros. Notice that each sets SNAP to an appropriate value for its scale. But many other settings are also scale-dependent. To include every scale-dependent setting and command in each scale macro would create a lot of repetition in your menu. It would be hard to update and maintain. So we use setq to save a variable, DSCALE, with the scale value. This DSCALE variable is used repeatedly by the [**GO**] macro, which each scale macro prompts you to select. Before we examine the [**GO**] macro and prompt function, let's test the menu. Now, in the drawing editor, load the menu and try it.

Testing the IA-SETUP Menu

Command: **MENU**   Load IA-SETUP and try it.

Select [24 x 36]   And you see:

```
Command: (setq x 36.0) 36.0
Command: (setq y 24.0)
Lisp returns: 24.0
```

Select [HALF]   And you get:

```
Command: (setq dscale 2.0) 2.0

Command: SNAP
Snap spacing or ON/OFF/Aspect/Rotate/Style <1.0000>: .25
Command: (prompt "Select [**GO**]...

1> ")
```

```
Select [**GO**]...            This is the prompt from the [HALF] macro.
Lisp returns: nil

Select [**GO** ]              And all the settings scroll by.
                              If you have a printer attached, you can hit <^Q> to echo it to print.
                              The last part looks like:

Command: ZOOM
All/Center/Dynamic/Extents/Left/Previous/Window/<Scale(X)>: .75X
Regenerating drawing.

Command: REGENAUTO ON/OFF <On>: OFF

Command: VIEW ?/Delete/Restore/Save/Window: S  View name to save: ALL
Command: LTSCALE New scale factor <1.0000>: (* 0.375 dscale)
Command: MENU Menu file name or . for none <IA-SETUP>: IA-ACAD

Command: QUIT                 Don't save this test drawing.
```

Your menus should look like those in the following screen shots when you test the menu. Your finished screen will be zoomed to an oversize view called ALL, with a grid covering the reset limits.

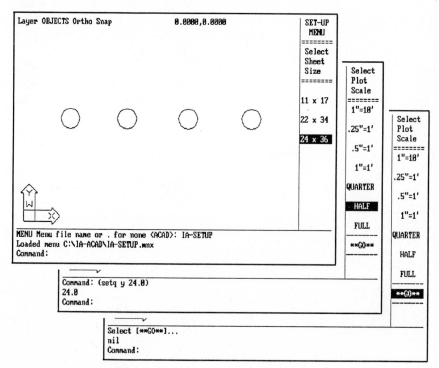

The Setup Screen Menus

The [**GO**] macro may look intimidating, but it is only a series of AutoCAD commands, a few getvar and setvar expressions, and some simple calculation functions. Remember, we saved the scale value as DSCALE. The first two lines of [**GO**] just use this value to set proper grid, axis, dimscale, and textsize (text height) values.

```
[ **GO** ]^c^c^cGRID !dscale ^GAXIS (/ dscale 2) AXIS OFF;+
(setvar "DIMSCALE" dscale) (setvar "TEXTSIZE" (* 0.125 dscale));+
```

Grid is simple, it just uses the !variable format, !dscale. Then the ^G characters toggle grid off until later to save redraws. Axis requires a bit of calculation, using the divide function in the expression (/ dscale 2) to divide dscale by two. The AutoLISP setvar function is used to set DIMSCALE and TEXTSIZE. The AutoCAD SETVAR command could have been used just as easily. The next two lines (not shown here) are the familiar [*RESET*] macro code. Then it continues with the setting of limits, zooming, saving a view, setting LTSCALE, and loading a menu.

```
LIMITS 0,0 (list (* x dscale) (* y dscale));+
REGENAUTO ON ZOOM W 0,0 (getvar "LIMMAX") ZOOM .75X REGENAUTO OFF;+
VIEW S ALL LTSCALE (* 0.375 dscale) MENU IA-ACAD ^GAXIS ON
```

Limits uses the AutoLISP multiply function *, but it needs a coordinate pair, X and Y. In AutoLISP, coordinate points are lists of two or three values, so we use the list function to combine the values. The first zoom retrieves these new limits from the LIMMAX system variable with the getvar function. The second zoom expands the generated area to give elbow room to avoid unwanted regenerations. The last ^G toggles the grid back on.

You can adapt this simple two-page setup menu by adding any other settings or commands that you need. You could add an expression similar to (setq border "SHT-B") to each of the sheet size selections. This expression could save the name of one of a set of standard borders. If you create borders and titleblocks at 1:1 scale in drawing files with names, like SHT-B.DWG, you can add an INSERT command to the [**GO**] macro to insert the border drawing. For example, you would add the following to the [**GO**] macro.

```
INSERT !border 0,0 !dscale ;;
```

You also can make this menu the default menu in the prototype drawing by editing your prototype, loading IA-SETUP.MNU and ENDing it.

How to Add Prompts to Macros

The prompt functions in the scale selections of the menu add prompts to your macros using a very simple text function. It takes one argument, the prompt string:

```
(prompt string)
```

All this does is display its string and return nil. In the menu examples, a ^M (code for <CTRL-M>, the <RETURN> character) is used to force the prompt to a new line.

```
[  HALF  ](setq dscale 2.0) SNAP .25 (prompt "Select [**GO**]...^M");
```

Outside menus, the AutoLISP \n newline code forces a new line:

```
(prompt "\nThis will appear on a new line.\n...and another!")
```

But in macros, the backslash interferes and causes a pause. Use the prompt form shown in the example in your menu macros.

Stopping Point

This completes a first tour of AutoLISP. You have seen that you can enhance your menu macros by just using a few AutoLISP functions, like getvar and setvar to get and set system variables. You can manipulate input values in AutoCAD commands, like dividing a circle diameter value to get a circle's radius value, using built-in math functions in AutoLISP. It doesn't take much to get started with AutoLISP. Just look for the variables or expressions that you need to give your macros an extra push, or to make them one or two steps easier!

This is a good stopping point. If you are going to take a break, END your drawing and save your IA-SETUP menu. In the next series of exercises, you will learn how to enhance your macros by using AutoLISP to get drawing input, and how to create and store an AutoLISP command.

Using Get Functions for Macro Input

One area where AutoLISP can enhance your macros is to get (and control) the input for macro commands. Use the GET family of AutoLISP functions to get drawing input. There is a get function for each major data type. All of the arguments to get functions are optional. The get functions can have a prompt argument to ask a question, or to give an instruction. The prompt can be any string value. All the get functions pause for input. In a menu macro, they require backslashes.

Here is the complete list of get functions that you have to work with:

```
(getangle basept promptstring)        Returns angle from 2 points or typed input.
(getcorner basept promptstring)       Returns 2nd corner of a rubber-banded
                                      rectangle.
(getdist basept promptstring)         Returns distance from 2 points or
                                      typed input.
(getint promptstring)                 Integer.
(getkword promptstring)               Returns one of a list of predefined
                                      key words.
(getorient basept promptstring)       Like GETANGLE but handles non-East base
                                      angle setting.
(getpoint basept promptstring)        Point.
(getreal promptstring)                Real.
(getstring flag promptstring)         String. If FLAG is True, it accepts
                                      <SPACES> in string and requires
                                      <RETURN> to enter.
```

If you were to look at your original HOLE command yet once more, you'd see that you've used the getdist function: (getdist "\nDiameter: ").

```
(defun C:HOLE () (setq rad (/ (getdist "\nDiameter: ") 2))
(while T (command "CIRCLE" pause rad)))
```

The backslash pauses for the input. The "\nDiameter:" is the prompt string. Try a couple of other input functions to get the hang of it. Type the input at the command line.

Using Get Functions for Input to Macros

Enter selection: **1**   Begin a NEW drawing, again named LISPTEST.

Command: **(getangle "Enter angle: ")**
Enter angle: **30**   Or you pick two points to show an angle.
Lisp returns: 0.523599   AutoLISP uses and returns angles in Radians, not degrees.
                               There are 2 x PI Radians in 360 degrees. One degree = 180/PI.

Command: **(* (getangle "Enter angle: ") (/ 180 pi))**   PI is predefined.
Enter angle: **30**
Lisp returns: 30.0

Command: **(setq pt1 (getpoint "Enter point: "))**   Save a point.
Enter point: Pick a point.
Lisp returns: (2.0 2.0 0.0)

Command: **(getangle pt1 "Enter angle: ")** Use it as a basepoint for rubber-banding.
Enter angle: Pick a point.
Lisp returns: 0.96007

```
Command: (getangle pt1 "Enter angle: ")
Enter angle: 30                                    Or you can type it.
Lisp returns: 0.523599

Command: (getstring "Enter word: ")
Enter word: This                                   The first <SPACE> enters it.
Lisp returns: "This"

Command: (getstring T "Enter sentence: ")          T is predefined.
Enter sentence: This is a sentence.                It allows <SPACES>.
Lisp returns: "This is a sentence."

Command: (getcorner pt1 "Enter other corner: ")    Use the base point.
Enter other corner: (5.4375 4.875 0.0)             It rubber bands a rectangle.
```

If you followed the sequences, you noticed that the input automatically becomes the data type requested. Invalid responses that are not the requested data type are rejected. Getstring will accept numbers as string data, and getreal will accept integers, but converts the integers to floating point reals. Using getdist is better than using getreal because you can enter the distance either by picking points, with optional rubber-banding, or by typing values. Getdist treats the distance as a real data type. You can input either decimal or current units, but the input is automatically converted to decimal.

If you use an integer, like 96, within an AutoLISP expression where it expects a real, like 96.0, AutoLISP converts it to 96.000000. If you give an AutoLISP getreal or getdist function input like 96.0, 96. or 96, AutoLISP accepts and converts these values to 96.000000. However, if you use a real within an AutoLISP expression that expects an integer, like the ITOA function, it will cause an error.

Getpoint accepts point input in X and Y coordinates. A Z coordinate is optional. You must initialize getpoint with initget to accept Z values. Recall, that a point (for AutoLISP) is simply a list of two (or three) reals.

How to Use Base Point Arguments and Rubber-Banding in Macros

The getdist, getangle, getorient and getpoint functions can use an optional base point argument. Getcorner must have a base point. AutoCAD uses rubber band lines when you (as a user) show a distance or angle by selecting points. Rubber-banding lets you dynamically display a distance in the coordinates box of the screen. Recall that the distance<angle is displayed in the relative distance coords mode. The getdist, getangle, getorient and getpoint functions all rubber band input

when two points are input or a base point is set. Use an optional base point if you need to tie the point down.

Placing a get function without a base point in the middle of an ordinary AutoCAD command interferes with the normal command's rubber-banding. Try this:

Testing Getpoint Function

```
Command: LINE
From point:                          Pick a point.
To point: (getpoint "Pick it: ")     And your rubber-banding disappears.
```

When you use the keyboard, the get functions automatically pause for input. However, you need to use the backslash character \ to pause the macro for input. Two AutoLISP get functions pose a problem when you use the backslash method of pause control. The getdist and getangle functions offer the user the choice of picking or typing the distance<angle. Typing the input requires only one backslash. If you pick two points, you need two backslashes. If you use these functions, you need to plan ahead and prompt for the input format expected. Base points help avoid this because they need only one pick point or typed input.

Using Get Functions to Enhance a Menu Macro

When you built (or used) the original [RECT:] macro to draw a rectangle, you may have felt the drawing logic was circuitous:

```
[RECT:    Draw rect by 2 corner pts.]^C^C^C^P+
ORTHO OFF LINE;\\;SETVAR MENUECHO 3 SELECT L;;+
ARC @ C MID,QUI @ A 180 ID END,QUI @ ERASE P ;+
COPY L ;@ CEN,QUI @ ID CEN,QUI @ SCALE P L ;@ 2;+
PLINE @ .X @ CEN,QUI @ ;PEDIT L E I ;^C+
PLINE @ .Y @ CEN,QUI @ ;PEDIT L E I ;^CID CEN,QUI @;+
PLINE @ .X @ CEN,QUI @ ;PEDIT L E I ;^CID CEN,QUI @;+
ERASE P ;PEDIT L J M @ @ ;;C ;ORTHO ON SETVAR MENUECHO 0
```

[RECT:] accomplished its goal of drawing a rectangle with only two input points. But it required a lot of trickery, such as using arcs to find the corner points. Why not just *get* the corner points? You can with AutoLISP!

Let's revisit the [RECT:] macro and make it clean and efficient with AutoLISP, using getpoint and getcorner to get the corner points, and listing functions to build the rectangle.

If you are using the IA DISK, you have the new [RECT:] macro in the menu file called IA-LISP.MNU. Copy this file to the IA-ACAD directory, and look at it with your text editor. If you are not using the disk, you will need to create the file and the macro.

Using Get Functions to Make an Improved [RECT:] Macro

Command: **SHELL**   Start your text editor with IA-LISP.MNU.
DOS Command: **NE IA-LISP.MNU**   Starts our editor, NE.
                                                Use *your* editor to create or look at IA-LISP.MNU.

 You have the improved rectangle macro. Just look at it.

 Create the macro by typing into the file.

```
[RECT:    Draw rect by 2 corner pts.]^C^C^C^P+
(setq ortho (getvar "ORTHOMODE")) (setvar "ORTHOMODE" 0);+
(setq ll (getpoint "Enter corner: "));\+
(setq ur (getcorner ll "Other corner: "));\+
(setq ul (list (car ll) (cadr ur))) (setq lr (list (car ur) (cadr ll)));+
(setq menuecho (getvar "MENUECHO")) (setvar "MENUECHO" 3);+
PLINE !LL W 0 ;!LR !UR !UL C;+
(setvar "ORTHOMODE" ortho) (setvar "MENUECHO" menuecho);
+
```

Save IA-LISP.MNU and exit to AutoCAD.

Let's examine the AutoLISP version of [RECT:]. In the first line we make sure ortho is on, using setvar. But whenever you change a system variable you should restore it, so we first get ORTHOMODE with getvar and save it as the variable ORTHO with setq. Next, getpoint gets the first (lower left) corner and setq saves it as LL. Then getcorner gets the opposite (upper right) corner, using LL as the anchor for a rubber band rectangle. It is saved as UR.

The other two corners have to be constructed from these two points. LR (lower right) uses the (first) X coordinate of UR and the (second) Y coordinate of LL. UL similarly uses the X of LL and the Y of UR. Since AutoLISP points are lists of two (2D) or three reals, we use the car, cadr and list functions to construct the points. Car is the function that extracts the first element of a list and cadr the second. The list function then combines these extracted values into new point lists that are saved by setq as UL and LR.

```
(setq ul (list (car ll) (cadr ur))) (setq lr (list (car ur) (cadr ll)));+
```

The rest of the new [RECT:] is similar to the old. We save, change and restore MENUECHO to suppress screen clutter, and restore ORTHOMODE. The PLINE command itself is identical to the old macro. Now try making a few rectangles with it.

Testing an Enhanced [RECT:] Macro

```
Command: MENU
Menu file name or . for none <ACAD>: IA-LISP
Compiling menu C:\IA-ACAD\IA-LISP.MNU...              Loads the new menu.


Select [RECT: ]                         The SETVARs return a few 0's and you get:


Command:
Enter corner:                           Pick a point for (getpoint "Enter corner: ").
           @COM PMT-L = Lisp returns: (7.0 4.5 0.0)
Command:
Other corner:                           Pick a point for (getcorner ll "Other corner: ").
Lisp returns: (8.6875 5.75 0.0)
Command: (7.0 5.75 0.0)     (list (car ll) (cadr ur)) calculates Upper Left.
Command:
Lisp returns: (8.6875 4.5) (list (car ur) (cadr ll)) calculates Lower Right.
Command: 0                              Saves MENUECHO and returns 0.
Command:
Lisp returns: 3                         Sets MENUECHO.


           Then PLINE !LL W 0 ;!LR !UR !UL C; draws the Pline rectangle:


Current line-width is 0'-0.0000"
Lisp returns: 0                         Resets ORTHOMODE.
Lisp returns: 0                         Resets MENUECHO.
```

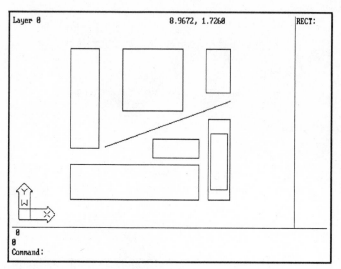

Rectangles Drawn With [RECT:]

The list, car and cadr functions in the new [RECT:] macro are used to build the upper left and lower right corner points. Remember in AutoLISP, points are lists, so let's look at lists to see how they work.

How AutoLISP Lists Work

A LIST is a group of elements of any data type, treated as one expression and stored as a single variable. An AutoLISP list may contain any number of reals, integers, strings, variables, or even other lists. Anything between an opening parenthesis and closing parenthesis is a list. If this sounds hauntingly familiar, it is. An expression is a list! You use lists to organize and process groups of information. Several system variables are lists. The LIMMAX (upper right Limits) system variable, for example, is a list.

Points Are AutoLISP Lists

```
Command: (getvar "LIMMAX")
Lisp returns: (12.0 9.0)    The upper right point of the limits.
```

Other examples of AutoLISP lists are ("A" "B") and ("NAME" 10.0 "DESK" "WS291A").

How to Use List Functions

AutoLISP has many list manipulation functions. [RECT:] uses the functions list, car and cadr. List is simple. It just makes a list of its arguments. Since a list is a group of elements, you need a way to extract the element that you want. Car is shorthand for the first element of a list, and cadr is the second element.

```
(setq ll (getpoint "Enter corner: "));\+
(setq ur (getcorner ll "Other corner: "));\+
(setq ul (list (car ll) (cadr ur))) (setq lr (list (car ur) (cadr ll)));+
```

In the [RECT:] example (list (car ll) (cadr ur))), list created a new point from the car of LL and the cadr of UR. The car function extracted the X coordinate of the lower left LL getpoint and the upper right UR getcorner points. Cdr returns a list of all elements, *except* the first element.

Using the Quote Function

The QUOTE function, which can be abbreviated as a single quotation mark ', is also important. The list function evaluates its contents, then forms a list. The quote function suppresses the evaluation of its expression(s). When it forms a list, it includes its contents literally. Let's look again at list, car, cadr, the similar cdr, and at the quote function. Type the input at the command line to see how these functions work.

Manipulating Lists

Command: **(setq test (list 1 2 3.0))**   Make a list.
Lisp returns: (1 2 3.0)

Command: **(car test)**
Lisp returns: 1   The first element.

Command: **(cdr test)**
Lisp returns: (2 3.0)   The rest of the list. All but the first element.

Command: **(cadr test)**   The 2nd element ...
Lisp returns: 2   the CAR of the CDR.

Command: **(nth 2 test)**
Lisp returns: 3.0   The 3rd element.

Command: **(setq test (list a b c))**   Evaluates A, B and C which are all unassigned
                                                   symbols (variables) with value nil.
Lisp returns: (nil nil nil)   Then it makes a list of three nils.

Command: **(setq test (quote (a b c)))**   Returns the unevaluated symbols.
Lisp returns: (A B C)

Command: **(setq test '(a b c))**   Quote abbreviated.
Lisp returns: (A B C)

AutoLISP has other functions, called caar, caddr, cadar, Nth, and more to manipulate lists. You can use the Nth function to access any element of a list, but watch the numbering. Nth counts 0, 1, 2, 3 ... (*not* 1, 2, 3 ...). This is typical computer counting. Watch your 0's and 1's carefully with AutoLISP functions. All AutoLISP functions do not count the same way.

Other List Functions

AutoLISP has several other functions that you can use to manipulate lists. These are: last, reverse, length, append, and cons. Last will give you the last element of a list. Reverse flips the order of the list. Length returns its length. Append takes any number of arguments, each a list, and merges them into a single list. Cons adds a new first element to a list. See INSIDE AutoLISP (New Riders Publishing) to see how to use these and the other list functions.

How to Create Functions in AutoLISP

You can define your own functions in AutoLISP. You already created a new AutoLISP function called C:HOLE with DEFUN (DEFine-FUNction). Defun defines a function by constructing a structured list of the program statements. Your AutoLISP functions create a local self-contained environment. Data passes into the function's local environment, your program statements use and manipulate the data, then pass the data back to the general AutoLISP-AutoCAD environment.

Before we define a new function, take another look at the first, simple version of C:HOLE.

```
(defun C:HOLE ()
  (setq rad (/ (getdist "\nDiameter: ") 2))
  (while T (command "CIRCLE" pause rad))
)
```

The general form of DEFUN, using HOLE as an example, is:

```
(defun NAME (ARGs / LOCALS)
   PROGRAM STATEMENTS...
)
```

You can make the NAME of a function any name that you wish, with upper and/or lower case characters. Use the same rules that you use for variables. Like variable names, you must avoid using reserved names from the atomlist. If you use a reserved name, you will redefine the original AutoLISP function and the original meaning will be unavailable until you start a new drawing!

C:HOLE has no *args* (arguments) or declared *locals*. We will look at arguments soon. Let's look at the program statements first.

Program statements like (setq rad ...) and (while T ...) are the core of your function. Program statements follow the general rules of AutoLISP evaluation, left to right and inside to out. The results of the last evaluated statement are returned to the global AutoLISP-AutoCAD environment.

You can use your own functions just like you use AutoLISP's built-in functions. This lets you make your programs modular, reusing subroutines. The BOLT function you are about to create is an example of a function using a subroutine, controlled by and receiving its input from another calling function.

AutoLISP's File Format

Sooner or later, you will want to store your functions in external files. You can store AutoLISP expressions and functions in disk files, just as you store menu files. You assign a file extension of .LSP to these files. The .LSP file may contain any number of function definitions and other expressions.

Unlike menus, when you write .LSP files, you do not have to worry about device or page sections, or <SPACES>. Extra lines do not act like <RETURN>s and you do not need the plus sign to continue line characters. Semicolons do not cause <RETURN>s, but indicate comments you can insert for your own information. Precede your headers, comments and explanations with semicolons.

Enhancing the [BOLT:] Macro

Create a BOLT function in a .LSP file. This BOLT function is an improvement on the [BOLT:] macro that you created two chapters ago. The following BOLT.LSP program isn't as complicated as it looks. Half of the code (the parts after the semicolons) are explanatory comments. If you are using the IA DISK, you have this program on disk as BOLT.LSP. You also need the HEAD.DWG and NUT.DWG block files, either from the IA DISK, or from chapter 18. Look at the file with your text editor, then load the file. If you are not using the disk, create the file. You can skip typing the non-bolded comments.

Making and Using an AutoLISP File

Command: **SHELL**	Start your text editor with BOLT.LSP.
DOS Command: **NE BOLT.LSP**	Starts our editor, NE.
	Use *your* editor to create or look at BOLT.LSP.

 You have the BOLT.LSP file to examine.

 Create the BOLT.LSP file.

```
; Draws filled Bolt using HEAD and NUT blocks.
(defun BOLT (diam)
   (setq pt1 (getpoint "\nHead point: "))          ;Get Insert pt.
   (setq pt2 (getpoint pt1 "\nNut point: "))       ;Get Insert pt.
   (command "INSERT" "HEAD" "S" diam pt1 pt2        ;Insert HEAD.
            "INSERT" "NUT"  "S" diam pt2 pt1        ;Insert NUT.
            "PLINE" pt1 "W" diam "" pt2 "W" 0 "" "" ;Draw Pline shaft
   )
);BOLT

(prompt "\nBOLT.LSP loaded.\n")

; end of BOLT.LSP
```

Save BOLT.LSP and exit to AutoCAD.

BOLT.LSP is actually quite straightforward. The diameter is fed to the function as the argument diam. It gets the two endpoints with getpoint, and saves them as PT1 and PT2 with setq. The PT2 getpoint uses PT1 as a base point to drag a rubber band reference line for PT2. Once we have the points and diameter, the rest of the function simply uses AutoLISP's command function to pass the INSERT and PLINE commands, parameters, diameter, and points to the AutoCAD command line.

Function Arguments

Function arguments are variable names you use to refer to the data passed into the function's environment. The number of arguments must match the number of pieces of data passed to the function. The BOLT function has only one argument, DIAM. You execute BOLT by typing (**bolt 1.25**), or any other reasonable value, and the function sets DIAM to 1.25. Multiple arguments are assigned to input in a 1:1 order.

How to Format and Document Your AutoLISP Programs

The indented format in the BOLT example is typical for typing AutoLISP programs, but AutoLISP doesn't care how you format white space (<SPACE>s, <TAB>s and <RETURN>s). The comments following the semicolons show how to document programs so you can still understand them next year. Programs are easier to read if all opening parentheses are either on the same line or vertically aligned with their matching closing parentheses.

Loading an AutoLISP Function

AutoLISP's LOAD function loads the function file much like the MENU command loads menu files. While loading, AutoLISP reads the function definitions and stores them in memory. Other expressions, like the prompt (prompt "\nBOLT.LSP loaded.\n"), are executed while loading. AutoLISP's LOAD automatically assumes the file extension .LSP unless you give it another extension. (AutoLISP does not execute user-defined functions until you execute them.) To load the BOLT.LSP file, type **(load "bolt")**. Try loading and testing the BOLT function.

Using AutoLISP's Load Function

```
Command: (load "bolt")
BOLT.LSP loaded.
Lisp returns: nil
Command: (bolt 0.5)
Head point:
Nut point:
```
Load the file.
The prompt.
The last evaluated expression. PROMPT always returns nil.
Execute the BOLT function, with the #DIAM argument 0.5.
Pick point.
Pick point.
The Inserts and a Pline command scroll by as the HEAD and NUT are inserted and the filled shaft is drawn.

```
Command: !PT1
Lisp returns: (2.37922 7.30479 0.0)
```
Look at the values of the variables.

```
Command: !PT2
Lisp returns: (2.37922 4.43836 0.0)
```

```
Command: !DIAM
Lisp returns: nil
```

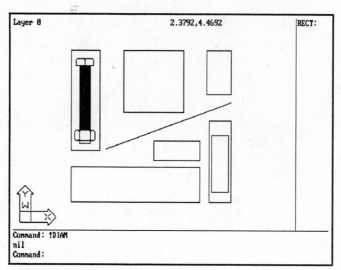

Inserted Head and Nut

If all went well, you should have a screen with an Inserted Head and Nut. You must type the argument as **0.5**, not .5 or you will get an "error: invalid dotted pair" message.

➡ *NOTE: Don't confuse AutoLISP's load function with the LOAD command. AutoCAD's LOAD command loads SHAPE definitions.*

➡ *NOTE: AutoLISP has a feature similar to DOS's AUTOEXEC.BAT files. If AutoCAD finds an AutoLISP file named ACAD.LSP in its program directory, it automatically loads it each time you start a new or existing drawing. Any expressions in the file are executed while loading, and you can define a special S::STARTUP function to autoexecute AutoCAD commands.*

Local vs. Global Arguments

Arguments and other variables used within functions can be *local* or *global*. Locals are variables that you need and use only within the function. Variables must be declared (listed) in the parentheses following the function name in the DEFUN to be local. AutoLISP makes a small localized environment which stores values of the locally defined variables. You usually don't want your function's variables to be global. In most cases, you'll want to put all your internal variables on the local list. Arguments like DIAM are always local whether you like it or not. Local variables have no value outside their parent function, unless they were also set outside the function. If a variable with the same name as a local variable exists outside the function, its value is unaffected by the function and the function is unaffected by it. If you want an argument's value available outside the function, you have to use a different name.

Globals are variables that have a value outside of the function in which they were created, as well as within the creating function. Every variable or function that you create, global or local, goes on the atomlist during the current drawing session. Except for arguments, variables are global unless you declare them local.

➡ *TIP: Use a standard prefix, like #, to indicate global variables.*

Later you'll revise BOLT to make PT1 and PT2 locals, and add a # to DIAM (making it #DIAM) as a global default value for repeated uses of the function. This will give you a working example of local and global variables.

AutoLISP's Command Function Transfers Data to AutoCAD

In the [CH:LAYER] macro, you used the AutoLISP expression (getvar "CLAYER") to return its value directly to AutoCAD. In the AutoLISP revised [RECT:] macro you used !variables in the line

```
PLINE !LL W 0 ;!LR !UR !UL C;
```

to feed saved variable point values to AutoCAD. AutoLISP's COMMAND function provides a much better way of feeding AutoCAD. AutoLISP can instruct AutoCAD to draw, or do anything else you can type. The key is the COMMAND function. It lets you run AutoCAD commands within an AutoLISP statement. Command's format is:

```
(command arg1 arg2 arg3 ... )
```

AutoLISP takes each item of the command's argument list and sends it to AutoCAD. If the argument is an AutoLISP variable or expression, it is first evaluated and then the results are passed to AutoCAD. Variables can be used anywhere in the statement to supply AutoCAD with data. Words within quotation marks are taken as "literal strings" by AutoCAD. Put AutoCAD commands, parameters and text in quotes. Unquoted words are read as AutoLISP variables. You can use other built-in AutoLISP functions within the command function.

There are restrictions on using the command function:

■ You cannot use get input functions within a command.

■ You cannot precede variable names with an exclamation point.

■ You cannot use C: commands (see the next section) in a command function.

Of course, AutoCAD will reject the command input if there are any errors in syntax or data type.

Each argument in the command list must be one complete instruction to AutoCAD. You cannot enter an X value, and later add the Y coordinate. You also must treat each instruction separately. For example, AutoCAD will treat (command "CIRCLE 5,5 0.25") as one erroneous instruction, not as three instructions. You also can make command functions pause for direct user input. You did this in the original HOLE command:

```
(command "CIRCLE" pause rad)
```

The function issues "CIRCLE" then pauses for the centerpoint before issuing the value of RAD as the radius. If you use pause in a command function within a menu, you also must supply the appropriate menu backslashes.

How to Add AutoLISP Commands to AutoCAD

Besides defining local and global variables, you can make your AutoLISP functions as easy to use and as clean in their screen appearance as a factory-defined AutoCAD command. You can make AutoLISP function names into AutoCAD commands by adding the function names to AutoCAD's command list. Precede the function name with a C: to add it to the list.

Try enhancing the BOLT function. It currently requires the awkward function argument form of diameter input. The following exercise pulls together an enhanced BOLT command that is defined as a C: defun that functions like a regular AutoCAD command. It adds prompting for the diameter and saves the diameter as a default for repeated executions. This enhanced BOLT, called EBOLT, has error handling added to its GET input functions. It is also an example of global and local variables, and a conditional if . . . then construction.

If you are using the IA DISK, this enhanced command is in the file EBOLT.LSP. If you are not using the disk, read along to see how it works. Then, come back later and type it in if you want to create and save the command. You don't need to type the non-bolded comments.

An Enhanced BOLT Command

Command: **SHELL**
DOS Command: NE EBOLT.LSP

Start your text editor with EBOLT.LSP.
Starts our editor, NE.
Use your editor to create or look at EBOLT.LSP.

You have the EBOLT.LSP file to examine.

Create the EBOLT.LSP file.

```
; Draws filled Bolt using HEAD and NUT blocks.
(setq #diam 0.25)                         ;Preset diameter to 0.25
(defun C:EBOLT ( / diam pt1 pt2 prmpt)
  (setq cmdecho (getvar "CMDECHO"))       ;saves command echo
  (setvar "CMDECHO" 0)                    ;echo off
  (if (> #diam 0)                         ;IF #DIAM is greater than 0
    (setq diam #diam)                     ;THEN set default to it
    (setq diam 0.25)                      ;ELSE set default to .25
  )
  (setq prmpt                             ;Set PRMPT to a string
    (strcat                               ;combine the strings
      "Bolt diameter <"                   ;beginning of prompt string
      (rtos diam)                         ;convert Real TO String for default
      ">: "                               ;end of prompt string
    )
  )
  (initget 6)                             ;initialize GET to no 0, no negative
  (if (setq #diam (getdist prmpt))        ;IF new value is entered at GETDIST
    nil                                   ;THEN do nothing - use new #DIAM
    (setq #diam diam)                     ;ELSE use old default
  )
  (setq pt1 (getpoint "\nHead point: "))              ;Get Insert pt
  (setq pt2 (getpoint pt1 "\nNut point: "))           ;Get Insert pt
  (command "INSERT" "HEAD" "S" #diam pt1 pt2          ;Insert HEAD
           "INSERT" "NUT"  "S" #diam pt2 pt1          ;Insert NUT
           "PLINE" pt1 "W" #diam "" pt2 "W" 0 "" ""   ;Draw Pline shaft
  )
  (setvar "CMDECHO" cmdecho)                          ;Restore setting
);EBOLT

(prompt "\nEBOLT.LSP loaded.\n")

; end of EBOLT.LSP
```

Save EBOLT.LSP and exit to AutoCAD.

The argument list of the defun line lists the local arguments. But C: functions can't take input arguments, so #DIAM is handled by a getdist. This function lets #DIAM exist as a global variable so that the previous value can be used as a default in repeated uses. So before getting diameter, EBOLT checks for a default value.

```
(if (> #diam 0)                 ;IF #DIAM is greater than 0
  (setq diam #diam)             ;THEN set default to it
  (setq diam 0.25)              ;ELSE set default to .25
)
```

After checking the default, EBOLT builds a prompt string that includes the default, converted to a string.

```
(setq prmpt                     ;Set PRMPT to a string
  (strcat                       ;combine the strings
    "Bolt diameter <"           ;beginning of prompt string
    (rtos diam)                 ;convert Real TO String for default
    ">: "                       ;end of prompt string
  )
)
```

Then the getdist uses this prompt string to see if you want to specify a new diameter, using initget to filter the input.

```
(initget 6)                     ;initialize GET to no 0, no negative
(if (setq #diam (getdist prmpt)) ;IF new value is entered at GETDIST
  nil                           ;THEN do nothing - use new #DIAM
  (setq #diam diam)             ;ELSE use old default
)
```

The rest of the function is essentially unchanged from the previous BOLT.LSP version.

You cannot use AutoLISP-defined C: commands as AutoCAD commands in a command function. You cannot enter a DEFUNed AutoLISP function when another function is active. C: functions *never* have arguments, but they can (and should) have variables declared as local variables.

Initializing Get Functions

EBOLT uses the initget function in conjunction with the getdist function to get a diameter value. Initget initializes the next following get function, controlling its input. It can refuse to accept 0 (zero), negatives, or null input (a <RETURN> instead of input). It can ignore limits, cause 3D points to be returned, or cause rubber-banding to use a dashed line. If a disallowed value is input to an initget-primed get function, it politely reprompts. For more about initget see INSIDE AutoLISP (New Riders Publishing). Try using the enhanced bolt command.

Using the EBOLT Command

```
Command: (setq pt1 nil pt2 nil)        Clear the old global variable values.
Lisp returns: nil
```

```
Command: (load "ebolt")
EBOLT.LSP loaded.
Lisp returns: nil
```

```
Command: EBOLT                 Try it like any other command.
Bolt diameter <0.2500>: .75            In commands, a leading 0 like 0.75 isn't needed.
Head point:                    Pick point.
Nut point:                     Pick point.
                               The PLINE draws the shaft:
```

```
Command: EBOLT                 Try it again. See how the default diameter prompt changes.
```

Strings

The "Bolt diameter .2500":" is the default prompt that the strcat function made in the example above. When you enter a value, it becomes the next default prompt. Strcat is a function that combines (concatenates) any number of strings into a single string. All its arguments must be strings, so the function used the rtos function to convert the real value of #DIAM to a string value. Rtos can take optional arguments to control precision and the type of units used. Otherwise, it defaults to the current units and their precision. There are several other string handling and associated functions:

```
ITOA          Converts Integers TO Strings.
STRCASE       Converts UPPER/lower case.
SUBSTR        Extracts portions of strings.
STRLEN        Returns the length of a string.
ANGTOS        Converts ANGles TO STRings.
ATOF          Converts an ASCII string representation of a real TO
              Floating point (a real).
ATOI          Converts an ASCII representation of an integer TO an
              Integer.
ASCII         Returns the ASCII value of the first character of a
              string.
CHR           Converts the integer value of an ASCII character to
              a string consisting of that character.
```

Adding Logic to Your Macros

Every program has a flow, direction, or logic which it follows. You can use a branch in your macros to direct your AutoLISP program to execute in a predictable order. Conditional statements are your branching tools for controlling your AutoLISP programs. The following overview will give an idea of the kinds of decisions you can have your programs make and react to.

Conditional Program Branching

AutoLISP has two branching functions, *if* and *cond*. You used the if in BOLT. All branching conditions need a conditional test to perform a branch. These conditional test expressions usually use *logical* and *relational* operators, like the greater than symbol > in the enhanced BOLT command. A conditional test may use any AutoLISP expression, like the (setq #diam (getdist ...) in BOLT.

Using Nil and Non-Nil in Conditional Tests

Remember, everything in AutoLISP is either True or nil. If something has no value, it's nil. If it has a value, it's True (non-nil). AutoLISP's conditional functions work on a nil or a non-nil basis. Non-nil means that as long as there is some value, the condition *passes* the test. Since everything is either nil or T, any expression can act as a conditional test.

Logical Operators

A logical operator is a function that determines how two or more items are compared. The basis for comparison is whether something is nil or non-nil. Logical operators return either a T (non-nil) or a nil (false) condition. The basic functions available for logical operations are:

```
AND     OR     NOT
```

The table below gives examples for the logical operations. As you look at the table, A and B are True (non-nil) and C is nil.

EXAMPLES	RETURN
(and a b c)	nil
(and a b)	T
(and b (getpoint "Pick: "))	Depends on input
(or c a b)	T
(or c)	nil
(not (or a b))	nil
(not c)	T

Both the *and* and the *or* functions can take any number of arguments. The and function returns nil if any of its arguments are nil, otherwise, it returns T. The or function returns True if any of its arguments are non-nil, otherwise it returns nil. Reading this carefully explains why, with no arguments, (and) is T, but (or) is nil!

Or stops evaluating and returns T as soon as it sees the first non-nil atom. In the same way, *and* quits evaluating and returns nil as soon as it encounters a nil argument. You need to be careful when you put other functions inside *and* or *or*. Whether an argument is evaluated depends on the values of preceding arguments.

Not is simple. Not takes a single argument and returns the opposite. Not returns T if its argument is nil, or returns nil if its argument is non-nil.

Relational Operators

A *relational* operator is a function that evaluates the relationship between two or more items. Relational operators include: *less than, greater than, equal to,* and *not equal to.*

The BOLT command function used (#diam 0) to determine whether a default value existed. The basis for comparison is whether something is nil or non-nil. Relational operators return either a T if the expression is true (non-nil), or return nil if the expression is false. The greater than and less than functions take any number of arguments. The first argument is compared to each following argument. Other relationals take only two arguments. Generally, the arguments may be any data type; the arguments are compared to see if they are numerically greater than, less than, or equal to.

In the following examples, X is '(A B C), Y is 1.5 and Z also is '(A B C).

EXAMPLE	READ AS	RETURNS
(< 2 y)	2 is less than Y -- false	nil
(> 2 y 3)	2 is greater than Y or 3 -- false	nil
(<= 1.5 y)	1.5 is less than or equal to Y	T
(>= 2 y)	2 is greater than or equal to Y	T
(= 1.5 y)	1.5 is equal to Y	T
(equal 1.5 y)	1.5 evaluates to same as Y	T
(eq z x)	Z is identical to X -- false	nil
(equal z x)	Z evaluates to same as X	T
(/= 2 y)	2 is not equal to y	T

Except for eq, equal, = and /=, these operations may have multiple arguments, comparing the first argument to all other arguments. Use the eq function to test lists to see if they are setqed (bound) to the same object. Eq generally is equivalent to the = and equal functions for numerical and string comparisons.

How to Use the If Structure

The simplest and most frequently used program branch is the *if* structure, sometimes called *if-then-else*. In plain English, AutoLISP thinks, "If the condition is T, then execute the first expression, else (if it is nil) execute the second expression." Here is the BOLT example:

```
(if (setq #diam (getdist prmpt))      ;IF
    nil                                ;THEN
    (setq #diam diam)                  ;ELSE
)
```

If has two possible paths in the example. Assume getdist was primed with (initget 6), so it will accept only positive or null values. If you just hit a <RETURN>, getdist returns nil. The if condition test is false and the else is executed. The else execution sets #DIAM to the default DIAM. If a valid value is input, the then step is executed. This does nothing, leaving #DIAM set to the value input to the getdist.

The Progn Structure

Limiting if statements to only a single then and a single else statement is confining. If you want to execute several statements, AutoLISP provides progn. Progn groups multiple AutoLISP expressions into one expression, notifying AutoLISP to treat the next series of statements as one statement. It always returns the last atom evaluated by the last expression within it. Progn's structure is:

```
(progn arg1 arg2 arg3 ... )
```

where the arguments can be any number of valid AutoLISP expressions.

The Cond Structure

Cond works much like if, except cond can evaluate any number of test conditions. You can think of cond as a kind of multiple if routine. Once cond finds the first condition that is non-nil, it processes the statements associated with that condition. Cond only processes the first non-nil condition.

The general format is shown below.

```
(cond
  (first test-condition  first statements ... )
  (second test-condition 2nd statements ... )
  ... more tests and statements ...
  (T last-statements ... )
)
```

Cond takes any number of lists as its arguments. Each argument must be a list containing a test followed by any number of expressions to be evaluated. Cond interprets the first item of each list as that list's test condition. It evaluates all of the expressions within the first non-nil list.

Since cond looks for the first non-nil condition, you want to make sure you test the most likely conditions before you test the least likely conditions. Putting your most likely non-nil conditions first increases your program's speed. The cond function is a good way to make programs branch based on a series of conditions. You can make the last test a test that is always non-nil, like the symbol T. Its expression will be evaluated if none of the others are non-nil. This is good for error prompts.

Program Looping Structures

Like many other programming languages, AutoLISP has several methods to cause a series of program steps to loop, executing over and over again. You can use these looping structures to reduce the number of statements in the program, continue a routine until a user action terminates it, converge on a mathematical solution, or batch process a list of data. We will mention two of these tools: the repeat and while structures.

The Repeat Structure

AutoLISP's *repeat* is a simple looping structure. Consider using repeat if your macros need to repeat some task. The repeat function executes any number of statements a specific number of times. All of its expressions get evaluated, but they get evaluated once each loop. Repeat returns the value of the last expression on the last loop.

Here is the general format and an example.

```
(repeat number    statements to repeat ... )
```

You can type a simple repeating statement at the AutoCAD command line.

Using a Repeat Loop in AutoLISP

```
Command: (repeat 5 (prompt "\nDo some stuff"))
Do some stuff
Do some stuff
Do some stuff
Do some stuff
Do some stuffnil

Command:
```

The While Program Structure

The function *while* loops like repeat, except while is open-ended, terminated by a conditional test. While continues to loop through its series of statements until the condition is nil:

```
(while condition    statements to execute ... )
```

Unlike the if function, while does not have an alternate else set of statements to execute if the condition fails the test. However, like cond and repeat, while lets you include an unlimited number of statements in the loop. While allows an indefinite but controllable number of loops. Each loop of a while function tests the condition and, if non-nil, evaluates each of the statements included within the closing parenthesis. While returns the last evaluation of the last completed loop. If no loops are completed, it returns nil. Although you may not have been aware of it at the time, you used a while to indefinitely repeat the first simple HOLE command:

```
(while T (command "CIRCLE" pause rad))
```

While is good for validating input, looping until the input meets the test. You also can use the function for program iteration. Iteration means that a loop is continued until the results of one or more expressions, calculated within the loop, determine whether the loop is terminated. The conditional test for an iteration usually contains some variable whose value gets changed during the course of the loop. Try the following at the keyboard.

Using a While Loop Function

```
Command: (setq count 0)
Lisp returns: 0

Command: (while (< count 10) (princ count) (setq count (1+ count)))
0123456789                      And AutoLISP returns 10.
```

➡ *TIP: GET functions are often put in a while loop to test input, for example, to see if the input is a member of a list.*

A Little Entity Access

Some of AutoLISP's more powerful customization features come from its access to AutoCAD's drawing database. Let's take a quick peek at AutoCAD's database using AutoLISP's entity access.

Every AutoCAD entity, whether a line, arc, or circle, has a name that is recognized by AutoCAD. Since the names change every time a drawing is entered from the main menu of AutoCAD, you don't even want to try to remember them. Instead, use AutoLISP's entity functions to ask for the names of entities from the database. Getting entity data lets you manipulate the data directly or use the data in your macros. Type the following input at the command line.

Using Entlast and Entget Functions to Get Entity Data

```
Command: LAYER                    Make layer OBJECTS and leave it current.
                                  Turn layer 0 off.
Command: TEXT                     Enter this text at height .125 and point 8.5,2.25:
Text: This is text.

Command: (setq ent (entlast))     Get the last entity's "name" with entlast.
Lisp returns: <Entity name: 60000A14>    Yours may be different.

Command: (setq edata (entget ent))    Look at its data with entget.
```

```
Lisp returns: ((-1 . <Entity name: 60000A14>) (0 . "TEXT") (8 . "OBJECTS") (10
8.5 2.25) (40 . 0.125) (1 . "This is text.") (50 . 0.0) (41 . 1.0) (51 . 0.0) (7
. "STANDARD") (71 . 0) (72 . 0) (11 0.0 0.0) (210 0.0 0.0 1.0))
```

The entity name lets AutoLISP refer to and manipulate the entity. The entget function looks up the data associated with the name you provide. You can even erase entities that you can't see by feeding AutoCAD entity names. AutoCAD's standard object selection depends on visibility, but you can bypass visibility using entity names.

How Entity Data Is Stored

Entity data is returned in a list format with special groups of DXF (Drawing eXchange Format) codes that flag which type of data is contained in the sublist. Each sublist has two parts. The first part is the DXF code, and the second is the data value. The integer 0 is a code for the entity type in the example above. You can see that the type is listed as TEXT. The 8 is a code for layer, and the layer is listed as OBJECTS. The 10 is the code for the start (insert) point which is 8.5 2.25 and the 11 is the code for the text alignment point. For entities like lines, the 10 and 11 codes are the start and endpoints. The 40 code is the height, the 1 code is the text value, the 50 is the rotation, the 41 is the width factor, the 51 is the oblique angle, the 7 is the style, the 71 and 72 codes are text justification and generation flags, and the 210 is for 3D.

These codes have differing meanings with different entities. Generally, any default data is not stored or listed. The leading integers in the parentheses are used to identify the type of data so that AutoLISP can process it. You can grab and manipulate any part of any drawing entity's data. The sky's the limit. That is why AutoLISP is such a powerful tool. It gives you direct access to the AutoCAD drawing database.

Extracting Entity Data

The DXF code (always an integer) allows you to access the inner parts of an entity list by association. In effect, you say, "Give me the sublist that has a 10 DXF code." AutoLISP will look at the entity list, find the sublist that has the matching 10 code and return that sublist. AutoLISP's assoc function gives you the ability to associate lists. Try extracting some data by typing the following input:

Using the Assoc Function to Extract Entity Data

Command: **(assoc 1 edata)**   Get the text group.
Lisp returns: (1 . "This is text.")

Command: **(cdr (assoc 1 edata))**   Extract the data from the text group.
Lisp returns: "This is text."

Since the association list still contains the DXF code, you need to strip this code before passing the list to AutoCAD. The cdr (the list less the first item) function is perfect for this.

Getting Data From AutoCAD's Tables

AutoCAD keeps items like block, layer, style, linetype and view names in reference tables. AutoLISP's tblsearch function can look through a table and return information from it.

The tblsearch function takes two pieces of information: the table to search and the name of the item to look for. Try two searches.

Using Tblsearch for a Quick Look at AutoLISP Table Access

Command: **(tblsearch "LAYER" "OBJECTS")**
Lisp returns: ((0 . "LAYER")(2 . "OBJECTS")(70 . 64)(62 . 3)(6 . "CONTINUOUS"))

Command: **(tblsearch "STYLE" "STANDARD")**
Lisp returns: ((0 . "STYLE") (2 . "STANDARD") (70 . 64) (40 . 0.0) (41 . 1.0) (50 . 0.0) (71 . 0) (42 . 0.125) (3 . "TXT") (4 . ""))

Command: **ERASE**   Erase the text.

➥ *NOTE: If you select a block insert, you get the information for the insert, not the entities within it.*

The Last Exercise

Working with AutoLISP can get intense. Let's finish up with some real fun. It is time to sit back, relax and look at one last AutoLISP file.

If you are using the IA DISK, get the AutoLISP file called THATSALL.LSP. It's a simple and fun example of entity modification through entity access. If you don't have the disk, you can create it or just read along.

That's All Folks

Here's the contents of the THATSALL.LSP file, if you need to create it. By now, you know how:

```
; THATSALL, an example of entity access and modification.

(defun C:THATSALL ()
  (command "TEXT" "M" (getvar "VIEWCTR") ;Middle justified text at screen center
    (setq ht2 0.05) (setq rot2 0) "That's All Folks!"   ;Height, 0 rotation
  )
  (setq                                  ;Set variables
    edata (entget (entlast))             ;Get entity data list
    ht (assoc 40 edata)                  ;Get height assoc list
    rot (assoc 50 edata)                 ;Get rotation assoc list
    incang (* 0.125 pi)                  ;1/16 of 360 degrees
  )
  (repeat 16                             ;Increase ht and angle in 16 increments
    (setq
      ht2 (+ ht2 0.05)                   ;Set new height
      rot2 (+ rot2 incang)               ;New angle
    )
    (entmod                              ;Modify the text entity
      (subst                             ;Substitute
        (cons 50 rot2)                   ;this new rotation assoc list
        rot                              ;for this old list
        (subst                           ;in this data list, which
          (cons 40 ht2)                  ;similarly substitutes new height
          ht                             ;for original height list
          edata                          ;in the original data list
        ) );close both subst
    );close entmod
  );close repeat
  (repeat 17                             ;similarly reverse height to 0
    (setq ht2 (- ht2 0.05))
    (entmod (subst (cons 40 ht2) ht edata))
  )
);close defun

;end of THATSALL.LSP
```

To test THATSALL, just load it and run it:

```
Command: (load"thatsall.lsp")
Lisp returns: C:THATSALL
```

```
Command: THATSALL             And if you run it, you see:
TEXT Start point or Align/Center/Fit/Middle/Right/Style: M
Middle point:
Height <0.0500>: 0.050000000000000
```

```
Rotation angle <0>: 0
Text: That's All Folks!
Lisp returns: ((-1 . <Entity name: 60000180>) (0 . "TEXT") (8 . "0") (10 6.14713
4.47 5 0.0) (40 . 1.38778e-17) (1 . "That's All Folks!") (50 . 0.0) (41 . 1.0)
(51 . 0.0) (7 . "STANDARD") (71 . 0) (72 . 4) (11 6.49713 4.5 0.0) (210 0.0 0.0
1.0))

Command:
```

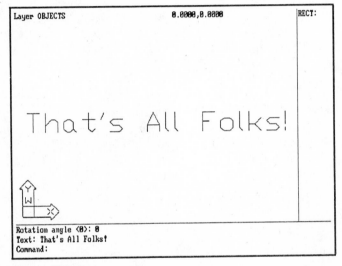

That's All Folks

This was the *last* exercise.

AutoLISP Summary

When you think about improving your macros with AutoLISP, use our examples as idea lists. Here are some of the ideas presented in the chapter.

You can use AutoLISP variables to eliminate menu selections that depend on drawing scale. Use AutoLISP to create intelligent macros to replace repetitive menu macros. When possible, use AutoLISP to calculate values to feed to AutoCAD commands, rather than pause the commands for input. Use AutoLISP to add prompts to menu macros to clarify the macro's use. Coordinate input with backslashes.

Use GET functions to obtain user input. Use AutoLISP's command function to send instructions to AutoCAD. Remember that you can add

AutoLISP C: commands to AutoCAD's command list. Use *and* and *or* functions for conditional prompts. Think about using *while* to filter and validate macro input. You also can make looping programs to construct data lists using the *repeat* function.

Where to Go From Here

We've only scratched the surface of AutoLISP's capabilities, trying to give you an overview of AutoLISP's logical structure, and a quick look at using AutoLISP in menu macros and entity access. To really tap into AutoLISP's power, see the New Rider's book, INSIDE AutoLISP. INSIDE AutoLISP covers the full scope of AutoLISP and will give you the tips and techniques that you need to help you customize your drawing commands.

Author's Farewell

AutoCAD is a powerful tool. But it is only that — a tool. The real inspiration and talent comes from the user. That would be you. We've explored AutoCAD's capabilities; now it's time for you to explore your own. Good luck. We hope to see you again when the next revision comes out.

AutoCAD Commands

MS-DOS and Configuring AutoCAD

What This Appendix Covers

AutoCAD has grown as a computer program. It is supported on a wide variety of computers. This appendix explains the assumptions the book makes about your AutoCAD workstation. In addition, the appendix provides:

■ Recommendations for setting up your hard disk and automating your MS-DOS system environment.

■ A discussion of common MS-DOS problems encountered in setting up and running AutoCAD.

■ A discussion of setting up AutoCAD and AutoLISP, and some common errors and problems.

MS-DOS and Setting Up AutoCAD

Getting AutoCAD going is similar to starting any other computer program. You must turn on the computer, load the operating system from disk, then initiate the AutoCAD program from an operating system prompt. The book assumes you have the hardware and software configuration described in this appendix. If your workstation setup is different, take a moment now to get familiar with the differences between the book's setup and yours.

Recommended INSIDE AutoCAD Teaching Configuration

The book assumes that you are running AutoCAD Release 10 or a later version on an MS-DOS computer with a hard disk. New Riders Publishing stocks other versions of this book to match most earlier releases of AutoCAD. Release 9, 10, and later versions require a math co-processor.

The book assumes you are using a pointing device, either a tablet cursor (stylus or puck) or a mouse, and a single screen color monitor. The exercises using AutoShade assume you have an AutoShade-supported video board and monitor. The plotting exercises are set up for a plotter, but are easily adapted to a printer/plotter.

We recommend the following minimum configuration:

- An 80286 or 80386 processor-based computer.

- 640K Memory plus 1MB or more EXTended or EXPanded RAM.

- Hard Disk with 20MB or more disk capacity.

- One or more diskette drives with 360K or more capacity.

- PC or MS-DOS Version 3.0 or later (3.3 is recommended) program files loaded on a hard disk directory called C:\DOS.

- AutoCAD program files loaded on a hard disk directory called C:\ACAD.

- AutoCAD configuration files loaded on a second hard disk directory called C:\IA-ACAD. These files are ACAD.CFG, ACADPP.OVL, ACADPL.OVL, ACADDG.OVL, and ACADDS.OVL.

Creating a separate directory, IA-ACAD, lets you work through the book's exercises without interfering with your normal AutoCAD use. See chapter 1 for details.

One Important Note

Make copies of the original disks that contain your operating system and AutoCAD. Do not use the originals.

Operating System

AutoCAD provides you with a set of drawing tools. The operating system works behind the scenes with AutoCAD as a task manager to manage and maintain your files.

The book assumes MS-DOS or PC-DOS, but nearly all material applies to any operating system. If you have OS2, you need an OS2 version of AutoCAD or you need to run AutoCAD in a DOS compatibility box.

Files are collections of commands and/or data on a disk. MS-DOS (and AutoCAD) files are recognized by their name extensions. The DOS name extension is the last three characters after the period in the DOS file name.

MS-DOS files have the file extension .COM (or EXE). The DOS system is composed of the file COMMAND.COM and two hidden files. These three files boot the computer system, run the AutoCAD program, and contain common file management commands like the DIR (Directory) command.

To execute the command, you type the command name at the DOS prompt followed by a <RETURN>. DIR <RETURN> executes the DIRectory command which gives a list of the DOS files in the current directory.

Other Common DOS Commands

Commands which are resident within COMMAND.COM, like the DIR command, are called *internal* DOS commands. Besides the DIR command, other important internal DOS commands that you will use are the MD (Make Directory) command, the CD (Change Directory) command, the COPY (file) command, the REN (Rename file) command, and the DEL (Delete file) command. Make sure you are familiar with these file management commands before you attempt any extensive work with AutoCAD.

Besides these DOS resident file management commands, DOS also has other *external* file management commands which you use in setting up and maintaining your files on disk. These also have the name extension .COM. For example, FORMAT.COM is the DOS command for formatting a data disk to accept DOS files. See your DOS manual for details.

AutoCAD Files

AutoCAD has three main types of files: program files (.EXE and .OVL files, for example), support files like help (.HLP), text (.SHX), pattern files (.PAT), and, of course, drawing files (.DWG). AutoCAD's default drawing file is called ACAD.DWG.

AutoCAD Program and Support Files

AutoCAD is a big program, one of the biggest running on microcomputers. The ACAD.EXE file executes AutoCAD and loads core functions, but most of AutoCAD's program code is contained in several overlay files (ACADx.OVL). In addition, AutoCAD uses several support files for data such as text fonts, linetypes, and hatch patterns. If you are unfamiliar with AutoCAD's file structure, take a look at the program files list in the AutoCAD Installation and Performance Guide that accompanied your software.

AutoCAD's file-naming conventions are easy to follow. It is not hard to deduce file functions by looking at the name extension. ACAD.MNU is the standard menu file. It is in the \SOURCE subdirectory on one of the support disks. (The compiled version is .MNX.) Driver files (the files that control the video display, digitizer, or plotter) have the extension .DRV. AutoCAD's configuration is stored in the ACAD.CFG file.

Preloaded AutoCAD Files

To run AutoCAD from a hard disk, you format the hard disk to receive DOS files, transfer the MS-DOS program files to the hard disk, and transfer the AutoCAD program and support files to the hard disk.

If your workstation has been prepared for you by a dealer, as required by Autodesk, these steps already have been done. If not, see your AutoCAD Installation and Performance Guide for complete installation and configuration instructions. Once properly installed and powered on, the machine will perform a hardware self-check, search for the operating files on the hard disk, and load the operating system. It is common practice for dealers to include an automatic date and time setting in the startup procedure. If this has been done, or after you enter the date and time, you should see the DOS operating system prompt C:> on your display screen.

An ACAD Directory

AutoCAD program files are usually placed in a directory called C:\ACAD. If the AutoCAD files were placed in this directory, you can change to it and start AutoCAD by typing ACAD <RETURN> at the C:> prompt. As soon as you type ACAD, the AutoCAD program takes over your computer and displays its Main Menu for you. The Main Menu gives you the choice of creating or editing drawings, plotting drawings, installing AutoCAD, or calling special utilities.

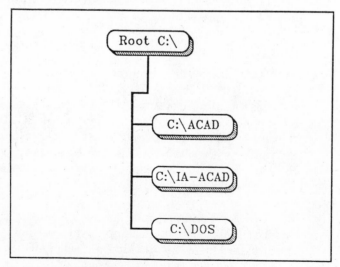

Inside AutoCAD Directory Structure

If you are working from another directory, like C:\IA-ACAD, you can still start AutoCAD by typing ACAD if C:\ACAD is included in your DOS PATH. If you are using DOS 3.0 (or a later DOS version), you can start AutoCAD by typing C:\ACAD\ACAD from another directory.

Configuring AutoCAD

If AutoCAD was not configured on your workstation, the AutoCAD Configuration Menu will sequentially prompt you to identify the types and selected parameters for your video display, digitizer, plotter, and printer/plotter which make up your workstation configuration.

Looking at Your AutoCAD Configuration

If AutoCAD was loaded and your workstation is already configured, you can look at your configuration by selecting **5** from the Main Menu. AutoCAD will display your current configuration and prompt you with the Configuration Menu.

Looking at Your AutoCAD Configuration

From the Main Menu.

```
Enter your selection: 5

Configure AutoCAD

Current AutoCAD configuration

Video display:                    Lists display type.
Axis drawn Inside the graphics area
Digitizer:                        Lists digitizer type.
Plotter:                          Lists plotter type.
Printer plotter:                  Lists printer type.
Press RETURN to continue: <RETURN>
```

Pressing <RETURN> gets you AutoCAD's Configuration Menu:

```
Configuration menu

0. Exit to Main Menu
1. Show current configuration
2. Allow I/O port configuration
3. Configure video display
4. Configure digitizer
5. Configure plotter
6. Configure printer plotter
7. Configure system console
8. Configure operating parameters

Enter selection:
```

Configuring or Reconfiguring Your System

Using the Configure AutoCAD utility is simple and straightforward. AutoCAD asks you several questions about your hardware setup and you respond with answers or a number selection from a list of choices that AutoCAD provides. Configuration is dependent on your hardware.

AutoCAD supports a number of computers and peripherals. We will not try to duplicate the large number of possible combinations. AutoCAD supplies a separate Installation and Performance Guide for configuring your computer workstation. The guide lists the displays and peripherals supported for each computer. We will show you the main features of configuration; see your Installation and Performance Guide for details and instructions.

To configure or reconfigure your system, you select a menu number. The number puts you in a submenu for each device-type and/or operating parameter. AutoCAD supplies a numbered list of devices it supports. You select the individual device by number and AutoCAD prompts you for information to configure its support of the device.

Hardware Options

Here are the book's hardware assumptions for displays and peripherals:

- Option 3 configures the video display. The book assumes AutoCAD's default values for a single video display, but dual screen systems can also be used. You should have at least 640 x 350 pixels (EGA) resolution.

- Option 4 configures the digitizer. The book assumes you have selected and configured a brand name digitizer from the option list under Option 4, but most of the exercises also work with a mouse.

- Option 5 configures the plotter. The book assumes you have selected and configured a brand name plotter from the option numbers listed under Option 5.

- Option 6 configures a printer/plotter. Few exercises in the book require a printer/plotter.

- Option 7 configures the system console.

- Option 8 configures selected operating parameters. The submenu lets you exit to the configuration menu, set an alarm for error messages, set up default prototype drawings, set drive/directory and file name prefix for use with temporary files, set the name and directory for plot-to-file, and set up AutoLISP features.

ADI Drivers

ADI drivers are memory resident (Terminate and Stay Resident) device driver programs for plotters, printers, digitizers and video cards. If you are using an ADI (Autodesk Device Interface) driver, you must install this type of driver prior to starting AutoCAD. You can install an ADI driver in your CONFIG.SYS file, AUTOEXEC.BAT file, or your AutoCAD startup batch file. Examples of both files are shown in this appendix.

ACAD.CFG

After exiting AutoCAD's configuration menu, you return to AutoCAD's Main Menu. Your configuration is kept in a file called ACAD.CFG and in the four ACAD??.OVL device driver files.

When you are through checking your system configuration, you can exit AutoCAD by selecting Option 0 Exit AutoCAD from the Main Menu. Option 0 gets you back to the MS-DOS operating system.

The Prototype Drawing

When you configure AutoCAD, it uses a standard prototype drawing as its initial drawing environment. AutoCAD's default drawing is called ACAD.DWG. This is your drawing setup until you change the initial values in ACAD.DWG, or until you change your prototype drawing.

Back to the Main Menu

Main Menu Options 1, 2, 3, and 4 are where the AutoCAD action is — we spend most of the book on what goes on inside these options.

Automating Your AutoCAD and AutoLISP Setup

To follow the menu macros and AutoLISP exercises in the book, you need to check your AutoLISP and DOS systems' environment, and you need to check your text editor.

AutoLISP Version

To check your version of AutoLISP, all you need to know is how to start up AutoCAD. AutoLISP should be loaded. Make sure your system doesn't have any custom menu or custom ACAD.LSP file installed.

Checking Your Version of AutoLISP

```
Enter selection:                 Begin a NEW drawing named INTRO=.
                                 The = forces all ACAD default settings.

Command: (ver)                   Type (ver) and hit <RETURN>.
"AutoLISP Release 10"            Or your version number.
```

If you got "AutoLISP Release 10," you're in great shape. If you didn't get at least "AutoLISP Release 9.0," then you need to look at your AutoCAD system. You must have AutoLISP 9.0 or later to follow the advanced material in this book. If you got an "Unknown command" or other error, check to see that you have Release 9 or 10 with ADE3. Then check to see that AutoLISP is not disabled by insufficient memory or the Configuration Menu item, Configure operating parameters.

Selecting Text Editors

You need to be sure that you have a text editor that will work for menu and AutoLISP development. Norton's Editor, Sidekick, PC Write (a "shareware" editor), Wordstar in non-document mode, the Word Perfect Library Program Editor, and the DOS program EDLIN all produce the standard ASCII file format that you will need. EDLIN is awkward and we recommend its use only as a last resort.

Make a copy of your text editor in your IA-ACAD directory and permanently configure it for nondocument mode so that you can use it without switching directories. If your text editor stores any of its format settings or modes, you need a separate non-document configured copy in your IA-ACAD directory. This avoids any conflicts in the text files that you will create for your development application. If your text editor insists on Microsoft mouse mode (Norton's does), you'll have to configure your mouse driver and AutoCAD accordingly.

Your editor must create standard ASCII files. We assume that you have a suitable editor at hand. Then, if you have doubts about its ability to produce ASCII files, test your editor with the following steps.

Text Editor Test

Install and configure a copy of your editor in the \IA-ACAD directory.

Load your text editor. Get into its edit mode and make a new file named TEXT.TXT.

Write a paragraph of text and block copy it to get a few screens full.

Save the file and exit to DOS. Then test it:

```
C:\> CD \IA-ACAD
C:\IA-ACAD> COPY TEXT.TXT CON
```
All the text you entered scrolls by if your editor produced a standard ASCII file.

```
C:\IA-ACAD> DEL TEXT.TXT
```

Your text editor is OK if COPY TEXT.TXT CON showed text identical to what you typed in your editor, no extra åÇäÆ characters or smiling faces! If you got any garbage, particularly at the top or bottom of the COPY, then your text editor is not suitable, or not configured correctly for use as a development editor.

The DOS Bootup Environment

When DOS boots ups, it reads COMMAND.COM and two hidden files named IBMBIO.COM and IBMDOS.COM. Then, it looks around for some more information. It gets its DOS environment information from two important files: CONFIG.SYS and AUTOEXEC.BAT.

We recommend a CONFIG.SYS file and an AUTOEXEC.BAT file, like those shown below, as a minimum base for using the advanced exercises.

CONFIG.SYS

CONFIG.SYS is the place to install *device drivers* that tell the computer how to talk to devices like disk drives, RAM disks and unusual video cards. It is also the place to put instructions that will improve your system performance and increase your DOS environment space for customization.

CONFIG.SYS must be located in the root directory. It is read automatically when your computer boots up. You may never even know it is there. We recommend that your file include the following lines. If you have a CONFIG.SYS file, display your file.

CONFIG.SYS

```
C:\IA-ACAD> CD \
C:\> COPY CONFIG.SYS CON
```
This assumes your drive is C:
Copies the file to the CONsole, the screen.

The CONFIG.SYS file contains:

```
BUFFERS=32
FILES=24
BREAK=ON
SHELL=C:\COMMAND.COM /P /E:512
```
Use a number from 20 to 48.

Allows <^C> and <BREAK> to break whenever possible.
/E:512 is for DOS 3.2 or 3.3.
Use E:32 for DOS 3.0 or 3.1.

> Edit your existing CONFIG.SYS file. If you do not have a
> CONFIG.SYS file, we recommend you create one.

Edit or create your CONFIG.SYS in your root directory using your tested ASCII text editor. Include lines similar to those above. Use the discussion below to help you in any modifications.

The BUFFERS line allocates more RAM to hold your recently used data. If a program frequently accesses recently used data, buffers reduce disk accesses and increase speed. Each two-buffer increment steals 1K from the DOS memory available to your programs. You may have to use a smaller number if AutoCAD runs short of memory.

The FILES line allocates more RAM to keep recently used files open. This reduces directory searching and increases data access speed. FILES uses very little memory, a large value helps with AutoCAD and AutoLISP.

The SHELL line ensures that you have adequate space for DOS environment variables. DOS allocates a small portion of RAM to store environment variable settings and information. AutoCAD and AutoLISP use several of these. You will need at least 256 bytes. We recommend allocating at least 512 bytes with DOS 3.2 and DOS 3.3.

AUTOEXEC.BAT File

AUTOEXEC.BAT is a batch file like any other, with one important exception: it is automatically executed every time the system is booted. Like CONFIG.SYS, it must be in the root directory.

The AUTOEXEC.BAT file is the place to install your TSR (Terminate and Stay Resident) programs like Prokey, Sidekick, and Superkey. It also is the place to install the other setup commands and DOS environment settings that you need to complete an application environment. Examine your AUTOEXEC.BAT file. We recommend that it include the following lines.

Examining the AUTOEXEC.BAT file

Be sure you are in the root C:\ directory.

`C:\>COPY AUTOEXEC.BAT CON`   Examine it.

> The following are DOS environment modifiers.

```
PROMPT $P$G
PATH C:\;C:\DOS
```

Other information may follow. Your path may include other directories.

Edit your AUTOEXEC.BAT file. If you do not have one, create one.

Edit or create your AUTOEXEC.BAT in your root directory, using your tested ASCII text editor. Include lines similar to those above. Use the discussion below to help you with any modifications.

PROMPT PG is extremely valuable. It causes the DOS prompt to display your current directory path so you don't get lost.

PATH is essential for automatic directory access to programs and DOS commands. The C:\ root and C:\DOS paths are essential to the book's recommended setup. If your DOS files are in a different directory, include the directory.

You should use whatever is relevant to your setup. It is more than likely that your path contains additional directories. The CONFIG.SYS and AUTOEXEC.BAT changes do not take effect until you reboot your computer.

Reboot

Reboot to test your configuration and batch file.

➡ *TIP: It helps to keep each program that you use, like AutoCAD, in its own subdirectory. File access is faster, you don't get files mixed up, and it is easier to install future program upgrades.*

➡ *TIP: Update your DOS to at least Version 3.1. It is easy to remember to keep AutoCAD software up to date, but it is easy to forget to update PC-DOS, or MS-DOS. DOS Versions 3.1 and later offer valuable features for a customizing environment, including a better ability to deal with space limitations. We recommend updating your DOS to 3.3.*

The PGP File

You can run other programs, utilities or DOS commands without ending AutoCAD or reloading your drawing. A few predefined *External Commands* are included with AutoCAD to do this. They are set in a file, ACAD.PGP. PGP stands for ProGram Parameter file. To see how SHELL fits into AutoCAD, look at the system organization illustration at the beginning of the appendix.

AutoCAD's standard SHELL features are set in the ACAD.PGP file, giving direct access to DOS commands. This access can be general purpose access or predefined access to jump out and run a specific DOS command or program. Copy the ACAD.PGP file from your \ACAD directory.

Try SHELL with some standard DOS commands. Start with a simple directory command.

PGP Going Outside AutoCAD

```
C:\> CD \IA-ACAD
```
Change to the book's directory.

```
C:\IA-ACAD> COPY \ACAD\ACAD.PGP
```
Copy your original PGP file.

```
C:\IA-ACAD> \ACAD\ACAD
Enter selection:
```
Start up AutoCAD.
Begin a NEW drawing named TEST.

```
Command: SHELL
DOS Command: DIR ACAD*.*
```
The general SHELL DOS access command.

```
Volume in drive C is HR-AT
Directory of C:\IA-ACAD
```
The files you copied.

```
ACADPP   OVL    1314   7-06-87  11:53a
ACADPL   OVL    9555   7-16-87   8:22p
ACADDG   OVL    2461   9-04-87   4:07p
ACADDS   OVL   13842   9-14-87   5:21p
ACAD     CFG    1516   9-14-87   5:28p
ACAD     PGP     501  10-19-87   9:00a
```

And possibly other files.

```
6 File(s)    2838528 bytes free
```

The PGP File

AutoCAD freed some memory, permitting DOS to run the DIR command. Although the DIR command is not a true AutoCAD command, you can enter it as if it were. Its execution is enabled by its definition in the ACAD.PGP file.

Take a look at the contents of the PGP file with another PGP command, using the DOS command TYPE:

Examining the ACAD.PGP File

```
Command: TYPE
File to list: ACAD.PGP

CATALOG,DIR /W,30000,*Files: ,0
DEL,DEL,30000,File to delete: ,0
DIR,DIR,30000,File specification: ,0
EDIT,EDLIN,42000,File to edit: ,0
SH,,30000,*DOS Command: ,0
SHELL,,127000,*DOS Command: ,0
TYPE,TYPE,30000,File to list: ,0
```

If your ACAD.PGP listing does not include the SHELL line, you need to find and copy the ACAD.PGP file from your original AutoCAD diskettes.

Each line in the file defines one PGP command, and uses five fields of information. Each field is a piece of information separated by a comma. Look at the last line, which defines the TYPE command. Let's examine the parts of the PGP specification.

TYPE is the AutoCAD command. The first field tells AutoCAD what name you want to use for the command at the AutoCAD command prompt.

TYPE is the External Command. The second field is what AutoCAD feeds to the DOS command line prompt, but it is not displayed inside AutoCAD. The external command field may include spaces. If the external command field is blank, as it is in the SH line and the SHELL line, it is not fed to DOS. DOS is fed only what you enter as input in response to the prompt.

30000 is the Memory Reserve. This number sets the amount of memory (in bytes) that you want AutoCAD to release for DOS use. Depending on your DOS version, it requires 25000 bytes or more. Memory reserve is the total RAM available under AutoCAD, less a few Kbytes. UNIX systems ignore the memory reserve setting and can run larger programs. The ACAD default is 30000.

File to list: is the prompt. AutoCAD uses the fourth field as a prompt for user input. It adds the input to the external command field and feeds the combined string to DOS. If an asterisk precedes the prompt, AutoCAD accepts spaces in the input line, but it requires an actual <RETURN> to enter the input.

Return Code: is the final item. It tells AutoCAD which screen to return to in a single screen system. A 0 returns to the text screen, while a 4 returns to whatever screen was displayed just before the PGP command was issued. For information on the other return codes, see the AutoCAD Reference Manual.

So, when you entered TYPE and hit <RETURN>, AutoCAD put away 30000 bytes of its memory, jumped out to DOS and issued the text string TYPE ACAD.PGP, exactly as if you had typed it at the C:\IA-ACAD> DOS prompt. Then, AutoCAD returned directly to the AutoCAD text screen.

Most PGP commands jump into DOS and back to AutoCAD and you never see a DOS C:\> prompt. If you use the SHELL command, SH and SHELL, and hit a <RETURN>, you simply get a DOS C:\>> with a subdirectory. The double >> indicates that AutoCAD still lurks in the background. You can run as many DOS commands and programs as you want before you go back to AutoCAD with EXIT.

Modifying the PGP File

You can modify the PGP file by adding new utility commands. For more information on modifying the PGP file, see CUSTOMIZING AutoCAD.

The \ACAD\ACAD.PGP is the factory standard file. AutoCAD only recognizes the name ACAD.PGP, so your modified file needs to have the same name. Be careful not to mix your files. Keep backup copies of PGP files under unique, unusable names like ACAD-10.PGP for the Release 10 standard.

AutoCAD loads the PGP file when it starts a drawing. If you modify the PGP file, you have to force AutoCAD to reload the new PGP file to test it. Quit your drawing, then come back to test the file.

Avoiding ACAD.LSP Conflict

Your system may have a modified ACAD.LSP file. If it does, AutoCAD automatically loads it at the start of each drawing edit session. If you wish to play it safe with the book's AutoLISP exercise, make a dummy ACAD.LSP file in your IA-ACAD directory.

Making a Dummy ACAD.LSP File

Create an ACAD.LSP file in your C:\IA-ACAD directory.
Enter the following line:

> (prompt "IA empty ACAD.LSP...")

Save the "empty" file and exit back to AutoCAD.

This empty dummy ACAD.LSP will load instead of any other ACAD.LSP file.

Using a Startup Batch File

AutoCAD lets you preset several of its startup settings. These control its memory usage and support file search order. You created the book's simple IA.BAT startup batch file in chapter 1. It simply changed directories and started AutoCAD. A startup batch file can also set memory allocations and file search order. The following is an example of a more involved startup batch file. You could create a file like this for each of your jobs or applications, each with a unique name.

The STARTUP.BAT file assumes your AutoCAD path is \ACAD. If not, substitute your path.

An Example STARTUP.BAT File

```
SET ACAD=\ACAD
SET ACADCFG=\IA-ACAD
SET ACADFREERAM=20
SET LISPHEAP=20000
SET LISPSTACK=8000
C:
CD \IA-ACAD
\ACAD\ACAD %1 %2
CD\
SET ACADCFG=
SET ACAD=
```

Here is a brief discussion of the settings in the STARTUP.BAT file. See CUSTOMIZING AutoCAD (New Riders Publishing), your AutoCAD Reference Manual, and the AutoCAD Installation and Performance Guide for more details.

SET ACAD= tells AutoCAD where to look if it doesn't find a needed support file in the current directory.

SET ACADCFG= tells AutoCAD where to look for configuration files. Creating several configuration directories and startup batch files is useful if you need to support more than one environment or if you need to support more than one device, like different plotters.

SET ACADFREERAM= reserves RAM for AutoCAD's working storage. The default is 24K, the maximum depends on the system, usually about 30K.

SET LISPHEAP= allocates memory for AutoLISP functions and variables (nodes). If you use many programs, or if you use large programs, you may need to increase this value. VMON (Virtual Memory ON) in AutoLISP makes AutoLISP page functions to disk or EXTended/EXPanded RAM. More HEAP space increases AutoLISP speed by reducing the swapping (paging) of functions. If you have Extended AutoLISP installed, you do not need to set this.

SET LISPSTACK= defines AutoLISP's temporary working data area during execution. Complex AutoLISP programs may require more stack space.

HEAP and STACK space combined cannot exceed 45000 bytes unless you have Extended AutoLISP installed. They reduce memory that otherwise is available to AutoCAD for free RAM and I/O page space. If you encounter problems running large programs, you have to adjust these settings to achieve a working balance. Don't be alarmed. It isn't hard. Change your settings until it works.

These SET environment settings do not affect memory outside of AutoCAD.

That is all there is to settings. The rest of the batch file is made up of straightforward startup DOS commands.

C: ensures that you are on the right drive. Substitute another letter if your hard drive isn't drive C:.

CD \IA-ACAD changes the working directory to \IA-ACAD.

\ACAD\ACAD %1 %2 executes ACAD. If \ACAD is on your PATH, you could use ACAD alone here, but specifying the directory avoids having DOS search the PATH. The %1 and %2 are replaceable parameters that you can enter when you run the STARTUP.BAT batch file. For example, to run a script with the name, NAME, you would enter STARTUP X

NAME and the batch file would execute this line as \ACAD\ACAD X NAME, running the script.

When you exit AutoCAD, CD\ returns you to the root directory. SET ACADCFG= and SET ACAD= clear their settings.

If you have Extended AutoLISP, you can install it in the startup batch file. The startup file can also include settings for control of extended memory (SET ACADXMEM=), expanded memory (SET ACADLIMEM=), and extended AutoLISP memory allocation (SET LISPXMEM=). If your system has more than 2MB of extended or expanded memory, you may find that limiting its use may improve performance. AutoCAD must use normal memory to implement extended or expanded. Too much extended or expanded memory starves the system for normal I/O page space and free RAM, and can actually reduce performance. See your Installation and Performance Guide for more information.

More DOS Tips and Techniques

Here are tips on organizing your DOS and AutoCAD environments.

❏ Customize your ACAD.PGP file by adding additional DOS commands, utilities, or programs that you would like to access from AutoCAD.
❏ Use SET ACAD= and SET ACADCFG= to clear any SET ACAD=name and SET ACADCFG=name settings that you make in a startup batch file, like IA.BAT. If you do not clear your settings, your other AutoCAD applications will find the settings and be directed to the wrong configuration and support files.
❏ Run CHKDSK /F at the DOS prompt on a regular basis. It will verify your hard disk file structure and free up *lost clusters*. Lost clusters are created when programs crash. Answer N when it asks if you want to convert the clusters to files. Do not run CHKDSK /F in AutoCAD.
❏ Use a disk optimizer or defragmentation program frequently to speed up file access on your hard disk. See any software dealer for recommendations.

Common Problems Encountered Running AutoCAD

Here are some common DOS problems encountered in setting up and running AutoCAD.

Common Problems With CONFIG.SYS

If your CONFIG.SYS settings do not run smoothly, your only indication may be that some things don't work. If you get the error message:

```
Bad or missing FILENAME
```

DOS can't find the file as it is specified. Check your spelling, and provide a full path.

```
Unrecognized command in CONFIG.SYS
```

means that you made a syntax error, or your version of DOS doesn't support the configuration command. Check your spelling.

Watch closely when you boot your system. These error messages flash by very quickly. If you suspect an error, temporarily rename your AUTOEXEC.BAT so that the system stops after loading CONFIG.SYS. You also can try to send the screen messages to the printer by hitting <CTRL-PRINTSCREEN> as soon as DOS starts reading the CONFIG.SYS file. Another <CTRL-PRINTSCREEN> turns the printer echo off.

Problems With ADI Drivers

If you have a problem with a device that uses an ADI driver, suspect the driver first.

Common Problems With AUTOEXEC.BAT

Errors in AUTOEXEC.BAT are harder to troubleshoot. There are many causes. Often, the system just doesn't behave as you think it should. Here are some troubleshooting tips:

■ Isolate errors by temporarily editing your AUTOEXEC.BAT. You can disable a line with a leading colon, for example:

```
: NOW DOS WILL IGNORE THIS LINE!
```

■ Many AUTOEXEC.BAT files have echo to the screen turned off by the command ECHO OFF or @ECHO OFF. Disable echo off to see what they are doing. Put a leading : on the line.

■ Echo to the printer. Hit <CTRL-PRINTSCREEN> while booting to see what is happening.

■ Make sure PROMPT, PATH and other environment settings precede any TSR (memory resident) programs in the file.

■ Check your PATH for completeness and syntax. Unsophisticated programs that require support or overlay files in addition to their .EXE or .COM files may not work, even if they are in the PATH. Directories do not need to be in the PATH unless you want to execute files in them from other directories.

- APPEND (DOS 3.3 or later) works like PATH to let programs find their support and overlay files in other directories. It uses about 5K of RAM. All files in an APPENDed directory are recognized by programs as if they were in the current directory. If you use APPEND, use it *cautiously*. If you modify an appended file, the modified file will be written to the current directory, NOT the APPENDed directory. Loading an AutoCAD.MNU file from an APPENDed directory creates a .MNX file in the current directory. AutoCAD searches an APPENDed directory before completing its normal directory search pattern, so appended support files will get loaded instead of those in the current directory.

- SET environment errors are often obscure. Type SET <RETURN> to see your current environment settings. If a setting is truncated or missing, you probably are out of environment space. Fix it in your CONFIG.SYS file. Do not use extraneous spaces in a SET statement.

- If your AUTOEXEC.BAT doesn't seem to complete its execution, you may have tried to execute another .BAT file from your AUTOEXEC.BAT file. If you nest execution of .BAT files, the second one will take over and the first will not complete. There are two ways to nest .BATs. With DOS 3.0 and later, use:

```
COMMAND /C NAME
```

where NAME is the name of the nested .BAT file. With DOS 3.3, use:

```
CALL NAME
```

- If you are fighting for memory, insert temporary lines in the AUTOEXEC.BAT to check your available memory. Once you determine what uses how much, you can decide what to sacrifice. Use:

```
CHKDSK
PAUSE
```

at appropriate points. Reboot to see the effect. Remove the lines when you are done.

- If you have unusual occurrences or lockups, and you use TSRs, suspect the TSRs as your problem source. Cause and effect may be hard to pin down. Disable TSRs one at a time in your AUTOEXEC file. Reboot and test.

These are the most common problems. See a good DOS book if you need more information.

Common Problems With DOS Environment Space

Running out of space to store DOS environment settings may give the error:

```
Out of environment space
```

An environment space problem also may show up in unusual ways such as a program failing to execute, AutoLISP not having room to load, or a block insertion not finding its block. This occurs because the PATH, AutoCAD settings limiting extended/expanded memory, and AutoCAD configuration, memory and support file settings are all environment settings.

You need to increase your environment setting in your CONFIG.SYS file. See CUSTOMIZING AutoCAD (New Riders Publishing) for more information on DOS environment settings.

Using AutoCAD With a RAM Disk

Running AutoCAD from a RAM disk can be even more efficient than using extended/expanded memory for I/O page space. If you want to run AutoCAD from a RAM disk, there are three things that you want to look at: AutoCAD's program files, temporary files, and the drawing itself. See CUSTOMIZING AutoCAD.

Finding Support Files

When you ask AutoCAD to find a support file like a menu file, it searches in a particular order. A typical search order is:

```
"STUFF.mnu":  Can't open file
  in C:\PROJECT (current directory)      First the current directory.
  or C:\SUPFILES\           Then the directory designated by SET ACAD=.
  or D:\                    Then the .OVL directory found on the PATH, if any.
  or C:\ACAD\               Last the program directory, home of ACAD.EXE.

Enter another menu file name (or RETURN for none):
```

If you keep AutoCAD's search order in mind, it will help you avoid errors in finding the wrong support files. A common cause of finding the wrong support files is setting ACAD=somename in a startup batch file. Make sure to SET ACAD= to clear it at the end of the batch file. Clear your SET ACADCFG= settings. Remember that APPENDed directories are always searched first.

Current Directory Errors

If you use SHELL to CD (Change Directories) from inside AutoCAD, you may get strange results. AutoCAD is not consistent. New drawings will not default to the changed current directory, yet SAVE defaults to save files in the changed current directory. Subsequent attempts to load support files, such as .MNX files, can crash AutoCAD.

If you must CD on SHELL excursions, automate it with a batch file that also changes back to the original directory.

SHELL Errors

Here are some common errors encountered in using SHELL:

```
SHELL error swapping to disk
```

is usually caused by insufficient disk space. Remember that the temporary files used by AutoCAD can use up a megabyte of disk space.

```
SHELL error: insufficient memory for command
```

may be caused by an ill-behaved program executed during a previous SHELL, or before entering AutoCAD. Some ill-behaved programs leave a dirty environment behind that causes AutoCAD to erroneously believe insufficient memory exists.

```
Unable to load XYZABC: insufficient memory
Program too big to fit in memory
```

If SHELL got this far, these are correct messages. You need to modify your ACAD.PGP to allocate more memory space.

```
SHELL error in EXEC function (insufficient memory)
```

can be caused by the default (24000) byte "SH" SHELL memory allocation being too small to load DOS. Exactly how much memory you need to allocate depends on your versions of DOS and AutoCAD, and on what you have in your CONFIG.SYS file. Recall that DOS 3.2 and later DOS versions must have at least 25000 bytes allocated in the ACAD.PGP. Use 30000 to give a little cushion.

Common AutoLISP Errors

The AutoLISP Programmer's Reference gives a complete listing of error messages. The following list gives a few hints of where and how to look for some other causes.

```
error: invalid dotted pair
error: misplaced dot
```

Look for a missing or an extra quotation mark " above the apparent error location.

Look for " imbedded in a string where it should be   \".

Look for strings that exceed 132 characters. STRCAT two strings if you need to.

n>   prompts such as   **3>**

Look for the same quotation mark error as shown in the dot errors example, or look for a missing closing parenthesis.

If the error occurs while you are LOADing a .LSP file, look in the file.

```
Unknown command
```

May be caused by AutoLISP, if you have a COMMAND function containing a "". The "" tries to repeat the last command entered at the ACAD prompt, not the last command sent to ACAD via the COMMAND function.

Miscellaneous Problems

If you run under a multi-tasking environment like CAROUSEL or DESKVIEW, you may get an error claiming a file should be in a directory it never was in. For example, you may get:

```
Can't find overlay file D:\ACAD\ACAD.OVL
Retry, Abort?
```

Or any other .OVL or ACAD.EXE. Don't type an A until you give up. Try an R to retry. If that doesn't work, copy the file to the directory listed in the error message. Flip partitions. You may need to hit another R during the flip. Copy the file, flip back and R again.

```
Expanded memory disabled
```

When you start ACAD from DOS, this error message can be caused by a previously crashed AutoCAD. Sometimes a crashed AutoCAD does not fully clear its claim on expanded memory. This causes the program to think none is available. Reboot to clear it.

Tracing and Curing Errors

You are your best source of error diagnosis. When problems occur, log them so you can recognize patterns to cure them. Here are some tips and techniques:

■ Use screen capture programs to document the text screen.

■ Dump the screen to the printer.

■ Write down what you did in as much detail as possible, as far back as you can.

■ Dump a copy of AutoCAD's STATUS screen to the printer.

■ Dump a copy of the screen of the DOS command SET to check settings.

Avoidance is the best cure.

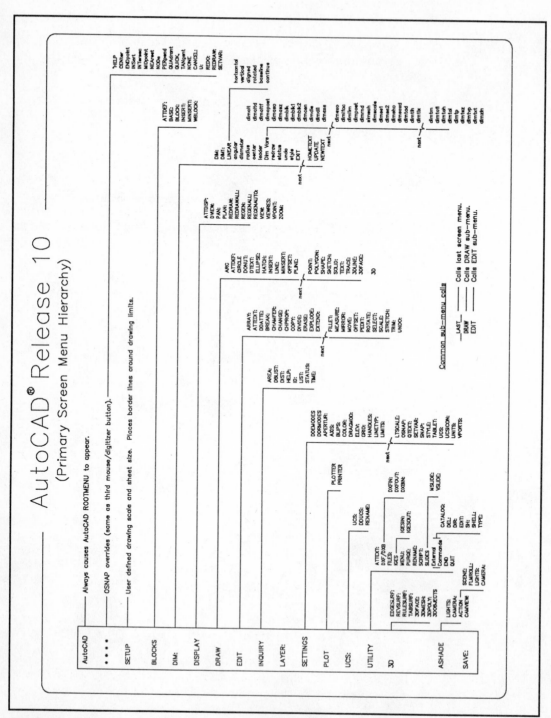

AutoCAD Standard Screen Menus

AutoCAD Menus and System Variables

AutoCAD Screen and Pull-Down Menus

AutoCAD comes from the factory with a preset structure of screen menus, pull-down menus, and a standard tablet menu. These menus list keys or commands that you use during an AutoCAD drawing editor session. The word AutoCAD is at the top of the standard AutoCAD screen *root menu*. The root menu list contains commands (words followed by a colon, like [DIM:] or [LAYER:]) and several keys (like [BLOCKS], [EDIT], [SETTINGS]) which call other screen menus.

This appendix shows the primary keys and commands of the standard AutoCAD screen menus in the AutoCAD Standard Screen Menus illustration (Release 10 version). The keys and commands are grouped by menus linked back to the AutoCAD root menu. The pull-down menus are shown in the chapter 1 facing page illustration, AutoCAD Release 10 Pull-Down Menu.

Remember, menus are simply for convenience in grouping commands. As additional features are added to AutoCAD, the screen menus and pull-down menus change. If you have additional features, or if customized commands have been added to your screen menus, write the screen menu words at the appropriate place in the menu list to get a complete list.

AutoCAD's Standard Tablet Menu

AutoCAD Release 10 comes with a standard tablet menu, including a plastic template for an 11" x 11" digitizer tablet. To use the standard AutoCAD tablet menu, you fix the AutoCAD standard plastic template to your digitizer, and use the AutoCAD TABLET command to let the program know where the tablet *boxes* are located.

The TABLET.DWG Drawing

AutoCAD also comes from the factory with a drawing file named TABLET.DWG. This is a drawing file like any other AutoCAD drawing file. You can view it on the screen, edit it, and plot it. You also can use this drawing to create a template drawing for your digitizer.

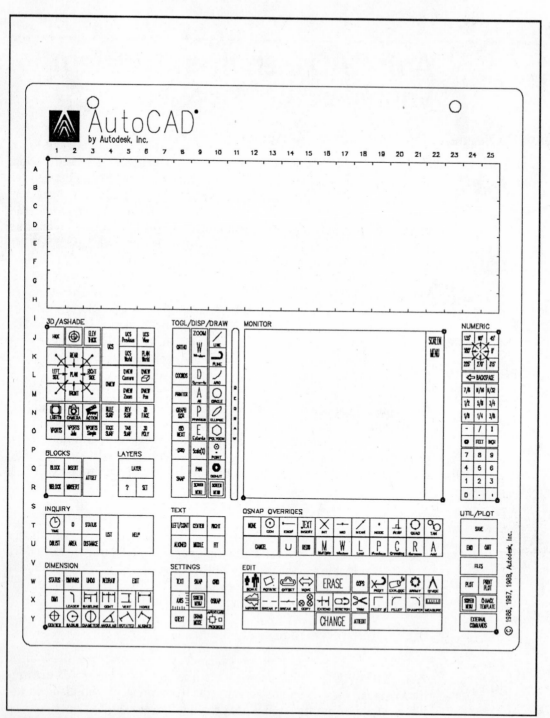

AutoCAD Standard Tablet Menu

Once you know how to edit drawings and customize the tablet menu, you can make your own tablet drawing, supporting the menu with your own tablet menu programs. If you customize your tablet menu, we suggest you first make a copy of TABLET.DWG, call it MYTABLET.DWG, and make your changes to the copy, not the original.

Configuring Your Tablet Menu

We assume that you are using an 11" x 11" digitizer that has been set up according to AutoCAD's Installation and Performance Guide. We also assume that you have already configured your system (Appendix B), and have loaded AutoCAD.

If you are using the AutoCAD template, place it on your digitizer. If you are using the plotted TABLET drawing, trim the drawing, leaving about a 1/2-inch border, and tape it to your digitizer. Since every tablet is different and since every user trims and tapes differently, you have to let AutoCAD know exactly where the tablet commands are located on the surface of the tablet.

You use the TABLET command from inside the drawing editor to configure the tablet. AutoCAD provides a series of tablet pick points on the drawing (or template) as a guide to loading each of the four menu areas prompted by the TABLET command. These are donut points on the menu.

The standard menu is divided into four menu areas by columns and rows. Look at the Standard Tablet Menu illustration. The columns are numbered 1 to 25 across the top. The rows are lettered A to Y on the left. Menu area 1 is the top rectangular area which is left for customization. The first "donut" pick point is near A and 1 in the top left corner. Menu area 1 has 25 columns and 9 rows of menu "boxes."

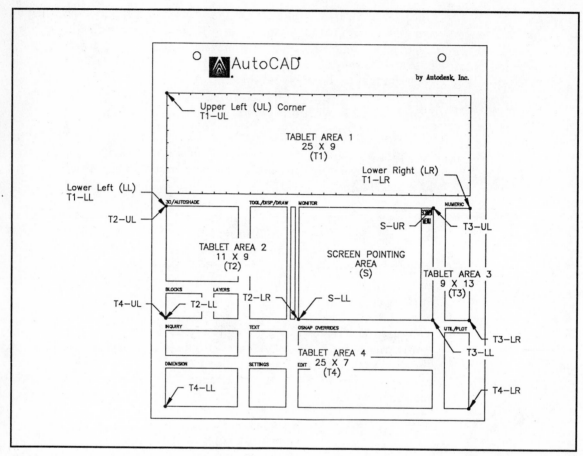

Configuring the AutoCAD Standard Tablet Menu

To configure the tablet, you pick three points for each menu area, and enter the number of columns and rows. Use the illustration, Configuring the AutoCAD Standard Tablet Menu, as a guide for picking points.

Configuring the AutoCAD Tablet Menu

Go to the Main Menu.

```
Enter selection: 1
Enter NAME of drawing : TEST
```

The drawing screen appears with the screen menu.

```
Command: TABLET
Option (ON/OFF/CAL/CFG): CFG
Enter the number of tablet menus desired (0-4) <4>: <RETURN>
```

```
Digitize the upper left corner of menu area 1:      Pick point.
Digitize the lower left corner of menu area 1:      Pick point.
Digitize the lower right corner of menu area 1:     Pick point.
Enter the number of columns for menu area 1: 25
Enter the number of rows for menu area 1: 9

Digitize the upper left corner of menu area 2:      Pick point.
Digitize the lower left corner of menu area 2:      Pick point.
Digitize the lower right corner of menu area 2:     Pick point.
Enter the number of columns for menu area 2: 11
Enter the number of rows for menu area 2: 9

Digitize the upper left corner of menu area 3:      Pick point.
Digitize the lower left corner of menu area 3:      Pick point.
Digitize the lower right corner of menu area 3:     Pick point.
Enter the number of columns for menu area 3: 9      Yes, that is 9.
Enter the number of rows for menu area 3: 13

Digitize the upper left corner of menu area 4:      Pick point.
Digitize the lower left corner of menu area 4:      Pick point.
Digitize the lower right corner of menu area 4:     Pick point.
Enter the number of columns for menu area 4: 25
Enter the number of rows for menu area 4: 7

Do you want to respecify the screen pointing area (Y) <RETURN>

Digitize lower left corner of screen pointing area:  Pick point.
Digitize upper right corner of screen pointing area: Pick point.
Command: QUIT
Do you really want to discard all changes ? Y
```

Main Menu appears. Select 0 to exit AutoCAD.

The standard AutoCAD tablet menu is configured for your digitizer and the configuration parameters are stored on your disk in a file.

AutoCAD System Variables

This appendix contains a table of AutoCAD system variables. Use this table to find AutoCAD's environment settings and their values. The table presents all the variable settings available through AutoCAD's SETVAR command or AutoLISP's setvar and getvar functions. The system variable name and the default AutoCAD prototype drawing (ACAD.DWG) settings are shown. A brief description is given for each variable, and the meaning is given for each code flag. All values are saved with the drawing unless noted with <CFG> for ConFiGuration file, or <NS> for Not Saved. Variables marked <RO> are read only, meaning you can't use SETVAR or the setvar function to change them.

AutoCAD System Variables

VARIABLE NAME	DEFAULT SETTING	DEFAULT MEANING	COMMAND NAME	VARIABLE DESCRIPTION
ACADPREFIX	"C:\ACAD\"			AutoCAD directory path **<NS>,<RO>**
ACADVER	"10"			AutoCAD release version **<RO>**
AFLAGS	0		ATTDEF	Sum of: Invisible=1 Constant=2 Verify=4 Preset=8
ANGBASE	0	EAST	UNITS	Direction of angle 0
ANGDIR	0	CCW	UNITS	Clockwise=1 Counter clockwise=0
APERTURE	10	10	APERTURE	Half of aperture height in pixels **<CFG>**
AREA	0.0000		AREA,LIST	Last computed area **<NS>,<RO>**
ATTDIA	0	PROMPTS		Insert uses: DDATTE dialogue box=1 Attribute prompts=0
ATTMODE	1	ON	ATTDISP	Attribute display Normal=1 ON=2 OFF=0
ATTREQ	1	PROMPTS		Insert uses: Prompts=1 Defaults=0
AUNITS	0	DEC. DEG.	UNITS	Angular units Dec=0 Deg=1 Grad=2 Rad=3 Survey=4
AUPREC	0	0	UNITS	Angular units decimal places
AXISMODE	0	OFF	AXIS	Axis ON=1 Axis OFF=0
AXISUNIT	0.0000,0.0000		AXIS	Axis X,Y Increment
BACKZ	0.0000		DVIEW	Back clipping plane offset - See VIEWMODE **<RO>**
BLIPMODE	1	ON	BLIPMODE	Blips=1 No Blips=0
CDATE	19881202.144648898		TIME	Date.Time **<NS>,<RO>**
CECOLOR	"BYLAYER"		COLOR	Current entity color **<RO>**
CELTYPE	"BYLAYER"		LINETYPE	Current entity linetype **<RO>**
CHAMFERA	0.0000		CHAMFER	Chamfer distance for A
CHAMFERB	0.0000		CHAMFER	Chamfer distance for B
CLAYER	"0"		LAYER	Current layer **<RO>**
CMDECHO	1	ECHO	SETVAR	Command echo in AutoLISP Echo=1 No Echo=0 **<NS>**
COORDS	0	OFF	[^D] [F6]	Update display Picks=0 ON=1 Dist>Angle=2
CVPORT	1		VPORTS	Identification number of the current viewport
DATE	2447498.61620926		TIME	Julian time **<NS>,<RO>**
DIMALT	0	OFF	DIMALT	Use alternate units ON=1 OFF=0
DIMALTD	2	0.00	DIMALTD	Decimal precision of alternate units
DIMALTF	25.4000		DIMALTF	Scale factor for alternate units
DIMAPOST	""	NONE	DIMAPOST	Suffix for alternate dimensions **<RO>**
DIMASO	1	ON	DIMASO	Associative=1 Line,Arrow,Text=0
DIMASZ	0.1800		DIMASZ	Arrow Size=Value (also controls text fit)
DIMBLK	""	NONE	DIMBLK	Block name to draw instead of arrow or tick **<RO>**
DIMBLK1	""	NONE	DIMBLK1	Block name for 1st end, see DIMSAH **<RO>**
DIMBLK2	""	NONE	DIMBLK2	Block name for 2nd end, see DIMSAH **<RO>**
DIMCEN	0.0900	MARK	DIMCEN	Center mark size=Value Add center lines=Negative
DIMDLE	0.0000	NONE	DIMDLE	Dimension line extension=Value
DIMDLI	0.3800		DIMDLI	Increment between continuing dimension lines
DIMEXE	0.1800		DIMEXE	Extension distance for extension lines=Value
DIMEXO	0.0625		DIMEXO	Offset distance for extension lines=Value
DIMLFAC	1.0000	NORMAL	DIMLFAC	Overall linear distance factor=Value
DIMLIM	0	OFF	DIMLIM	Add tolerance limits ON=1 OFF=0
DIMPOST	""	NONE	DIMPOST	User defined dimension suffix (eg: "mm") **<RO>**
DIMRND	0.0000	EXACT	DIMRND	Rounding value for linear dimensions
DIMSAH	0	OFF	DIMSAH	Allow separate DIMBLKS ON=1 OFF=0
DIMSCALE	1.0000		DIMSCALE	Overall dimensioning scale factor=Value
DIMSE1	0	OFF	DIMSE1	Suppress extension line 1 Omit=1 Draw=0
DIMSE2	0	OFF	DIMSE2	Suppress extension line 2 Omit=1 Draw=0
DIMSHO	0	OFF	DIMSHO	Show associative dimension while dragging
DIMSOXD	0	OFF	DIMSOXD	Suppress dim. lines outside extension lines Omit=1 Draw=0
DIMTAD	0	OFF	DIMTAD	Text above dim. line ON=1 OFF(in line)=0

VARIABLE NAME	DEFAULT SETTING	DEFAULT MEANING	COMMAND NAME	VARIABLE DESCRIPTION
DIMTIH	1	ON	DIMTIH	Text inside horizontal ON=1 OFF(aligned)=0
DIMTIX	0	OFF	DIMTIX	Force text inside extension lines ON=1 OFF=0
DIMTM	0.0000	NONE	DIMTM	Minus tolerance=Value
DIMTOFL	0	OFF	DIMTOFL	Draw dim. line even if text outside ext. lines
DIMTOH	1	ON	DIMTOH	Text outside horizontal ON=1 OFF(aligned)=0
DIMTOL	0	OFF	DIMTOL	Append tolerance ON=1 OFF=2
DIMTP	0.0000	NONE	DIMTP	Plus tolerance=Value
DIMTSZ	0.0000	ARROWS	DIMTSZ	Tick size=Value Draw arrows=0
DIMTVP	0.0000		DIMTVP	Text vertical position
DIMTXT	0.1800		DIMTXT	Text size=Value
DIMZIN	0		DIMZIN	Controls leading zero (see AutoCAD manual)
DISTANCE	0.0000		DIST	Last computed distance **<NS>,<RO>**
DRAGMODE	2	AUTO	DRAGMODE	OFF=0 Enabled=1 Auto=2
DRAGP1	10		SETVAR	Drag regen rate **<CFG>**
DRAGP2	25		SETVAR	Drag input rate **<CFG>**
DWGNAME	"TEST"			Current drawing name **<RO>**
DWGPREFIX	"C:\IA-ACAD\"			Directory path of current drawing **<NS>,<RO>**
ELEVATION	0.0000		ELEV	Current default elevation
EXPERT	0	NORMAL	SETVAR	Suppresses "Are you sure" prompts (See AutoCAD Reference Manual)
EXTMAX	-1.0000E+20,-1.0000E+20			Upper right drawing extents X,Y **<RO>**
EXTMIN	1.0000E+20,1.0000E+20			Lower left drawing extents X,Y **<RO>**
FILLETRAD	0.0000		FILLET	Current fillet radius
FILLMODE	1		FILL	Fill ON=1 Fill OFF=0
FLATLAND	0		SETVAR	Temporary 3D compatibility setting act like Release 9=1 R10=0
FRONTZ	0.0000		DVIEW	Front clipping plane offset - See VIEWMODE **<RO>**
GRIDMODE	0	OFF	GRID	Grid ON=1 Grid OFF=0
GRIDUNIT	0.0000,0.0000		GRID	X,Y grid increment
HANDLES	0		HANDLES	Entity handles Enabled=1 Disabled=0 **<RO>**
HIGHLIGHT	1		SETVAR	Highlight selection ON=1 OFF=0 **<NS>**
INSBASE	0.0000,0.0000		BASE	Insert base point of current drawing X,Y
LASTANGLE	0		ARC	Last angle of the last arc **<NS>,<RO>**
LASTPOINT	0.0000,0.0000			Last @ pickpoint X,Y **<NS>**
LASTPT3D	0.0000,0.0000,0.0000			Last @ pickpoint X,Y,Z **<NS>**
LENSLENGTH	50.0000		DVIEW	Length of lens in perspective in millimeters **<RO>**
LIMCHECK	0	OFF	LIMITS	Limits error check ON=1 OFF=0
LIMMAX	12.0000,9.0000		LIMITS	Upper right X,Y limit
LIMMIN	0.0000,0.0000		LIMITS	Lower left X,Y limit
LTSCALE	1.0000		LTSCALE	Current linetype scale
LUNITS	2	DEC.	UNITS	Linear units: Scientific=1 Dec=2 Eng=3 Arch=4 Frac=5
LUPREC	4	0.0000	UNITS	Unit precision decimal places or denominator
MENUECHO	0	NORMAL	SETVAR	Normal=0 Suppress echo of menu items=1 No prompts=2 No input or prompts=3 **<NS>**
MENUNAME	"ACAD"		MENU	Current menu name **<RO>**
MIRRTEXT	1	YES	SETVAR	Retain text direction=0 Reflect text=1
ORTHOMODE	0	OFF	[^O] [F8]	Ortho ON=1 Ortho OFF=0
OSMODE	0	NONE	OSNAP	Sum of: Endp=1 Mid=2 Cen=4 Node=8 Quad=16 Int=32 Ins=64 Perp=128 Tan=256 Near=512 Quick=1024
PDMODE	0	POINT	SETVAR	Controls style of points drawn
PDSIZE	0.0000	POINT	SETVAR	Controls size of points
PERIMETER	0.0000		AREA,LIST	Last computed perimeter **<NS>,<RO>**

VARIABLE NAME	DEFAULT SETTING	DEFAULT MEANING	COMMAND NAME	VARIABLE DESCRIPTION
PICKBOX	3		SETVAR	Half the pickbox size in pixels **<CFG>**
POPUPS	1			AUI Support=1 No Support=0 **<NS>, <RO>**
QTEXTMODE	0	OFF	QTEXT	Qtext ON=1 Qtext OFF=0
REGENMODE	1	ON	REGENAUTO	Regenauto ON=1 Regenauto OFF=0
SCREENSIZE	570.0000,410.0000			Size of display in X,Y pixels **<NS>, <RO>**
SKETCHINC	0.1000		SKETCH	Recording increment for sketch
SKPOLY	0	LINE	SETVAR	Polylines=1 Sketch with Line=0
SNAPANG	0		SNAP	Angle of SNAP/GRID rotation
SNAPBASE	0.0000,0.0000		SNAP	X,Y base point of SNAP/GRID rotation
SNAPISOPAIR	0	LEFT	SNAP [^E]	Isoplane Left=0 Top=1 Right=2
SNAPMODE	0	OFF	SNAP [^B] [F9]	Snap ON=1 Snap OFF=0
SNAPSTYL	0	STD	SNAP	Isometric=1 Snap standard=0
SNAPUNIT	1.0000,1.0000		SNAP	Snap X,Y increment
SPLFRAME	0		SETVAR	Display spline frame ON=1 OFF=0
SPLINESEGS	8		SETVAR	Number of line segments in each spline segment
SPLINETYPE	6	CUBIC	SETVAR	Pedit spline generates: Quadratic B-Spline=5 Cubic B-Spline=6
SURFTAB1	6		SETVAR	Rulesurf and tabsurf tabulations, also revsurf and edgesurf M density
SURFTAB2	6		SETVAR	Revsurf and edgesurf N density
SURFTYPE	6	CUBIC	SETVAR	Pedit smooth surface generates: Quadratic B-Spline=5 Cubic B-Spline=6 Bezier=8
SURFU	6		SETVAR	M direction surface density
SURFV	6		SETVAR	N direction surface density
TARGET	0.0000,0.0000,0.0000		DVIEW	UCS coords of current viewport target point **<RO>**
TDCREATE	2447498.61620031		TIME	Creation time (Julian) **<RO>**
TDINDWG	0.00436285		TIME	Total editing time **<RO>**
TDUPDATE	2447498.61620031		TIME	Time of last save or update **<RO>**
TDUSRTIMER	0.00436667		TIME	User set elapsed time **<RO>**
TEMPPREFIX	""			Directory location of AutoCAD's temporary files, defaults to drawing directory **<NS>, <RO>**
TEXTEVAL	0	TEXT	SETVAR	Evaluate leading "(" and "!" in text input as: Text=0 AutoLISP=1 **<NS>**
TEXTSIZE	0.2000		TEXT	Current text height
TEXTSTYLE	"STANDARD"		TEXT,STYLE	Current text style **<RO>**
THICKNESS	0.0000		ELEV	Current 3D extrusion thickness
TRACEWID	0.0500		TRACE	Current width of traces
UCSFOLLOW	0		SETVAR	Automatic plan view in new UCS=1 Off=0
UCSICON	1		UCSICON	Sum of: Off=0 On=1 Origin=2
UCSNAME	""		UCS	Name of current UCS Unnamed="" **<RO>**
UCSORG	0.0000,0.0000,0.0000		UCS	WCS origin of current UCS **<RO>**
UCSXDIR	1.0000,0.0000,0.0000		UCS	X direction of current UCS **<RO>**
UCSYDIR	0.0000,1.0000,0.0000		UCS	Y direction of current UCS **<RO>**
USERI1 - 5	0			User integer variables USERI1 to USERI5
USERR1 - 5	0.0000			User real variables USERR1 to USERR5
VIEWCTR	6.2518,4.5000		ZOOM,PAN,VIEW	X,Y center point of current view **<RO>**
VIEWDIR	0.0000,0.0000,1.0000		DVIEW	Camera point offset from target in WCS **<RO>**
VIEWMODE	0		DVIEW,UCS	Perspective and clipping settings, see AutoCAD Reference Manual **<RO>**
VIEWSIZE	9.0000		ZOOM,PAN,VIEW	Height of current view **<RO>**
VIEWTWIST	0		DVIEW	View wist angle **<RO>**
VPOINTX	0.0000		VPOINT	X coordinate of VPOINT **<RO>**
VPOINTY	0.0000		VPOINT	Y coordinate of VPOINT **<RO>**

VARIABLE NAME	DEFAULT SETTING	DEFAULT MEANING	COMMAND NAME	VARIABLE DESCRIPTION
VPOINTZ	1.0000		VPOINT	Z coordinate of VPOINT **\<RO\>**
VSMAX	12.5036,9.0000,0.0000			ZOOM,PAN,VIEW
				Upper right of virtual screen X,Y **\<NS\>,\<RO\>**
VSMIN.	0.0000,0.0000,0.0000			ZOOM,PAN,VIEW
				Lower left of virtual screen X,Y **\<NS\>,\<RO\>**
WORLDUCS	1		UCS	UCS equals WCS=1 UCS not equal to WCS=0 **\<RO\>**
WORLDVIEW	1		DVIEW,UCS	Dview and VPoint coordinate input: WCS=1 UCS=0

\<NS\> Not Saved   **\<CFG\>** Configure File   **\<RO\>** Read Only

Index

Q

New Riders Library

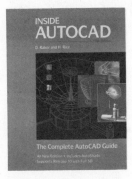

INSIDE AutoCAD   **Fifth Edition**
The Complete AutoCAD Guide

D. Raker and H. Rice
750 pages, over 400 illustrations
ISBN: 0-934035-49-0 **$29.95**

INSIDE AutoCAD, the best selling book on AutoCAD, is entirely new and
rewritten for AutoCAD's 3D Release 10. This easy-to-understand book serves
as both a tutorial and a lasting reference guide. Learn to use every single
AutoCAD command as well as time saving drawing techniques and tips.
Includes coverage of new 3D graphics features, AutoShade, and AutoLISP.
This is the book that lets you keep up and stay in control with AutoCAD.

INSIDE AutoLISP
The Complete Guide to Using AutoLISP for AutoCAD Applications

J. Smith and R. Gesner
672 pages, over 150 illustrations
ISBN: 0-934035-47-4, **$29.95**

Introducing the most comprehensive book on AutoLISP for AutoCAD Release
10. Learn AutoLISP commands and functions and write your own custom
AutoLISP programs. Numerous tips and tricks for using AutoLISP for routine
drawing tasks. Import and export critical drawing information to/from Lotus
1-2-3 and dBASE. Automate the creation of scripts for unattended drawing
processing. *INSIDE AutoLISP* is the book that will give you the inside track
to using AutoLISP.

INSIDE AutoSketch
A Guide to Productive Drawing Using AutoSketch

By Frank Lenk
240 pages, over 120 illustrations
ISBN: 0-934035-20-2, **$17.95**

INSIDE AutoSketch gives you real-life mechanical parts, drawing schematics,
and architectural drawings. Start by learning to draw simple shapes such as
points, lines and curves, then edit shapes by moving, copying, rotating and
distorting them. Explore higher-level features to complete technical drawing
jobs using reference grids, snap, drawing layers and creating parts. *INSIDE
AutoSketch* will let you draw your way to success!

For fast service, call a New Riders Sales Representative
at (818) 991-5392

New Riders Library also includes products on Desktop Publishing

Style Sheets for Technical Documents

320 pages, over 100 illustrations
ISBN: 0-934035-31-8 Book/Disk Set **$39.95**

Get the maximum out of Xerox Ventura Publisher with these advanced, high-performance technical document style sheets

Style Sheets for Newsletters

320 pages, over 100 illustrations
ISBN: 0-934035-29-6 Book/DiskSet **$39.95**

Have immediate impact with these sophisticated professionally designed one-, two-, three-, four-, and five- column layouts. Choose from two dozen attractive newsletters for Xerox Ventura Publisher.

Style Sheets for Business Documents

320 pages, over 100 illustrations
ISBN: 0-934035-22-9 Book/Disk Set **$39.95**

Contains more than 30 top-quality business documents for Xerox Ventura Publisher. Put the power of sophisticated graphics design to work for your company.

Inside Xerox Ventura   Second Edition

496 pages, over 250 illustrations
ISBN: 0-934035-59-8 **$24.95**

The finest reference guide to Xerox Ventura Publisher has been completely rewritten for Version 2.

Publishing Power With Ventura   Second Edition

624 pages, over 400 illustrations
ISBN: 0-934035-61-X, **$27.95**

Unlock the inner secrets of Xerox Ventura Publisher Version 2. The only learning guide available with in-depth, step-by-step instructions for creating newsletters, flyers, books, and more! The optional disk makes learning even easier. Other books talk about productivity—this book delivers it!

Desktop Manager

Manual 220 pages
ISBN: 0-934035-34-2, Manual/Disk **$99.95**

The desktop accessory software that lets you manage your Xerox Ventura documents. *DESKTOP MANAGER* runs transparently from within the Xerox Ventura Publisher environment, providing these features; file management, timed backup, document control, style sheet settings, and report generation status, schedule dates.

Managing Desktop Publishing

A Style Guide for Desktop Publishing

By Jesse Berst
240 pages
ISBN: 0-934035-27-X, **$9.95**

The essential handbook for the modern writer or editor. Save production time by using your word processor to pre-format desktop publishing documents for Word, Word Perfect, Xerox Ventura Publisher and Pagemaker. Learn how to use DOS to organize your electronic files. Numerous tips on usage and lists of design rules that will make your writing more consistent and more correct.